T0257662

IET COMPUTING SERIES 62

Explainable Artificial Intelligence (XAI)

Other volumes in this series

Explainable Artificial Intelligence (XAI)

Concepts, enabling tools, technologies and applications

Edited by
Pethuru Raj, Utku Köse, Usha Sakthivel,
Susila Nagarajan and Vijanth S. Asirvadam

The Institution of Engineering and Technology

Published by The Institution of Engineering and Technology, London, United Kingdom

The Institution of Engineering and Technology is registered as a Charity in England & Wales (no. 211014) and Scotland (no. SC038698).

First published 2023

The Institution of Engineering and Technology
Futures Place
Kings Way, Stevenage
Hertfordshire SG1 2UA, United Kingdom

www.theiet.org

British Library Cataloguing in Publication Data
A catalogue record for this product is available from the British Library

ISBN 978-1-83953-695-3 (hardback)
ISBN 978-1-83953-696-0 (PDF)

Typeset in India by MPS Limited
Printed in the UK by CPI Group (UK) Ltd, Eastbourne

Credit for Prelims: "Cover Image: Yuichiro Chino / Moment via Getty Images

Contents

About the editors

Pethuru Raj is the chief architect and Vice President in the Site Reliability Engineering (SRE) division of Reliance Jio Platforms Ltd., Bangalore, India. He focuses on emerging technologies including Internet of Things (IoT), artificial intelligence (AI), big and fast data analytics, blockchain, digital twins, cloud native computing, edge and fog clouds, reliability engineering, microservices architecture (MSA), and event-driven architecture (EDA). He previously worked at IBM global Cloud Center of Excellence (CoE), Wipro Consulting Services (WCS), and Robert Bosch Corporate Research (CR). He has authored and edited 34 books. He is a member of ACM. He holds a PhD degree in Formal Language Theory and Finite Automata from Anna University, Chennai, India.

Utku Köse is an associate professor at Suleyman Demirel University, Turkey, and a visiting researcher at University of North Dakota, USA. His research interests include artificial intelligence, machine ethics, optimization, chaos theory, distance education and e-learning, computer education and computer science, and biomedical applications. He has more than 200 scientific publications including articles, proceedings, and reports. He has authored and edited several books. He is a member of ACM, an IEEE senior member, and member of IEEE Systems Man and Cybernetics Society, and IEEE Young Professionals. He received his PhD degree in Computer Engineering from Selcuk University, Turkey.

Usha Sakthivel is currently working as a professor, Dean, and Head of the Department of Computer Science and Engineering at Rajarajeswari College of Engineering, Bangalore, India. She has 25 years of experience and graduated from Manonmanium Sundaranar University, in Computer Science and Engineering in 1998. She obtained her master's degree in computer science and engineering and PhD degree from Sathyabama University in the area of mobile ad hoc networks in 2013. She has 70 publications in international and national conferences and 45 publications in national and international journals in the area of mobile ad hoc networks, IoT, and wireless security. Most of the publications are having impact factor cited in SCI, Google Scholar, Scopus (h index and i10index), Microsoft, and others. She received funding from AICTE under NCP scheme, MODROBS, TGS, VTU TEQIP, and SERB (DST). She received the best teacher award from Lions Club in 2010 and 2012. She received the best paper award in many conferences. She received the women researcher award from Elsevier in 2020. She developed the Centre of Excellence Lab in IoT with industry collaboration and organized many international and national conferences including ICICN'16, ICRTCET'18, ICACT2020, ICETEMT 2022, FDPs, and Technical Talks. She is associated with ISTE, CSI, IEEE, IAENG, IDES, and IACSIT. She has reviewed papers in Springer journals, IGI global, IJCs, and CIIT journals. She acted as a TPC member in MIRA'14, IoT BDS'17, and IoTBDS'18 in Portugal. She chaired sessions in FCS'14, ICISC'13, ICCCT'15, ICCCT'17, and IoTBDS'18. She is local chapter Active SPOC for NPTEL, the college website coordinator, and NBA co-coordinator at college level. She is the program coordinator for CoE on Women Empowerment in collaboration with Honeywell Corporation and Capgemini. She has published four patents including one granted patent. She has authored two books and edited one book.

Susila Nagarajan is currently working as a professor and Head of the Department of Information Technology at Sri Krishna College of Engineering and Technology, Coimbatore, India. She has 21 years of experience and graduated from Periyar Maniammai College of Technology for Women, Bharathidasan University in 2001 with a bachelor's degree in computer science. She completed her master's degree in computer science and engineering from Sathyabama Institute of Science and Technology in 2005 as a 9th Rank Holder.

She completed her PhD in the field of information and communication engineering in the area of cloud computing in 2017. She has published various papers in international journals and conferences. She has submitted various project proposals under various schemes of DST STI Hub, FITST, SATYAM, SERB, AQIS (AICTE), WOS, WTP, and TIDE. She has published over 30 papers in referred national and international journals and conferences and published 5 patents. She is an Innovation Ambassador of the Institution Innovation Council, Ministry of Education, and a NITTTR mentor. She has received various awards including National Cloud Champion Coordinator by AWS Educate, National Winner Coordinator, Learnathon, Best Coordinator, and Skill Edge Technological Foundation Courses. She has authored various books and books chapters with Elsevier, CRC Press, IET, IGI Global, and others. She has received grants from various funding agencies like AICTE, ICMR, and DXC Technologies for organizing national and international level conferences, workshops, and women empowerment program. She has mentored a project titled "INTELLBOT" for the 2000–2004 batch students, which won the FIRST PRIZE in Indian National Academy of Engineering (INAE), Delhi. She has mentored a project titled "Voice Based Automated Wheelchair for Handicapped" for the 2009 batch students, which was awarded a grant from the Tamil Nadu State Council for Science and Technology. She has received "Best Faculty Award" for the year 2015 at Sri Krishna College of Engineering and Technology. She has organized various workshops, faculty development programs, and national level conference: NCCCIS, NCRAC in association with IEEE, AICTE, ICMR, etc. She has organized the first edition of TEDX SKCET in the Institution. As the college level ICT academy coordinator, she has organized various Power seminars, FDP's, Learnathon contests, and initiated different Center of Excellence in association with Dell EMC, VMware, Zoho, RHA, etc. She has mentored the team AGCoderz who got the First Prize in the Zoho Appathon Contest. She is a reviewer for several international journals including *Expert Systems*, Wiley. She served as Academic Jury Member for Youth Talk – ICT Academy and Session Chair for various national and international conferences. She has obtained various universal certifications from different forums like Nasscom Future Skills, Coding Ninjas, Edx, and Coursera.

Vijanth S. Asirvadam is an associate professor in the Department of Electrical and Electronics Engineering at the Universiti Teknologi PETRONAS (UTP), Malaysia. He was previously a system engineer in the industry. His research interests include computing techniques in signal, image and video processing, linear and nonlinear system identification, unconstraint optimization, and model validation. He is a member of IEEE and IET. He has published over 200 articles in proceedings and journals in the fields of computing and control. He holds a PhD degree on the topic of "Online and Constructive Neural Learning methods" from Queen's University Belfast, UK.

Preface

Explainable artificial intelligence (XAI) is a set of promising algorithms and approaches that empower users to comprehend why and how AI models reach a particular decision. These AI models must be penetrative, pervasive and persuasive, trustworthy, and transparent. XAI plays a significant role in ensuring a heightened confidence in the recommendations made by AI systems.

A growing number of AI models are being built and transitioned into microservices, which are front ended with flexible application programming interfaces (APIs). They are increasingly used to automate several essential activities (personal, social, and professional). They are being exposed as a service to be publicly discoverable, network-accessible, accessed, assessed, and leveraged by a bevy of service clients running across a variety of input and output devices. They provide scores of next-generation services including prediction, recommendation, detection, recognition, translation, summarization, and classification. Besides empowering software products and services to exhibit intelligent behaviors, AI is also becoming essential in IT infrastructure modules, platform software, middleware solutions, database systems, electronic devices, machineries in manufacturing floors, medical instruments, defense equipment, wares, and merchandizes to be cognitive in their operations, outputs, and offerings.

But there are several possibilities for an AI decision to go irreparably wrong. Mitigation strategies include a proper feature selection; a careful choice of the AI algorithm to train and create an AI model, the detailed monitoring and observation of the AI models to check for drift or degradation; the choice of parameter and hyperparameter values; and a variety of investigations to understand whether there are any problems with the input data.

XAI is the way forward to explain how AI models perform data processing and reach a decision by bringing interpretability and explainability. It is predominantly used to describe an AI model and its inner functioning so that users can better understand if there are any deviations and deficiencies in the model's decision-making process thereby ensuring accuracy, fairness, and positive outcomes. With XAI in place, there is also an increased awareness for AI engineers and data scientists to adopt a more responsible approach to AI development.

With a series of distinct advancements in the AI paradigm, we now have access to complex AI models. Deep neural networks (DNNs) employ multiple hidden layers between their input and output layers for tackling complicated requirements such as face recognition, object detection, and speech recognition. Deep learning (DL) algorithms are increasingly important for example in healthcare for cancer diagnosis and medication to better understand the implications of a DL algorithm's diagnosis. With an increased number of hidden layers, the visibility and controllability of the inner processing of the models become more complex. Understanding and explaining how such black-box models work and contribute are a difficult proposition.

AI systems are becoming more sophisticated as they continuously learn by ingesting data to deliver correct predictions. Businesses increasingly rely on competent AI systems to make decisions that can significantly affect individual rights, human safety, and critical business operations. XAI is therefore critical for global enterprises and governments to deliver trustworthy and transparent services to their citizens, constituents, and consumers. In this book, we present the noteworthy contributions of AI algorithms, models, and systems across several industry verticals. We describe prominent and dominant AI challenges and explain the concept of XAI and why it is now getting a lot of attention including XAI algorithms, tools, libraries, frameworks, and platforms.

The Book Editors: Dr Pethuru Raj, Dr Utku Köse, Dr Usha Sakthivel, Dr Susila Nagarajan, and Dr Vijanth Sagayan Asirvadam

## Chapter 1

An overview of past and present progressions in XAI

Shweta Shankar Shete[1], M.S. Rachana[2], A.P. Jyothi[3] and S. Usha[4]

Deep learning [1] has gained a huge commitment to the new headway in man-made brainpower. In contrast with conventional artificial intelligence (AI) techniques, for example, choice trees and backing vector machines, profound learning strategies have accomplished considerable improvement in different forecast assignments. Notwithstanding, deep neural networks (DNNs) are similarly powerless in clarifying their derivation cycles and eventual outcomes. In some certifiable applications, for example, business choice, process advancement, clinical determination, and venture suggestion, reasonableness and straightforwardness of our AI frameworks become especially fundamental for their clients, for individuals who are impacted by AI choices, and besides, for the scientists and designers who make the AI arrangements. This chapter gives an insight into explainable AI, the new and trending current technology used for diverse modern-day applications.

1.1 Introduction

(A) Explainable AI (XAI) is man-made consciousness that is modified to portray its motivation, reasoning, and dynamic cycle in a way that can be perceived by the normal individual. XAI is in many cases examined according to profound learning and assumes a significant part in the FAT ML model (reasonableness, responsibility, and straightforwardness in AI).

XAI gives general data about how an AI program settles on a choice by uncovering:

1. The program's assets and shortcomings.
2. The particular standards the program uses to show up at a choice.
3. Why a program goes with a specific choice rather than options.

[1]Symbotic LLC, Wilmington, MA, USA
[2]Department of CSE, RVITM, Bengaluru, India
[3]Department of CSE, RUAS, Bengaluru, India
[4]Department of CSE, RRCE, Bengaluru, India

4. The degree of trust that is proper for different sorts of choices.
5. What kinds of blunders the program is inclined to.
6. How blunders can be amended.

A significant objective of XAI is to give algorithmic responsibility. Up to this point, AI frameworks have basically been secret elements. Regardless of whether the data sources and results are known, the calculations used to show up at a choice are much of the time restrictive or not handily perceived, notwithstanding when the internal operations of the writing computer programs are open source and made uninhibitedly accessible.

(B)   Explainable man-made brainpower (XAI) is a bunch of cycles and strategies that permit human clients to understand and believe the outcomes and results made by AI calculations. Reasonable AI is utilized to portray an AI model, its normal effect and likely inclinations. It portrays model [2] precision, reasonableness, straightforwardness, and results in AI-fueled navigation. Logical AI is significant for an association in incorporating trust [3] and certainty while putting AI models into creation. AI reasonableness additionally assists an association with taking on a capable way to deal with AI advancement [4].

As AI turns out to be further developed, people are tested to grasp and backtrack how the calculation came to an outcome. The entire estimation process is transformed into what is ordinarily alluded to as a "black box" that is difficult to decipher. These black-box models are made straightforwardly from the information. Also, not even the specialists or information researchers who make the calculation can comprehend or make sense of what precisely is occurring inside them or how the AI calculation showed up at a particular outcome.

There are many benefits to understanding how an AI-empowered framework has prompted a particular result. Reasonableness can assist engineers with guaranteeing that the framework is filling in true to form, it very well may be important to satisfy administrative guidelines, or it very well may be significant in permitting those impacted by a choice to challenge or change that result. Research interest of XAI over time is shown in Figure 1.1.

A definitive logical objective of AI is to develop a proper model of the mind that completely makes sense of the movement of "reasoning" as it is performed by people. The procedure of AI research directs that such a model must be approved assuming that it is made functional. Hence, AI is midway worried about building functional frameworks that show ways of behaving that outline the frameworks' capacity to "think". According to a functional viewpoint, robotized thinking frameworks vow to be very helpful, e.g., as advisors to human specialists, as independent substances that persistently screen and control complex modern cycles, as a situation that thoroughly investigates the potential outcomes in a planned space, as robots that insightfully investigates actual conditions that are excessively unforgiving for sensible investigation by people, and so forth. In view of this impression of utility, the logical undertaking of AI has produced a designing discipline whose essential objective is to construct helpful frameworks that consolidate the procedures for executing shrewd normal ways of behaving that have

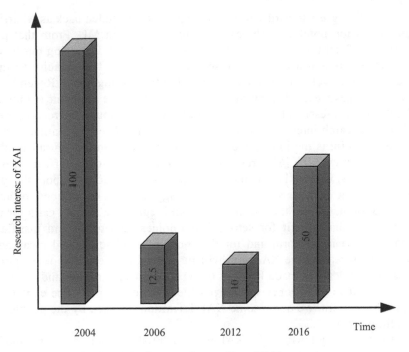

Figure 1.1   Research interest of XAI over time

risen up out of AI research. Now, AI has created methods that render the most crude of such frameworks practical. People display clever ways of behaving in plenty of exercises. To seek the objective of computerizing astute thinking, AI specialists have investigated a significant number of these various exercises and endeavored to assemble frameworks that effectively execute the exercises. This has led to a subdivision within the field of AI that is dedicated to exploring the "types of reasoning" that underlie distinct forms of human intelligence and behavior. According to the designing point of view, each unique sort of insightful movement can be utilized as the reason for various helpful applications that require particular execution strategies. A portion of the significant canny exercises that AI has investigated, and is proceeding to investigate, are summed up below [5].

1.2   Background study

Getting XAI: A contextual definition XAI is an examination field that expects to make AI frameworks' results more reasonable to people. The term was first begat in 2004 by Van Lent *et al.* to portray the capacity of their framework to make sense of the way of behaving of AI-controlled elements in reproduction games' application. While the term is generally new, the issue of logic has existed since the mid-1970s when analysts read up on clarification for master frameworks. In any case, the speed of progress toward settling such an issue has dialed back as AI arrived at an expression point with the astounding advances in ML. From that point forward, the focal point of AI research has moved toward carrying out models and calculations that accentuate prescient power while the capacity to make sense of choice cycles has taken a rearward sitting arrangement. Recently, the topic of XAI has regained renewed attention from both the academic community and industry professionals. Figure 1.1 outlines the astounding resurgence of XAI term research interest utilizing Google patterns. The reappearance of this exploration point is the immediate aftereffect of the relentless entrance of AI/machine learning (ML) [6] across businesses and its essential effect on basic dynamic cycles, without having the option to give itemized data about the chain of thinking that prompts specific choices, suggestions, expectations, or activities made by it. Hence, the social, moral, and legitimate tension calls for new AI strategies that are fit for settling on choices reasonable and justifiable. Actually, there is no norm and for the most part acknowledged meaning of logical AI. In reality, the XAI term will in general allude to the development, drives, and endeavors made because of AI straightforwardness and trust concerns, more than to a proper specialized idea. Hence, to put some explanation around this pattern, we quote some XAI definitions as seen by the people who are calling for it.

As indicated by DARPA [7], XAI plans to "produce more reasonable models, while keeping an elevated degree of learning execution (expectation precision); and empower human clients to comprehend, fittingly, trust, and successfully deal with the arising age of misleadingly clever accomplices". The objective of empowering logic in ML, as expressed by FAT* [1], "is to guarantee that algorithmic choices as well as any information driving those choices can be cleared up for end users and different partners in non-specialized terms" [8,9].

Interpretability and reasonableness of ML calculations have consequently become major problems: who is responsible on the off chance that things turn out badly? Could we at any point make sense of why things turn out badly? Assuming things are functioning admirably, do we have at least some idea why and how to use them further? Many articles have proposed various measures and structures to catch interpretability, and the subject of reasonable man-made brainpower (XAI) has turned into an area of interest in ML research local area. Famous DL libraries have begun to incorporate their own XAI libraries, like Pytorch, Captum, and tensorflow. Its application can be found in the healthcare domain [10], IOT applications [11], data transmission [12], and energy efficiency in WSN [13].

Moreover, the implementation of interpretability evaluation criteria, including factors like reliability, causality, and usability, aids the machine learning community in tracking how algorithms are used and how their application can be enhanced, offering valuable guidance for future developments. Specifically, it has been exhibited that perception is equipped for assisting scientists with recognizing wrong thinking in ordering issues that numerous past specialists potentially have missed [14,15].

1.2.1   Key-related ideas of XAI

- Interpretable ML:
  An interpretable framework [16] is a framework where a client cannot see yet additional study and comprehend how sources of info are numerically planned to yield. This term is preferred over "reasonable" in the ML setting where it alludes to the ability to get the working rationale in ML calculations. Scientists frequently utilize the two terms "interpretability" and "reasonableness" interchangeably [17,18]. Despite the fact that there is an affirmation of the need for an unmistakable scientific categorization. Different creators utilize different terms, for example, understandability or conceivability to allude to a similar issue, while some industrials favor the term coherent AI [19].

- Black-box problem:
  In science, processing, and designing, the terms black box, dark box, and white box are utilized for various degrees of conclusion of the part's inner substance. Specifically, a black-box part uncovers nothing about its interior plan, design, and execution, though on the contrary, a white-box part is totally presented to its client. In the middle, there might exist various degrees of dim-box parts relying on how many subtleties are accessible. Monetarily, the "black-box" idea has been taken advantage of by mechanical ventures, generally in their endeavors to safeguard protected innovation and keep up with seriousness. In AI, the trouble for the framework to give a reasonable clarification on how it showed up at a response is alluded to as "the black-box issue" [8].

- Dependable AI:
  Dependable AI is an AI that considers cultural qualities and moral contemplations. Capable AI has three fundamental points of support: accountability, responsibility, and transparency. Together, these contemplations structure the ART standards for AI [20]: accountability alludes to the need to clear up and legitimize one's choices and activities for its accomplices, clients, and others with whom the framework cooperates. Obligation alludes to the job of individuals themselves and to the ability of AI frameworks to deal with one's choice and recognize blunders or unforeseen outcomes. Straightforwardness alludes to the need to depict, review, and recreate the components through which AI frameworks [21] simply decide and figure out how to adjust to its current circumstance, and to the administration of the information utilized made. Different drives center around a few extra contemplations like decency and morals in characterizing responsible AI [8]. Exact AI's precision is an exhibition metric that alludes to the number of right expectations made by the model (normally an ML model) over a wide range of forecasts made.

- Information science:
  AI models for the most part require getting a preparation and testing set of data. Information science is a field that brings together insights, information investigation, AI, and their connected strategies to comprehend and dissect real peculiarities with information [8].

Sociology explanation is, above all else, a type of social collaboration. The overall discipline of sociology is worried with society and the connections among people inside the general public. A few intriguing sociologies speculations incorporate causality, methodical mental predispositions, contrastive clarification, and argumentation [8].

1.3   Overview of XAI

Somewhat recently, AI has accomplished an eminent force that might convey the best of assumptions over numerous application areas across the field. For this to happen, the whole local area remains before the obstruction of reasonableness, an intrinsic issue of AI methods [22] brought by sub-imagery (e.g., troupes or deep neural networks) that was absent in the last promotion of AI. Standards fundamental to this issue fall inside the supposed XAI field, which is recognized as a critical element for the pragmatic sending of AI models. This outline inspects the current writing in the field of XAI, including a possibility toward what is yet to be reached. We sum up past endeavors to characterize reasonableness in ML, laying out an original definition that covers earlier applied suggestions with a significant spotlight on the crowd for which logic is looked for. We then propose and examine a scientific categorization of ongoing commitments connected with the logic of various ML models, including those focused on deep learning strategies for which a subsequent scientific categorization is fabricated. This writing examination fills in as the foundation for a progression of difficulties looked at by XAI, like the junction between information combination and logic. Our possibilities lead toward the idea of responsible AI, specifically, a strategy for the enormous scope execution of AI techniques in genuine associations with decency, model logic, and responsibility at its center. Our definitive objective is to furnish novices to XAI with a reference material to animate future exploration progresses, yet additionally to energize specialists and experts from different disciplines to embrace the advantages of AI in their action areas, with practically no earlier predisposition for its absence of interpretability [23,24].

Ongoing advancements in AI that are acquainting new ML procedures will take care of progressively muddled issues with higher prescient limits. Nonetheless, this prescient power accompanies a rising intricacy that can bring about troubles to decipher these models. Regardless of the way that these models produce exceptionally precise outcomes, there should be a clarification to comprehend and trust the model's choices. This is the place where XAI makes that big appearance.

There is a wide assortment of techniques utilized for XAI; however, since it is an extremely new field, there is definitely not a laid-out agreement based on the conditions and the scientific categorization yet. Subsequently, there can be alternate points of view on sorting these techniques. The following are three unique methodologies of categorization:

1. **Categorization in view of the strategy's pertinence to various models:**
    The main methodology depends on the strategy's materialness to various models. Whenever we are ready to apply the clarification technique to any

model after it is prepared, we can call it a model-freethinker. As models acquire prescient power, they can lose their straight forwardness; consequently, applying the technique after the preparation cycle forestalls forfeiting the prescient power for interpretability. This should be visible as a benefit when contrasted with model-explicit strategies that are restricted to just a single explicit model, nonetheless, it implies that one is generally worse than the other. Model-explicit methodologies are likewise called inherent techniques since they approach the internals of a model, for example, the loads in a straight relapse model.

2. **Categorization in view of the extent of the clarification:**
    One more methodology is categorization in view of the extent of the clarification. Clarification may be required at the occurrence level or the model level. Neighborhood interpretability expects to make sense of the choices a model makes about an occasion. Then again, worldwide clarifications mean to address the subject of what the boundaries of a model mean for its choices. Accordingly, when the model has numerous boundaries, worldwide reasonableness can be hard to accomplish.

3. **Categorization in view of the stage that we apply the logic strategies:**
    The third methodology is categorization in view of the stage that we apply the reasonableness strategies. These stages are pre-demonstrating, in-displaying. and post-displaying (post-hoc). The point of pre-displaying logic is more toward investigating and understanding the dataset. For in-demonstrating, it is to foster models that are self-making sense of or completely discernible. The greater part of the logical exploration connected with XAI centers around the post-hoc techniques which intend to make sense of mind-boggling models after the preparation interaction. Since model-skeptic techniques are likewise applied in the wake of preparing the model, they are post-hoc strategies by their temperament also.

The assemblage of XAI writing is not just immense yet additionally developing at a high speed with the terms, make sense of, decipher, and see frequently utilized reciprocally. To address the absence of straightforwardness in ML and the subsequent requirement for additional confirmation (see Section 1.1), the XAI research region, with a staggering spotlight on ML interpretability, looks to make AI frameworks more human-understandable, along these lines empowering trust-working as well as consistency. The assignment of making ML frameworks straightforward is intrinsically troublesome inferable from the high intricacy of the information and calculations included. As a matter of fact, figuring out a solitary through the meaning of substantial framework human clarifications stays tested. To effectively increment client trust in AI, the avocation should match the space as well as the intricacy or understandability of the client. This has driven specialists to address this test according to alternate points of view, coming about in assorted XAI approaches and ensuing clarification types. A few endeavors to give a scientific categorization to XAI techniques have previously been made. In light of these arrangements, the most unmistakable properties of XAI strategies are summed up in Table 1.1.

Table 1.1   *Important properties of XAI approaches*

S. no.	Properties
1	Interpretability
2	Scope
3	Mode
4	Supported data types
5	Mechanism

Since there is no XAI approach that works for all clients, relying upon explicit use-case prerequisites, these properties can direct the determination of the most suitable methodologies. Most of the XAI research has taken an algorithmic concentration. While some ML techniques, like direct relapse, are inherently straightforward, most XAI strategies give interpretability post-hoc for example as an assistant part [25]. The techniques may likewise vary in scope—the model might be made sense of (worldwide) or a particular forecast (nearby) or both. The cutting-edge clarification instruments can be comprehensively ordered to highlight attribution strategies, proxy models, counterfactuals, delegate instances of classes (models), case-based clarifications, causal components (e.g., rules), literary or just visual. These portrayals are, in any case, not liberated from cross-over—models, counter models, or element attributions, for example, might be introduced in a visual way. A large portion of these XAI strategies predominantly take care of explicit information types like pictures, and hence when applied to time-series information, do not completely work with expanded human comprehension. For example, notwithstanding LIME being a famous model-freethinker XAI method, it was displayed to yield terribly showing on time-series information, probably attributable to the high dimensionality of the information and its utilization of a direct classifier. The deficiencies of these XAI techniques for fleeting information make them intrinsically challenging to apply to most utilizing cases emerging in the process industry [26,27].

1.4   History of XAI

During the 1970s–1990s, emblematic thinking frameworks, like MYCIN [28], GUIDON [29], SOPHIE, and PROTOS, were investigated that could address, reason about, and make sense of their thinking for symptomatic, informative, or AI (clarification based learning) purposes. MYCIN, created in the mid-1970s as an exploration model for diagnosing bacteremia contaminations of the circulatory system, could make sense of which of its hand-coded rules added to a determination in a particular case. Research in astute coaching frameworks created frameworks, for example, SOPHIE, that could go about as an "eloquent master," making sense of critical thinking procedures at a level the understudy could comprehend, so they would realize what move to make straightaway. For example, SOPHIE could make sense of the subjective thinking behind its gadgets investigating, despite the fact that it at last depended on the SPICE circuit test system. Essentially, GUIDON added instructional exercise rules to enhance MYCIN's area level standards so it could make sense of procedure for clinical findings. Emblematic ways to deal with AI, particularly those depending on clarification-based learning, like PROTOS, unequivocally depended on portrayals of clarifications, both to make sense of their activities and to gain new information.

During the 1980s through mid-1990s, truth upkeep frameworks (TMS) were created to expand the abilities of causal-thinking, rule-based, and rationale-based induction frameworks. A TMS acts to expressly follow substitute ways of thinking, legitimizations for ends, and thought processes that lead to logical inconsistencies, permitting future thinking to stay away from these impasses. To give clarification, they follow thinking from ends to suppositions through rule tasks or legitimate inductions, permitting clarifications to be created from the thinking that follows. For instance, take a rule-based problem solver with only a few choices concerning Socrates, which leads to the conclusion that he has succumbed to poison.

Simply by following through the reliance structure, the issue solver can develop the accompanying clarification: "Socrates kicked the bucket since he was mortal and drank toxin, and all humans bite the dust when they drink poison. Socrates was mortal since he was a man and all men are mortal. Socrates drank poison since he held dissenter convictions, the public authority was moderate, and those holding moderate protester convictions under moderate states should drink poison".

By the 1990s, scientists likewise started concentrating on whether it was feasible to definitively extricate the non-hand-coded rules being produced by hazy prepared brain organizations. Specialists in network-powered decision support systems for clinicians have strived to develop robust explanations that enhance the trustworthiness and reliability of these advancements in practice. During the 2010s, public worry about racial and other inclinations in the utilization of AI for criminal condemning choices and discoveries of financial soundness might have prompted expanded interest in straightforward counterfeit intelligence. As an outcome, numerous scholastics and associations are creating instruments to assist with distinguishing predisposition in their frameworks.

Marvin Minsky *et al.* raised the issue that AI can work as a type of reconnaissance, with the inclinations inborn in observation, proposing humanistic intelligence (HI) as a method for making an all the more fair and adjusted "human-tuned in" AI.

Current complex AI strategies, for example, profound learning and hereditary calculations are normally opaque. To tackle this challenge, various new techniques have emerged to enhance the transparency and interpretability of current complex AI strategies, such as deep learning and genetic algorithms. These methods include approaches like layer-wise significance propagation (LRP), which helps identify the input features that contribute most significantly to the outcome of a neural network. Different strategies have been created to make sense of one specific expectation made by a (nonlinear) black-box model, an objective alluded to as "neighborhood interpretability". It is significant that the simple rendering of the ideas of nearby interpretability in a far-off setting (where the black-box model is executed by an outsider) is presently under a magnifying glass.

Moreover, there has been work on making glass-box models that are more straightforward to review. This incorporates choice trees [30], Bayesian organizations, scanty direct models, and more. In 2018, an interdisciplinary meeting called FAT* (Fairness, Accountability, and Transparency) was laid out to concentrate on straightforwardness and logic with regard to socio-specialized frameworks, a large number of which incorporate man-made brainpower.

A few procedures permit representations of the information sources that individual neurons answer most unequivocally. A few gatherings have observed that neurons can be amassed into circuits that fill human-understandable roles, some of which dependably emerge across various organizations prepared freely.

At a more significant level, different methods exist to extricate compacted portrayals of the elements of given inputs, which can then be investigated by standard grouping strategies. On the other hand, organizations can be prepared to yield semantic clarifications of their way of behaving, which are then straightforwardly human-interpretable. The conducted model can likewise be made sense with regard to preparing information for instance, by assessing which preparing inputs affected a given way of behaving the most.

1.5   Top AI patterns

The focal point of AI reception is confined to working on the proficiency of tasks or the adequacy of activities. It tends to be utilized to further develop the partner insight too. Allow us to investigate the top patterns expected in 2021.

1. **More noteworthy cloud and AI joint effort**
   Rico Burnett, the overseer of client advancement at lawful administrations supplier Exigent, says that AI will assume a critical part in the expansive reception of Cloud Solutions in 2021. Through the sending of man-made consciousness, it will be feasible to screen and oversee cloud assets and the immense measure of accessible information.

2. **Simulated intelligence answers for IT**
   The quantity of AI arrangements that are being produced for IT will increment in 2021. Capgemini's Simion predicts that AI arrangements that can recognize normal IT issues all alone and self-right any little glitches or issues will see an expansion in the impending years. This will diminish personal time and permit the groups in an association to chip away at high-intricacy tasks and concentrate somewhere else.

3. **AIOps turns out to be more famous**
   In the course of the most recent couple of years, the intricacy of IT frameworks has expanded. Forrester as of late said that merchants would need stage arrangements that consolidate more than one checking discipline like application, framework, and systems administration. IT activities and different groups can work on their key cycles, navigation, and undertakings with

AIOps arrangements and further developed investigation of the volumes of information coming in its direction. Forrester encouraged the IT chiefs to find AIOps suppliers who will engage the get group joint effort through start to finish advanced encounters, information relationship, and incorporation of the IT activities into the executives' toolchain.

4. **Man-made intelligence will help in organizing information**

   Later on, we will see that more unstructured information is organized with normal language handling and AI processes. Associations will use these advancements and make information so that RPA or mechanical cycle robotization innovation can involve when they need to computerize value-based action in an association. RPA is one of the quickest developing regions in the product business. The main constraint that it faces is that it can utilize organized information. With the assistance of AI, unstructured information can without much of a stretch be changed over into organized information, which can give a characterized yield.

5. **Man-made reasoning ability will stay tight**

   The stock of ability is supposed to be an issue in taking on man-made consciousness in 2021. There has been a diligent hole in AI ability, and associations have at long last understood this potential. It is fundamental to address this hole and guarantee that a more extensive gathering learns computerized reasoning. Guaranteeing that a more extensive arrangement of clients approach man-made brainpower to zero in on innovation, learning systems, and supporting an adjustment of the fundamental in 2021 to the workplace.

6. **Enormous scope reception of AI in the IT business**

   We have seen ceaseless development in the reception of AI inside the IT business. Notwithstanding, Simion predicts that associations will involve AI underway and begin utilizing them at an enormous scope. With the assistance of man-made reasoning, an association can get ROI continuously. This implies that associations will see their endeavors being paid off.

7. **Man-made intelligence ethics is the concentration**

   Natalie Cartwright, prime supporter and COO of Finn AI, an AI banking stage, predicts that in 2021, associations will convey mastery of the most proficient method to use man-made consciousness against major worldwide issues, invigorate development and monetary development, and guarantee incorporation and variety. As AI morals become more vital to associations, straightforwardness of information and calculation reasonableness are two of the issues that are at the center of attention.

8. **Expanded processes become progressively famous**

   Man-made consciousness and information science will end up being a piece of a greater picture with regard to advancement and robotization in 2021. Information environments are adaptable, lean, and furthermore give information on schedule to heterogeneous sources. Notwithstanding, it is important to give an establishment to adjust and encourage development. As indicated by Ana Maloberti, a major information engineer at Globant, organizations will go above and beyond in improving their increased business and improvement processes. Utilizing AI, programming advancement cycles can be upgraded, and we can search for a more extensive aggregate knowledge and further develop joint effort. We should encourage an information-driven culture and outgrow the trial stages to move into a feasible conveyance model.

9. **Computerized reasoning will turn out to be more logical**
   The ranking executive of an item at the client information center point, Tealium and Dave Lucas, expresses that there will be a greater spotlight on reasonableness. As more information guidelines become possibly the most important factor, the confidence in AI will be essential. To plainly comprehend and explain how every trademark will add to the end forecast or the aftereffect of the AI model.

10. **Voice and language-driven knowledge**
    Especially in client care focus, the expansion in remote working has driven an incredible chance to take on NLP or ASR (mechanized discourse acknowledgment) capacities. Under 5% of all client contacts are regularly checked for quality input by ISG's Butterfield. Because of the absence of one-on-one instruction, associations can utilize man-made consciousness to finish routine quality, keep an eye on client understanding, and can aim to guarantee consistency.

11. **Man-made intelligence for security and surveillance**
    Man-made intelligence strategies have proactively been applied to confront acknowledgment, voice recognizable proof, and video investigation. These strategies structure the best combo for reconnaissance and biometric validation. Along these lines, in 2022, we can anticipate the escalated abuse of AI in video observation.

    Man-made reasoning is gainful for an adaptable arrangement of safety frameworks. Beforehand, engineers invested a ton of energy designing the framework since it was enacted when a particular number of pixels on a screen changed. Along these lines, there were such a large number of deceptions. These alerts were brought about by falling leaves or a running creature. On account of AI, the security framework recognizes objects, which adds to a more adaptable arrangement.

    Simulated intelligence in video reconnaissance can identify dubious actions by zeroing in on strange ways of behaving, not faces. This capacity empowers making safer spaces, both public and private, through recognizing possible dangers. Such AI-driven video arrangements could be likewise valuable for operations, retail, and assembling.

    Another specialty that gives promising points of view to the AI application is voice acknowledgment. Advancements connected with voice acknowledgment can decide the character. By character, we mean the age of an individual, orientation, and enthusiastic state. The standards on what voice acknowledgment for observation is based can be equivalent to on account of Alexa or Google Assistant. An element that is appropriate for security and reconnaissance is an inherent enemy of the mocking model that identifies combined and recorded voices. One of the most urgent innovations for security is biometric face acknowledgment. Different noxious applications attempt to deceive security frameworks by giving phony photographs rather than genuine pictures. To guard against such cases, different enemies of parodying methods are being created and utilized at a large scale.

12. **AI progressively video handling**

The test for handling constant video transfers is dealing with information pipelines. Engineers mean to guarantee precision and limit the inactivity of video handling. Furthermore, AI arrangements can assist with accomplishing this objective.

To execute an AI-based approach in live video handling, we want a pre-prepared brain network model, a cloud foundation, and a product layer for applying client situations. Handling speed is significant for constant streaming, so this multitude of parts ought to be firmly coordinated. For quicker handling, we can parallelize processes or further develop calculations. Process parallelization is accomplished through document parting or utilizing a pipeline approach. This pipeline engineering is the most ideal decision since it does not diminish a model's exactness and takes into account the utilization of an AI calculation to handle video continuously with practically no intricacies. Likewise, for pipeline design, it is feasible to apply unexpected impacts inferring face location and obscuring. You can observe more data regarding the matter in our article devoted to AI continuously video handling.

Current ongoing stream handling is inseparably connected to the utilization of foundation expulsion and obscure. The interest in these instruments has expanded in view of COVID-19 commitment to the rise and advancement of recent fads in video conferencing. What's more, these patterns will be effectively evolved in light of the fact that, as indicated by Globe Newswire, the worldwide video conferencing market is supposed to develop from USD 9.2 billion in 2021 to USD 22.5 billion by 2026.

There are various ways of creating devices for foundation evacuation and obscure in a constant video. The test is to plan a model fit for isolating an individual from the edge of the foundation. The brain network that can complete such an assignment could be found on existing models like BodyPix, MediaPipe, or PixelLib. Whenever the model is picked, the test stays for its combination with a proper structure and coordinating the ideal execution process through the use of Web Assembly, WebGL, or WebGPU. Creating obscure or foundation expulsion apparatuses is depicted in our examination.

1.6 Conclusion

XAI has diffused into numerous regions of our private and expert life. It henceforth impacts how we live and function. In addition, it is progressively utilized in basic circumstances with possibly serious ramifications for individual people, organizations, and the general public overall. In outcome, new moral inquiries emerge that challenge important tradeoffs between an open improvement of AI-put together advancements and guidelines. Right now, seeing one more raise of consideration for AI, we accordingly require a logic research in data frameworks using XAI. In rundown, it tends to be reasoned that XAI is a focal issue for data frameworks research, which opens up a huge number of intriguing yet additionally provoking inquiries to examine.

References

[1] B. Zhou, D. Bau, A. Oliva, and A. Torralba, Interpreting deep visual representations via network dissection. *IEEE Trans. Pattern Anal. Mach. Intell.*, vol. 41, no. 9, pp. 2131–2145, 2019.

[2] Z. C. Lipton, The Mythos of model interpretability. *CoRR*, vol. abs/1606.03490, pp. 1–8, 2016. http://arxiv.org/abs/1606.03490.

[3] M. T. Dzindolet, S. A. Peterson, R. A. Pomranky, L. G. Pierce, and H. P. Beck, The role of trust in automation reliance. *Int. J. Hum.–Comput. Stud.*, vol. 58, no. 6, pp. 697–718, 2003.

[4] Ethics Guidelines for Trustworthy AI, Nov. 2019. https://ec.europa.eu/digital-single-market/en/news/ethics-guidelinestrustworthy-ai.

[5] V. Bellotti and K. Edwards, Intelligibility and accountability: human considerations in context-aware systems. *Hum. Comput. Interact.*, vol. 16, pp. 193–212, 2009.

[6] T. Kulesza, M. Burnett, W. Wong, and S. Stumpf, Principles of explanatory debugging to personalize interactive machine learning. In *Proceedings of the 20th International Conference on Intelligent User Interfaces* (ACM, 2015), pp. 126–137.

[7] D. Gunning, Explainable artificial intelligence (XAI), DARPA/I2O; www.cc.gatech.edu/~alanwags/DLAI2016/(Gunning)%20IJCAI-16%20DLAI%20WS.pdf.

[8] H. H. Clark and S. E. Brennan, Grounding in communication. In *Perspectives on Socially Shared Cognition*, L. B. Resnick, J. M. Levine, and S. D. Teasley (eds.). (American Psychological Association, 1991), pp. 127–149.

[9] F. K. Dosilovic, M. Brcic, and N. Hlupic, Explainable artificial intelligence: a survey. In *Proceedings of the 41st International Convention on Information and Communication Technology, Electronics and Microelectronics (MIPRO)*, May 2018, pp. 210–215.

[10] A. P. Jyothi, C. Megashree, S. Radhika, and N. Shoba, Detection of cervical cancer and classification using texture analysis. *J. Contemp. Issues Bus. Govern.*, vol, 27, no. 3, 2021.

[11] U. Sakthivel, A. P. Jyothi, N. Susila, and T. Sheela, Conspectus of k-means clustering algorithm. In *Applied Learning Algorithms for Intelligent IoT* (Auerbach Publications, 2021), pp. 193–213.

[12] A. P. Jyothi and U. Saktivel, Technique to Balance Energy Efficient Clustering with Data Transmission in Large Scale Sensor Network.

International Journal of Advanced Networking & Applications (1st International Conference on Innovations in Computing & Networking (ICICN16), CSE, RRCE), pp. 107–113, 2016.

[13]   A. P. Jyothi and U. Sakthivel, Trends and technologies used for mitigating energy efficiency issues in wireless sensor network. *Int. J. Comput. Appl.*, vol. 111, no. 3, pp. 32–40, 2015.

[14]   O. Biran and C. Cotton, Explanation and justification in machine learning: a survey. Paper presented at the IJCAI-17 Workshop on Explainable AI (XAI), Melbourne, Australia, 20 August 2017.

[15]   A. Vellido, The importance of interpretability and visualization in machine learning for applications in medicine and health care. *Neural Comput. Appl., early access*, Feb. 1, 2019, doi:10.1007/s00521-019-04051-w.

[16]   T. Miller, Explanation in artificial intelligence: insights from the social sciences. *Artif. Intell.*, vol. 267, pp. 1–38, 2018.

[17]   F. Doshi-Velez and B. Kim, Towards a rigorous science of interpretable machine learning, 2017, arXiv:1702.08608. http://arxiv.org/abs/1702.08608.

[18]   S. Tonekaboni, S. Joshi, M. D. McCradden, and A. Goldenberg, What clinicians want: contextualizing explainable machine learning for clinical end use. *CoRR*, vol. abs/1905.05134, pp.1–12, 2019. http://arxiv.org/abs/1905.05134.

[19]   C. Olah, A. Satyanarayan, I. Johnson, *et al.*, The building blocks of interpretability. Tech. Rep., Jan. 2020. https://distill.pub/2018/building-blocks/.

[20]   S. R. Soekadar, N. Birbaumer, M. W. Slutzky, and L. G. Cohen, Brain–machine interfaces in neurorehabilitation of stroke. *Neurobiol. Disease*, vol. 83, pp. 172–179, 2015.

[21]   O. Çiçek, A. Abdulkadir, S. S. Lienkamp, T. Brox, and O. Ronneberger, 3D U-Net: learning dense volumetric segmentation from sparse annotation. *CoRR*, vol. abs/1606.06650, pp. 6–7, 2016. http://arxiv.org/abs/1606.06650.

[22]   G. Montavon, W. Samek, and K.-R. Müller, Methods for interpreting and understanding deep neural networks. *Digit. Signal Process.*, vol. 73, pp. 1–15, 2018.

[23]   W. Samek, T. Wiegand, and K. Müller, Explainable artificial intelligence: understanding, visualizing and interpreting deep learning models. *CoRR*, vol. abs/1708.08296, pp. 1–6, 2017. http://arxiv.org/abs/1708.08296.

[24]   S. M. Lundberg and S.-I. Lee, A unified approach to interpreting model predictions. In *Advances in Neural Information Processing Systems 30*, I. Guyon, *et al.* (eds.), (Red Hook, NY: Curran Associates, 2017), pp. 4765–4774.

[25]   L. H. Gilpin, D. Bau, B. Z. Yuan, A. Bajwa, M. Specter, and L. Kagal, Explaining explanations: An overview of interpretability of machine learning. In *Proceedings of the IEEE 5th International Conference on Data Science and Advanced Analytics (DSAA)*, Oct. 2018, pp. 80–89.

[26]   D. Wang, Q. Yang, A. Abdul, and B. Y. Lim, Designing theory-driven user-centric explainable AI. In *Proceedings of the 2019 CHI Conference on Human Factors in Computing Systems* (ACM, 2019), Paper no. 601.

[27] A. B. Arrieta, N. Díaz-Rodríguez, J. D. Ser, *et al.*, Explainable artificial intelligence (XAI): concepts, taxonomies, opportunities and challenges toward responsible AI. *Inf. Fusion*, vol. 58, pp. 82–115, 2020.

[28] S. Lapuschkin, S. Wäldchen, A. Binder, G. Montavon, W. Samek, and K.-R. Müller, Unmasking Clever Hans predictors and assessing what machines really learn. *Nature Commun.*, vol. 10, no. 1, p. 1096, 2019.

[29] M. T. Ribeiro, S. Singh, and C. Guestrin, 'Why should I trust you?': Explaining the predictions of any classifier. In *Proceedings of the 22nd ACM SIGKDD International Conference on Knowledge Discovery and Data Mining*, New York, NY: Association Computing Machinery, Aug. 2016, pp. 1135–1144.

[30] R. R. Selvaraju, A. Das, R. Vedantam, M. Cogswell, D. Parikh, and D. Batra, Grad-CAM: Why did you say that? Visual explanations from deep networks via gradient-based localization. *CoRR*, vol. abs/1610.02391, pp. 1–21, 2016. http://arxiv.org/abs/1610.02391

Chapter 2

Demystifying explainable artificial intelligence (EAI)

B. Narendra Kumar Rao[1] and Sailaja[1]

Today, artificial intelligence (AI) permeates nearly every aspect of our personal and professional life. It is the most extensive information base and common-sense reasoning system. When examining a dataset, the era of automated decision-making, such as profiling, necessitates the correct knowledge and skills. Modern systems frequently suffer from a lack of transparency [1] and interpretability. Due to these problems, explainable AI (EAI) has become a hot topic in academia. The term "explainable AI" (EAI), also known as "interpretable AI," is a term used to describe machine learning and deep learning methods that can justify decisions that people can understand. In this work, we demonstrate how our EAI technique can be used to analyze the model's real-time decisions [2,3], identify trends in the model's overall behavior, and aid in the identification of potential flaws [4] in the model's evolution. Furthermore, in order to ensure that the explanations are reliable and useful, we objectively test their consistency across a wide range of EAI metrics [5,6]. EAI strives to demystify the reasoning that underlies an algorithm's output.

2.1 Introduction

2.1.1 An overview of artificial intelligence

Artificial intelligence (AI) has exhibited signs that were previously difficult to resolve. However, over the last 10 years, there has been significant and ongoing progress, which has led to an increase in the use of its methods [such as machine learning (ML) algorithms] for tackling a variety of problems, as well as an increase in model complexity and the use of opaque black-box AI models. As a result, it is critical to consider arrangements that can contribute to tending to such a test, which could help grow the use of computer-based intelligence frameworks [2,4] in basic and delicate spaces (e.g., medical care and security areas) where different standards must be met other than high precision. It has become a fundamental component of

[1]School of Computing, Mohan Babu University, Tirupati, India

some genuine applications [5]. The accompanying variables are driving the multiplication of AI-based algorithmic dynamics across many disciplines:

1. The interest in handling a great many a lot of information.
2. High-performance computing resources exist (e.g., Cloud computing, GPU computing, etc.).
3. Algorithms that are powerful and novel.

In any case, the majority of useful man-made information-based models are "black box" in nature, making understanding how the model or calculation works and making decisions difficult.

Furthermore, human cognizance of situation choices impacts human interests, incredible opportunities, and lives. Thus, the choice is critical for high-stakes applications. For example, credit support in finance, automated machines in protected methodology, obstruction disclosure through network security, and so on system framework, interference disclosure through network assurance, and so on. New laws are being introduced by regulators, such as the European Union's General Data Protection Regulation (GDPR), also known as the "right to explanation", the US government's "Algorithmic Accountability Act of 2019" [1,5,7], or the US Department of Defense's Ethical Principles for Artificial Intelligence (DFP-AI) to use automated decision-making systems to address primarily fairness, accountability, and transparency risks.

2.1.2   Introduction to explainable AI

Explainable AI (EAI) has been proposed as a solution for moving toward more transparent AI and avoiding limiting AI adoption in critical domains. EAI aims to develop explainable techniques to assist end-users comprehend, trust, and manage a new era of AI systems. The need for explanations can be traced back to early expert systems and Bayesian network research. Deep learning, on the other hand, has transformed EAI into a thriving research field.

2.2   Concept of XAI

EAI encompasses AI (ML) or man-made intelligence frameworks/devices for demystifying dark model internals (e.g., what the models have realized) as well as making sense of individual expectations. In general, the reasonableness of a man-made intelligence model's expectation is the degree of adaptable subjective comprehension of the relationship among model data and forecast (i.e., specific/reasonable purposes of the event) in a beneficiary well-disposed way. The terms "reasonableness" and "interpretability" are used interchangeably throughout the text. As a result of a clever framework (i.e., an AI-based framework) [8], in terms of significance, fulfillment, and consistency of pre-word usage, it is clear that reasonableness is more than interpretability. As a result, we will use these terms wherever appropriate.

Due to the growing number of EAI approaches, it has become difficult to realize the pros, cons, and comparative advantages associated with the various

Figure 2.1   Explainable AI

domains [1]. The Explainable AI, tools and frameworks to deploy interpretable and inclusive machine learning model listed in Figure 2.1. Additionally, there are many differences between EAI methodologies, such as whether a methodology is ante-hoc (involved in pre-training), post-hoc (works on already trained item models), surrogate (deploys a simple model to emulate the prediction of the underlying model), or limited (explains prediction or decision of an instance). Despite numerous reviews on EAI methods [2,7], there is still a lack of comprehensive EAI technique when it emanates from these methods and perspectives. The image is a visual representation of EAI and how it may affect the end-user. Despite numerous reviews on EAI methods, there is still a lack of comprehensive EAI technique when it emanates from these methods and perspectives. The image is a visual representation of EAI and how it may affect the end-user.

2.3   Explainable AI (EAI) architecture

EAI assists developers, decision-makers, consumers, and other stakeholders in understanding why and how an AI prediction came to be EAI refers to ML and deep learning strategies that can make sense of their choices for humans.

The goal of EAI is to make the reasoning behind a calculation justifiable to humans. For example, many simulated intelligence calculations use deep learning, in which calculations figure out how to distinguish designs based on massive amounts of preparation data [3,7,8].

In the above scenario, the EAI system could assist with adjusting model execution to clinical rules and goals to anticipate disease at the beginning phases [4]. It is among the most valuable man-made intelligence applications in medical care that offers a customized insight to patients as far as dealing with their well-being and disposing of their queries.

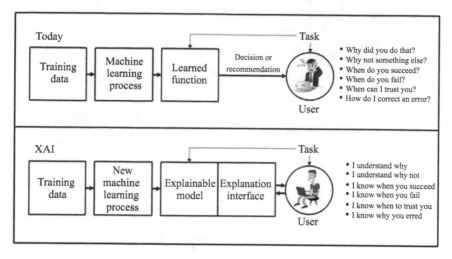

Figure 2.2   AI vs. EAI

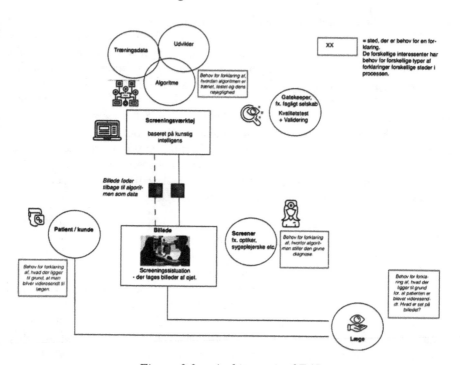

Figure 2.3   Architecture of EAI

EAI would help to facilitate the implementation of AI/ML in the health domain in general, and especially transparency and trust. Understanding why a model makes certain predictions can be as difficult when determining the accuracy of those predictions in many applications of AI in health [6].

2.4 Learning techniques

ML is a subset of AI that solves problems using data. These solvers are trained models that can learn based on the information provided. This data comes from the probability theory and linear algebra [5,6]. ML algorithms use our data to learn and solve predictive tasks automatically.

Deep learning: it is a branch of ML and uses multilayered neural networks to accomplish these objectives.

2.5 Demystifying EAI methods

According to John McCarthy, "...it is the science and engineering of creating intelligent machines, particularly intelligent computer programmes." It is similar to

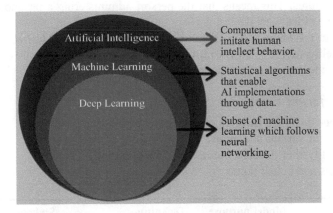

Figure 2.4   AI vs. ML vs. deep learning

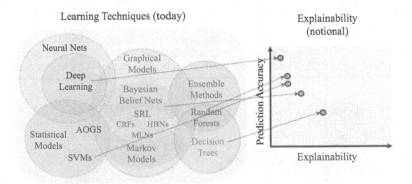

Figure 2.5   Learning techniques

the usage of computers to sort out human understanding, yet AI does not need to restrict itself to normally apparent techniques in the presence of computerized navigation, including profiling, and, at least, significant data about the rationale in question [7,8], as well as the importance and expected consequences for data subject. To prevent the information subject privileges, opportunities, and real interests, the information regulator should make suitable strides.

2.5.1   Clever Hans

Clever Hans was utilized to exhibit a creature's high-level degree of number sense. Hans was the horse of Wilhelm von Osteen, an exercise room science educator, beginner horse mentor, phrenologist, and spiritualist. It is a psychological term that describes when an animal or a person senses what someone wants them to do even when no signals are given to them. When testing the intelligence of animals or humans, it is critical to consider this effect.

Clever Hans exemplifies an important concept in psychology: "double blind" testing procedures. This means that the person administering a psychological test should have no idea what the test is about or what the "correct" answers are [1,2,6]. Examiners in the know can manipulate a test to produce the desired results; not only for intelligent horses but also for humans. An unintentional smile or frown can easily persuade someone to respond in a particular way.

2.5.2   Different users and goals in EAI

ML engineer/designer (master client):
- Conduct in various situations
- Test and further develop framework (investigating)
- Qualities and cutoff points

Domain	Model purpose	Technique	Stakeholders
Finance	Loan repayment	Highlight significance	Credit officials
Insurance	Risk assessment	Highlight significance	Risk analysis
Content moderation	Malicious reviews	Highlight significance	Content moderators
Finance	Cash distribution	Highlight significance	ML specialists
Facial recognition	Smile detection	Highlight significance	ML engineers
Content moderation	Sentiment analysis	Highlight significance	QA/ML engineers
Healthcare	Medical access	Counterfactuals	ML specialists
Content moderation	Object detection	Adversarial perturbation	QA ML engineers

Figure 2.6   Clever Hans

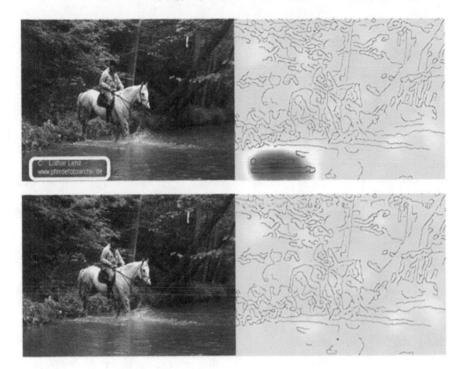

Figure 2.7   Clever Hans's phenomenon: communication with horse and man

2.5.3   EAI as quality assurance

2.5.3.1   Various clients – various objectives

(a)   Developer and terminal:
- Trust in the framework – even in unexpected situations.
- Decision-making and reasoning

(b)   Description of outcomes that differ from expectations
- Is it virtuous to use the system or stakeholder?
- Ethical or legal constraints
- Adherence

2.5.3.2   Different objectives for utilizing EAI

1.   Verification: Is the outcome produced in view of known speculations?
2.   Additional data:
    (a)   Result is one of the numerous factors in a decision cycle
    (b)   Hypothesis can "fix" poor choices
    (c)   Outcome should be made sense of additional (specialist – diagnosis, scheduler – administration representative, expert – enterprise designer)
3.   Model-based simplification.

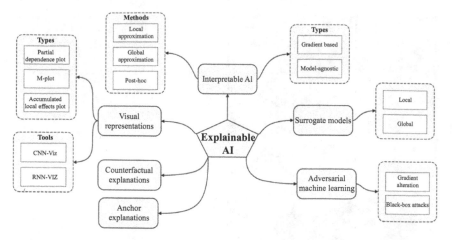

Figure 2.8   Taxonomy of EAI methods

2.6   Implementation: how to create explainable solutions

2.6.1   Method taxonomy

A scientific categorization of EAI strategies that joins terms and thoughts from the writing and that assists with separating and assessing EAI techniques.

Metrics:

- Practically grounded measurements (autonomous of human judgment)
- Human-grounded measurements (abstract judgment required)
- Application-grounded (full human–man-made intelligence framework required).

2.6.2   Rules – intrinsic local explanations

Intrinsically motivated (or interest-driven) learning is another exploration region in AI and robotics technology that means to make specialists that can master general abilities or ways of behaving and can be utilized to further develop execution in outward errands [3,8] like asset securing.

The study of intrinsically motivated learning as a method for autonomous, deeply ingrained learning in computers and unconditional learning in computer game characters. When the agent understands a meaningful abstract representation, a concept of distance between two representations can be used to gauge novelty, allowing the agent to efficiently explore its environment. Despite the inspiring success of deep learning in specific domains [4,5] (e.g., AlphaGo), many in the field (e.g., Gary Marcus) have pointed out that the ability to generalize remains a fundamental challenge in AI.

While promising in terms of developing objectives from the design of the climate without remotely forced exercises, intrinsic motivation learning still faces the same generalization challenge: instructions to reuse strategies [6,8] or activity successions, how to compress and represent persistent or complex state spaces, and how to hold and reuse notable elements learned.

2.6.3 Prototypes

Neural Prototype Tree (ProtoTree) for commonly interpretable fine-grained picture acknowledgment plan with beginning to end getting ready philosophy upgrades interpretability by organizing the models in a multi-evened [1,4] out tree structure. It divides the thinking system into small steps, which improves model perception and error examination while decreasing the number of models.

Examples

2.6.4 Learned representation

Representation learning is a type of AI technique that enables a framework to familiarize itself with the Representation, which is necessary for emphasizing discovery or characterization from sparse data [3]. Allowing a machine to learn involves applying those concepts to a specific movement, which reduces the need for manual component design.

Figure 2.9   Prototype examples

Figure 2.10   Learned representation

2.6.5   Partial dependence plot – global post-hoc explanations

The partial dependence plot (abbreviated PDP or PD plot) illustrates the insignificant impact of two or three components on the anticipated effects of AI. If the objective part relationship is linear, monotonic, or more ambiguous [3,7], a partial dependence plot can demonstrate this. The partial dependence function for regression is defined as:

$$\hat{fS}(x_S) = EXC\left[\hat{f}(x_S, X_C)\right] = \int \hat{f}(x_S, X_C)dP(X_C)$$

The X_S are the highlights for which the fractional reliance capability ought to be plotted and X_C are different elements utilized in the AI model f^, which are here treated as arbitrary factors. Typically, there are only a couple of highlights in the set. The feature(s) in S are those for which we need to know the impact on the expectation. The component vectors X_S and X_C consolidated make up the complete element space x.

Partial dependence continues to work by underrating the machine learning model's result over the selection of the elements in set C, allowing the capability to show the relationship between the highlights in set S we are interested in and the expected result [1,7]. By minimizing various elements, we get a capability that relies solely on highlights in S, with communications with various elements included.

2.6.6   Feature attribution (importance)

Feature attribution is a critical component of post-modeling (also known as post-hoc) explanation generation and facilitates such goals. A feature attribution technique is a function that accepts model inputs and outputs a per-feature attribution score depending on how much each feature contributed to the model's output.

Feature distribution drift	Feature attribution drift	What might be going on?	Next step
No	Yes	Feature likely interacts with one or more other features and the joint distribution of the combination has drifted	Examine drift in correlation between this feature and other features
Yes	No	Feature drifts in a manner that does not affect contribution to the model This may happen because: • Drift is specifically in the distribution of out-of-vocab values (these are all treated similarly by the model and therefore there is no attribution drift)	Examine the global importance of the feature. If the feature is important, debug where the drift is concentrated

(Continues)

(Continued)

Feature distribution drift	Feature attribution drift	What might be going on?	Next step
Yes	Yes	• Feature is overall unimportant to the model Feature drifts in a manner that does affect contribution to the model This may happen because: • Coverage of the feature has changed i.e., fraction of null values has changed • Some other non-trivial change in the feature's distribution	Examine features in order of attribution drift. Check if there is substantial change in the coverage of the feature

2.7 Applications

Learning tool

EAI has worked with the handling of a lot of information and its application in the industry. The quantity of apparatuses and systems accessible to information researchers and designers has been developed to pair with the progression of AI and ML [1]. Sample feedback is shown in Figure 2.11.

AI tools and frameworks

• List of AI tools and frameworks
  ✓ CNTK
  ✓ Open neural network (NN)

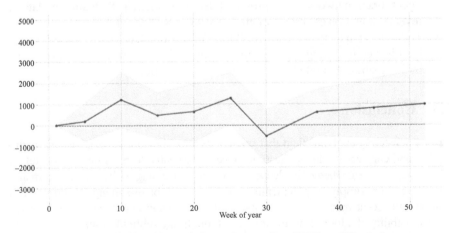

Figure 2.11   Partial dependence plot (PDP or PD plot)

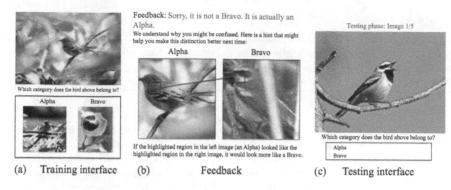

(a)   Training interface   (b)   Feedback   (c)   Testing interface

Figure 2.12   Feedback

- ✓ Scikit learn
- ✓ Tensor flow
- ✓ Google ML kit
- ✓ Theano
- ✓ PyTorch
- ✓ Caffe
- ✓ H20: Open Source AI Platform
- ✓ Keras
- ✓ Auto ML
- ✓ MxNet

(a)   Interface agents are computer programmed that use AI techniques to assist a user when interacting with a specific computer application. The paper discusses an interface agent that is based on the metaphor of a personal assistant.

(b)   Feedback networks, otherwise called repetitive brain organizations or intelligent brain networks, are profound learning models that stream data in reverse. It empowers criticism circles in the organization.

(c)   Today's UI testing technologies, like Test Complete, have started to use intelligence in testing to ease some of the difficulties that testers experience by integrating AI and object recognition capabilities.

2.8   Conclusion

AI is a constantly evolving field that weaves its way through logic, statistics, mathematics, and engineering. Its applications have the potential to transform every field in which they are used, whether by deepening our understanding of the world, automating procedures, or simply supplementing our own problem-solving abilities [1,7]. Throughout recent many years, technological advances in computational power and the accessibility of a lot of information have brought the subfield of machine learning, especially deep learning to the consideration of the overall population [3,5].

EAI is a preeminent path for responsible AI, serving in resolving ambiguity where system decisions are unforeseen. EAI must meet the demands for understandable, transparent, interpretable, and (as a result) trustworthy AI-based solutions in order to achieve this [8]. The time has come to recognize the importance of developing AI solutions that are grounded in explanation. Demystify has created a sophisticated AI solution that explains and validates any machine learning model.

References

[1]   Adam Zewe | MIT News Office "Demystifying machine-learning systems," A new method automatically describes, in natural language, what the individual components of a neural network do. Publication Date: January 27, 2022.

[2]   De Carolis, B. and Rossano, V. A team of presentation agents for edutainment. In: *Proceedings of the 8th International Conference on Interaction Design and Children*, pp. 150–153. IDC 2009, ACM, New York, NY, 2009.

[3]   Hoffman, R.R., Mueller, S.T., Klein, G., and Litman, J. Metrics for explainable AI: challenges and prospects, arXiv:1812.04608, 2018.

[4]   Gilpin, L.H., Bau, D., Yuan, B.Z., Bajwa, A., Specter, M., and Kagal, L. Explaining explanations: an approach to evaluating interpretability of machine learning. In: *The 5th IEEE International Conference on Data Science and Advanced Analytics (DSAA 2018)*, 2018.

[5]   Miller, T. Explanation in artificial intelligence: insights from the social sciences. *Artificial Intelligence*, 267, 2018, 1–38.

[6]   Schneider, J. and Handali, J. Personalized explanation in machine learning: a conceptualization, 2019. arXiv preprint arXiv:1901.00770.

[7]   Explainable AI Driving business value through greater understanding, PwC https://www.pwc.co.uk/audit-assurance/assets/explainable-ai.pdf.

[8]   Wachter, S., Mittelstadt, B., and Russell, C. Counterfactual explanations without opening the black box: automated decisions and the GDPR. *Harvard Journal of Law & Technology*, 31(2), Spring 2018, 844.

Chapter 3

Illustrating the significance of explainable artificial intelligence (XAI)

Pethuru Raj[1] and Chellammal Surianarayanan[2]

3.1 Introduction

Artificial intelligence (AI) is turning out to be an indispensable paradigm for businesses and individuals. AI is automating and accelerating a specific set of everyday problems such as classification, regression, clustering, detection, recognition, translation, etc. AI can classify whether an incoming e-mail is spam or real, recognize a person's face in an image, understand a speech and convert it into text, create an appropriate caption for a scene, etc. The scope of AI is fast expanding. Industry verticals are keenly exploring and experimenting with different things. Business processes are being automated and optimized through the smart leverage of all kinds of noteworthy advancements happening in the AI space. Increasingly AI takes the center stage in business operations across the globe. There is a dazzling array of integrated platforms, frameworks, toolsets, libraries, and case studies and hence the adoption of AI algorithms and models is picking dramatically in the recent past. However, there are a few critical challenges to be surmounted before the widespread usage of AI models in mission-critical domains such as healthcare, security, retailing, supply chain, and infrastructure management. That is, business executives and IT experts insist on trustworthy and transparent decision-making by AI models.

This chapter is to explain the brewing challenges in the AI field and how they can be surmounted through competent technology solutions. Especially how the fast-emerging explainable AI (XAI) is a set of methods and software libraries that allow human users to comprehend and trust the results created by AI models. XAI is to describe an AI model and how it arrived at a particular decision. XAI is to explain the AI model's implications and potential biases. It helps in understanding model accuracy and fairness. XAI turns out to be a crucial cog for mission-critical enterprises to embark on the AI paradigm with all the clarity and confidence. With the maturity of the XAI concept, the AI adoption happens in a responsible manner across industry verticals.

[1]Edge AI Division, Reliance Jio Platforms Ltd., Bangalore, India
[2]Centre of Distance and Online Education, Bharathidasan University, Tiruchirappalli, India

3.2   The growing power of AI

Having understood the strategic significance of AI technologies and tools, business houses and AI organizations are keen to embrace this emerging digital technology to envisage sophisticated business workloads and IT services. The AI-powered empowerment helps enterprising businesses to explore fresh avenues to increase both bottom- and top-line revenues. Businesses can easily retain their customers' loyalty by providing premium and path-breaking capabilities. Business houses can add additional clients through the delectable contributions of AI, which is famous for pinpointing hidden patterns in datasets. Creating actionable insights out of big data is the principal goal of the AI paradigm. By disseminating the discovered knowledge to business and IT applications, the target of making software applications and services intelligent in their operations, outputs and offerings is being elegantly fulfilled. Besides software systems, all kinds of input/output systems such as wearables, mobiles, portables, hearables, and implantable, fixed, nomadic, and wireless devices in our everyday environments such as homes, hotels, and hospitals are readied to be smart.

All kinds of devices, instruments, equipment, appliances, wares, utilities, machineries, etc. in our personal, social, and professional places are being astutely empowered to exhibit a cognitive and conscious behavior through the incorporation of distinct AI power. Thus, in the increasingly digital era, there is a massive amount of multi-structured digital data. When AI models are supplied with digital data, the key aspect of knowledge generation happens. With the AI-enabled transformation, every tangible object in our midst becomes smart, every electronic device becomes smarter and every human being, who is being digitally assisted and augmented by multiple devices, will become the smartest. To fulfill the dream of setting up and sustaining intelligent environments and enterprises, the contributions of AI methods are becoming hugely critical. Preciously speaking, AI is the core and central aspect of the dream of intelligent societies. Leading market analysts, researchers, and watchers have forecast for huge market for the AI phenomenon. Technology experts, evangelists, and exponents are in unison in articulating and accentuating the wherewithal of AI in smoothening and strengthening the journey toward the vision of an industrialized and intelligent world.

3.3   The challenges and concerns of AI

In the previous section, we have pronounced the growing greatness of the AI conundrum. There is a surge in embracing the AI mechanism across the world for a variety of reasons. A variety of business operations are being augmented and automated through the AI distinctions. With the flourish of AI-centric processing units as hardware accelerators, end-to-end integrated platforms for AI model engineering, evaluation, optimization, and deployment, facilitating frameworks, specialized engines, enabling toolkits and software libraries, and other enablers, the AI adoption and adaptation are picking up fast. Every process and data-intensive problems are being attempted to be solved through a host of innovations in the AI space. AI brings in the much-needed efficacy and affordability. The hugely complicated process of transitioning raw data collection into information and into knowledge to be consciously used by decision-makers, leaders, stakeholders, and executives is greatly simplified through the inherent strength of AI algorithms and models. In a nutshell, making sense out of data mountains is being facilitated by AI techniques and tools. Producing intelligence at the right time at the right place for the right people is the core and central aspect of the AI paradigm. There are case studies and proof-of-concepts (PoCs) in plenty illustrating the utility and universality of the AI phenomenon.

In the midst of surging popularity, there are a few critical concerns being expressed by AI practitioners. With a series of remarkable advancements in the AI landscape, it becomes difficult to comprehend how a particular AI model has arrived at a decision. AI models, especially deep neural network (DNN) architectures, and models are hard to retrace how the inference is made. Therefore, AI systems are termed as a black box. It is opaque even for data scientists and engineers to understand the route taken by AI algorithms to land in an inference. There are several hidden layers between the input and the output layer. It is incomprehensible how the trained, tested, and validated AI model reacts to fresh data. It becomes a tough affair and assignment for professionals to interpret and explain the result of black-box AI models. There are issues of biases in taking decisions. AI researchers are, therefore, keen to bring forth enabling techniques to explain why and how an AI algorithm makes certain decisions on new data. Thus, in the recent past, with the increased usage of AI systems across several mission-critical domains, the new notion of XAI is grasping the attention of many in the AI field.

Machine learning (ML) algorithms are being leveraged to detect whether a person is infected with COVID virus. Epidemiologists are extensively using AI to monitor the spread of a disease in a particular locality. Drug discovery is being speeded up through the leverage of AI methods. For example, AI helped to arrive at appropriate vaccines quickly for COVID virus attacks. It would have taken several years for genetics and molecular biology experts to come out with vaccines without the services of AI. Thus, AI is occupying a prominent and dominant spot in many fields. AI adoption is expected to grow dramatically in the years to unfurl. Therefore, the need for XAI libraries and toolsets is to grow considerably in the days to come.

3.4 About the need for AI explainability

With the interest in embracing and employing newer technologies to avail deeper and decisive automation in our personal and professional assignments is growing steadily, there is a need for evaluating the pros and cons of each technology. As discussed above, AI is the most promising technology for the future of the world. AI has all the power and virtue to thrive in the years to come. Yet there is a need to keep an eye on its functioning and contributions across industry verticals. When AI is being used for advancing and automating healthcare operations, it is imperative to analyze and understand how AI arrives at certain decisions. Because even if there is a small deviation in AI's recommendations, there is a possibility for risks to human lives. Therefore, technocrats and business leaders insist on evolving viable methods to gain enhanced understanding of how AI algorithm and models work to decide something. AI inferences have to be unambiguously explained to end-users and service providers. Deep neural networks in the AI domain are typically black-box systems. There is no transparency on how DNN architectures calculate and throw out inferences. The challenge at hand is to move toward gray-box systems, which are visible for human eyes and minds to perceive what is happening in the hidden layers of DNNs.

XAI ensures utmost transparency and can support iterative models that ensure correct outcomes. The long-pending goals of correct diagnoses of diseases and the right medication are being fulfilled through XAI in an exemplary manner. When AI is used for the identification of high-risk patients for specific diseases, it is vital to understand which factors or features contribute to the identification decision. XAI comes in handy in taking a few more relevant facets and facts into consideration to explain the AI decision. The scope of XAI expands further. With the unique contributions of the XAI paradigm, other verticals are exploring and experimenting with the strategically sound power of XAI. Financial services providers use XAI to review fraudulent transactions and claims to sharply reduce operational costs.

Drug manufacturers leverage XAI to fast-track the process of end-to-end drug discovery to control a pandemic. Thus, with enhanced trust in AI, timely and automated intervention is to pick up in the days to come. Human involvement is bound to go down with the delectable advancements being accomplished in the XAI space.

As accentuated above, AI is not an infallible technology. Due to various reasons, the performance and prediction power of AI models may degrade. That is, AI models may result in biased and unfair decisions. XAI has the wherewithal to point out the discrimination thereby any untoward incident can be stopped forthwith. Wrong data can lead to wrong decisions. The features of AI models may be wrongly selected and weighted. Thus, possibilities for arriving and articulating incorrect inferences are there.

In short, explainability is a sincere attempt through technological advancements to infuse trust in AI predictions. The aspect of explainability is to considerably enhance the understanding of both the inputs and outputs of a model. With unsupervised ML, there is not much input information to create ML models. If a human data scientist gets involved in providing insights into input data, there is a possibility of arriving at biased inferencing. Thus, for making perfect decisions, automated solutions are mandated.

The facet of XAI models is that humans have to understand the outcome of XAI models. In the case of black-box ML models, there are no explicit insights into what goes into the machines and what the machines learn and predict. Therefore, the help of a human subject matter expert (SME) is needed to understand how machines produce the result. The human experts have to study the result and ought to re-enact the whole process and retrace the results to get a better understanding of the decisions articulated by ML models. In a nutshell, model explainability mainly deals with the knowledge of the input parameters thereby the model output can be properly explained. XAI is being touted as the most important requirement to fulfill the target of trustworthy AI. The trust in AI models and their predictions has to be substantially improved with explainability techniques and tools. Users can understand what the model is learning. This knowledge helps to fulfill the goals of transparency, trustworthiness, fairness, and accountability of the AI system.

With XAI models, it is easier for providers and subscribers to put the trust and act upon on the predictions made by XAI. Therefore, there are clarion calls to produce regulatory mechanisms for controlled AI usage. AI governance is gaining the importance of considering the overwhelming adoption of AI algorithms and models.

3.5   The importance of XAI

Software engineers can easily retrace to understand and explain how a particular software application outputs a result. However, that is not the case with AI engineers because of the extreme complexity of AI models. The functioning of AI models is not easy to understand. The human understanding of software packages and AI models is essential to gain the confidence of these automated systems. To give 100% control to AI systems, it should be easy and essential to know how the AI computation happens. Such a grasp on any booming technology allows us to measure, manage, and enhance it further to tackle varying demands. Precisely speaking, the overwhelming approach to fulfill the emerging requirements such as interpretability and explainability of black-box AI models is to move over to white-box AI models. Omitting the aspect of explainability in life-critical domains such as healthcare poses a threat and hence it takes a very careful and calculated move on embracing AI. Notwithstanding, AI is penetrative, pervasive, and persuasive.

AI is increasingly ingrained with our daily walks and works. Nevertheless, understanding how AI arrives at a decision is hard to fathom. Especially understanding the decision-making routes of complex AI models is a really tough affair and hence sophisticated AI models are being termed as black boxes. The requirement at hand is to transition complex AI programs into gray or glass boxes so that humans can understand how and why AI algorithms arrive at such a particular decision. The decision pathways are visible to humans. The AI systems can explain the decision-making process and humans can easily interpret AI's decisions. The functioning of AI programs is transparent to users and hence the trustworthiness of AI systems can go up sharply. All kinds of biases and deviations can be eliminated so that the decisions are fair and acceptable.

The aspect of explainability has acquired a special importance in the mission-critical domains such as healthcare. Any imprecision in AI models can result in an irreparable situation. For boosting the confidence of users in AI systems, the trust in AI has to go up drastically. AI systems should not be influenced by age, gender, culture, race, abilities, etc. AI decisions are crucial for healthcare service providers and patients. All should be able to avail the distinct benefits of the ever-growing AI systems. There should not be any partiality and preferences. As patients are not typically proficient in AI technologies and tools, there is a need getting imposed on AI systems to clearly yet concisely explain their decisions. Thereby, all kinds of decisions and deeds across industry verticals hereafter will be information-backed. The intuition-based deals will go away soon.

Precisely speaking, explainability turns out to be the cornerstone to securing and strengthening users' trust in AI systems. By knowing an AI system's internal processes, end-users can easily comprehend its pros and cons clearly. A clear-cut understanding of any AI system helps to remove any fear about it and to know its distinct features and functionalities. Such a deeper understanding can facilitate to envisage and incorporate fresh capabilities toward delighting patients and care-givers. There are powerful tools emerging and evolving for enabling a standard reporting of AI models. The report can include the type of model, the details on the dataset on which the AI model gets trained and tested, what is the performance level? and any impending risks, etc.

As described in the other chapters, there are easy-to-understand and use frameworks and tools to help the system's users to understand and interpret the results. The tools provide scores for each factor and feature, which influences the final outcome. This helps to reflect the patterns identified by the model in the data. That is, the significance of different features in arriving at decisions can be quantified. In computer vision examples, heatmaps (referred to as saliency maps) come handy in expressing and exposing which parts of pixels of the image have contributed more to the final result. This gives the cue that a certain factor has played a crucial role in shaping up the prediction. But there is no clarity on why that factor has induced the result. In other words, there is still no answer to the why-question. For example, chest X-ray images typically help doctors to diagnose diseases. In that images, certain regions would have played a role in influencing the final prediction of the AI system. But the doctor does not know why those portions influence the result. That is, the humans ought to get the answer to the why-question.

XAI models bring forth viable solutions and structures so that data scientists and users can correctly understand and explain why they came to a particular decision. The model's analytical logic and internal operations are fully transparent and interpretable. That is, even non-experts can easily get to know the model's internal functioning.

Thus, XAI plays an important role in mission-critical fields. As inscribed at the beginning of this chapter, there are severe issues emanating from AI models' bad predictions. AI models recommend an action but the action does not make any sense for people. Therefore, experts and industry leaders favor of strengthening the brewing idea of XAI. XAI models self-explain the reason behind the recommendation. In short, the aspect of explainability is very much indispensable for people to have the confidence and clarity on the decisions. Trust is essential for any technology domain to flourish. Any mistake by AI systems can be life-threatening or affect the livelihood of people. Thereby the field of XAI draws a greater attention as it can provide explanations in natural language and facilitate easy interpretation. Such an empowerment does a lot of good for decision-makers and end-users alike.

The AI adoption is increasing day by day. A myriad of industry verticals is immensely benefiting out of all the praiseworthy improvisations happening in the enigmatic AI space. Especially in the healthcare domain, AI is used to accelerate and automate a variety of manual tasks, which are typically error-prone. AI models with the explainability feature can contribute in many ways including detecting anomaly or outlier by scanning medical images and other sensor data, pinpointing useful patterns in data heaps, in empowering caregivers with medication recommendation, helping in articulating and accentuating risk-mitigation mechanisms, etc. Experts have come out with certain scenarios wherein the XAI capability is being insisted. When fairness in AI decisions is indispensable, the importance of XAI is critical. If any decision results in an irreparable situation, then the aspect of XAI is crucial. AI learns and comes out with new hypotheses. For establishing the truthfulness of any hypothesis proposed by AI models, subject matter experts (SMEs) depend on the power of XAI.

3.6 The importance of model interpretation

Any ML model has a predictive function, which untangles distinct relationships and patterns in input data and exposes it to automated systems, decision-makers, and executives. The model brings forth a function between the independent (input) variables and the dependent (target or response) variable(s).

When a model finds something useful and usable in the incoming data, it helps people and systems to take decisions correctly. The model interpretation is all about simplifying the process of understanding and explaining how and why these decisions are arrived. The overall idea behind this is to ensure the transparency of the working condition of the model. Also, the common people have to easily understand the model's recommendations, suggestions, inferencing, etc. Like software systems, models too have a few important non-functional requirements (NFRs). A model has to have a better interpretability just like maintaining a good performance level. We all know that the prominent performance indicators/metrics of ML models are precision, accuracy, recall, etc. However, performance metrics are typically fixed at the beginning. However, metrics do not tell everything about a model's predictions. The performance may degrade due to various reasons such as model concept drift, data drift, etc. Hence, it is paramount to understand how and why a model takes certain decisions.

3.6.1 Model transparency

An ML model is getting created by leveraging an ML algorithm on data features. That is, an ML model is a representation mapping inputs to potential outputs. In other words, an ML model is a mathematical formula or equation to accurately map input independent variables (inputs) to dependent variables (responses).

The bewildering idea behind model transparency is to gain a clear-cut understanding of how models are being derived and what are the things that directly or indirectly influence model decisions. The coefficients in linear equations/ models, weights of a neural network, etc. play a vital role in shaping up model decisions.

XAI experts have pointed out a series of steps to be considered to simplify the process of model interpretation.

3.6.2   Start with interpretable algorithms

As indicated elsewhere, the smartest way to embark on model interpretation is to use easily interpretable algorithms like linear and logistic regression. Tree-based algorithms are also recommended. Some experts even recommend k-nearest neighbors (KNN) and Naive Bayes.

3.6.3   Standard techniques for model interpretation

The interpretability is to guarantee the much-needed fairness, accountability, and transparency. Such an additional facility boosts the confidence of decision-makers and end-users to leverage AI models more for a variety of business and personal requirements. The proven techniques are given below.

1. There are exploratory data analysis (EDA) and data visualization techniques simplifying the complex task of model interpretation.
2. There are also dimensionality reduction techniques, which reduce the feature space so that visualizing and understanding what factors are influencing a model to take certain decisions. The well-known reduction techniques include principal component analysis (PCA) and self-organizing maps (SOM). Further on, there is another method of **nonlinear dimensionality reduction** (also known as **manifold learning**). This aims to project high-dimensional data onto lower-dimensional latent manifolds.
3. There are well-known model performance evaluation metrics such as accuracy, precision, and recall. Further on, there are receiver operating characteristic (ROC) curve and the AUC algorithm for classification models

3.6.4   ROC curve

This is a ROC curve illustrating the performance of a classification model at all classification thresholds. This plots two parameters: True Positive Rate (TPR) (TPR is synonymously termed as recall) and False Positive Rate (FPR). The area under the ROC curve (AUC) is an efficient and sorting-based algorithm to compute the points in an ROC curve. AUC provides an aggregate measure of performance across all possible classification thresholds.

Similarly, for regression models, the standard performance evaluation metrics are mean squared error (MSE) and root mean squared error (RMSE), and mean absolute error (MAE) for regression models.

3.6.5 Focus on feature importance

Features are critical for making correct prediction. Therefore, the domains of feature engineering, optimization, and selection are getting a lot of attention these days as they are to achieve the intended success. Understanding and articulating those features, which contribute considerably to taking certain decisions or making recommendations, or performing inferences or articulating specific outcomes, etc. ultimately help in model interpretation. Skater (https://oracle.github.io/Skater/) is an open-source unified framework to enable model interpretation. Skater supports algorithms to demystify the learned structures of a black-box model both globally (inference on the basis of a complete data set) and locally (inference about an individual prediction).

Figure 3.1 is a standard example of a feature importance plot from Skater on a census dataset.

Looks like Age and Education-Num are the top two features, where Age is responsible for model predictions changing by an average of 14.5% on perturbing the Age feature. A feature's importance is calculated based on the increase of the model's prediction error after perturbing the feature. A feature is important if perturbing its values increases the model error. A feature is unimportant if perturbing its values keeps the model error unchanged.

3.6.6 Partial dependence plots (PDPs)

A PDPs makes the marginal impact of a feature on model prediction by keeping other features in the model constant. The derivative of partial dependence can describe the impact of a feature. PDPs can also show whether the relationship between the target and a feature is linear or complex. PDP is a global method. That

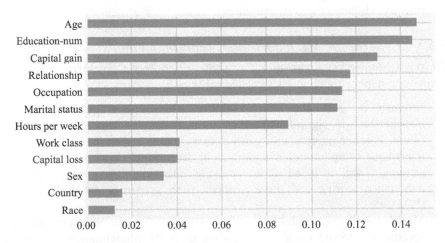

*Figure 3.1   The features and their importance for model prediction (reference:
https://towardsdatascience.com/explainable-artificial-intelligence-
part-2-model-interpretation-strategies-75d4afa6b739)*

is, the PDP method takes into account all instances and makes a statement about the global relationship of a feature with the predicted outcome.

3.6.7   Global surrogate models

Previously we have discussed how to simplify model interpretability by leveraging easily interpretable ML models, feature importance scoring methods, and PDPs. But there is a need to interpret complex models. One viable and venerable solution approach is to use global surrogate models. A global surrogate model is an interpretable model that is trained to approximate the predictions of a black-box model, which can be essentially any model derived out of any training algorithm. That is, global surrogate models are model-agnostic.

Generally, the process is to create an interpretable surrogate model from the base and black-box model. A surrogate model is model-agnostic since it requires no information about the inner workings of the black-box model. Just the relation of input and predicted output is used. Tree-based models are found to be good for building surrogate models. The main steps for building surrogate models are explained in this book (https://christophm.github.io/interpretable-ml-book/global.html).

1. Choose a dataset: This could be the same dataset that was used for training the black-box model or it can be a new dataset from the same distribution. It is also OK to choose a subset of the data.
2. For the chosen dataset, get the predictions of the base and black-box model.
3. Choose an interpretable surrogate model (linear models or tree-based models).
4. Train the interpretable model on the dataset and its predictions.
5. Measure how well the surrogate model replicates the prediction of the black-box model.
6. Interpret/visualize the surrogate model.

3.6.8   Criteria for ML model interpretation methods

Christoph Molnar has authored a few well-written books on interpretable ML (https://christophm.github.io/interpretable-ml-book/).

- **Intrinsic or post hoc interpretability**: This is leveraging intrinsically interpretable ML algorithms such as linear, parametric, and tree-based algorithms. Post hoc interpretability means first creating a black-box model, which is prepared using ensemble algorithms or deep neural network (DNN) architectures. Then, it is all about applying interpretability methods (feature importance scoring and other methods such as partial dependency plots (PDP), etc.
- **Model-specific or model-agnostic**: Model-specific interpretation tools are specific to intrinsic model interpretation methods. Model-agnostic tools are relevant to post hoc methods. These agnostic methods usually operate by analyzing feature input and output pairs. That means these methods do not have access to any model internals such as weights and constraints.

There are two types. Model explanation (i.e., global explanation for the whole model) and explanation for instance-specific prediction (that means local explanation). The global explanation is to focus on the whole model and to explain the operational logic. The local explanation is to explain the model's prediction for individual instances. Explanations come in the form of rules, feature importance, counterfactuals, plots, visualization, etc.

Global interpretability is to understand and explain model decisions based on interactions between the predictor features (input) and responses (output). Gaining a deeper understanding of feature interactions and the importance of facilitating the global interpretability. However, visualizing features with more than two dimensions and analyzing their conditional interactions are beset with many practical challenges. Therefore, the focus gets turned towards understanding subsets of features. Such modularization ultimately leads to global interpretability.

For local interpretability, it is sufficient to understand prediction decisions for a single datapoint. That is, the focus is on that datapoint and the idea is to understand the prediction made by the model by looking at a local subregion in the feature space around that point.

Local data distributions and feature spaces may give accurate explanations. The LIME framework (discussed below) can be used for model-agnostic local interpretation. The best practice is to use both global and local interpretations to explain model decisions not only for one instance but also for a group of instances.

Primarily deep learning (DL) models are inherently complex due to the participation of hundreds and even thousands of hidden layers in between the input and the output layers. Thus, DL architectures are being termed as black-box systems as in Figure 3.2. Further on, to finetune the prediction accuracy, ensemble models are being used. Ensemble models are being built by aggregating multiple AI models. Therefore, AI experts recommend to leverage simple AI algorithms such as decision trees and regression models, thereby the opaqueness of AI decisions can be avoided. The model performance is good when going for simple and well-understood algorithms. How XAI emerges as a solace and silver bullet for industries to benefit from the extreme power of AI is vividly illustrated in Figure 3.2.

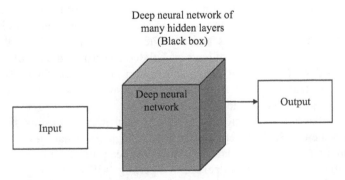

Figure 3.2   Eliminating the opaqueness of AI decisions with an ensemble of simple models

As machine and DL models are being represented through complex mathematical formulae, there is a need for competent approaches to reduce the model complexity. When the model complexity goes down, then understanding models' decisions and recommendations becomes easy for data scientists, business executives, and even end-users. As indicated above, calculating feature importance and tools-based model explainability are being seen as the way forward to nullify any bad implications of AI models.

3.7   Briefing feature importance scoring methods

In the literature, there are several proven and potential feature importance scoring methods such as mean decrease impurity (MDI), mean decrease accuracy (MDA), and single feature importance (SFI). These methods are good at producing a feature score, which clearly articulates the feature's impact on the predictive quality of ML models. However, it is important to know a specific feature's contribution to influencing the prediction. In the recent past, there came a few ML techniques that facilitate the detection of a feature's contribution. Such methods ultimately simplify and streamline the easy interpretability of model's decision. The insights being shared by such ML techniques empower business leaders and data scientists to understand and reveal the criteria used while arriving at decisions. Financial and insurance industries are acquiring immense benefits through such measures. An in-depth explanation can be given to customers, who seek the basis on which certain decisions (approval or rejection) are being taken. Similarly, pharmaceutical and healthcare industries get the boost through the self-explanatory capability of recent-day and tools-assisted ML models.

Besides understanding the importance of every feature in decision-enablement, the aspect of feature selection contributes to the easy interpretability of AI decisions. Throwing out insignificant features is important. Feature selection also tackles the curse of dimensionality. The problem of model overfitting is also minimized through appropriate feature selection. Thus, feature engineering involving selection, optimization, etc. turns out to be a constructive factor. Fortunately, there are a few competitive feature selection techniques. There are articles on different feature selection methods and also there are Python implementations for each of the methods. Experts also have articulated the pros and cons of each of the methods based on their practical implementation difficulties. They also indicate that calculating feature importance scores using analytical methods as opposed to statistical and embedded methods can.

In short, the key motivation for XAI is to transition black-box systems into glass-box systems. Such an empowerment through the smart leverage of XAI libraries and packages helps data scientists to check and fix biases. The much-needed fairness in arriving at decisions is getting fulfilled through XAI. There are two widely interested explainability algorithms: the LIME and SHAPE algorithms.

3.8   Local interpretable model-agnostic explanations (LIMEs)

The key motivations for the LIME method are given below. This is based on the research paper published and made available on page https://arxiv.org/pdf/1602.04938.pdf. First, we probably accept that a linear ML model is more interpretable than a complicated ML model. However, the following linear model is not easily interpretable as it has several variables.

$$Y = 1.50 + 3.3X_1 + 25.4X_2 + 312X_3 + 32X_4 + 436X_5 + 9.33X_6 + 2.3X_7 + 4.9X_8 + 0.3X_9$$
$$+40.2X_{10} + 4.33X_{11} + 6.1X_{12} + 873X_{13} + 1.3X_{14} + 4.5X_{15} + 73.2X_{16} + 0.53X_{17} + 0.61$$
$$X_{18} + 9.2X_{19} + 453X_{20} + 8.32X_{21} + 25.4X_{22} + 7.31X_{23} + 30.32X_{24} + 23.6X_{25} + 5.32X_{26}$$
$$+3.0X_{27} + 90.1X_{28} + 4.2X_{29} + 893X_{30} + 53.0X_{31} + 13.3X_{32} + 2.5X_{33} + 7.6X_{34} + 6.35X_{35}$$
$$+5.13X_{36} + 0.32X_{37} + 49.1X_{38} + 3.2X_{39} + 1.8X_{40}$$

Second, for an individual prediction, only a few variables play a significant role in arriving at a prediction. Other variables are not contributing much to an individual prediction. The interpretation should make sense from an individual prediction's view. This is being termed as local fidelity. Globally important features may be irrelevant in the local context. Thus, even if a model has hundreds of variables, only a few variables directly contribute to a local (individual) prediction.

Having understood the growing requirements, the authors have come out with LIME, which makes it easy to interpret any model. LIME enables local fidelity (locally interpretable). The authors of LIME insist to build two types of trust for confidently using a model.

- Trusting an individual prediction: Users must trust an individual prediction act upon that prediction with all the confidence and clarity.
- Trusting a model: Once the model is trained, tested, and validated, then it goes to a production environment. There are performance evaluation metrics such as accuracy, precision, recall, etc. If there is a need to visualize the performance of any multi-class classification problem, we use the area under the curve (AUC) and receiver operating characteristics (ROC) curve. This has emerged as an important evaluation metric for checking any classification model's performance. ROC is a probability curve and AUC represents the degree or measure of separability. AUC tells how much the model is capable of distinguishing between classes. With the higher AUC, the model is good at predicting 0 classes as 0 and 1 classes as 1.

LIME is a popular algorithm for model explanation. LIME explanations are primarily based on local surrogate models. As written before, surrogate models are interpretable models that are typically learned on the predictions of the original black-box model. An example is given in Figure 3.3 where the prediction of a disease arrived based on symptoms is being explained by an explainer.

Local interpretability can answer the question like "Why is the model behaving in a specific way in the locality of a data point x?"

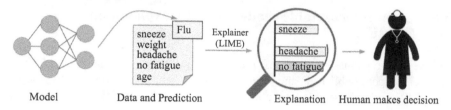

Figure 3.3   Prediction is explained by an explainer (reference: https://www. oreilly.com/content/introduction-to-local-interpretable-model- agnostic-explanations-lime/)

LIME tests out what happens to the original black-box model's predictions when some variations or perturbations are made on the dataset of the black-box model. Typically, LIME generates a new dataset consisting of perturbed samples and the associated black-box model's predictions. On this dataset, LIME then trains an interpretable model based on the proximity of the sampled instances to the instance of interest. Here is a high-level workflow as articulated by the book author.

- Choose the instance of interest for which you want to get an explanation of the predictions of your black box model.
- Perturb your dataset and get the black-box predictions for these new points.
- Weight the new samples by their proximity to the instance of interest.
- Fit a weighted, interpretable (surrogate) model on the dataset with the variations.
- Explain prediction by interpreting the local model.

This supplies all the insights on how much each feature has contributed to the ML model for an individual prediction. This algorithm operates and delivers in a model-agnostic manner. That is, this algorithm can be applied to any black-box ML model. This also works for different neural network (NN) architectures. This algorithm works by leveraging the prominent technique of surrogate models. That is, instead of explaining the black-box ML model directly, it uses a local surrogate model to provide the required explanations.

The surrogate model is being prepared in a phase manner. First, the LIME algorithm creates a new proxy data set by making some permutations to the feature values of the available dataset. Second, each of these samples is assigned a particular weight value that is proportional to its similarity with respect to the instance, which has to be explained. Finally, leverage a surrogate ML model, which is an easily explainable model like decision tree, linear regression, etc. on the weighted proxy data set.

The LIME algorithm creates a local surrogate model, which can be used to supply model explanations. This technique works even when there are complex black-box models. Further on, there is no need to train the local surrogate model on the same features that were used to train the black-box model.

The main limitation is the need for the creation of a local surrogate model that has to explicitly define the similarity metric to the sample, which ought to be explained. Because determining this similarity metric is not easy and the metric values vary from case to case. If the similarity metric is not properly chosen, then there is a possibility for instable explanations. That is, the explanation of nearly identical samples may differ from each other a lot. There are several implementations of this algorithm using multiple programming languages. The Python-centric LIME package is available for practitioners. Interested readers can get sample LIME implementations at Introduction to XAI using LIME – GeeksforGeeks and explain your model predictions with LIME | Kaggle.

3.9 SHAP explainability algorithm

Shapley additive explanation (SHAP) is a model explainability algorithm. This operates on the single prediction level not at the global ML model level. The algorithm derives its technique from the cooperative game theory. That is, it is able to determine the payout for each player within a cooperative coalition.

The payout for each player is being calculated based on the magnitude of the SHAP value that is associated with that player. The magnitude value is identified by the player's contribution. The Shapley value actually represents the feature's contribution to the final prediction. Thus, when the SHAP algorithm is used on a particular instance, there will be many Shapley values.

Each value is associated with one of the instance's features.

The final prediction can be calculated by adding a baseline value, which is constant for each ML classifier/regressor. The magnitude and the sign of the Shapley value can determine the contribution of a feature in arriving at the final prediction. High absolute Shapley values indicate that the feature is important. The sign of the Shapley value conveys the direction. For a binary classifier, a negative sign means that the feature has pushed down the prediction to 0 label. Besides knowing the importance of individual features, it is important to know the importance of a collection of features. The question is to understand how each feature value contributes to the prediction compared to the average prediction. The effect of each feature is the weight of the feature times the feature value minus the average effect of all apartments. This is a linear model. For complex models, a solution comes from cooperative game theory. SHAP, which is based on the concept of cooperative game theory, is the way forward. The SHAP algorithm is model-agnostic. However, its computational time is on the higher side. Especially if it has to handle complex ML models with many features, the time complexity is high. The workaround for this limitation is to leverage a package that allows one to define the used ML model.

The Tree Explainer is an implementation of the SHAP package. This does a good job for tree-based algorithms such as random forest, decision tree, and Gradient Boost.

The DeepExplainer package can explain DL models, which are basically complex. Here is an example. This package can provide the explanation of a DL image classification model that was trained to recognize a series of animals. The SHAP explainability algorithm can detect which pixels together caused the algorithm to decide a certain animal class. Further on, the SHAP algorithm can provide explanations for natural language processing (NLP) problems. This is through the package's Kernel Explainer (https://pub.towardsai.net/explain-your-machine-learning-predictions-with-kernel-shap-kernel-explainer-fed56b9250b8). This is model-agnostic and can handle any type of ML algorithms. Thus, the feature importance techniques (LIME and SHAP) emerge as a new category of enabling tools for data scientists.

Here are some domains wherein the power of XAI is keenly sought.

- **Healthcare**: This is a life-critical domain and hence any wrong decision can have a bad and sad impact. XAI comes in handy for surgeons, doctors, clinicians, and caregivers as it can explain the medication recommendations to patients by providing insights into the variables that took part in the decision-making process.
- **Finance**: This is another prospective domain for XAI. Important financial decisions are being taken through AI models these days. Herein, any mishap can result in catastrophic situations. Thus, the AI model has to throw light on what prompted it to arrive at such a decision.
- **Recruitment**: Selecting appropriate resumes for further review is being automated through AI. Now the capability of XAI can tell us why a candidate's resume was selected or not selected. This nullifies any sort of bias and unfairness.
- **Fraud detection**: There is no doubt that fraudulent and suspicious transactions have to be correctly captured and alerted in time. Similarly, fake product identification is another crucial element. On the other hand, any wrong identification can be a huge inconvenience for service providers and consumers. Therefore, for boosting the confidence on AI decisions, the aspect of XAI is a definite value-addition to nullify any bias and discrimination.

3.9.1 AI trust with symbolic AI

This is another recent approach for incorporating the much-needed trust in AI algorithms and models. With the widespread adoption of AI capabilities, appropriate regulatory actions are being confabulated. AI service providers are forced to take right and relevant measures to embed more trust into their AI initiatives. The simple and straightforward way to accomplish this is by using a rule-based approach (symbolic AI) to develop any AI model.

With symbolic AI, the relationship between concepts is predefined and hence how the model works and contributes becomes easy to understand for anyone. This rule-based approach is better than creating XAI models. The control is with the AI engineer not on the AI model. With the rule-based approach, any undesirable or biased results can be easily traced back to the root cause and insightfully fixed. Thus, to develop and run fully XAI models, without an iota of doubt, the rule-based approach is the way forward. As inscribed above, certain sectors insist on explainability. Any compromise on the aspect of explainability may be catastrophic. Without formal explanations, even legal complications or financial repercussions may emerge to haunt AI solution and service providers. But for complicated and sophisticated business problems, symbolic AI turns out to be a difficult affair. Therefore, the automated feature engineering is being widely recommended. Thus, the hybrid AI approach is preferred. In a hybrid approach, explainability can be imparted in multiple ways as indicated below.

• We can use symbolic AI to make the feature engineering process explainable. Symbolic AI helps to extract the most relevant features and use them to bring forth competent AI models.
• The other recommendation is to annotate a massive amount of unstructured data and then a human well-versed in data engineering can validate them for their correctness. Finally, training an AI model can be initiated.
• Another possibility is to develop an AI model to automate the process of creating well-defined and comprehensive symbolic AI rules by taking annotations as the input.

In summary, with AI, it is possible for engineers to enable ML/DL algorithms to extract actionable insights out of data heaps. AI algorithms have the wherewithal to find useful and usable patterns in datasets. The knowledge discovered gets disseminated to business and IT systems to do the right and relevant tasks in time. Thus, insights-driven jobs can be accomplished in an automated manner. Also, multiple systems get integrated and there are business processes for orchestrating multiple services and systems to do complicated tasks with all the clarity and alacrity. Thus, AI-powered automation in association with integrated systems and optimized processes is being seen as a game-changer for the forthcoming era of knowledge.

3.10   The growing scope of XAI for the oil and gas industry

AI solutions are extensively used for solving complicated problems across mission-critical industries. The AI journey is literally mesmerizing. We have generative AI, industrial AI, and real-time AI, explainable, edge, and efficient AI, responsible, trustworthy, and transparent AI, etc. Google has introduced Compose AI in the Gmail application. Thus, there are a series of innovations in the AI. Enterprises keenly leverage the distinct capabilities of AI to envisage and realize enterprise-class systems to retain their consumers and to obtain new customers. In short, AI aids enterprising businesses across the globe to produce and offer pioneering and premium services to their esteemed end-users. A plethora of innovations, disruptions, and transformations are being enabled through AI. For AI to survive and thrive, the main contribution is none other than the huge accumulation of digital data. AI has laid down a stimulating foundation for making sense out of data heaps quickly. That is, transitioning digital data to information and to knowledge is being provided by AI algorithms and models. In the digital era, AI helps to make more value out of data.

AI supports the optimization and automation of business processes. AI provides visibility into business operations and such an understanding helps decision-makers and experts to strategize and plan ahead with all the clarity and alacrity. Important sectors such as the oil and gas industry are gaining more through AI. There are powerful AI solutions by Oil & Gas Solutions – beyond.ai for the oil and gas industry. In other chapters, we have detailed how AI contributes immensely to accelerating and automating a variety of upstream, midstream, and downstream activities. The role of AI in the oil and gas industry is growing rapidly with more understanding of the transformative power of AI technologies and tools. There are several product vendors and solution providers unearthing and providing competent solutions for empowering the oil and gas industry, which is incidentally facing numerous challenges from green activists.

3.10.1   XAI for the oil and gas industry

In high-risk and high-value industries such as oil and gas, healthcare, and finance, it is essential to know what the machine is learning from the data and articulate its findings. But AI models (machine and deep learning models) have to explain why they arrive at a suggestion. The sections below will explain why the XAI is important. For AI to be a trusted advisor and human-like decision-maker, XAI turns out to be an important contributor.

3.11   Conclusion

Previously we were using easily interpretable ML algorithms such as linear, logistic, and polynomial regression decision trees. But nowadays we have bigger problems at hand. This forces us to leverage high-end machine and DL algorithms to create highly accurate problem-solving models. For example, random forest (RF) is an ensemble ML algorithm, which is a combination of multiple decision tree algorithms. The accuracy goes up significantly with the RF algorithm but everything comes with a price. It is quite difficult to interpret the internal functioning of these hugely complicated algorithms and there is no clarity on how the algorithm arrived at such a suggestion, recommendation, detection, summarization, and knowledge discovery. When we humans take a decision, we can clearly explain on what basis we arrived at the conclusion. What prompted to take such a result can be meticulously articulated but that is not the case of automated algorithms and systems. This insists on embedding the interpretability and self-explanatory capabilities into the algorithms to gain back the trust of people on AI-powered systems. Calculating the feature importance is one simple and straightforward approach to simplify the interpretability of AI decisions.

Bibliography

[1] Explainable AI (XAI) by IBM https://www.ibm.com/watson/explainable-ai

[2] XAI making Machine Learning Models Transparent and Understandable https://www.geeksforgeeks.org/explainable-artificial-intelligencexai/

[3] XAI: Tools and frameworks to understand and interpret your machine learning models https://cloud.google.com/explainable-ai/

[4] Explainable artificial intelligence: a comprehensive review https://link.springer.com/article/10.1007/s10462-021-10088-y

[5] Explainable Artificial Intelligence for Medical Applications https://www.hindawi.com/journals/jhe/2022/9087776/

[6] Explainable AI – how humans can trust AI, https://www.ericsson.com/en/reports-and-papers/white-papers/explainable-ai–how-humans-can-trust-ai

[7] Explainable Artificial Intelligence by James Thorn, https://towardsdatascience.com/explainable-artificial-intelligence-14944563cc79

[8] The Main Characteristics of Engineering Application of Artificial Intelligence by Shahab Mohaghegh https://medium.com/geekculture/explainable-artificial-intelligence-xai-67444ed64a38

[9] XAI Research Papers https://paperswithcode.com/task/explainable-artificial-intelligence

[10] XAI Adoption and Advocacy https://ejournals.bc.edu/index.php/ital/article/view/14683/11243

Chapter 4

Inclusion of XAI in artificial intelligence and deep learning technologies

*M. SureshKumar[1], S.I. Vishwa Raviraaj[1] and
R. Sukhresswarun[1]*

4.1 Introduction

As technology has advanced over the past few decades, the complexity of artificial intelligence (AI) systems has increased rapidly. While these systems can provide impressive results, they can also be difficult to understand, even for experts in the field. Explainable AI (XAI) is an emerging field of research focused on making AI systems more transparent and interpretable. In this article, we will explore what XAI is, why it matters, and how it works.

XAI is an emerging field of research that aims to make AI systems more transparent, interpretable, and accountable. In recent years, AI has made significant advances in fields such as natural language processing, image recognition, and game playing. However, as AI systems become more complex and ubiquitous, it becomes increasingly important to ensure that they are used ethically and responsibly.

One of the main challenges with AI is that it can be difficult for humans to understand how the system arrived at a particular decision. For example, a deep learning algorithm might be able to identify objects in an image with incredible accuracy, but it may not be clear how the system arrived at its conclusion. This can lead to a lack of trust in the system, particularly in high-stakes domains such as healthcare, finance, and criminal justice.

Technically, XAI refers to a set of methods and techniques that enable AI systems to provide human-understandable explanations of their decisions, predictions, and actions. XAI utilizes various approaches such as rule-based systems, decision trees, and model-based techniques to produce explanations that can be interpreted and verified by humans. XAI aims to address the lack of transparency and accountability in traditional black-box AI systems referred in Figure 4.1, which can make it difficult for developers and users to understand and trust these systems. By providing interpretable explanations, XAI can increase the effectiveness, reliability, and trustworthiness of AI systems in a variety of applications.

[1]Department of Information Technology, Sri Sairam Engineering College, Chennai, India

Figure 4.1   Black box

4.2   What is XAI?

XAI refers to AI systems that can be easily understood and explained by humans. It is an approach to building AI systems that prioritizes transparency, interpretability, and accountability. XAI systems aim to provide users with a clear understanding of how they work, how they make decisions, and how they can be improved. In contrast, traditional, AI systems often operate as "black boxes," meaning that the inner workings of the system are not visible or understandable to humans.

While XAI has the potential to provide many benefits, there are also several challenges that must be addressed. One of the main challenges is complexity. AI systems can be incredibly complex, with millions or even billions of parameters. This can make it difficult to provide clear and concise explanations for their decisions.

Another challenge is the trade-off between explainability and accuracy. In many cases, making an AI system more interpretable may require sacrificing some level of accuracy or performance. This can be particularly problematic in high-stakes applications, where accuracy is critical.

Bias and fairness are also important challenges in XAI. AI systems can perpetuate and even amplify biases that exist in the data they are trained on. This can lead to unfair or discriminatory decisions. For example, a facial recognition system that is trained on a dataset that is not representative of the population may have higher error rates for certain groups of people.

Privacy is another concern in XAI. XAI systems may require access to sensitive personal data, such as health records or financial information. This raises concerns about privacy and security, particularly in light of recent high-profile data breaches and hacks.

Finally, there is currently a lack of standardization and regulation around XAI. As XAI is a rapidly evolving field, there is no universally accepted set of standards or guidelines for how XAI systems should be designed, evaluated, and deployed. This can lead to inconsistency and confusion in the development and implementation of XAI systems.

Despite these challenges, there are many potential benefits to XAI. One of the main benefits is improved accuracy and performance. By incorporating human feedback and oversight into the AI system, XAI can help ensure that the system is making decisions that are aligned with human values and preferences. This can lead to more accurate and reliable outcomes.

Another benefit of XAI is improved trust and transparency. XAI can help build trust in AI systems by providing clear and concise explanations for how the system arrived at a particular decision. This can help ensure that the system is being used ethically and responsibly.

XAI also has the potential to improve accountability and regulation. By incorporating data provenance and human oversight into AI systems, XAI can help ensure that decisions are made fairly and in accordance with regulations and standards.

Overall, XAI is an important and rapidly evolving field that has the potential to make AI systems more transparent, interpretable, and accountable. While there are many challenges that must be addressed, including complexity, accuracy, bias, and privacy, there are also many potential benefits to XAI, including improved accuracy, trust, and accountability. As AI continues to become more pervasive in our lives, XAI will become increasingly important in ensuring that these systems are used ethically and responsibly.

4.3 Why is XAI important?

The importance of XAI stems from the fact that AI systems are increasingly being used in high-stakes applications, such as healthcare, finance, and criminal justice. In these domains, the decisions made by AI systems can have serious consequences for individuals and society as a whole. Therefore, it is critical that AI systems be transparent and accountable. Additionally, XAI can help build trust in AI systems and ensure that they are used ethically and responsibly.

XAI is important for several reasons. One of the main reasons is that it helps build trust and transparency in AI systems. As AI systems become more complex and ubiquitous, it becomes increasingly important to ensure that they are used ethically and responsibly. By providing clear and concise explanations for how the system arrived at a particular decision, XAI can help build trust in the system and ensure that it is being used in a fair and ethical manner.

Another important reason for XAI is that it can help improve accuracy and performance. By incorporating human feedback and oversight into AI systems, XAI can help ensure that the system is making decisions that are aligned with human values and preferences. This can lead to more accurate and reliable outcomes.

XAI is also important for improving accountability and regulation. By incorporating data provenance and human oversight into AI systems, XAI can help ensure that decisions are made fairly and in accordance with regulations and standards. This can help prevent the use of AI systems in ways that may be harmful or discriminatory.

One of the main challenges with AI is that it can be difficult for humans to understand how the system arrived at a particular decision. This can lead to a lack of trust in the system, particularly in high-stakes domains such as healthcare, finance, and criminal justice. XAI aims to address this challenge by prioritizing transparency and interpretability in AI systems. XAI techniques can take many forms, including explainability techniques, interpretable models, human-in-the-loop systems, data provenance, and adversarial testing.

As AI is increasingly integrated into our daily lives, it is important to understand how these systems make decisions, especially in high-stakes situations such as healthcare, finance, and criminal justice.

Traditional AI systems operate as a "black box," meaning that their decision-making processes are opaque and difficult to interpret. XAI seeks to address this issue by developing AI models that can provide clear, transparent explanations for their actions, allowing users to understand and trust the decisions being made.

There are several approaches to developing XAI, including rule-based systems, model inspection and visualization, and natural language generation. Rule-based systems rely on explicit rules and logic to make decisions, while model inspection and visualization use techniques such as decision trees and heatmaps to help users understand how an AI model is making decisions. Natural language generation involves generating human-readable explanations for AI decisions. XAI has the potential to improve the transparency and accountability of AI systems, increasing user trust and improving outcomes in high-stakes domains. However, there are also challenges to developing XAI, including the trade-off between transparency and performance, and the difficulty of developing explanations that are both accurate and understandable to non-experts.

4.4   How does XAI work?

XAI systems are designed to provide transparency and interpretability for AI models and their decisions. There are several approaches to building XAI systems, including explainability techniques, interpretable models, human-in-the-loop systems, data provenance, and adversarial testing [1].

One approach to XAI is *explainability techniques*. These involve using algorithms and tools to extract information from AI models that can help humans understand how the model arrived at a particular decision. For example, one approach is to identify which features of an input were most important in making the decision. This can help humans understand what factors the model considered and how it weighed them. Another approach is to provide visualizations that show how the model arrived at a particular decision, such as heatmaps that highlight the regions of an image that was most important in making a classification.

Another approach to XAI is *interpretable models*. These are models that are designed to be inherently transparent and interpretable. For example, decision trees and linear regression models are often more interpretable than deep neural networks. However, interpretable models may not always be the best choice for a particular application, as they may sacrifice accuracy for interpretability.

Human-in-the-loop systems involve incorporating human feedback and oversight into the AI system. For example, a radiology AI system might flag potential abnormalities in a scan, but a human radiologist would ultimately make the final diagnosis. This approach can help ensure that the AI system is making decisions that are aligned with human values and preferences. It can also help identify errors or biases in the AI model that may have been overlooked.

Data provenance involves tracking the origin and lineage of data throughout the AI system. This can help ensure that the data being used to make decisions is accurate and unbiased. It can also help identify sources of error or bias in the system. For example, data provenance could be used to track the source of training data used to build a facial recognition model. If the training data was biased toward a particular demographic, this could lead to biased decisions when the model is deployed.

Adversarial testing involves intentionally manipulating the input to an AI system to identify weaknesses or vulnerabilities. For example, an image recognition system might be tested by adding small amounts of noise to an image to see if it can still correctly identify the object in the image. This can help identify potential sources of error or bias in the system. Adversarial testing is particularly important for systems that are used in safety-critical applications, such as self-driving cars or medical diagnosis systems.

To build an XAI system, it is important to start by selecting an appropriate approach that is tailored to the specific application and use case. Different approaches may be more or less effective depending on the complexity of the model and the requirements for transparency and interpretability.

Once an approach has been selected, it is important to design the XAI system to integrate seamlessly with the underlying AI model. This may involve modifying the architecture of the model or adding additional layers to provide transparency and interpretability [2]. It is also important to ensure that the XAI system can scale to handle large volumes of data and complex models.

4.5 Role of XAI in machine learning and deep learning algorithm

XAI, or explainable AI, is becoming increasingly important as machine learning and deep learning algorithms are being used in more critical applications, such as healthcare, finance, and autonomous vehicles. XAI refers to the ability of an AI system to explain its decision-making process in a way that humans can understand.

The role of XAI in machine learning, deep learning, and AI algorithms is to provide transparency and interpretability. By understanding how an AI system is making decisions, humans can better trust and validate its outputs [3]. This is especially important in cases where the AI system is making decisions that have significant consequences, such as in healthcare or autonomous vehicles.

XAI techniques can be applied at different stages of the machine learning pipeline, such as during data preprocessing, model training, and post-processing of results. Some common XAI techniques include feature importance analysis, decision tree analysis, and model-agnostic methods like LIME and SHAP.

XAI is also important for regulatory compliance, as many industries require that AI systems be able to explain their decisions. In the European Union, for example, the General Data Protection Regulation (GDPR) requires that individuals have the right to explanation for automated decision-making systems.

The primary purpose of XAI is to provide human-understandable explanations for the predictions or decisions made by AI algorithms. Here are some of the ways in which XAI helps in these areas:

1. Transparency: XAI provides transparency in the decision-making process of AI algorithms. It helps to identify the factors that influence the outcome and allows users to understand why a particular decision was made.
2. Trustworthiness: XAI promotes the trustworthiness of AI algorithms. By providing explanations for the decisions made by AI, it helps users to have confidence in the algorithm's performance.
3. Accountability: XAI ensures accountability in the decision-making process of AI. It helps to identify the sources of errors and biases in the algorithm and enables users to hold the algorithm and its designers responsible.
4. Optimization: XAI can be used to optimize the performance of AI algorithms. By identifying the factors that contribute most to the outcome, XAI can help developers to improve the algorithm's accuracy and efficiency.
5. Compliance: XAI can help ensure compliance with regulations and ethical standards. By providing explanations for the decisions made by AI, XAI can help developers and users to ensure that the algorithm's actions are in line with legal and ethical guidelines.

In Figure 4.2, (A) today's AI models are often considered black boxes, because they take an input and provide a prediction without saying how and why they arrived at it. (B) Recent XAI methods redistribute the output back to input space and explain the prediction in terms of a "heatmap," visualizing which input variables were decisive for the prediction. (C) This allows to distinguish between meaningful and safe prediction strategies, for example, classifying rooster images by detecting the roster's comb and wattles or classifying cat images by focusing on the cat's ears and nose, and so-called Clever Hans predictors, for example, classifying horse images based on the presence of a copyright tag.

In summary, XAI plays a crucial role in the development and deployment of machine learning, deep learning, and AI algorithms. By providing human-understandable explanations for the decisions made by these algorithms, XAI promotes transparency, trustworthiness, accountability, optimization, and compliance.

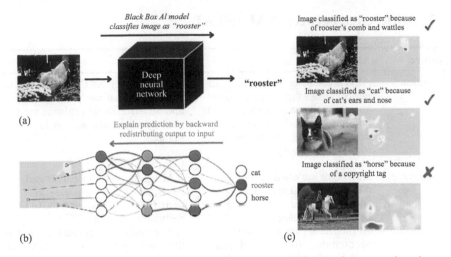

*Figure 4.2   Models A, B, and C denote how AI models are often considered as a
black box*

Overall, XAI is a crucial component in the development and deployment of AI
systems that are transparent, trustworthy, and effective.

4.6   Applications of XAI in machine learning in deep learning

XAI has a wide range of potential applications in machine learning in deep learning, including:

1. Healthcare: XAI can be used to help doctors and nurses make more accurate
    diagnoses and treatment decisions. For example, an XAI system could help
    identify patients at risk of developing sepsis, a life-threatening condition that
    can be difficult to diagnose.
2. Finance: XAI can be used to help identify fraud and make more accurate
    investment decisions. For example, an XAI system could analyze credit card
    transactions to identify patterns of fraudulent activity.
3. Criminal justice: XAI can be used to help judges and parole boards make more
    informed decisions about sentencing and parole. For example, an XAI system
    could analyze criminal records and other data to predict the likelihood of
    reoffending.
4. Transportation: XAI can be used to improve traffic flow and reduce accidents.
    For example, an XAI system could analyze traffic patterns and suggest the best
    routes for drivers to take.
5. Customer service: XAI can be used to provide more personalized and effi-
    cient customer service. For example, an XAI system could analyze customer
    data and provide tailored recommendations or solutions to their inquiries.

4.7   Difference between XAI and AI

Feature	AI	XAI
Definition	AI is a computer system that can perform tasks that usually require human intelligence, such as visual perception, speech recognition, decision-making, and language translation, without explicit instructions.	XAI stands for XAI, which refers to AI systems that can provide clear and understandable explanations of their decisions and actions to humans.
Transparency	AI models are often opaque and difficult to understand, making it challenging to identify the reasoning behind their decisions.	XAI models are transparent and explainable, making it easy to understand how they arrived at a particular decision.
Accountability	AI models are typically not accountable for their decisions, as they lack transparency and explainability.	XAI models are accountable for their decisions, as they provide clear and understandable explanations of their reasoning.
Bias	AI models can be biased due to the data they are trained on, which can result in unfair or discriminatory decisions.	XAI models can identify and mitigate bias in the data they are trained on, resulting in more fair and equitable decisions.
Adoption	AI is widely adopted across various industries, including healthcare, finance, and manufacturing.	XAI is still in its early stages of adoption, but it is gaining traction in industries where transparency and accountability are critical, such as healthcare and finance.

4.8   Challenges in XAI

While XAI has the potential to provide many benefits, there are also several challenges that must be addressed. Some of the main challenges include:

1. Complexity: AI systems can be extremely complex, making it difficult to provide clear and concise explanations for their decisions.
2. Trade-off between explainability and accuracy: In many cases, making an AI system more interpretable may require sacrificing some level of accuracy or performance.
3. Bias and fairness: AI systems can perpetuate and even amplify biases that exist in the data they are trained on. This can lead to unfair or discriminatory decisions.
4. Privacy: XAI systems may require access to sensitive personal data, raising concerns about privacy and security.
5. Lack of standards: Currently, there are no widely accepted standards or guidelines for XAI, making it difficult to evaluate and compare different systems.

XAI has emerged as an important area of research and development in recent years, with the goal of improving the transparency, interpretability, and accountability of AI systems. However, despite its promise, there are several challenges that must be addressed to realize the full potential of XAI.

One of the main challenges with XAI is that it is not always clear what "explainability" means in practice. There are many different techniques and algorithms that can be used to make an AI system more explainable, but it is not always clear which techniques are most effective for a given application or domain. This can make it difficult to evaluate and compare different XAI systems and to determine which ones are most appropriate for a particular use case.

Another challenge with XAI is that there is often a trade-off between accuracy and interpretability. Some of the most accurate AI models, such as deep neural networks, are also some of the most complex and difficult to interpret. Conversely, simpler and more interpretable models may sacrifice accuracy to provide better explanations. This trade-off can make it difficult to strike the right balance between accuracy and interpretability in a given application.

Another challenge with XAI is related to the scalability of XAI techniques. While XAI techniques have shown promise in relatively simple and controlled environments, it is not yet clear how well they will scale to more complex and dynamic real-world environments. In particular, it may be difficult to develop XAI techniques that can adapt to changing circumstances or that can provide accurate and timely explanations in real-time.

Another challenge with XAI is related to the difficulty of incorporating human feedback and oversight into AI systems. While human feedback and oversight can be valuable for improving the transparency and accountability of AI systems, it can also be difficult to incorporate effectively.

For example, humans may have biases or inconsistencies in their feedback, or they may not be able to provide meaningful feedback in real-time.

Yet one more challenge with XAI is that it can be difficult to define and measure the "explainability" of an AI system. There is no universally accepted definition of explainability, and different stakeholders may have different requirements and expectations for what makes an AI system explainable. This can make it difficult to develop and evaluate XAI systems that meet the needs of all stakeholders.

In addition, XAI faces challenges related to the complexity and heterogeneity of data. AI systems often rely on large amounts of complex and heterogeneous data, which can make it difficult to understand how the system is making decisions. This can be especially challenging when the data is noisy, incomplete, or biased, as this can lead to incorrect or misleading explanations.

Finally, XAI faces challenges related to the regulatory and ethical considerations associated with AI. As AI becomes more pervasive in our lives, it is increasingly important to ensure that these systems are being used ethically and responsibly. However, it can be difficult to develop regulations and ethical frameworks that are appropriate for the rapidly evolving field of AI, particularly given the complexity and heterogeneity of AI systems.

To address these challenges, researchers and practitioners in the XAI community are working to develop new techniques and algorithms that prioritize transparency, interpretability, and human feedback. These include techniques for explaining the decisions made by complex AI models, approaches for incorporating human feedback and oversight into AI systems, and methods for evaluating and comparing different XAI systems. By addressing these challenges, XAI has the potential to transform the field of AI and to help ensure that these systems are being used in a fair, transparent, and accountable manner.

4.9   Advantages of XAI

XAI has several advantages over traditional black-box AI systems, including:

1. *Improved transparency*: One of the key advantages of XAI is that it provides increased transparency into how an AI system is making decisions. Traditional black-box AI systems can be difficult to interpret and understand, which can make it challenging to identify errors or biases in the system. XAI systems, on the other hand, provide explanations for their decisions, which can help users understand why the system is making certain recommendations or predictions.

2. *Increased trust*: Another advantage of XAI is that it can increase user trust in AI systems. When users understand how an AI system is making decisions, they are more likely to trust the system and its recommendations. This can be especially important in high-stakes applications, such as healthcare or finance, where trust is critical.

3. *Better performance*: XAI can also lead to better performance in AI systems. When users can understand how an AI system is making decisions, they may be able to provide feedback or corrections that can help improve the system's accuracy and reliability. In addition, XAI techniques such as feature importance analysis can help identify which features or variables are most important for making accurate predictions, which can help optimize the system's performance.

4. *Regulatory compliance*: XAI can also help organizations comply with regulatory requirements related to AI. Many regulatory frameworks, such as the General Data Protection Regulation (GDPR) in Europe, require that organizations be able to explain the decisions made by their AI systems. XAI can provide a way for organizations to meet these requirements and demonstrate compliance.

5. *Better human–AI interaction*: XAI can also improve the interaction between humans and AI systems. When users can understand how an AI system is making decisions, they may be more likely to engage with the system and provide feedback or corrections. This can lead to a more collaborative and effective relationship between humans and AI.

6. *Improved fairness and accountability*: XAI can also help improve the fairness and accountability of AI systems. By providing explanations for their decisions, AI systems can help identify and mitigate biases and errors in the

system. In addition, XAI can help ensure that AI systems are being used in an ethical and responsible manner, which is increasingly important as AI becomes more pervasive in our lives.

Overall, XAI has several advantages over traditional black-box AI systems, including increased transparency, improved trust, better performance, regulatory compliance, better human–AI interaction, and improved fairness and accountability. As XAI continues to evolve and mature, it has the potential to transform the field of AI and to help ensure that these systems are being used in a fair, transparent, and accountable manner.

4.10 Disadvantages of XAI

While XAI has several advantages, it is not without its disadvantages. Some of the main disadvantages of XAI include:

1. *Increased complexity*: XAI systems are often more complex than traditional black-box AI systems. This complexity can make it more difficult to implement and maintain XAI systems. In addition, the explanations provided by XAI systems may be difficult for non-technical users to understand, which can limit their usefulness.
2. *Trade-offs between explainability and performance*: XAI techniques often involve trade-offs between explainability and performance. For example, some XAI techniques may sacrifice performance to provide more interpretable explanations. This can be problematic in applications where accuracy is critical, such as medical diagnosis or financial forecasting.
3. *Limited applicability*: XAI techniques may not be applicable to all types of AI systems. For example, XAI may be less effective in applications where the underlying algorithms are highly complex or where the data is noisy or incomplete. In addition, XAI techniques may be less effective in applications where the decisions made by the AI system are highly context dependent.
4. *Limited scope of explanations*: XAI techniques may be limited in the scope of explanations they can provide. For example, some XAI techniques may only be able to explain the overall decision made by the AI system, without providing details about how specific features or variables influenced the decision. This can limit the usefulness of XAI in applications where detailed explanations are required.
5. *Increased computational overhead*: XAI techniques often require additional computational resources compared to traditional black-box AI systems. This increased computational overhead can make XAI systems more expensive to implement and maintain.
6. *Difficulty in maintaining consistency*: XAI techniques can also be difficult to maintain consistency across different systems or versions of the same system. This is because the explanations provided by XAI systems may be highly dependent on the specific data and algorithm used to generate the explanation.

Figure 4.3   Explainability of XAI

As a result, it can be challenging to ensure that the explanations provided by different systems or versions of the same system are consistent.

7. *Ethical concerns*: Finally, XAI systems can raise ethical concerns related to fairness, bias, and accountability. For example, if an XAI system is used to make decisions about hiring, lending, or medical diagnosis, the explanations generated by the system may need to be audited to ensure that the decisions are fair and unbiased. In addition, XAI systems may be held to higher standards of accountability than traditional black-box AI systems, which can create additional challenges for developers and users.

In summary from Figure 4.3, we can infer that while XAI has several advantages, it is important to be aware of the challenges and limitations of these systems. Researchers and practitioners in the field of XAI must work to develop techniques that balance explainability and performance are applicable to a wide range of AI systems, and are consistent and fair across different versions of the same system. By addressing these challenges, XAI has the potential to make AI systems more transparent, trustworthy, and useful in a wide range of applications [4].

XAI has several disadvantages that can limit its effectiveness in certain applications. These disadvantages include increased complexity, trade-offs between explainability and performance, limited applicability, limited scope of explanations, increased computational overhead, and difficulty in maintaining consistency. It is important for researchers and practitioners in the field of XAI to be aware of these disadvantages and to develop strategies for mitigating them to ensure that XAI systems are effective and useful in a wide range of applications.

4.11   Future scope of XAI

The field of XAI has gained significant attention in recent years due to the need for transparency and accountability in AI systems. As AI continues to become more pervasive in our daily lives, it is crucial that we are able to understand how these systems are making decisions and to ensure that they are making fair and ethical decisions. In this essay, we will explore the future of XAI, including current challenges and future developments.

XAI refers to the ability of AI systems to provide explanations for their decisions and actions, in a way that can be understood by humans. There are many reasons why XAI is important, including:

1. Transparency: XAI helps to provide transparency into how AI systems are making decisions, which is essential for ensuring accountability and fairness.
2. Trust: By providing explanations for their decisions, AI systems can help to build trust with users and stakeholders.
3. Ethics: XAI can help to ensure that AI systems are making ethical decisions, by providing explanations for why certain decisions were made.
4. Compliance: In some industries, such as finance and healthcare, there are regulations that require systems to be explainable, so XAI is necessary to comply with these regulations.

Despite the importance of XAI, there are many challenges that must be addressed to fully realize its potential. One of the biggest challenges is the complexity of AI systems. Many AI systems, such as deep learning neural networks, are highly complex and difficult to understand, even for experts in the field. This makes it challenging to provide explanations that can be understood by non-experts.

Another challenge is the trade-off between accuracy and interpretability. In many cases, more accurate AI models are less interpretable, while more interpretable models may sacrifice some accuracy. This trade-off must be carefully considered when designing AI systems.

Despite these challenges, there are many exciting developments in the field of XAI that will shape its future. One of the most promising developments is the use of natural language explanations. Rather than providing visualizations or other forms of explanation, AI systems can provide explanations in natural language that can be easily understood by humans.

Another promising development is the use of counterfactual explanations. Counterfactual explanations show how a decision would have been different if certain factors had been changed. This can help users to understand why a certain decision was made and how it could be changed in the future.

There are also many efforts underway to develop standards and best practices for XAI. The IEEE Global Initiative on Ethics of Autonomous and Intelligent Systems has developed a set of standards for AI transparency, which includes recommendations for explainability. Other organizations, such as the Partnership on AI, are also working to develop best practices and guidelines for XAI.

4.12 Conclusion

Explainable AI is an emerging field of research that aims to make AI systems more transparent and interpretable. XAI is important for ensuring that AI systems are used ethically and responsibly, particularly in high-stakes domains like healthcare, finance, and criminal justice. While XAI has the potential to provide many benefits, there are also several challenges that must be addressed, such as complexity, bias, and privacy concerns. As XAI continues to evolve, it will be important to establish standards and guidelines to ensure that these systems are used in a safe and effective manner.

In conclusion, XAI is a rapidly growing field that has the potential to address some of the limitations and concerns associated with traditional black-box AI systems. By providing interpretable explanations of how AI systems arrive at their decisions, XAI can increase transparency, trust, and accountability in these systems. XAI can also improve the overall performance and reliability of AI systems by enabling developers and users to identify and correct errors, biases, and other issues.

However, XAI also faces several challenges and limitations, including increased complexity, trade-offs between explainability and performance, limited applicability, limited scope of explanations, increased computational overhead, difficulty in maintaining consistency, and ethical concerns. These challenges must be addressed through ongoing research and development in the field of XAI to ensure that these systems are effective, useful, and fair.

Despite these challenges, XAI has already made significant contributions to a wide range of fields, including healthcare, finance, transportation, and more. As XAI techniques continue to evolve and improve, we can expect to see even more applications and benefits of this technology in the years to come. By working to address the challenges and limitations of XAI, we can create AI systems that are transparent, trustworthy, and effective, and that enable us to harness the full potential of AI for the betterment of society.

References

[1] S. Kaur, *Explainable AI: Building Interpretable Models,* https://medium. com/@supreetkaur_66831/explainable-ai-xai-building-interpretable-models-d616b0fccd33

[2] H. Chad Lane, Domain Independence XAI Architecture, https://www. researchgate.net/figure/Domain-Independent-XAI-Architecture_fig2_228572498

[3] R. Inam, A. Terra, A. Mujumdar, and E. Fersman, *Explainable AI – How Humans can Trust AI*, https://www.ericsson.com/en/reports-and-papers/ white-papers/explainable-ai--how-humans-can-trust-ai

[4] S. Mohehhegh, *Explainable Artificial Intelligence (XAI)*, https://medium. com/geekculture/explainable-artificial-intelligence-xai-67444ed64a38

Chapter 5

Explainable artificial intelligence: tools, platforms, and new taxonomies

*Ghulam E. Mustafa Abro[1], Parteek Kumar[2],
Vijanth Sagayan Asirvadam[1], Nirbhay Mathur[1] and
Fawad Salam Khan[3]*

Recent advances in machine learning (ML) strategies have introduced several artificial intelligence (AI)-based systems. These AI systems have the capability to perceive, learn, smartly decide, and act quickly on the given situation. Apparently, this is the requirement from such systems but after witnessing their performance, it has been noticed that these systems are unable to explain their actuation to users (humans). This constraint has been taken into consideration by several researchers later, after all this is the main thing required to make our autonomous systems more intelligent and robust. At this instant, researchers felt the need for explainable AI (XAI) that may make the verifiability of taken decision essential. This will increase the demand for an ability to question, understand, and above all generate a trust level over artificial intelligence systems. There are several models but still there is no consensus on the assessment of explainability. Thus, this chapter presents a comprehensive review of current state-of-the-art over the XAI that have a societal impact. In addition to this, one may find the drivers and tools for XAI. Last but certainly not the least is the complete literature review that provides the future research directions for researchers in this area.

5.1 Introduction

With the evolution of ML algorithm and the modern demands, the explainable AI (XAI)-based systems are getting a lot of attention by the researchers. These researchers are indulged in improving the ML algorithms and model in terms of

[1]Department of Electrical and Electronic Engineering, Universiti Teknologi PETRONAS, Seri Iskandar, Perak, Malaysia
[2]Second Company Department, Telecom SudParis, 5 Rue Charles Fourier Evry, France
[3]Faculty of Electrical and Electronics (FKEE), Universiti Tun Hussein Onn Malaysia, Parit Raja, Malaysia

better explainability and performance metrics. Looking at the significance of this area, one must put more focus on the convergence of scientific knowledge. Thus, this chapter aims to present all relevant literature review on the explainability of artificial intelligence (AI). Besides quoting all previous research contributions, it supports the idea that explainability of AI algorithms is one of the important aspects. One may also be able to study fundamental concepts that are related to this area. Unlike other research manuscripts, this chapter focuses on the societal impact of the XAI and the performance metrics. There is an increment observed in heterogeneous sort of data as well as in computational power and this led ML algorithms to be more predictive in nature as compared to previous ones. The systems nowadays are more complex for instance and to handle them there is a need for more efficient techniques such as deep residual networks (RESNETs) [1] initiated for the first time in 2016. It has more than 200+ layers and has outclassed human performance already in recognizing the patterns or objects. With such extraordinary performance, ML-based systems have been accepted by all in huge numbers and in several daily life services and products. Either one is opting for any movie suggestions to voice assistants or in any other domains where decisions may key impact thing, i.e., health care decisions during the COVID-19 era. Our society now cannot deny the utilization and importance of AI [2].

As per the international data corporation (IDC), AI has to grow from US $30 billion to US $80 billion between the epoch of 2018 and 2023 which means the compound annual growth rate (CAGR) will be almost 40% [3]. In addition to this, there are several market intelligence firms such as Tractica that have already predicted that AI-based systems and software solutions may give rise to global revenue from US $9.0 billion to US $102.5 billion by the end of 2025 [4]. To strengthen the same idea, Gartner which is one of the famous research companies has quoted AI as one of the top three strategic technology trends in the year 2019 [5]. This shows that AI has a great impact over society right now and in the future this will grow more [2].

Till now, it seems that ML algorithms to implement AI solutions are powerful enough, but they have some constraints and limitations as well. In the list of such constraints, one may see a transparency lack [6] that is associated with black-box ML models. The term black box itself shares the idea that the internal structure will be hidden from users and therefore there are some disadvantages as well. For example, it will prevent a human from understanding the logic behind the system on which it is deciding the things [7]. In simple words, one may say that the black-box model is a complex system to understand [8]. This is the issue with several ML-based models [9] such as deep neural networks (DNN). As ML-based models are nowadays studied and implemented in several domains such as healthcare, courts, and other sensitive and regulated domains, one must be aware of the explainability of AI behind these high-stakes decisions.

To address this limitation of understanding, the logic behind ML-models enabled researchers to bring the concept of XAI that majorly focuses on the interpretability of AI algorithms and systems. The main objective behind introducing this area is to create models with more interpretability with high predictiveness [2].

This term explainable artificial intelligence (XAI) has been proposed for the first time in [10] to define the ability of a system to brief the behavior of AI-controlled applications. Initially, it was discussed in a minor context in the early 1970s to draw the attention of researchers and experts [11–13], and later researchers continued their work until neural networks had been introduced [14]. Later, the progress was somehow sluggish in the early 2000s [15,16]. During this development, the focus of AI has been moved toward the models and improvising the algorithms whereas the interpretability was not into consideration yet. In recent times, when people witnessed the ML-based complex systems that were behaving just like a black box, the need for this topic emerged a lot [17].

The chapter has been structured as follows. In Section 5.2, one may find social and industrial awareness about ML-based systems, and Section 5.3 shares the challenges of the XAI. Furthermore, one may find the societal concerns and regulations within this section. Whereas the literature review regarding the concepts is mentioned in Section 5.4. Section 5.5 deals with the study of existing strategies to improve the XAI. Lastly, but certainly not the least, Section 5.6 concludes the chapter.

5.2   ML-based systems and awareness

The most famous term in this field is DARPA which stands for Defense Advanced Research Project Agency which is an entity dully funded by the Department of Defense of the United States of America. This project has initiated XAI and led to the acquisition of funding for 11 U.S. research labs [18] for the same project. Their main aim was to address the interpretability of AI-based systems with a high predictiveness level and gain the trust among society for understanding the systems in a better way [19]. Later, it was observed that the White House Office of Science and Technology Policy also shared a report "Preparing for the future of AI" showing the public focus that the AI systems will be now more open, understandable, and more transparent so that people may understand the logics and assumptions behind them [20]. Moreover, USACM that stands for U.S. Public Policy Council for Computing Machinery also shared a report titled "Statement on Algorithmic Transparency" in 2017.

This report also highlighted the seven principles for algorithmic transparency and accountability [21]. Along with the United States, other countries also realized the same need which can be seen in the Dutch AI Manifesto in 2018. This manifesto explains how a system can take decisions [22], and the French Strategy for AI was introduced in 2018 by the French President to develop such transparent algorithms that may explain the models and provide an easy user interface [23]. Similarly, the Royal Society of United Kingdom Academy of Sciences initiated the same thing in 2017 recognizing the importance of interpretability and sharing AI as one of the promising solutions for social issues [24].

Moreover, transparency and interpretability will bring more confidence among society and can easily be deployed. In Portugal, the National Initiative on Digital Skills also endorsed the same concept in their official document of AI Portugal 2030 vision. The entire document is all about innovation and further growth strategy using AI in Portugal and in the context of Europe [25]. It also emphasizes that AI can ensure ethics and societal safety if AI-made decisions are improved in terms of explainability. So, this is the common context of several countries that AI systems must be produced in a way that may give freedom to humans to understand and in this way the risk of bias error will also be reduced [26]. Keeping the same idea the European Commission proposed and implemented a pilot project of 16 months in the year 2018 popularly known as Algorithmic Awareness Building (AAB) [27–29]. There are several such documents that have instructed such ideas including the seven key essentials for AI systems to be transparent, accountable, and trustworthy.

Discussing the AI-based companies such that Google has declared their practices publicly that advocates the idea of interpretability and user experience as well [30]. There is an automated ML platform titled "H2O" which is a driverless AI that shares the interpretability as one of its features [31]. One may see DataRobot which is one of the familiar and commercial ML-solution so far and results in human interpretability [32]. Discussing further, one may see that IBM presents a business AI Platform titled "IBM Watson AI OpenScale" [32]. Apart from all, Kyndi also shared a XAI platform for several public, private, financial, and healthcare domains [33].

Discussing the research firms and project, one may see the example of FICO, which is an analytics software company that is focused on the ML interpretability and shared one white paper on XAI toolkits [34] which turned this idea into analytics workbench product later [35]. The research team at FICO has been involved in developing transparent credit Risk Scorecards which is one of the better examples to understand the concept of an explainable artificial intelligence approach [36]. This work also clinched the best paper award in the year 2018 under the category of data Analytics in 2018 [37].

Social sites such as Facebook in association with Georgia Tech shared a publication that highlights DNN models [38]. Similarly, Uber, like applications have a model agnostic visual debugging tool for ML [39]. This XAI is defined as a two-way communication between humans as the user and a computing gadget as an ML model executer. Within this relation, there are three research areas that can be considered to improve things such as:

- Data Science (DS)
- Human Science (HS)
- Human Computer Interaction (HCI)

ML algorithms are of no use without data and their predictiveness and accuracy depend on both the quantity as well as the quality of the data. Similarly accurate explanation depends on accurate predictions, so Data Science is a strongly interlinked concept. Whereas to study how humans understand the explanation and consider the working of a model is known as the Human Science (HS). Lastly, HCI stands for Human Computer Interaction is the area where one must deal with user comprehension along with trust in the system. Researchers have considered that the user must be given this freedom to derive the outcome

Table 5.1   Workshops and sessions on interpretability from 2014 to 2022

Name of sessions	Year
CVPR Session on XAI [41]	2019–2022
AAAI-19 Network Interpretability for deep Learning [42]	2019
ICAPS [43,44]	2018–2019
Session on Explainable Smart Systems [45,46]	2018–2019
CD-MAKE Workshops [47,48]	2018–2019
IPMU Session 2018 [49]	2018–2019
MLCN, DLF Sessions [50]	2018
Session on IJCAI Workshop [51,52]	2017–2018
IJCNN Explainability [53]	2017
XCI Session [54]	2017
NIPS Symposium [55]	2017
NIPS Symposium on complex system [56]	2016
ICML Workshop [57–59]	2016–2018
DTL and KDD Session [60]	2014–2018

based on priority [17] and knowledge from the related data/field. This can help in improving the XAI systems.

Furthermore, it is suggested that researchers from the cognitive science and psychology domain may come forward to improvise the ML-based system for interpretability issues and bridging data science with human sciences [40]. Some of the sessions were conducted over the same topic and are quoted in Table 5.1. This shows the progress already initiated for the same cause.

The above number of symposiums and sessions shows the increasing interest of people around the globe for explainable AI (XAI) [41–60]. There are several competitions as well to showcase the better solutions from renowned institutions such as a joint collaboration among Oxford, MIT, Google, and FICO to introduce the first explainable ML challenge in the year 2018 where teams were instructed to not only produce models with accuracy but also do create it in terms of fine interpretability [61]. There are several other world institutions such as the Institute for Ethical AI and Machine Learning UK, which is considered as one of the research centers for ML provided the eight principles for responsible development of ML systems [62] after going through research work.

This term explainable AI has been outlined by various research centers and institutions [63–66] but in practical scenarios, explainability and interpretability are connected topics. It is said that interpretable systems are explainable if and only if their operations within the system can be understood completely by the users [2] and therefore the term of interpretability has been used a lot more than explainability.

5.3   Challenges of the time

This section shares the main reasons why the topic of XAI has attracted the audience of today. Moreover, one may find challenges associated with this field.

5.3.1   Requirement of explainability

If any model is utilized and has a good predictiveness level and is acceptable, still one has some risks related to the acceptability of that model to take some decisions. The issue is all about metrics that are classification of accuracy for instance, one may not be dependent on this for solving the real issues of the world [40].

Therefore, it is important to consider the predictiveness, accuracy, and explainability as well to completely depend over any model [40,67,68] but at the same point, it is said there are certain situations where the explainability can be ignored. Such situations are divided into two categories as mentioned below:

- First one is where no important influence occurs due to incorrect results.
- Second is the situation where the issue is studied in depth, and one may trust already the decision given by the system even if the system is not that much perfect.

The first category refers to low-risk systems where any mishandling may not harm [69] whereas the second situation refers to any system where the entire calculation is dependent on the system itself such as an automated bottle-filling plant that has been given the instructions for the day and that will do the job for the rest without any intervention of human being.

5.3.2   Impact of high-stake decisions

In this sub-heading, it is to share the importance of such cases where there is a huge impact of decisions on our society. For example, in the health care and financial service domains. These are the domains where the wrong decisions may bring imbroglio [9] and in real such situations have increased the need for explainability. To realize the seriousness of such decisions, the manuscript would like to quote some of the examples. Let us say that if people are denied parole incorrectly [70,71], bail given to dangerous criminals or pollutants are not detected [72], and the model is quoting an unsafe situation as a safe one [73]. There are several incidents where the decision was made in the wrong way such as a mortgage crisis [74] and the reason was the same which is a lack of transparency in the same system.

5.3.3   Concerns of society

Discussing the details of wrongly taken decisions as it is very sensitive matter and leads to serious impacts over the society. One of the popular examples is the criminal risk assessment algorithm known as correctional offender management profiling for alternative sanctions (COMPAS) where biased decisions and non-reliable outcomes have damaged several minority groups [75,76]. It was also seen that COMPAS was more difficult to understand the logic and audit as well [75]. This is the reason, the chapter supports the significance of interpretability/explainability of ML-based systems [77] so that one audits the system and may understand the internal logic.

It is an admitted fact that these ML-based systems do not provide 100% perfect results and judgment but still it is one of the better ways to derive solutions. The only thing such a system requires is detailed data. More data will bring more accuracy to the decision. With more data the model will be trained in a better way to return better predictions, but if it is not taken into consideration, then it may lead to the discrimination of several minority groups [78].

Some of the researchers argued and compared human-made decisions with computer-made decisions and claimed that due to the involvement of humans in computer-made decisions, the results were improved, and the right measures were taken. These researchers have quoted several systems [79] that never comment on the future but rather than the past-related data which means they did not have learning ability, and this is the reason one should derive the way that may comment over the biasness and explainability of the system.

Researchers have used the knowledge of psychology [80] and proposed several amendments in the light of incompleteness and explanations. To optimize and understand the explainability one must keep the below points in mind [40]:

• Fairness and insurance of predictions
• Keeping the privacy of the data
• Ensuring the interaction between human and ML systems

5.3.4   Regulations and interpretability issue

Due to such consequences and incidents, society raises the need for such ML systems that may have an element of explainability. In addition to this, there is a need to introduce some new regulations for the verifiability of such algorithmic decisions. One of the examples is protection regulations set by Europe known as "European General Data Protection Regulation (GDPR)" which is ISO/IE 27001 certified [81–83]. It was introduced in 2018 and shares the explanation aspects of algorithmic decisions [84]. This emerges the obligation to explain the ML-based system [85] so that one may audit it easily which is no doubt a challenging task so far [86]. In addition to this, one should know when and what sort of explanation is needed [87,88].

In simple words, the model must explain how the prediction process is executed because in this way, one may solve the original issue. As far as incompleteness is considered, there should be some specifications included such as safety, ethics, optimizing mismatched objectives, and trading off between multi-object [89]. Since interpretability and explainability are the subject sort of constraint and therefore it remains unsolved so far [90]. It relies on several factors such as context and other types of explanatory factors [91].

5.4   State-of-the-art approaches

Explainability or interpretability is something that cannot be defined in terms of mathematical context, but it is defined in non-mathematical context as the degree at which one may understand the logic or cause of a decision taken by the ML-based system [92–95]. This means that the level of the model must be higher so that a person may predict the results easily.

The ability to explain the understandable logic behind any model is the latest definition referred nowadays [40] and the better model is the one that may define the reasons for the derived outcome better [69]. Moreover, interpretability is something that is associated with the understanding of how one may understand the idea of the model and may also be able to digest the reasons behind the decisions. To resolve the curiosity of one human being and make him able to learn is the prime objective of explainability [94]. In most of the general cases, it has been observed that humans are not concerned with what is going on behind the computer, but this situation is really changed when they get an unexpected outcome. This thing creates curiosity and stimuli humans to know the reason behind such unexpected outcomes.

These curios incidents are more frequent during the study of ML models and their trainings as they react like a black-box model that provides predictions without detailed and easy explanations [69]. Discussing the perks of explainability, one may use them to resolve the world issues [94] and this impacts a lot on social life. These unexpected outcomes are very common in the study of ML models, thus researchers can minimize the gap between expectation and reality by meeting the criteria of explanation. Quoting an example where an ML model of the bank can easily reject the loan application. In a such scenario, the loaner must know why his application has been rejected or what grounds the ML algorithm scrutinizes his application. The level of explainability is decided as per some of the decision factors [88] which are quoted by the European General Data Protection Regulatory (GDPR).

In addition to this, if we see the example of getting meaningful information about the different products and movie recommendations; people who like the same type of movies will get suggestions for similar movies [95]. This example also witnesses the acceptance of society in our daily routine and this is the core thing required for the integration of ML-based systems in daily life. This is commonly intuitive that our society will accept ML-based algorithms if they are explainable [96,97]. It is likewise really well worth noting that factors are used to control social interactions. By growing a shared means of something, the explainer affects the actions, feelings, and ideals of the recipient of the rationalization. More specifically, for a system to correctly engage with people, it is able to want to form people's feelings and ideals via persuasion, so as to attain their meant goal [69]. Another critical price empowered via way of means of interpretability is safety [94]. Interpretability permits MLs fashions to be tested, audited, and debugged, which is a route in the direction of growing their safety, especially for domain names wherein mistakes will have extreme consequences. For example, which will keep from self-using motors strolling over cyclists, a proof would possibly display that the maximum essential function to perceive bicycles is the two wheels, and this rationalization facilitates to consider part cases, along with while wheels are included via way of means of facet bags [69]. Interpretability additionally permits detection of defective version behavior, via debugging and auditing. An interpretation of a faulty prediction facilitates to apprehend the reason for the error. It can provide a course on the way to repair the machine and, thereby, boom its safety.

For example, in a husky versus wolf photo classifier, interpretability might permit to discover that misclassification passed off due to the fact the version found out to apply snow as a function for detecting wolves [69].

As per [40], an ML model and its decision must provide a proper way so that the infrastructure of an ML-based system may be verified. This also includes factors such as integrity, confidentiality, and above all the fairness of the system. From an other perceptive, explainability turns it depending on the data only. Thus, for ML models, one must have enough data. The completeness of the model is all about how one has done the parameterization of the data. Let us have the same example of the bank model where its main aim is to provide loan to those people who may return in a specific time and may repay, but there are other parameters that a bank looks at before providing the loan such as the obligation to not discriminate over the demographics [69]. This is good to see that the ML-based black-box models have solved several issues with large datasets. Explainability shares the main way to extract the data from the model thus, the better way or definition to define explainability depends on the field of application and context [78]. Researchers have defined this concept already. It states that the explanation of any ML-based system must answer to the logic behind the decisions. Indeed the main aim of explainability is to clear the doubts and make things easy to understand. So, when the explanation term is concerned it indicates toward the characteristic values of an individual that correspond to the prediction and of course, it is humanly understandable [69]. To acquire the better or the best explanation, it is very important to understand the ML model completely. There are some explanatory theories quoted in [96] as mentioned below:

- *Non-pragmatic hermeneutics:* It is the explanation related to the right answers associated with why questions.
- *Pragmatism of interpretation:* This is the explanation that is a good reply for why questions for the generic audience. The important difference between both theories is that there is no chance for the audience in non-pragmatic theories. Because they are not most of the cases the right explanation. This means whether a person understands it or not, this is no longer a concern in non-pragmatic theories whereas pragmatic is vice versa and are allied naturally with an idea that it may have multiple meanings and explanations [97]. Literature says it has been argued that XAI and pragmatic theories are more suitable as compared to non-pragmatic theories. It is because they are as per the practicality, legal and ethical demands of companies. Whereas the researchers are developing XAI-based ML systems as per the expectations of humans. It shows that the main goal is to make the audience in a state of understanding these algorithms, not to answer them correctly [94].
- *Cognitive dimension:* This dimension deals with knowledge acquisition and deriving the factual explanation through active inferences. The idea is to identify the cause of the main event and then the subset of the causes to provide a better explanation.
- *Social dimension*: This dimension deals with the process that is referred to as a specific interaction. This interaction is between the social interaction,

knowledge acquisition, and later transformed to the interpreter from explainer. The main objective is to acquire more detailed information from the explainer to understand the method to derive the decision. Moreover, the interpreter discussed here can be anyone, i.e., a machine or a human. It is to emphasize more the need for interpretation as well [98].

- *Expressive power*: It is known as an explanatory structure or language which can set of rules, or decision trees.
- *Opacity:* This shows the dependency of explanatory methods over the internal working of any ML model and its parameters. As a result, the model diagnostic methods have no transparency.
- *Portability:* It defines the range of ML-based models where the explanatory strategy is implemented. Moreover, one may say that it is the exact opposite of opacity. It means if there is high opacity then there will be low mobility or portability and vice versa.
- *Algorithm complexity:* It is linked with the computational subject of the proposed method. It is a significant property that must be taken into consideration, especially during the computation time. Furthermore, this is evaluated in several conditions for instance with respect to randomness and in terms of a few explanatory methods that may lead to low stability of XAI. It is also noted that there are some methods and strategies where the results are depending on several choices, for instance, the number of time intervals, sampling of data as well as significance of feature. To provide a clearer view of the content of this literature review, Table 5.2 presents a summary of the literature review.

Table 5.2   Summary of literature review

Section	Content
Explainability Goals	Accuracy
	Efficiency
Explainability Evaluation	Human level
	Functional level
Human Friendly Explainability	Selectivity, social, truthful, and consistent
Properties of XAI	Accuracy
	Fidelity
	Consistency
Scope of XAI	Algorithm transparency
	Global and local model explainability
Taxonomy of XAI	Pre in and post model study
	Results explanation
Significance of Explainability	Satisfy the curiosity
	Scientific finding
	Find meaning
	Safety
	Acquire knowledge

5.5 Assessment approaches

After stating the need for explainability in several aspects, one may think of the assessment approaches to how explainability can be measured. A similar ambiguity has been mentioned in [40] that however model and their classes are explainable and expressible? In addition to this if one is going to compare the methods of different models with each other, then is it necessary to have the same explainability need? Such questions are equally important for explanation methods whereas the progress in this regard is still on its way and researchers are more titled toward the task of increasing the predictive accuracy. After seeing so much growth in the methods to improve the ML explainability and XAI, very less focus has been set on the development of measures that assess the explainability of the model.

There are a few advancements such as opting for the most appropriate explanation and metrics so that one may quantify these methods [78,99]. As per the survey, 5% of the literature addresses the issue of assessing the explainability methods [2]. Thus, this section shares a focus on this idea. Research contributions have proven that there are two main indicators for assessment such as qualitative and quantitative indicators. After reviewing these indicators, it is observed to establish a linkage between both indicators. This has been illustrated in Table 5.3.

5.6 Drivers for XAI

XAI is essential when people are to comprehend, appropriately trust, and successfully govern the outcomes of AI algorithms for commercial benefits, ethical considerations, and supervisory concerns. The literature that has been looked into indicates that there are at least four possible motivations for the passion for explaining AI algorithms (see Figure 5.1). Although there may seem to be a

Table 5.3 *Relation between explanation properties and quantitative explainability indicators*

Factors [100]	Research contribution [101]	Research contribution [78]	Research contribution [64]
Representative	NA	NA	Completeness
Novelty	NA	Separability, identity	NA
Significance	NA	NA	NA
Certainty	NA	Stability	NA
Comprehension	NA	NA	Compactness
Stability	NA	NA	NA
Consistency	Invariance	NA	Yes
Fidelity	Sensitivity	NA	Corrections
Accuracy	NA	NA	Corrections

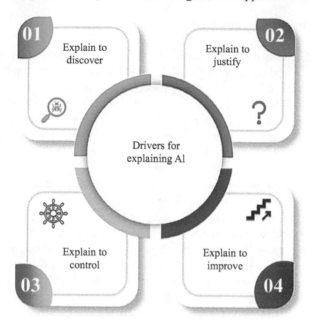

Figure 5.1   Drivers of explaining AI

connection between these motivations, it is important to keep in mind that they represent the numerous motivations for XAI.

Asking for clarifications is an effective way to discover underlying knowledge and learn about the underlying problem. Only explainability can offer a strong tool for confirming and gaining fresh perspectives on the current conundrum, which will eventually lead to a more dependable AI solution. Thus, it is anticipated that XAI algorithms will one day assist domain specialists in revealing hitherto unknown theories and laws in the fields of chemistry, physics, biology, medicine, and nanoscience. The information gathered by XAI can be used to better understand how AI algorithms behave when exposed to various learning methodologies, data formats, architectural designs, parameters, etc.

There have been numerous discussions in the literature about AI solutions producing arbitrary or unfair results. This suggests that there is an increasing need for justifications to ensure the accuracy of the judgments made by AI algorithms. Instead of discussing the internal mechanics or the thinking logic at the heart of the decision-making system, explanations of AI-driven findings frequently imply the necessity for motives or rationalizations for that conclusion. In this situation, XAI can be used to provide the necessary information to justify results, particularly in cases of unforeseen judgments. Additionally, it ensures that a testable and verifiable procedure supports decisions as being fair and rational, fostering trust.

Contrary to popular belief, the answer goes beyond justifying the results of AI algorithms. It can, however, also help prevent things from going wrong. In fact, having a better understanding of how the system operates allows you to spot potential flaws and vulnerabilities earlier and makes it easier to quickly identify and correct errors in less critical situations. The management of the AI-based system can be improved by establishing a set of control rules based on this information.

The need to constantly improve AI algorithms' performance is another reason to explain them. It is widely acknowledged that XAI algorithms can be strengthened more firmly. Users will know the ideal method to make a production brighter once they are aware of the motivations for its creation. As a result, XAI may serve as the foundation for further advancement between machines and humans. In turn, this will open the door for improving learning outcomes in dynamic and changing situations.

5.6.1 Tools and frameworks

With the importance of XAI growing every day, it is crucial for the research community to establish a set of tools and frameworks that will make it easier to implement and reproduce various explainability approaches for investors at various levels. As a result, this section of the book lists the typical open-source XAI frameworks (see Figure 5.2).

- AIX3601: This open-source toolkit, which was described in [102,103], provides a cogent, accommodating, and straightforward programming interface in addition to a corresponding software architecture to implement various explainability approaches required by a range of stakeholders. A few quantitative criteria were provided by the AIX360 to serve as substitutes for the "excellentness" of a given local explanation.

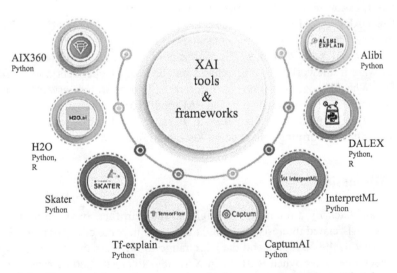

Figure 5.2   Frameworks and common tools for comprehensible artificial intelligence

- H2O: It represents another intriguing toolbox for deciphering AI systems, offering both intrinsic local and global explanations based on rules.
- It is an integrated, open-source Python framework called Skater that is used to implement model interpretation for many ML modes in practical issues. In either regression or classification problems, it enables the local and global demystification of the learned structures of a black-box model.
- Tf-explain is a framework for deriving explanations for TensorFlow models based on gradient and activation maps.
- Ethical ML-XAI is an ML tool that uses model and data analysis to create fundamental explainability in AI solutions.
- An open-source framework for PyTorch model interpretability is CaptumAI. It breaks down the different explanation techniques into three categories: primary attribution, layer attribution, and neuron attribution. It can handle several data modalities and is easily extensible with new features and algorithms.
- Glass-box ML models built for interpretability and black-box explainability approaches for elucidating current AI solutions are provided by the InterpretML free Python module.
- DALEX: It is put out by [104] to facilitate the creation of responsible AI solutions that integrate various methodologies and close the gap currently separating black-box models from XAI. It provides an interactive explanation of the concept based on a model-neutral user interface and many fairness indicators. There are two versions of DALEX: one for R programming and the other for Python programming. It has been tailored for tabular data and can support numerous visualization plots.
- Alibi is an open-source Python framework that is designed to deal with many types of data (such as tabular, text, and picture data) under both regression and classification models. It was first introduced in [105].
- The DARPA XAI program created the Explainable AI Toolkit (XAITK), an open-source toolkit that helps consumers, academics, and technicians understand complex AI solutions. The toolkit combines a more unified, well-liked software framework with a searchable database of independent non-profits.
- The What-If Tool is a framework for providing a straightforward graphical user interface from which an opaque AI model for classification or regression can be understood. It enables users to directly visualize the results in various ways after performing inference on a sizable number of samples.

5.7   Discussion

Let us stand back for a moment. Although the three artifacts ought to be adequate for many XAI-related interests, they might fall short in some circumstances. Due to the intricacy of the XAI area and the wide range of interests that researchers from other disciplines have when working in XAI, it is likely that some circumstances will be too unique for one of our solutions to be effective. We will briefly examine a few methods that might work in this section.

5.7.1 For researchers outside of computer science: taxonomies

Each of the studied taxonomies has a certain purpose, as was previously said. However, as we have argued, these taxonomies are not appropriate for all goals that a taxonomy could be used for. For instance, when assessing the caliber of these taxonomies, we have occasionally employed the criterion of newcomer-friendliness. Here, one may argue that many of these taxonomies are not intended for XAI beginners, at least not ones who aren't computer scientists. Even with our idea, we must acknowledge that it is just the beginning of facilitating multi-disciplinary research. In light of this, it might be advantageous to create taxonomies specifically for researchers outside of the field of computer science.

Tim Miller's influential book "Explanation in Artificial Intelligence: Insights From the Social Sciences" [106] contains one suggestion in this regard. To enlighten computer scientists about explanation research, he surveyed the literature in philosophy, cognitive science, and psychology for this project. He was inspired by the realization that there is no consensus in the XAI literature regarding what constitutes a good explanation; he and his colleagues found that many authors just put forth what they believe to be satisfactory explanations without providing any supporting evidence [100,107]. Miller identified four qualities that explanations should include in his review [106]: they should be contrastive, chosen for the situation at hand, not contain possibilities, and respect social elements (e.g., take into account a person's background knowledge). Additionally, he discovered that various explanation styles each had advantages and disadvantages of their own. Some are better than others, for instance, when it comes to inspiring understanding. Therefore, it would be useful to create a taxonomy of explainability approaches based on the type of produced explanation.

Different kinds of explanations are a professional issue for philosophers and psychologists in particular. In light of this, an explanation-based taxonomy could aid those from various disciplines in beginning to use XAI. With the help of such a taxonomy, psychologists could, for instance, carry out research to determine what kind of explanations are most appropriate in certain situations (see, for instance, [108–110] for such studies in employment scenarios).

5.7.2 Taxonomies and reviews focusing on specific aspects

To solve missing cases, taxonomies for specific application domains may be created. In fact, there are some works out there that go this route. For example, Müller *et al.* [111] provide a taxonomy specifically for the field of computational pathology, and Tjoa and Guan [112] created one specifically for the field of medicine.

In other studies, explainability summaries for certain domains are presented instead of taxonomies. Examples are Nunes and Jannach [112] who concentrate on the explainability of recommender systems, Anjomshoae *et al.* [113] who concentrate on the explainability of robotics and human-robot interaction, Abdul *et al.* [114] who concentrate on the human-computer interaction (HCI) domain, and Mathews [115] who concentrates on the classification of biomedicine and malware.

Likewise, evaluations that concentrate on a single class of explainability techniques might also be beneficial to cover situations in which our suggestions might not work. For instance, Ivanovs *et al.* [116] examine perturbation-based explainability techniques for DNNs, highlighting their differences as well as their similarities.

5.7.3   Fresh perspectives on taxonomy

The absence of crucial elements may also contribute to the formation of scenarios that our recommendations do not address. With the help of the dimension fidelity [117], we shall demonstrate this concept. The problem with many post-hoc explainability methods is that the explanation they produce does not always correspond to what is happening in the model they are explaining [118].

The internals of the models they explain are not taken into account by model-agnostic explainability methods, which are the focus of this issue. In this aspect, model-specific explainability approaches perform better since they build explanations by using a model's internals. The explanations' level of adherence to the models they describe, however, still falls on a continuum. As a result, approaches could be taxonomized according to how faithful they are. The following is one justification for such a dimension: various scenarios have various stakes. The ability to get a trustworthy explanation in case of failure is crucial, especially when the stakes are high. As Rudin contends [119], there might in some circumstances be no alternative to utilizing ante-hoc explainability methodologies.

5.7.4   Taxonomy levels at new levels

The addition of new levels to the taxonomy is the final strategy we want to cover to meet situations that our artifacts might not be able to resolve. We will talk about this in terms of the outcome dimension. Let us go back to the techniques TCAV [118] and counterfactual explanations [120], which were previously categorized inconsistently, for this purpose. In theory, our taxonomy can adequately classify them. Both fall within the category of feature importance in terms of the outcome.

The traits that they measure, meanwhile, are significantly different in terms of semantics. Counterfactual explanations explain what modifications to the input values would be necessary to produce a specific output value. On the other hand, TCAV determines if certain user-defined ideas are pertinent to a specific classification class.

There is nevertheless a distinction between using existing features (as provided by the input variables) and using freshly generated ones (as defined by the user), even though some of these semantic differences may be attributable to the difference in scope (counterfactual explanations are local, but TCAV is global). Therefore, one may add additional subcategories for feature relevance approaches to account for this distinction. These subcategories might be relevant to the (kind of) feature being looked at. Such subcategories exist in some of the analyzed taxonomies, for example [121,122]. However, compared to the taxonomies' more basic categories, the incongruity for these ones is even more obvious. As a result, there is still much to learn about this.

5.8 Conclusion

As seen in this chapter, the main reason why the interpretability problem remains unresolved is that interpretability is a very subjective concept and, therefore, difficult to formalize [90]. Although some of the work presented is done for general purposes, interpretability is a domain-specific concept [90,91], and therefore no universal definition is possible [9]. This means that when it comes to the interpretability of ML, it is necessary to consider the application domain and use case for each specific problem. Although there has been useful work in the assessment of interpretability, the field of ML interpretability research needs to focus more on comparing existing methods of interpretation rather than new-only: with interpretability assessment only, including metrics that help measure interpretability, and context definitions help to compare different use cases, we can know which direction interpretation methods should aim. In addition, interpretability assessment should be a contextualized process: the scope and use cases of the current problem should be considered, as well as the type of audience asking about the model's decisions. These are requirements to ensure proper interpretability. Ultimately, the long-term solution would be a model-agnostic framework (which we have not yet developed at the time of this writing) that is likely to provide the best explanation of all possible solutions available while taking into account the problem domain, the use case, and enter of the user.

This is clear that the amount of XAI research is increasing. In this book chapter, one may also explore several contemporary explainability method taxonomies and new levels. We have noted, among other things, that the discrepancies and inconsistencies between different taxonomies may prevent us from seamlessly obtaining a clear image of the XAI landscape. But such a detailed picture is essential for XAI to reach its full potential. Interdisciplinary research is frequently necessary to solve the issues that XAI should focus on [123–125]. In theory, explainability makes it possible to prevent discrimination [126], increase trustworthiness [127], distribute responsibility [128], and generally promote human well-being [129–132]. This is true if researchers from various fields can collaborate on the problem. As a result, uncertainty in the industry could delay the potentially enormous social advantages that XAI promises.

We proposed and discussed three artifacts—a taxonomy combining elements of the reviewed ones, a database of explainability methods, and a decision tree to assist in determining which (type of) method is required—based on our analysis of the research field and its issues. Future investigation into these three artifacts, in our opinion, will serve as a useful starting point for other XAI-related studies, particularly interdisciplinary ones.

Acknowledgments

The authors would like to thank the Center for Graduate Studies, University of Teknologi, PETRONAS, Malaysia, for providing state-of-the-art research facilities to carry out this work. The authors also thank the co-authors for the opportunity to work in collaboration with Telecom SudParis, France. Last, but certainly not least, I thank the Department of Electrical and Electronics Engineering UTP and CGS UTP for the opportunity during the 03 months Research Mobility Program to study at Telecom SudParis to do the work under Erasmus+ program.

Author contributions

Conceptualization, G.M.A. and V.S.A.; methodology, G.M.A. and P.K.; resources, G.M.A., P.K., and F.S.K.; writing—original draft preparation, G.M.A. and P.K.; writing—review and editing, P.K. and G.M.A.; visualization, V.S.A. and G.M.A.; supervision, G.M.A. and V.S.A.; project administration, V.S.A.

Funding

This research received no external funding.

Conflicts of interest

The authors declare no conflicts of interest.

References

[1] He, K., Zhang, X., Ren, S., *et al.* Deep residual learning for image recognition. In *Proceedings of the IEEE Conference on Computer Vision and Pattern Recognition*, Las Vegas, NV, 27–30 June 2016; pp. 770–778.

[2] Adadi, A. and Berrada, M. Peeking inside the black-box: a survey on Explainable Artificial Intelligence (XAI). *IEEE Access* 2018, 6, 52138–52160.

[3] International Data Corporation. Worldwide Spending on Cognitive and Artificial Intelligence Systems Forecast to Reach $77.6 Billion in 2022. *According to New IDC Spending Guide*. Available online: https://www.idc.com/getdoc.jsp?containerId=prUS44291818 (accessed on 1 June 2022).

[4] Tractica. *Artificial Intelligence Software Market to Reach $105.8 Billion in Annual Worldwide Revenue by 2025*. Available online: https://www.tractica.com/newsroom/pressreleases/artificialintelligence-software-market-to-reach-105-8-billion-in-annual-worldwide-revenue-by-2025/ (accessed on 1 June 2022).

[5] Gartner. *Gartner Top 10 Strategic Technology Trends for 2019*. Available online: https://www.gartner.com/smarterwithgartner/gartner-top-10-strategic-technology-trends-for-2019/ (accessed on 1 June 2022).

[6] Du, M., Liu, N., and Hu, X. Techniques for Interpretable Machine Learning, 2018. *arXiv*, arXiv:1808.00033.

[7]　Montavon, G., Lapuschkin, S., and Binder, A., *et al.* Explaining nonlinear classification decisions with deep Taylor decomposition. *Pattern Recognit.* 2017, 65, 211–222.

[8]　Golovin, D., Solnik, B., Moitra, S., *et al.* Google vizier: a service for black-box optimization. In *Proceedings of the 23rd ACM SIGKDD International Conference on Knowledge Discovery and Data Mining*, Halifax, NS, Canada, 13–17 August 2017; pp. 1487–1495.

[9]　Rudin, C. Please stop explaining black box models for high stakes decisions, 2018. *arXiv*, arXiv:1811.10154.

[10]　Van Lent, M., Fisher, W., and Mancuso, M. An explainable artificial intelligence system for small-unit tactical behavior. In *Proceedings of the National Conference on Artificial Intelligence*, San Jose, CA, 25–29 July 2004; AAAI Press: Menlo Park, CA; MIT Press: Cambridge, MA, 2004; pp. 900–907.

[11]　Swartout, W.R. *Xplain: A System for Creating and Explaining Expert Consulting Programs; Technical Report*; University of Southern California, Information Sciences Institute: Marina del Rey, CA, 1983.

[12]　Van Melle, W., Shortliffe, E.H., and Buchanan, B.G. EMYCIN: a knowledge engineer's tool for constructing rule-based expert systems. In *Rule-Based Expert Systems: The MYCIN Experiments of the Stanford Heuristic Programming Project*; Addison-Wesley Reading: Boston, MA, 1984; pp. 302–313.

[13]　Moore, J.D. and Swartout, W.R. *Explanation in Expert Systems: A Survey; Technical Report*; University of Southern California, Information Sciences Institute: Marina del Rey, CA, 1988.

[14]　Andrews, R., Diederich, J., and Tickle, A.B. Survey and critique of techniques for extracting rules from trained artificial neural networks. *Knowl. Based Syst.* 1995, 8, 373–389.

[15]　Cramer, H., Evers, V., Ramlal, S., *et al.* The effects of transparency on trust in and acceptance of a content-based art recommender. User Model. *User Adapt. Interact.* 2008, 18, 455.

[16]　Herlocker, J.L., Konstan, J.A., and Riedl, J. Explaining collaborative filtering recommendations. In *Proceedings of the 2000 ACM Conference on Computer Supported Cooperative Work*, Philadelphia, PA, USA, 2–6 December 2000; pp. 241–250.

[17]　Abdul, A., Vermeulen, J., Wang, D., *et al.* Trends and trajectories for explainable, accountable and intelligible systems: an HCI research agenda. In *Proceedings of the 2018 CHI Conference on Human Factors in Computing Systems*, Montreal, QC, Canada, 21–26 April 2018; p. 582.

[18]　Gunning, D. *Explainable Artificial Intelligence (XAI)*, Defense Advanced Research Projects Agency: Arlington, VA, 2017; Volume 2.

[19]　Gunning, D. *Explainable Artificial Intelligence (XAI), 2019*. Available online: https://www.darpa.mil/program/explainable-artificial-intelligence (accessed on 22 January 2019).

[20]   Committee on Technology National Science and Technology Council and Penny Hill Press. Preparing for the Future of Artificial Intelligence; *CreateSpace Independent Publishing Platform: Scotts Valley*, CA, 2016.

[21]   ACM US Public Council. Statement on Algorithmic Transparency and Accountability. 2017. Available online: https://www.acm.org/binaries/content/assets/public-policy/2017_usacm_statement_ algorithms.pdf (accessed on 22 January 2019).

[22]   IPN SIG AI. *Dutch Artificial Intelligence Manifesto*, 2018. Available online: http://ii.tudelft.nl/bnvki/wpcontent/uploads/2018/09/Dutch-AI-Manifesto. pdf (accessed on 22 January 2019).

[23]   Cédric Villani. *AI for Humanity—French National Strategy for Artificial Intelligence*, 2018. Available online: https://www.aiforhumanity.fr/en/ (accessed on 22 January 2019).

[24]   Royal Society. *Machine Learning: The Power and Promise of Computers that Learn by Example*, 2017. Available online: https://royalsociety.org/topics-policy/projects/machine-learning/ (accessed on 3 May 2019).

[25]   Portuguese National Initiative on Digital Skills. *AI Portugal 2030*, 2019. Available online: https://www.incode2030.gov.pt/sites/default/files/draft_ai_portugal_2030v_18mar2019.pdf (accessed on 3 May 2019).

[26]   European Commission. *Artificial Intelligence for Europe*, 2018. Available online: https://ec.europa.eu/digital-single-market/en/news/communication-artificial-intelligence-europe (accessed on 3 May 2019).

[27]   European Commission. *Algorithmic Awareness-Building*, 2018. Available online: https://ec.europa.eu/digital-single-market/en/algorithmic-awareness-building (accessed on 3 May 2019).

[28]   Rao, A.S. *Responsible AI & National AI Strategies,* 2018. Available online: https://ec.europa.eu/ growth/tools-databases/dem/monitor/sites/default/files/4%20International%20initiatives%20v3_0.pdf (accessed on 22 January 2019).

[29]   High-Level Expert Group on Artificial Intelligence (AI HLEG). *Ethics Guidelines for Trustworthy Artificial Intelligence*, 2019. Available online: https://ec.europa.eu/futurium/en/ai-alliance-consultation/guidelines (accessed on 3 May 2019).

[30]   Google. *Responsible AI Practices—Interpretability.* Available online: https://ai.google/education/ responsible-ai-practices?category=interpretability (accessed on 18 January 2019).

[31]   H2O.*ai. H2O Driverless AI.* Available online: https://www.h2o.ai/products/h2o-driverless-ai/ (accessed on 18 January 2019).

[32]   DataRobot. *Model Interpretability.* Available online: https://www.datarobot.com/wiki/interpretability/ (accessed on 18 January 2019).

[33]   Kyndi. *Kyndi AI Platform.* Available online: https://kyndi.com/products/ (accessed on 18 January 2019).

[34]   Flint, A., Nourian, A., and Koister, J. *xAI Toolkit: Practical, Explainable Machine Learning.* Available online: https://www.fico.com/en/latest-thinking/white-paper/xai-toolkit-practical-explainablemachine-learning (accessed on 18 January 2019).

[35] FICO. *FICO Makes Artificial Intelligence Explainable,* 2018. Available online: https://www.fico.com/en/newsroom/fico-makes-artificial-intelligence-explainable-with-latest-release-of-its-analytics-workbench (accessed on 18 January 2019).

[36] Fahner, G. Developing transparent credit risk scorecards more effectively: an explainable artificial intelligence approach. *Data Anal.* 2018, 2018, 17.

[37] FICO. *FICO Score Research: Explainable AI for Credit Scoring,* 2019. Available online: https://www.fico.com/blogs/analytics-optimization/fico-score-research-explainable-ai-and-machinelearning-for-credit-scoring/ (accessed on 5 February 2019).

[38] Kahng, M., Andrews, P.Y., Kalro, A., *et al.* ActiVis: visual exploration of Industry-scale deep neural network models. *IEEE Trans. Vis. Comput. Gr.* 2018, 24, 88–97.

[39] Zhang, J., Wang, Y., Molino, P., *et al.* Manifold: a model-agnostic framework for interpretation and diagnosis of machine learning models. *IEEE Trans. Vis. Comput. Gr.* 2019, 25, 364–373.

[40] Doshi-Velez, F. and Kim, B. Towards a rigorous science of interpretable machine learning, 2017, *arXiv,* arXiv:1702.08608.

[41] CVPR. *CVPR 19—Workshop on Explainable AI.* Available online: https://explainai.net/ (accessed on 12 July 2019).

[42] Zhang, Q., Fan, L., and Zhou, B. *Network Interpretability for Deep Learning.* Available online: http://networkinterpretability.org/ (accessed on 22 January 2019).

[43] ICAPS. *ICAPS 2018—Workshop on Explainable AI Planning (XAIP).* Available online: http://icaps18.icapsconference.org/xaip/ (accessed on 12 July 2019).

[44] ICAPS. *ICAPS 2019—Workshop on Explainable AI Planning (XAIP).* Available online: https://kcl-planning.github.io/XAIP-Workshops/ICAPS_2019 (accessed on 12 July 2019).

[45] Lim, B., Smith, A., Stumpf, S., *et al.* 2018: Workshop on Explainable Smart Systems. In CEUR Workshop Proceedings; City, University of London Institutional Repository: London, UK, 2018; Volume 2068. Available online: http://openaccess.city.ac.uk/20037/ (accessed on 12 July 2019).

[46] Lim, B., Sarkar, A., Smith-Renner, A., *et al.* ExSS: Explainable smart systems 2019. In *Proceedings of the 24th International Conference on Intelligent User Interfaces*: Companion, Marina del Ray, CA, USA, 16–20 March 2019; pp. 125–126.

[47] Holzinger, A., Kieseberg, P., Tjoa, A.M., *et al.* (eds.). Machine Learning and Knowledge Extraction: Second IFIP TC 5, TC 8/WG 8.4, 8.9, TC 12/WG 12.9 International Cross-Domain Conference, CD-MAKE 2018, Hamburg, Germany, August 27–30, 2018, Proceedings; Springer: Berlin, Germany, 2018; Volume 11015.

[48] CD-MAKE. *CD-MAKE 2019 Workshop on EXPLAINABLE ARTIFICIAL INTELLIGENCE.* Available online: https://cd-make.net/special-sessions/make-explainable-ai/ (accessed on 12 July 2019).

[49]   IPMU. *IPMU 2018—Advances on Explainable Artificial Intelligence*. Available online: http://ipmu2018.uca.es/submission/cfspecial-sessions/special-sessions/#explainable. (accessed on 12 July 2019).

[50]   Stoyanov, D., Taylor, Z., Kia, S.M., *et al.* Understanding and interpreting machine learning in medical image computing applications. In First International Workshops, MLCN 2018, DLF 2018, and iMIMIC 2018, Held in Conjunction with MICCAI 2018, Granada, Spain, September 16–20, 2018; Springer: Berlin, Germany, 2018; Volume 11038.

[51]   IJCAI. *IJCAI 2017—Workshop on Explainable Artificial Intelligence (XAI)*. Available online: http://home.earthlink.net/~dwaha/research/meetings/ijcai17-xai/ (accessed on 12 July 2019).

[52]   IJCAI. *IJCAI 2018—Workshop on Explainable Artificial Intelligence (XAI)*. Available online: http://home.earthlink.net/~dwaha/research/meetings/faim18-xai/ (accessed on 12 July 2019).

[53]   IJCNN. *IJCNN 2017 Explainability of Learning Machines*. Available online: http://gesture.chalearn.org/ijcnn17_explainability_of_learning_machines (accessed on 22 January 2019).

[54]   Pereira-Fariña, M. and Reed, C. *Proceedings of the 1st Workshop on Explainable Computational Intelligence (XCI 2017)*; Association for Computational Linguistics (ACL): Stroudsburg, PA, 2017.

[55]   Caruana, R., Herlands, W., Simard, P., *et al. Proceedings of NIPS 2017 Symposium on Interpretable Machine Learning*, 2017. *arXiv*, arXiv:1711.09889.

[56]   Wilson, A.G., Kim, B., and Herlands, W. *Proceedings of NIPS 2016 Workshop on Interpretable Machine Learning for Complex Systems*, 2016. *arXiv*, arXiv:1611.09139.

[57]   Kim, B., Malioutov, D.M., and Varshney, K.R. *Proceedings of the 2016 ICML Workshop on Human Interpretability in Machine Learning (WHI 2016)*, 2016. *arXiv*, arXiv:1607.02531.

[58]   Kim, B., Malioutov, D.M., Varshney, K.R., *et al. Proceedings of the 2017 ICML Workshop on Human Interpretability in Machine Learning (WHI 2017)*, 2017. *arXiv*, arXiv:1708.02666.

[59]   Kim, B., Varshney, K.R., and Weller, A. *Proceedings of the 2018 ICML Workshop on Human Interpretability in Machine Learning (WHI 2018)*, 2018. *arXiv*, arXiv:1807.01308.

[60]   FAT/ML. *Fairness, Accountability, and Transparency in Machine Learning*. Available online: http://www.fatml.org/ (accessed on 22 January 2019).

[61]   FICO. *Explainable Machine Learning Challenge*. 2018. Available online: https://community.fico.com/s/explainable-machine-learning-challenge (accessed on 18 January 2019).

[62]   Institute for Ethical AI & Machine Learning. *The Responsible Machine Learning Principles*. 2019. Available online: https://ethical.institute/principles.html#commitment-3 (accessed on 5 February 2019).

[63]   Lipton, Z.C. *The Mythos of Model Interpretability*, 2016. *arXiv*, arXiv:1606.03490.

[64] Silva, W., Fernandes, K., Cardoso, M.J., *et al.* Towards complementary explanations using deep neural networks. In *Understanding and Interpreting Machine Learning in Medical Image Computing Applications*; Springer: Berlin, Germany, 2018; pp. 133–140.

[65] Gilpin, L.H., Bau, D., Yuan, B.Z., *et al. Explaining Explanations: An Approach to Evaluating Interpretability of Machine Learning*, 2018. *arXiv*, arXiv:1806.00069.

[66] Doran, D., Schulz, S., and Besold, T.R. *What Does Explainable AI Really Mean? A New Conceptualization of Perspectives*, 2017. *arXiv*, arXiv: 1710.00794.

[67] UK Government House of Lords. *AI in the UK: Ready, Willing and Able?* 2017. Available online: https://publications.parliament.uk/pa/ld201719/ldselect/ldai/100/10007.htm (accessed on 18 January 2019).

[68] Kirsch, A. Explain to whom? Putting the user in the center of explainable AI. In *Proceedings of the First International Workshop on Comprehensibility and Explanation in AI and ML 2017 Co-Located with 16th International Conference of the Italian Association for Artificial Intelligence (AI* IA 2017)*, Bari, Italy, 16–17 November 2017.

[69] Molnar, C. *Interpretable Machine Learning*, 2019. Available online: https://christophm.github.io/ interpretable-ml-book/ (accessed on 22 January 2019).

[70] Temizer, S., Kochenderfer, M., Kaelbling, L., *et al.* Collision avoidance for unmanned aircraft using Markov decision processes. In *Proceedings of the AIAA Guidance, Navigation, and Control Conference*, Toronto, ON, Canada, 2–5 August 2010; p. 8040.

[71] Wexler, R. When a computer program keeps you in jail: how computers are harming criminal justice. *New York Times*, 13 June 2017.

[72] McGough, M. *How Bad Is Sacramento's Air, Exactly? Google Results Appear at Odds with Reality, Some Say*, 2018. Available online: https://www.sacbee.com/news/state/california/fires/article216227775.html (accessed on 18 January 2019).

[73] Varshney, K.R. and Alemzadeh, H. On the safety of machine learning: cyber-physical systems, decision sciences, and data products. *Big Data* 2017, 5, 246–255.

[74] Donnelly, C. and Embrechts, P. The devil is in the tails: actuarial mathematics and the subprime mortgage crisis. *ASTIN Bull. J. IAA* 2010, 40, 1–33.

[75] Angwin, J., Larson, J., Mattu, S., *et al. Machine Bias*. 2016. Available online: https://www.propublica.org/article/machine-bias-risk-assessments-in-criminal-sentencing (accessed on 18 January 2019).

[76] Tan, S., Caruana, R., Hooker, G., *et al. Detecting Bias in Black-Box Models Using Transparent Model Distillation*, 2017. *arXiv*, arXiv:1710.06169.

[77] Doshi-Velez, F., Kortz, M., Budish, R., *et al. Accountability of AI Under the Law: The Role of Explanation*, 2017. *arXiv*, arXiv:1711.01134.

[78] Honegger, M. *Shedding Light on Black Box Machine Learning Algorithms: Development of an Axiomatic Framework to Assess the Quality of Methods that Explain Individual Predictions*, 2018. *arXiv*, arXiv:1808.05054.

[79]   O'Neil, C. *Weapons of Math Destruction: How Big Data Increases Inequality and Threatens Democracy*; Broadway Books: Portland, OR, 2017.

[80]   Keil, F., Rozenblit, L., and Mills, C. What lies beneath? Understanding the limits of understanding. In *Thinking and Seeing: Visual Metacognition in Adults and Children*; MIT Press: Cambridge, MA, 2004; pp. 227–249.

[81]   Holzinger, A., Langs, G., Denk, H., *et al.* Causability and explainabilty of artificial intelligence in medicine. In *Wiley Interdisciplinary Reviews: Data Mining and Knowledge Discovery*; Wiley: Hoboken, NJ, 2019; pp. e1312.

[82]   Mueller, H. and Holzinger, A. *Kandinsky Patterns*, 2019. *arXiv*, arXiv: 1906.00657.

[83]   European Commission. *General Data Protection Regulation*, 2016. Available online: https://eur-lex.europa.eu/legal-content/EN/TXT/PDF/?uri=CELEX:32016R0679 (accessed on 18 January 2019).

[84]   Weller, A. *Challenges for Transparency*, 2017. *arXiv*, arXiv:1708.01870.

[85]   Holzinger, A., Biemann, C., Pattichis, C.S., *et al. What Do We Need to Build Explainable AI Systems for the Medical Domain? 2017. arXiv*, arXiv: 1712.09923.

[86]   Wachter, S., Mittelstadt, B., and Russell, C. Counterfactual explanations without opening the Black Box: automated decisions and the GDPR. *Harv. J. Law Technol.* 2017, 31, 841.

[87]   Goodman, B. and Flaxman, S. *EU Regulations on Algorithmic Decision-Making and a "Right to Explanation"*, 2016. *arXiv*, arXiv:1606.08813.

[88]   Wachter, S., Mittelstadt, B., and Floridi, L. Why a right to explanation of automated decision-making does not exist in the general data protection regulation. *Int. Data Priv. Law* 2017, 7, 76–99.

[89]   Hardt, M., Price, E., and Srebro, N. Equality of opportunity in supervised learning. *In Advances in Neural Information Processing Systems*; MIT Press: Cambridge, MA, 2016; pp. 3315–3323.

[90]   Rüping, S. *Learning Interpretable Models*. Ph.D. Thesis, University of Dortmund, Dortmund, Germany, 2006.

[91]   Freitas, A.A. Comprehensible classification models: a position paper. *ACM SIGKDD Explor. Newslett.* 2014, 15, 1–10.

[92]   Case, N. How to become a centaur. *J. Des. Sci.* 2018.

[93]   Varshney, K.R., Khanduri, P., Sharma, P., *et al.* Why Interpretability in Janis Klaise, Arnaud Van Looveren, Giovanni Vacanti, and Alexandru Coca. 2021. *Alibi explain: Algorithms for explaining machine learning models. J. Mach. Learn. Res.* 2021, 22, 1–7.

[94]   Mach. Learn. Res. 22, (2021). Machine learning? An answer using distributed detection and data fusion theory, 2018. *arXiv*, arXiv: 1806.09710.

[95]   Miller, T. Explanation in Artificial Intelligence: insights from the social sciences. *Artif. Intell.* 2018, 267, 1–38.

[96]   Kim, B., Khanna, R., and Koyejo, O.O. Examples are not enough, learn to criticize! Criticism for interpretability. *In Advances in Neural Information Processing Systems*; MIT Press: Cambridge, MA, 2016; pp. 2280–2288.

[97]   Heider, F. and Simmel, M. An experimental study of apparent behavior. *Am. J. Psychol.* 1944, 57, 243–259.

[98]   Ribeiro, M.T., Singh, S., and Guestrin, C. "Why Should I Trust You?": explaining the predictions of any classifier. In *Proceedings of the 22nd ACM SIGKDD International Conference on Knowledge Discovery and Data Mining*, San Francisco, CA, 13–17 August 2016; pp. 1135–1144.

[99]   Kim, B. and Doshi-Velez, F. Introduction to interpretable machine learning. In *Proceedings of the CVPR 2018 Tutorial on Interpretable Machine Learning for Computer Vision*, Salt Lake City, UT, 18 June 2018.

[100]   Miller, T, Howe, P., and Sonenberg, L. Explainable AI: beware of inmates running the asylum. Or: how i learnt to stop worrying and love the social and behavioural sciences. In *Proceedings of the IJCAI 2017 Workshop on Explainable Artificial Intelligence (Melbourne, Australia) (IJCAI XAI 2017)*, D. W. Aha, T. Darrell, M. Pazzani, D. Reid, C. Sammut, and P. Stone (eds.), 2017. 36–42. arXiv:1712.00547

[101]   Tukey, J.W. *Exploratory Data Analysis*; Pearson: London, UK, 1977; Volume 2.

[102]   Sundararajan, M., Taly, A., and Yan, Q. *Axiomatic Attribution for Deep Networks*, 2017. *arXiv*, arXiv:1703.01365.

[103]   Vijay, A., Bellamy, R.K.E., Chen, P.-Y., *et al. AI Explainability 360: Impact and Design*, 2021. (September 2021). Retrieved from http://arxiv.org/abs/2109.12151.

[104]   Mojsilovic´, A., Mourad, S., Pedemonte, P., *et al. One Explanation Does Not Fit All: A Toolkit and Taxonomy of AI Explainability Techniques*, 2019. (September 2019). Retrieved from http://arxiv.org/abs/1909.03012.

[105]   Nothdurft, F., Richter, F., and Minker, W. Probabilistic human-computer trust handling. In *SIGDIAL2014–15th Annual Meeting of the Special Interest Group on Discourse and Dialogue, Proceedings of the Conference*, 2014, pp. 51–59, https://doi.org/10.3115/v1/w14-4307

[106]   Miller, T. Explanation in Artificial Intelligence: insights from the social sciences. *Artif. Intell.* 2019, 267, 1–38. https://doi.org/10.1016/j.artint.2018.07.007

[107]   Miller, T. Contrastive explanation: a structural-model approach. *Knowl. Eng. Rev.* 2021, 36, Article e14, 22. https://doi.org/10.1017/S0269888921000102

[108]   Langer, M., Baum, K., König, C.J., *et al.* Spare me the details: how the type of information about automated interviews influences applicant reactions. *Int. J. Select. Assess.* 2021, 29(2), 154–169. https://doi.org/10.1111/ijsa.12325

[109]   Langer, M., König, C.J., and Fitili, A. Information as a double-edged sword: the role of computer experience and information on applicant reactions towards novel technologies for personnel selection. *Comput. Hum. Behav.* 2018, 81, 19–30. https://doi.org/10.1016/j.chb.2017.11.036

[110]   Truxillo, D.M., Bodner, T.E., Bertolino, M., Bauer, T.N., and Yonce, C.A. Effects of explanations on applicant reactions: a meta analytic review. *Int. J. Select. Assess.*, 2009, 4, 346–361. https://doi.org/10.1111/j.1468-2389.2009.00478.x.

[111]   Tjoa, E. and Guan, C. A survey on Explainable Artificial Intelligence (XAI): toward medical XAI. *IEEE Trans. Neural Netw. Learn. Syst.*, 2021, 11, 4793–4813. https://doi.org/10.1109/TNNLS.2020.3027314.

[112]   Nunes, I. and Jannach, D. A systematic review and taxonomy of explanations in decision support and recommender systems. *User Model. User-Adapt. Interact.*, 2017, 27(3–5), 393–444. https://doi.org/10.1007/s11257-017-9195-0.

[113]   Anjomshoae, S., Najjar, A., Calvaresi, D, *et al.* Explainable agents and robots: results from a systematic literature review. In *Proceedings of the 18th International Conference on Autonomous Agents and Multi Agent Systems* (Montréal, Québec, Canada) (AAMAS 2019), E. Elkind, M. Veloso, N. Agmon, and M.E. Taylor (Eds.). International Foundation for Autonomous Agents and Multiagent Systems, Richland County, SC, 2019; pp. 1078–1088. https://doi.org/10.5555/3306127.3331806.

[114]   Ashraf Abdul, J. Vermeulen, D., Wang, B.Y., *et al.* Trends and trajectories for explainable, accountable and intelligible systems: an HCI research agenda. In *Proceedings of the 2018 Conference on Human Factors in Computing Systems* (Montréal, Québec, Canada) (CHI 2018), R.L. Mandryk, M. Hancock, M. Perry, and A.L. Cox (Eds.). Association for Computing Machinery, New York, NY, 2018, Article 582, 18 pages. https://doi.org/10.1145/3173574.3174156

[115]   Mathews, SM. Explainable artificial intelligence applications in NLP, biomedical, and malware classification: a literature review. In *Intelligent Computing – Proceedings of the Computing Conference* (London, England, United Kingdom) (CompCom 2019), K. Arai, R. Bhatia, and S. Kapoor (Eds.). Springer International Publishing, Cham, CH, 2019; pp. 1269–1292. https://doi.org/10.1007/978-3-030-22868-2_90.

[116]   Maksims Ivanovs, R.K. and Ozols, K. Perturbation-based methods for explaining deep neural networks: a survey. *Pattern Recogn. Lett.* 2021, 150, 228–234. https://doi.org/10.1016/j.patrec.2021.06.030

[117]   Langer, M., Baum, K., Hartmann, K., Hessel, S., Timo, S., and Jonas, W. Explainability auditing for intelligent systems: a rationale for multi-disciplinary perspectives. In *29th IEEE International Requirements Engineering Conference Workshops (Notre Dame, Indiana, USA) (REW 2021)*, Tao Yue and Mehdi Mirakhorli (Eds.). IEEE, Piscataway, NJ, 2021; pp. 164–168. https://doi.org/10.1109/REW53955.2021.00030

[118]   Kim, B., Wattenberg, M., Gilmer, J., *et al.* Interpretability beyond feature attribution: Quantitative Testing with Concept Activation Vectors (TCAV). In *Proceedings of the 35th International Conference on Machine Learning (Stockholm, Sweden) (ICML 2018)*, J.G. Dy and A. Krause (Eds.). Microtome Publishing, Brookline, MA, USA, 2018; pp. 2668–2677. http://proceedings.mlr.press/v80/kim18d.html

[119]   Rudin, C. Stop explaining Black Box Machine Learning models for high stakes decisions and use interpretable models instead. *Nat. Mach. Intell. 1, 2019,* 5, 206–215. https://doi.org/10.1038/s42256-019-0048-x

[120] Wachter, S., Mittelstadt, B., and Russell, C. Counterfactual explanations without opening the Black Box: automated decisions and the GDPR. *Harv. J. Law Technol. 31*, 2017, 2, 841–887. https://doi.org/10.2139/ssrn. 3063289.

[121] Arrieta, A.B., Natalia Díaz-Rodríguez, J.D. Ser, Adrien Bennetot, S.T., *et al.* Explainable Artificial Intelligence (XAI): concepts, taxonomies, opportunities and challenges toward responsible AI. *Inf. Fusion* 2020, 58, 82–115.

[122] Speith, T. A review of taxonomies of explainable artificial intelligence (XAI) methods. In *2022 ACM Conference on Fairness, Accountability, and Transparency*, 2022, pp. 2239–2250.

[123] Saraswat, D., Bhattacharya, P., Verma, A., *et al.* Explainable AI for healthcare 5.0: opportunities and challenges. *IEEE Access* 2022, 10, 84486–84517.

[124] Langer, M., Oster, D., Speith, T., *et al.* What do we want from Explainable Artificial Intelligence (XAI)?–A stakeholder perspective on XAI and a conceptual model guiding interdisciplinary XAI research. *Artif. Intell.* 2021, 296, 103473.

[125] Dodge, J., Vera Liao, Q., Zhang, Y., Bellamy, R.K.E., and Dugan, C. Explaining models: an empirical study of how explanations impact fairness judgment. In *Proceedings of the 24th International Conference on Intelligent User Interfaces*, 2019; pp. 275–285.

[126] Holzinger, A., Goebel, R., Fong, R., *et al.* (eds.). *XxAI-Beyond Explainable AI: International Workshop, Held in Conjunction with ICML 2020, July 18, 2020, Vienna, Austria, Revised and Extended Papers.* Vol. 13200. Springer Nature, 2022.

[127] Panesar, A. and Panesar, A. "Ethics of intelligence." In *Machine Learning and AI for Healthcare: Big Data for Improved Health Outcomes,* 2019, pp. 207–254.

[128] Luciano, F., Cowls, J., Beltrametti, M., *et al.* AI4People—an ethical framework for a good AI society: opportunities, risks, principles, and recommendations. *Minds Mach.* 2018, 28, 689–707.

[129] Markus, A.F., Jan A.K., and Peter R.R. The role of explainability in creating trustworthy artificial intelligence for health care: a comprehensive survey of the terminology, design choices, and evaluation strategies. *J. Biomed. Inf. 2021,* 113, 103655.

[130] IBM. *Trust and Transparency in AI.* Available online: https://www.ibm. com/watson/trust-transparency (accessed on 18 January 2019).

[131] Arya, V., Bellamy, R. K. E., Chen, P.-Y., *et al.* AI Explainability 360 Toolkit. In *Proceedings of the 3rd ACM India Joint International Conference on Data Science & Management of Data (8th ACM IKDD CODS & 26th COMAD)*, pp. 376–379, 2021.

[132] Kevin, B., Mantel, S., Schmidt, S., *et al.* From responsibility to reason-giving explainable artificial intelligence. *Philos. Technol.* 2022, 35(1), 12.

Chapter 6

An overview of AI platforms, frameworks, libraries, and processes

Sruthi Anand[1], Ram Gurusamy Raja[2] and T. Sheela[3]

6.1 Introduction to AI

Artificial intelligence (AI) is a sophisticated software-based technology that combines complex computer programming with aspects of human intelligence in a variety of ways to do a wide range of tasks that were previously thought to be only humanly feasible. The invention of electronic computers with stored programs gave rise to the idea of AI. At a meeting held at Dartmouth College in 1956, computer scientist John McCarthy first used the phrase "Artificial Intelligence".

A branch of computer science that has grown over time is AI. It involves replicating human cognitive processes using machines, notably computer systems. The phrase "artificial intelligence" (AI) is frequently used to describe a project that aims to create systems that are capable of doing activities that typically require human intelligence, such as decision-making, visual perception, language comprehension, and speech recognition. AI systems routinely operate by consuming vast amounts of trained and labeled data, scanning it for correlations and patterns, and then using those patterns to predict future events.

AI is concerned with the development and use of computer systems that can solve issues that often call for human intelligence. Such issues are related to jobs that are naturally occurring, such as eyesight or natural language interpretation, or both. Typically, they cannot be resolved using traditional algorithmic techniques. AI systems handle symbolic information rather than only numerical data, as is customary in computer science, to solve them. AI uses several different types of knowledge about an application area. Therefore, important to AI research and development are the issues of knowledge representation, acquisition, and usage. One of the most active subfields is the deployment of knowledge-based systems.

[1]Department of Information Technology, Vasavi College of Engineering, Osmania University, Hyderabad, India
[2]Reiter Affiliated Companies, Oxnard, CA, USA
[3]Department of Information Technology, Sri Sairam Engineering College, Anna University, Chennai, India

6.2   Role of AI in the 21st century

AI, the most popular and dynamic technological phrase of the 21st century, has begun to rule the global stage with its clever functions. There is no denying that AI is improving global productivity and workflow across a wide range of sectors. However, there is still ongoing worry about future employment chances for people. Organizations have gradually wake up to the fact that AI has to work with humans, and many career possibilities are emerging for that. Organizations are gaining a competitive edge thanks to this cutting-edge technology in the fiercely competitive IT sector. Industries are benefiting from the most well-known disruptive technologies in ways that were unimaginable a decade ago. AI enters the tech-driven future.

6.2.1   The 2000s

Traditionally, autonomous robots were designed to operate independently of humans. They were created to carry out dangerous and time-consuming tasks. However, in the new millennium, an interest in expanding artificially intelligent bots sparked a series of remarkable developments. Researchers began focusing on developing robots that could interact and cooperate with people rather than simply taking orders from them. In the early 2000s, Honda took the lead in demonstrating the world's first two-legged, walking humanoid. ASIMO was created as an entirely new type of robot that could function in society and serve as a human partner. The next stage of humanoid robots added social abilities. MIT researchers created a smart bot that can socially interact with people.

6.2.2   The 2010s

The first intelligent personal assistant was introduced to the world in 2010. According to a study conducted by NPR and Edison Research, 16% of Americans, or approximately 39 million people, own a smart speaker. The capabilities of these intelligent assistants have advanced in recent years, allowing the average person to transform their entire home into an intelligently connected hub. Now that Alexa and Google Home are available, a simple "good morning" statement can activate your coffee maker, play your favorite song, and provide you with the weather forecast. AI for business has shown significant benefits in addition to personal use. Chatbots encourage the use of messenger to improve customer experience and engagement across a variety of platforms [1].

6.2.3   The future

Massive advancements in AI's capacity for human communication will occur in the future. AI and robotics will become more user-friendly and functional through advancements in machine learning (ML) and recognition. For instance, the newly unveiled Google Duplex technology enables AI to speak like a person and even place calls on the customers' behalf. Future AI robots are much more anticipated now that the technology is already being developed. Regarding future AI, the influence on the global labor force is further anticipated. The majority of manual work in businesses will likely be eliminated by smart automation as it develops. According to Justin Fier, Head of Cyber Intelligence and Analysis at Darktrace, AI will operate as a force multiplier, assisting people in properly allocating resources and setting priorities, enhancing rather than replacing human labor. There is no way to minimize the influence that AI has had to date or the implications it will have going forward. Technology is developing at a rate that has never been seen before, and the future is certain to usher in some great technologies thanks to the continuous support of some of the biggest organizations in the world for AI research [2].

6.3 How AI transformed the world

To further comprehend how AI is changing the world, seek cloud AI services consultancy. So much so that implementation, acceptance, and integration are happening across several sectors, including the following.

6.3.1 Transportation

The two key technologies that are pushing the use of AI in transportation are autonomous cars and drone delivery systems. To adjust to changing conditions, it makes use of high-performance computing, deep learning systems, and cutting-edge algorithms. AI gives automobiles the ability to examine the data gathered by other autonomous vehicles over a network and gain knowledge from their mistakes. According to current weather forecasts or prevailing road conditions, it modifies the directions.

6.3.2 Finance

By evaluating finely parsed data to uncover trends and anomalies, AI improves financial decision-making. For instance, high-frequency trading bots are used in the financial markets to enhance investment analysis and decision-making. Fraud detection is a further use of AI in banking. It makes it easier to spot fraudulent activity before it has an impact on your company. It signals abnormal behavior that needs further inquiry. Financial analysts are able to identify issues before they become apparent.

6.3.3 Healthcare

Healthcare services are being revolutionized by AI. It offers resources for data analysis and problem prediction. It entails patient education, sensitization, and other preventative efforts that aid in preventing hospitalizations. Deep learning algorithms can be used by healthcare practitioners to address medical issues. It offers continual training options to improve pattern recognition and data management.

6.3.4 Intelligent cities

AI is at the forefront of these initiatives as modern governments strive to be proactive in the provision of services. Large volumes of data may be gathered and analyzed by businesses to enhance resource management, energy efficiency, environmental planning, and crime prevention.

6.3.5   Security

A layered approach to cybersecurity is provided by AI leveraging cloud-based cognitive systems. Companies may improve network security by routinely educating AI models to address known threats. DNA-level code analysis can be used as a security mechanism to identify and thwart malicious code that is being sent from outside the system [3].

6.4   AI process

We can define an AI engineering process or AI process (AP) which can be used to solve almost any AI problem.

Define the problem: This step includes the following tasks: defining the scope, value definition, timelines, governance, and resources associated with the deliverable.

Dataset selection: This step can take a few hours or a few months depending on the project. It is crucial to obtain the correct and reliable dataset for an AI/ML project.

Data description: This step includes the following tasks: describe the dataset including the input features and target feature(s) and include summary statistics of the data and counts of any discrete or categorical features including the target feature.

Data preparation: This step includes the following tasks: data pre-processing, data cleaning, and exploratory data analysis (EDA).

Feature engineering: This step includes the following tasks: quantization or binning; mathematical transforms; scaling and normalization; convert text data features into vectors; modify and/or create new features.

Design: This step includes the following tasks: feature selection, decomposing the problem, and building and evaluating models. We can use AutoML or create a custom test harness to build and evaluate many models to determine what algorithms and views of the data should be chosen for further study.

Training: This step includes building the model which may include cross-validation.

Evaluation: This step includes the evaluation of well-performing models on a hold-out test dataset and model selection.

Tuning: This step involves algorithm tuning of the few selected well-performing models which may include evaluation of ensembles of models to obtain further improvement in accuracy.

Finalize: This step is to finalize the chosen model by training using the entire dataset and making sure that the final solution meets the original business requirements for model accuracy and other performance metrics.

Deployment: The model is now ready for deployment. There are two common approaches to the deployment of ML models to production: embed models into a web server or offload the model to an external service. Both model-serving approaches have pros and cons.

Monitoring: This is the post-deployment phase which involves observing the model and pipelines, refreshing the model with new data, and tracking success metrics in the context of the original problem [4].

6.5   TensorFlow

TensorFlow is an open-source software library launched by Google in November 2015. It is one of the most widely used deep learning and ML frameworks for numerical computation, which speeds up and simplifies the use of neural networks and ML. It can be used for a variety of applications but focuses particularly on training and inference. It supports data preparation, feature engineering, and model serving in addition to training. Python, JavaScript, C++, and Java are just a few of the programming languages that support TensorFlow.

TensorFlow is compatible with both common CPUs and specialized AI accelerators like GPU and TPU. It may be used with 64-bit Linux, macOS, Windows, and mobile operating systems like iOS and Android. TensorFlow models can be used to deploy models on PCs, browsers, edge computing hardware, and even microcontrollers.

6.5.1   Installation

TensorFlow is simple to install on Linux, Mac OS, and Windows machines. It is always preferable to set up separate TensorFlow environments. The installation links for Linux-based machines and Mac OS are: https://www.tensorflow.org/install/install_linux and https://www.tensorflow.org/install/install_mac [5].

6.5.2   TensorFlow basics

6.5.2.1   Tensor

A tensor is a multidimensional array of numbers. Vectors and matrices can be thought of as 1D and 2D tensors, respectively. Tensors are commonly used for data storage and processing.

Example An RGB image is stored in a 3D tensor, with the horizontal axis along one dimension and the vertical axis along the other, and the third dimension corresponding to the three color channels, namely Red, Green, and Blue.

6.5.2.2   Tensor data types

A tensor can have the following data types:

- bool
- int32

- float32 (default)
- complex64
- String

6.5.2.3   Tensorflow.js

A JavaScript library for defining and using tensors is called TensorFlow.js.

The Python-based TensorFlow library was created with the same functionality as Tensorflow.js.

6.5.2.4   Basic TensorFlow commands

1. Import TensorFlow and Numpy Library
     import tensorflow as tf
     import numpy as np
2. Activate a TensorFlow Interactive Session
     tf.InteractiveSession()
3. Define Tensors
     x = tf.zeros((2,2))
     y = tf.ones((2,2))
4. Check the Shape of the Tensor
     x.get_shape()
5. Reshape a Tensor
     tf.reshape(x,(1,4)).eval()
6. Define TensorFlow Constants
     a = tf.constant(1) b = tf.constant(5) c= a*b
7. Define TensorFlow Variables
     w = tf.Variable(tf.ones(2,2),name='weights')

6.5.2.5   Optimizers in TensorFlow

TensorFlow has a large library of optimizers for cost functions. The optimizers are all gradient-based, with a few exceptions for dealing with local minima problems.

1. **GradientDescentOptimizer:**
   The basic full-batch gradient-descent technique is implemented by GradientDescentOptimizer, which also accepts the learning rate as an input. Since the gradient-descent technique does not automatically loop over iterations, this logic must be stated in the implementation.
   Usage:
   train_op = tf.train.GradientDescentOptimizer(learning_rate).minimize(cost)
   where learning_rate is the constant learning rate and the cost is the cost function that needs to be minimized through gradient descent
2. **AdagradOptimizer:**
   AdagradOptimizer is a first-order optimizer similar to gradient descent but with a few differences. Rather than having a single global learning rate, the

learning rate is normalized for each dimension on which the cost function is dependent.

This is a useful optimizer to employ in applications with sparse data such as natural language processing and image processing.

Usage:

train_op=tf.train.AdagradOptimizer.(learning_rate=0.001, initial_accumulator_value=0.1)

where learning_rate represents η and initial_accumulator_value represents the initial non-zero normalizing factor for each weight

3. **AdadeltaOptimizer**:

AdadeltaOptimizer is a less aggressive variant of AdagradOptimizer in terms of lowering the learning rate. Adadelta's complete elimination of the learning-rate constant is a key benefit.

Usage:

train_op = tf.train.AdadeltaOptimizer(learning_rate=0.001, rho=0.95, epsilon=1e-08)

where rho represents γ, epsilon represents ϵ, and η represents the learning rate.

4. **AdamOptimizer**:

Similar to Adagrad, Adam, or the Adaptive Moment Estimator, is another optimization technique that has an adaptable learning rate for each parameter or weight.

5. **Usage:**

train_op=tf.train.AdamOptimizer(learning_rate=0.001,beta1=0.9,beta2=0.999, epsilon=1e-08). minimize(cost)

where learning_rate is the constant learning rate η and cost C is the cost function that needs to be minimized through AdamOptimizer. The parameters beta1 and beta2 correspond to $\beta1$ and $\beta2$, respectively, whereas epsilon represents ε [6].

6.6   Scikit learn

One of the most essential and vital Python frameworks for data science and ML is scikit-learn. It uses a wide variety of ML algorithms to achieve classification, clustering, regression, and other important ML techniques. This library effectively implements many of the widely used ML techniques, including support vector machines, logistic regression, random forests, K-means clustering, hierarchical clustering, and many more.

6.6.1   Features

- Easy and effective to use.
- Built using NumPy, SciPy, and matplotlib.
- Accessible to everybody and reusable in various contexts.
- Open source, commercially usable.

6.6.2   Installation

1. Using pip
    pip install -U scikit-learn
2. Using Conda
    conda install scikit-learn

6.6.3   Scikit modeling

1. **Dataset loading:**
    A dataset is a collection of data.
    It has two components:
    * Feature
    * Response

    Features:
    * The variables of data are called their features.
    * They are also known as predictors, inputs, or attributes.
    * A feature matrix is a collection of features, in case there is more than one.
    * A feature name is the list of all the names of the features.

    Response:
    * It is the output variable that basically depends upon the feature variables.
    * They are also known as target, label, or output.
    * A response vector is used to represent the response column. Generally, we have just one response column.
    * Target names are used to represent the possible values taken by a response vector.

    CODE:
    ```
    from sklearn.datasets import load_iris
    iris = load_iris()
    X = iris.data
    y = iris.target
    feature_names = iris.feature_names
    target_names = iris.target_names
    print("Feature names:", feature_names)
    print("Target names:", target_names)
    print("\nFirst 10 rows of X:\n", X[:10])
    ```

    OUTPUT:
    The output for the above code is shown in Figure 6.1.

2. **Data preprocessing**:
    Data preprocessing is a process of preparing the raw data and making it suitable for an ML model. It is the first and most important step in developing an ML model.

```
Feature names: ['sepal length (cm)', 'sepal width (cm)', 'petal length (cm)', 'petal width (cm)']
Target names: ['setosa' 'versicolor' 'virginica']

First 10 rows of X:
[[5.1 3.5 1.4 0.2]
 [4.9 3.  1.4 0.2]
 [4.7 3.2 1.3 0.2]
 [4.6 3.1 1.5 0.2]
 [5.  3.6 1.4 0.2]
 [5.4 3.9 1.7 0.4]
 [4.6 3.4 1.4 0.3]
 [5.  3.4 1.5 0.2]
 [4.4 2.9 1.4 0.2]
 [4.9 3.1 1.5 0.1]]
```

Figure 6.1   Output on loading dataset and assigning labels

- Binarization:
  When we need to convert numerical values into Boolean values, we use this preprocessing technique.
- Mean removal:
  With this method, the mean is removed from the feature vector, leaving each feature centered on zero.
- Scaling:
  This preprocessing technique is used to scale the feature vectors. Scaling feature vectors is critical because features should not be artificially large or small.

3. **Splitting the dataset:**
   To test the accuracy of our model, divide the dataset into two parts: training and testing. Train the model with the training set and test it with the testing set.

   CODE:
   ```
   from sklearn.datasets import load_iris
   iris = load_iris()
   X = iris.data
   y = iris.target
   from sklearn.model_selection import train_test_split
   X_train, X_test, y_train, y_test = train_test_split(
   X, y, test_size = 0.3, random_state = 1)
   print(X_train.shape)
   print(X_test.shape)
   print(y_train.shape)
   print(y_test.shape)
   ```

Figure 6.2   Output

Figure 6.3   Output for accuracy

OUTPUT:
Figure 6.2 shows the output for the code that splits the dataset into training and testing data.

4. **Training the model:**
   ```
   from sklearn.datasets import load_iris
   iris = load_iris()
   X = iris.data
   y = iris.target
   from sklearn.model_selection import train_test_split
   X_train, X_test, y_train, y_test = train_test_split(
   X, y, test_size = 0.4, random_state=1
   )
   from sklearn.neighbors import KNeighbors Classifier
   from sklearn import metrics
   classifier_knn = KNeighbors
   Classifier(n_neighbors = 3)
   classifier_knn.fit(X_train, y_train)
   y_pred = classifier_knn.predict(X_test)
   print("Accuracy:", metrics.accuracy_score(y_test, y_pred))
   ```

   OUTPUT:
   Figure 6.3 shows the output of the accuracy of the model.

6.6.4   Data representation in scikit

Representation of data in scikit learn can be done in the following ways:

(I) **Data as tables:**
    Tables are the best way to represent data in Scikit-learn. A table is a 2D grid of data, with rows representing individual elements of the dataset and columns representing quantities related to those individual elements. Figure 6.4 depicts how data is represented and interpreted in a table format.

```
import seaborn as sns
iris = sns.load_dataset('iris')
iris.head()
```

	sepal_length	sepal_width	petal_length	petal_width	species
0	5.1	3.5	1.4	0.2	setosa
1	4.9	3.0	1.4	0.2	setosa
2	4.7	3.2	1.3	0.2	setosa
3	4.6	3.1	1.5	0.2	setosa
4	5.0	3.6	1.4	0.2	setosa

Figure 6.4   Loading the dataset and interpreting it as tables

(II) **Data as feature matrix:**

A feature matrix is a table layout in which information is represented as a 2D matrix. It is saved in the variable X and is assumed to be 2D with the shape [n samples, n features]. It is usually stored in a NumPy array or a Pandas DataFrame. As previously stated, the samples always represent the individual objects described by the dataset, and the features represent the distinct observations that quantitatively describe each sample.

(III) **Data as target array:**

In addition to the Features matrix, denoted by X, we have a target array. It is also known as a label. It is represented by the letter y. Typically, the label or target array is one-dimensional and has a length of n samples. It is generally contained in NumPy array or Pandas Series. The values in the target array can be both continuous numerical values and discrete values [7].

6.6.4.1   How do target array and feature matrix differ?

The target array is typically the number we wish to predict from the data, making it the dependent variable in statistical language. This is how we may differentiate between the two.

Example:

```
import seaborn as sns
iris = sns.load_dataset('iris')
%matplotlib inline
import seaborn as sns; sns.set()
sns.pairplot(iris, hue='species', height=3);
```

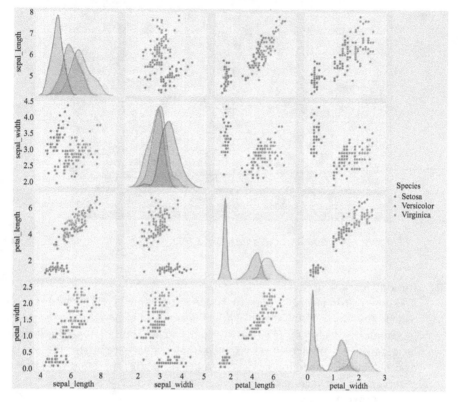

Figure 6.5   Visualizing the dataset

6.7 Keras

An open-source, Python-based high-level neural network framework called Keras is able to run on Theano, TensorFlow, or CNTK. Francois Chollet, a Google developer, was the one who created it. To enable quicker experimentation with deep neural networks, it is made user-friendly, expandable, and modular. It supports both Convolutional and Recurrent Networks separately as well as in combination.

It uses the Backend library to resolve low-level computations because it is unable to handle them. As a high-level API wrapper for the low-level API, the backend library enables it to run on TensorFlow, CNTK, or Theano. Figure 6.5 show how a dataset can be visualized.

6.7.1 Features

1. **Modularity:**
   Keras has modularity. It takes into account models that take the shape of graphs or sequences. You can save the model you're working on with Keras.

For saving the current model, Keras offers the save() method. The model can even be applied later.

2. **Large dataset:**
A sizable pre-defined dataset is included in Keras. It offers you a selection of datasets. This dataset is available for immediate import and loading.

Consider the IMDB DATA. There are almost 25k reviews of the films there. To evaluate each video, this dataset contains binary numbers (0 and 1). Positive emotion is represented by 1, while negative emotion is represented by 0.

You can load IMDB DATA as:
From   keras.datasets   import   imdb
(x_train,y_train),(x_test,y_test)=imdb.load_data()

3. **Train from numpy data:**
NumPy array is used by Keras to train and assess the model.

Fit() is used in this sentence. The model is fitted to the training data using the fit() technique. It can take some time to complete this training. The fit() method used three arguments: epochs, batch size, and validation data.

NumPy array is used by Keras to train and assess the model. Fit() is used in this sentence. The model is fitted to the training data using the fit() technique. It can take some time to complete this training. The fit() method used three arguments: epochs, batch size, and validation data.

4. **Evaluation and validation:**
Both evaluate() and predict() are available in Keras. Several techniques can make use of the NumPy dataset. The evaluation of the outcome is completed when the data have been tested. These techniques are employed to assess our models.

5. **Pre-defined models in Keras:**
There are several pre-trained models in Keras. You can import these models from keras.applications. These models can be adjusted and used to extract features. VGG16, VGG19, Xception, and other weights for image classification are contained in the Keras.application module.

6. **Encoding in Keras:**
You can use the encoding feature on Karas. Encoding is possible in Keras thanks to the one hot() function. You can use it to quickly encode integers. You can tokenize the data using it as well. The text is converted to lowercase, the white spaces are removed, and the punctuation is removed using this function.

7. **Layers in Keras:**
In Keras, there are several layers and parameters. There are numerous techniques included in each Keras layer. These layers are helpful in building, configuring, and training the data. The dense layer helps with operation implementation.

The input is flattened using flatten. Dropout enables input dropout. The output can be reshaped using the Reshape tool. A Keras tensor is started using input.

```
keras.layers.Reshape(target_shape)
kera.layers.Flatten(data_format=none)
keras.layers.Dropout(rate,noise_shape=none,seed=none)
```

8. **Keras is Python-native library:**
   A comprehensive Python library is Keras. It employs all of the accepted Python concepts. It is a library created in the Python programming language. Keras offers you a user-friendly environment because it is Python-oriented.

9. **Pre-processing of data:**
   You can preprocess data using a number of the functions offered by Keras. Among these is the ImageDataGenerator function. You may import it by using the command:
   import ImageDataGenerator from keras.preprocessing.image.

6.7.2   Building a model in Keras

1. **Build a network:**
   At this stage, you specify the various model layers and their interconnections. Sequential and functional models are the two main model categories in Keras. Afterwards, you specify the dataflow between the models you have chosen.

2. **Compile a network:**
   Compiling code entails transforming it into a format that a machine can understand. This task is carried out via the model.compile() method in Keras. We specify the loss function that calculates the losses in our model, the optimizer that decreases the loss, and the metrics that are used to determine the accuracy of our model to build the model.

3. **Fit the network:**
   After compiling, we used this to fit our model to the data. The model is trained using our data in this manner.

4. **Evaluate the network:**
   We must assess our model's inaccuracy after we have fitted it.

5. **Make predictions:**
   We use model.predict() to make predictions using our model on new data.

6.7.3   Applications of Keras

- Deep models can be produced using Keras and then deployed on mobile devices.
- Deep learning model distributed training also uses Keras.
- Companies like Netflix, Yelp, Uber, and others employ Keras.
- Moreover, Keras is frequently used in deep learning contests to develop and deploy quick functional models.

6.8   Open NN

OpenNN (Open Neural Networks Library) is a software library that implements neural networks, a key field of deep learning research. It was built in the C++ programming language.

Why Open NN?

It is written in C++ for better memory management and faster processing speed, and it uses CUDA and openMP for GPU acceleration as well as CPU parallelization. openNN was created using ANSI C++. This implies that the library can be easily built on any system. For example, the software tool natural designer is for sophisticated analytics. It was created using OpenNN and has a graphical user interface that makes data entering and result interpretation straightforward.

History

The development began in 2003 at the International Center for Numerical Methods in Engineering as part of the RAMFLOOD research project, which was sponsored by the European Union (Risk Assessment and Management of FLOODs). It then continues as a part of subsequent initiatives. The startup business Artelnics is now working on developing OpenNN.

Characteristics

For supervised learning, the program implements any number of layers of nonlinear processing units. The creation of neural networks with universal approximation capabilities is made possible by this deep architecture. It enables OpenMP multiprocessing programming to improve computer speed.

ML algorithms are included in OpenNN as a collection of functions. Using an application programming interface, they can be integrated with other software tools to do predictive analytics activities. Although a graphical user interface is absent in this case, specialized visualization tools can support some functions.

Use cases of OpenNN

Collaboration promotes innovation through open-source licensing. Many of the modern technologies we take for granted would not exist today without them or would be hidden behind the restrictions of the patent system. Technology has advanced so quickly over the last few decades because of the open-source movement.

Advantage of OpenNN

- Cost Effective
- Reliability
- Flexibility
- Error Free
- User Friendly
- Security

6.8.1   Application

A software program for general-purpose AI is called OpenNN. It uses ML strategies to complete predictive analytics tasks in many industries. For instance, the library has been used in the chemistry, engineering, and energy fields. The library is open source, hosted at SourceForge, and licensed under the GNU Lesser General Public License.

6.8.2   RNN

A recurrent neural network (RNN) is a kind of artificial neural network mainly used in speech recognition and natural language processing (NLP). It is utilized in the creation of models that replicate the activity of neurons in the human brain. Recurrent networks are made to identify patterns in data sets, including text, genomes, handwriting, spoken language, and more. It is a type of deep learning-oriented algorithm, which follows a sequential approach. Recurrent networks are also distinguished by the fact that they share parameters among all of their layers.

Why RNN?

RNN were created because there were a few issues in the feed-forward neural network:

- Cannot deal with sequential data
- Only takes into account the current input
- Cannot recall previous inputs

The RNN is the solution to these problems.

Working of RNN

RNNs are a particular kind of neural network in which the results of one step are fed into the current step as input. RNN operates on the principle that each layer's output is saved and fed back into the system's input to forecast that layer's output. They are distinguished by their "memory," which allows them to influence the current input and output by using information from previous inputs. Figure 6.6 depicts the layers involved in the working of RNN.

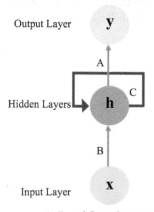

A, B, and C are the parameters

Figure 6.6   Layers of RNN

In this case, "x" represents the input layer, "h" represents the hidden layer, and "y" represents the output layer. The network parameters A, B, and C are used to improve the model's output.

The input layer "x" receives the neural network's input, processes it, and sends it to the middle layer. The middle layer "h" can be made up of several hidden layers, each with its own activation functions, weights, and biases.

The RNN will standardize the various activation functions, weights, and biases, resulting in the same parameters for each hidden layer. Then, rather than creating multiple hidden layers, it will create one and loop over it as many times as necessary. The recurrent network first converts independent activations into dependent ones. It also assigns the same weight and bias to all layers, reducing the RNN's parameter complexity.

To compute the current state

$h_t = f(h_{t-1}, X_t)$

where h_t denotes the current state; H_{t-1} denotes the previous state; X_t = input condition

To apply the activation function tanh, we have

$ht = \tanh(W_{hh}h_{t-}1 + W_{xh}X_t)$

where W_{hh} is the weight of the recurrent neuron and W_{xh} is the weight of the input neuron.

The formula for calculating output:

$Y_t = W_{hy}h_t$

Training through RNN

- The network performs a single time step on the input.
- We can calculate the current state using the current input and the previous state.
- Now, the current state is through h_{t-1} for the next state.
- There are n steps, and at the end, all of the information can be combined.
- The final step is to calculate the output after all of the previous steps have been completed.
- Finally, we compute the error by calculating the difference between the actual and predicted output.
- The error is back-propagated to the network to adjust the weights and produce a better result.

Application of RNN

1. **Speech recognition:**
   Traditional speech recognition models based on Hidden Markov Models have been replaced by RNNs. These RNNs are more capable of classifying speeches and converting them into text without losing context.

2. **Sentiment analysis:**
   We use sentiment analysis to determine whether a sentence is positive, negative, or neutral. As a result, RNNs are best at handling data sequentially to find sentence sentiments.
3. **Generating image descriptions:**
   To provide a description of what is happening inside an image, a combination of CNNs and RNNs is used. CNN does the segmentation, and RNN reconstructs the description using the segmented data.
4. **Text summarization:**
   This application can be of great assistance in summarizing content from literature and customizing it for delivery within applications that cannot handle large amounts of text.
5. **Call center analysis:**
   This is one of the most important applications of RNNs in audio processing. Customer metrics are based on the outcome of the call rather than the call itself.

Advantages of RNN

➢ An RNN remembers every piece of information it encounters over time. It is only useful in time series prediction because it remembers previous inputs.
➢ The main advantage of RNN is that it can model a set of records so that each pattern is assumed to be dependent on previous ones.

Disadvantages of RNN

➢ Training an RNN is a very difficult task.
➢ The computation of the neural network is slow.
➢ If you are using the activation functions, then it becomes very tedious to process long sequences.

6.9   Theano

6.9.1   An overview

We can analyze mathematical operations, including multi-dimensional arrays, so effectively thanks to the Theano Python module. It is primarily employed for creating deep learning projects.

On a graphics processing unit (GPU) as opposed to a CPU, it operates much more quickly. For issues involving a lot of data, Theano's rapid speeds put C implementations in a tough fight. It can utilize GPUs, which under some specific conditions allows it to perform orders of magnitude better than C on a CPU.

It is capable of taking structures and turning them into extremely effective code that makes use of native libraries like Numpy. It is primarily made to manage the several kinds of processing needed for deep learning's massive neural network algorithms. Because of this, it is a very well-liked library in the deep learning community.

6.10 Why go for Theano Python library?

Theano is an attempt to combine Sympy and Numpy into one potent library. It is something of a cross between the two. Figure 6.7 illustrates the use of Theano and its advantages.

6.10.1 PROS

- On top of Theano, open-source deep libraries like Keras, Lasagne, and Blocks have been developed.
- Graph computation is a nice abstraction.
- Raw Theano is a little bit basic.
- It has some high-level wrappers such as Keras and Lasagne which increase its usability.

6.10.2 CONS

- It can be deployed on single GPU.
- On AWS, it may be problematic.
- Large models can demand long compile times.
- The use of error messages for debugging is limited.

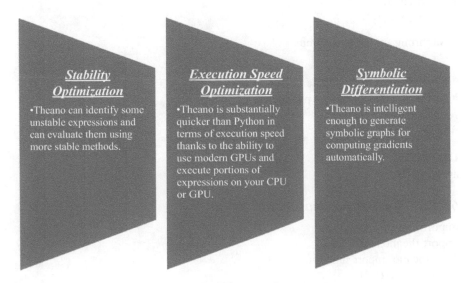

Figure 6.7   Theano advantages

6.11   Basics of Theano

6.11.1   Subtracting two scalars

```
import Theano
from theano import tensor
# Declaring variables
a = tensor.dscalar()
b = tensor.dscalar()
# Subtracting
res = a − b
# Converting it to a callable object
# so that it takes matrix as parameters
func = theano.function([a, b], res)
# Calling function
assert 20.0 == func(30.5, 10.5)
```

OUTPUT:
It will not provide any output as the assertion of two numbers matches the number given, hence it results in a true value.

6.11.2   Adding two scalars

```
import numpy
import theano.tensor as T
from theano import function

# Declaring two variables
x = T.dscalar('x')
y = T.dscalar('y')

# Summing up the two numbers
z = x + y

# Converting it to a callable object
# so that it takes matrix as parameters
f = function([x, y], z)
f(5, 7)
```

OUTPUT:
array(12.0)

6.11.3   Adding two matrices

```
import numpy
import theano.tensor as T
from theano import function
x = T.dmatrix('x')
y = T.dmatrix('y')
```

$z = x + y$
f = function([x, y], z)

f([[30, 50], [2,3]], [[60, 70], [3,4]])

OUTPUT:
array([[90., 120.],[5., 7.]])

6.11.4   Logistic function

Logistic curve is given by,

$$s(x) = \frac{1}{1 + e^{-x}}$$

```
import theano
from theano import tensor

# Declaring variable
a = tensor.dmatrix('a')

# Sigmoid function
sig = 1 / (1 + tensor.exp(−a))

# Now it takes matrix as parameters
log = theano.function([a], sig)

# Calling function
print(log([[0, 1], [−1, −2]]))
```

OUTPUT:
[[0.5 0.73105858
0.26894142 0.11920292]]

References

[1]   https://www.pro-sapien.com/blog/how-ai-has-advanced-during-21st-century-and-where-its-headed/
[2]   https://basis.net/blog/gentle-introduction-artificial-intelligence
[3]   https://sdsclub.com/21st-century-ai-biggest-achievements/
[4]   https://towardsai.net/p/l/the-ai-process
[5]   https://www.tutorialspoint.com/scikit_learn/scikit_learn_introduction.html
[6]   https://github.com/aniruddhachoudhury/Data-Science-Books/blob/master/Pro%20Deep%20Learning%20with%20TensorFlow%20-%20A%20Mathematical%20Approach%20to%20Advanced%20Artificial%20Intelligence%20in%20Python.pdf
[7]   https://www.javatpoint.com/tensorflow

Chapter 7

Quality framework for explainable artificial intelligence (XAI) and machine learning applications

Muthu Ramachandran[1,2]

Artificial intelligence (AI) and machine learning (ML) applications are applied in many applications and devices, and it is expected to grow by 15 trillion dollars by 2030 [1,2]. There are more demands for explainable AI (XAI) for its improvement in explainability attributes of the AI quality. Software quality is defined as the product meets its required product specification and is expected to behave as it is expected by the stakeholders. Furthermore, we need a systematic approach to the design, development, implementation, and testing of AI products. Therefore, this chapter proposes a software engineering framework for AI and ML applications (SEF—AI and ML) supporting the complete XAI application development phases including a reference architecture to standardize across XAI applications. The framework has been validated through a case study involving an explainable Chatbot using business process modeling notations (BPMN), modeling, and simulation. The results demonstrate a 98% utilization rate and improved time efficiency, confirming the validation of performance and resource requirements for cloud-driven AI Chatbot services. Therefore, SEF—AI and ML has the potential to be a standard framework for AI and ML applications to achieve the desired quality and certainty of AI products and services.

7.1 Introduction

AI and ML have evolved rapidly into all mainstream software applications including healthcare and mobile apps. Many AI products rely largely on the data that we create in our daily usage and experiences we gain from using various online tools and mobile apps in addition to traditional knowledge and wealth we have created for centuries since human evolution. The data we feed to AI and ML is the backbone of AI products. AI and ML have the potential to change the way we

[1]AI Tech, Public Intelligence, Leeds, UK
[2]School of Electronics and Computer Science, University of Southampton, Southampton, UK

operate, make decisions, and do business. PwC [2] estimates that AI's impact on the global economy could be worth $15 trillion by 2030. Probably, the biggest revolution in the field of AI has been deep learning (DL) and it has grown by 38–50% over the last decade [3]. The robust survey found that four overall awareness of AI among companies is however high across the EU, standing at 78% (Digibyte). In addition, most AI applications have adopted natural language processing (NLP) as the front-end user interface as found in most Chatbot applications.

Unfortunately, and like nearly all other technologies, AL, ML, DL, and NLP-driven and integrated applications can fail—whether by unintentional misuse or intentional abuse [4]. Mcgregor [4] reports that avoiding repeated AI failures requires making past failures known. Therefore, they have introduced a systematized collection of incidents where intelligent systems have caused safety, fairness, or other real-world problems: the AI Incident Database [5]. As of today, the Partnership on AI Incident Database (AIID) holds over 1,000 public reports of algorithmic discrimination, data privacy violations, training data security breaches, and other harmful failures [5]. Therefore, we have the right to ask for transparency, accountability, and a systematic approach to designing and developing AI applications by openly declaring the source of data, the process and techniques adopted in how AI applications were designed and developed, and on any autonomic decision to be made by AI-driven products such as applications such as self-driving cars and financial.

One of the aims of this chapter is to provoke an important thought on Software Engineering challenges for AI and ML applications development, data and model development validation and verification. Some of those challenges are different from traditional software development that we have seen so far for the past 50 years or so as follows:

1. Learning from real-time data which will be fed back to ML and AI models is difficult to predict and specify its behaviors.
2. Difficult to test data, debug AL, ML, and DL (AMD) systems.
3. Even more challenging is DL, where not only the number of parameters can be of the order of millions, but where, typically, the representation of the data is learned separately from the inferential models and can consist of different nested levels of abstraction.
4. What is the Software Engineering process for developing and delivering AMD applications?
5. Some of the key attributes of AI quality are fairness, accountability, explainability, responsibility, transparency, and how do we specify and validate all the attributes?

In general, there are five key pillars of AI systems: *categorization, classification, machine learning, collaborative filtering, and recommendations.* In addition, the current AI system has been considered as a Blackbox which provides recommendations and decisions as its main output to end users and communities. However, the general AI systems have limitations in explaining their automated decision and recommendations. Therefore, XAI is gathering momentum in a huge way to address the key attributes of explainability characteristics of AI software systems [6]. Goel *et al.* [6] explain that the XAI is a Whitebox system with explanation when requested to the following questions:

- Which feature is dominant among all available features?
- Can it provide a correlation among a set of features?
- Why does the model predict this instead of others?
- What data stream is being used at any particular point during training or during testing?

In summary, we need to know how AI systems were designed and developed and any process and standard adopted for gathering, and verifying AI requirements, design method adopted, test strategies adopted, quality verification conducted, etc.

Section 7.1 introduces SE for AMD and also identifies a list of challenges and research needed for developing AMD systems. Section 7.2 provides a comprehensive guide to the literature survey and critical evaluation. Section 7.3 provides an integrated approach to developing AMD systems. Section 7.4 provides AMD requirements engineering process and techniques which is the most important part of any development lifecycle as the requirements engineering (RE) ensures earlier identification of the problem analysis, resource constraints and requirements, and performance evaluation including testing and quality requirements for validation and verification. In addition, RE is also known as the contractual document between development organizations and their clients. Section 7.5 introduces a systematic Software Engineering Framework (SEF4AIML) for AI and ML applications which includes a service-based reference architecture and a case study on an explainable Chatbot application that has been introduced to evaluate the architecture using BPMN simulation for performance requirements on execution time, cloud resources, and cost.

7.2   Background

Traditional quality management (QM) concepts emerged from manufacturing and have been actively applied to the software development process. QM can be defined as the process of making sure that the defined policy, process, product specification, development standards, plan, and budget are measured and controlled to meet the required user level of satisfaction. IEEE [7] defines *software quality as the degree to which a system, component, or process meets customer or user needs or expectations* whereas one of the current studies defines *AI quality as a set of observable attributes of an AI system that allows you to assess, over time, the system's real-world success* [8].

One of the aims of the research question is to identify if this definition is still applicable to AI quality. In addition, [9] defines several quality attributes such as safety, security, understandability, portability, testability, usability, reliability, adaptability, reusability, resilience, modularity, efficiency, robustness, complexity, and learnability as shown in Figure 7.1.

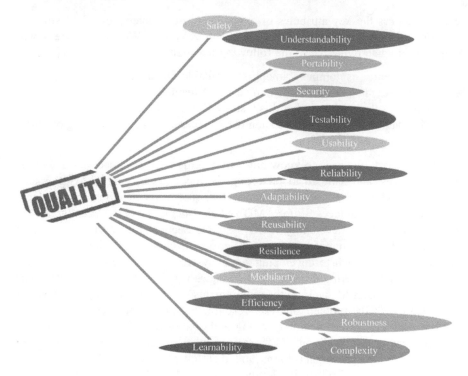

Figure 7.1   Software quality attributes

Furthermore, software quality consists of the quality process, QM, and quality assurance. This combined effort is also known as software quality assurance (SQA) and software QM (SQM). It is a parallel activity across the software development lifecycle to make sure the functional as well as non-functional and performance requirements have been met as specified and the chosen process has been followed systematically. Therefore, software quality has two distinct activities: process quality and product quality. The process quality is a set of conformance activities to make sure the chosen software process (Waterfall Method, Agile Method, or any other process paradigm such as Service-Oriented) has followed according to a standard such as IEEE and ISO. To this end, IEEE [7] defines the scope of SQA as:

• To assess the chosen software development process artifacts
• To evaluate the conformance to software processes
• To evaluate the effectiveness of the software processes

These activities also ensure that a standard template is used for software specification, software design, software coding, and software testing, and include software maintenance activities to be performed to make sure the developed system performs as expected over time. A typical software quality plan is presented as follows:

As shown in Figure 7.2, the SQA plan consists of several activities and documenting them systematically to achieve the required quality to satisfy stakeholders

Software Product Introduction and Scope;
Risks and Risk Management
Software Process Descriptions;
Software Quality Goals & Quality Standards Chosen (IEEE and ISO ISO 9001:2015, etc.);
Software Product Plans and Specification:
    Software Requirements Specification
    Software Design Specification
    Software Implementation Specification Algorithms and Pseudocodes (Coding)
    Software Testing Specification & Test Driven Development Plans
Product Release and Closing Project Plan Procedures

Figure 7.2   SQA plan structure

and end-users. It starts with software product introduction and scope, analysis of risks and risk management (Risk Register), and Software Quality Goals and Standards chosen to follow as required by the stakeholders. A major step in the process is to develop software product requirements specification, design specification, and detailed implementation specification using algorithmic approaches such as pseudocode and test specification.

However, the traditional attributes may not be all suitable and may even be more complex for modern and emerging applications such as AI, ML, DL, RL, and service-oriented systems. Therefore, a new perspective is presented in quality engineering fields by Breu *et al.* [10] which consists of four fields to measure quality such as knowledge management, automation, data analysis, and collaborative processes. In addition, they insist on continuous delivery as a mandatory attribute for business agility. Surprisingly, more recently, the term assurance has changed its meaning completely for modern complex systems and disruptive technologies such as AI and ML. Bloomfield *et al.* [11] define assurance as the claims, arguments, and evidence (CAE) framework as they define claims are assertions put forward for general acceptance. Another biggest property of any disruptive technologies such as AI and ML systems is the behavioral uncertainty in a real-time scenario, bias based on existing data, safety in self-driving cars, etc. Al Alamin and Uddin [12] present ML application development from a software development perspective and highlight standards, data, and practices. They also have identified ambiguous ML requirements, bias and lack of fairness, privacy concerns, lack of standard testing specification, non-deterministic integration of modules using ML models, insufficient MLOps support into the traditional DevOps process, lack of adversarial robustness due to data dependency, lack of scalability in real-world scenarios, elevated complexity in ML configuration management, and inadequate standard regulation/compliance.

This sets a scene for further research and exploration and has created awareness for integrated research between AI/ML and software engineering communities. Therefore, the following section presents an integrated framework taking into consideration of AI subfields such as XAI, responsible AI, conversational AI, and human-centered AI.

7.3   Integrated framework for AI applications development

AI applications have evolved into more specialized subsets such as responsible AI, XAI, human-centered AI, and cognitive and conversational AI. Hence, there is a need for an integrated framework to capture the commonality and variability of features. Martínez-Fernández *et al.* [13] discuss the interplay between AI4SE and SE4AI that has emerged over the past 30 years or so. In addition, Data Science for Software Engineering (DS4SE) and Software Engineering for Data Science (SE4DS) have also evolved [14]. For example, AI4SE activities include *collecting expert knowledge on best software practices for knowledge discovery, reasoning, learning, planning, natural language processing, perception, or supporting decision-making.* SE4AI activities include requirements engineering for AI, structuring data collecting, and cleaning processes such as the CRISP method, specification for AI applications using formal and semi-formal notations, implementing AI systems with DevOps and DevSecOps (Agile practices), and deployment using continuous delivery and monitoring. These are the adaptation of modern software engineering practices into producing quality and sustainable AI systems. In addition, SE has a wealth of knowledge and techniques that evolved over the past 50 years which allows one to choose and select appropriate methods, tools, and techniques.

Software engineering has evolved over the past 50 years with several development processes, methods, techniques, and tools. Erdogmus *et al.* [15] have summarized several developments in software engineering as follows:

- 60 software development methodologies
- 50 static analysis tools
- 40 software design methods
- 37 benchmark organizations
- 25 size metrics
- 20 kinds of project management tools
- 22 kinds of testing and dozens of other tool variations.
- There are a minimum of 3,000 programming languages software, and only 100 are frequently used. New programming languages are announced every 2 weeks, and new tools are out more than once each month. Every 10 months new methodologies are discovered.

With the above achievements in software engineering, key challenges in the years to come include:

- How can we adopt software engineering best practices for the benefits and sustainability of AI applications?

- How do we assess the suitability of SE practices for AI application development?
- What is the popular AI/ML approach?
- How application has been developed in the context of AI software development?

In addition, Nascimento *et al.* [16] have identified classification and regression-based applications accounts for 31% of AI/ML applications, 40% of the applications developed using neural network and DL, 6% of the applications developed using probabilistic graphical model, and others account for 23%. They have also reported that 58% of them have adopted an in-house research process and the rest of them have developed using ad-hoc processes. They have also found out that most challenges are the lack of software testing and quality of AI applications at present.

Therefore, it sets a scene for applying to all AI- and ML-intensive applications to make sure that these systems have been developed systematically with state-of-the-art software engineering. Menzies [17] discusses five laws of AI namely SE applies to AI and AI software systems need software engineers in addition to AI modelers, better SE leads to better AI, and SE needs a special kind of AI to solve SE problems.

However, AI systems have themselves been more specialized with several distinct classes as shown in Figure 7.3, an integrated framework for all classes of AI systems at present.

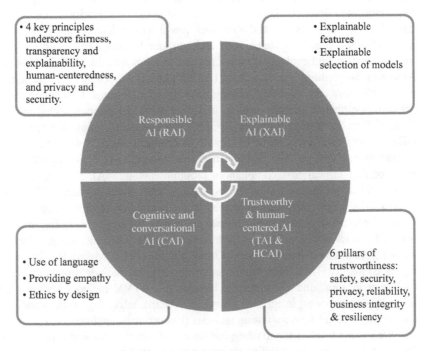

Figure 7.3   Integrated framework for AI

As shown in Figure 7.3, an integrated approach to AI, AI systems have emerged into several distinct classes:

1. *XAI* aims to provide explainability of the services offered concerning features, data, and models adopted in executing services. XAI should provide explainable features and reasoning when requested for any disadvantages and consequences of its actions and any decisions made. XAI should explicitly provide support for businesses, end users, stakeholders, and regulating committees. XAI should also be explainable for the selection of ML models, training datasets, etc. XAI should also be explainable what-if scenarios to be verified formally and can also be validated using requirements simulation models such as BPMN.
2. *Responsible AI (RAI)* aims to provide support for accountability, fairness, security, safety, trustworthiness, and explainability.
3. *Trustworthy and human-centered AI (TAI and HCA)* aims to provide Build Ethics In (BEI) with six pillars of trustworthiness such as safety, security, privacy, reliability, business integrity and resiliency, and formalized and standardized ethical and risk assessment.
4. *Cognitive and conversational AI and ethical AI* aim to provide conversational AI systems with that of Humans. This approach has extended Chatbot applications with advancements in conversational AI systems.
5. *BEI* aims to build ethics right from requirements, and design, to implementation, testing and evaluation. This involves the ethics development lifecycle of identifying ethical requirements from various stakeholders involved, mapping ethical requirements to design and architecture, validating the authenticity of source data, data cleaning, AI decisions, and outcomes how it will be handled from an ethical perspective by the AI systems with and without human participation, and to implementation and evaluation with a particular focus on ethical requirements.
6. *AI testing, verification, and validation* (ATVV) best practices include user testing, testing, cleaning and validating training datasets. In addition, ATVV recommends performance testing, security testing, and regulatory compliance testing such as General Data Protection Regulation (GDPR). Regulatory compliance testing for GDPR is now mandatory in the EU for all AI products. Furthermore, as per trends in current research, ATVV best practices recommends AI ethics by design by incorporating ethical and compliances requirements into AI development lifecycle: ethical requirements, ethics by design, and ethics testing. ATVV also recommends a new technique known as smart interaction testing which involves testing for smart devices if this delivered as an app. Smart device testing includes testing for voice-activated devices (Siri, Alexa, Google Assistant), Large Language Models, Augmented Reality (AR), Virtual Reality (VR), Mixed Reality (MR), Extended Reality (XR). Furthermore, smart devices may include drones, driverless cars, mobile apps, and E-commerce. In addition, ATVV includes testing cloud services, web services, integration testing of systems, edge, fog services and their connections. Cloud services testing includes data services, application as a service, real-life testing, black-box and white-box testing. There is also a new type of testing known as back testing is a testing technique to test predictive models based on the historical model as this is important to identify AI bias on historical data.

Table 7.1   Critical evaluation of AI approaches: XAI, RAI, HCAI, CAI, and TAI

AI characteristics	XAI	RAI	CAI	TAI	HCAI
Safety	✔	✔	✔	✔	✔
Robustness					
Reliability	✔	✔	✔	✔	✔
Correctness					
Fairness	✔	✔	✔	✔	✔
Accuracy	✔	✔	✔	✔	✔
Consistency					
Model relevance	✔	✔	✔	✔	✔
Security					
Privacy and data privacy	✔	✔	✔	✔	✔
Efficiency					
Interpretability	✔				
Adaptability					
Scalability					
Algorithm Accountability	✔	✔	✔	✔	✔
Ethics					
Explainability	✔				
Transparency	✔				
Understandability	✔				
Comprehensibility	✔				
Blackbox Implementation		✔	✔	✔	✔
Whitebox Implementation	✔				

Table 7.1 provides a critical evaluation of AI classes: XAI, responsible AI (RAI), cognitive and conversational AI (CAI), trustworthy AI (TAI), and human-centered AI (HCAI), and from the existing literature [18–20] some of the common characteristics are important across all AI categories with exception and more emphasis is given to certain characteristics such as interpretability and interactivity are the most important characteristics when designing XAI and CAI.

It is the foundation for understanding the characteristics of AI systems and their behaviors as the key input for any requirements phase of the software development lifecycle, clear, consistent, and validated requirements can save effort and improve the quality of the AI applications.

7.4   AI systems characteristics vs. SE best practices

There are several characteristics of AI applications that we need to study as SEs to map best practices to tackle and provide appropriate solutions to those characteristics. For example, if AI systems require safety and reliability for a robotic application then there are plenty of solutions that exist from the past 50 years of software engineering that have been successful and well-established. In this instance, Martinez-Fernandez *et al.* [13] recommend verification and validation techniques to solve safety and reliability and there are several techniques to adopt such as fault-tree analysis.

It is important to identify some of the characteristics of the AI systems and then match them against a list of SE best practices. To this end, Martínez-Fernández *et al.*

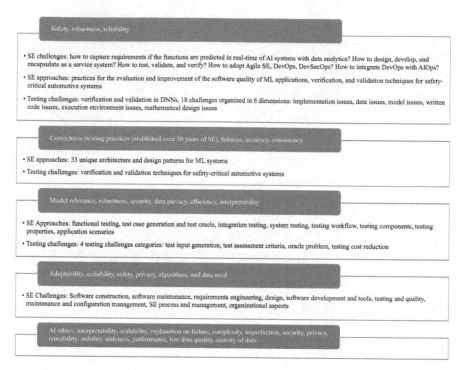

Figure 7.4　AI and ML systems characteristics vs. SE best practices

[13] have identified several characteristics of AI systems which have been refined and are shown in Figure 7.4. For example, one of the AI and ML characteristics is safety, robustness, and reliability (SRR) which can be handled and addressed with several goods and established software engineering practices such as capturing requirements on SRR explicitly and specifying those requirements and should be modeled and simulated using use cases and BPMN process models. SRR can also be verified and validated using formal methods and techniques.

Identify AI services level requirements and a set of key non-functional requirements such as validation and verification of fairness, robustness, causality, accountability, trustworthiness, counterfactual reasoning, transparency, reinforcement learning, explainability, responsibility, and probabilistic models.

7.4.1　Explainable AI characteristics

Explainable AI emerged to address the limitations discovered in traditional AI systems. XAI is focused to address the key principle of the explainability attribute of the AI system for its automated decisions and to interact with humans as expected as discussed in Section 7.1.3 of this chapter. XAI is considered to be the whitebox approach. Furthermore, Nazar *et al.* [20] recommend that human–computer interaction is more important in XAI in particular they have adopted this approach in healthcare applications. Nazar *et al.* [20] recommend XAI some additional characteristics on

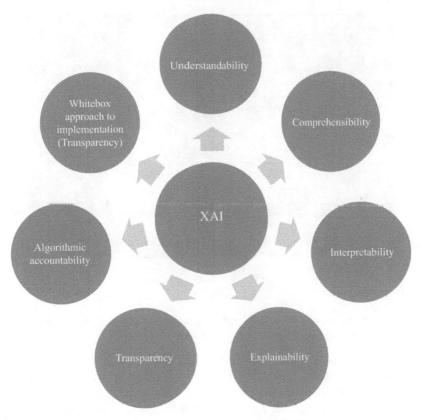

Figure 7.5   Characteristics of XAI

trustworthiness, causality, transferability, informativeness, confidence, accessibility, fairness, interactivity, and privacy awareness. Some of the characteristics found in the existing literature [18] are shown in Figure 7.5 as follows:

1. Understandability aims to provide how the AI system works and how it took a particular decision without details of the internal implementation, etc.
2. Comprehensibility aims to be able to explain learned knowledge from the trained data in a manner by which humans should be able to understand.
3. Interpretability intends to explain and provide meaning in understandable terms to a human.
4. Explainability explains the AI system's automated decisions made using the trained data to humans interactively.
5. Transparency defines a set of characteristics to be able to explain and provide reason to three categories of the models: simulate models, decomposable models, and algorithmic transparency models (how a particular algorithm has been chosen given the current situation).
6. Algorithmic accountability aims to adopt the current legislation which has been proposed in the US Senate [21].

XAI System Introduction and Scope;
    Specification of Risks, Risk Management, Understandability,
    Comprehensibility, Interpretability, Explainability, Transparency
    and Algorithmic Accountability Plans
AI System Development Process Descriptions;
AI System Plans and Specification;
    AI System Requirements Specification
    AI System Design Specification
    AI System Implementation Specification Algorithms and
    Pseudocodes (Coding and Algorithmic Accountability to specify
    chosen ML models)
    AI System Testing Specification & AI System Test Driven
    Development Plans
AI System Release and Closing Project Plan Procedures

Figure 7.6   AQA structure

7. Whitebox approach to implementation (transparency) defines its implementation and algorithms' accountability and explainability.

Furthermore, to achieve AI quality, it is important to specific AI quality assurance (AQA) structure as shown in Figure 7.6 which is an extended version of the SQA plan structure presented in Figure 7.2. It is noticeable that, in this research, it has been chosen to use the term AI system instead of software since it may contain various types of AI products such as mobile apps, API, cloud and IoT services, and data and streaming services, and a multitude of devices. It consists of several activities such as XAI system introduction and scope which requires specifying in detail how XAI characteristics (specification of risks, risk management, understandability, comprehensibility, interpretability, explainability, transparency, and algorithmic accountability plans) will be achieved and evaluated. Followed by the AI system development process, plans, and specifications including algorithmic accountability as it is now a legal requirement by the Governments.

This leads to an understanding of how AMD and RL (AMDRL) models have been developed versus the Agile Software Engineering development process in the following section.

7.5 ML lifecycle (model, data-oriented, and data analytics-oriented lifecycle)

Modern software engineering offers a wealth of Agile methodologies to choose from including SCRUM, XP, Lean, etc. In addition to traditional SE practices and methodologies, Agile Software Engineering offers several successful software development methods such as SCRUM one of the most popular Agile methodologies. They offer a short lead time in capturing and managing AI requirements efficiently. Agile Software Engineering also offers the concepts of DevOps which have been adopted in AI and are known as MLOps and AIOps. Figure 7.7 shows a comparative stage of development phases in Agile Software Engineering versus ML development phases. Agile SE starts with identifying software-specific requirements for AI and ML whereas AI and ML lifecycle starts with identifying business and AI and ML model requirements and their suitability, etc.

An important phase in any software engineering lifecycle is the requirements engineering as it has been a well-known fact in the success of 50 years of SE is the

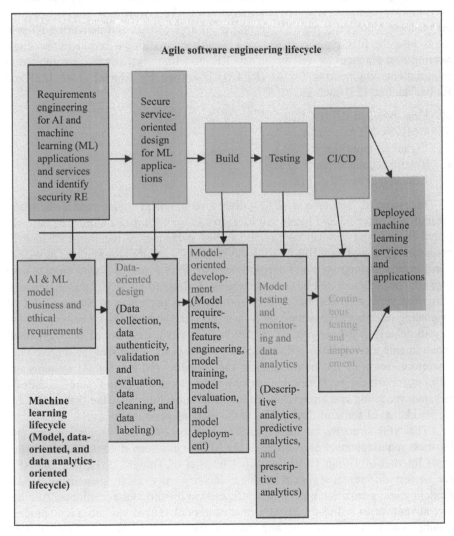

Figure 7.7   Agile vs. AI and ML lifecycle

ripple effect (also known as the Iron Law of SE) of any change at the later part of the lifecycle (code and delivery) will cost you more to fix it.

7.6   AI/ML requirements engineering

Software and systems requirements are categorized into two known as functional requirements which identify the functional aspects (e.g., the user can open and close an account, etc.) of the system, and non-functional requirements which identify constraints imposed on the system such as quality and reusability. Eliciting, specifying, modeling, and validating requirements for AI systems benefit performance, cost, and resource requirements for AI software as well as making the AI business much clear before investing in AI applications and delivering AI products into the marketplace. There is a wealth of traditional requirements engineering best practices as well as the new RE modeling practices that are applied in requirements engineering for AI (RE4AI) identified by Ahmad *et al.* [22] and Ramachandran [23] such as:

- Goal-oriented RE (GORE)
- UML/SysML/use cases
- Signal temporal logic (STL)
- Traffic sequence charts (TSC)
- Conceptual model (CM)

Furthermore, Bencomo *et al.* [24] discuss requirement engineering as the secret weapon for better AI and better software. In addition, Ramachandran [23] has proposed BPMN and simulations to validate key performance requirements such as resource, effort, and cost. BPMN allows us to identify service requirements as well as non-function requirements and decision points at a business level with emphasis on organizational factors and business strategies. A detailed BPMN requirement modeling and simulation for the Chatbot application is presented in Section 7.5.2 of evaluating reference architecture for AI and ML (RE for AI & ML). I believe that the key to achieving the desired AI quality is to identify key sets of non-functional requirements that exhibit AI characteristics that are identified in Figure 7.5. Therefore, some of the non-functional requirements (NFRs) for AI systems are fairness, robustness, explainability, responsibility, etc. as shown in Figure 7.8. BPMN is visual modeling and simulation requirements modeling language that allows for the validation of some of these NFRs at the early stage in the lifecycle.

The NFR structure can be expanded based on evolving AI applications and business requirements. For example, if the AI data has been streamed from a large-scale Internet of Things (IoT), Industrial Internet of Things (IIoT), then the NFR can be very different and should be able to identify and evaluate them using BPMN modeling and simulation and other verification and validation techniques. Another key advantage of using the BPMN process model is that we can adopt process mining, knowledge discovery, and patterns for the reuse of requirements from existing requirements.

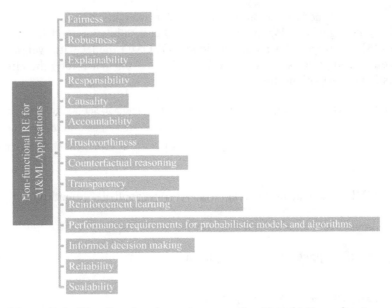

Figure 7.8   *Non-functional requirements for AI and ML applications*

7.7   Software effort estimation for AMD, RL, and NLP systems

Software cost estimation techniques are the key to achieving software projects delivered on time and within budget. Traditionally, a unit of software measure is based on several lines of code (LOC). The question is how could we estimate the size of software during requirements or business requirements when you have your first business meeting scheduled with stakeholders? To this end, there are several estimation techniques emerged, one of which is a function point estimation which can be calculated using several business services or several software features identified, and another technique is based on an expert judgment which is driven by previous knowledge of software cost. Third, software cost estimation is based on the application of ML methods and existing datasets to predict software development costs and effort.

However, the current challenge for software engineering for AI/ML is how do we adopt a software cost estimation technique for AI and ML. Most of the AI/ML applications utilize the cloud, data science, IoT, IIoT, and edge. Therefore, this paper has identified a combination of traditional methods along with constant factors for cloud, edge, IoT, and AI and ML algorithmic complexity.

7.7.1   Modified COCOMO model for AI, ML, and NLP applications and apps

It is important to calculate the effort required for specified AI applications. In the era of cloud and mobile computing, most AI applications are integrated with a cloud and social media. Therefore, we can adopt weighting factors identified for cloud computing when adopting the COCOMO cost estimation model. In addition, Guha [25] has proposed a modified cloud COCOMO model with weighting for service-oriented projects $a = 4$, $b = 1.2$, $c = 2.5$, $d = 0.3$. Therefore, the effort and cost estimation equations are:

$$\text{AI/ML project effort applied(EA)} = a \times (\text{number of AI and ML service points})^{b}$$
$$\times (\text{number of automated AI and ML decesion points})$$
$$\times (\text{number of human decision points}) \text{ (human months)}$$

$$(7.1)$$

$$\text{AI/ML development time(DT)} = c \times (\text{effort applied})^{d} \text{ (months)} \qquad (7.2)$$

Number of AI and ML and software engineers required

$$= \text{effort applied(EA)}/\text{development time(DT)} \qquad (7.3)$$

$$\text{AI and ML size} = \sum_{0}^{N} \text{AI and ML features}$$

$$\times \text{ cloud constants(modified COCOMO)}$$

$$\times \sum_{0}^{N} \text{AI and ML automated decision points}$$

$$\times \sum_{0}^{N} \text{human decision points}$$

$$\times \text{ AI and ML algorithmic complexity} \qquad (7.4)$$

Equations (7.1)–(7.4) provide cloud project effort and cost estimations based on AI service points which is the sum of all interface AI service function points. Equation (7.1) provides an estimation of project effort (EA) which includes constants applied to cloud-driven AI/ML applications as a service. The constant a is multiplied by the number of AI/ML service points which is based on several AI/ML features which are accessible to end users including API which is also multiplied by several automated decisions taken by AI/ML services and multiplied by several human decision points where human interventions are required. Eq. (7.2) provides an estimation of AI/ML development time (DT) which consists of a constant c multiplied by EA to the square of a constant d. Eq. (7.3) provides several AI and ML and SE experts required based on the multiplication of EA and DT. Eq. (7.4) is an interesting and quite important aspect of complex analysis which consists of a summation of all AI/ML features times a summation of all automated decision points times a summation of all human decision points times AI and ML algorithmic complexity. Therefore, it is important to adopt a complete Software Engineering Lifecycle for AI systems. The following section provides a complete software engineering framework for AI and ML applications.

7.8 Software engineering framework for AI and ML (SEF4 AI and ML) applications

The software engineering framework for AI and ML (SEF4 AI and ML) consists of several stages as shown in Figure 7.9 starting with identifying AI strategies, applying ontologies to identify AI requirements, identifying information architecture, domain-specific modeling, and identifying business risk analysis. The second stage is to identify AI classes/types as shown in Figure 7.3 and is CHERT: Conversational AI, Human-Centred AI, Explainable AI, Responsible AI, and Trustworthy AL. The AI classes/types may expand as further research and application evolves and explodes over the coming years.

Third, to adopt a software engineering lifecycle for AI application development as shown in Figure 7.7 based on business needs and applications a choice

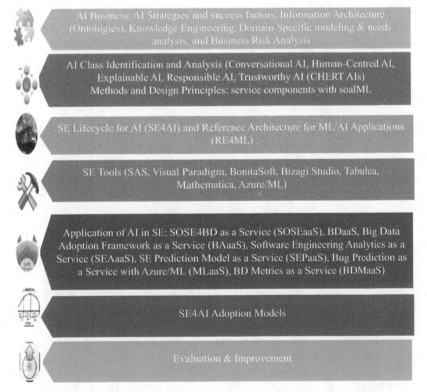

Figure 7.9   Software Engineering Framework (SEF) for AI and ML

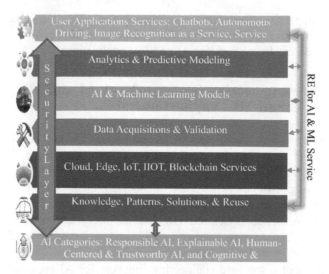

Figure 7.10   Reference Architecture (REF) for AI & ML

between a traditional SE lifecycle vs. Agile SE. During this stage of the framework, one can also identify a reference architecture for AI and ML (RE for AI & ML) for a chosen AI business as shown in Figure 7.10 which consists of seven layers and is customizable based on the nature of the domain and its application characteristics.

7.9   Reference Architecture for AI & ML

A reference architecture, in general, provides a standardized framework and structure for holding software components and assets, and, for AI and ML applications, this is critically important to place software assets and data in a specified structure as the AI and ML systems are more dynamic and are scalable in real-time. Therefore, as one of the key contributions toward a strategic software engineering framework, this paper has evolved a reference architecture for AI and ML applications known as RE4AI which consists of seven layers as shown in Figure 7.10, namely AI categories: XAI, RAI, CAI, etc. which drive the layers above and can be customized and simplified. The layers above aim to provide support for reusable knowledge, assets, patterns, and problem-solving solutions in combination with the Cloud, Edge, IoT, IIOT, blockchain (CEIIB) paradigm of services, and so on. The layer above this is known as the data acquisition and validation layer, where data are acquired from all sources. In addition to acquiring the data, this layer conducts data transformation, cleaning, and validation. The acquired data is then securely stored for access by AI and ML services.

The layer above is known as the AI and ML models and algorithms and is cataloged based on algorithmic classification such as ML, DL, and RL. The layer above is known as the analytics and predictive modeling layer where results are visually presented, and decisions are taken by either automated or humans as we have already identified the expected behaviors during requirements engineering for the AI and ML phase of the lifecycle presented in Section 7.4.2. The top layer is known as the user service layer where interaction with end users takes place and the data flow to the layer below for any actions and decisions by the analytics and AI layers. Our next big challenge is to validate the architecture and the flow of information across the elements and layers. The other two layers shown on both sides are the security layer and a RE for AI & ML service bus as the current and future generations of AL and ML applications are service driven. Therefore, a reference architecture should follow service-oriented principles of scalability, reusability, composability, and extensibility. This is extremely useful for testing AI and ML applications to achieve expected quality and safety. This is presented with a case study on Chatbot applications as part of a conversational AI.

7.10   Evaluation of Reference Architecture (REF) for AI & ML: explainable Chatbot case study

AI and ML Chatbot is one of the popular and demonstrated applications of conversational AI and ML found in all commercial websites, automated help systems, automated telephone systems, chat online with customer services teams, etc. Chatbots are also known as virtual agents, and they learn from conversations from the types of natural language queries and answers. Chatbots are developed using data, ML, DL techniques, and NLP. Chatbot also helps ML and DL algorithms to learn about user intent and to better understand the human language and accents as found in voice-activated Chatbots in Sri (Apple), Alexa (Amazon), and Google Assistant. [26] predicts that *"approximately $12 billion in retail revenue will be driven by conversational AI in 2023."* Figure 7.8 shows BPMN requirements modeling and simulation for a Chatbot application which consists of user interaction (100 users used for initial simulation), starting with user identification and authentication service, followed by branching into automated AI decision service, Chatbot service, and ML analytics service, and all the services located across the reference architecture as lanes and pools in BPMN.

   The tool used for modeling and simulating BPMN is known as Bizagi which is a cloud-driven low-cost process automation platform. This tool is easy to use to model and simulate BPMN processes and activities in a short time leading to validate key performance characteristics of the AI applications and any organizational processes [27]. Figure 7.11 shows the Chatbot activities run-time simulation for 100 users accessing this simulated Chatbot which took approximately 0.17 sec. These are useful performance requirements to validate before the design and implementation as we know the efficiency of the services on-the-fly and in the cloud.

   Existing Chatbot applications seem to lack explainability, user interface, transparency, use of language, empathy, emotions, and conversational decisions [28]. Therefore, we take such characteristics to design explainable AI Chatbots for

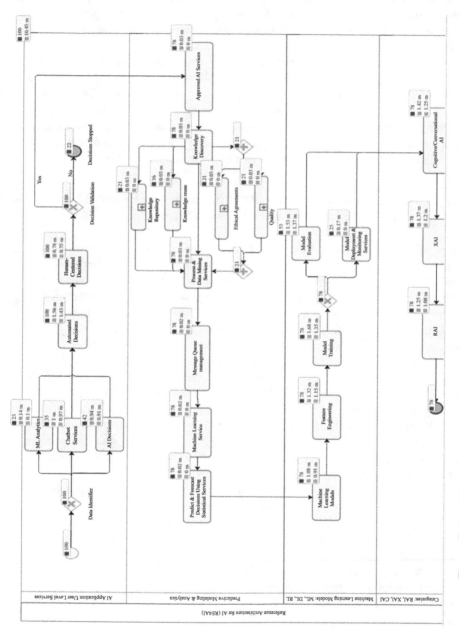

Figure 7.11   BPMN process simulation of RE4AI for a Chatbot conversational AI application

all types of applications. There is an emerging need for XAI Chatbots in critical applications such as healthcare [28]. Therefore, we believe that this can only be achieved by adopting the SEF—AI and ML framework that considers a complete lifecycle, and validation and verification of such conversations using requirements simulation with BPMN process modeling notation which is presented in Figure 7.11. In addition, Figure 7.12 shows resource utilization graphs for each task and the time it took. The vertical axis represents a reference architecture for AI as a pool (RE4AI) and lanes represent the layers of the reference architecture in the pool as shown in Figure 7.10. Typically, in BPMN, a pool represents the overall process of an organization and lanes represent the activities of the departments. We have used it to represent the reference architecture for artificial intelligence applications and lanes to represent the layers of the architecture such as user applications services (top layer), analytics and predictive modeling (the layer below the top), AI and ML models, data acquisitions and validation, Cloud, edge, IoT, IIOT, blockchain services, knowledge, patterns, solutions, and reuse, AI categories: RAI, XAI, HCAI and TAI, and CAI as shown in the vertical axis. The horizontal axis shows the application services as activities in BPMN modeling for the explainable Chatbot application case study. In each lane, application services are shown as activities in BPMN. In the case study, it shows the Chatbot application activities start from user activity shown in a green circle which is validated using user authentication activity known as object identifier followed by three choice services presented to the user level as ML analytics (ML analytics), Chatbot services, and AI decisions which then takes the user to a service AI service known as automated decisions based on the query asked by the user, followed by the user selected decisions (human-centred decision), followed by decision validation services, and a decision stopped service by the AI Chatbot application.

For example, ML analytics shows that it has handled 23 user requests, and the total time it took was 0.14 m, and spent 0.1 m on each request. Figure 7.12 shows the resource utilization graph for the Chatbot application using the BPMN simulation tool Bizagi [29].

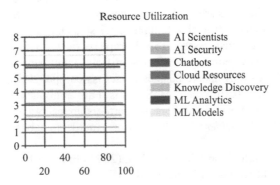

Figure 7.12   Resource utilization for the Chatbot services with BPMN simulation

In addition, there is a promising result that shows about 98% of resource utilization for most of the tasks of AI scientists, AI security, Chatbots, cloud resources, knowledge discovery, ML analytics, and AI models. In addition, we can also use the BPMN models in our cost–effort estimation equations to see the exact complexity and cost–benefit analysis.

7.11   Conclusions and further research

AI and ML applications have reached their adaptation maturity as we have witnessed in all applications and devices we use. However, we need a systematic approach to the design, development, implementation, and testing of AI products. Hence, this chapter proposes a SEF—AI and ML applications. The framework has been validated using a case study on Chatbot a conversational AI using BPMN modeling and simulation and the results show validation of performance and resource requirements for AI Chatbot cloud-driven services with 98% utilization and time efficiency. The results show a promising outcome for the application of systematic software engineering principles to achieve the desired AI quality. However, there are several research challenges in the validation and verification of AI requirements such as fairness, unbiasedness, and other characteristics discussed in this chapter. Further research is also required in applying the NLP for eliciting, capturing, verifying, and validating AI and ML application requirements. There is an immediate need for software engineering for AI and AI for software engineering throughout the lifecycle. There is also further research required in AISecOps and MLSecOps, for designing and delivering explainable applications, etc.

References

[1]   Holmes, F. (2019) AI Will Add $15 Trillion To The World Economy By 2030, https://www.usfunds.com/resource/ai-will-add-15-trillion-to-the-world-economy-by-2030/

[2]   PwC (2022) *Sizing the Prize*, https://www.pwc.com/gx/en/issues/data-and-analytics/publications/artificial-intelligence-study.html, Accessed on 2.11.2022.

[3]   Digibyte (2020) Artificial Intelligence: first quantitative study of its kind finds uptake by businesses across Europe is on the rise, Digibyte, https://digital-strategy.ec.europa.eu/en/news/artificial-intelligence-first-quantitative-study-its-kind-finds-uptake-businesses-across-europe, 28 July 2020

[4]   Mcgregor, S. (2020) When AI Systems Fail: Introducing the AI Incident Database, November 18, 2020, https://partnershiponai.org/aiincidentdatabase/

[5]   AIID (2022) *AI Incident Database*, https://incidentdatabase.ai/, Accessed on 28.11.2022.

[6]   Gohel, P., Singh, P., and Mohanty, M. (2021) Explainable AI: current status and future directions, arXiv:2107.07045.

[7]   IEEE (2014) IEEE Standard for Software Quality Assurance Processes, IEEE Std 730^{TM}-2014.

[8] Data, A. (2022), What is AI Quality, https://truera.com/what-is-ai-quality/#:~:text=AI%20Quality%20is%20the%20set,the%20organization%20and%20broader%20society, Accessed on 3.12.2022

[9] Sommerville, I. (2016) *Software Engineering*, 10th ed., Pearson.

[10] Breu, R., Kuntzmann-Combelles, A., and Felderer, M. (2014) New perspective on software quality, *IEEE Software*, January/February 2014.

[11] Bloomfield, R., *et al.* (2019) Disruptive Innovations and Disruptive Assurance: Assuring Machine Learning and Autonomy, *IEEE Computer*, August 2019.

[12] Al Alamin, A. Md. and Uddin, G. (2021) Quality assurance challenges for machine learning software applications during software development life cycle phases, In: *2021 IEEE International Conference on Autonomous Systems (ICAS)*, 11–13 August 2021, IEEE Proceedings, Montreal, QC, Canada.

[13] Martínez-Fernández, S., *et al.* (2021) Software Engineering for AI-Based Systems: A Survey, https://arxiv.org/abs/2105.01984

[14] Ramachandran, M. (2019) SOSE4BD: Service-oriented software engineering framework for big data applications. In: *Proceedings of the 4th International Conference on Internet of Things, Big Data and Security –* Vol. 1: IoTBDS. SciTePress, pp. 248–254. ISBN 9789897583698; doi: https://doi.org/10.5220/0007708702480254.

[15] Erdogmus, H., Medvidovic, N., and Paulisch, F. (2018) 50 Years of Software Engineering, Special Issue, *IEEE Software*, September/October 2018

[16] Nascimento, E., *et al.* (2020) Software engineering for artificial intelligence and machine learning software: A systematic literature review, https://arxiv.org/abs/2011.03751

[17] Menzies, T. (2020) The Five Laws of SE for AI, SE for AI, *IEEE Software*, JANUARY/FEBRUARY 2020.

[18] Barredo, A., *et al.* (2019) Explainable Artificial Intelligence (XAI): Concepts, Taxonomies, Opportunities and Challenges toward Responsible AI, 26 Dec 2019, *arXiv:1910.10045v2 [cs.AI]*.

[19] Hall, P., *et al.* (2022) Machine Learning for High-Risk Applications: Techniques for Responsible AI, O'Reily.

[20] Nazar, M., *et al.* (2021) A systematic review of human–computer interaction and explainable artificial intelligence in healthcare, *IEEE Access*, doi:10.1109/ACCESS.2021.3127881.

[21] Congress.gov (2022) H.R.6580 - Algorithmic Accountability Act of 2022, 117th Congress (2021-2022).

[22] Ahmad, K., *et al.* (2021) What's up with requirements engineering for artificial intelligence systems? In: *2021 IEEE 29th International Requirements Engineering Conference (RE)*, 20–24 September 2021, Notre Dame, IN.

[23] Ramachandran, M. (2013) *Business Requirements Engineering for Developing Cloud Computing Services, Software Engineering Frameworks for Cloud Computing Paradigm* (Mahmood, Z and Saeed, S, eds.), Springer.

[24] Bencomo, N., *et al.* (2022) *The Secret to Better AI, IEEE Software, SE for AI*, January/February 2022.

[25] Guha, R. (2013) Cloud COCOMO/Modified COCOMO for Cloud Service Cost and Effort Estimation Technique: Impact of Semantic Web and Cloud Computing Platform on Software Engineering, Mahmood, Z and Saeed, D (eds.) (2013) *Software Engineering Framework for Cloud Computing Paradigm*, Springer, 2013.

[26] Bishop, C. (2022) Zendesk Blog, Chatbots vs. conversational AI: What's the difference?

[27] Dumas, M., *et al.* (2018) *Fundamentals of Business Process Management*, 2nd Edition, Springer.

[28] Jovanovic, M., *et al.* (2021) Chatbots as Conversational Healthcare Services, *IEEE Internet Computing*, May/June 2021.

[29] Bizagi (2022) Low-Code Process Automation Platform, https://bizagi.com/

Chapter 8

Methods for explainable artificial intelligence

Sajid Ali[1]

Artificial intelligence (AI) has become an integral part of our society as it assists various sectors in dealing with difficult issues and revamping outdated methods. Many organizations are actively attempting to incorporate AI into their workflows due to its exceptional performance, which rivals human performance in a wide range of tasks [1]. However, the increasing complexity of AI models has made it challenging to understand how they make decisions, creating a lack of transparency and resulting in potential trust and ethical issues. At the annual Neural Information Processing Systems Conference in December 2018, a case was presented to the attendees as an example [2]. The scenario involved displaying two images on a screen—one of a patient being operated on by a human surgeon, with a caption indicating a 15% risk of mortality during surgery, and the other of a robotic arm with a failure rate of only 2%. The audience was then asked to vote on their preferred surgeon. Interestingly, despite the lower risk of death associated with the robotic arm, all but one of the attendees voted in favor of the human surgeon. This raises questions about why the audience chose the less accurate model over the more reliable one. This example highlights the importance of trust in AI systems, particularly in situations where human lives are at stake, in addition to issues of accuracy.

The need for transparency and interpretability in AI models has prompted the development of explainable AI (XAI), a field that focuses on developing methods and tools to explain the decision-making processes of AI models to humans. XAI provides users with insights into how AI models work and why they make certain decisions, enhancing trust, accountability, and transparency. For instance, a study conducted by IBM Watson Health found that providing physicians with explanations of how an AI system arrived at a particular recommendation could help build trust and improve acceptance of AI-driven decision-making in healthcare [3]. In addition, XAI can also help identify and correct biases in AI models, making them more equitable and inclusive. Therefore, the importance of XAI in enhancing trust, accountability, and transparency in AI models cannot be overstated.

[1]Department of Electrical and Computer Engineering, College of Information and Communication Engineering, Sungkyunkwan University, Suwon, South Korea

Furthermore, XAI has gained significant attention across multiple application domains, resulting in a proliferation of XAI tools and techniques proposed in both industry and academia [4]. The current XAI systems offer a diverse range of dimensions and functionalities, spanning from simple exploratory data analysis to understanding complex AI models. As a result, choosing the appropriate method for a given set of requirements necessitates a clear understanding of the various methods and fundamental differences among the different XAI approaches.

In this chapter, we delve into a detailed discussion of more comprehensive methods for XAI. We aim to explore approaches that can analyze the methods used in XAI and help us better evaluate the results produced by intelligent systems. To accomplish this, we divide this chapter into four distinct perspectives:

- an initial study,
- the importance of XAI,
- an overview of XAI techniques, and
- a taxonomy of popular XAI methods.

We conclude this chapter with a summary of discussed methods. By examining these perspectives in depth, we hope to provide a more comprehensive understanding of XAI and its potential applications.

8.1   Preliminarily study

The literature on XAI has been categorized into various areas, including XAI applications, social science and argumentation, and multidisciplinary fusion for explanation improvement. In this section, we review the existing literature on these areas.

Application concerns: Meske *et al.* [5] explored the impact of explainability on AI trust and demonstrated the use of XAI in medical diagnosis. They employed CNN and MLP models to identify malaria from thin blood smear slide images. Additionally, the authors emphasized the necessity of explainability and highlighted the risks of black-box AI. Islam *et al.* [6] presented a case study on credit default prediction, demonstrating the effectiveness of XAI techniques in gaining a competitive advantage from both local and global perspectives.

Social science and argumentation concerns: Miller [7] incorporated articles from the social sciences and discussed how XAI incorporates ideas from philosophy, cognitive science, and social psychology to produce good explanations of its results. Mueller [8] discussed psychological theories of explanation, stressing the definition of a good explanation. Vassiliades *et al.* [9] investigated the connection between argumentation and XAI, exploring interpretable prediction models that integrate ML and argumentation theory. Hussain *et al.* [10] used an engineering approach to explain XAI concepts by giving mathematical outlines of the methods used.

Multidisciplinary fusion concerns: Scientists have attempted to develop transparent models to decipher the inner workings of black-box systems. Liu *et al.* [11] proposed an interactive visualization method that aids in the diagnosis, comprehension, and refinement of AI systems and associated data mining issues. Zhang *et al.* [12] focused on the interpretability of CNNs' middle-layer representations, while Ras *et al.* [13] investigated the explainability of certain systems in terms of dataset bias. Montavon *et al.* [14] provided an overview of the interpretability problem and discussed the layer-wise relevance propagation (LRP) method.

XAI has been used in studies on supervised ML, unsupervised ML, and RL. Puiutta *et al.* [15] published the first review on XRL and provided an overview of the problem and definitions of key terms. Burkart and Huber [16] discussed XSML principles and techniques and provided a taxonomy of interpretable model learning, surrogate models, explanation types, and data explainability. Gerlings *et al.* [17] identified four thematic arguments motivating the need for XAI, completeness vs. interpretability dilemma, human explanations, and technologies producing XAI, which are essential to how XAI handles the black-box issue.

8.2 Importance of XAI for human-interpretable models

XAI aims to create ML models that are understandable to humans, particularly in sensitive industries like the military, banking, and healthcare, where experts require assistance in solving problems more effectively, and need meaningful results that they can comprehend and rely on. Not only is it essential for specialists to be able to evaluate appropriate outputs, but it also benefits developers to identify incorrect results, prompting them to scrutinize the system further. AI techniques can be used to assess current knowledge, advance knowledge, and develop new assumptions or theories, as stated in the demonstration of XAI [18].

Researchers aim to achieve several goals through XAI methods, including justification, control, improvement, and discovery. These objectives can enhance the transparency of black-box systems and provide several benefits. The benefits of XAI can be summarized as follows [19]:

- It empowers individuals to counteract any negative impacts of automated decision-making.
- It assists individuals in making more informed choices.
- It exposes and safeguards security vulnerabilities.
- It integrates algorithms with human values, which is an important objective.
- It enhances industry standards for the development of AI-powered products, thus increasing consumer and business confidence.
- It enforces the Right of Explanation policy.

For a model to be accepted by both end-users and industries, it must be trustworthy. However, building a reliable model is a challenging task. The trustworthiness of a model is influenced by several factors, including fairness, robustness, interpretability, and explainability/interpretation. Among these, explainability is considered to be one of the most significant aspects. Previous studies have mainly focused on improving the quality of explanations and insights for future research [20]. Researchers have proposed various approaches to qualitatively explain AI models using comprehensible text, mathematics, or visualizations.

8.3   Overview of XAI techniques

The field of XAI encompasses a wide range of techniques with varying scopes and applications, which are outlined in this section. A summary of the taxonomies covered in this section can be found in Figure 8.1, which can be broadly categorized into scoop-based, model-based, complexity-based, and methodology-based approaches. Although there exist numerous techniques for achieving explainability, this section will discuss them in detail in the following paragraphs. It is worth noting that, in the context of ML algorithms, the term "interpretability" is often used interchangeably with "explainability" in many papers.

Scoop-based explainers: Feature importance analysis is a commonly employed method for understanding the relationship between model outputs and inputs, whether for a single prediction or the model as a whole. The type of analysis conducted can be classified as either a local or global method, depending on the importance of the feature being examined. *Local explainers*, as the name suggests, are tailored to a specific decision or instance [21], meaning that their explanations are limited to a single case. A well-known example of a local explainer is LIME [22]. On the other hand, *global explainers* offer explanations that apply to the entire dataset [21], maintaining consistency across the entire range of observations. However, certain global explainers are also capable of providing localized explanations, such as SHAP, which can deliver both local and global explanations [23]. Table 8.1 presents a detailed outline of scoop-based XAI methods, including their definition, scope, interpretation, technique, application, and limitations.

Complexity-based explainers: The degree of interpretability of an AI model is typically inversely related to its complexity. Generally, the more complex a model, the more difficult it is to comprehend and explain. *Intrinsic interpretability* refers to the ability to construct self-explanatory models with built-in interpretability. It is often achieved through the use of simple model structures, which can come at the expense of accuracy in many cases [21]. Alternatively, a high-accuracy model with high complexity can be built, and a different set of methods can be utilized to provide necessary explanations without understanding the original model's inner workings. This class of techniques provides *post-hoc explanations* [24], usually by constructing a second model, often as a surrogate of the original

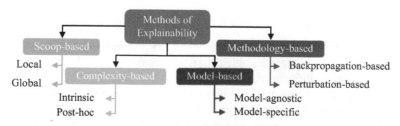

Figure 8.1   Taxonomies of XAI methods into scoop-based, model-based, complexity-based, and methodology-based approaches

Table 8.1 A comprehensive overview of scoop-based XAI methods

Criteria	Local	Global
Definition	Explainability focused on individual decisions made by a model	Techniques perturbation-based methods, LIME, anchor, SHAP, etc.
Scope	Provides information about the reasoning behind specific predictions	Application useful for situations where individual predictions need to be explained, such as in healthcare or legal domains
Interpretation	Provides an interpretation of the model's reasoning for a specific input	
Limitations	May not provide a complete picture of the model's behavior and may be sensitive to input perturbations	Explainability focused on overall model behavior Provides information about how the model works in general Provides an interpretation of the model's structure and overall behavior Model-based methods, decision trees, rule lists, sensitivity analysis, etc. Useful for model validation and improvement, or in cases where a model is being used to inform policy decisions May not provide insights into individual predictions, and may be computationally expensive for complex models

model (e.g., TREPAN [25]), to provide users with explanations. Table 8.2 provides an elaborate summary of the complexity-based XAI techniques, encompassing their definition, model design, performance, data requirement, implementation, and examples.

Model-based explainers: One way to categorize existing interpretability strategies is by distinguishing between model-agnostic and model-specific methods [21]. A *model-specific* [26] method, as the name suggests, is only applicable to particular types of models. Intrinsic methods are model-specific by definition. In contrast, *model-agnostic* [27] methods are not dependent on the type of ML model used. There has been a recent surge of interest in model-agnostic interpretability techniques since they are model-free. Model-agnostic methods offer post-hoc interpretability and are often used as local or global explainers to interpret ANNs. The model-based XAI techniques, including their definition, scope, implementation, and examples, are presented in detail in Table 8.3.

Methodology-based explainers: XAI core algorithms can be categorized into two main groups, based on the implemented methodology: backpropagation-based or perturbation-based methods. The former, also known as *gradient-based*

Table 8.2   A comprehensive overview of complexity-based XAI methods

Criteria	Intrinsic interpretability	Post-hoc interpretability
Definition	Models are inherently interpretable	Models are made interpretable after training
Model design	Interpretable models are designed from scratch	Pre-existing models are made interpretable
Performance	May have lower performance	Maintains the original model's performance Data requirements
May require less data	Relies on the same data as the original model	
Implementation	May require specialized implementation	Can be added as a layer to existing models
Examples	Decision trees, rule-based systems	LIME, SHAP

Table 8.3   A comprehensive overview of model-based XAI methods

Criteria	Model-agnostic	Model-specific
Definition	Explainable independent of any specific ML model.	Explainable for a particular ML model only.
Scope	Can be applied to any black-box model.	Specific to the model's architecture and design.
Implementation	Does not require any information regarding the underlying model.	Relies on the internal details of the model.
Examples	LIME, SHAP, anchors.	Layer-wise relevance propagation, DeepLIFT, integrated gradients.

techniques, utilize backpropagation to transmit a significant signal from the output to the input, starting from the output of the network and assigning weights to each intermediate value calculated during the forward pass. These techniques utilize a gradient function to differentiate the network output with respect to each intermediate parameter and update the weights of each parameter to align the output with the ground truth.

Examples of backpropagation-based methods include saliency maps and class activation maps (CAM) [20].

On the other hand, *perturbation-based algorithms* use a range of techniques, including occlusion, masking, conditional sampling, filling operations, or generative algorithms, to partially replace features in a given input instance, and assess the impact of these changes on the network output. Unlike backpropagation-based methods, perturbation-based algorithms do not require backpropagating gradients, as a single forward pass is sufficient to comprehend how the perturbed component in the input instance contributes to the network output [20,28]. Table 8.4 provides a comprehensive overview of methodology-based XAI techniques, along with their respective definitions, advantages, and limitations.

Table 8.4   A comprehensive overview of methodology-based XAI methods

Criteria	Backpropagation-based	Perturbation-based
Description	These methods use the gradient of the model's output with respect to the input to identify which features have the greatest impact on the output.	These methods alter the input in some way and observe how the output changes to understand which features have the greatest impact. Model-agnostic.
Advantages	Can be applied to any model that uses backpropagation. Fast and efficient. Can provide more robust explanations.	Can provide both global and local explanations. Do not require access to the model's internal workings.
Disadvantages	Can be computationally expensive for larger models. Only provide explanations for models that use backpropagation. Can be less robust to adversarial attacks.	Can be computationally expensive if perturbations need to be applied multiple times. Can be less precise than backpropagation-based methods. Can be more susceptible to noise in the data.

In the subsequent section, we present a comprehensive overview of several widely used techniques for elucidating intricate models. It is anticipated that this compilation will aid both experts in selecting suitable methods for model explication and developers of XAI methods in recognizing the inadequacies of the presently existing methods.

8.4   Taxonomy of popular XAI methods

A comprehensive range of various XAI methods and approaches have been developed by the global community. To assist engineers and students in selecting the most suitable approach, a detailed analysis and discussion are presented in this section. The commonly used XAI methods are categorized into backpropagation-based, perturbation, influence, knowledge extraction, concept, visualization, and example-based, as depicted in Figure 8.2.

8.4.1   Backpropagation-based methods

These methods calculate attribution values for input features through a forward and backward pass in a deep neural network (DNN). These methods are typically faster and less computationally expensive than perturbation approaches and may require multiple passes in certain cases. However, their results are not always directly correlated with output variation [29]. This section discusses various backpropagation approaches, which are summarized below.

Gradient-only methods focus solely on the gradient when determining the effect of a pixel change on the final prediction. Examples of such methods include

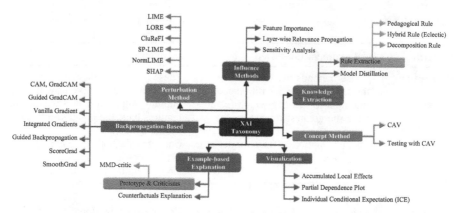

Figure 8.2   A proposed taxonomy for XAI. Definition of acronyms: LIME, locally interpretable model-agnostic explainer; LORE, local rule-based explanation; CluReFI, cluster representatives with LIME; SP LIME, submodular pick LIME; CAM, class activation map; MMD, maximum mean discrepancy; CAV, concept activation vector; SHAP, Shapley additive explanation.

Grad-CAM [30] and Vanilla Gradient [31]. These methods operate on the principle that altering a pixel in the input image will either increase or decrease the predicted probability of the class. The CAM method and its variations are explained first, followed by Vanilla-based gradient approaches.

CAM: It is a technique for visualizing the discriminative image areas detected by a convolutional neural network. The CAM was first introduced by Zhou *et al.* [32], who built upon the work of Lin *et al.* [33] in utilizing global average pooling (GAP) as a structural regularizer in CNNs. It was developed by modifying the GAP method to efficiently produce a weighted activation map for each feature map in a single forward pass. The CAM is created by calculating the spatial average of the feature maps using the GAP layer immediately before the SoftMax layer and then passing the weight matrix back to the last convolutional layer to produce the CAM. The process is depicted in Figure 8.3.

The activation map of the eth neuron from the last convolutional layer at a specific location (x,y) is denoted as $M_e(x, y)$. The GAP is computed by summing the values of $M_e(x, y)$ for all values of x and y. Let w^C be the weight matrix for the class C at the eth neuron. The SoftMax layer uses $\sum_e w^C \cdot GAP$ as an input for class C, and outputs the probability P_C.

$$\frac{\exp\left(\sum_e W_e^C \cdot GAP\right)}{\sum_c\left(\exp\left(\sum_e W_e^C \cdot GAP\right)\right)} \tag{8.1}$$

The weight matrix w^C is passed to the feature maps of the last convolutional layer to obtain the CAM which is defined as

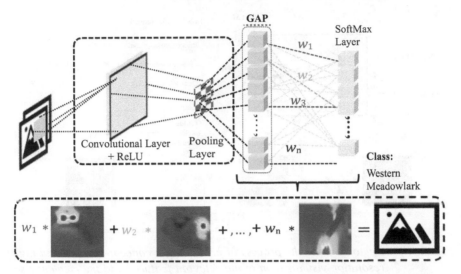

Figure 8.3 *The GAP generates the spatial average of each unit's feature map from the last possible convolutional layer. A weighted sum of the spatial data is then used to generate the final result. The CAM highlights the discriminative areas that are unique to each class.*

$$C A M_c(x,y) = \sum_e w_e^C \cdot M_e(x,y) \qquad (8.2)$$

GradCAM: It is providing visual explanations for any model in the convolutional neural network family without architectural modifications or retraining [30]. This method assigns significance ratings to each neuron for the given target class using the gradient information backpropagated to the final convolutional layer. GradCAM is based on the idea that CNN layers are capable of capturing both spatial information and high-level semantics, and the final CNN layer may have the optimal composition for extracting important data. The input image is passed through a CNN module and uses task-specific calculations to get a raw score for a particular category. A non-zero signal is backpropagated to a set of rectified convolutional feature maps (RCFMs), which are combined to produce the GradCAM map of the target class.

The GradCAM localization map, denoted as $M^C \in R^{bxt}$, is a representation of the underlying patterns within a neural unit for class C.

$$M_{GradCAM}^C = ReLU \left(\sum_k w_k^c m_k \right) \qquad (8.3)$$

Before going through the SoftMax function, the class score S_C is used to compute the gradient of the RCFM m_k with respect to S_C. This gradient, denoted as γ_k, is then passed to the GAP layer to obtain the significant weights matrix.

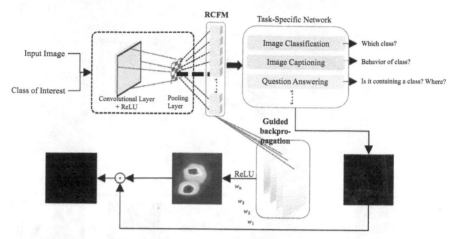

Figure 8.4   Demonstrating the process of producing a concept-specific and high-resolution visualization of the relevant features and the elementwise multiplication of the heatmap of the GradCAM with guided backpropagation to produce the guided GradCAM

Guided GradCAM: The technique is a class-discriminative method used to locate target class areas, but it has a limited capacity to highlight fine-grained features compared to pixel-space gradient visualization methods like DeconvNet [34] and guided backpropagation [35]. Guided backpropagation highlights gradients in relation to the input image by suppressing negative gradients when backpropagating via ReLU layers. This technique aims to capture pixels that are sensed by neurons rather than those that inhibit neurons. The combination of guided backpropagation and GradCAM visualization methods produces guided GradCAM, as illustrated in Figure 8.4.

Vanilla gradient: The technique of visualizing the representations of AI models, specifically DNNs, to explore the underlying patterns within neural units is a natural concept. The Vanilla Gradient method, also known as *Saliency Maps*, calculates the gradient of the loss function with respect to the input pixels and generates saliency maps that highlight areas with a significant impact on the model's prediction [31]. However, this method has been criticized for focusing only on the input and failing to explain how the model makes its decision.

In the context of image classification, a saliency map is a visual representation of the significance of each pixel in an image. The saliency score is calculated by a linear model that consists of the image's weight vector and bias:

$$Sc(I) = bc + Iw \tag{8.4}$$

In the case of a non-linear DNN, the saliency score calculation becomes non-linear:

$$Sc(I) \approx bc + Iw \tag{8.5}$$

However, by taking the derivative of the score function with respect to the image, the weight vector can still be obtained. Uncertainty in the gradient calculation arising from non-linear units like ReLU is resolved by considering the derivative of the output of the previous layer multiplied by an indicator function of the output of the current layer:

$$\frac{\partial F}{\partial N_L} = \frac{\partial F}{\partial N_{L+1}} \cdot I(N_L > 0) \tag{8.6}$$

The saliency map is derived from the weight vector by taking the absolute value of each weight value and mapping it back to its corresponding pixel in the image:

$$M_{ij} = |w_{idx(i,j)}| \tag{8.7}$$

For RGB images, the maximum value across all color channels is considered to generate a single saliency map.

Integrated gradients: This approach to understanding DNNs is by visualizing their representations. Sundarajan *et al.* [36] propose that integrated gradients combine gradient implementation invariance (GII) with the sensitivity of LRP or DeepLift techniques. Integrated gradients calculate gradients along inputs, which are on a straight line between a baseline image and the input image, to suppress noise:

$$IG_k(I) = \left(I_k - I_k'\right) \times \int_{\beta=0}^{1} \frac{\partial F(I' + \beta(I - I'))}{\partial I_k} d\beta \tag{8.8}$$

The integrated gradients along the *k*th dimension are defined using an integral approximation.

Guided backpropagation: The technique calculates the gradient of the desired output concerning the input by ignoring the backpropagation of ReLU functions, allowing only non-negative gradients to be backpropagated. In guided backpropagation, the ReLU function is applied to the input gradients, and in deconvolution, the ReLU function is applied to the output gradients, which are then directly backpropagated. However, both methods produce imputed versions of the gradient rather than the true gradient, according to the DeconvNet and guided backpropagation approaches [35].

ScoreGrad: It is a visualization technique that utilizes gradient information and an increase of confidence concept to prioritize activation maps [37]. The model takes an input image *I* and produces logits F' using a convolutional layer N_L. The contribution of the *i*th channel of N_L to F' is calculated using the Cont function,

$$Cont(A_{NL}^i) = F^c(I \times H^i) - F^c(I_b), \tag{8.9}$$

where I_b is the baseline image for class category *c*. The Score-CAM is obtained by applying ReLU to the sum of the multiplication of β^c, which is calculated using Cont for each activation map, and A^i.

$$L_{scoreCAM}^c = ReLU\left(\sum_i \beta_i^c A_{NL}^i\right) \tag{8.10}$$

Upsampling and normalization are applied to each element of A^i before calculating the Score-CAM.

SmoothGrad: The technique of sensitivity maps can produce noisy results due to fluctuations of partial derivatives, and it may not indicate the correlations between highlighted pixels and input labels [38]. To address this issue, the method of SmoothGrad uses a Gaussian kernel to smooth the gradients, which involves adding various forms of Gaussian noise to the input image and averaging sensitivity maps [39]. The resulting definition of SmoothGrad involves the input image, Gaussian noise, and the number of instances used in the process:

$$\widehat{M}_{sm}(I) = \frac{1}{n}\sum_{1}^{n} M_n\left(I + G\left(0, \sigma^2\right)\right) \tag{8.11}$$

There are two smoothing methods that can enhance gradient-based sensitivity maps [39]. First, averaging the maps generated from multiple small perturbations of an input image has a significant smoothing effect. Second, if the training data is distorted with random noise, this effect can be further amplified.

8.4.2   Perturbation methods

The perturbation-based methods compute the importance of a particular feature in a training instance by modifying it through deletion, masking, or alteration, followed by a forward pass on the modified input, and comparing the resulting output with the original output. Although these methods enable direct evaluation of the marginal impact of a feature, they tend to become computationally intensive as the number of features to be evaluated increases [40].

LIME: It is a local surrogate method that utilizes proxy models to interpret individual predictions of black-box ML techniques. LIME generates a new dataset by perturbing input instances and utilizing the black-box model's predictions. The perturbed dataset is used to build an interpretable model that approximates the ML model's predictions locally [22]. The model's local fidelity is evaluated using a proximity measure between the perturbed sample and the original instance. LIME is model-agnostic, allowing it to be used with any ML model. The data variation method utilized by LIME depends on the type of data being analyzed, with images and text often using on/off methods, while tabular data utilizes perturbations of each feature independently.

The LIME model is defined as a function that minimizes a loss function that measures the unfaithfulness of the interpretable model in approximating the ML model's predictions locally, plus a complexity measure of the interpretable model:

$$\Theta(\phi) = \arg\min_{F \in B} L\left(f, F, \Pi_\phi\right) + \omega(F) \tag{8.12}$$

LORE: It is a method that generates trustworthy and interpretable explanations in an agnostic manner. It does so by constructing a simple and interpretable predictor using a genetic algorithm to generate a balanced set of neighboring instances of a given instance x, from which a decision tree classifier is extracted. The resulting decision tree is then used to infer a local explanation [41]. The local explanation is represented as a pair of objects, where the first object is a binary predictor p used to make a decision y, and the second object is a set of counterfactual rules that represent the minimum changes required to the feature x values to cause the predictor to reverse its decision as defined as follows:

$$e = \langle r = p \rightarrow y \phi \rangle, \tag{8.13}$$

CluReFI: It is an extension of LIME, which is used for visualizing the representation of a cluster after data clustering. Once an unknown data instance is assigned to the nearest cluster, the cluster assignment is explained through per-feature validity visualization. CluReFI provides a visualization of the feature validity ranges for the most significant features that contribute to a specified class for each cluster [42]. In contrast to LIME, CluReFI presents users with the crucial aspects that contribute to the class for their representation.

SP-LIME: It is a technique used to identify crucial events for examining a model's predictions, as it is infeasible to examine all predictions under typical conditions [22]. By using the explanations for the selected subset, users can decide whether or not to trust the model's behavior. The problem of choosing a set of events that provides maximum coverage within a certain budget is known as the pick set problem as shown below:

$$PickSet(RS, I) = \arg \max_{D, |D| \leq B} C(D, RS, I) \tag{8.14}$$

A greedy approach is used to solve this NP-hard problem, where the coverage is defined as the overall relevance of features that appear at least once in the selected subset for instance with local importance scores given by RS for instance I.

NormLIME: It is a method used to determine the importance of a feature for a particular input in an interpretable way. This approach involves training an interpretable model F that is local to the region surrounding a certain input x_0. A Gaussian probability distribution is used to sample the data around x_0. The resulting dataset is then used to develop a sparse LR $F(x', x_0) = w^T x'$, where w_{x0} represents the importance of each feature. The method involves minimizing the loss function $L(f, F, \pi_{x0})$ subject to an upper limit K on the number of non-zero components in w_{x0}. Although the optimization is difficult, it may be approached by choosing the top K features using LASSO regression and then carrying out regression exclusively on those features.

SHAP: It is a technique proposed by Lundberg and Lee [23] in 2017 for explaining the output of any ML model. It uses the Shapley value approach, which is a coalitional game theory-based method for measuring the contribution of each feature in a prediction. The explanation is given in terms of a linear model that calculates the feature attribution for each feature. The SHAP explanation is given as follows:

$$g\left(\widehat{Z}\right) = \Phi_0 + \sum_{i=1}^{M} \Phi_i \widehat{Z}_{ij} \tag{8.15}$$

SHAP has properties such as local accuracy, missingness, consistency, efficiency, symmetry, dummy, and additivity. KernelSHAP and TreeSHAP are alternative estimation strategies based on Shapley values that are efficient for different types of models. SHAP values can provide both local and global interpretabilities. The former allows for the localization and comparison of the impacts of each feature on a prediction, while the latter can show how much each feature contributes to the target variable, positively or negatively.

8.4.3   Influence methods

Methods that analyze the impact of changes in input or internal elements on model performance can help to assess the significance of a feature in ML models [43]. This allows for debugging and improving the explanation of ML model behavior and predictions by identifying influential training examples. The literature suggests three techniques for determining input variable significance: feature importance, LRP, and sensitivity analysis.

Feature importance: The calculation of feature importance is determined by the change in a model's error when features are permuted. A feature is considered important if permuting its values results in an increase in the model's error. Conversely, if permuting a feature has no effect on the model's error, it is considered irrelevant. Various methods exist for computing feature importance, such as *Leave-One-Covariate-Out* (LOCO) [44] inference and *Model Class Reliance* (MCR) [45]. The MCR algorithm uses mean squared error (MSE) to measure the error of the original model and estimates the permuted feature importance by dividing the permuted error by the original error.

LRP: It is a relevant computation method that has demonstrated its versatility and high performance in benchmark experiments. LRP redistributes the prediction functions in reverse order by backpropagating from the output layer to the input layer, while conserving relevance. The method assumes that the classifier is composed of several layers of computation [46]. During a forward pass through the network, the activations at each layer are recorded, and using specific rules, a score at the output layer is backpropagated. The redistribution of relevance from neuron k to neuron j in successive layers is defined as $RS_{j \leftarrow k}$, while the relevance of neuron k is defined as RS_k. The conservation property requires that $\sum_j RS_{j \leftarrow k} = RS_k$, and the contribution of higher-layer relevance to a lower-layer neuron is aggregated to produce the lower-layer neuron's relevance. By combining these equations, the relevance conservation property between two layers can be obtained, and the whole network's relevance conservation sequence can be expressed as

$$\sum i = 1^d \, RS_i = \ldots = \sum_j RS_j = \sum_k RS_k = \ldots = F(x), \qquad (8.16)$$

where $F(.)$ is the function that encodes the output neuron's concept, and x is the input data.

Sensitivity analysis: It is a method for identifying important input features in ML and DL models. This technique perturbs the input data and examines the resulting changes in the model output to determine which features have the greatest impact on the output [47]. It has been successfully applied in various fields such as medical diagnosis, ecological modeling, and image classification. It is considered a model-agnostic explanation method that can help assess the model's stability and confidence in results. It is defined formally in terms of a relevance score as follows, based on the local gradient x of model F:

$$RS_i(x) = \left(\frac{\partial F}{\partial x_i}\right)^2 \tag{8.17}$$

The above relevance scores are decomposed into the gradient square norm as follows:

$$\sum_{i=1}^{d} R_{i(x)} = \|\nabla \cdot F(x)\|^2 \tag{8.18}$$

Sensitivity analysis generates relevance scores based on the local gradient of the model, and it is often used to identify or remove irrelevant input features. However, it does not provide an explanation itself but rather shows variations in explanations [48].

8.4.4 Knowledge extraction

Extracting explanations from black-box ML models, such as ANNs, is a challenging task since their internal behavior is difficult to interpret. ANNs may alter the filter or kernel in the hidden layer, leading to complex internal representations of the entire network. To provide human-understandable explanations for ANNs, two techniques are commonly used: rule extraction and model distillation. Both techniques aim to retrieve the knowledge learned by individual layers during training and present it in a more interpretable format.

Rule extraction: According to Craven [49], rule extraction is a process of producing a simplified approximation of a neural network's behavior from training data and the trained ANN. There are several types of rule extraction techniques available, including IF-THEN rules, M-of-N rules, and decision trees. These rules can be categorized into propositional/Boolean logic and non-conventional logic. Rule extraction algorithms, such as fuzzy modeling, genetic programming, and Boolean rule extraction, have been developed over time. Three distinct types of methods for extracting rules based on the trained NN architecture are decompositional, pedagogical, and eclectic methods. These methods operate on the neuron level, disregarding the NN architectural design or combining decompositional and pedagogical methods, respectively.

The ultimate goal of rule extraction is to gain insight into highly complex ML models.

Model distillation: It is a method of transferring knowledge from a teacher network to a student network through model compression. This approach is used to improve the explainability of complicated models by translating them into interpretable ones. It was first proposed to decrease a model's runtime computing cost but has since been used for knowledge extraction purposes. Interpretable Mimic Learning and DarkSight are two examples of model distillation techniques for generating robust predictions while imitating the performance of black-box deep learning models. For more information on the model distillation approach, interested researchers can refer to the works by [50,51].

8.4.5   Concept methods

The importance of addressing bias in ML is widely recognized, and the need to address it is even greater in the case of AI. Concept-based methods have been proposed as a means to increase the transparency and trustworthiness of AI systems.

CAV: Kim *et al.* [52] proposed the CAVs method to provide human-friendly explanations of the internal states of neural networks globally. This approach involves an explanation function, g, included in the model to produce human-understandable concepts (C) as explanations. CAVs are orthogonal to a hyperplane that separates instances without a concept from instances with a concept in the layer activations, using a binary classification task to distinguish between the layer activation of two sets. CAVs have been extended further in numerous research articles, such as automatic concept-based explanations (ACE), causal concept effect (CaCE), ground truth CaCE (GT-CaCE), variational auto encoders-based CaCE (VAE-CaCE), and ConceptSHAP.

Testing with CAV: The use of CAVs for testing AI models is known as testing CAVs (TCAVs), which assesses the sensitivity of a model using directional derivatives. The sensitivity of a model is determined by shifting the input in a direction toward the concept for a particular layer, and the sensitivity of all classes of inputs can be computed with TCAV techniques. If we have an input x, the gradient logit of layer n for class c can be denoted as $H_c(x)$. Using this, we can compute the conceptual sensitivity of class c to C at layer n by calculating the directional derivative with respect to a concept vector vC^n:

$$S_{Cc,n} = \lim_{\epsilon \to 0} \frac{H_{n,c}\left(F_n(x) + \epsilon\, v_c^n\right) - H_{n,c}(F_n(x))}{\epsilon} = \nabla H_{n,c}(F_n(x)) \cdot v_n^c. \qquad (8.19)$$

Additionally, TCAV techniques enable the computation of sensitivity for all input classes. For a given class c within the entire dataset X, TCAV can be defined as:

$$TCAV_{Cc,n} = \frac{\left|\{x \varepsilon X_c : S_{Cc,n} > 0\}\right|}{|X_c|} \qquad (8.20)$$

8.4.6   Visualization methods

The concept of visualizing representations of a DNN to gain insights into the patterns learned by the model is widely used. This technique is mainly used for supervised learning models, and the following paragraphs will cover various visualization methods used with DNNs, along with their respective strengths and weaknesses.

Accumulated local effects: It is a visualization technique that avoids erroneous extrapolation with associated predictors. Accumulated local effects average and accumulate changes in predictions over a grid in graphs. The formula for accumulated local effects shows three differences from the partial dependence plot:

$$\hat{f}_{x_p} = \int E_{x_0 \| x_p} \left[\hat{f}(x_0, x_p) | x_p = x_0 \right] dx_p - const \tag{8.21}$$

$$= \int \left(\int \hat{f}(x_p, x_0) dp(x_0 \| x_0 = x_p) \right) dx_p - const \tag{8.22}$$

First, it averages prediction changes instead of the predictions themselves. Second, it determines the effect of a feature on a prediction by adding up the local partial derivatives across the range of features in set X. Third, it subtracts a constant from the result to center the accumulated local effects plot, ensuring that the average effect across the data is zero. This method is defined as the integral of the expected prediction of a model over a region in the feature space and is useful for visualizing the relationship between a single feature and the model's prediction.

Partial dependence plot: It is a method to analyze the relationship between a feature and a model's prediction [53]. The partial dependence plot shows the average prediction of a black-box model as an individual feature is changed throughout its range. The partial dependence plot can visualize how a single feature influences the global model's prediction. Krause *et al.* [54] extended the partial dependence plot by adding a partial dependency bar that shows a colored depiction of the prediction value across the range of input values that a feature may take. For regression, the partial dependency function is estimated using the Monte Carlo technique. The partial dependence plot is calculated for a subset of features P and other features O using the model $\hat{f}$:

$$\hat{f}_{x_p}(x_p) = E_{x_0} \left[\hat{f}(x_p, x_0) \right] = \int \hat{f}(x_p, x_0) dp(x_0) \tag{8.23}$$

The PDP estimates the average function $\hat{f}_x(x_P)$ by calculating the average prediction for all the samples in the dataset:

$$\hat{f}_{x_p}(x_p) = \frac{1}{n} \sum_{i=1}^{n} \hat{f}(x_p, x_0^i) \tag{8.24}$$

Individual conditional expectation: This technique is an extension of partial dependence plots, which are used to show the relationship between a single feature and the target. The individual conditional expectation plot provides a visualization of how the target function changes for each instance, whereas the partial dependence plot shows the average relationship between the feature and the target [55]. The combination of individual conditional expectations and partial dependence plots allows for the identification of heterogeneity and interactive effects. Individual conditional expectation plots are drawn for each example $\hat{f}^{(i)}$ is drawn against $x^{(i)}$, with $x^{(i)}$ remaining the same. Centered and derivative individual conditional expectation plots are further extensions of the standard individual conditional expectation plot, which can be used to explore the presence of inter-acting effects.

8.4.7   *Example-based explanation*

Example-based explanations, also known as case-based explanations, can be gen-erated using various techniques such as prototypes and criticisms, and counter-factuals. Each of these methods has its advantages and disadvantages. The strengths and limitations of these methods will be discussed in the following paragraphs.

Prototypes and criticisms: Prototypes refer to individual instances that repre-sent a set of data instances, while criticisms are data instances that are distinct enough not to be included in the prototype set [56]. Prototypes and criticisms can be used to describe data and make black-box models interpretable. The maximum mean dis-crepancy (MMD-critic) method [57] is a popular approach that integrates prototypes and criticisms. This method uses a kernel function to analyze data densities, a witness function to identify criticisms, and a greedy search technique for prototype and cri-ticism selection. The equation below is used to calculate the squared MMD measure:

$$MMD^2 = \frac{1}{p^2} \sum_{i,j=1}^{p} \mathbf{k}(z_i, z_j) - \frac{2}{pn} \sum_{i,j=1}^{p,n} \mathbf{k}(z_i, x_j)$$

$$+ \frac{1}{n^2} \sum_{i,j=1}^{n} \mathbf{k}(x_i, x_j). \tag{8.25}$$

The *witness* estimator is defined as follows:

$$witness(x) = \frac{1}{n} \sum_{i=1}^{n} k(x, x_i) - \frac{1}{p} \sum_{j=1}^{p} k(x, z_j) \tag{8.26}$$

In this context, an interpretable model is defined as:

$$\hat{f}(x) = \arg \max_{i \in S} k(x, x_i)$$

The MMD-critic method helps in better understanding data distributions, con-structing understandable models, and making black-box models interpretable. An interpretable model is defined as the prototype that has the highest value of the kernel function.

Counterfactuals: These are synthetic examples that are different from actual training set instances and can be generated to explain a model's decision. The idea of counterfactual explanations was introduced by Wachter *et al.* [58] and involves optimizing a loss function that takes an instance of interest, a counterfactual, and the desired outcome. The loss function is optimized to get the best counterfactual explanation as follows:

$$L(x, x', y', \lambda) = \lambda \cdot \left(\hat{f}(x' - y')\right)^2 + d(x, x') \tag{8.27}$$

The multi-objective counterfactuals (MOC) approach [59] allows for more detailed post-hoc explainability by minimizing four objective losses simultaneously. To do this, the authors simultaneously minimize four objective losses (O_1, O_2, O_3, O_4):

$$L\left(x, x', y', X^{obs}\right) = \left(O_1\left(\hat{f}(x'), y'\right), O_2(x, x'), O_3(x, x'), O_4\left(x', X^{obs}\right)\right) \quad (8.28)$$

Suffian *et al.* [60] proposed generating counterfactual explanations with user feedback to enhance automated explanations. It is also possible to generate linguistic counterfactuals using fuzzy sets and systems, as proposed by [61].

8.5 Conclusion

As AI models are becoming increasingly regulated by governments, it has become crucial to provide explanations for their decisions. The emergence of XAI has helped us to better understand AI systems and move towards models that can offer human-friendly explanations. However, it remains unclear whether the growing range of XAI methodologies and tools is enough to provide practical support in the risky scenarios that regulatory stakeholders are concerned about. For instance, can an intelligent model be used for a medical diagnosis simply because of the availability of score-CAM [37] or GradCAM [30]? The answer is a resounding "NO" because there are no established risk-aware scenarios that can guide the research community on the requirements for implementing XAI-supported AI models in real-world contexts. Therefore, society needs approaches that recognize XAI tools as necessary but insufficient steps toward assessing the trustworthiness of AI-based systems for specific tasks.

References

[1] Enholm IM, Papagiannidis E, Mikalef P, and Krogstie, J. Artificial intelligence and business value: a literature review. *Information Systems Frontiers.* 2021; 24(5):1709–1734.

[2] Rudin C and Radin J. Why are we using black box models in AI when we don't need to? A lesson from an explainable AI competition. *Harvard Data Science Review.* 2019;1(2):1–9.

[3] Vroegindeweij R and Carvalho A. Do healthcare workers need cognitive computing technologies? A qualitative study involving IBM Watson and Dutch professionals. *Journal of the Midwest Association for Information Systems (JMWAIS).* 2019;2019(1):4.

[4] Islam MR, Ahmed MU, Barua S, *et al.* A systematic review of explainable artificial intelligence in terms of different application domains and tasks. *Applied Sciences.* 2022;12(3):1353.

[5] Meske C and Bunde E. Transparency and trust in human–AI-interaction: the role of model-agnostic explanations in computer vision-based decision support. In: *International Conference on Human–Computer Interaction.* Springer; 2020. p. 54–69.

[6]   Islam SR, Eberle W, Ghafoor SK, *et al.* Explainable artificial intelligence approaches: a survey. *CoRR.* 2021.

[7]   Miller T. Explanation in artificial intelligence: insights from the social sciences. *Artificial Intelligence.* 2019;267:1–38.

[8]   Mueller ST, Hoffman RR, Clancey W, *et al.* Explanation in human-AI systems: a literature meta-review, synopsis of key ideas and publications, and bibliography for explainable AI, 2019. *arXiv preprint arXiv:190201876.*

[9]   Vassiliades A, Bassiliades N, and Patkos T. Argumentation and explainable artificial intelligence: a survey. *The Knowledge Engineering Review.* 2021;36:e5.

[10]   Hussain F, Hussain R, and Hossain E. Explainable Artificial Intelligence (XAI): an engineering perspective, 2021. *arXiv preprint arXiv:210103613.*

[11]   Liu S, Wang X, Liu M, *et al.* Towards better analysis of machine learning models: a visual analytics perspective. *Visual Informatics.* 2017;1(1):48–56.

[12]   Zhang Q and Zhu SC. Visual interpretability for deep learning: a survey. *Frontiers of Information Technology and Electronic Engineering.* 2018;19:27–39.

[13]   Ras G, van Gerven M, and Haselager P. Explanation methods in deep learning: users, values, concerns and challenges. In: *Explainable and Interpretable Models in Computer Vision and Machine Learning.* Springer; 2018. p. 19–36.

[14]   Montavon G, Samek W, and Müller KR. Methods for interpreting and understanding deep neural networks. *Digital Signal Processing.* 2018;73:1–15.

[15]   Puiutta E and Veith EM. Explainable reinforcement learning: a survey. In: *International Cross-Domain Conference for Machine Learning and Knowledge Extraction.* Springer; 2020. p. 77–95.

[16]   Burkart N and Huber MF. A survey on the explainability of supervised machine learning. *Journal of Artificial Intelligence Research.* 2021;70:245–317.

[17]   Gerlings J, Shollo A, and Constantiou I. Reviewing the Need for Explainable Artificial Intelligence (XAI). HICSS. 2021.

[18]   Rieg T, Frick J, Baumgartl H, *et al.* Demonstration of the potential of white-box machine learning approaches to gain insights from cardiovascular disease electrocardiograms. *PLoS One.* 2020;15(12):e0243615.

[19]   Guidotti R, Monreale A, Ruggieri S, *et al.* A survey of methods for explaining black box models. *ACM Computing Surveys (CSUR).* 2018;51 (5):1–42.

[20]   Das A and Rad P. Opportunities and challenges in explainable artificial intelligence (XAI): a survey, 2020. arXiv preprint arXiv:200611371.

[21]   Adadi A and Berrada M. Peeking inside the black-box: a survey on explainable artificial intelligence (XAI). *IEEE Access.* 2018;6:52138–52160.

[22]   Ribeiro MT, Singh S, and Guestrin C. "Why should I trust you?" Explaining the predictions of any classifier. In: *Proceedings of the 22nd ACM SIGKDD International Conference on Knowledge Discovery and Data Mining*; 2016. p. 1135–1144.

[23] Lundberg SM and Lee SI. A unified approach to interpreting model predictions. In: *Proceedings of the 31st International Conference on Neural Information Processing Systems*; 2017. p. 4768–4777.

[24] Lipton ZC. The mythos of model interpretability. *Communications of the ACM.* 2018;61(10):36–43.

[25] Craven MW and Shavlik JW. Extracting tree-structured representations of trained networks. In: *Proceedings of NIPS*; 1995. p. 24–30.

[26] Hu ZF, Kuflik T, Mocanu IG, *et al.* Recent studies of XAI-review. In: *Adjunct Proceedings of the 29th ACM Conference on User Modeling, Adaptation and Personalization*; 2021. p. 421–431.

[27] Zafar MR and Khan N. Deterministic local interpretable model-agnostic explanations for stable explainability. *Machine Learning and Knowledge Extraction.* 2021;3:525–541.

[28] Ivanovs M, Kadikis R, and Ozols K. Perturbation-based methods for explaining deep neural networks: a survey. *Pattern Recognition Letters.* 2021;150:228–234.

[29] Ancona M, Ceolini E, Öztireli C, *et al.* Towards better understanding of gradient-based attribution methods for deep neural networks. In: *ICLR 2018 Conference*, 2018.

[30] Selvaraju RR, Cogswell M, Das A, *et al.* Grad-cam: visual explanations from deep networks via gradient-based localization. In: *Proceedings of the IEEE International Conference on Computer Vision*; 2017. p. 618–626.

[31] Simonyan K, Vedaldi A, and Zisserman A. Deep inside convolutional networks: visualising image classification models and saliency maps. In: *Workshop at International Conference on Learning Representations.* Citeseer; 2014. p. 1–8.

[32] Zhou B, Khosla A, Lapedriza A, *et al.* Learning deep features for discriminative localization. In: *Proceedings of the IEEE Conference on Computer Vision and Pattern Recognition*; 2016. p. 2921–2929.

[33] Lin M, Chen Q, and Yan S. Network in network. In: *International Conference on Learning Representations.* 2013.

[34] Zeiler MD and Fergus R. Visualizing and understanding convolutional networks. In: *European Conference on Computer Vision.* Springer; 2014. p. 818–833.

[35] Springenberg JT, Dosovitskiy A, Brox T, *et al.* Striving for simplicity: the all convolutional net, 2014. arXiv preprint arXiv:14126806.

[36] Sundararajan M, Taly A, and Yan Q. Axiomatic attribution for deep networks. In: *International Conference on Machine Learning.* PMLR; 2017. p. 3319–3328.

[37] Wang H, Wang Z, Du M, *et al.* Score-CAM: score-weighted visual explanations for convolutional neural networks. In: *Proceedings of the IEEE/CVF Conference on Computer Vision and Pattern Recognition Workshops*; 2020. p. 24–25.

[38] Baehrens D, Schroeter T, Harmeling S, *et al.* How to explain individual classification decisions. *The Journal of Machine Learning Research.* 2010;11:1803–1831.

[39]   Smilkov D, Thorat N, Kim B, *et al.* Smoothgrad: removing noise by adding noise. In: *Workshop on Visualization for Deep Learning, ICML*, 2017.

[40]   Zintgraf LM, Cohen TS, Adel T, *et al.* Visualizing deep neural network decisions: prediction difference analysis. In: *ICLR Conference*, 2017.

[41]   Guidotti R, Monreale A, Ruggieri S, *et al.* Local rule-based explanations of black box decision systems, 2018. arXiv preprint arXiv:180510820.

[42]   El Bekri N, Kling J, and Huber MF. A study on trust in black box models and post-hoc explanations. In: *International Workshop on Soft Computing Models in Industrial and Environmental Applications*. Springer; 2019. p. 35–46.

[43]   Linardatos P, Papastefanopoulos V, and Kotsiantis S. Explainable AI: a review of machine learning interpretability methods. *Entropy.* 2021;23 (1):18.

[44]   Lei J, G'Sell M, Rinaldo A, *et al.* Distribution-free predictive inference for regression. *Journal of the American Statistical Association.* 2018;113 (523):1094–1111.

[45]   Fisher A, Rudin C, and Dominici F. Model class reliance: variable importance measures for any machine learning model class, from the Rashomon. *Perspective.* 2018;68:13–22.

[46]   Bach S, Binder A, Montavon G, *et al.* On pixel-wise explanations for non-linear classifier decisions by layer-wise relevance propagation. *PLoS One.* 2015;10(7):e0130140.

[47]   Zurada JM, Malinowski A, and Cloete I. Sensitivity analysis for minimization of input data dimension for feedforward neural network. In: *Proceedings of IEEE International Symposium on Circuits and Systems-ISCAS'94.* vol. 6. IEEE; 1994. p. 447–450.

[48]   Sung A. Ranking importance of input parameters of neural networks. *Expert Systems with Applications.* 1998;15(3–4):405–411.

[49]   Craven MW. Extracting comprehensible models from trained neural networks. The University of Wisconsin-Madison; 1996.

[50]   Tan S, Caruana R, Hooker G, *et al. Distill-and-Compare: Auditing Black-Box Models Using Transparent Model Distillation.* Association for Computing Machinery, 2018.

[51]   Tan S. Interpretable approaches to detect bias in black-box models. In: *Proceedings of the 2018 AAAI/ACM Conference on AI, Ethics, and Society*; 2018. p. 382–383.

[52]   Kim B, Wattenberg M, Gilmer J, *et al.* Interpretability beyond feature attribution: quantitative testing with concept activation vectors (TCAV). In: *International Conference on Machine Learning.* PMLR; 2018. p. 2668–2677.

[53]   Goldstein A, Kapelner A, Bleich J, *et al.* Peeking inside the black box: visualizing statistical learning with plots of individual conditional expectation. *Journal of Computational and Graphical Statistics.* 2015;24(1):44–65.

[54]   Krause J, Perer A, and Ng K. Interacting with predictions: visual inspection of black-box machine learning models. In: *Proceedings of the 2016 CHI Conference on Human Factors in Computing Systems*; 2016. p. 5686–5697.

[55]   Hyvärinen A, Hurri J, and Hoyer PO. Independent component analysis. In: *Natural Image Statistics*. Springer; 2009. p. 151–175.

[56]   Kim B, Rudin C, and Shah JA. The Bayesian case model: a generative approach for case-based reasoning and prototype classification. In: *Advances in Neural Information Processing Systems*; 2014. p. 1952–1960.

[57]   Kim B, Khanna R, and Koyejo OO. Examples are not enough, learn to criticize! criticism for interpretability. *Advances in Neural Information Processing Systems*. 2016;29:1449–1457.

[58]   Wachter S, Mittelstadt B, and Russell C. Counterfactual explanations without opening the black box: automated decisions and the GDPR. *Harvard Journal of Law and Technology*. 2017;31:841.

[59]   Dandl S, Molnar C, Binder M, *et al.* Multi-objective counterfactual explanations. In: *International Conference on Parallel Problem Solving from Nature*. Springer; 2020. p. 448–469.

[60]   Suffian M, Graziani P, Alonso-Moral JM, *et al.* FCE: feedback based counterfactual explanations for explainable AI. *IEEE Access*. 2022;10: 72363–72372.

[61]   Stepin I, Catala A, Pereira-Fariña M, *et al. Factual and Counterfactual Explanation of Fuzzy Information Granules*. Springer-Verlag; 2021.

Chapter 9

Knowledge representation and reasoning (KRR)

Syed Muzamil Basha[1] and Naif K. Al-Shammari[2]

Knowledge representation and reasoning (KRR) is a key research area in artificial intelligence that deals with the design and development of methods to represent, manipulate, and reason with knowledge in computer systems. KRR techniques are used to develop intelligent systems that can reason about complex domains, make decisions, and provide explanations for their actions. The present research aims to understand the process of representing knowledge and reasoning with different domains, including agriculture, education, healthcare, and business. Different techniques, such as ontologies, semantic networks, frames, rule-based systems, description logics, first-order logic, and Bayesian networks, have been developed to facilitate the representation and reasoning of knowledge. In the present research, different techniques for representing and reasoning with knowledge are used in two different domains: academic knowledge and farmer knowledge. The study examines the strengths and weaknesses of each technique and provides insights into which techniques are most suitable for different types of KRR tasks. The results of this study can help practitioners and researchers to choose the most appropriate technique for their specific KRR needs.

9.1 Introduction

Knowledge representation and reasoning (KRR) is an essential aspect of developing intelligent systems that can reason and make decisions. It is concerned with how to represent knowledge about the world in a way that allows intelligent systems to make inferences and draw conclusions based on that knowledge. The primary goal of KRR is to provide a formal framework for representing knowledge that can be used to support automated reasoning. KRR is used in a wide range of applications, including natural language processing (NLP), expert systems, decision support systems, robotics, and many others [1].

[1]School of Computer Science and Engineering, REVA University, Bangalore, India
[2]Department of Mechanical Engineering, College of Engineering, University of Ha'il, Ha'il, Saudi Arabia

There are several key concepts that are fundamental to KRR, including ontology, inference, and logic. Ontology is the study of how to represent the knowledge about a domain. Inference refers to the process of deriving new knowledge from existing knowledge. Logic provides a formal framework for reasoning about knowledge. In recent years, there has been a significant progress in the development of KRR techniques and tools. Some of the key areas of research in KRR include ontologies, knowledge graphs, semantic web technologies, and machine learning (ML) for KRR. KRR is a crucial area of research for developing intelligent systems that can reason and make decisions in complex environments. By providing a formal framework for representing and reasoning about knowledge, KRR enables intelligent systems to operate more efficiently and effectively in a wide range of applications. The contribution of the present research is to list out the challenges involved in various tools and techniques available for representing knowledge, such as ontologies, semantic networks, frames, rule-based systems, description logics (DL), first-order logic, and Bayesian networks along with its advantages and drawbacks.

9.2   Methodology

A formal framework for representing knowledge refers to a structured method for representing information and knowledge in a way that can be processed by a machine. This framework is designed to support automated reasoning and inference, allowing intelligent systems to draw logical conclusions based on the knowledge they possess. In the context of KRR, such frameworks may include logical formalisms such as predicate logic, modal logic, DL, and many others. Such formal frameworks for representing knowledge are essential for building intelligent systems that can reason about complex domains, make informed decisions, and provide insights into complex problems. By using these frameworks, we can model complex relationships and dependencies among objects, concepts, and events, making it possible to develop sophisticated reasoning algorithms that can solve complex problems in a wide range of applications.

9.2.1   Reference model

The reference model for KRR is a conceptual model that outlines the key elements and processes involved in representing and reasoning about knowledge in intelligent systems. This model consists of three main components: knowledge representation, reasoning mechanisms, and inference procedures.

The knowledge representation component specifies how knowledge is encoded in a formal language or data structure, such as ontologies or knowledge graphs. The reasoning mechanisms component outlines the methods and algorithms used to manipulate and reason with the knowledge represented, such as rule-based reasoning, logic-based reasoning, or ML-based reasoning. The inference procedures component specifies how to draw new conclusions or make predictions based on the existing knowledge and the results of the reasoning process.

Designing a reference model for KRR involves several steps, including [2]:

1. Identify the purpose and scope: Define the specific domain and application for which the reference model is being designed.
2. Define the conceptual model: Develop a conceptual model that represents the key concepts, relationships, and constraints in the domain.
3. Identify the representation formalisms: Identify the appropriate representation formalisms (e.g., ontologies, logic-based languages, graph-based models) that will be used to represent the concepts and relationships in the domain.
4. Define the inference mechanisms: Define the inference mechanisms (e.g., deductive reasoning, probabilistic reasoning) that will be used to reason over the knowledge represented in the model.
5. Identify the knowledge sources: Identify the sources of knowledge that will be used to populate the model, including experts in the domain, existing ontologies and knowledge bases, and relevant literature.
6. Evaluate and refine the model: Evaluate the model against specific criteria, such as completeness, consistency, and efficiency, and refine it as necessary.
7. Implement and test the model: Implement the model in software, and test it against a range of scenarios to ensure that it meets the desired performance criteria.
8. Document and disseminate the model: Document the reference model and make it available to other researchers and practitioners in the field.

By following these steps, a well-designed reference model can provide a structured and systematic approach to KRR in a given domain, enabling more efficient and effective decision-making and problem-solving.

9.2.2   Ontologies

Ontologies are a formal way to represent knowledge by specifying a set of concepts, properties, and relationships that describe a particular domain of interest. They are often used in KRR to facilitate sharing and reuse of knowledge across different systems and applications. An ontology provides a structured and organized representation of the concepts and relationships within a domain, allowing for more efficient and accurate reasoning about that domain. It also allows for the creation of a common vocabulary and shared understanding among people and systems working within that domain.

Ontologies can be created manually or automatically through various methods such as text mining, NLP, or ML. They can be expressed in various formal languages such as Web Ontology Language (OWL), resource description framework (RDF), or RDFS. Ontologies are widely used in various fields such as healthcare, finance, and e-commerce to provide a common vocabulary and structure for data and knowledge representation. They also play an important role in the development of intelligent systems such as expert systems, recommender systems, and semantic search engines.

9.2.3   Knowledge graphs

Knowledge graphs are a type of knowledge representation that represents information as a graph structure, with nodes representing entities and edges representing relationships between them. Knowledge graphs are widely used in applications such as search engines, recommender systems, and question–answer systems. In knowledge graphs, entities are represented as nodes, and relationships between entities are represented as edges. Each entity and relationship is assigned a unique identifier, and additional information can be attached to the nodes and edges as attributes.

The graphical structure of knowledge graphs allows for efficient querying and reasoning over large amounts of data and enables the discovery of new insights and relationships. Knowledge graphs can be constructed automatically using ML techniques, or curated manually by experts in a particular domain.

9.2.4   Semantic web technologies

Semantic web technologies are a set of standards and technologies designed to enable machine-readable data on the web. They provide a common framework for representing and sharing data, enabling automated processing and reasoning by machines [3]. Some of the key semantic web technologies for KRR include the following:

RDF: RDF is a standard for describing resources on the web, including their properties and relationships. It provides a flexible, extensible framework for representing knowledge in a machine-readable format.

OWL: OWL is a language for representing ontologies on the web. It provides a rich set of constructs for defining classes, properties, and relationships between them, allowing for complex reasoning and inference.

SPARQL: SPARQL is a query language for querying RDF data. It provides a powerful and flexible mechanism for querying and retrieving data from knowledge graphs.

Linked data: Linked data is a set of best practices for publishing and linking data on the web. It provides a standardized way of representing and linking data, enabling more efficient and effective data integration and discovery.

Together, these technologies provide a powerful framework for representing and reasoning about knowledge on the web, enabling a wide range of applications in areas such as NLP, knowledge management, and intelligent systems.

9.2.5   ML

ML is a subfield of artificial intelligence (AI) that can be used for KRR. In ML, algorithms are trained on data to recognize patterns and make predictions. The resulting models can be used to represent knowledge, and reason over it. For example, in NLP, ML techniques can be used to learn patterns in text data, such as word embedding, which can then be used to represent the meaning of words in a knowledge base. ML algorithms can also be used to learn rules or decision trees that can be used to reason over the knowledge base.

In addition, ML techniques can be used to automatically learn ontologies or taxonomies from data, which can help to organize and represent knowledge. ML techniques are especially useful when dealing with large and complex datasets, where the manual duration of the data and the knowledge base may be difficult or impossible.

9.2.6   Tools and techniques

There are various tools and techniques used for KRR, some of which include:

1. Semantic networks: A graphical representation that depicts relationships between concepts.
2. Frames: A structured representation that organizes knowledge around a central concept or "frame."
3. Rule-based systems: A set of rules and logical statements used to represent and reason about knowledge.
4. DL: A formal language for representing knowledge, often used in ontology development.
5. First-order logic: A formal system used to represent and reason about knowledge.
6. Bayesian networks: A probabilistic graphical model used to represent and reason about uncertain knowledge.
7. Neural networks: A ML technique used to represent and reason about patterns in data.
8. Fuzzy logic: A mathematical framework for representing and reasoning about uncertainty.
9. NLP: Techniques for representing and reasoning about language-based knowledge.
10. Graph databases: A type of database designed to store and query graph-structured data, often used for knowledge graph applications.

These tools and techniques can be used in combination to represent and reason about knowledge in a variety of domains, including AI, expert systems, and knowledge management.

Semantic networks are a graphical representation of knowledge that show the relationships between concepts. Some advantages of using semantic networks for knowledge representation include the following:

1. Easy to understand: Semantic networks are simple and intuitive, making them easy to understand and interpret. They are often used in NLP and information retrieval systems to represent knowledge in a way that is easily accessible to humans.
2. Efficient: Semantic networks are often more efficient than other knowledge representation methods because they require less storage space and can be quickly searched to retrieve information.
3. Flexibility: Semantic networks can be used to represent a wide range of knowledge domains and can be easily extended to accommodate new concepts and relationships.

However, there are also some drawbacks to using semantic networks for knowledge representation, such as the following:

1. Limited expressiveness: Semantic networks are not always expressive enough to capture all the nuances and complexities of a particular domain, especially when dealing with abstract concepts or complex relationships.

2. Scalability: As the size of the network grows, it becomes more difficult to manage and navigate, and it may become unwieldy and difficult to use.
3. Lack of formalism: Semantic networks lack a formal logical foundation, which can make it difficult to reason about the relationships between concepts or to ensure consistency and correctness.

Some of the challenges in using semantic networks for KRR include [4] the following:

1. Scalability: As the number of nodes and edges in the semantic network grows, the complexity of maintaining and querying the network can become prohibitively high.
2. Ambiguity: Semantic networks rely on the accurate definition of concepts and their relationships. However, in natural language, the meanings of words can be ambiguous, leading to potential errors in the representation.
3. Inference: Semantic networks often require some form of inference mechanism to derive new knowledge from existing knowledge in the network. Designing an effective inference mechanism can be challenging, particularly when dealing with large and complex networks.
4. Maintenance: Semantic networks require ongoing maintenance to ensure that the knowledge they contain remains accurate and up-to-date. This can be a time-consuming and resource-intensive process.
5. Integration: Combining information from multiple semantic networks can be challenging, as different networks may use different vocabularies and conceptual models.
6. Interpretability: Semantic networks can become complex and difficult to interpret, particularly when dealing with large and interconnected networks. This can make it difficult for users to understand the reasoning processes that underpin the network's decision-making.
7. Representation bias: The choice of how to represent knowledge in a semantic network can have a significant impact on its effectiveness. Different representation choices may introduce biases or limitations that impact the accuracy or completeness of the knowledge represented.

Frames are a type of knowledge representation technique used in AI, which represents concepts or objects as structured frames consisting of slots and fillers. Some of the challenges in frames include [4] the following:

1. Knowledge acquisition: The process of creating a frame-based representation requires knowledge acquisition, which can be time-consuming and costly. Expert knowledge is required to create the frames, which may be difficult to obtain.
2. Maintenance: Frames require maintenance and updating as new information becomes available. As the knowledge base grows, it becomes more difficult to manage and maintain consistency.
3. Hierarchy: Frames are often organized hierarchically, which can be challenging to design and implement. The hierarchy must be carefully designed to ensure that it accurately reflects the relationships between concepts.

4. Interoperability: Frames can be difficult to integrate with other knowledge representation techniques. Integrating frames with other knowledge representation techniques may require a significant amount of effort.
5. Inference: Inference in frames can be complex, as the system must be able to reason about the relationships between concepts and fillers in the frames.

Rule-based systems are widely used for KRR in various applications. However, they also face several challenges. Some of the major challenges in rule-based systems are the following:

1. Scalability: As the number of rules and the size of the knowledge base increase, the performance of the rule-based system may deteriorate, making it difficult to scale up the system.
2. Knowledge acquisition: Knowledge acquisition is a crucial step in rule-based systems, and it involves capturing knowledge from domain experts and converting it into a set of rules. This process can be time-consuming, expensive, and error-prone, especially for complex domains.
3. Rule conflicts: In some cases, rules may conflict with each other, leading to uncertainty and ambiguity in the inference process. Resolving rule conflicts can be challenging and may require the use of advanced techniques such as fuzzy logic or probabilistic reasoning.
4. Maintenance: Rule-based systems require frequent updates and maintenance to ensure that they remain accurate and up-to-date with the latest knowledge in the domain. This can be a challenging and time-consuming task, especially for large and complex knowledge bases.
5. Interpretability: Rule-based systems are often criticized for their lack of interpretability, as the inference process can be opaque and difficult to understand. This can be a significant drawback in applications such as healthcare or finance, where the reasoning process needs to be transparent and explainable.
6. Expressiveness: Rule-based systems may not be expressive enough to represent complex and nuanced knowledge in some domains, such as NLP or image recognition. In such cases, other techniques such as deep learning or neural networks may be more suitable.

Overall, rule-based systems offer a powerful and flexible approach to KRR, but they also face several challenges that need to be addressed to improve their effectiveness and applicability in real-world applications.

DL is a family of knowledge representation formalisms that are widely used in AI applications, such as semantic web technologies, ontologies, and NLP. Some of the challenges in DL include the following:

1. Complexity: DL reasoning can be computationally expensive, and can require complex algorithms and data structures to achieve efficient and scalable reasoning.
2. Scalability: The size and complexity of knowledge bases can present significant challenges for DL reasoning, particularly when dealing with large-scale data sets.

3. Expressiveness: The expressiveness of DLs can be limited and may not be able to represent certain types of knowledge or relationships between concepts.
4. Interoperability: DLs may not be fully interoperable with other systems or data sources, which can make it difficult to integrate knowledge from multiple sources.
5. Uncertainty: DLs may struggle with representing and reasoning with uncertain or incomplete information.
6. Maintenance: Knowledge bases may require frequent updates and maintenance to ensure that they remain accurate and up-to-date, which can be time-consuming and resource-intensive.

The first-order logic, also known as predicate logic, is a formal system that is widely used for KRR in AI. Some of the challenges in the first-order logic are [5] the following:

1. Complexity: The first-order logic can become computationally expensive when dealing with complex statements or large knowledge bases, which can make it impractical for certain applications.
2. Incompleteness: The first-order logic cannot express all aspects of human knowledge and reasoning, and there may be situations where it falls short or is incomplete.
3. Uncertainty: The first-order logic does not have a formal way to represent uncertainty, which is a key aspect of many real-world problems.
4. Inconsistency: In some situations, the use of first-order logic can lead to inconsistencies or contradictions within a knowledge base.
5. Interpretation: The first-order logic requires a precise interpretation of its symbols and syntax, which can be a challenge in some applications.

Overall, despite these challenges, the first-order logic remains a powerful tool for KRR in AI and continues to be an active area of research.

Some of the challenges in Bayesian networks include [6] the following:

1. Complexity: Bayesian networks can become very complex when dealing with large amounts of data or complex relationships between variables.
2. Data availability: Bayesian networks require large amounts of data to build accurate models, and getting access to high-quality data can be a challenge.
3. Domain knowledge: Building accurate Bayesian networks requires expert knowledge of the domain being modeled, which may be difficult to obtain.
4. Interpretation: The results of Bayesian network analysis can be difficult to interpret, especially for non-experts.
5. Computational resources: Bayesian network analysis can be computationally intensive, requiring powerful computers or high-performance computing clusters.
6. Overfitting: There is a risk of overfitting the model to the training data, which can result in poor performance when applied to new data.
7. Sensitivity to prior probabilities: Bayesian networks are sensitive to the choice of prior probabilities, which can be subjective and may not always reflect real-world data.

9.3   Results and discussion

One potential case study could involve the development of a knowledge management system for a large technology company. The company has a diverse range of products and services, and its employees need to have access to accurate and up-to-date information about these offerings. The company wants to use a KRR system to capture this information and make it easily accessible to employees.

To accomplish this, the company could use a combination of tools and techniques, such as ontologies, semantic networks, and rule-based systems. They could develop an ontology to capture the different types of products and services offered by the company and use semantic networks to represent the relationships between these different offerings. Rule-based systems could be used to capture business rules and logic for different scenarios.

However, the development of such a knowledge management system would present several challenges. One challenge would be developing an effective ontology that captures all the relevant information about the company's products and services. This would require input from subject matter experts across the organization, as well as ongoing maintenance to ensure the ontology stays up to date.

Another challenge would be ensuring that the system is easily accessible and usable by employees. The company would need to develop an intuitive interface and ensure that employees can easily search and find the information they need. The company would need to ensure that the KRR system is scalable and can handle the large amounts of data and information associated with the company's diverse offerings. This would require careful design and testing to ensure the system can handle different scenarios and use cases. The development of a KRR system for a large technology company presents both significant opportunities and challenges. By leveraging a combination of tools and techniques, the company could develop an effective system for managing their knowledge assets and improving employee productivity and performance.

9.3.1   *Case study: using different techniques for representing medical knowledge [7]*

A team of medical professionals and computer scientists have come together to develop a system that can aid in diagnosing rare genetic disorders. The system is intended to assist medical professionals in the diagnosis of rare genetic disorders by providing a knowledge representation system that can process medical data and provide recommendations.

To accomplish this task, the team has decided to use a combination of different techniques for representing knowledge. The following is a breakdown of the techniques used and their specific applications:

Ontologies: The team has developed a comprehensive ontology of rare genetic disorders. The ontology includes a taxonomy of genetic disorders, symptoms, causes, and treatments. The ontology is used as a reference for identifying rare genetic disorders based on the symptoms exhibited by a patient.

Semantic networks: The team has developed a semantic network that links symptoms to the genetic disorders that cause them. The semantic network is used to infer the presence of a genetic disorder based on the symptoms exhibited by a patient.

Frames: The team has developed a frame-based system that models the symptoms and treatments of rare genetic disorders. Each frame corresponds to a specific genetic disorder and includes information about the symptoms, causes, and treatments associated with the disorder. The frame-based system is used to provide recommendations for the treatment of rare genetic disorders.

Rule-based systems: The team has developed a rule-based system that uses expert knowledge to infer the presence of a genetic disorder based on the symptoms exhibited by a patient. The rule-based system uses a set of rules to identify the genetic disorder that is most likely to be causing the symptoms.

DL: The team has used DL to represent the knowledge contained in the ontology and the frame-based system. The DL are used to reason about the relationships between symptoms, genetic disorders, and treatments.

Bayesian networks: The team has used Bayesian networks to model the probabilistic relationships between symptoms and genetic disorders. The Bayesian network is used to calculate the probability of a patient having a specific genetic disorder based on the symptoms exhibited by the patient.

Using this combination of different techniques for representing knowledge, the team has developed a system that can aid medical professionals in the diagnosis of rare genetic disorders. The system is currently being tested in a clinical setting to evaluate its effectiveness. Future work will focus on improving the accuracy and speed of the system, as well as expanding its capabilities to cover additional rare genetic disorders.

9.3.2   Case study: using different techniques for representing academic knowledge [8]

A university wants to develop a knowledge base to capture and manage academic knowledge across various departments. The knowledge base should be able to store information about courses, faculty, research topics, publications, and other related information. To accomplish this, the university has decided to explore different techniques for representing knowledge, such as ontologies, semantic networks, frames, rule-based systems, DL, first-order logic, and Bayesian networks.

9.3.2.1   Ontologies

The university decides to use ontologies to represent knowledge about courses, faculty, and research topics. They create a hierarchy of classes and subclasses to represent different courses, faculty members, and research areas. They also define properties to describe the characteristics of each class, such as the name, description, prerequisites, and course materials.

9.3.2.2   Semantic networks

To represent relationships between courses, faculty, and research topics, the university decides to use semantic networks. They create nodes for each entity and connect them with edges to represent relationships such as "teaches", "belongs to", and "publishes".

9.3.2.3 Frames

The university decides to use frames to represent knowledge about publications. They create a frame for each publication and define slots to describe its attributes, such as the title, author, publisher, and publication date.

9.3.2.4 Rule-based systems

The university decides to use a rule-based system to represent knowledge about course prerequisites. They define rules that specify the prerequisites for each course based on the courses taken by the student.

9.3.2.5 DL

The university decides to use DL to represent knowledge about the requirements for a degree program. They create a set of axioms that describe the relationships between courses, prerequisites, and degree requirements.

9.3.2.6 First-order logic

To represent more complex relationships between entities, the university decides to use first-order logic. They create logical statements that describe relationships such as "All faculty members who teach computer science courses have a PhD".

9.3.2.7 Bayesian networks

Finally, the university decides to use Bayesian networks to represent knowledge about student performance. They define variables such as "grades", "study habits", and "attendance" and create a network of conditional probabilities to predict student success.

By using different techniques for representing academic knowledge, the university can create a comprehensive knowledge base that can be used by students, faculty, and administrators. However, there are trade-offs to consider when selecting a technique, such as the complexity of the representation, the ease of maintenance, and the ability to support inference and reasoning. Therefore, it is important to carefully evaluate the requirements and constraints of the knowledge base before choosing a technique for knowledge representation.

9.3.3 Case study: using different techniques for representing farmer knowledge [9]

In this case study, we will explore how different techniques for representing knowledge, such as ontologies, semantic networks, frames, rule-based systems, DL, first-order logic, and Bayesian networks can be used for representing farmer knowledge.

Background: Farmers have a vast amount of knowledge about various crops, their growth patterns, diseases, and ways to prevent them. This knowledge is usually passed down from generation to generation and learned through practical experience. With the advent of technology, it has become possible to capture and represent this knowledge in a structured and organized manner.

Approach: To represent farmer knowledge, we can use various techniques, such as the following:

Ontologies: Ontologies can be used to represent the domain knowledge of agriculture, including crops, soils, weather patterns, and other relevant information. An ontology can provide a standardized vocabulary for describing these concepts and their relationships, making it easier to share and reuse knowledge.

Semantic networks: Semantic networks can be used to represent the relationships between different concepts in agriculture. For example, we can create a semantic network of the different types of crops, their growth patterns, and the pests and diseases that affect them. This network can help farmers identify the best crops to plant in a particular season and the best ways to protect them from pests and diseases.

Frames: Frames can be used to represent the knowledge of specific crops. For example, we can create a frame for tomato plants that includes information on their growth patterns, nutritional requirements, common diseases, and the best ways to prevent them.

Rule-based systems: Rule-based systems can be used to represent the knowledge of how to prevent and treat crop diseases. For example, we can create a rule-based system that provides advice on how to prevent tomato plants from getting blight, including specific actions to take at different stages of the plant's growth.

DL: DL can be used to represent the knowledge of specific crops and their properties. For example, we can use DL to represent the properties of tomato plants, such as their size, color, and nutritional value.

First-order logic: First-order logic can be used to represent the knowledge of the relationships between different concepts in agriculture. For example, we can use the first-order logic to represent the relationship between soil nutrients and plant growth.

Bayesian networks: Bayesian networks can be used to represent the probabilities of different events occurring in agriculture. For example, we can create a Bayesian network that predicts the probability of a crop failing due to a specific disease based on factors such as weather patterns and the presence of pests.

Outcome: Using these techniques, we can represent farmer knowledge in a structured and organized manner. This can help farmers make better decisions about which crops to plant and how to protect them from pests and diseases. It can also help researchers identify new ways to improve agricultural practices and develop new crop varieties that are more resistant to disease.

Challenges: However, there are several challenges to representing farmer knowledge using these techniques. One of the main challenges is that the knowledge is often based on practical experience rather than scientific evidence, making it difficult to formalize and represent it in a structured manner. Another challenge is that farmers may have different ways of representing their knowledge, which can make it difficult to create a standardized representation. Finally, these representations can be complex and difficult to understand for people who are not familiar with the domain of agriculture.

Conclusion: Despite these challenges, using different techniques for representing knowledge can be a valuable tool for capturing and sharing farmer knowledge. By creating structured and organized representations of this knowledge, we can help farmers make better decisions, improve agricultural practices, and ultimately increase crop yields and food security.

9.3.4   Case study: social media knowledge representation techniques [10]

9.3.4.1   Problem statement

A social media company wants to develop a knowledge representation system to extract, store, and analyze data from various social media platforms. They want to explore different techniques for representing social media knowledge and identify the most suitable technique for their needs.

9.3.4.2   Approach

The company can explore various techniques for representing social media knowledge, including the following:

Ontology-based approach: In this approach, the company can create an ontology that represents the concepts and relationships relevant to their domain. They can use a tool like Protégé to build and maintain the ontology. The ontology can be used to extract and organize data from various social media platforms.

Graph-based approach: In this approach, the company can represent social media data as a graph, where nodes represent entities (e.g., users, posts, hashtags) and edges represent relationships between entities. They can use a graph database like Neo4j to store and analyze the graph data.

ML-based approach: In this approach, the company can use ML algorithms to extract and represent social media knowledge. For example, they can use NLP techniques to extract entities and relationships from social media text, and then represent the extracted knowledge using a structured format like RDF.

Hybrid approach: The company can also explore a hybrid approach that combines two or more of the above techniques. For example, they can use an ontology to represent the domain concepts and relationships, and then use ML algorithms to extract and populate the ontology with social media data.

9.3.4.3   Evaluation

To identify the most suitable technique, the company can evaluate each approach based on the following criteria:

Data complexity: Some social media platforms may have complex data structures that may be difficult to represent using certain techniques. The company should evaluate each approach's ability to handle the complexity of their data.

Scalability: The company should evaluate each approach's ability to scale to handle large volumes of data.

Performance: The company should evaluate each approach's performance in terms of processing speed and memory usage.

Ease of use: The company should evaluate each approach's ease of use, including the ease of implementation, maintenance, and querying.

Based on the evaluation, the company can choose the most suitable technique for their needs.

9.3.4.4   Conclusion

Representing social media knowledge using different techniques can provide various benefits, such as improved data organization, better insights, and faster analysis. The company should evaluate each approach's strengths and weaknesses and choose the most suitable technique for their specific needs.

9.3.5   *Case study: using different techniques for representing cyber security knowledge [11]*

9.3.5.1   Problem statement

A large cybersecurity company is struggling to effectively represent and communicate its vast amount of knowledge and expertise to its clients and employees. They want to find a solution that can efficiently convey complex cybersecurity concepts in a clear and easy-to-understand manner.

9.3.5.2   Solution

The cybersecurity company decides to explore different techniques for representing cybersecurity knowledge, including the following:

Visual representations: The company creates a series of visual diagrams, charts, and infographics that help illustrate complex cybersecurity concepts. For example, they create a diagram that shows the different layers of security in a network, or a flowchart that outlines the steps in a cybersecurity incident response plan. These visual representations help simplify complex information and make it more accessible to non-technical stakeholders.

Storytelling: The company also creates a series of case studies and narratives that describe real-world cybersecurity incidents and the steps taken to mitigate them. These stories help illustrate the importance of cybersecurity and provide concrete examples of how the company's expertise can be applied in practical situations.

Gamification: The company develops a cybersecurity training game that teaches employees how to identify and respond to common cybersecurity threats. The game is designed to be fun and engaging, but also educational, and helps reinforce important cybersecurity concepts in a memorable way.

Interactive tools: The company creates interactive tools, such as a vulnerability scanner or a phishing email simulator, that allow clients and employees to test their own security measures and identify potential weaknesses. These tools provide hands-on experience with cybersecurity concepts and help individuals better understand the importance of good cybersecurity practices.

9.3.5.3   Results

After implementing these different techniques for representing cybersecurity knowledge, the cybersecurity company sees several positive outcomes:

Improved client communication: The visual representations and storytelling techniques help the company communicate complex cybersecurity concepts more effectively to non-technical stakeholders, improving client understanding and trust.

Increased employee engagement: The gamification and interactive tools help make cybersecurity training more engaging and interactive, leading to improved retention and application of cybersecurity knowledge.

Stronger cybersecurity practices: The interactive tools help identify potential weaknesses in clients' security measures, leading to improved overall cybersecurity practices and risk mitigation.

Overall, by using a combination of visual representations, storytelling, gamification, and interactive tools, the cybersecurity company was able to more effectively represent and communicate its vast amount of knowledge and expertise to both clients and employees, leading to improved cybersecurity practices and overall organizational success.

9.4 Conclusion and future work

As we have seen, KRR is crucial for developing intelligent systems that can solve complex problems and reason about uncertain information. There are various tools and techniques available for representing knowledge, such as ontologies, semantic networks, frames, rule-based systems, DL, first-order logic, and Bayesian networks. Each of these approaches has its advantages and drawbacks, and the choice of which to use depends on the specific problem domain and the requirements of the application. However, despite the progress made in this field, there are still many challenges that need to be addressed, such as the scalability and complexity of KRR systems, the lack of standardization and interoperability among different approaches, and the difficulty of handling uncertainty and incomplete information. Future work in this area could focus on developing more efficient and scalable algorithms for KRR, as well as on improving the interoperability and standardization of different approaches. Additionally, there is a need for more research on handling uncertainty and incomplete information, as these are common problems in many real-world applications. With continued research and development in this field, we can expect to see even more sophisticated and intelligent systems in the future.

References

[1] Dadure, P., Pakray, P., and Bandyopadhyay, S. (2023). Challenges and opportunities in knowledge representation and reasoning. In *Encyclopedia of Data Science and Machine Learning*, IGI Global, pp. 2464–2477.

[2] Sassanelli, C. and Terzi, S. (2022). The D-BEST reference model: a flexible and sustainable support for the digital transformation of small and medium enterprises. *Global Journal of Flexible Systems Management*, 23(3), 345–370.

[3]   Lan, G., Liu, T., Wang, X., Pan, X., and Huang, Z. (2022). A semantic web technology index. *Scientific Reports*, *12*(1), 3672.

[4]   Han, J., Sarica, S., Shi, F., and Luo, J. (2022). Semantic networks for engineering design: state of the art and future directions. *Journal of Mechanical Design*, *144*(2), 1–11.

[5]   Akama, K. and Nantajeewarawat, E. (2022). Knowledge-representation-logic: an extension of first-order logic. *International Journal of Innovative Computing, Information and Control*, *18*(4), 1055–1069.

[6]   Hassan, S., Wang, J., Kontovas, C., and Bashir, M. (2022). An assessment of causes and failure likelihood of cross-country pipelines under uncertainty using Bayesian networks. *Reliability Engineering & System Safety*, *218*, 108171.

[7]   Nadimi-Shahraki, M. H., Zamani, H., and Mirjalili, S. (2022). Enhanced whale optimization algorithm for medical feature selection: a COVID-19 case study. *Computers in Biology and Medicine*, *148*, 105858.

[8]   Li, K., Hou, Y., Andersen, P. S., Xin, R., Rong, Y., and Skov-Petersen, H. (2022). An ecological perspective for understanding regional integration based on ecosystem service budgets, bundles, and flows: a case study of the Jinan metropolitan area in China. *Journal of Environmental Management*, *305*, 114371.

[9]   Abbasi, R., Martinez, P., and Ahmad, R. (2022). An ontology model to represent aquaponics 4.0 system's knowledge. *Information Processing in Agriculture*, *9*(4), 514–532.

[10]   Messaoudi, C., Guessoum, Z., and Ben Romdhane, L. (2022). Opinion mining in online social media: a survey. *Social Network Analysis and Mining*, *12*(1), 25.

[11]   Xiong, W., Legrand, E., Åberg, O., and Lagerström, R. (2022). Cyber security threat modeling based on the MITRE Enterprise ATT&CK Matrix. *Software and Systems Modeling*, *21*(1), 157–177.

Chapter 10

Knowledge visualization: AI integration with 360-degree dashboards

K. Sasikala Rani[1] and Chandrasekar Nagarajan[2]

The main intention of visualization is to enhance the ability of understanding and creating a new vision of the problem given. This chapter focuses on knowledge visualization. With technology advancements, visual images play a major role in representing data. We will cover different tools and technologies to gather visual data and how to convert it into a knowledge-level presentable form.

10.1 Introduction

According to the Cambridge Dictionary, visualization is "the act of visualizing something or someone" or "forming a picture of it in your mind."

The human brain processes visual information more efficiently compared to written information: when the same information is provided both in the written and in the visual form (such as with a keyword and a corresponding icon), performances are enhanced. The working memory of a common person is limited in capacity to retain information for a long period while performing analysis on that information mentally. The working memory of a single person to store information is limited in capacity as well as in time information. Visualizations may help to reduce the cognitive load and enhance the processing abilities by visualizing abstract relationships. They allow to externalize knowledge for example to share it with others or to get an overview about the big picture of the field of interest.

Due to the tremendous revolution in technology, the impact of visualization has become more significant. Visualization enables through creative power of imagery in contrast to text-based knowledge. It is possible to rearrange visualized knowledge easily by visualizing the ideas with sketches through visualization than text.

Information visualization refers to the representation of data in a meaningful way that users can interpret and easily comprehend. This includes the concepts of data visualizations and dashboards. Data visualization is the presentation of data in

[1]Tata Consultancy Services, Asia Pacific Pte. Ltd., Singapore
[2]Department of Computer Science and Engineering, Sri Krishna College of Engineering and Technology, Coimbatore, India

a pictorial or graphical format. It is easy to identify patterns and make decisions based on that by the stakeholders by seeing the analytics graphically/pictorially. They can further use interactive visualization technology to drill down into charts and graphs for more detail to learn about the data we see and how it is processed. It helps in communicating complex findings faster and constructively. It often facilitates new discussions and brainstorming.

Knowledge visualization is the process of expressing information in formats like infographics, dashboard systems, diagrams, pie charts, bar graphs, sketches, and illustrations. Knowledge visualization is a blended combination of information visualization, didactic techniques, visual cognition, and more practical applications like business diagramming or visual programming languages. This chapter discusses the need for knowledge visualization and the role of knowledge visualization in design thinking, machine learning, and tools for creating knowledge visualization.

10.2   Information visualization vs. knowledge visualization

Information visualization investigates enormous volumes of abstract data and derives new insights but knowledge visualization enriches their knowledge by providing the best means of expressing their ideas. Information visualization aids to enhance information retrieval, access, manipulation, and presentation of voluminous data sets and knowledge visualization mainly focuses on knowledge-augmented communication between users by relating new perceptions to the existing concepts.

Knowledge visualization finds its applications in various industry sectors where raw data can be presented in a structured way that is easily understandable. In the case of visualizing a world map to identify the boundaries of countries, mountains, oceans, forests, etc., knowledge visualization plays a role in creating neat shapes and different colors can be used to highlight different geographical areas.

Another prominent example of visualization is the dashboard which reflects the pattern of success and failure of an ad campaign. It expresses pertinent information about the performance of an ad. For example, Google AdWords, Facebook Ad Campaigns, etc. follow trends of knowledge visualization.

10.3   Knowledge visualization in design thinking

The use of visualization in design thinking is fundamental as it helps in communication and sharing ideas to arrive at a common understanding in turn helps to catalyst the design thinking process and also turns ideas into action. Visualizations contain the following social, cognitive, and emotional purposes which are highly useful for design thinking teams.

Emotional purposes:

- Generating participation and commitment.
- Supporting shared appreciation.
- Displaying interdependencies.

Social purposes:

- Incorporating divergent viewpoints.
- Further thorough assessments.
- Easier recollection.

Cognitive purposes:

- Allowing new standpoints
- Further thorough assessments
- Easier recollection.

Visualization plays a major role in various design thinking phases as follows

Empathize phase: The main function of this phase is for the design thinking team to perceive and involve with the user and their experiences. In this phase, the design thinking team needs to understand the client/stakeholder to make the context clearer and more tangible so that they will not create any incomplete design for a solution.

While verbal and textual information is abstract, visualization makes concepts more concrete and thus manageable. Considering stakeholders and systems as a part of context and communication using stakeholder maps with other stakeholders enables them to give feedback and contributions. It helps to do modifications and additions in a collaborative mode which in turn will lead to creative ideas and options. The system can be visualized using conceptual diagrams using computer software like PowerPoint or physical aids like white paper, board, flipchart, etc.

Define phase: The main function is to analyze and channelize the feedback of the previous phase into insights into a meaningful design challenge using Matrix and Venn diagram. This phase can be visualized using a 2-by-2 matrix as a template using PowerPoint.

Ideate: This phase focuses on generating ideas by exploring wide solution spaces. Ideate phase can be visualized using metaphoric hand drawings and post-it-notes using whiteboard, paper, or flipchart.

Prototype: The ideas generated during the Ideate phase are converted into physical world tangible products during the prototype phase. The visualization in this phase should create a scene/environment where the user can experience the application and understand the roles of people associated with the prototype. The visualization can be done using conceptual and metaphoric hand drawings.

Test phase: The objective of this phase is to put to real life and test. This can be visualized with a conceptual hand drawing on whiteboard, paper, or flipchart with post-it-notes.

10.4   Visualization in transferring knowledge

Knowledge visualization enables the swift transfer of knowledge between individuals or groups. The relevant information for different stakeholders must be identified and based on that the depth of information to be transferred can be decided depending on the time and caliber of the recipients. The challenge is that some recipients may be decision-makers who may not understand the modern visualization tools. The next major challenge is information overload which may cause an increase in quantity leading to a decrease in quality.

This may create a problem in identifying the ability to identify the essential information. Hence, it becomes necessary to strategize the information concerning quality and relevance. Another major problem associated with this is if the decision-makers cannot interpret the information, then they may take wrong decisions or transfer wrong information/knowledge. Hence, visualization tools may mislead due to lack of visualization competency. This challenge can be addressed by using specialized tools for each specific problem [1].

10.5   The knowledge visualization model

According to Burkhard [2], research outcomes can be represented as a knowledge visualization model. The research model if transferred as such a researcher to the receiver, the receiver can integrate his/her background knowledge about the received information. Visualizations can be added to the research model as complementary to make the research information complete.

Even if a portion of the knowledge is transferred from the sender to the receiver, the knowledge can be expressed as visualizations. The receiver can try to understand the sent information with his/her understanding and knowledge. The clarifications/doubts can be sent back to the sender. The sender can append appropriate modifications to the visualizations so that the receiver can understand the model still better. Burkhard proposes a specific substructure of the visual knowledge representation.

The attention of the receiver should be achieved in a way that it must first attract the receiver by using an image to represent the visualization. Next the context in which the information is represented needs to be clearly illustrated so that the receiver can clearly understand the importance of the knowledge. The final stage is the actual presentation of the knowledge.

10.5.1   Knowledge visualization framework

These perspectives answer three key questions with regard to visualizing knowledge, namely:

1.   What type of knowledge is visualized?
2.   Why should that knowledge be visualized?
3.   How is the knowledge visualized?

The **Knowledge Type (What) Perspective** aims to identify the type of knowledge to be transferred whether it is declarative knowledge (know-what), procedural knowledge (know-how), experimental knowledge (know-why), orientational knowledge (know-where), individual knowledge (know-who) [3].

The visualization motive perspective aims to find the reason why knowledge representation is used. Motives for knowledge visualization use that can be anticipated are knowledge sharing through visual means, knowledge crafting or creation, learning from visuals, codifying past experiences visually for future users, or mapping knowledge [4] so that experts, for example within a large organization, can be more easily identified.

The **Visualization Format Perspective (how)** groups visualization as the following: heuristic sketches, conceptual diagrams, visual metaphors, knowledge animations, knowledge maps, and scientific formats.

Heuristic sketches: Characterizes the main idea and aids to visualize an idea, providing an unstable format for unstable knowledge. Heuristic sketches take an individual's interpretation by accepting their arguments and suggestions.

Conceptual diagrams: They are highly structured and can be used to represent knowledge that is more analytical that explores structural relationships among parts using abstract and schematic representations. They help to reduce complexity, amplify cognition, explain causal relationships, and structure information.

Visual metaphors: Represent a hybrid combination of heuristic sketches and conceptual diagrams that use graphic metaphors to structure information and convey standards through the implications of the metaphor used. Thus, procedural knowledge is expressed and the base of visual metaphor is the application of knowledge.

Knowledge animations: Represent procedural knowledge dynamically through interactive animations where static representation will not help. Knowledge maps use cartographic conventions to represent knowledge. Scientific charts display content scientific knowledge like publications and bring out the relationships in terms of mutual influence.

10.6 Formats and examples of knowledge visualization

Having outlined the key questions of knowledge visualization, we show in this section how they can be answered for specific application contexts.

10.6.1 Conceptual diagrams

Graphical representations of abstract ideas using conventional shapes like arrows, circles, pyramids, or matrices can be used to standardize the information and depict their relationships. EdrawMax tool can be used to create a conceptual framework as in Figure 10.1.

An example of a knowledge-intensive diagram is the Toulmin chart (Figure 10.2) based on the argumentation theory of Steven Toulmin [5,6]. Such a chart helps to break down an argument into different parts (such as claim, reasons, and evidence) which is useful when evaluating the validity of a claim.

Claim: Conclusions or viewpoints one tries to convince others to agree with.

Ground: Facts used to play as a foundation for the claim.

Warrant: General or hypothetical statements, acting as bridges between data and claim.

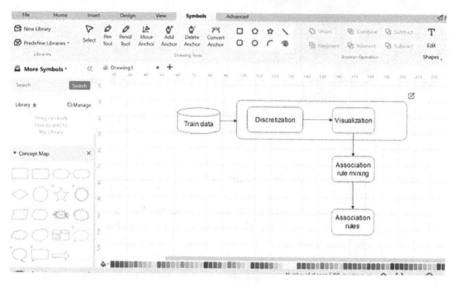

Figure 10.1   Steps in data mining using EdrawMax tool

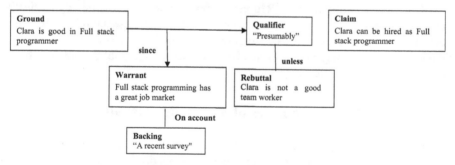

Figure 10.2   Toulmin chart

Qualifier: Indicating the strength granted by the warrant to support its claim.

Rebuttal: Conditions in which the warrant is not applicable. As a result of a rebuttal, the consequential conclusion can be overturned.

Backing: Demonstrating the validity of warrant.

10.6.2   Visual metaphors

A visual metaphor can be defined as an illustration of anything of physical existence or idea by using a visual image that indicates a particular association. Visual metaphors can be natural things available or man-made artificial things. Their main feature is that they organize information meaningfully. In doing so, they fulfill a dual function [6].

Visual metaphor performs the following activities:

1. They place information graphically in a proper position to have a proper structure and organization.
2. They give a deep insight and give an inference about the main characteristics of the metaphor that is used.

Four major classifications of visual metaphors can be grouped into four generic groups based on their root domain as the following:

1. **Natural phenomena** like sunrise, ocean, tornado, lightning, cloud, trees, etc.
2. **Artificial objects**: lime car, table, computer, computer virus, road, temple, bridges, etc.
3. **Activities like** walking, eating, driving, fishing, jumping, typing, pouring, fencing, etc.
4. **Abstract concepts**: family, law, argument, chaos, fractal, sustainability.

The major idea behind metaphors is that graphic depictions that are not a part of the discussed domain of unrelated graphic shapes can be summarized and can be used to convey the underlying idea by relating it to a concrete phenomenon.

10.6.3 Knowledge animation

They can be defined as computer-aided interactive visualizations given to the users to manage, interact, and manipulate a variety of data and information that promotes knowledge generation and transfer of knowledge. Knowledge visualization facilitates better understanding, improved recall, more engaging, deeper insights, and a faster knowledge transfer. The various applications include project management, brainstorming, process mapping, budgeting, etc.

Novel animated visual metaphors as the Infoticle metaphor allow new, instructive ways to interact with information. In contrast to static visualizations or applications in the field of information visualization, where users interact with data, in the Infoticle application data-driven particles (= Infoticles), help to explore large time-varying datasets with reoccurring data objects that alter in time. Animating these Infoticles leads to a knowledge animation which allows seeing the behavior of individual data entries or the global context of the whole dataset [7].

10.6.4 Knowledge maps

Knowledge maps [1] are graphic formats that follow cartographic conventions to reference relevant knowledge. A knowledge map comprises a ground layer representing the context for the mapping and the individual elements that are mapped within the given context. The ground layer typically consists of the mutual context that all employees can understand and relate to.

10.6.4.1 Knowledge map types

- **Procedural knowledge maps:** Many companies have properly documented procedures for the activities of the company and the documents will be communicated across the organization. For instance, if a new employee joins the company, the employee can be made aware of the organization by giving them a proper knowledge transfer using the knowledge maps. Then the employee can be properly onboarded into the process and they can be more productive. It will be very helpful for the contractual employees also. Knowledge maps will also be useful in situations where some tasks occur in some irregular intervals like system threats and breaches.

- **Conceptual knowledge maps:** These maps can be used to represent the extension of any ideas. These maps start with a central idea and show the various issues related to the central idea by creating subtopics. Example: customer complaints can be resolved using the conceptual knowledge maps.
- **Competency knowledge maps:** This maps help to illiterate behavior. Mapping students competency shows their skills in analytical, technical, and soft skills to train students based on their requirements identified. Knowledge maps can be mapped to visual tool that can be used to identify the skill gaps and giving right training at the right time to the right people.

10.6.4.2 Tool for knowledge mapping

MindManager can be used for creating complex knowledge maps easily. Figure 10.3 depicts the features of MindManager tool.

10.6.5 Knowledge domain visualization

Achievements in information visualization and in studying scientific literature were the foundation for a new knowledge visualization direction, which is called knowledge domain visualization (KDViz) or visual co-citation analysis.

Visual interfaces for the exploration of digital libraries: With an increasing number of digital documents, new information retrieval paradigms become decisive. The need for improved search result visualizations is described in an empirical

Figure 10.3 Features of MindManager tool

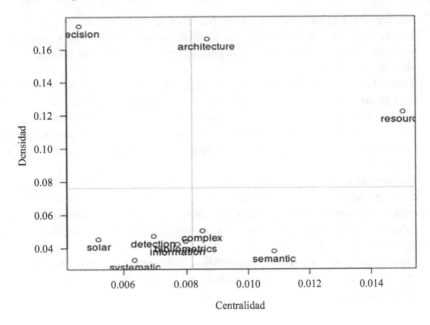

Figure 10.4   KDViz tool

evaluation of an information retrieval system [8]. Traditional text-based retrieval systems are effective for specific searches, but for exploratory tasks, users need new and more effective approaches.

Tool for KDViz performs knowledge visualization using mpa co-words method as the word clustering method and network graphs with D3.js library as visualization tool. Figure 10.4 depicts KDViz tool.

10.7   Types and usage of knowledge visualization tools

- **Attention-grabbing tools:** The tools are so very important since it is very essential to grab the attention of the audience so that knowledge transfer can be done effectively. Some of the popular attention-grabbing tools are Flipchart sketches, PowerPoint presentations, Physical or virtual whiteboards
- **Tools for knowledge expansion:** Visual representation paves the way to widen the scope of the knowledge so that different instances and outcomes can be analyzed. Knowledge expansion can be done effectively using the following tools: physical models, exploratory sketches and diagrams, knowledge maps.
- **Memory aid tools:** I hear and I forget. I see and I remember – Confucius. As the saying goes, visualization enabled the user to remember, learn, and analyze. Some of the popular memory aid tools are Infographics, Spider diagrams, Software-based visual maps.

- **Motivational tools:** Tools are also available to make the recipients become active, inspired, and group members alike. Some of the known motivation tools are Short, punchy videos, Concept diagrams, and Idea maps that encourage brainstorming.
- **Tools that promote insight:** It is very important that the users visualizing the data should be able to analyze and should be able to create deep insights by demonstrating the relationships between the data presented, data flow, and workflow. Some of the tools that can help us for the mentioned purpose are the following: Data plotting charts or graphs, Matrix diagrams, and Swimlane diagrams.
- **Collaboration tools:** The shared information needs to be coordinated so that the information can be utilized effectively. This is a major benefit of knowledge visualization. Some of the illustrative tools that aid in enhancing group collaboration include the following: Directional diagrams, Flowcharts, Funnel diagrams, or charts
- **MindManager knowledge visualization software**: The visualization tools can be put together and provided with an all-in-one interface like MindManager.

10.8   Knowledge visualization templates

10.8.1   Mind maps

They can be considered as logical organization tools. It can be considered as graphic representations of logic connections between ideas and concepts. These tools will help us to structure the knowledge in a way similar to how we naturally think. It almost simulates our brain process in structuring and arranging the knowledge. Some mind map tools are Coggle, GetMind, Canva, InfoRapid KnowledgeBase Builder, Scapple, and Wondershare EdrawMind.

10.8.1.1   Mindmomo

Mindmomo is a mind mapping software that helps to create mind maps with many built-in layouts. It is platform independent and gives flexible online and offline syncing. The presentations may be embedded with Hyperlinks & Attachments, web images, multimedia files, mind-mapping tools, hashtags, spell checkers, etc. Figure 10.5 shows features of Mindmomo and Figure 10.6 shows mind mapping for a company structure.

10.8.1.2   MindMeister

With MindMeister's mind map editor, the mind maps can be created, shared using the available browser, and need not download the application and do the updates manually. The maps created are stored in the cloud, which can be accessed from Mac, Windows PC, Linux computer, Chromebook, or mobile device. Figure 10.7 shows the MindMeister—Mind map templates and Figure 10.8 shows the mind map of a student.

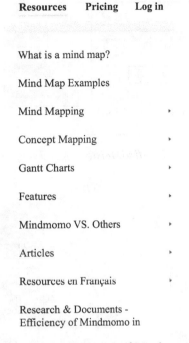

Resources   Pricing   Log in

What is a mind map?

Mind Map Examples

Mind Mapping   ›

Concept Mapping   ›

Gantt Charts   ›

Features   ›

Mindmomo VS. Others   ›

Articles   ›

Resources en Français   ›

Research & Documents -
Efficiency of Mindmomo in

Figure 10.5   Features of Mindmomo

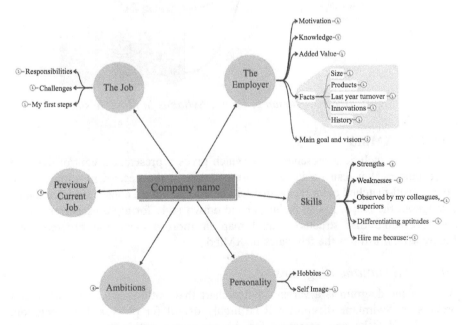

Figure 10.6   Mind mapping for a company structure

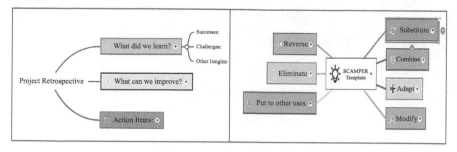

Figure 10.7   MindMeister—Mind map templates

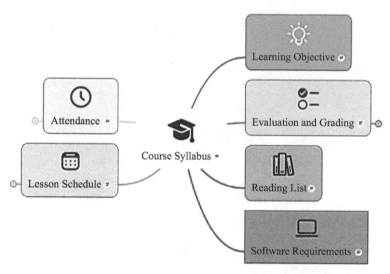

Figure 10.8   Mind map of Course Syllabus in MindMeister

10.8.1.3   XMind

The features include a presenter view which gives a presenter a control over the presentation. They can navigate the presentation in the desired position. It also gives a well-matched color theme that will help to achieve a consistent color theme throughout the maps. It also includes hand drawn style for more user-friendliness and tree table that structures mind map in more logical and ordered way. Figure 10.9 illustrates the templates of XMind.

10.8.2   Swimlane diagrams

A Swimlane diagram is a variant of flowchart that outlines who does what in a process. A Swimlane diagram will be highly useful for process documentation, since shared tasks and processes for sub-operations within a business process involve multiple departments.

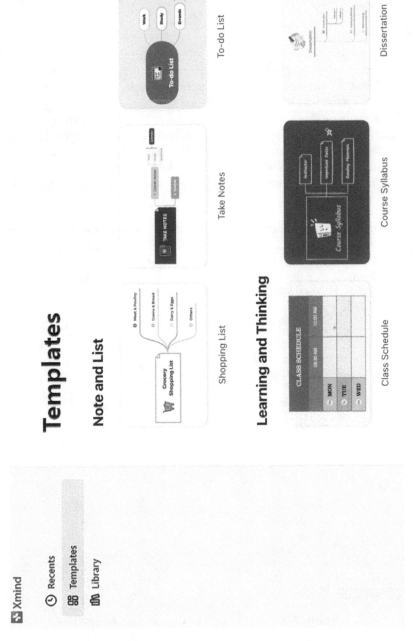

Figure 10.9   Templates of Xmind

Some of the tools to create Swimlane diagrams are the following:

- Zenkit.
- Office Timeline.
- Monday.
- Smart draw.
- Lucidchart, etc.

10.8.2.1   Lucidcharts

Lucidchart is a tool based on cloud-based solution where users can collaboratively work in real-time while building UML diagrams. Lucidchart is extremely user friendly thanks to the drag-and-drop feature available. Drag and drop is less restrictive and makes creating diagrams more seamless and less time consuming. The advantages of using Lucidcharts are easy-to-style shapes, keyboard shortcuts, and organizing diagrams using containers that include links and layers for easy-to-read diagrams, good collaboration, polished slide presentation, and publishing the diagram. It can be integrated with the software like MS Office, Salesforce for Sales Cloud, GitHub, Jira, etc. Figure 10.10 shows the swim lane creation in Lucidcharts.

10.8.2.2   Zenkit tool

Kanban board is a visual management tool that helps visualizing a work progress. They can be used in physical or virtual mode. The basic three-column structure, "To-Do, In progress, Done" is of great use in teams. This shared visual management tool helps to monitor everyone involved and track their work progress and provides transparency in taking decisions. Figure 10.11 shows the three-column structure of Zenkit tool.

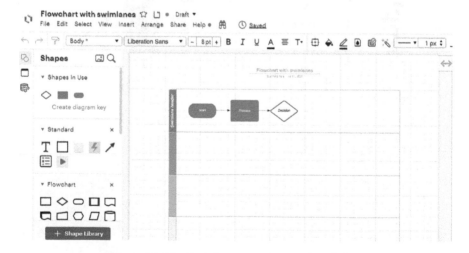

Figure 10.10   Swimlane creation in Lucidcharts

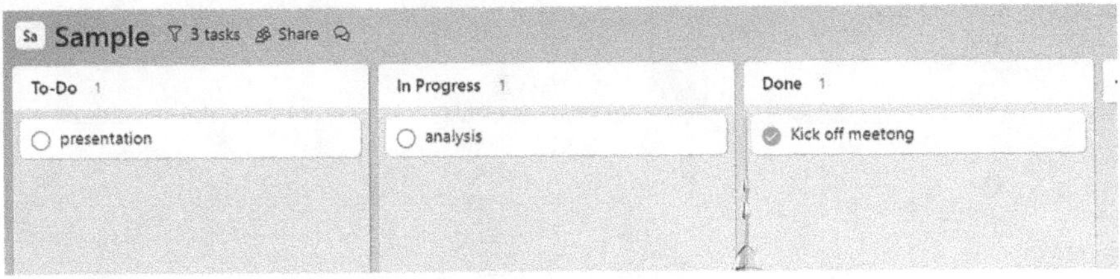

Figure 10.11   Three-column structure of Zenkit tool

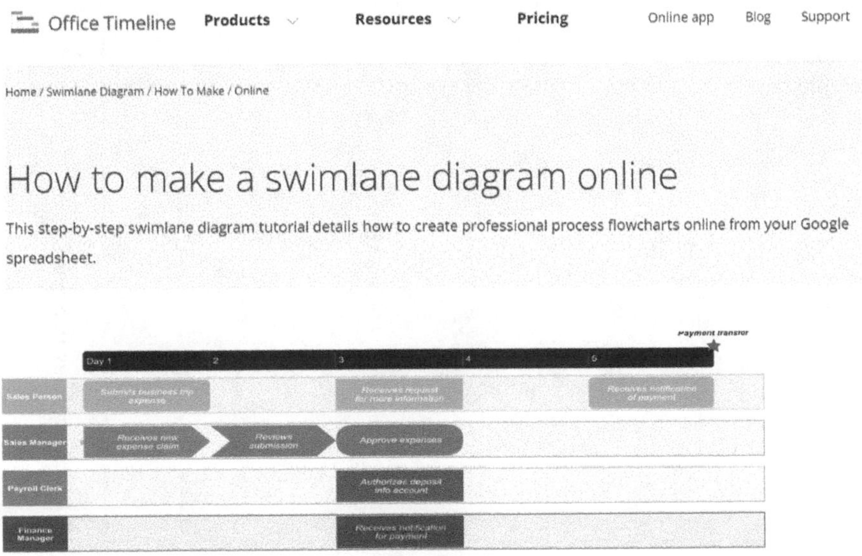

Figure 10.12   Creation of Swimlane diagram using Office Timeline

10.8.2.3   Office Timeline

Office Timeline has smart design tools and powerful automation features to simplify project management and come up with impressive presentations. It offers several free timeline templates for various project tasks and work schedules. The templates feature different visual styles, colors, and content that can be customized. Office Timeline integrates with other applications such as Excel, Wrike, and Smartsheet for importing and exporting data files. Figure 10.12 depicts a creation of Swimlane diagram using Office Timeline.

10.8.2.4   SmartDraw

SmartDraw provides an easier way to create swim lane diagrams. The usage of this tool is much easier and comfortable because of the inbuilt drawing that SmartDraw has. Swim lane diagram can be started with a flowchart template and required symbols can be taken from the extensive library of symbols available with the tool. Figure 10.13 shows the templates in SmartDraw.

Figure 10.13   Templates in SmartDraw

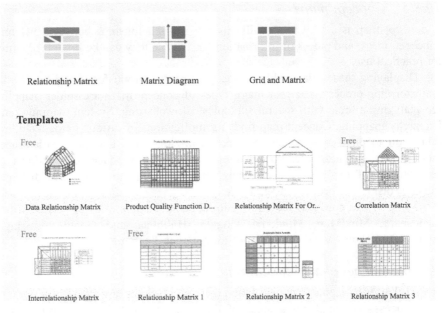

Figure 10.14   Sample matrix diagram templates in EdrawMax

10.8.3   Matrix diagrams

A matrix diagram is a project management and planning tool to analyze and visualize the relationships between data sets. Matrix diagrams or matrix charts provide a clear visualization of complex information which may give a deep insight which might not be possible otherwise.

Matrix diagrams can be used to visualizing complex relationships for identifying problems and growth opportunities, comparing potential solutions, and reviewing performance.

EdrawMax aids the users to create stories in the form of engaging diagrams, charts, presentations, infographics, and other visual content. EdrawMaxcan be used to create more than 280 types of diagrams, from technical diagrams to infographics. Figure 10.14 shows sample matrix diagram templates in EdrawMax.

10.8.4   Flowcharts

As a visual map of a process or workflow, flowcharts help you lay down knowledge in a series of sequential stages. By using a symbol to represent each step—and linking those steps with directional arrows—flowcharts are especially valuable for explaining complex concepts and communicating processes without the need for tech-heavy language.

Some of the best tools for creating flowcharts are the following:

Lucidchart, Miro, Creately, Whimsical, ConceptDraw Diagram, Cacoo, VisualParadigm Online, Edraw Max, SmartDraw, and Gliffy.

10.8.5   Concept maps

A concept map is a way to visually display the relationships between different concepts, ideas, and pieces of information, and hence they can be organized better for practical use.

Displaying these relationships visually improves group focus and boosts the brainstorming process. The four major types of concept maps are spider mapping for analyzing a topic with several subtopics, Flowcharting, System mapping, and Hierarchy mapping. Concept map finds its applications in various fields including Education to plan complex curriculum, organizing study materials with proper prerequisites, Business to explore market situations to introduce new products, to perform SWOT analysis of a company, and Individual to brainstorm different career paths, to perform self-assessment.

Some of the powerful tools to create concept maps are MindMeister, Miro, Lucidspark, MindMup, Mindomo, Coggle, Bubbl.us, and Google drawings. Figure 10.15 shows MindManager tool for concept diagram.

10.8.6   Funnel charts or diagrams

Funnel chart is a graphical representation that demonstrates how data flows through in a process. The application areas of funnel charts include representing sales funnels, recruitment, and order fulfillment processes. Figure 10.16 shows the funnel diagram depicting the percentage of users visiting a shopping website, adding products to cart, and purchasing a product. The funnel chart clearly depicts the percentage of conversion of number of visitors of the site to buyers of products from the site

Figure 10.15   MindManager tool for concept diagram

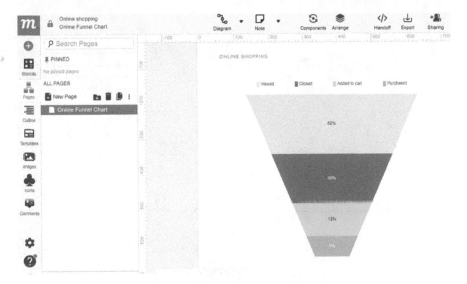

Figure 10.16 Funnel diagram for online shopping application

10.9 Visualization in machine learning

For visualizing classification data, decision trees, production rules, and decision graphs are used widely. The knowledge visualization techniques are useful to analyze the dataset easily and discover new properties of the dataset [9,10].

Using the following ways, visualization can be applied to machine learning.

10.9.1 Decision trees

Decision trees are used in machine learning for decision making by using branching in a tree structure. Decision trees are a type of machine learning where the tree structure branches according to a certain parameter. The tree contains two entities: decision nodes and leaves. The data is split based on the parameters in the decision nodes and the leaves have the final outcomes or the decision. Some of the major tools for creating decision trees are Weka, KNIME, Rapid miner, SilverDecisions, etc.

10.9.1.1 Weka

Weka is a workbench containing machine learning algorithms for data-mining tasks. The workbench contains algorithms for data preparation, knowledge visualization, classification, and clustering.

Sample decision tree created using WEKA to visualize airline reservation is shown in Figure 10.17.

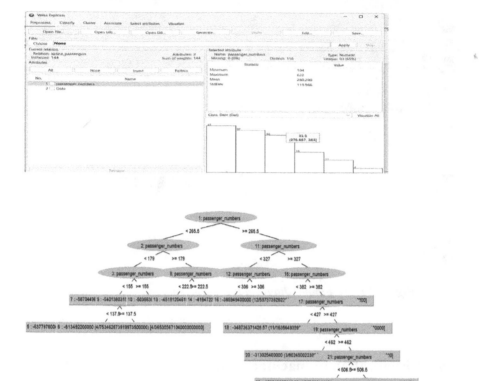

Figure 10.17   Decision tree for airline reservation created using Weka

10.9.1.2   KNIME

The key features of KNIME tool are modular workflow approach where documents are analyzed, and it stores the analysis process in the order it was conceived and implemented, while ensuring that intermediate results are always available. Figure 10.18 depicts KNIME dashboard.

10.9.1.3   RapidMiner

RapidMiner provides drag-and-drop features to design the analytics process. The major advantage is its compatibility with the existing database software like Oracle, SQL, Excel, etc. It has a repository that can hold the data sets that we use to experiment and it also has a rich set of public data sets for experimental purposes. Figure 10.19 shows RapidMiner dashboard.

10.9.1.4   SilverDecisions

It is a free and open-source tool for manually creating and analyzing decision trees. The SilverDecisions application gives an interface in a browser that provides a rich

Figure 10.18   KNIME dashboard

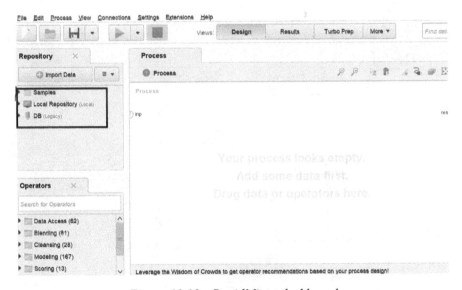

Figure 10.19   RapidMiner dashboard

set of layout, graphics, and export options and functionalities. Figure 10.20 shows the creation of decision tree using SilverDecisions.

10.9.2   Decision graph

Decision graph (DG) is a generalization of the conventional decision tree algorithm, extending the tree structure to a directed acyclic graph [11]. Similar to the sequential inference process in DTs, the test samples in a DG start from the root

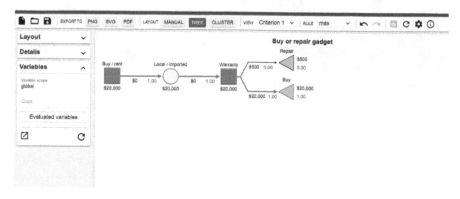

Figure 10.20   Creation of decision tree using SilverDecisions

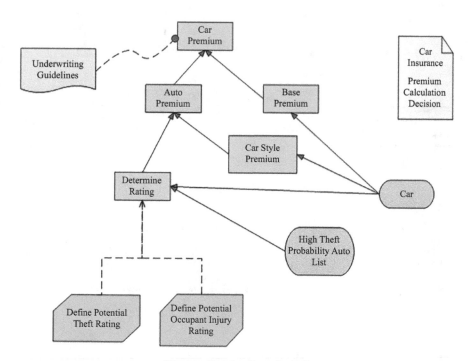

Figure 10.21   Sample DG

and successively select a path at the internal nodes until a leaf node is reached. The main difference between binary DTs and DGs is: In DTs, each child node has one parent node. However, DGs allow multiple parent nodes to share the same child node (Figure 10.21).

DG elements

S. no.	Notation	Description
1	Decision	The act of determining an output from a number of inputs, using decision logic which may reference one or more business knowledge models
2	Business Knowledge	A function encapsulating business knowledge, in the form of business rules, decision tables or an analytic model. Some of the tools may not support this element. In such cases, the decision logic is directly linked to the decision rather than the business knowledge model
3	Knowledge Source	The authority for a business knowledge model or decision
4	Input Data	Information used as an input by one or more decisions. It also denotes the parameters of a business knowledge model
5	⟶	Information—input data or decision output—required for a decision
6	– – – – –⟶	The invocation of a business knowledge model
7	– – – – –●	Showing the knowledge source of an element or the dependency of a knowledge source on input data

10.10   Conclusion

Knowledge visualization is powerful, as we discussed in this chapter. With technology advancements, visual images play a major role in representing data. In this chapter, we have highlighted the knowledge visualization and the differences between information and knowledge visualization. We have covered different tools and technologies to gather visual data and how to convert it into a knowledge-level presentable form. The role of knowledge visualization in design thinking, machine learning, and the frameworks for the same is highlighted. This chapter also covered the knowledge visualization templates, frameworks, and the tools to create the same.

References

[1]   Vande Moere, A. and Purchase, H. On the role of design in information visualization. *Information Visualization*. 2011;10(4):356–371.

[2]   Mayer, R. and Lfe Medieninformatik. *"Knowledge Visualization"*, 2009.

[3]   Alavi, M. and Leidner, D. Knowledge management and knowledge management systems: conceptual foundations and research issues. *MIS Quarterly*, 2001;1(10):107–136.

[4]   Eppler, M. and Burkhard, R. (2004). *Knowledge Visualisation: Towards a New Discipline and Its Fields of Application.*

[5]   Kernbach, S. and Nabergoj, A.S. Visual design thinking: understanding the role of knowledge visualization in the design thinking process. In: *22nd International Conference Information Visualisation (IV)*, July 2018.

[6]   Wang, W., Arya, D., Novielli, N., Cheng, J., and Guo, J.L.C. ArguLens: anatomy of community opinions on usability issues using argumentation models. In: *CHI '20: Proceedings of the 2020 CHI Conference on Human Factors in Computing Systems, April 2020*, pp. 1–14. https://doi.org/10.1145/3313831.3376218.

[7]   Eppler, M. *The Image of Insight, the Use of Visual Metaphors in the Communication of Knowledge*, 2003. http://www.alexandria.unisg.ch/Publikationen/54880.

[8]   Eppler, M.J. and Mengis, J. The concept of information overload: a review of literature from organization science, accounting, marketing, MIS, and related disciplines. *The Information Society*. 2004;20(5):325–344. doi: 10.1080/01972240490507974.

[9]   Sutcliffe, A., Bruijn, O., Thew, S., *et al.* Developing visualization-based decision support tools for epidemiology. *Information Visualization*. 2012; 13:13–17. doi:10.1177/1473871612445832.

[10] Humphrey, M., Cunningham, S.J., and Witten, I.H. Knowledge visualization techniques for machine learning. *Intelligent Data Analysis*, 1998;2:333–347.

[11] Sudo, H., Nuida, K., and Shimizu, K. An efficient private evaluation of a decision graph. In: *International Conference on Information Security and Cryptology*. Springer, 2018, pp. 143–160.

Web references

https://www.makeuseof.com/tag/8-free-mind-map-tools-best-use/
https://silverdecisions.pl/SilverDecisions.html?lang=en
https://resource.flexrule.com/knowledge-base/decision-graph/#decision-graph-elements
https://neptune.ai/blog/visualizing-machine-learning-models
https://www.mathworks.com/help/deeplearning/ug/deep-learning-visualizationmethods.html#responsive_offcanvas

Chapter 11

Empowering machine learning with knowledge graphs for the semantic era

Pethuru Raj[1] and G. Jaspher Willsie Kathrine[2]

11.1 Introduction

The widely used relational database model organizes data in the format of tables with columns and rows. By checking the tables, the relationship amongst the different data points can be identified. This has been doing well for business operations automation as the data volume is growing slowly. For complicated operations (which involve identifying relationships amongst data points kept in different tables), the relational database model is found inefficient and inadequate. There are other inadequacies in the hugely popular and widely relational database systems (RDBS). Therefore, there is a clarion call for pioneering database solutions for the impending knowledge era. Graph databases are being proclaimed as the one with all the

On the other side, with the rising need for creating and managing intelligent devices and software products for business transformation, the role and responsibility of artificial intelligence (AI) methods go up significantly. Machine learning (ML) and deep learning (DL) algorithms play a very vital role in producing sophisticated AI systems and services. For AI algorithms to do their tasks, they need a lot of correct and cleaned data. Right data is to result in highly accurate predictions/inferences/conclusions.

Data typically gets collected from different sources and cleansed. There are several dissimilar data formats and transmission protocols greatly complicating the goal of data integration. Therefore, there are insistences for competent data integration and virtualization technologies and tools, which play a very vital role in visualizing and realizing profoundly impactful AI systems. That is, there is a need for a fresh and flexible approach to fulfilling the complicated requirement of data integration. The need for data integration has given rise to many research works and thought processes into working out the best possible way to collect, store, manipulate, and maintain digital data. Knowledge graphs (KGs) are the graph

[1]Edge AI Division, Reliance Jio Platforms Ltd., Bangalore, India
[2]Department of Computer Science and Engineering, Karunya Institute of Technology and Sciences, India

databases emerging and getting established as the next-generation data management system for speeding up knowledge engineering and extraction towards digitally transformed businesses and societies. The popularity of KGs is increasing due to their potential and flexibility in dealing with complex and interrelated data.

In a KG, the data is stored and information is depicted in a graphical format. This methodology in KGs can be applied to create a graphical representation of the relationships amongst all of its data points. Hence, even if the data points do not fit neatly together into a table, the associations between the data points can be evaluated fast and with much less computation power which is the explicit advantage over relational database.

Formally, a KG is a directed labelled graph that intrinsically and illustratively represents relations between data points. A node of the KG represents a data point. The entity of this data point could be a person, a place, or a webpage, and an edge represents the relationship between a pair of data points.

11.2   Tending towards digitally transformed enterprises

Without an iota of doubt, the greatest trial for enterprise IT team is connecting disparate and distributed digital data because unconnected data does not serve any useful purpose. Thus, linking digital data to squeeze out data-driven insights is turning out to be a prime target for businesses to march ahead. In a nutshell, it is an overwhelmingly accepted truth that the faster adoption of digitization and digitalization technologies and tools helps to create a lot of digital data and to convert it into actionable insights quickly. Company executives can then convincingly embark on insights-driven decisions and actions. Industries become productive, offer premium services, reduce wastage, delight their consumers, and increase their revenues. The real and sustainable business transformation is getting fulfilled through the smart leverage of potential digital technologies and tools. Connected assets and data are the prime requirements for initiating and implementing digitally inspired transformations. That is, all kinds of silos have to be eliminated through sophisticated technologies to have modernized systems in place.

Data has to be integrated to set up a flourishing foundation for a dazzling array of business innovations and disruptions. Besides data virtualization techniques, data fabric, and mesh products are gaining immense attention for simplifying and speeding up data integration. Data analytics and AI methods are getting bigger market and mind shares in transitioning data to knowledge. To smoothen the process of knowledge discovery and dissemination, KGs are being pronounced as the most important factor and facet. Digital transformation attains the intended success through rapid and ready insights from disparate digital data. Data fabrics offer a flexible data integration solution, which facilitates the dynamic delivery of semantically enriched data. KG is the key technology to transform existing data infrastructure into a data fabric. This chapter is fully dedicated to explain the nitty-gritty of KGs and why it is being portrayed as the key ingredient to attain the intended success of the AI paradigm. KGs are destined to play a critical role in shaping up the digital transformation initiatives.

11.3 The emergence of KGs

For any business and government organization to grow and glow, effective and efficient data collection, analytics, and management are very much indispensable. With the fast proliferation of unstructured data, deriving knowledge from data becomes a tough task. Semantic tools are being recommended as the way forward for surmounting data management issues. Semantic KGs are the main driver behind knowledge maintenance and discovery.

There have been many sincere attempts to improve RDBMSs to fully accomplish the ideals of digital transformation initiatives. The surging popularity of NoSQL databases and distributed SQL databases to beneficially tackle fast-growing digital data is well known. On the other side, graph databases especially KGs quickly grow in stature due to their extreme flexibility and their intrinsic capability to deal with complex and interrelated data in an adaptive and adroit manner.

There are a few interesting advantages of graph databases when compared with older relational databases. Through graph databases, the associations between all data points can be computed quickly while consuming less computation power. Graphs are generally visual. Vertices are represented by entities such as people and accounts. Edges vividly and visually represent the relationship between entities. Such a setup simplifies a lot of things including knowledge discovery and dissemination. A basic graph is shown in Figure 11.1.

In the given basic graph, there exist two different nodes namely, Node A and Node B. The relationship between the two nodes is represented by an edge. This is also known as a **triple**. The importance lays in identifying the methodology by which information is implanted in these graphs. If Node A = Biden and Node B = USA, then it is quite expected that the edge would be "president of" as shown in Figure 11.2.

A node or an entity can have many relations: Joe Biden is not only the President of the United States, he also chaired the Senate judiciary committee from

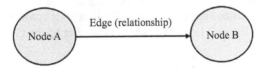

Figure 11.1 Basic graph

Figure 11.2 Node relations

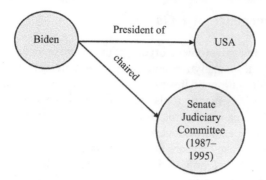

Figure 11.3   Multiple node relations

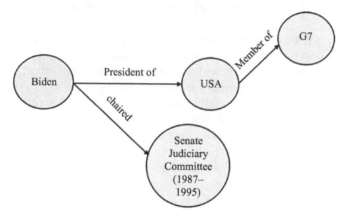

Figure 11.4   Multiple node relations with new relations

1987 to 1995. This information about Biden can be depicted in the KG. One more node is added for the new entity, Senate judiciary committee.

A new association need not emerge from the first node but from any other node in a KG as depicted in Figure 11.4. The USA is a member of the Group of Seven (G7).

11.4   Briefing the concept of KGs

Generally, the human brain acquires knowledge by building connections between neurons. For AI systems also to learn and understand, they have to establish and enrich connections between data. KGs come in handy here to empower AI.

A KG typically characterizes a network of real-world entities (people, places, events, business domains, technical concepts, etc.) and their relationships. These details are optimally getting stored in a graph database and are visually presented in the graph format. Nodes, edges, and labels are the three main components of KGs. Any real-world entity can be represented through a node. An edge

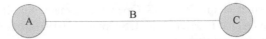

Figure 11.5 Representation of edge

connecting nodes is to illustrate the association between the entities. For example, a node could be a service provider and a service consumer. An edge is to categorically articulate the relationship between the nodes as vividly illustrated through Figure 11.5.

A represents the head/subject, C represents the tail/object, and B represents the relationship/predicate. In short, a KG is the grouping of interconnections amongst real-world entity descriptions such as products, events, services, locations, and people. A KG brings out the context information through coupling and by attaching semantic metadata. Such a competency makes KGs a perfect platform for simplifying data integration and analytics. Resultantly, the knowledge representation, discovery, and dissemination acts get streamlined.

11.5 Formalizing KGs

A KG can be defined as **G**={**E, R, T**}, where labelled and directed multi-graph is denoted by **G**, and **R, T, E** represent the edges, triples, and nodes, respectively.

The triple is formalized as (**u, e, v**) ∈ **T**. The head and tail nodes are defined as u, v respectively. The head node is denoted as **u** ∈ **E** and the tail node is denoted as **v** ∈ **E**. The variable **e** ∈ **R** is the edge connecting the nodes **u** and **v**. A triple is formalized in the semantic regime (u, e, v). **u, e,** and **v** correspond to **s, r, o. s,** and **o** represent two entities, the subject and the object of the fact and **r** is the relation that connects **s** and **o**.

In the statement: "Socrates influenced Plato.", the graph perspective called as the triple will include "Socrates" and "Plato" as two nodes of the graph. The edge between these two nodes is "influenced." From a semantic viewpoint, the statement includes "Socrates" and "Plato" as two entities, with "influenced" as the relation between the two entities. The terms of the statement are entities and relations.

Building a KG manually is not easy. Going through thousands of documents and extracting all the entities with the correct relations between them is not easy. Compute machines are assigned the entity identification and relation actions to perform this herculean task. The machines have a challenge of not being able to understand natural language. Hence, the way forward is to add the natural language processing (NLP) techniques such as dependency parsing, sentence segmentation, entity recognition, and parts of speech (POS) tagging.

Sentence segmentation: The beginning step in constructing a KG is to split the text document or article into sentences. Only those sentences in which there is exactly 1 subject and 1 object that are shortlisted.

In the given set of lines, "Indian tennis player Sumit Nagal moved to the top 200 on 29 July 2019 after qualifying in Hamburg. The 24-year-old recently won the opening round match at the 2020 US Open tournament. Sumit Nagal made his Grand Slam debut against Federer in the US Open of 2019. Sumit Nagal did win the first set.", the sentence split are,

1. Indian tennis player Sumit Nagal moved to the top 200 on 29 July 2019 after qualifying at Hamburg.
2. The 24-year-old recently won the opening round match at the 2020 US Open tournament.
3. He made his Grand Slam debut against Federer in the 2019 US Open.
4. Sumit Nagal did win the first set.

Out of the given four sentences, the 1 subject and 1 object sentences are the second and the fourth sentence and they are shortlisted. In the second sentence, the subject is "24-year-old" and the object is "US Open tournament". In the fourth sentence, "Sumit Nagal" is the subject and the object is "first set". This is shown in Table 11.1.

The challenge is to make the computer to understand the context of the text, particularly in the cases of multi-word subject and object cases. Tracing the objects in both the sentences above is highly complicated.

Entities extraction: The mining of a single-word entity from a sentence is quite easy. Such an extraction can be performed with POS tags. Mostly nouns and proper nouns are considered to be entities. When an entity extends across multiple words, then POS tags alone are not sufficient. Parsing the dependency tree of the sentence is required.

Traditionally, there are two types of graphs. The first one is semantic graphs inspired by resource description framework (RDF) and there are labelled property graphs. In property graphs, it is possible for users to add properties or attributes about data. This is adding metadata for simplifying the search activity. On the other hand, semantic graphs simplify data preparation to empower data analytics. KGs actually get originated with semantic graphs to make logical inferences from their data.

The property graph data model has three elements such as the following:

*   Nodes for representing the entities in the graph.
*   Edges for representing the relationships between entities
*   Properties represent the attributes associated with a node or with an edge.

The knowledge (RDF) graph model has two element nodes and edges. In contrast to the property graph data model, in the KG, the nodes can be values

Table 11.1   Sentence, subject, and object

Sentence	Subject	Object
The 24-year-old recently won the opening round match at the 2020 US Open tournament	24-year-old	US Open Tournament
Nagal won the first set	Nagal	First Set

with literal strings, integers, or resources with unique identifiers or anything that can be related. The edges (predicates or properties) are the directed links between nodes. The subject is the "from node" of an edge. The object is the "to node." When two nodes are connected with an edge, a subject–predicate–object statement is formed and it is called as Triple. Navigation and querying of edges can be done in either direction. Hence, a directed graph of triple statements is called as a KG.

The World Wide Web Consortium (W3C) manages the KGs. It indicates that a property graph is less interoperable but the strong standardization used in KGs enables the addition of knowledge toolkits.

The RDF is the core technology for the vision of semantic web (SW). SW has a purpose to realize a web-scale data infrastructure that is in readable and understandable format by machines. To accomplish this vision, the adopted web technologies include uniform resource identifiers (URIs) and the hypertext transfer protocol (HTTP) protocol. But more technologies are required to fully implement this SW vision.

A formal notion of meaning (semantics) that set up the basis for founded deductions is provided by RDF. The RDF graph can be depicted in various formats like N-Triples, N3, XML, JSON, and Turtle. The example "Plato influenced Aristotle" can be translated into RDF and serialized in N-Triples as follows:

<http://dbpedia.org/resource/Plato>
<http://dbpedia.org/ontology/influenced>
<http://dbpedia.org/resource/Aristotle>.

Using a serialization like Turtle, the RDF can be more compactly declared employing the so-called prefixes. Hence, the example can be rewritten as

@prefix dbo: <http://dbpedia.org/ontology/>.
@prefix dbr: <http://dbpedia.org/resource/>.
dbr:Plato dbo:influenced dbr:Aristotle.

In the view of SW, the terms **dbr:Plato** and **dbr:Aristotle** are known as resources. A relation between two different resources (**dbo:influenced**) is known as predicate or property.

RDF permits not only to represent relations between entities but also represents specific information related to a single entity. In the RDF statement

dbr:Plato dbo:birthDate -428-0-0^^xsd:date,

the literal value is the object and it is not an entity. It is a specific data type defined using the XML schema datatypes (XSD). In the perspective of a graph, a literal value is considered as a leaf node of the KG. Beginning from the RDF representation, quantified statements are added to denote the semantics of relations and entities relations.

The two different language models that assist in the construction of quantified statements in the form of RDF graphs are the RDF schema (RDFS) and Web Ontology Language (OWL).

Ontologies are the backbone of the formal semantics of a KG. This can be seen as the data schema of the graph. It serves like a formal contract between the users and the developers of the KG concerning the meaning of the data in it. A human being or a software application can be considered as a user who wants to interpret the data in a precise and reliable manner. Ontologies make sure the existence of a shared understanding of the data and its meanings.

There are a number of representation and modelling instruments when formal semantics are used to express and interpret the data of a KG.

- **Classes**: An entity description most often comprises a classification of the entity in relation to a class hierarchy. In the case of dealing with business information, there will be classes: Person, Location, and Organization. A common superclass for Persons and organizations is Agent. Location can have numerous sub-classes, like Populated place, City, Country, etc. The concept of class is borrowed from object-oriented design, where each entity usually fits into exactly one class.
- **Relationship types**: The relationships among entities are usually labelled with types, which provide information about the nature of the relationship, e.g., relative, friend, competitor, etc. Formal definitions can have relationship types like that parent-of is inverse relation of child-of, they both are special cases of relative-of, which is a symmetric relationship. Sub-region and subsidiary are transitive relationships.
- **Categories**: An entity can be related with categories, which describe some feature of its semantics, e.g., "Big four accountants" or "20th century composers". A book can belong simultaneously to more than one category like "Books about India", "Bestseller", "Books by French authors", "Books for children", etc. The categories are defined and well-ordered into a taxonomy.
- **Free text descriptions**: A "human-friendly text" description is often provided to clarify design intentions for the entity and to improve search.

To gain a correct understanding of KGs, there is a need to get to know its basic unit ("fact"). A fact is the most basic block that can be elegantly stored in a KG. Facts can be represented in the form of triplets such as

HRT: <head, relation, tail>
SPO: <subject, predicate, object>

So, facts contain three elements that help in the intuitive representation of facts in any KG. Head and tail nodes encode entities that are real-world objects or abstract concepts. The relation is to denote the connection between entities. Edges form the relationships. Here is a simple KG example. One example of fact could be <BoB, is_interested_in, The_Mona_Lisa>. Bob is the head and Mona Lisa is the tail and the interest is the relationship. Thus, a KG is a collection of facts as shown in Figure 11.6.

It has to be noted that there are no limitations on the data type of the fact stored in KG. In Figure 11.6, the persons are persons like Bob, Alice, paintings (Mona Lisa), dates, etc.

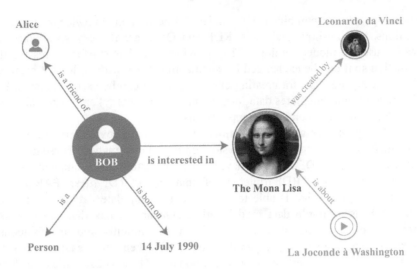

Figure 11.6   KG

11.6   Creating custom KGs

The growing relevance of KGs has been articulated and accentuated. Experts and practitioners have come out with proven techniques and tips to build and deploy KGs. Further on, domain-specific KGs are being built and deployed. KGs get created from the base data, which could be tabular, graphical, or text blob. The complete KG creation process can be divided into two steps:

- **Facts creation:** Herein, it is all about parsing the text (sentence by sentence) and extracting facts in triplet format like <H, R, T>. As text is processed, the prominent pre-processing steps such as tokenization, stemming, or lemmatization to clean up the text can be leveraged. The next step is to extract the entities and relations (facts) from the text. For entities, named entity recognition (NER) algorithms can be used. For relation, sentence dependency parsing techniques can be used to find the relationship between any pair of entities.
- **Facts selection:** The first step results in a large number of facts. Then there is a need to remove duplicated facts to arrive at the right and relevant facts that could be added to a KG. There are viable and venerable techniques (entity and relation disambiguation) to easily identify duplicates. This involves a consolidation of the same facts. For example, "Albert Einstein" can also be written as "Albert E." or "A. Einstein" in the text. Finally, a set of rules can be had to decide which triplet has to be added to the KG or which one could be ignored. There could be redundant and irrelevant information.

KG ontology: An ontology is a model of the world listing the types of entities, the relationships that connect them, and constraints on the ways that entities and relationships can be combined. Ontologies define domain knowledge, including definitions, relationships, and rules. RDF and OWL are the key vocabulary frameworks used to model ontology. They provide a mechanism for expressing this information so it can be exchanged between applications without loss of meaning. RDF provides languages for creating ontology, which can be used to create a KG. A KG acquires and integrates data into an ontology (or many) and then makes that knowledge available to enterprise applications.

Hosting property and RDF graphs: As indicated above, there are property graphs such as Neo4j and OrientDB to store graphical information. These graphs do not directly support RDF files and have their own custom query language. On the other hand, there exists "RDF triplet stores" that support RDF files. SPARQL is an RDF query language that is able to retrieve and manipulate data stored in RDF format. RDF is a simple data model with a standard syntax that can represent information of any form. RDF has the ability to explicitly and unambiguously capture meaning (semantics) in the data itself. RDF helps to create vocabularies that define and describe every element in a domain. These vocabularies are shared and accessible across systems.

- Ontotext GraphDB (https://www.ontotext.com/products/graphdb/): GraphDB allows the user to link diverse data and index it for semantic search. It can be enriched via text analysis to build big KGs. This provides frontend (visualization) and backend (server) services to see and query hosted KGs.
- Virtuoso (https://virtuoso.openlinksw.com/) provides backend services to query-hosted KG. Virtuoso's core SQL & SPARQL power many enterprise KG initiatives similar to powering DBpedia and a majority of nodes in the Linked Open Data Cloud – the world's largest publicly accessible KG.

Compared to normal graphs, KGs can accommodate heterogeneous data. KGs typically model real-world information and perform logical reasoning. Further on, KGs guarantee structured representation, remove redundancy, and query complex information. In the case of SQL databases, there are occasions such as doing a number of Join operations in a SQL query. Thus, KGs carry a number of technical advantages to simplify and speed up business transformation.

KGs are being explored for a variety of use cases such as logical reasonable, explainable, or interpretable AI (XAI), deeper and decisive data analytics. As accentuated elsewhere, KGs are bound to play a greater and grandiose role in shaping up the impending AI era. KGs will contribute as an infrastructure layer for simplifying AI processes. KGs are increasingly adopted and adapted by technology giants as a prominent part of their digital transformation goals.

Precisely speaking, technology-inspired connections between diverse and distributed data sources can create linked-in/integrated data points, which is to serve as a stimulating environment for a dazzling array of digital innovations and disruptions. These illustrated connections are critically contributing to assisting humans and machines in arriving at context-aware and cognitive decisions.

KG eases the complicated process of collecting, enriching, storing, searching, and navigating through a lot of diverse information such as text matters, images, videos, and audios. The information may be domain-specific or agnostic. Thus, the growing perception about KG is to accomplish a smart search of big data and to readily uncover actionable relationships hidden among two or more entities.

How a KG works?: KGs are typically made up of datasets from different and distributed sources, which generally differ in structure. Therefore, well-defined schemas, identities, and context details are made to work together to bring forth structure to disparate data. Schemas typically provide the framework for the KG. The participating nodes are classified through identities appropriately and the context determines the setting in which that knowledge exists. These components come in handy in distinguishing words with multiple meanings. Such an empowerment allows search engines, expert systems, and question and answer (Q/A) systems to unambiguously determine the difference between apple, the fruit and Apple, the brand.

In the recent past, KGs are artistically empowered through powerful ML algorithms. ML is an emerging field of study and research. The ML domain is a growing collection of self-learning algorithms to arrive at accurate predictions from data. It is a generally accepted truth that with more data, the prediction accuracy is bound to go up. The challenge is to collect and clean a vast amount of data from disparate sources. In the recent past, DL, a subset of ML, is gaining immense momentum.

The NLP capability, which is being accomplished through DL algorithms, is to construct a comprehensive view of nodes, edges, and labels through a process called semantic enrichment. When new data gets ingested, this process of semantic enrichment enables KGs to unambiguously identify individual objects and to understand the unique relationships between different objects. This acquired knowledge is used when integrating other similar datasets. Such an arrangement eliminates manual data collection and the integration work needed to support business decision-making. The data integration endeavours while forming KGs, actually simplify the creation of new knowledgebase and establishing connections between data points.

Why KGs?: Graphs organize data and highlight relationships between data points. A graphical representation looks like a network of interconnected data points. A KG contributes to transitioning data into machine-understandable knowledge through data connection and enrichment. Typically, real-world knowledge is

• **Situational**: Knowledge gets changed depending on circumstances.
• **Layered**: The associations between concepts permit for nuanced and neat understanding.
• **Changing**: Novel discoveries promptly change meanings.

The context details are generally missing in the data. Attempting to capture context by traditional data management systems makes them fail. This drawback acts against a decisive and deeper understanding of data. KGs are therefore purpose-built for flexibly incorporating the value-adding context information into the data to enable machines to correctly understand data and act accordingly.

A KG is being viewed as a reusable and responsible data layer for linking data silos and for answering complex queries. KGs have the intrinsic power to represent contextualized data and can accommodate the ever-changing nature of knowledge. That is, KGs easily accept new data, definitions, and requirements.

A KG with its inherent ability to embed real-world context into data is touted as the ideal tool for accomplishing data integration, which is turning out to be a complicated thing in the deeply distributed world. Data gets unified using the graph's native ability to link concepts instead of integrating data by combining tables. Thus, KGs connect data silos and produce a flexible data layer for the strategic enterprise transformation.

In short, a KG helps to express and expose relationships between data. KGs can help bridge data silos and contribute as a viable and venerable data fabric to accelerate data integration.

11.7 Characterizing KGs

KGs are gaining market and mind shares quickly. In data science, the common use cases are around adding identifiers and descriptions to multimodal data with the intention of enabling sense-making, integration, and explainable analysis. In the field of AI, KGs simplify and speed up ML activities. KGs

- decrease the need of large-labelled datasets;
- simplify transferring of learning and explainability;
- encode task, domain, and knowledge application as it is very difficult to learn manually from data alone.

Integrating and publishing data into KGs is definitely a complex process. This requires extracting and merging information from heterogeneous sources. In the case of structured sources, such as tables (CSV, HTML tables, relational databases, etc.) and tree-based structures (XMLs, JSONs, etc.), the integration strategy is to map their local schemas to the global schema represented by the target ontologies.

Unlike other sources, such as plain texts, structured information can be mapped to KGs through a semantic integration process. The common strategy adopted by the SW community to apply this process is to use reference ontologies as global schemas. Then, mappings are constructed to describe the relationships between the global schema and the local schema of the target data source. The data integration performance depends upon the consistency and the expressiveness of the ontology adopted as a global schema.

A KG is used to organize and integrate data according to an ontology. The ontology is the schema of the KG which applies a reason to derive new knowledge. Domain experts can create KGs from scratch. Unstructured or semi-structured data sources can be used to form KGs. KGs can also be assembled from existing KGs with the help of automated data or semi-automatic validation and integration mechanisms.

KGs are

- **Graphs**: KGs are basically a graph. Nodes represent entities of interest and their types. Edges represent relationships between and attributes of the nodes. Graphs make it easy to integrate new datasets and formats. Edges in graphs support exploration by assisting in navigating from one part of the graph to the other through links.
- **Semantic**: The meaning of the data is encoded in an ontology. Ontology describes the types of entities in the graph and their characteristics. In short, it is all about capturing the semantics of data with graph-based structures. Organization and storing of data is done in a graph.

    KGs are effective tools for capturing and structuring a large quantity of multi-relational data, which can be explored through query mechanisms. KGs have become the backbone of semantic search engines, question and answer (Q&A) systems, expert and recommendation systems, and conversational bots. A formal framework for the semantic interpretation of the data is provided by the semantic-based perspective. This is important to do deductive reasoning.
- **Extensible**: KGs arc bendable in terms of the types of data and schemas they can support. KGs and their schemas evolve to reflect changes in the domain. Every new data added to the graph is reflected once becomes available.

KGs are primarily relationship-driven: A KG mainly couples data points to express and expose relations and comprehensively describe any worthwhile domain. It is destined to reveal beneficial relationships between different entities through the structures (nodes, edges, and labels). In the beginning of this chapter, the distinct contributions of nodes, edges, and labels have been highlighted. How a fact is being represented through such triples. The brewing idea is how to enable machines with a suite of technologies to accurately and artistically interpret data. As articulated elsewhere, different mechanisms such as taxonomies and ontologies are being considered to empower KGs to interpret data correctly.

Ontology and taxonomy bring forth the hierarchical and structural organization of data. KGs exhibit correlations between data points. Consider the word "lavender". A KG would illustrate the relationship of lavender to multiple entities such as plant, colour, and scent. Further on, lavender gets linked up with objects like shoes, scented candles, and wildflowers. KGs help in establishing connections between entities like "bird feeder", "birdbath", "birdcage", and so on.

KGs turn data into knowledge: KGs are more precise and perfect in defining entities and their innate relationships, reasoning, proposing new theories, untangling hidden patterns, and extracting knowledge can be done by machines with heightened accuracy. Further on, as indicated above, KGs solve the data quality issues such as data ambiguity and incompleteness. KGs also play an important role in bringing in semantic structure to unstructured data. Such an empowerment presents KGs as the core and central piece of innovation for the AI field to survive and thrive.

Articulating and addressing the data challenges towards accelerated ML: A term can have multiple meanings and, on the other side, multiple terms can have the same meaning. In the increasingly unstructured data era, knowledge systems can be in trouble in unambiguously understanding a term's meaning. For example, the word, "apple", can mean the apple fruit, but it can also mean the trillion-dollar technology company.

There are hundreds of human communication languages, which are not formal languages such as programming languages such as Java, Python, C, and C++. On informal languages, it is quite difficult to precisely interpret the meaning of words. Understanding the underlying context/situation is mandatory to gain a decisive and deeper understanding of terms. Thus, an unambiguous understanding of data is essential towards knowledge creation and communication.

Semantic KGs are being touted as the perfect answer to these data-related challenges.

Terms, documents, etc. are generally classified into a hierarchical system to form a workable taxonomy. Taxonomies are all set to enable precise organization and management of data. Data organization and management are crucial for making sense out of data.

There are a number of automated tools emerging and evolving to pull key terms and terminologies from a large text content. Entity extraction is a crucial activity here. This allows users to take advantage of synonyms and multilingual labels to avoid the widely reported term-ambiguity problems. Language discrepancies are also being eliminated through such a proven and potential approach.

Existing business workloads and IT services are significantly enhanced through KGs and a host of advanced tools. For example, on a B2C e-commerce application, a semantic search can produce results that match the meaning of a user query instead of focusing on the exact words. That is, a search engine can understand user intent to make search experiences pleasant.

Employees' profiles with all the technical competencies can be semantically searched to find and form a group of right and relevant people for performing certain mission-critical projects. Question and answering systems are being accordingly empowered to generate structured search results from the organic text.

As indicated above, KGs empower the flourishing domain of ML remarkably. KGs are destined to supply correct data with contextual details to ML algorithms. This is to sharpen the prediction accuracy being made by ML models for a variety of everyday problems. The problems of data missing and quality are being elegantly surmounted through KGs. KGs help in minimizing all kinds of data management risks. Enterprise knowledge gets generally prepared and represented through well-defined business rules, which are formally expressed through an ontology. All these formalities and identities come in handy for ML algorithms to bring forth accurate predictions.

KGs are being pronounced as the central and core contributor for the intended success of the AI paradigm. KGs act as a well-oiled data fabric facilitating data interoperability between the departments of large enterprises. That is, enterprise data availability and accessibility are guaranteed for smoothening ML. The context and labels inscribed in KGs ultimately help supervised ML.

NLP and entity extraction help organizations to quickly create training sets. Thus, semantic KG hugely simplifies data preparation and provision thereby ML/DL aspects get speeded up towards knowledge discovery and dissemination.

11.8 Use cases of KGs

Since KGs contain a large quantity of curated and connected information, question–answering is the most appropriate use case. KGs help in searching and retrieving right details to insightfully assist users in their everyday tasks.

With the greater awareness of KGs and their distinct contributions, worldwide organizations are embarking on building and sustaining them. Wikidata (https://www.wikidata.org/wiki/Wikidata:Main_Page) is a well-known KG. Google KG is represented through Google Search Engine Results Pages (SERPs), serving information based on what people search. This KG is comprised of over 500 million objects, sourcing data from various sources such as Freebase (https://dbpedia.org/page/Freebase_(database)) and Wikipedia (https://en.wikipedia.org/wiki/Main_Page). Other domains such as healthcare, retail, finance, entertainment, and entertainment are also accordingly strengthened through appropriate KGs.

As noted down, Google extensively uses the growing and glowing idea of KGs to simplify and speed up searching. Facebook also relies on this graph phenomenon to keep track of networks of people and the connections between them. This helps in recommending new friends.

Netflix uses the proven KG technology to organize information on its movies, TV programs, etc. Further on, it incorporates their actors, directors, etc. Also, it establishes the connexions between them. Such an organization helps Netflix to predict which customers would prefer which movies at what point in time. Netflix deploys a KG to stockpile the vast quantities of information for its recommendation system.

Electronics and manufacturing giant Siemens use KGs to build viable models enabling an easy and elegant access to all of its data. Such a setup goes a long way in having risk management and process monitoring capabilities. Further on, building and enhancing digital twins for a variety of mission-critical physical assets are being facilitated through KGs. As known to everyone, digital twins are primarily being used to design, prototype, and test hugely complicated machineries and equipment to pinpoint any inherent risks and fresh possibilities and opportunities.

In the case of the supply chain domain, KGs can be used to keep track of inventories of different packages, parcels, and parts. Companies can precisely track inventories of various components, cadre involved, time, etc. Companies therefore gain the capability of taking informed decisions and shipping items rapidly and cost-effectively.

The other use cases lie in data discovery, data management, and data analytics. Data discovery is an important use case for KGs. Data management use cases focus on data validation, aggregation, and governance. The other use cases include data assurance, data catalogues, data lineage and provenance, compliance, risk management, and data fabric. Through data assurance, KGs provide increased trust and explainability.

Data analytics is about discovering and analysing data to extract actionable insights. KGs simplify data discovery and analytics. ML algorithms train the data discovered to bring forth viable insights. A variety of predictive, prescriptive, personalized, and prognostic analytics get accomplished through KG-enabled ML models. Decision science gains the boost with the faster maturity and stability of KG technologies and tools.

Thus, every worthwhile business domain is seriously exploring and experimenting with the flourishing idea of KGs to be right and relevant to their constituents and consumers. As indicated above, KGs are popular for data integration and interoperability. Linking distributed and disparate data gets hugely simplified through KGs and this unique attribute greatly facilitates knowledge extraction and exposition. Property graphs generally function as silos. This distinction is the main reason for presenting and promoting KGs as data fabrics. Within a single source or department, property graphs contribute immensely in making sense out of data. But for large enterprises with multiple departments, property graphs are found wanting.

KGs adroitly amass enterprise information and their relationships to offer enterprise knowledge management. With KGs and AI capabilities in place, it is possible to search and deliver the right knowledge at the right point. This knowledge may be templates, best practices, key guidelines, project information, etc. Further on, organizations can improve the KG search by leveraging NLP. The connections between documents, projects, and people are helpful in building a network of connected assets. Thus, knowledge capture and delivery get streamlined and speeded up.

11.9   ML and KGs

ML is being applied across industry verticals. ML is used in healthcare to detect cancerous tumours. To find factors that positively and negatively impact business, ML is used in supply chain functions. In the financial services industry, ML comes handy for investors to identify new opportunities and possibilities. ML heavily depends on data. With more data, the prediction accuracy is bound to go up. Unfortunately, ML processes miss out on contextual evidence since connections and data structures are difficult to process and pinpoint. However, KGs are elegant in capturing, persisting, and making contextual information usable. In a nutshell, contextualized AI is reliable, resilient, interpretable, responsible, and trustworthy.

Due to a lack of contextual information, classical AI systems are not sophisticated enough and not contributing convincingly to solving complex problems. As discussed above, KGs are a logical way to accurately identify data relationships and deliver their meaning. Hence, KGs drive intelligence into the data and provide context to AI. And hence these two are termed as the most powerful combination spurring an enigmatic interest in contextual AI.

With a bevy of noteworthy advancements in the ML space, everyday machines and devices are intrinsically enabled to self-learn from data. That is, business workloads and IT services are to exhibit cognitive behaviour. A variety of domain-specific expert systems, context-aware workloads, intelligent devices, adaptive services (business and IT), and cognitive software solutions exist. Thus, ML algorithms and models are to bring forth a paradigm shift for IT and business domains. With KGs in place, the ML algorithms get succulently empowered to fulfil the long-pending goal of providing enhanced prediction accuracy. KGs are touted as a right step towards enabling machines at our homes, hotels, and hospitals to more deeply understand multimedia and multimodal data such as still and dynamic images, audio, and text. With a deeper and greater understanding, envisaging and implementing next-generation capabilities become simpler and quicker. Accommodating video, audio, and text into the columns and rows of a relational database is a tedious and time-consuming affair. But neatly fitting them in graph databases is a simpler and smart move.

In short, the integration of ML and KGs is being seen as a positive signal to achieve bigger and better things for worldwide business enterprises.

KGs are to empower the AI domain comprehensively. KGs have the inherent power in capturing context details by unambiguous understanding of any hidden relationships between data. KGs assemble all data at the enterprise level. Such a capability accelerates building ML/DL models, which contribute in speedy realization of predictive and prescriptive insights. Additionally, KGs become the fundamental and foundational element to contribute as a data fabric for data integration.

KGs harmonize data across sources, structures, and locations. In short, graphs are turning out to be an optimal option for accomplishing data integration. Integrating datasets is essential for unearthing hidden insights. Data is a primary requirement for creating path-breaking AI models for solving a variety of business and technical problems. KGs gain prominence across industry verticals as they emerge as a unified platform to represent, prepare, and connect all of the data. Thus, KGs serve as an important ingredient in transitioning data to information and to actionable insights.

On the other hand, ML empowers the domain of KGs. By feeding the predictions being extracted and supplied by ML models, businesses can considerably increase their knowledge-driven capabilities, which, in turn, leads to the visualization of fresh possibilities and opportunities and enables the ready realization of deeper and decisive automations. The seamless and spontaneous integration of ML and KGs is being touted as a trendsetter for the ensuing digital era.

An ML algorithm has to be provided with training data to train an ML model. The training data must include decisive features to learn a function for making accurate predictions. However, ML models without context require extensive training and a set of predictive and prescriptive rules. Also, such models are primarily problem-centric. By adding KGs, which supply the much-needed context,

ML models are guaranteeing better predictions. KGs also allow for graph feature engineering using complex graph algorithms and simple graph queries. By using connected and contextual features, it is possible to maximize the predictive power of ML models. Graph technologies-based KGs can exhibit noteworthy advantages as graphs have the innate strength to spontaneously represent and examine connections and associations among data. Graph algorithms are precisely developed to understand the topology of data through connections. This has resulted in many peculiar use cases such as finding communities, uncovering influential components, and inferring patterns and structure. Including KGs in ML increases the accuracy.

KG augments ML substantially. This integrated feature provides the ability to learn generalized and predictive features directly from within the graph. Feature engineering and selection are not straightforward. Herein, this combination comes in handy in choosing the most predictive features. Companies, having understood the strategic importance of this combination, are increasingly leveraging the unique combination to envisage and implement fresh use cases.

A global e-commerce leader has created a shopping bot, which is sufficiently empowered through a KG. This is to add the much-needed context details to ML models to make better heuristic decisions about user intent. For another example, a well-known construction-equipment manufacturer successfully utilizes the KG-inspired ML capability towards predictive maintenance, which, in turn, improves equipment life. Herein, millions of warranty and service documents have to be parsed for identifying subjects and objects in the text and they get added into a KG for describing the context. This helps ML models to learn, understand, and predict the required maintenance. Then appropriate remediation can be considered and completed in time.

The future potential of ML approaches can be augmented by bringing KG and ML technology together. Another use case is that the knowledge-filled graphs facilitate the production of the labels. This is mandatory for accomplishing supervised learning. Precisely speaking, implementing, and attaching a KGs is a first and foremost requirement for neatly guaranteeing the success of the AI paradigm.

KGs explicitly represent the rich associations between data. A KG adds context to data by establishing connections among data. This enables software agents to exhibit intelligent behaviour. By adding associations to data and enhancing it with semantics, KGs drive the transition of data into intelligence. Thus, data becomes information and knowledge gets simplified through the enigmatic KG concept.

In short, to deal with large-scale KGs, ML not only helps to quickly build and structure KGs but also infers links between data points. On the other hand, ML is getting benefits from KGs to deeply understand data such as text, image, video, and audio, that cannot be fitted comfortably into the relational database. KGs are used on top of ML models to make AI systems more transparent and interpretable. KGs also bring in the ability to develop the ability to understand images, retrieve information, and answer queries. A hybrid of KG and ML systems can understand the world better, organize, and infer missing knowledge.

KGs are to be used for knowledge generation and not just querying. Today most knowledge work is siloed and over-specialized. Researchers and technocrats miss out on valuable connections between concepts in different fields. KGs come as a solace to pinpoint promising connections between disparate ideas and domains. For example, a medical doctor and an engineer team up to design a new medical device and to develop a large graph that includes their knowledge together. Many others can be accommodated in a KG. Such a combination might create opportunities for new links between concepts to be uncovered, and new solutions to be developed.

11.10   KGs for explainable and responsible AI

For AI models to make intelligent decisions in time, context information is essential. KGs have to natively represent the associations, complexity, and the context of data. Linked data facilitates easy capturing of hidden relationships between the data. Data's semantics and its relationships create a contextual knowledge. Such a representation enables AI systems to arrive at intelligent conclusions and inferences. By storing information as a graph of nodes and edges, context is an inevitable consequence compared to information getting stored in a traditional relational database.

Human intelligence is definitely non-linear and generally takes multiple perspectives before taking a decision. So, the schema-less nature of KGs guarantees the much-needed suppleness by not being strictly enforcing types on data. Schema-based representation of data is possible through KG. The representation is not compulsory as in traditional relational databases.

AI systems are expected to be fair, unbiased, understandable, ethical, explainable, and interpretable to be overwhelmingly accepted and used. In other words, for gaining wider acceptance and adoption, AI systems have to be fair and not to be skewed in their decisions. Further on, they have to self-explain why they have arrived at a particular prediction. There are many possibilities for AI models to take wrong decisions, which may eventually lead to wrong actions. Ideating and implementing viable and venerable techniques and tools for ensuring responsible AI are therefore gaining the attention of AI researchers.

KGs are designated as the most pivotal and paramount ones for guaranteeing the much-needed AI fairness. The rules-based approach generally provides highly traceable explanations for AI decisions. The explainability of AI inferences is also simplified through rules, which are easily encoded in KGs.

KGs are also presented as a fertile and flexible environment for storing ML models, their training and testing data, and their predictions. Such metadata turns out to be invaluable for providing the widely insisted interpretability.

KGs aggregate enterprise knowledge, connect disconnected, and disparate data from geographically distributed sources, and prepare data for smoothening the ML process. The distinct analytical capabilities of ML are being facilitated through

KGs. In a nutshell, KGs are projected as the important ingredient for the intended success of the AI era.

In conjunction with the mesmerizing AI implementation technologies (ML and DL algorithms), KGs are capable of opening up fresh opportunities and possibilities for the ensuing knowledge era. KGs are all set to be a prime technology for setting up and sustaining modern data systems. A KG provides deep semantic context to data so machines can read and understand data to predict accurately. KGs can enrich data sets and produce real-world facts that ML algorithms can succulently use to improve ML model performance.

KGs improve the way information is searched and ease the complex process of searching and exploration in the era of big data which is in the form of multi-structured data (audios, videos, and images about a user, entity, or object) that emerges and evolves fast. KGs have the core and critical asset for knowledge representation and reasoning (KRR).

11.11   Stardog enterprise KG platform

Today's data landscape is becoming complicated and distributed. With the faster proliferation of zillions of Internet of Things (IoT) devices and sensors, there is a dramatic and drastic rise in multi-structured data. Besides massive data volumes, data velocity, viscosity, variety, and value vary sharply. Thus, for the big data world, there is a need for highly adaptive data management solutions in order to facilitate data analytics. As indicated above, uniting data from different sources and breaking data silos through data virtualization solutions for unleashing data insights gain momentum these days. KG is being proclaimed as the best-in-class approach for linking data and subsequently enriching data with context details. KGs are to simplify and speed up knowledge engineering.

Stardog allows for the connection of data silos irrespective of their structure, speed, scope, and size, SPARQL, the Stardog's query language, can help in for-mulating complex queries, in piercing through data silos, and in coming out with correct and composite answers.

The Stardog KG platform can represent structured, semi-structured, and unstructured data in the graph to create a uniform data layer, enriched with the full context of data from every source. KG administrators and knowledge workers can use Stardog Studio to model data, write queries, and view data sources. Data sci-entists and analysts can use Stardog's powerful BI/SQL server to point to Tableau, PowerBI, Qlik, or any other SQL-based visual analytics tool to quickly build reports, dashboards, and derive actionable insights.

Unlock the power of Data Lakes: Data lakes emerge as the data store for the big data world. Data lakes could stock a massive amount of multi-structured data. Data scientists benefit immensely out of data lakes in their everyday assignments. However, companies struggle to gain business value from data lakes. They have to do a lot to make data accessible and queryable. This ultimately delays data analy-tics activities. Data preparation consumes a lot of talent, time, and treasure. This

KG platform makes it easy to connect data lakes and semantically enrich and query datasets for enabling data analytics.

Enrich knowledge: The flexible semantic data layer incorporated in this platform enables the user to endlessly link and network the complex relationships contained within the data lakes without changing the underlying data, enriching the semantic meaning of the data. And our best-in-class inference engine and built-in ML easily interprets the data and uncovers new relationships and patterns in an easy to explain way, reducing time to insight.

Semantic search and query: Semantic search enables searching data lakes by meaning, scanning the KG to uncover all layers of connections across the search terms, ensuring that no results are left out. By using SPARQL, it is possible to answer complex analytic questions from data stored across multiple data lakes.

Unleash data analytics: Stardog's Enterprise KG makes it easy to connect, contextualize, and discover new insights from any data source and structure so teams can deliver better, faster, and lower-cost analytic solutions to their customers.

Improve access: The certified connectors enable easy access to the full breadth of unified data. And with enterprise-grade data virtualization, data can be accessed without moving or copying it and share any combination of virtualized or persisted data through KG, empowering data and analytics teams to operate with greater efficiency and at lower cost.

An Enterprise KG platform such as Stardog augments and intensifies RDF graph into something more relevant than the consolidation of its parts. It is done by adding a knowledge toolkit to a Graph Database. A suite of tools and connectors are required additionally to make it easy to connect, model, and map all the data that is required, regardless of its structure. The Enterprise KG platform supports a wider and deeper range of services by integrating all the required features inside a graph database.

11.12   What CANNOT be considered a KG?

Every RDF graph is not a KG: For example, a set of statistical data, e.g., the GDP data for countries, characterized in RDF is not a KG. Representation of data in graph form is often useful, but it might not be required to capture the semantic knowledge of the data. It is sufficient for an application to have a string "USA" associated with the string "GDP" and a number "65 trillion" without the requirement of defining the meaning of countries and Gross Domestic Product (GDP) of a country. The connections and the graph make the KG and not the language used to represent the data.

Not every knowledge base is a KG: Interlinking the entity descriptions amongst themselves is a key feature of a KG. The description of one entity will include another entity. A graph is formed by this process of linking (e.g. A linked to B, B linked to C, C linked to D implies A linked to D). Knowledge bases are without formal structure and semantics. For example, the Q&A "knowledge base" about a software product does not represent a KG. An expert system that has a collection of data organized in a format that is not a graph can facilitate analysis using automated deductive processes such as a set of "if–then" rules.

11.13   Conclusion

A KG is a semantic network and characterizes a network of real-world entities. KGs represent "realism" as a combination of objects, events, concepts, or situations by taking into account the relationship between them. All this information is stored in the graph database and viewed as a graph structure. The heart of the KG is a knowledge creation, representation, persistence, and exchange model. KGs add context to data thereby making sense out of data gets hugely simplified and speeded up. RDF-based representation of KGs provides the best framework for data integration, analytics, and reuse since they combine the following:

- **Expressivity**: The SW, OWL, and stack (RDFs) standards allow for a fluent representation of various types of data and content like data schema, vocabularies, and taxonomies, all sorts of metadata, master data, and reference. The extension of RDF makes it easy to model provenance and other structured metadata.
- **Performance**: It allows for the efficient organization of graphs of billions of facts and its properties.
- **Interoperability**: A variety of specifications for data serialization query through SPARQL, management through SPARQL Graph Store and federation. The usage of globally unique identifiers (URIs) facilitates data integration and publishing facilities.

KGs and ML are the two inseparable strands in the double helix that forms the DNA for any intelligent system across industry verticals. Both will continue to evolve further to bring in deeper and decisive automations for the ensuing knowledge era.

Bibliography

[1] Lecue F. On the role of knowledge graphs in explainable AI. *Semantic Web*, 2020;11(1):41–51.
[2] Bhatt S.P., Sheth A., Shalin V., and Zhao J. Knowledge graph semantic enhancement of input data for improving AI. *IEEE Internet Computing*, 2020;24(2):66–72. doi:10.1109/MIC.2020.2979620.
[3] Grainger T., Aljadda K., Korayem M., and Smith A. The semantic knowledge graph: a compact, auto-generated model for real-time traversal and ranking of any relationship within a domain. In *2016 IEEE International Conference on Data Science and Advanced Analytics (DSAA)*, 2016, pp. 420–429. doi:10.1109/DSAA.2016.51.

[4] Shaoxiong J., Shirui P., Erik C., Pekka M., and Philip S.Y. A survey on knowledge graphs: representation, acquisition and applications. *IEEE Transactions on Neural Networks and Learning Systems*, 2022;33(2):494–514. doi:10.1109/TNNLS.2021.3070843.

[5] Vetle R., Ahmet S., and Dumitru R. Building semantic knowledge graphs from (semi-)structured data: a review. *Future Internet,* 2022;14:129. https://doi.org/10.3390/fi14050129.

Chapter 12

Enterprise knowledge graphs using ensemble learning and data management

Janson Luke Ong Wai Kit[1], Vijanth Sagayan Asirvadam[2] and Mohd. Fadzil B. Hassan[1]

Ensemble model is made of a set of models that integrate various type supervised for form classifier to increase or boast prediction consistency. This chapter introduced improved algorithm framework for supervised learning which takes the best three classifiers out of six and combine to produce enhanced ensemble model using uniform voting approach. The proposed technique is tested on PIMA Indian Diabetes dataset and showed superior performance compared to classification tree-based extended techniques (e.g., Random Forest and AdaBoost). The new structured formulated ensemble framework introduced also tend to be invariant to size of fold during validation process (k-fold validation).

12.1 Introduction

Ensemble modeling applications are widely used for their prediction persistency and have been effectively implemented in areas such as medicine, manufacturing, finance, and many other industries [1]. By merging two or more models, the ensemble model produces better predictions than a single model [2]. This research provides a predictive modeling framework based on enhanced ensemble models. Ensemble modeling refers to the integration or combining machine learning models to develop an enhanced ensemble alternative structure [3]. Thus, this model integration will improve predictive modeling by utilizing the ensemble model, which has the potential to improve prediction accuracy [4]. The proposed enhanced ensemble model framework is also validated by utilizing six or more algorithms selection and assessment models. As a result, by choosing three models with high confidence ratings and ensemble them together. By entailing training datasets as part of the machine learning models, the datasets will be subjected to ensemble model assessments through the comparison stages [5].

[1]Department of Computer and Information Sciences, University Teknologi Petronas, Perak, Malaysia
[2]Department of Electrical and Electronic Engineering, University Teknologi Petronas, Perak, Malaysia

The results of the model experiment will be used to integrate or combine three best fit models with high confidence levels and this study, the ensemble model on diabetes database.

This research is organized into five sections as follows: Section 12.2 discussed on the current ensemble model learning and Section 12.3 will go through the related work and literature review. Section 12.4 discussed the enhanced ensemble model methodology; Section 12.5 covers the datasets disease diagnostics used for this study which is inclusive of the results and discussion; and finally Section 12.6 on the conclusion of this work.

12.2   Current ensemble model learning

Ensemble model learning is an approach or method for learning a target function by training multitude individual learners and integrating their learnings to prediction [6]. The concept of ensemble techniques may be related to real-life scenarios. When making significant judgments, it is common to consider the opinions of numerous experts rather on single judgment. Using ensemble model for prediction, it yields better outcomes than predicting from using a single model [7], although ensembles have been proved to be more accurate than individual classifiers in many circumstances, combining models does not always yield good results [8]. A voting or averaging technique is frequently used to integrate the results of many classifier models that have been trained [9]. Here, three popular ensemble models will be emphasized namely Bagging, Boosting, Random Forest, and their methods on combining their outputs for predictions [10]. This section next will explain further the techniques including the proposed enhanced ensemble model.

12.2.1   Bagging

The process of bagging is based on the Bootstrap sampling approach with each cycle generating a new set of bootstrap samples for generating the individual classifier of the same method [11]. The Bootstrap sampling methodology replaces the data item at random, some instances may be repeated, while others may be overlooked throughout the sampling process [12]. The next stage in the bagging process is to aggregate all of the classifiers that were created in the previous phase. To create a final prediction, bagging combines the results of the classifiers with the aid of voting [13].

12.2.2   Boosting

Boosting raises the poor classifier's performance to that of a strong classifier [14] by resampling (reweighing) the data instances, it creates sequential learning classifiers [15]. At first, all of the occurrences are given the same uniform weights. During each learning phase, a new hypothesis is stated, and the examples are reweighted such that successfully categorized examples have lower weights and the system may focus on cases that were incorrectly categorized during this phase, which have greater weights. It chooses the incorrectly categorized instances so that they can be correctly categorized during the following learning stage. This procedure is repeated until the final classifier is constructed and the results of all the classifiers are pooled using majority voting [16].

12.2.3 Random Forest

Random Forest is a tree-specific algorithm. The tree is induced using a mixture of bagging and the random subspace approach [17]. It is similar to bagging, only each model is a random tree instead of a single model, and each tree is built according to the training set's bootstrap sample to N [18]. To separate each node, another random step is needed. To separate each node, another random step is needed. Rather than examining all potential splits N, a small subset of feature n is randomly picked ($n<N$), and the optimal split is picked from this subset. The final categorization is determined by a majority vote across all trees [19].

12.3 Related work and literature review

The literature review on the ensemble models' methods, techniques, and comparison are studied widely by researchers. Various studies are conducted as to work on the best ensemble models for applications to improve the machine learning results using only a singular machine learning algorithm for the prediction modeling. In this study, we have reviewed the literature on comparison study and design of ensemble model. Thus, it is an interesting research area targeted by many ensemble model scholars to work on the best model. Many researchers focus on using the existing models such as Bagging, Boosting, Stacking, and Random Forest in building the ensemble model for predictive modeling either on prototyping model or on conducting empirical study. Actual studies on ensemble model and method are working on a comparative study on existing ensemble models and discussed about the results outcome from the experiment. The aim of this study is to develop an enhanced ensemble model using pre-ensemble model analysis where to study which algorithm is the best for ensemble model and compute the best three algorithms for ensemble model that will discuss in section three later.

The work by S. Wan and H. Yang on the theory and in practice, Bagging, Boosting, Stacking, and Random Forest are compared. Only 31 datasets were included in the comparative analysis, which focused on four current ensemble models [20]. Also, M. Pandey and S. Taruna work focuses on a comparison study of four current ensemble models only for performance modeling on student academic results, including Bagging, Boosting, Random Forest, and Rotation Forest. No work on assessing own ensemble model algorithm [21].

Other research by N. Muhammad Baba *et al.* working on getting a higher performance rate, an ensemble technique is utilized to compare and search for appropriate classifiers from a collection of models that would be utilized as a model for forecasting water quality. The literature did not go over the proposed model in detail or provide any empirical experiments to back it up [22]. According to S. Lee *et al.* work on performance comparison of ensemble model, this study compares decision trees using ensemble approaches (Random Forests, Bagging, and Boosting) with k-NN using ensemble approaches (bagging and boosting) and linear regression using ensemble approaches for estimating movie box-office revenue (bagging and boosting). The ensemble model has limitations because the study is confined to small datasets [23].

While on the financial management credit scoring literature by Y. Li and WS. Chen, the results of a comparison research and experiment on five commonly used baseline classifiers: neural network, decision tree, logistic regression, naive Bayes, and support vector machine. With the exception of AdaBoost, the experiment shows that ensemble learning outperforms individual learning. This chapter examines the causes behind some algorithms' poor performance and makes recommendations for credit scoring model selection [24]. Other research by Ghodselahi on Support Vector Machine (SVM) classifiers are used as members of the ensemble model in the hybrid model, which combines clustering and classification approaches. It is disputed if using ensemble in a hybrid model improves classification performance because it is limited to credit scoring [25].

Nora El-Rashidy *et al.* work on various COVID-19 datasets, however, only touch based on concept for machine learnings and deep learning model on conceptual approach. It is also discussed that machine learning is not really implemented in clinics, hospitals, and medical services and with the introduction of ensemble models and enhanced ensemble models, it can bring more capabilities on tackling the COVID-19 pandemic or perhaps other shortfall pandemics [26].

Azam Naghavi *et al.* research on suicide ideation or behavior diagnosis using ensemble model based on Bagging-Bootstrap sampling approach with only three-fold cross-validations where testing and training of the models could be debatable on the accuracy of the predictions. This research would be better if empirical experiments can be done on various Bagging, Boosting, Random Forest, or perhaps an enhanced ensemble model to justify the predictive results for suicide ideation or behavior diagnosis [27].

To conclude the literature review assessment, there is many ensemble model and methods to propose on researching the best ensemble model. Thus, a number of existing research works are primarily focused on literature review analysis on datasets and applications. Most research works focus on model study and empirical analysis and evaluated the existing ensemble model using the bagging model. Also, there is less study on ensemble models working or researching about improving the existing methods of pre-ensemble model rather than focus directly on ensemble the model.

12.4   Methodology

The enhanced ensemble model framework is introduced with a model, flowchart, and explaining algorithm stages. This section discusses on performance evaluation and comparison using an experimental method using the datasets on medical applications.

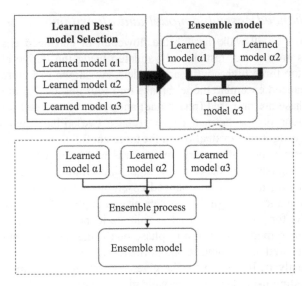

Figure 12.1　Ensemble model paradigm

12.4.1　Enhanced ensemble model framework

To increase the accuracy of predictive analytics applications, ensemble modeling is adopted by taking two or more related but separate predictive models and then integrating the results into a single model [28]. The accuracy tends to be greater and more improved than the classic model technique provided a well-chosen group of multiple strong models is chosen [29]. Figure 12.1 shows an example of ensemble model, in which three models, $\alpha 1$, $\alpha 2$, and $\alpha 3$, are selected from the training data and ensembled together, then utilized as inputs and trained at the next layer.

12.4.2　Training and testing datasets

The proposed predictive techniques improve ensemble models and consists of three steps which are as follows:

- Raw Dataset Preparation illustrates how to prepare raw datasets, and in this study will use Excel files to experiment with datasets.
- Training and Testing/Validation Data covers the learning stage where it consists of six classification algorithms that will be used for model evaluation; the best three model's selection is represented by $\alpha 1$, $\alpha 2$, and $\alpha 3$.
- The predictive modeling framework for enhanced ensemble model architecture. The framework consists of raw datasets, training, and data testing/validation. During the training data phases, it will assess the datasets to determine which methods have a high confidence level for integrating them into an ensemble model and therefore employing the ensemble model.

12.4.3   Enhanced ensemble model and algorithm

In this section, we will walk through the flowchart of enhanced ensemble model where datasets are trained, tested, and validated using the define algorithm, and ensemble the top three high confidence models. As shown in Figure 12.2, on the flowchart, enhanced ensemble model breaks into four phases that are as follows:

Dataset phase are prepared (phase one) and ready to proceed for training and testing/validations on the defined dataset (phase two). Phase two will start the execution of the algorithm evaluation on the three confidence out given assessment. If the experiment is not satisfactory, the process will be repeated. Thus, in phase three, upon getting best confidence on the algorithm evaluation, this is then mapped as example $\alpha 1$, $\alpha 2$, $\alpha 3$ and the enhanced ensemble models are created based on this. The training and testing of the datasets placed in phase four, and the enhanced ensemble model for prediction is used to validate its performance.

The ensemble model algorithm in phase one using medical datasets is where the data is prepared by summarizing, normalizing, and separating the required variables for analysis. In phase two, the given datasets will split into 80% training set and 20% testing using k-fold cross-validations requirement. Next, we will start evaluating and compare the model.

After the 80–20 testing and validations of the datasets, we will begin with the evaluation of the algorithm to calculate the top three confidence levels. This step

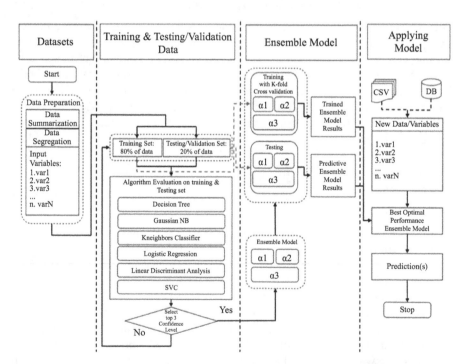

Figure 12.2   Detailed algorithm steps for enhanced ensemble model

will build and test the models using six algorithms namely Classification and Regression Trees, Gaussian Naive Bayes, K-Nearest Neighbours, Linear Discriminant Analysis, Logistic Regression, and Support Vector Machines.

12.5　Experimental setup and enterprise dataset

The PIMA Indian Diabetes datasets is used as benchmark database provided and made available by University of California Machine Learning Repository. The dataset contains 768 women from a population with diabetes in which 258 show diabetes positive and 500 show negative measurement. It consists of nine attributes as shown in Table 12.1. For every training instance, it includes eight fields and an outcome or response field that serves as the training instance's label with class binary of 0 representing as healthy person or 1 representing a patient with diabetes.

12.5.1　Ensemble models performance evaluation using enterprise knowledge graph

We conducted a performance and precision evaluation on the current ensemble models using Bagging, Boosting, and Random Forest [30] to gauge which of the proposed ensemble model's results are superior to those of the enhanced ensemble models. The datasets that will be evaluated using the current ensemble models that is Bagging, Boosting, and Random Forest together with the enhanced ensemble model, are covered and the performance of ensemble models will be evaluated using k-fold cross-validations as seen in Figure 12.3. Here we performed assessment and evaluation of the existing benchmark and enhanced ensemble models.

k-fold cross-validation is a "resampling procedure" and wholesome testing procedures that are used to evaluate machine learning algorithm on a given datasets [31]. K-fold cross-validation having one parameter known as "K" refers to the number of group dataset splits. When k is selected, it is used as refereeing to the model for example when we imply $k=10$, k will be experiment 10-fold (or times) cross-validations on the given datasets (90% training and 10% test dataset).

Table 12.1　Diabetes disease datasets descriptions

Fields	Attributes	Data range
Pregnancies	No. of times pregnant	0–17
Glucose	Plasma glucose concentration 2 hours in an oral glucose tolerance test	0–199
Blood pressure	Diastolic blood pressure	0–122
Skin thickness	Triceps skin fold thickness	0–99
Insulin	2-Hour serum insulin	0–846
BMI	Body mass index	0–67.1
Diabetes Pedigree Function	Diabetes pedigree function	0.078–2.42
Age	Age (years)	21–81
Outcome	Class (0 or 1)	Tested positive for diabetes = 1

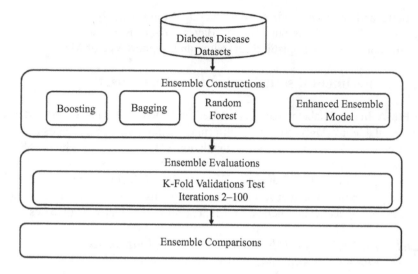

Figure 12.3 Build, evaluate, test, and select best model

k-Fold cross-validation is popularly used in performance assessment in machine learning algorithm to evaluate the unknown dataset by normalizing datasets to estimate how the machine learning algorithm perform on the predictions on the defined datasets that is not used during the model training (known as testing dataset) [32]. It is a widely used method because of its simplicity on performance and precision evaluation for experiment.

12.5.2 Tree classification as knowledge graph

Bagging works best with algorithms with a lot of variation such as decision trees and Random Forest is one example of improved bagging technique with resampling.

Boosting ensemble algorithms generate a series of models that seek to repair the errors of the models that came before and then used to construct predictions, which are weighted and merged to provide a final output forecast e.g., AdaBoost Classifier.

Bagged decision trees are extended into Random Forest with the training dataset that is sampled using replacement, but the trees are built in such a way that the correlation between individual classifiers is reduced. Instead of picking the optimal split point in the tree building greedily, just a random selection of characteristics is examined for each split.

12.6 Result and discussion

The training and testing and validation datasets utilized in the experiment will be subsequently used for model assessment on the pre-selection procedure for enhanced ensemble models indicated as for example $\alpha 1$, $\alpha 2$, and $\alpha 3$. In Figure 12.4, a boxplot chart was utilized to provide a clearer statistical perspective of the top three models that might be utilized to build the ensemble model using 2-, 4-, 5-, and 10-fold.

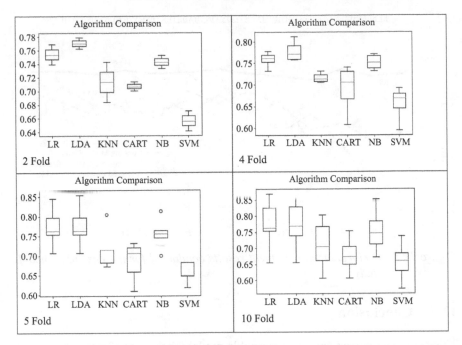

*Figure 12.4   Algorithm evaluation results using 2-, 4-, 5-, and 10-fold confidence
level for enhanced ensemble model*

The enhanced ensemble model using a combination of LR (α1), LDA (α2), and NB (α3) gives the outcome of >0.77 by using uniform voting (or equal weightage). The equal voting strategy is adopted looking into traditional supervised classifiers such Logistic Regression, Linear Discriminant and Naive Bayesian that seem to show comparable results based on cross-validation analysis. Adopting hard or soft weightage on ensemble framework may bias towards the better model thus providing uniform momentum, which will be a better choice.

Using *k*-fold cross-validations approaches on the ensemble models which include Tree-based (which is supervised form in nature) Bagging, Boosting, and Random Forest as benchmark comparison, the proposed enhanced ensemble framework results are compared and depicted in Figure 12.5 using PIMA Indian Diabetes datasets. The goal of this assessment is to make comparison to show the performance of structured ensemble models using different folds 2–100 (*k*-fold validation). The proposed ensemble model not only performed better but invariant to the numbers of fold using *k*-fold validations.

- Bagging Results: (0.696615–0.765139);
- Boosting Results: (0.730469–0.762237);
- Random Forest Results: (0.699214–0.768148);
- Enhance Ensemble Result: (0.768305–0.775101).

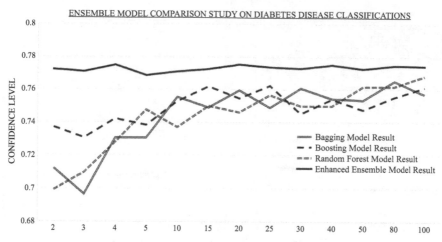

Figure 12.5   Performance assessment results conducted for the ensemble models study

12.7   Conclusion

This study presents an enhanced ensemble model for the classification by proposing a new enhanced structured ensemble model. The proposed model is compared with using classical ensemble models such as Bagging, Boosting, and Random Forest (Bagging with weightage resampling). The enhanced ensemble model introduced in this chapter selects the optimal three models out of six traditional supervised classification algorithms and combine using uniform voting technique then train and test/validate on PIMA Indian Diabetes Datasets. The enhanced ensemble supervised classifier models recorded the highest classification accuracy and invariant to cross-validation fold.

References

[1]   Brazdil, P., Giraud Carrier, C., Soares, C., Vilalta, R., Meta learning: *Applications to Data Mining.* 1 ed.; Springer-Verlag Berlin Heidelberg: 2009.
[2]   Caruana, R., Munson, A., Niculescu-Mizil, A. In Getting the Most Out of Ensemble Selection, *Sixth International Conference on Data Mining (ICDM'06), 18-22 Dec. 2006*; 2006; pp 828–833.
[3]   Waleed M, Um T-W, Kamal T, Usman SM. Classification of Agriculture Farm Machinery Using Machine Learning and Internet of Things. *Symmetry.* 2021;13(3):403. PubMed PMID: doi:10.3390/sym13030403.
[4]   Trawiński, B., Lasota, T., Kempa, O., Telec, Z., Kutrzyński, M. In *Comparison of Ensemble Learning Models with Expert Algorithms Designed for a Property Valuation System*, Cham, Springer International Publishing: Cham, 2017; pp 317–327.

[5]   Rahimi N, Eassa F, Elrefaei L. An Ensemble Machine Learning Technique for Functional Requirement Classification. *Symmetry*. 2020;12(10):1601. PubMed PMID: doi:10.3390/sym12101601.

[6]   Zheng C, Wang C, Jia N. An Ensemble Model for Multi-Level Speech Emotion Recognition. *Applied Sciences*. 2020;10(1):205. PubMed PMID: doi: 10.3390/app10010205

[7]   Hsu, Y.-F., Lee, W.-P., Evaluation of the going-concern status for companies: An ensemble framework-based model. *Journal of Forecasting* 2020, 39 (4), 687–706.

[8]   Lu Z, Xia J, Wang M, Nie Q, Ou J. Short-Term Traffic Flow Forecasting via Multi-Regime Modeling and Ensemble Learning. *Applied Sciences*. 2020;10 (1):356. PubMed PMID: doi:10.3390/app10010356.

[9]   Bauer, E., Kohavi, R., An Empirical Comparison of Voting Classification Algorithms: Bagging, Boosting, and Variants. *Machine Learning* 1999, 36 (1), 105–139.

[10]   Chen, K. L., Lee, H., Shing, C.-C., Yang, J. In An Analysis of Algorithms Used by Business Intelligence Software, *Proceedings of International Conference on Pacific Rim Management*, San Francisco, California USA, San Francisco, California USA, 2009; pp 36–39.

[11]   Coelho, A. L. V., Nascimento, D. S. C., On the Evolutionary Design of Heterogeneous Bagging Models. *Neurocomputing* 2010, 73 (16), 3319–3322.

[12]   Pham, H., Olafsson, S., Bagged ensembles with tunable parameters. *Computational Intelligence* 2019, 35 (1), 184–203.

[13]   Collell, G., Prelec, D., Patil, K. R., A Simple Plug-in Bagging Ensemble Based on Threshold-moving for Classifying Binary and Multiclass Imbalanced Data. *Neurocomputing* 2018, 275, 330–340.

[14]   Zhang, C., Zhang, Y., Shi, X., Almpanidis, G., Fan, G., Shen, X., On Incremental Learning for Gradient Boosting Decision Trees. *Neural Processing Letters* 2019, 50 (1), 957–987.

[15]   Oza, N. C. In Online bagging and boosting, *2005 IEEE International Conference on Systems, Man and Cybernetics, 12-12 Oct. 2005*; 2005; pp 2340–2345 Vol. 3.

[16]   Konstantinov, A. V., Utkin, L. V., Interpretable Machine Learning with an Ensemble of Gradient Boosting Machines. *Knowledge-Based Systems* 2021, 222, 106993.

[17]   Parmar, A., Katariya, R., Patel, V. In A Review on Random Forest: An Ensemble Classifier, *International Conference on Intelligent Data Communication Technologies and Internet of Things (ICICI) 2018, Cham, 2019*; Hemanth, J., Fernando, X., Lafata, P., Baig, Z., (eds.), Springer International Publishing: Cham, 2019; pp 758–763.

[18]   Breiman, L., Random Forests. *Machine Learning* 2001, 45 (1), 5–32.

[19]   Wu, Z., Lin, W., Zhang, Z., Wen, A., Lin, L. In An Ensemble Random Forest Algorithm for Insurance Big Data Analysis, *2017 IEEE International Conference on Computational Science and Engineering (CSE) and IEEE*

International Conference on Embedded and Ubiquitous Computing (EUC), 21-24 July 2017; 2017; pp 531–536.

[20]   Wan, S., Yang, H., Comparison among Methods of Ensemble Learning. *In Proceedings of the 2013 International Symposium on Biometrics and Security Technologies, IEEE Computer Society*: 2013; pp 286–290.

[21]   Pandey, M., Taruna, S., A Comparative Study of Ensemble Methods for Students' Performance Modeling. *International Journal of Computer Applications* 2014, 103, 26–32.

[22]   Muhammad Baba, N., Makhtar, M., Fadzli, S. A., Awang, M. K., Current Issues in Ensemble Methods and Its Applications. *Journal of Theoretical and Applied Information Technology* 2015, 81.

[23]   Lee, S., Kc, B., Choeh, J. Y., Comparing Performance of Ensemble Methods in Predicting Movie Box Office Revenue. *Heliyon* 2020, 6 (6), e04260.

[24]   Li, Y., Chen, W., A Comparative Performance Assessment of Ensemble Learning for Credit Scoring. *Mathematics* 2020, 8(10), 1756.

[25]   Sun, Q., Pfahringer, B. *In Bagging Ensemble Selection*, Berlin, Heidelberg, Springer Berlin Heidelberg: Berlin, Heidelberg, 2011; pp 251–260.

[26]   El-Rashidy, N., Abdelrazik, S., Abuhmed, T., Amer, E., Ali, F., Hu, J.-W., El-Sappagh, S. Comprehensive Survey of Using Machine Learning in the COVID-19 Pandemic. *Diagnostics* 2021, 11, 1155. https://doi.org/10.3390/diagnostics11071155

[27]   Naghavi, A., Teismann, T., Asgari, Z., Mohebbian, M.R., Mansourian, M., Mañanas, M.Á. Accurate Diagnosis of Suicide Ideation/Behavior Using Robust Ensemble Machine Learning: A University Student Population in the Middle East and North Africa (MENA) Region. *Diagnostics* 2020, 10, 956. https://doi.org/10.3390/diagnostics10110956

[28]   Seufert, A., Schiefer, J. In Enhanced business intelligence - supporting business processes with real-time business analytics, *16th International Workshop on Database and Expert Systems Applications (DEXA'05), 22-26 Aug. 2005*; 2005; pp 919–925.

[29]   ZHANG, C.-X., ZHANG, J.-S., A Survey of Selective Ensemble Learning Algorithms. *Chinese Journal of Computers* 2011, 1399–1410.

[30]   Hussain, S., Keung, J., Khan, A. A., Bennin, K. E., Performance Evaluation of Ensemble Methods For Software Fault Prediction: An Experiment. *In Proceedings of the ASWEC 2015 24th Australasian Software Engineering Conference*, Association for Computing Machinery: Adelaide, SA, Australia, 2015; pp 91–95.

[31]   Refaeilzadeh, P., Tang, L., Liu, H., Cross-Validation. In *Encyclopedia of Database Systems*, Liu, L., Özsu , M. T., (eds.), Springer US: Boston, MA, 2009; pp 532–538.

[32]   Krstajic, D., Buturovic, L. J., Leahy, D. E., Thomas, S., Cross-validation Pitfalls When Selecting and Assessing Regression and Classification Models. *Journal of Cheminformatics* 2014, 6 (1), 10.

## Chapter 13

Illustrating graph neural networks (GNNs) and the distinct applications

Pethuru Raj[1], N. Susila[2] and S. Usha[3]

13.1 Introduction

The fledgling concept of graph neural network (GNN) has gained a greater acceptance and adoption in the recent past across domains such as social and transport networks, knowledge graphs (KGs), recommendation, expert and question-answering systems, neurons in the brain, and life science that deals with molecular structure. The unique power of GNNs in modeling the intriguing and intimidating dependencies between nodes in a graph has laid down a stimulating environment for envisaging breakthrough results in the graph theory arena. GNN is a special but powerful type of neural networks. GNNs directly operate on the graph-structured data and are capable of assisting in implementing intelligent systems. In short, GNNs are being viewed as an enabling factor and facet of real digital transformation.

This chapter is to explain the distinct characteristics of GNNs and how they contribute to visualizing and realizing a variety of advanced applications for the impending knowledge era.

13.2 Briefing the distinctions of graphs

Graphs are emerging and evolving as a powerful language for describing and analyzing everyday entities along with their unique relations/interactions. Graphs are becoming prevalent these days. We often read about social networks, computer networks, transport networks, disease pathways, etc. Networks are also termed as graphs. Graphs are a highly flexible data structure that generalizes many other data structures. For example, if there are no edges, then it becomes a set. If there are

[1]Edge AI Division, Reliance Jio Platforms Ltd., Bangalore, India
[2]Department of Information Technology, Sri Krishna College of Engineering and Technology, Coimbatore, India
[3]Department of Computer Science and Engineering, Rajarajeswari Engineering College, Bengaluru, India

only "vertical" edges and any two nodes are connected by exactly one path, then we have a tree.

A network (or graph) is a representation of connections among a set of entities/ items. This representation is often written as G=(V,E), where V={V1,...,Vn} is a set of nodes / vertices and E={{Vk,Vw},..,{Vi,Vj}} is a set of two-sets (set of two elements) of edges / links. An edge represents the connection between two nodes in the set of vertices (V).

A graph (Figure 13.1) is often represented by **A**, an adjacency matrix. If a graph has **n** nodes, **A** has a dimension of **(n × n)**.

Sometimes the nodes have a set of features (for example, a user profile). If the node has **f** numbers of features, then the node feature matrix **X** has a dimension of **(n × f)**. Networks can also take multiple structures and attributes. There are multiple graph types as indicated below.

- Undirected graphs do not have direction. Such graphs are useful for cases where relationships are symmetric. Directed graphs have direction and are useful for asymmetrical relationships
- Cyclic graphs are paths starting and ending at the same node. On the other hand, in acyclic graphs, paths start and end at different nodes.
- In weighted graphs, not all relationships are equal. That is, some relationships carry more weight. On the other hand, in an unweighted graph, all relationships are equal.
- In sparse graphs, every node in the subset may not have a path to every other node. But in dense graphs, every node in the subset has a path to every other node

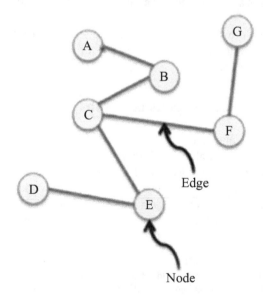

Figure 13.1   A graph structure

Networks have some basic properties and, from that, a variety of advanced techniques can be made and used for tackling complex business and technical problems. The prominent network-centric advancements and activities are illustrated below.

- **Network connectivity**: A connected graph is a graph wherein every pair of nodes has a path between them. In a graph, there can be multiple connected components.
- **Network distance**: The distance between two nodes is the length of the shortest path between them. The path length is typically identified by the number of steps it takes to traverse from a node y to x.
- **Network centrality**: Centrality is a way to think about the importance of nodes/edges in a graph. Some of the ways to quantify "importance" in a network are the amount of degree of connectivity, the average proximity to other nodes, the fraction of shortest paths that pass through nodes, etc.

The centrality measures help in

- finding the influential nodes in a social network
- identifying the nodes that disseminate information to many nodes or prevent epidemics
- pinpointing the hubs in a transportation network
- listing out the important pages on the web
- discovering the nodes that prevent the network from breaking up

Precisely speaking, the web of nodes and edges form a graph, which is a mathematical representation of the network structure of the data. Graph nodes and edges can optionally have a type. A graph with a single type of node and a single type of edge is called homogeneous. An example of a homogeneous graph is an online social network with nodes representing people and edges representing friendship, where the type of nodes and edges are always the same. On the other hand, a graph with two or more types of nodes and/or two or more types of edges is called heterogeneous. There are other applications such as degree centrality and network clustering.

Graph theory gains prominence and dominance due to its growing acceptance across. Also, there are a number of enabling technologies and tools emerging to easily make use of graphs as a sophisticated technical solution for a variety of personal, professional, and social requirements. Information/knowledge concepts and assets are increasingly organized and linked to prepare the world for the impending knowledge era. People are networked through social networks such as Facebook, professionals are being linked through professional networks such as LinkedIn, communication networks connecting people, properties, handhelds, wearables, fixed, portable and implantable devices, machineries, robots, drones, etc., critical and cyber infrastructures are being networked to automate and accelerate a variety of business operations, airports across the world are connected to ensure smooth travel, transport and trip across cities, counties, countries, and continents, functional interactions between genes and proteins are facilitated through a unique genetic structure, and so son. Hence, graphs have become an inseparable part of our lives.

Data representation through a graph, which is being pitched as a flexible and futuristic data structure for the knowledge era, enables embedding complex structural information as features. Such an empowerment is to yield higher performance in some domains. Besides a stronger feature representation, graph-based methods leverage representation learning to automatically learn features and represent them as an embedding. That means, a large amount of high-dimensional information can be encoded in a sparse space without any significant performance degradation. The application scope goes up remarkably as articulated by Dr. Leskovec.

- **Node-level tasks: node classification and regression**: This is to predict a label, type, category, or attribute of a node. Essentially, every node in the graph is supplied with a label and the need here is to predict the label of the nodes without any ground-truth. Ultimately this will predict a property of a node. This is also known as node attribute inference problem and is termed as the problem of inferring missing or incomplete attribute values of some nodes, given attribute values of other nodes in the network. The capability gives you the ability to bring in context and neighborhood information into your predictions. For example, in an online social network, there might be demands for predicting the music preferences of a user's friendship network. This helps to pinpoint fake accounts in a social network with millions of accounts.
- **Link prediction**: This is to predict if there are missing links between two nodes or finding hidden relationships between entities. It is important to predict missing relationships because some were hidden from us during data collection. There may be a need to predict how the network structure will evolve in the future through insertion or deletion of links, given its snapshot at the current time. In an online social network, we can use link prediction to suggest new friends to members. This is useful for KG completion and recommendation systems. E-commerce and social sites use this immensely.
- **Graph-level tasks: graph classification, regression, and clustering:** This is to categorize different graphs. This is the problem of discriminating between graphs of different classes. For an appropriate example, consider the representation of a chemical compound as a graph. In this graph, nodes are atoms, and edges are bonds between atoms. Given a set of chemical compounds and each compound is being represented as a graph. Now, we want to predict whether a compound is cancer-hindering or not. This is a graph classification problem. Given a graph representing the structure of a molecule, predict molecules' toxicity. Clustering is to detect whether nodes can form a community for a particular cause. Forming a knowledge community for a particular technology is accomplished through this application.

Another example is the segmentation of users of a social network into communities based on their hobbies, without having to explicitly ask each user if they are interested in that topic. There are many more powerful applications being derived from the growing and glowing power of graphs. The graph nodes and edges can also incorporate properties called attributes or features. In a social network, a node

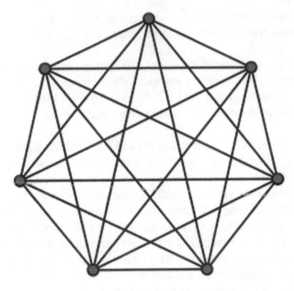

Figure 13.2   A complete graph

representing a person may have attributes for their age, salary, hobbies, and location. Similarly, an edge between two people nodes may have a date property establishing when the online relationship began. Other properties also can be attached to nodes and edges.

Graphs are also categorized as static or dynamic. Static graphs do not change with time but a dynamic graph changes its structure over time. That is, nodes and edges can be added and removed. As intricate real-life situations are being increasingly modeled using graphs, their evolution through time can be neatly captured with a dynamic graph. As we all know, social networks grow continuously with the addition and removal of new friends and peers (Facebook is a serious example). Social and professional networks are being exemplified as dynamic graphs.

A complete graph is the one in which each node is connected to all other nodes as vividly illustrated below (Figure 13.2).

In summary, these days, a lot of information is represented through graph structures. A graph consists of two main elements, nodes (vertices or points) and edges (links or lines) where the nodes are connected by edges. For example, in a chemical molecule that consists of multiple atoms, the atoms can be defined as nodes and the bond between atoms can be defined as edges. Another example is document citation networks. The nodes represent individual documents and each edge represents whether that document is cited by the other.

13.3   The challenges

Graphs are inherently complex but expressive. Non-uniformity is the main reason for graphs to be complicated in their structure and behavior. However, machine learning (ML) models on learning from graph-structured data are to leverage the additional features like the nodes' degree, their centrality, etc. to bring in deeper and decisive insights.

However, the graph structure is not straightforward for machine and deep learning (DL) algorithms. Neural networks (NNs) expect to receive their data in a uniform format. Convolutional NNs (CNNs) expect a grid that represents the different dimensions of the data they process (e.g., width, height, and color channels of images).

Graphs can come in different structures and sizes, which do not conform to the rectangular arrays that NNs expect. Graphs are "permutation invariant." That is, changing the order and position of nodes does not make any difference as long as their relations remain the same. In contrast, changing the order of pixels results in an altogether different image. To make graphs useful for various NNs, their input data must be transformed into a format that can be processed by an NN.

As described below, a graph can represent non-Euclidean data. That is, graphs are simply beyond any coordinate systems that we are accustomed to. This makes the interpretation of graph data a difficult process when compared with other well-known data types such as images, videos, and texts, which can be easily mapped to a 2D or 3D Euclidean space. Further on, a graph does not have a fixed form. There can be two graphs, which are structurally and visually different. But the two graphs can have the same adjacency matrix (if we don't consider the weight of edges).

Though graphs help to embed high-dimensional and highly related data to arrive at high-performance models for a variety of tasks, graphs can be exceedingly complex. Graphs are of arbitrary size and have complex topological structures. There is no fixed node ordering. Fortunately, there are statistical analysis methods and algorithms to assist and augment our ability to understand and reason from networks. Network models help in simulating the dispersion and cascade of information through a network due to its inherent relational structure. This gives tremendous and timely insights into how knowledge and information propagate across.

Why does data get structured as graphs?: Graphs are intrinsically excelling in providing a matured way of dealing with abstract concepts like relationships and interactions. They also natively assist in an easy and elegant visualization of these concepts. Graphs have gained the wherewithal to solve complicated problems through their inherent sophistications. They innately provide simpler representations for expressing, exchanging, and transforming problems.

Graph theory is now a matured and stabilized subject of study and research and there are a plethora of enabling tools, libraries, platforms, frameworks, and databases for deriving business and technical benefits out of graph representations of multi-structured data. With graph data structure gaining prominence and dominance across industry verticals, the aspect of graph data science is gaining momentum. Data scientists are increasingly representing a multitude of problems through multi-faceted and versatile graphs to immediately and immensely benefit. There are a variety of distinct advancements in the graph space such as KGs. In summary, for the AI era, graphs are bound to shine as an enabling technology.

13.4 ML algorithms

Undoubtedly, the flourishing field of ML is to play a key role in next-generation data analytics requirements. With more data getting generated, it becomes vital for collecting, cleaning, and crunching data from different data sources to facilitate knowledge discovery and dissemination. Extracting hidden insights out of growing data volumes in time is being viewed as the most important task for producing and sustaining sophisticated business workloads, premium IT services, domain-specific and agnostic expert and recommendation systems, cognitive applications such as natural language processing (NLP), and computer vision.

Considering its massive adoption, there are a number of enabling ML platforms, frameworks, libraries, applications, algorithms, and models. The ML research is fast expanding across. The number of research publications and white papers on ML is growing rapidly. ML experts, exponents, and evangelists meticulously focus on a variety of personal, professional, and social use cases for considerably boosting the leverage of ML capabilities across industry verticals.

The primary contribution of ML technologies and tools is to bring forth competent ML models for a variety of problems such as classification, regression, clustering, association, image recognition, object detection, and speech recognition. In short, prediction, inference, and conclusion/decision problems are artistically accomplished through ML models. Here is a formal definition from an ML expert. An ML model, a self-learning computer program, is to learn from experience E with respect to some task T and some performance measure P, if its performance on T, as measured by P, improves with experience E. This is the definition articulated by Tom Mitchell, Carnegie Mellon University.

So if you want your program/model to predict traffic patterns at a busy junction (this is a task), you can run the model with data about past traffic patterns (this is an experience E) and, if it has successfully "learned", it will then do better at predicting future traffic patterns (this is the performance measure P). Notably, ML solves problems that cannot be solved by numerical means alone. There are supervised, semi-supervised, unsupervised, and reinforcement ML types. Let us go a bit deeper into supervised learning.

Supervised ML: In the case of supervised ML applications, the ultimate goal is to develop a predictor function $h(x)$ (this is sometimes called the "hypothesis"). "Learning" consists of using sophisticated mathematical algorithms and statistical methods to iteratively optimize this function so that, given an input data x about a certain domain (say, square feet of a house), it will accurately predict some useful value $h(x)$ (say, market price for the house). Practically speaking, x always represents a series of data points. So, a housing-price predictor might take not only the total square feet ($x1$) of the house but also the number of bedrooms ($x2$), the house location ($x3$), an independent house ($x4$), and other decision-enabling attributes. The mathematical formula for a simple house-price predictor can be as follows:

$$h(x) = \theta_0 + \theta_1 x \tag{13.1}$$

where θ_0 and θ_1 are constants. The goal now is to find the perfect values of θ_0 and θ_1 to make the predictor work perfectly for newer sets of house data also.

Optimizing the predictor function $h(x)$ is being accomplished by using multiple training examples. For each training example, there is an input data value x and a known corresponding output, y. Now for each training experiment, we need to find the difference between the correct value and the predicted value. The training gives us an easy and quick way to measure the "wrongness or the weakness" of $h(x)$. We can then accordingly empower $h(x)$ by tweaking the values of θ_0 and θ_1 to minimize the error. The above example is technically a simple problem of univariate linear regression. However, consider a predictor that looks like this

$$h(x_1, x_2, x_3, x_4) = \theta_0 + \theta_1 x_1 + \theta_2 x_3^2 + \theta_3 x_3 x_4 + \theta_4 x_1^3 x_2^2 + \theta_5 x_2 x_3^4 x_4^2 \quad (13.2)$$

This function is a complicated one. Many modern ML problems take thousands or even millions of dimensions of data to build predictions using hundreds of coefficients. Fortunately, the iterative approach taken by ML systems is much more resilient in the face of such complexity.

Gradient descent for minimizing wrongness: As inscribed above, we need to make sure θ_0 and θ_1 are getting better with each step. The answer lies in measuring the wrongness. The wrongness measure is also known as the **cost or loss function** $J(\theta)$. The input θ represents all of the coefficients, which are being used in the predictor function. So θ is actually the pair θ_0 and θ_1. $J(\theta_0, \theta_1)$ gives a mathematical measurement of how wrong the predictor is when it uses the given values of θ_0 and θ_1. The cost function (θ_0, θ_1) computes an average penalty over all of the training examples. Thus, the goal is to find θ_0 and θ_1 for the predictor function $h(x)$ such that the cost function (θ_0, θ_1) is as minimum as possible. Consider the following plot of a cost function for an ML problem (Figure 13.3).

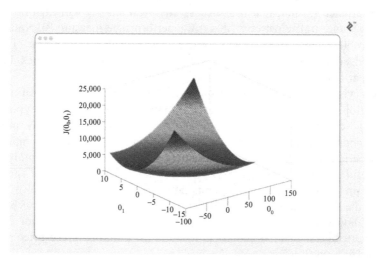

Figure 13.3   A cost function

The graph has a slight bowl to its shape. The bottom of the bowl represents the lowest cost, which the predictor can give us based on the given training data. The goal is to find the values of θ_0 and θ_1 corresponding to this point.

The solution approach is to take the gradient of (θ_0, θ_1), which is the pair of derivatives of $J(\theta_0, \theta_1)$ i (one over θ_0 and one over θ_1). The gradient will be different for every different value of θ_0 and θ_1, and tells us what the "slope of the hill is" and, in particular, "which way is down", for these particular θs. For example, when we plug our current values of θ into the gradient, it may tell us that adding a little to θ_0 and subtracting a little from θ_1 will take us in the direction of the cost function-valley floor. Therefore, we add a little to θ_0, and subtract a little from θ_1. After completing one round of learning, the updated predictor

$$h(x) = \theta_0 + \theta_1 x \tag{13.3}$$

will return better predictions than before. This process of calculating the current gradient and updating the θs from the results is known as gradient descent.

Classification problems in ML: Under supervised ML, two major subcategories are the following:

- **Regression ML systems:** Systems where the value being predicted falls somewhere on a continuous spectrum. These systems help with questions of "How much?" or "How many?"
- **Classification ML systems:** Systems for making a "yes or no" prediction, such as "Is this tumour cancerous?", "Does this cookie meet our quality standards?", and so on.

The major differences between classification and regression are the design of the predictor $h(x)$ and the design of the cost function $J(\theta)$. If the correct guess was 0 and we guessed 0, the cost function should not add any cost each time this happens. If the guess was right, but we were not completely confident (e.g. $y = 1$, but $h(x) = 0.8$), this should come with a very minimal cost, and if our guess was wrong but we were not completely confident (e.g. $y = 1$ but $h(x) = 0.3$), this should come with some significant cost, but not as if we were completely wrong. This behavior is captured by the following log function:

$$cost = \{-\log \log(h(x)) if \ y = 1 - \log \log(1 - h(x)) if \ y = 0 \tag{13.4}$$

Again, the cost function $J(\theta)$ gives us the average cost over all of the training examples. This illustrates how the predictor $h(x)$ and the cost function $J(\theta)$ differ between regression and classification problems but gradient descent still works the same.

More business and technical problems are being tried through the distinct power of ML. There are pioneering ML algorithms along with integrated platforms and frameworks for performing ML-based automated data analytics to derive predictive and prescriptive insights.

Unsupervised ML: The main aim of unsupervised ML is to find useful relationships within data. There are no training data sets. Instead, the system is innately empowered through a host of statistical methods to find usable patterns and cor-relations in a given data set. A good example is that Facebook, a leading social network application, uses this learning type to find closely knit friends based on certain criteria. Thus, in the ML world, supervised and unsupervised learning methods are contributing immensely to solving complex business problems.

13.5   DL algorithms

NNs are well suited to ML models where the number of inputs is literally mam-moth. DL algorithms are pitched as the appropriate ones for tackling large inputs. That is, deep NNs (DNNs) are doing yeomen services as competent DL models.

Perceptrons are a basic NN building block. If there are n points in the plane, labeled "0" and "1". We are given a new point and we want to guess its label. One approach is to look at the closest neighbor and return that point's label. But the best way is to pick a line that best separates the labeled data and use that as your classifier. In this case, each piece of input data would be represented as a vector $\mathbf{x} = (x\_1, x\_2)$ and the function would be something like "'0' if below the line, '1' if above". The separator can be defined by a vector of weights $\mathbf{w}$ and a vertical offset (or bias) b. Then, the predictor function would combine the inputs and weights with a weighted sum transfer function

$$f(x) = x \times w + b \tag{13.5}$$

The result of this transfer function would then be fed into an activation function to produce a labeling. In the example above, our activation function was a threshold cut-off (e.g., 1 if greater than some value)

$$h(x) = \{1: iff(x) = w \times x + b > 00: \textit{Otherwise} \tag{13.6}$$

The training of the perceptron consists of feeding it with ample training samples and calculating the output for each of them. After each sample, the weights w are adjusted in such a way so as to minimize the output error, defined as the difference between the desired (target) and the actual outputs. There are other error functions, like the mean square error, but the training process remains the same. The single perceptron approach to DL has one major drawback. It can only learn linearly separable functions. Thus, there is an insistence on multilayer perceptrons (feed-forward NN). That is, it is all about composing a bunch of single perceptrons together to create a more powerful multilayer perceptron for learning.

A feedforward NN is an artificial NN in which the connections between nodes do not form a cycle. The opposite of a feedforward NN is a recurrent NN (RNN), in which certain pathways are cycled. In the feedforward model, the data may pass through multiple hidden nodes, it always moves in one direction and never backwards. In this model, a series of inputs enter the layer and are multiplied by the weights. Each value is then added together to get a sum of the weighted input values. If the sum of the values is above a specific threshold, usually set at zero, the value produced is often 1, whereas if the sum falls below the threshold, the output value is -1.

Using a property known as the delta rule, the NN can compare the outputs of its nodes with the intended values. This allows the network to adjust its weights through training to produce more accurate output values. This process of training and learning produces a form of a gradient descent. In multi-layered perceptrons, the process of updating weights is defined as back-propagation. In such cases, each hidden layer within the network is adjusted according to the output values produced by the final layer.

If each of our perceptrons is only allowed to use a linear activation function, then the final output of the network will still be a linear function of the inputs. In other words, a linear composition of a bunch of linear functions is still just a linear function. If restricted to linear activation functions, then the feedforward NN is just another perceptron. The problem with the linear activation is that the gradient descent is constant. That is, during backpropagation, the rate of change of error is constant. The learning opportunities here are very few. Therefore, the non-linear functions are the widely used activation functions. It makes it easy for an NN model to adapt with a variety of data and to differentiate between the outcomes. The non-linear activation functions are mainly divided on the basis of their range or curves.

Sigmoid or logistic activation function: The sigmoid function curve (Figure 13.4) looks like an S-shape.

Sigmoid takes a real value as the input and outputs another value between 0 and 1. The sigmoid activation function translates the input range in $(-\infty, \infty)$ to the range in $(0,1)$. Therefore, it is especially used for models where we have to predict the probability as an output. The function is differentiable. That means, we can find the slope of the sigmoid curve at any two points. The softmax function is a more generalized logistic activation function which is used for multiclass classification.

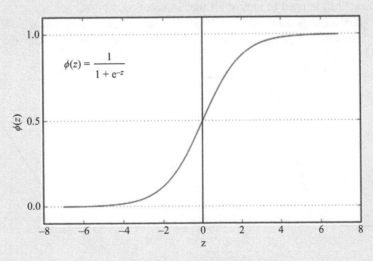

Figure 13.4   The sigmoid function curve

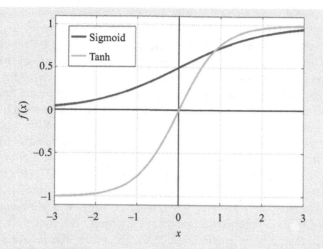

Figure 13.5   Hyperbolic tangent activation function

Tanh or hyperbolic tangent activation function (Figure 13.5): Tanh is also like a logistic sigmoid but it is better. Unlike a sigmoid function that will map input values between 0 and 1, the tanh will map values between −1 and 1. Similar to the sigmoid function, the derivative of tanh can be expressed in terms of the function itself.

The advantage is that the negative inputs will be mapped strongly negative and the zero inputs will be mapped near zero in the tanh graph. The tanh function is mainly used for classification between two classes. Both tanh and logistic sigmoid activation functions are used in feed-forward NNs.

Rectified linear unit (ReLU) activation function: The ReLU (Figure 13.6) is used in almost all the convolutional NNs.

The ReLU is half rectified (from bottom). $f(z)$ is zero when z is less than zero and $f(z)$ is equal to z when z is above or equal to zero. The range is

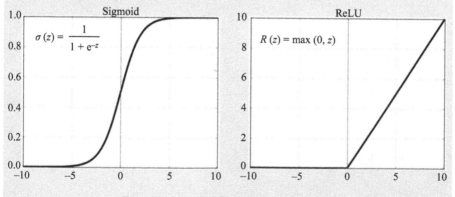

Figure 13.6   ReLU activation function

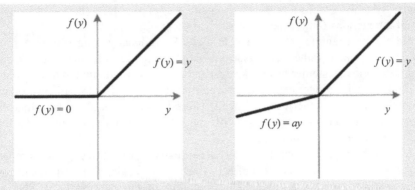

Figure 13.7   Leaky ReLU

[0 to infinity). The issue is that any negative input given to the ReLU activation function turns the value into zero immediately in the graph, which in turn affects the resulting graph by not mapping the negative values appropriately.

Leaky ReLU: This is an attempt to solve the dying ReLU problem. Figure 13.7 illustrates ReLU versus Leaky ReLU.

The leak helps to increase the range of the ReLU function. Usually, the value of **a** is 0.01 or so. When **a** is not 0.01, then it is called randomized ReLU. Therefore, the range of the Leaky ReLU is (−infinity to infinity). So most NNs use non-linear activation functions like the sigmoid, tanh, Softmax, ReLU, Leaky ReLU.

Thus, there are powerful ML/DL algorithms operating on Euclidean data to make accurate and timely predictions. There are transfer and activation functions. Further on, there are error or cost functions followed by gradient decent for bringing in the desired optimization. Precisely speaking, there are pioneering techniques and tips to enable machines to automatically learn from data. More details on ML algorithms and how to use them to bring forth predictive insights out of data heaps can be found on page https://www.toptal.com/machine-learning/machine-learning-theory-an-introductory-primer. Further on, here is a stimulating article on DL algorithms (https://www.toptal.com/machine-learning/an-introduction-to-deep-learning-from-perceptrons-to-deep-networks). With the surging popularity of ML and DL algorithms, producing, evaluating, optimizing, and transitioning them into network-accessible microservices, and deploying AI model microservices in IT environments are gaining speed and sagacity.

13.6   The emergence of GNNs

It is proven that the unique combination of graphical representation learning with the predictive power of DL models turns out to be a game-changer for the ensuing era of knowledge. Graphs emerge as a simple yet powerful tool to describe complex systems. Graphs represent a problem as a set of objects (nodes) along with a set of interactions (edges) between pairs of these objects.

Here is an example. The need is to classify products getting sold in a store. Typically, we would gather various details about the products (manufacturer name, place, date, price, customer feedback, etc.) and use them as an input to train a viable ML model. Each product can be represented as a node and each pair of products frequently bought together can be linked. There are other possibilities to link different products. Thus, a graph-based ML model supplies more intuitive and intimate information about the products.

Due to their extraordinarily powerful expressive capabilities, graphs are getting significant interest in the field of ML. Each node is paired with an embedding. This embedding establishes the node's location in the data space. GNNs are topologies of NNs that operate on graphs. A GNN architecture's primary goal is to learn an embedding that contains information about its neighborhood. We may use this embedding to tackle a variety of issues, including node labeling, node and edge prediction, and so on.

In other words, GNNs are a subclass of DL techniques that are specifically built to do inference on graph-based data. They are applied to graphs and are capable of performing prediction tasks at the node, edge, and graph levels.

13.7 Demystifying DNNs on graph data

In the recent past, NNs have gained a lot of minds and market shares and success. However, the early variants of NNs could only be implemented using Euclidean data. But a lot of data nowadays have underlying graph structures, which are non-Euclidean. Tasks such as face recognition, object detection, speech recognition, etc. are being increasingly accomplished through DL algorithms. DNN such as CNN and RNN are being leveraged to tackle such complex operations. DL is extremely good at capturing hidden patterns of Euclidean data (images, videos, and text).

But the challenge is how to approach applications where data is generated from non-Euclidean domains. Non-Euclidean data is usually represented as graphs with complex relationships and interdependencies between entities/objects. That's where GNNs come in. The most fundamental aspect of GNN is a graph and we have given a detailed account of graphs and its capabilities at the beginning of this chapter.

Graph data is naturally so complex and has therefore created a lot of challenges for classical ML and DL algorithms to consume and produce expert decisions. The reason is that conventional ML and DL algorithms are devised for receiving and processing simple and homogeneous data such as static and dynamic images, which carry the same structure and size. This is being thought of as fixed-size grid graphs. And text and speech are sequences and hence considered as line graphs.

GNNs can learn more and produce deeper decisions through the graph representation. The nodes can be represented as a table of user characteristics. In the node table, each row contains information about one entity (e.g., user, customer, bank transaction). The edges, the lines that connect the nodes, can be represented in the same way. Each row contains the IDs of the users and additional information such as date of friendship, type of relationship, etc. When this information is supplied to the NN, it can elegantly extract useful patterns and actionable insights, which is more valuable than the simple information contained in the individual components of the graph.

In a nutshell, a set of objects, places, people, and the connections between them is neatly and nicely describable through graphs. Most of the time, the input data for the classical ML algorithms is mainly structured or relational. Thus, the graph is being positioned and proclaimed as a supreme and sublime structure for clean and concise data representation. DNNs also receive and operate well on graph data structure. In the recent past, therefore, the aspect of GNNs gains a greater adoption for solving complicated business and social problems such as traffic prediction, fake news detection, modeling disease spread, physics simulations, etc.

GNNs are gaining the power to answer questions about individual as well as combined characteristics of these graphs. As articulated above, GNNs can be used at node, edge, and graph-level for accomplishing a variety of tasks including building next-generation networked systems.

The GNN receives the formatted graph data as an input and produces a vector of numerical values that represent relevant information about nodes and their relations. This vector representation is called "graph embedding". Embeddings are often used in ML to transform complicated information into a structure that can be leveraged and learned. For example, NLP systems use word embeddings to create numerical representations of words and their relations together.

When the graph data is passed to the GNN, the features of each node are combined with those of its neighboring nodes. This is called "message passing". If the GNN is composed of more than one layer, then subsequent layers repeat the message-passing operation, gathering data from neighbors of neighbors and aggregating them with the values obtained from the previous layer. For example, in a social network, the first layer of the GNN would combine the data of the user with those of their friends, and the next layer would add data from the friends of friends and so on. Finally, the output layer of the GNN produces the embedding, which is a vector representation of the node's data and its knowledge of other nodes in the graph.

The distinction of GNNs is that nodes are naturally defined by their neighbors and connections. That is, the neighbors of a node and all of the connections to its neighbors define the power of the node. We give every node a state (x) to represent its power. We can use the node state (x) to produce an output (o). The final state (x_n) of the node is normally called "node embedding". The task of a GNN is to determine the "node embedding" of each node, by looking at the information on its neighboring nodes. The combination of graph data and NNs has resulted in the advancement of GNNs. There are a few important variants such as graph convolutional networks (GCNs).

Translating graph into features for NNs: The brewing challenge how graphs can be shaped into features to be ingested into the NNs. To implement real-world GNNs, there is a need to represent the features as matrices. There are several matrices contributing to build a GNN.

- **Adjacency matrix (A)**: An adjacency matrix is an $N \times N$ matrix filled with either 0 or 1, where N is the total number of nodes. Adjacency matrices are able to represent the existence of edges that connect the node pairs through the value in the matrices. For example, if we have five nodes in our graph, then the shape of the matrix is [5, 5]. Matrix element A_{ij} is 1 if an edge exists between node i and j.

- **Node attributes matrix (X)**: This matrix (Figure 13.8) represents the features or attributes of each node. If there are N nodes and the size of node attributes is F, then the shape of this matrix is $N \times F$. In the example of the CORA dataset, we will have a corpus that contains words from all the documents. The node attributes would be bag-of-words that indicate the presence of a word in the document, while each document is represented by a node. In this case, F will represent the size of the corpus (the total number of unique words) while N is the total number of documents available.

- **Edge attributes matrix (E)**: Like nodes, edges can also have their own attributes. If the size of edge attributes is S and the number of edges available is n_edges, then the shape of this matrix is $n\_edges \times S$.

Graphs are becoming the new normal for representing complicated data points. In social networks, friend connections can be realized by a social graph. In speech

Document 1

Corpus: {i, like, hate, pizza, chicken, porridge}
Size of Corpus (F) = 6

"I like pizza".

	Document 1	Document 2
I	1	1
like	1	0
hate	0	1
pizza	1	0
chicken	0	1
porridge	0	1

Document 2

"I hate chicken porridge".

The shape of Node attributes matrix X is 2 x 6.

Figure 13.8   Node attributes matrix

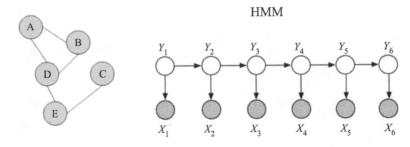

Figure 13.9   HMM

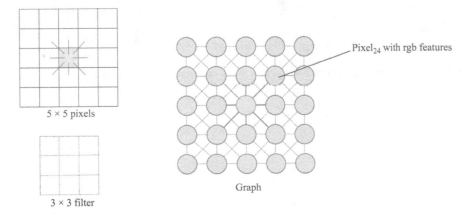

Figure 13.10   A CNN graph

recognition, the phoneme Y_i and the acoustic model x_i form a hidden Markov model (HMM) (this is a graph (Figure 13.9) for speech recognition).

Even on CNN, an input image can be modeled as a graph. For example, the right diagram (Figure 13.10) is the graph for a 5×5 image. Each node represents a pixel and for the case of a 3×3 filter, every node is connected to its eight immediate neighbors.

A large number of ML problems can be empowered to be efficient and effective when they are getting modeled by graph structures. When the relationships between neighboring nodes are irregular and multi-dimensional, there is a need to define them explicitly to arrive at efficient outputs. In CNN, we majorly work in a Euclidean space. But graphs can operate in non-Euclidean space. In general, NNs take an input x to predict z.

In a GCN, the input to the NN will be a graph (Figure 13.11). Also, instead of inferring a single z, it infers the value z_i for each node i in the graph. And to make predictions for Z_i, a GCN utilizes both X_i and its neighboring nodes in the calculation (Figure 13.12).

$$z = NN(x)$$

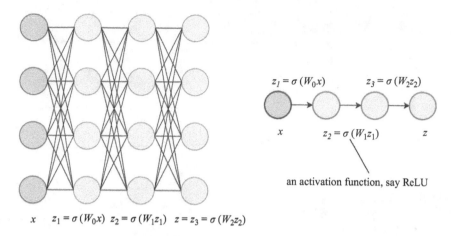

$$x \quad z_1 = \sigma(W_0 x) \quad z_2 = \sigma(W_1 z_1) \quad z = z_3 = \sigma(W_2 z_2)$$

This leads us to the important challenge of how an NN can process a graph directly

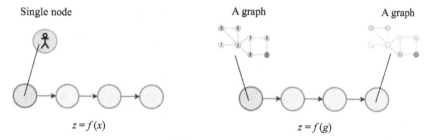

Figure 13.11   A CNN taking a graph as an input

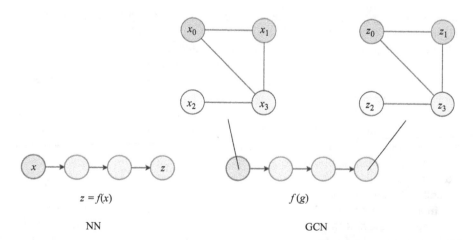

Figure 13.12   Comparing NN and GCN

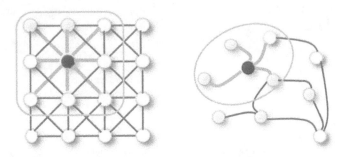

Figure 13.13   GCN is to apply convolution over a graph

The general idea of GCN is to apply convolution over a graph (Figure 13.13). Instead of having a 2D array as an input, GCN takes a graph as an input as vividly illustrated below.

The first diagram (the first row) below is the NN and the second diagram is the GCN with a graph containing four nodes as the input.

In the first NN, it contains multiple dense layers (fully connected layers). x is the input for the first layer and z_i is the output of layer i. For each layer, we multiply z (or x for the first layer) with the weight matrix W and pass the output to an activation function σ (ReLU). GCN is very similar, but the input to σ is $\hat{A}H^iW^i$ instead of $W_i z_i$, i.e. $\sigma(W_i z_i)$ versus $\sigma(\hat{A}H^iW^i)$ where z_i and H^i are the output vectors from the last hidden layer for NN and GCN, respectively. But W^i and W_i have different dimensions. And for the first layer in GCN, X contains an array of nodes instead of a single node x. X will be encoded as a matrix with each row containing the features of a node (Figure 13.14).

So what is $\hat{A}$? GCN introduces an adjacency matrix A. The element A_{ij} in A equals *1* if node i and j are connected. Otherwise, it will be zero. So $\hat{A}$ indicates the neighbors of a node. But we will make one more adjustment to indicate all nodes are self-connected. This indicates the output of a node in a hidden layer depends on itself and its neighbors. So, we convert all diagonal elements of A to 1 to form $\hat{A}$. Mathematically, $\hat{A}$ (Figure 13.15, equals $A + I$).

That comes to the output of the hidden layer to be $\sigma(\hat{A}H^iW^i)$. If we ignore W for a second, for each node in a hidden layer, $\hat{A}H^i$ sums up features on each node with its neighbors.

However, we may face the diminishing or exploding problem in an NN if we do not have certain control over the range of the hidden layer output. GCN wants $\hat{A}$ to be normalized to maintain the scale of the output feature vectors. One possibility is to multiple $\hat{A}$ with $\hat{D}^{-1}$, where $\hat{D}$ is the diagonal node degree matrix of $\hat{A}$ in measuring the degree of each node. At a high level, instead of summing up itself with its neighbor, multiplying the sum with the inverse $\hat{D}^{-1}$ sort of averages them. Specifically, $\hat{D}$ is a diagonal matrix with each diagonal element $\hat{D}_{ii}$ counts the number of edges for the corresponding node i. And the output for each hidden layer becomes $\sigma(\hat{D}^{-1}\hat{A}H^iW^i)$, instead of $\sigma(\hat{A}H^iW^i)$.

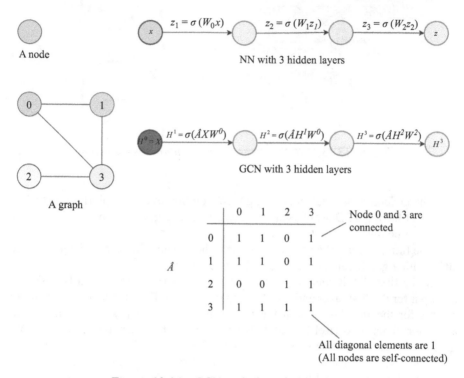

Figure 13.14   GCN with three hidden layers

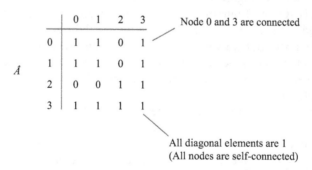

Figure 13.15   Converting all diagonal elements of A to 1 to form Â

Let us calculate $\hat{D}$ (Figure 13.16). For an undirected graph, the degree of a node is counted as the number of times an edge terminates at that node. So a self-loop will count twice. In our example, node 0 has 2 edges connecting to its neighbors plus a self-loop. Its degree equals 4 (i.e. 2 + 2). For node 3, its degree equals 5 (3 + 2).

A

	0	1	2	3
0	1	1	0	1
1	1	1	0	1
2	0	0	1	1
3	1	1	1	1

$\hat{D}$

	0	1	2	3
0	4	0	0	0
1	0	4	0	0
2	0	0	3	0
3	0	0	0	5

Figure 13.16   Transitioning from $\hat{A}$ to $\hat{D}$

$\hat{D}^{-1}$

	0	1	2	3
0	1/4	0	0	0
1	0	1/4	0	0
2	0	0	1/3	0
3	0	0	0	1/5

Figure 13.17   Finding the inverse of $\hat{D}$

And $\hat{D}^{-1}$ (Figure 13.17) equals.

In this example, it has three hidden layers and for each hidden layer, it computes its output as $\sigma(\hat{D}^{-1}\hat{A}H^{i}W^{i})$. The equation used to compute a hidden layer output from the last layer output is called the propagation rule.

Besides using $\sigma(\hat{D}^{-1}\hat{A}H^{i}W^{i})$, there are other choices. The propagation rule can be generalized as:

$$H^{(l+1)} = f(H^{(l)}, A) \tag{13.7}$$

Different choices of f result in different variants of the models. As per the research paper "Semi-Supervised Classification with Graph Convolutional

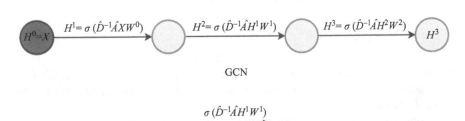

GCN

$$\overrightarrow{\sigma(\hat{D}^{-1}\hat{A}H^{1}W^{1})}$$

a layer-wise propagation rule

Networks," the following propagation rule is applied:

$$H^{(l+1)} = \sigma\left(\tilde{D}^{-\frac{1}{2}}\tilde{A}\tilde{D}^{-\frac{1}{2}}H^{(1)}W^{(1)}\right) \tag{13.8}$$

where

$$\tilde{A} = A + I_N \tag{13.9}$$

$$\tilde{D}_{ii} = \sum^{j} \tilde{A}_{ij} \tag{13.10}$$

Â and $\hat{D}^{-1}$ are calculated in the same way as before.

In the node classification problem setup, each node v is characterized by its feature x_v and associated with a ground-truth label t_v. Given a partially labeled graph G, the goal is to leverage these labeled nodes to predict the labels of the unlabeled. It learns to represent each node with a d-dimensional vector (state) h_v which contains the information of its neighborhood. Specifically,

$$h_v = f\left(X_v, X_{co[v]}, h_{ne[v]}, X_{ne[v]}\right) \tag{13.11}$$

where $x\_co[v]$ denotes the features of the edges connecting with v, $h\_ne[v]$ denotes the embedding of the neighboring nodes of v, and $x\_ne[v]$ denotes the features of the neighboring nodes of v. The function f is the transition function that projects these inputs onto a d-dimensional space. Since we are seeking a unique solution for h_v, we can apply Banach-fixed point theorem and rewrite the above equation as an iteratively update process. Such operation is often referred to as message passing or neighborhood aggregation.

$$H^{t+1} = F(H^t, X) \tag{13.12}$$

H and X denote the concatenation of all the h and x, respectively. The output of the GNN is computed by passing the state h_v as well as the feature x_v to an output function g:

$$o_v = g(h_v, X_v) \tag{13.13}$$

Both f and g here can be interpreted as feed-forward fully-connected NNs. The L1 loss can be straightforwardly formulated as the following:

$$loss = \sum_{i=1}^{p} (t_i - o_i) \tag{13.14}$$

which can be optimized via gradient descent. You can get more details on this from the paper titled as "Graph neural networks: A review of methods and applications" by Jie Zhoua and the team.

Convolution works well on images that are generally uniform grids. The process includes sliding the convolutional operator window across a 2D image and we compute some function over that sliding window. Then, we pass the learned function through many layers. The goal is to generalize the notion of convolution beyond these simple 2D lattices. The insight is that convolution takes a little sub-patch of the image (i.e., a little rectangular part of the image), applies a function to it, and produces a new part (a new pixel). The core concept behind convolutional NNs (CNNs) introduces hidden convolution and pooling layers to identify spatially localized features via a set of receptive fields in kernel form.

It is very difficult to perform CNN on graphs because of the arbitrary sizes of graphs. There are complex graphs without a fixed form and with a variable size of unordered nodes, which can have different amounts of neighbors.

GNNs are a class of DL methods designed to infer data described by graphs. GNNs provide an easy way to do node-level, edge-level, and graph level prediction tasks. GNNs can do what CNNs failed to do.

13.8   GNNs: the applications

Graph-structured data is prevalent these days. The following problems are being elegantly solved through GNNs.

- **Node classification:** The requirement here is to determine the labeling of samples (represented as nodes) by looking at the labels of their neighbors. Usually, a part of the graph is labeled.
- **Graph classification:** The task here is to classify the whole graph into different categories. The applications include determining whether a protein is an enzyme or not in bioinformatics, categorizing documents in NLP, doing social network analysis, etc.
- **Graph visualization:** This concerns the visual representation of graphs that reveal structures and anomalies that may be present in the data. This increases a deeper understanding of the graphs.
- **Link prediction:** This is to predict whether there is a connection between two entities.

GNNs in computer vision (CV): Through CNNs, machines can detect objects in images and videos. Still they do not have the power to gain the visual intuition of a human. That is, we do not know the relationships of the objects detected by a CNN-based object detector. But by employing GNN in CV, it is possible to model the relationships between objects. Then objects detected are fed into a GNN inference for relation prediction.

GNNs in CV generate images from graph descriptions. Traditionally images are generated from text using GAN or autoencoder. Instead of using text for image creation and description, graph-to-image generation provides more information on the semantic structures of the images. Thus, GNNs come in handy in scene graph generation models. The uniqueness of this model parses an image into a semantic graph that consists of objects and their semantic relationships. That is, given an image, scene graph generation models detect and recognize objects and predict semantic relationships between pairs of objects. The other famous applications include human–object interaction and few-shot image classification

GNNs in NLP: We know that the text is a type of sequential data and it can be ingested into an RNN or LSTM easily. However, graphs gain surging popularity in accomplishing NLP applications like text classification, exploiting semantics in machine translation, user geolocation, relation extraction, and question answering.

Text classification: GNNs shrewdly utilize the inter-relations of documents or words to infer document labels. GCN and GAT models first convert text to graph-of-words, and then use graph convolution operations to convolve the word graph. The graph-of-words representation of texts brings in the huge advantage of capturing non-consecutive and long-distance semantics.

Neural machine translation (NMT): Machine translation is the task of automatically converting source text in one language to text in another language. With DL, the aspect of neural machine translation has become the new normal to perform the translation task. Google Translate is a leading example of NMT. Typically massive datasets of translated sentences are used to train and produce a model capable of translating between any two languages. One established NMT version is the encoder decoder structure. This architecture is typically composed of two RNNs, which are used together in tandem to create a translation model. When this is coupled with the power of attention mechanisms, this architecture can guarantee impressive results.

The typical inputs to NMT systems are sentences in which words are represented as individual vectors in a word embedding space. This word embedding space does not show any connection among words within a sentence such as dependency or semantic role relationships. However, semantic information is essential to generate concise and appropriate translations in machine translation. The authors of this research paper "Improving Neural Machine Translation with AMR Semantic Graphs" have brought in the method of integrating abstract meaning representation (AMR) graphs (https:// amr.isi.edu) as additional semantic information into the current popular NMT systems such as Seq2Seq, ConvSeq2Seq, and Transformer. AMR graphs are rooted, labeled, directed, and acyclic graphs representing the entire content of a sentence. The point here is that the contributions of GNNs for machine translation are steadily growing.

GNNs in traffic forecasting: Traffic forecasting is an important ingredient for setting up and sustaining intelligent transportation systems (ITSs). Accurate traffic forecasting can guarantee better traffic management and alleviate traffic problems such as traffic congestion and pollution. Graphs can express traffic networks well and hence the flourishing graph model has more power to bring in a suite of innovations and disruptions in the field of traffic prediction. In the recent past, GNNs have become an emerging research issue for tackling the traffic forecasting problem. Specifically, one of the main types of GNNs is the spatial–temporal GNN (ST-GNN). This is being applied to various time-series forecasting applications. It is, therefore, logical to consider the traffic network as a spatial–temporal graph. In that graph, the nodes are sensors installed on roads and the edges represent the distance between pairs of nodes. And each node has the average traffic speed within a window as dynamic input features. There are several research publications clearly illustrating how GNNs can have a roller-coaster ride on traffic prediction.

GNNs in chemistry: Chemists can use GNNs to do advanced research on the graph structure of molecules or compounds. In these graphs, nodes are atoms, and edges are the chemical bonds. The other well-researched applications of GNNs include program verification, program reasoning, social influence prediction, recommender systems, electronic health records (EHR) modeling, brain networks, and adversarial attack prevention.

Another interesting use case is zero-shot learning (ZSL). This is all about trying to learn to classify a class given NO training samples of the target classes at all. If no training samples were given, we need to let the model "think" logically to recognize a target. For example, if we were given three images and told to find "okapi" among them. We may not have seen an "okapi" before. But if we were also given the information that an "okapi" is a deer-face animal with four legs and has zebra-striped skin, then it is quite easy for us to figure out which one is "okapi". There are methods for simulating this "thinking process" by converting the detected features into text. With traditional techniques, it is hard to model the relationships between the text descriptions. Graph representations aptly model these relationships.

Image classification is a basic computer vision task. Most of the models provide attractive results when given a huge training set of labeled classes. The focus is to make these models to perform well on zero-shot and few-shot learning tasks. As indicated above, GNN is the way forward. KGs can provide the necessary information to guide the ZSL task.

GNNs is an information-processing system that uses message passing among graph nodes. In recent years, GNN variants including graph attention network (GAT), GCN, and graph recurrent network (GRN) have shown revolutionary performance in computer vision applications using DL and artificial intelligence. These NN model extensions collect information in the form of graphs. GNN may be divided into three groups based on the challenges it solves: link prediction, node classification, graph classification. Machines can differentiate and recognize objects in image and video using standard CNNs.

Extensive amounts of research work need to be done before robots can have the same visual intuition as humans. GNN architectures, on the other hand, may be used to solve various image categorization and video challenges. The number of GNN applications in computer vision is not limited and continues to expand. Human–object interaction, active understanding, image categorization from a few shots and many more. In this paper, the use of GNN in image and video understanding, design aspects, architecture, applications, and implementation challenges towards computer vision is described. GNN is a strong tool for analyzing graph data and is still a relatively active area that needs further research attention to solve many computer vision applications.

13.9 The challenges for GNNs

From social science to biology, GNNs have been widely presented as the artistic way of learning from data. Researchers have indicated that graphs can facilitate the realization of robust and resilient AI models. However, building and sustaining GNNs to make sense out of graph data poses several theoretical and engineering challenges as articulated below.

- **Giant graphs—memory limitations**: Real-world networks can grow enormously in size. For example, Facebook has almost 3 billion active accounts. Each user is getting associated with a node in the graph. Each user is interacting with other users in a myriad of ways (liking, commenting, sharing, etc.). This results in billions of edges in the graph. Trying to train a GNN on such a colossal network consumes a lot of computational and storage resources. This is to waste a lot of precious energy and dissipate a large amount of heat into the fragile environment.
- **Sparse computations—hardware limitations**: Graphs are inherently sparse objects and GNNs have to leverage the sparsity for efficient and scalable computation. As we know that modern GPUs are designed to handle dense operations on matrices. Therefore, customized hardware accelerators for tackling sparse matrices could significantly boost the latency and scalability of GNNs.
- **Graph subsampling—reliability limitations**: The idea is to split large graphs into smaller subgraphs and train GNNs via the mini-batch gradient descent method. However, there is a catch. The datasets for ML are statistically independent. However, the relational structure of network data comes with a statistical dependence between samples. Thus, it is doubtful that the subgraphs retain the semantics of the full graph.

To surmount these issues, researchers are collaboratively working to unearth pioneering technologies and tools. A variety of methods are being circulated to overcome the above-mentioned challenges.

13.10   Conclusion

Connection-based data can be expressed and exposed as graphs. Graph structures are more complex than images (static and dynamic) and text due to the indisputable fact that connectivity happens at multiple levels. Graphs are innately completely irregular and unpredictable.

The roads to go from point A to point B constitute a graph. The links in a web page integrate the web page with several other web pages. This constitutes a graph. When your employer pays you, your payment goes through a graph of financial institutions. Graphs are touted as excellent tools to visualize relations between people, objects, and concepts. Lately, graphs emerge as a flexible and futuristic data source for ML models to be trained, refined, and deployed. DNNs are emerging as a transformative power center for a variety of business problems. DL models are being built and deployed in public, private, and edge cloud environments. There is a vast growth in the DL domain in the recent past. Primarily DL algorithms and models are meticulously applied to complicated tasks such as object identification and voice recognition through the use of techniques such as CNN, RNN, and autoencoders.

With data getting represented through highly efficient and effective graphs, GNNs are fast emerging and evolving to tackle some specific problems with all the alacrity and astuteness. Graph representation is expressive, visual, and extensible. GNNs can gain more through graphs. This chapter has detailed the nitty-gritty of GNNs and how GNNs can be artistically used to bring in robust and resilient solutions for a bevy of problems in the digital era.

Bibliography

[1] A. Madurkar, *Graph Learning with Python Part 1: Basics, Metrics, and Algorithms*, https://towardsdatascience.com/graph-machine-learning-with-python-pt-1-basics-metrics-and-algorithms-cc40972de113.

[2] *Challenges and Opportunities in Deep Reinforcement Learning with Graph Neural Networks: A Comprehensive Review of Algorithms and Applications*, https://arxiv.org/pdf/2206.07922.pdf.

[3] J. Hui, *Applications of Graph Neural Networks (GNN)*, https://jonathan-hui.medium.com/applications-of-graph-neural-networks-gnn-d487fd5ed17d.

[4] A. Menzli, *Graph Neural Network and Some of GNN Applications: Everything You Need to Know*, https://neptune.ai/blog/graph-neural-network-and-some-of-gnn-applications.

[5] I. Mayachita, *Understanding Graph Convolutional Networks for Node Classification*, https://towardsdatascience.com/understanding-graph-convolutional-networks-for-node-classification-a2bfdb7aba7b.

[6] P. Sharma, *What Are Graph Neural Networks, and How Do They Work?*, https://www.analyticsvidhya.com/blog/2022/03/what-are-graph-neural-networks-and-how-do-they-work/.

[7] *A Gentle Introduction to Graph Neural Networks*, https://distill.pub/2021/gnn-intro/.

Chapter 14

AI applications—computer vision and natural language processing

J. Granty Regina Elwin[1] and Vijayalakshmi Karunakaran[2]

Computer vision is a field of study that focuses on enabling computers to interpret and understand visual information from the world around us. Artificial intelligence (AI) has revolutionized computer vision by providing algorithms and models that can process, analyze, and classify images and videos. AI applications in computer vision have many real-world applications, including in healthcare, transportation, entertainment, and security. Some of the popular AI applications in computer vision include object detection and recognition, image segmentation, image restoration, pose estimation, scene understanding, augmented reality (AR), medical imaging, etc.

14.1 Object recognition

Object recognition has a wide range of applications across various fields, including computer vision, robotics, autonomous vehicles, healthcare, security, and entertainment. Object recognition is a critical component of computer vision. It helps in image and video processing by automatically identifying and labeling objects in an image or video. This technology is used in image and video search, face recognition, and tracking. Object recognition is used in robotics to enable robots to identify and locate objects in their environment. This technology is used in manufacturing, logistics, and agriculture to automate the picking and placing of objects. Object recognition is essential for the development of self-driving cars. It helps the car to recognize road signs, pedestrians, and other vehicles on the road, allowing it to make informed decisions about how to navigate the road safely. Object recognition is used in medical imaging to identify and diagnose medical conditions. For example, it can help detect tumors, lesions, and other abnormalities in medical images such as X-rays and MRIs. Object recognition is used in security systems to identify and track people and objects. This technology is used in surveillance

[1]Department of Information Technology, Sri Krishna College of Engineering and Technology, Coimbatore, India
[2]ABEAM Analytics PTE Ltd, Singapore

systems to identify potential threats and in biometric systems to verify the identity of individuals. Object recognition is used in the entertainment industry for various purposes, such as in gaming, virtual reality, and AR. It can help create realistic virtual environments and enable players to interact with virtual objects. Overall, object recognition has numerous applications in various fields, and it is a rapidly evolving technology that is opening up new possibilities and opportunities for innovation.

There are two main types of object recognition: static and dynamic. Static object recognition is the ability to identify an object that is not moving. Dynamic object recognition is the ability to identify an object that is moving.

Static object recognition in computer vision is the process of identifying and categorizing objects within a still image or a video frame. This process involves extracting features from the image or frame, analyzing them, and then matching them with a set of pre-defined object categories. Static object recognition is relatively easier when compared to dynamic object recognition. As an illustration, in the case of recognizing a car, the computer only has to take into account the car's physical structure. However, for identifying a person, the computer has to consider various factors such as the person's physical shape, motion, and facial expressions.

Dynamic object recognition identifies objects in a changing or dynamic environment, where objects may move, change position or orientation, or interact with each other. This requires real-time analysis of video frames, tracking objects, and detecting changes in their appearance and motion over time. In contrast, static object recognition involves identifying objects in a static or fixed environment, where objects are stationary and their appearance does not change over time. The main difference between dynamic and static object recognition is the level of complexity involved. Dynamic object recognition requires more sophisticated algorithms and techniques to handle the changing nature of the environment, while static object recognition is relatively simpler and can be accomplished using traditional computer vision techniques. However, dynamic object recognition has wider applications in fields such as surveillance, robotics, and autonomous vehicles, where real-time identification and tracking of objects are crucial.

The ability to identify objects based on their physical appearance, including recognizing familiar objects and identifying unfamiliar ones is referred to as object recognition. This cognitive process is crucial in trivial everyday activities, such as recognizing a friend in a crowded room. There exist various theories regarding how object recognition works, such as the mental template or prototype theory, which suggests that we have an idea of what an object should look like, and we compare it to the actual object to recognize it. Alternatively, the feature extraction theory suggests that we pick out certain important features of an object to recognize it. Nonetheless, object recognition plays a vital role in allowing us to interact with our environment and comprehend the world around us.

This task of object recognition which seemingly is simple and intuitive to us, humans is not so easy for the computer. To identify and classify objects in an image, a computer requires an understanding of the 3D structure of an object and its appearance from different angles. Thanks to recent progress in machine learning (ML), computers are now capable of achieving remarkable results in object recognition. This technology finds numerous applications, including security (e.g., identifying intruders or stolen items), self-driving vehicles (e.g., recognizing pedestrians or other cars), and retail (e.g., identifying products on store shelves). With object recognition systems becoming increasingly accurate, these applications are becoming more reliable and efficient.

To give more insight into how this technology works in real life, this section presents a list of the most interesting object detection applications.

14.2   AI-powered video analytics

AI-powered video analytics is a technology that uses AI algorithms and ML techniques to analyze video footage automatically. This technology enables computers to interpret visual data, identify objects and people, recognize patterns, and even detect anomalies or potential threats in real-time. Some of the applications of AI-powered video analytics include surveillance and security systems, traffic management, crowd monitoring, and retail analytics. By automating video analysis, this technology can save time and resources, reduce human error, and improve the accuracy and efficiency of video monitoring and analysis. Retail stores use this technology to monitor customer movement in large spaces and detect potential shoplifting incidents. This impressive technology allows stores to make changes in real-time and collect data on customer behavior over extended periods. Predicting and addressing unexpected threats has always been a challenge in creating safe environments. In the past, human workers were unable to monitor, process, and provide solutions in a short time frame. However, with video analytics, a space can be quickly scanned and potential problems can be detected within minutes, enabling timely action.

14.3   Contactless payments

Object recognition can be used in contactless payments to identify objects such as smartphones and payment cards, enabling transactions to occur without the need for physical contact between the device and the payment terminal. This technology allows for faster and more convenient transactions, as customers can simply wave their device or card near the terminal to initiate a payment. Object recognition in contactless payments relies on ML algorithms that can identify and authenticate the object being used for payment. This technology has become increasingly popular in recent years due to the growing demand for faster, safer, and more convenient payment options. In addition to object recognition, AI plays a critical role in contactless payments by enabling ML algorithms to analyze transaction patterns and detect potential fraud or security risks. By analyzing large volumes of data, AI can identify patterns and anomalies that may indicate fraudulent activity, such as unusual transaction amounts or suspicious transaction locations. This enables banks and payment providers to quickly detect and prevent fraud, improving the security and reliability of contactless payments. AI-powered chatbots and virtual assistants can also provide customer support and personalized recommendations, enhancing the overall user experience. As contactless payments continue to grow in popularity, AI will play an increasingly vital role in ensuring their security, reliability, and convenience.

Object recognition is a crucial component of fully automated checkout systems, which rely on computer vision technology to recognize and track the items being purchased by a customer. By using object recognition algorithms and ML techniques, these systems can quickly and accurately identify products, calculate their prices, and add them to the customer's bill. This technology enables customers to scan and pay for their purchases without the need for human interaction, reducing wait times and improving the shopping experience. Object recognition in automated checkout systems also reduces the risk of errors and theft, as the technology can detect discrepancies between the scanned item and its actual price or weight. As the demand for contactless and self-service shopping options continues to grow, object recognition technology in fully automated checkout systems is becoming increasingly important in the retail industry [1].

14.4   Foot tracking

Object recognition can be used in foot tracking to identify and track the movement of people's feet. This technology enables real-time monitoring and analysis of foot traffic in different locations, such as retail stores, airports, and public spaces. By using ML algorithms and computer vision technology, foot tracking systems can detect and identify individuals based on the unique patterns of their foot movements, and analyze their behavior to provide insights into their preferences, interests, and demographics. Foot tracking can also be used to optimize store layout and improve customer experience, by analyzing foot traffic patterns and identifying areas of high or low customer engagement. Additionally, foot tracking can be used in security applications, such as identifying and tracking suspicious individuals in crowded areas or detecting anomalies in foot traffic patterns. Foot tracking can be used to monitor foot traffic in stores, track customer behavior, and optimize store layout for better customer flow and engagement. As object recognition technology continues to advance, foot tracking is becoming an increasingly valuable tool for analyzing and understanding human behavior in different environments. In addition to its application in the Retail industry, foot tracking proves to be advantageous in various fields. Advertising: Foot tracking can be used to analyze customer demographics and interests, which can help advertisers tailor their campaigns to specific target audiences. In healthcare, foot tracking can be used to analyze gait patterns and detect abnormalities or injuries, which can aid in the diagnosis and treatment of certain conditions. In the sports industry, foot tracking can be used to monitor and analyze athlete performance, including running speed, foot placement, and gait analysis. Foot tracking can be used to monitor crowded areas and detect suspicious behavior, as well as monitor and control access to certain areas. In the field of transportation, foot tracking can be used to analyze and optimize traffic flow in busy areas, such as airports and train stations, to improve passenger experience and reduce congestion.

14.5   Animal detection

Object recognition is employed in animal detection to identify and track different species of animals in various environments. This technology relies on computer vision and ML algorithms to analyze images and videos and detect animals based on their unique visual features, such as color, shape, and texture. Object recognition in animal detection has many applications, including wildlife conservation, agriculture, and monitoring of invasive species. In wildlife conservation, object recognition technology can be used to monitor endangered species and track their movements in their natural habitats. This information can be used to understand their behavior, population dynamics, and habitat requirements, which can aid in conservation efforts. In agriculture, object recognition can be used to identify pests and diseases affecting crops and livestock, allowing farmers to take appropriate measures to mitigate damage and protect their yield. It can also be used to track the movements of livestock and monitor their health and well-being. In monitoring invasive species, object recognition technology can help detect and track the spread of invasive species, allowing for more effective management and control of these species. Object recognition in animal detection has the potential to greatly enhance our understanding and management of animal populations in various environments, and it can play an important role in conservation, agriculture, and wildlife management.

14.6   Airport facial recognition

Every time you visit an airport there seems to be a new technology that has been integrated into the check-in experience. Although it might seem like a hassle to have your face searched by a computer. It can save you time and make your trip more enjoyable. There are two reasons that airports have decided to use object detection software during departures. The first reason is that customers can go through check-in quickly. Another reason for facial recognition in airports is that it creates a safe and more secure environment for customers. This technology allows you to scan people's documents and research the data on border control agencies. A human would spend double the amount of time doing the same task if it was not for object detection.

14.7   Autonomous driving

Autonomous cars, which are designed to operate without human intervention, depend heavily on object recognition in addition to other technologies. In order for autonomous vehicles to navigate safely and effectively, they must be able to detect and recognize objects in their surroundings, including other vehicles, pedestrians, traffic signals, road signs, and obstacles. Object recognition technology in autonomous cars relies on a combination of sensors, including cameras, radar, lidar, and ultrasonic sensors, which provide the vehicle with a 360-degree view of its surroundings. Computer vision and ML algorithms analyze the data from these sensors in real-time to detect and identify objects, and the car's control system uses this information to make decisions about navigation, speed, and braking.

By using object recognition technology, autonomous cars can anticipate and respond to potential hazards more quickly and accurately than human drivers. This has the potential to greatly reduce the number of accidents on the road, as well as increase the efficiency of transportation systems. Object recognition in this field has the potential to revolutionize the way we think about transportation and mobility in the future.

14.8   Video surveillance

Object recognition in video surveillance is a common application of AI. AI algorithms can be trained to detect and recognize objects, people, and events in surveillance footage in real-time, which can help improve the efficiency and effectiveness of video surveillance systems. Various AI techniques are used for object recognition in video surveillance. Deep learning is a subset of ML that uses neural networks to learn and recognize objects in surveillance footage. Convolutional neural networks (CNNs) are a type of deep learning algorithm that is particularly well-suited for image and video recognition. They can be trained to recognize patterns and features in video frames and identify specific objects. Motion detection is a simple technique that involves detecting changes in pixel intensity over time. It can be used to detect moving objects in a video frame, which can then be classified using object recognition techniques. Intervention of AI for object recognition in video surveillance can help automate the process of monitoring and analyzing video footage, making it easier for security personnel to identify and respond to potential threats in real-time.

14.9   Healthcare medical detection

AI for object detection in the medical industry has the potential to improve diagnosis, treatment, and patient outcomes. Object detection algorithms can be trained to recognize specific objects or patterns in medical images, such as X-rays, CT scans, and MRIs. With the advent of AI, computer vision has made huge inroads in healthcare, with applications ranging from medical imaging analysis to patient monitoring. Computer vision algorithms can be used to analyze medical images such as X-rays, CT scans, and MRIs. These algorithms can help detect abnormalities and assist radiologists in making accurate diagnoses. Computer vision can assist surgeons in performing procedures by providing real-time feedback and guidance. For example, it can help surgeons locate tumors or other structures during minimally invasive surgeries. Computer vision can be used to detect and monitor certain diseases, such as skin cancer, by analyzing images of skin lesions. Computer vision can be used to monitor patients in hospitals or other healthcare settings, such as nursing homes, by analyzing video footage. For example, it can detect falls or other incidents and alert healthcare providers. Computer vision can be used to analyze large datasets of molecular structures and predict how certain compounds will interact with each other. This can help researchers identify new drugs and develop more effective treatments. AI algorithms can be trained to recognize patterns and markers associated with specific diseases, such as Alzheimer's, Parkinson's, and multiple sclerosis. Identifying and labeling specific anatomical structures in medical images, such as organs, bones, and blood vessels has been made possible through AI powered. This can help physicians and surgeons plan and execute procedures with greater precision and accuracy. This can help improve the accuracy of diagnosis and enable earlier intervention and treatment.

AI-enabled computer vision continues to transform healthcare by improving diagnosis accuracy, reducing the risk of errors, and enabling more personalized care.

Some common applications of AI for object detection in the medical industry include:

Tumor detection: AI algorithms can be trained to recognize and locate tumors in medical images. This can help radiologists and oncologists detect cancerous growths at an early stage and develop appropriate treatment plans.

Diagnosis of diseases: AI algorithms can be trained to recognize patterns and markers associated with specific diseases, such as Alzheimer's, Parkinson's, and multiple sclerosis. This can help improve the accuracy of diagnosis and enable earlier intervention and treatment.

Identification of anatomical structures: AI algorithms can be trained to identify and label specific anatomical structures in medical images, such as organs, bones, and blood vessels. This can help physicians and surgeons plan and execute procedures with greater precision and accuracy.

Detection of abnormalities: AI algorithms can be trained to identify abnormalities in medical images that may be missed by human observers. For example, AI can be used to detect lung nodules in chest X-rays that may be indicative of lung cancer.

14.10   Computer vision in agriculture

The application of computer vision to agriculture is growing [2]. The total performance of the agricultural sector has been enhanced by computer vision, from increased productivity to decreased production costs with automation. With its automation and detection skills, computer vision has begun to establish a firm presence in the agricultural industry. The computer vision-AI models have made several contributions to the agricultural business in areas like planting, harvesting, advanced weather analysis, weeding, and plant health detection and monitoring. The following are a few of the most significant contributions of the present.

14.10.1   Drone-based crop monitoring

The market share that drone technology has recently amassed is largely attributable to its capacity for autonomous flight. The use of drones in agricultural and precision agriculture has become crucial. Drones are aircraft that have a built-in camera and can fly, allowing them to collect enormous amounts of data. The computer vision-enabled camera may be trained to identify the soil conditions using its geo-sensing capabilities, as well as to identify unfavorable conditions, crop health information, and aerial views of the complete farming land. Techniques for locating and recognizing a certain object include semantic segmentation and picture annotations.

14.10.2   Yield analysis

Crop yield analysis uses a combination of deep learning approaches to create cutting-edge computational models. Drone-collected data, satellite photos, vital data on soil elements, moisture levels, and meteorological conditions are input into smart systems that have been taught to handle massive amounts of complex data. The results of such a study enable us to make crucial predictions in advance. Such a strategy is useful for managing people and being ready for unforeseen natural disturbances.

14.10.3   Smart systems for crop grading and sorting

Farming has a significant demand for computer vision machines driven by AI. Farming has benefited from the ability to automate tedious and time-consuming processes like separating the right from the wrong crops and identifying which ones are best for shipping. As smart systems can determine the longevity of the crops and the prevalence of viruses in the crops, resulting in less agricultural loss, it is evolving into a crucial component. The quality of the fruits and vegetables is rated to determine which batches of the product should be transported first and which ones may sustain for a longer period of time and can be shipped to distant locations.

14.10.4   Automated pesticide spraying

Spraying pesticides on crops is a frequent technique in agriculture. Equipment and drones that use computer vision are becoming more and more popular. These devices can keep an eye on the crop, spot diseased areas, and spray the necessary amount of pesticide. Because of these contributions, the workforce is now healthy and not exposed to any pesticides through breathing.

14.10.5   Phenotyping

In today's world, phenotyping is widely used to discover agricultural features for precision farming. Phenotyping is now a productive strategy thanks to sophisticated computer vision algorithms. To remove unnecessary crop data or information from the photos and retain only the pertinent information on precise measurements, computer vision algorithms are integrated with image processing characteristics.

Techniques like depth estimation, color enhancement, segmenting the region of interest, and identifying the region of interest are possibilities for producing trust-worthy results for future analysis with the collected data. The crop breeds have been greatly enhanced by this information.

14.10.6 Forest information

Computer vision-enabled drones and smart systems with aerial capabilities have made it possible to collect data about trees that are dispersed over a large area of land. The following probable detection-based activities include tree detection, tree classification and kind, stem analysis data, yield estimation, tree health, unused land, farming land borders, and drainage data.

14.11 Computer vision in transportation

AI-based computer vision is currently having a significant impact on how the authorities manage traffic laws. Computer vision technology is having a significant impact on the construction of secure transportation facilities by detecting violations of laws including following speed limits, stopping at stops, and wearing safety equipment like helmets and seatbelts. Following are a few of the key applications of computer vision in transportation systems.

14.11.1 Safety and driver assistance

According to a CDC survey, 1.35 million people are injured or killed in car accidents each year. There are numerous elements that contribute to these accidents. Some of these include mechanical difficulties, poor visibility, inattentiveness, and tired drivers. Sensors with data receptors are put in numerous locations across the world, particularly in smart cities. These sensors with cameras powered by computer vision are placed at major intersections and other highways. By keeping an eye on and supplying data on the distances between vehicles, pedestrians, and stationary objects on the road, these cameras aid in the regulation of safety measures. The motorist receives this information and can subsequently select a safer path. Municipalities and other public entities can also use the visual data gathered by the computer vision models. Visual data sensors can also prevent collisions by recognizing road signs, obstructions, and other information. Computer vision tools will assist agencies in tracking the routes with the most travelers. As a result, fuel and vehicle usage in public transportation can be managed.

14.11.2 Traffic control

A smart city's transportation system is influenced by its ease of mobility. For instance, it could be challenging for an ambulance or an emergency vehicle to get through if a patient needs to be transported swiftly to the hospital and must travel via some of the city's key intersections. In this case, traffic monitoring and communication are provided by smart transportation solutions driven by computer vision and IoT network devices. These devices can tell the drivers which lane to use for a simple commute to get there more quickly. Data receptors can be put on cars for this use. It is also possible to use mobile applications that support computer vision-based smart transportation. On roads and in automobiles, applications based on IoT and computer vision are also present. The driver of the vehicle and the traffic police will both be notified if it is discovered that the speed limit has been exceeded. To determine vehicle proximity and anticipated traffic density of a specific location, computer vision algorithms are also included in GPS, GIS, and radio-frequency sensors.

14.11.3   Driving autonomous vehicles

Several motor manufacturing businesses now live by the motto of driverless cars. These vehicles use computer vision in addition to a variety of other technologies to function. These automated driving systems, in contrast to manual driving, correct human errors and prioritize mobility, occupant and pedestrian safety, and fuel-related considerations. Even in limited visibility, the smart cameras placed in these vehicles will let the automobile locate various obstacles in front of it. For 3D mapping and decision-making about the route, driving speed, and parking, they rely on computer vision. By leveraging embedded technologies, two autonomous vehicles traveling along on the same course might anticipate a collision and decide whether to turn around. AI and computer vision are two key technologies for creating a reliable transportation network. Incorporating AI-based technology for infrastructure facilities will be an act of good governance as it values the wellbeing of the citizens given the rise in security concerns around transportation.

14.12   Computer vision in healthcare

The growth of AI has already had significant positive effects on the healthcare sector. The use of computer vision in healthcare is now advancing quickly to provide life-saving interventions. Doctors are able to diagnose their patients' illnesses more quickly and in the early stages. This makes it feasible for them to recommend the best course of action and keep track of the disease's development.

It aids in saving doctors valuable time that would otherwise be spent determining the condition based on the different symptoms. Computer vision is becoming more prevalent in a variety of fields. They include things like health monitoring, medical image analysis, and predictive analysis. The interpretation of photos and videos is a focus of computer vision. Among the tasks involved include segmentation, object recognition, and image categorization. Medical imaging can benefit greatly from recent developments in image categorization and object recognition. Numerous studies in pathology, radiology, and dermatology have produced positive results for difficult medical diagnostic tasks.

14.13   Benefits of computer vision in healthcare

14.13.1   Reliable image analysis

Medical image analysis calls for quick and precise analysis. Computer vision succeeds on both counts since it can identify patterns that aid in the earlier diagnosis of diseases by doctors. In healthcare, computer vision also limits the potential for human error. By analyzing mammograms, AI-based visual systems are skilled at detecting breast cancer. They also allow for quick analysis, which is essential for spotting diseases early.

14.13.2   Contemporary operating rooms

Systems for keeping an electronic health record (EHR) can be laborious, particularly when recording surgical operations. It necessitates a lot of human input, which frequently results in mistakes and delays. Computer vision solves this issue by automating the observation and recording of the entire process. By using this technology, medical professionals can do away with tedious manual labor and devote more time to patient care.

14.13.3   Improved patient identification

Healthcare institutions frequently see instances of patent identity errors. Although the majority of these cases are typically detected early, they nevertheless present a risk. Patients who receive the incorrect care and medications if it is not identified could die. Their health may deteriorate, and it may cause additional problems. Additionally, these mistakes may result in hospitals facing millions-dollar legal damage claims and a resulting loss of reputation. In healthcare, computer vision aids in overcoming all of these issues.

14.13.4   Faster medical research

Computer vision accelerates the process. As a result, diseases can be found by researchers considerably more quickly. To achieve good results, they can then better formulate medical treatments.

14.14   Computer vision in manufacturing

Over the past ten years, computer vision has become the most widely used technology, particularly in the industrial sector. The benefits of computer vision-enabled manufacturing include a decrease in production errors, an increase in product quality, a greater operational flexibility, a reduction in time and expense, and increased productivity. Some of the most effective computer vision application cases in the manufacturing industries are given below:

14.15   Predictive maintenance

The functioning of manufacturing organizations will be impacted by frequent or unexpected equipment failures. It interferes with manufacturing and has an effect on total sales results. IoT technology combined with AI and ML-powered predictive maintenance systems will track the operation of machinery, forecast device faults, and determine when overhaul services are required. The best applications of computer vision in manufacturing enable the producer to increase equipment lifetime and decrease performance.

14.16   Reading text and barcodes

It is a well-liked use of computer vision in the manufacturing sector. It is not always simple to recognize and understand text and barcodes. Modernized AI, ML, and computer vision-powered systems and apps are being used in "smart factories" to tackle this issue and signal "go" for industrial automation.

14.17   Inventory management

Computer vision systems may assist with stock counting, inventory management in warehouses, and automating and alerting managers if any manufacturing-related item is not in sufficient supply. When counting stock, computer vision technologies can reduce human error. It is challenging to locate merchandise in large warehouses. These systems can assist inventory managers in finding items in the warehouse using a computer vision system based on barcode data.

14.18   Defects reduction

Only a few machine vision inspection systems require the aid of the operator, but the majority of cutting-edge computer vision solutions do not. A surface inspection system called "WebSpecter" is used by Shelton, a renowned manufacturer in the United States, to find defects, save images, and record image-related metadata. Defects are graded and categorized according to their category when products enter the product line. The manufacturers will be able to discriminate between various fault kinds as a result, and only when faults are present do X numbers of Y types wish to stop the manufacturing line.

14.19   3D vision inspection

Several laser displacement sensors or cameras are typically used in 3D machine vision systems. The robot receives orientation information from two or more cameras that are mounted at various locations thanks to multiple camera 3D vision applications. On the production line, a computer vision inspection system was installed to look for tiny connector pins. Locating these pins is quite challenging for manual inspectors. The car owner and manufacturer are notified of the catastrophe if the faulty connection pin continues through the production cycle.

14.20   Computer vision in retail

Retailers may increase consumer loyalty by providing a better in-store experience using computer vision. By looking at client purchasing patterns, it can hasten the purchasing process. The arrangement of store shelves may be optimized using the data obtained by computer vision to speed up purchases. It is also a good option for enhancing in-store self-service and can deter theft and fraud. Faster than current equipment, automated visual inspection put in the aisles and at the register will catch shoplifters.

Some of the most effective computer vision application cases in the retail industry are given below.

14.21   Virtual mirrors and recommendation engines

Virtual mirrors in retail might be the next step in enhancing consumer experience and personalization. A regular mirror with a display mounted behind the glass is referred to as a virtual mirror. Virtual mirrors using computer vision cameras and AR may display a variety of contextual data that improve client engagement with the company. For instance, if someone puts on a hat in the dressing room, the virtual mirror will detect the hat and suggest a purse, jewelry, accessories, and other things that will go well with it.

14.22   Self-checkout

An increase in the usage of computer vision systems for automated checkout systems in retail outlets is also a result of the trend towards customer service automation. Computer vision systems enable in-store cameras and sensors to track products, shelves, and customers with accuracy. Upon leaving the store, the consumer is immediately charged for the marked items by the system based on CV and AI.

14.23   Inventory management

Computer vision is being used to improve efficiency in omnichannel retail systems. Smart cameras and sensor systems are used to track inventory levels and products on shelves in real-time. For example, Sam's Club, an American retail company, is using inventory scanning robots to track and share information on inventory levels, price accuracy, product location, etc.

14.24   Retail theft prevention

Computer vision systems also help in preventing shoplifting by tracking each product and the customer's behavior. For example, Vaak Eye is a shoplifting prevention system based on computer vision and is installed with retail store cameras. The system observes customer behavior to identify potential shoplifting activities. Walmart is also using AI-enabled surveillance cameras to eliminate shoplifting from their stores.

14.25   In-store advertisement

Computer vision in retail can also be used to identify certain customers when they enter the store and send them special discounts. They can also get recommendations on what to buy, depending on their purchase history.

14.26   Computer vision in sports

For decades, sports coaches have employed data science to enhance the performance of their teams. Sports analytics empowers coaches to make significant judgments with more assurance, while big data aids in real-time, split-second decisions. Every sport is benefiting from the use of computer vision, which also helps referees make the proper calls and enhances training sessions. Some of the most effective computer vision application cases in the sports industries are given below.

14.27   Detection of rule violations using computer vision in sports

Computer vision is also being used to assist in the discovery of rule violations in sports. For instance, FIFA (the football association) uses the Video Assistant Referee (VAR) system, a computer system, to assist officials in making decisions concerning contentious or game-changing occurrences. To assist referees in determining whether a goal has been scored, if a foul has been committed, or whether an offside has happened, this method uses video footage from the game. The precision of this method is far higher than the human eyes.

14.28   Object detection and ball tracking

Sports equipment is identified using real-time object detection, for instance, by using AI to trackballs. Sports like basketball, football, soccer, and others employ these programs. Algorithm-based ball tracking includes following a ball's movement and predicting its trajectory using ML algorithms. This data may be utilized to increase shooting and passing accuracy, as well as to aid coaches in developing game plans for sporting events.

14.29   Predicting the winner of a sporting event

By observing the participants' motions, ML algorithms may be utilized to forecast the outcome of a sporting event. A system that can anticipate the outcome of a match can be taught by examining the data gathered by computer vision. This data may be used to place bets or simply to provide a general impression of who is more likely to win statistically. Football match results may be predicted using systems based on deep neural networks (DNNs) and artificial neural networks (ANN) [3].

14.30 Injury detection with computer vision

Applications to identify and track injury risk variables increasingly rely on data science and computer vision. In both practices and games, the Detroit Pistons employ computer vision to monitor player movement. To enhance player performance and avoid injuries, performance data is employed. For instance, ankle sprain risk in aerobics is examined using computer vision.

14.31 AI batting and pitching performance

In sports involving bats and balls, including cricket and baseball, computer vision is beginning to take on a more significant role. The objective of these sports is to use a tool to strike a target (a ball) (a bat). The use of computer vision can help athletes become better at throwing or hitting. When batting, computer vision can track the ball's trajectory and forecast its location at the point of impact. The application of this knowledge can aid batters in modifying their swing.

14.32 Computer vision in education sector

Every student's participation in class may be easily tracked with the help of computer vision technology [4]. In the near future, it is hoped that computer vision will improve the capacity to identify, gauge, and react to the involvement levels of specific pupils. The following are some ways that computer vision will change education.

14.33 Applications of computer vision in the education sector

14.33.1 AI for security at schools

By scanning and analyzing video footage to find any suspicious activity, such as loitering, intrusion detection, or the detection of anomalous events, computer vision systems provide security at schools. By spotting possible threats before they have a chance to do damage, this contributes to the safety of both students and staff. The layout of the school campus can be improved for safety and efficiency by using computer vision systems to monitor traffic flow and parking lot congestion.

14.33.2 Conducting online exams

Online assessments can be helped by computer vision software for teachers. A camera, for example, is a vital tool that may be used to identify students. By continuously monitoring the pupils' movements, body language, and other activities, this can also work as an online surveillance agent. In addition to utilizing computer vision to identify students, it is necessary to examine candidates' online activity and microphone recordings to look for signs of fraud or unethical behavior.

14.33.3   Automated attendance monitoring

Deep face recognition systems can be used in attendance monitoring systems. The video of common inexpensive CCTV cameras can be analyzed with deep learning to automatically detect people and perform face recognition to identify students and register their attendance.

14.33.4   Facial emotion analysis

From face expression analysis, DNNs have been utilized to identify students' emotions. The knowledge of face expression recognition in education can assist teachers in modifying their lectures properly. Such a technique offers a quantitative, continuous, and automatic means to help assess the level of service a teacher gives. The technology is still in its infancy, so privacy protection must be included (using special cameras or edge AI for on-device ML).

14.33.5   Reduce fraud instances

By paying attention to the students' facial expressions and voice samples, cheating incidents on exams can be reduced whether they take place in a classroom or online. In reality, video proof of instances where students are discovered cheating is admissible. To analyze articles, computer vision and AI may be combined. Since these tools can function more quickly than humans, using them proves to be a time-efficient strategy. The use of technology allows for the classification of related student responses to open-ended questions. Teachers often check a significant number of papers, making it possible for these instances to go missed.

14.34   Natural language processing

Natural language processing (NLP) is a subfield of AI and computer science that focuses on the interaction between computers and human language. NLP involves developing algorithms and computational models that enable computers to understand, interpret, and generate human language. NLP is used in a variety of applications, such as machine translation, sentiment analysis, chatbots, speech recognition, and text summarization [5,6]. NLP techniques include parsing, part-of-speech tagging, named entity recognition, semantic analysis, and ML. NLP has made significant advancements in recent years due to the development of deep learning algorithms and the availability of large datasets. These advancements have led to the creation of intelligent virtual assistants such as Siri and Alexa, and have made it easier for machines to process and understand human language. The following section discusses the various AI applications in the field of NLP.

14.35   E-mail filtering

When you enable e-mail filtering, you allow the software to independently analyze incoming e-mails for red flags that indicate spam/phishing content and automatically move those e-mails to a separate folder. NLP techniques are used in email filtering to analyze the content of an e-mail, such as the subject line, body text, and sender information. Keywords, syntax, and semantic relationships between words are extracted and used to make a prediction about the e-mail's category. The predictions are then used to sort the e-mails into different folders or label them. In addition to spam filtering, NLP can be used to implement more advanced e-mail filtering systems that can automatically categorize e-mails based on their content and prioritize them based on their importance.

Multiple criteria are used by spam filters to evaluate an incoming email. They look for common trigger words, such as "free" and "earn money," that indicate an unwanted email attempting to sell you something. If the sender sends you an email using your e-mail address rather than your contact name, your spam filter may flag it because the sender is not in your contacts. Senders attempting to send you unsolicited content, such as newsletters, may be flagged as spam. Furthermore, if the sender's IP address has previously been flagged for spamming, another sender with the same IP address will almost certainly be flagged as well.

The e-mail's content and design can also set off a spam filter. Large fonts and large images are two of the most common layout triggers for spam. The criteria change if you enable software that detects phishing e-mails. While all of the above criteria may automatically raise an e-mail to the attention of a content filter, additional red flags will raise the attention of a phishing filter.

Phishing e-mails typically contain a link or an attached document containing malware used to hack into your network.

Senders who have been flagged for a history of sending malware may set off a phishing filter. E-mails from unknown senders with links or attached documents may also set off phishing filters. Phishing filters will typically move flagged e-mails to an additional inbox, sometimes labeled as "Other". Flagged e-mails in this inbox will be "on hold" until you release, block, or allow them. If you release an e-mail, it is sent to your normal inbox to be opened, but you must continue to approve e-mails from the sender in the future. If an e-mail is blocked, it is rejected, and the sender is now barred from sending you future e-mails.

14.36   Advantages of e-mail filtering using NLP

Increased productivity: E-mail filtering can assist in automating the process of sorting and categorizing e-mails, saving time, and increasing productivity.

Improved organization: NLP-based e-mail filtering can categorize e-mails, making it easier for users to locate and avoid missing important messages.

Reduced spam: NLP-based e-mail filtering can effectively identify and flag spam e-mails, reducing the number of unwanted messages in a user's inbox.

Personalized filtering: NLP-based e-mail filtering can be tailored to each user's-specific requirements and preferences, resulting in a more personalized experience.

14.37   Disadvantages of e-mail filtering using NLP

False positives: Because NLP-based e-mail filtering is not perfect, important e-mails may be mistakenly classified as spam.

False negatives: There may be times when spam e-mails are not detected and reach a user's inbox.

Limited understanding: NLP-based e-mail filtering relies on current technology's limited understanding of language and context, which can lead to incorrect categorization or classification.

Privacy concerns: Because NLP-based e-mail filtering involves the processing of personal and sensitive information, it may raise privacy concerns.

Technical complexity: Implementing an NLP-based e-mail filtering system can be technically challenging and may necessitate specialized knowledge and resources.

14.38   Different types of machine translation in NLP

There are four types of machine translation:

1. **Statistical machine translation or SMT**

    It works by referring to statistical models that are based on the analysis of massive amounts of bilingual content. It anticipates determining the correspondence between a word from the source language and a word from the target language. Google Translate is a real-world example of this.

    Currently, SMT is excellent for basic translation; however, its most significant disadvantage is that it does not consider context, which implies that translation is frequently incorrect or, in other words, does not expect high-quality translation. Statistical-based machine translation models are classified into four types: hierarchical phrase-based translation, syntax-based translation, phrase-based translation, and word-based translation.

2. **Rule-based machine translation or RBM**

    RBMT basically translates the fundamentals of grammatical rules. It directs a grammatical examination of the source and target languages to generate the translated sentence. However, RBMT necessitates extensive editing, and its heavy reliance on dictionaries implies that mastery takes time.

3. **Hybrid machine translation or HMT**

    HMT, as the name implies, is a hybrid of RBMT and SMT. It employs a translation memory, making it undeniably more successful in terms of quality. Nonetheless, even HMT has a number of drawbacks, the most significant of which is the need for extensive editing, as well as the use of human translators.

HMT approaches include multi-engine, statistical rule generation, multi-pass, and confidence-based.

4. **Neural machine translation or NMT**
    NMT is a type of machine translation that uses neural network models (based on the human brain) to build statistical models with the goal of translation as the end goal. The primary benefit of NMT is that it provides a single system that can be prepared to unravel both the source and target text. As a result, it does not rely on specific systems common to other machine translation systems, particularly SMT.

14.39   Computer vision in construction

Computer vision is making a huge impact on the construction industry. By automating tasks, reducing costs, and increasing accuracy, AI vision technology is changing the way construction projects are managed. Edge AI and computer vision are enabling new applications in the construction industry by providing real-time information and scalable, distributed intelligence at the project site. This allows construction managers to make better decisions, reducing waste and improving efficiency.

14.40   Construction equipment detection and tracking

By tracking the presence and movement of equipment, ML can recognize cranes, bulldozers, excavators, and loaders. Hence, construction managers can make sure that machines are being used efficiently and reduce waiting times in specific areas (regions of interest). Different variations of intelligent solutions use object detection algorithms to detect construction vehicles and prevent machinery from blocking walkways or exits.

14.41   Asset management and maintenance

Computer vision can be used to keep track of the condition of construction assets. This can help with asset management, as it allows managers to keep track of which assets need repairs or replacements. It can also help with maintenance, as it can alert workers when an asset is starting to wear down and needs to be repaired or replaced. By using AI vision intelligence, the lifetime of assets can be improved, waste is reduced, and expensive interruptions and delays can be reduced and shortened. In addition, maintenance is essential to meet safety standards and comply with legal requirements.

Automated quality control computer vision can be used for automated quality control for construction materials. By using camera sensors to detect and identify irregularities in the material, computer vision can be used to ensure that the construction process is as accurate as possible. This can help to reduce the number of errors and improve the overall quality of the finished product. This can help save time and money by catching errors early on in the production process. For example, a construction company can use AI vision to automatically inspect the quality of the concrete being used in a building project. If there are any defects identified, the company can then take corrective action before it causes further damage.

Examples of automated quality control for construction materials include:

- Using sensors to detect and identify irregularities in the material.
- Checking the consistency of the material.
- Monitoring the color of the material.
- Checking the dimensions of the material.
- Detecting and identifying defects in the material.
- Classifying the type of material.

14.42   Dangerous goods sign recognition

Dangerous goods sign recognition using computer vision algorithms is an effective way to identify hazardous materials in a fast and accurate manner. Through the use of deep learning algorithms, computer vision systems can be trained to detect and recognize and classify signs associated with hazardous materials and substances such as explosives, flammable liquids, radioactive substances, and corrosives. This technology allows for more efficient safety protocols and control of hazardous materials while reducing the potential for human error. Additionally, applying computer vision technologies for sign recognition helps in other safety-related tasks, such as monitoring hazardous areas, real-time risk assessment, and personnel tracking in facilities.

14.43   Automated inspection with AI vision

Computer vision can be used to automatically inspect personal protective equipment (PPE), inspect construction vehicles and machines, or detect environmental safety hazards at construction sites. This enables enormous time savings for construction companies, as it eliminates the need for manual inspection while ensuring consistent and subjective inspection results. Using intelligent vision analysis, companies can automatically evaluate the quality of materials and workmanship. This makes it possible to ensure that standards are met and reduces the chances of defects.

14.44   Process optimization and tracking

Computer vision technology can be used to track the progress of construction projects. This is immensely helpful for project managers, as it allows them to understand how the project is progressing and identify any potential issues early. This enables project managers to optimize the construction process and make sure that projects are completed on time and within budget. In construction, human–computer interaction (HCI) is used to help manage processes and monitor a wide range of tasks.

Examples include:

- Detecting when a worker breaks safety protocols.
- Ensure that the correct construction materials are used.
- Inspecting construction sites for safety hazards.
- Monitoring the color of construction materials.
- Dimension checking of construction materials.
- Detecting and identifying defects in construction materials.

14.45 Safety and security monitoring

Computer vision helps to increase safety and security in construction by monitoring the surroundings of workers at all times. Modern ML analysis automates the detection of anomalous events. This can be used to detect dangerous events such as people in close proximity to heavy construction machinery. Computer vision can also be used to ensure that construction projects meet all the required standards and enforce adherence to policies regarding equipment usage. This can help to save time and money on the safety examination process, as well as ensure that any issues are identified and rectified as soon as possible. In addition, security cameras can help to deter crime and vandalism on the construction site. Computer vision is widely used in security and surveillance applications, to monitor large sites and detect intruders or unauthorized activity on construction sites.

14.46 Computer vision in aviation

Computer vision is an application of AI that enables machines to interpret and understand digital images. The aviation industry has been quick to adopt computer vision technology to improve safety and efficiency. The fields of use are very broad and include recognition and detection of airplanes, airport security and management, plane identification, autonomous flying of drones, and even missile guidance systems.

14.47 Aircraft inspection and maintenance

Computer vision is also used in aviation for tasks such as aircraft inspection and maintenance. By using images of the aircraft, technicians use ML to detect problems and recognize damage patterns that may not be visible to the naked eye. AI vision inspection helps to improve safety and avoid potential accidents or downtime. In addition, computer vision can be used for the automatic examination of aircraft components to reduce the amount of time and labor required for manual inspection. It further helps to increase the objectivity and consistency of the assessment.

Examples of AI vision inspection applications include:

- Inspecting the body of the airplane for damages or problems.
- Checking the engine for fluid leaks or other damage.
- Looking for cracks or other damage on the wings or fuselage.
- Inspecting the landing gear for wear or damage.
- Analyzing the brakes and tires for wear or damage.

14.48   Intelligent baggage handling

Computer vision is being used more and more in airports for baggage handling. Deep learning systems can automatically read labels with machine vision (optical character recognition) to identify trolleys and their locations. This helps to improve the efficiency of the baggage handling process and reduces the chance of lost luggage. It further reduces the number of errors and makes it easier to find misplaced luggage. Computer vision systems use cameras to scan the tags on luggage and match them with the information in the airline's database. This allows airport workers to quickly identify which bag belongs to which passenger. One of the first airports to implement a machine vision system was London Heathrow in 2014. Since then, many other airports have followed suit. Another visual deep learning application helps to identify and localize ground vehicles and baggage tugs and carts at airports. This is important to increase the efficiency of managing and distributing baggage carts. In addition, vehicle identification and localization help to avoid ground vehicle collisions, which are a major cause of accidents at airports.

14.49   AI vision security at airports

Computer vision can also be used for security applications. By installing cameras at strategic locations, it is possible to track the movement of people and objects at airports. Real-time information and reports help to identify potential security threats and improve operational security. Surveillance use cases include fence-climbing detection, perimeter monitoring to detect trespassing, large-scale heat mapping, movement path analysis, and queue monitoring. Advanced applications involve emotion analysis and gaze estimation to evaluate the mood and attentiveness of people.

Important applications of AI vision monitoring with computer vision include:

- Tracking the movement of people and objects.
- Monitoring for potential security threats, and detection of abandoned objects.
- Implement real-time crowd monitoring and anomaly analysis.
- Reduce false positives and negatives in security checks.
- Automated fire and smoke detection.

14.50 Face recognition at airports

Computer vision-based facial recognition software is used to identify passengers at airports. Such AI software compares the passenger's face to a database of images that have been pre-loaded into the system. The system performs face detection and face recognition with common IP cameras. Face analysis technology is used to streamline the boarding process and to make sure that only passengers who are supposed to be on a particular flight are able to board. In some cases, facial recognition software is also used to identify suspected criminals or individuals that are on no-fly lists.

14.51 Computer vision in insurance

AI and computer vision will transform the whole future value chain of insurances. Use cases and opportunities abound everywhere. AI fosters more powerful risk assessment systems, gaining advantages from risk assessment, AI-triggered automation, and forward-looking analytics. New risk management systems can become so powerful and disruptive to change insurance business models upside down, from pooling to personalizing risks. Key AI insurance applications of computer vision include risk management of existing insurance contracts, risk estimation for new contracts, claims management, and asset or process monitoring in real-time.

14.52 AI technology trends for insurers

Digital transformation and value-creating AI are of rapidly increasing importance for the business model of insurance companies. In the insurance sector, innovation is driven by emerging AI technologies that impact the entire value chain. Hence, there is a huge interest in the leading insurers to push digitization to the next level by leveraging risk-relevant and behavioral data gathered with distributed sensors and ML.

14.53 Sensing the physical world

The complex and massive amount of data gathered by sensors such as cameras requires ML to process information. AI tech is applied to transform data into insights and automation to trigger efficiencies and new applications in insurance. Today, AI adoption in the insurance industry is still far beyond its full capabilities. An important reason is that ML applications rely on masses of data hardly available in insurance.

As we enter the era of the Internet of Things (IoT) and AI (AIoT), AI adoption in insurance will benefit tremendously from real-world data generated by connected sensors. Visual sensors such as cameras and on-device computer vision provide a highly scalable method for AI vision intelligence.

In general, computer vision works in three basic steps:

1. obtaining image data/video from a camera,
2. processing the image with AI models,
3. understanding the image.

14.54   Key technology trends in Insurtech

Digitalization in the insurance industry is driven by a range of emerging technologies such as the IoT and Big Data. The immense amount of data created at the edge (connected devices with sensors) requires AI to analyze and understand the data. Traditional, cloud-based web applications require centralized processing in the cloud (data offloading), limiting adoption because of limited reliability, security, privacy, performance, connectivity, latency, and scalability. Therefore, recent megatrends around Edge Intelligence (Edge AI) move AI processing tasks from the cloud towards the edge, in close proximity to the sensor that produces the data. This approach of on-device ML helps overcome the limits of cloud computing and enables the implementation of ubiquitous real-world AI solutions.

14.55   Top applications of computer vision in insurance

14.55.1   Risk assessment with computer vision

Computer vision technology is used to process real-world information to assess specific risks more precisely, faster, and more objectively than humans. AI can find patterns in various scenarios to use computer vision in risk assessment. A popular example is remote sensing, for example, to analyze flood risk.

AI vision is able to perform sentiment analysis for real-time risk scoring with deep learning. The data can be used for dynamic pricing based on individual risk factors.

While multiple academic examples have been discussed and implemented, insurers experience difficulties in realizing the opportunities in actual business processes yet. Only a few productive implementations are widely deployed as of today, something that is very likely to change in the near future.

14.56   AI in insurance for underwriting process automation

The value chain of office processes is often characterized by a variety of different software applications. Hence, underwriters spend a considerable amount of their time manually transferring data from one software application to another while spending only a little time with higher-value tasks such as reasoning from information, selling, or engaging with brokers.

About 80% of data in today's insurance companies is text. Hence, NLP is regarded as one of the most widely implemented AI technologies today. Here, AI is used for automated interactions, cognitive applications, and automatically providing relevant information using semi-structured information.

Since underwriting tasks involve a high volume of documents, often paper-based, the extraction of structured information from scanned documents plays an important role. Therefore, AI-enabled optical character recognition (OCR) is used to save time and manual labor. The extracted information can be used for creating recommendations for the underwriter, such as referring to similar cases.

14.57 AI to understand new and complex risks

According to the Allianz Risk Barometer, the most important global business risks of today are

- Cyber incidents.
- Business interruption.
- Natural catastrophes.
- Pandemic outbreak.
- Changes in legislation and regulation.
- Climate change.
- Fire, explosion.

The complexity of risks continuously increases, and new risks cause unprecedented levels of disruption to businesses and their supply chains. Emerging technology and AI will increase the interpretability of business risks by extracting patterns and making complex risks manageable.

Examples include intelligent systems to detect and mitigate factors of business interruption or natural catastrophes. Another example is the automated monitoring of compliance with guidelines such as social distancing or mask detection, where applications provide a risk score to quantify and track risks across multiple locations.

References

[1] V. Shankar, How artificial intelligence (AI) is reshaping retailing. *Journal of Retailing*, 2018;94(4):vi–xi, ISSN 0022-4359, https://doi.org/10.1016/S0022-4359(18)30076-9.

[2] R. Sharma, Artificial intelligence in agriculture: a review. In: *2021 5th International Conference on Intelligent Computing and Control Systems (ICICCS), Madurai, India*, 2021, pp. 937–942, doi:10.1109/ICICCS 51141.2021.9432187.

[3] G. Yair, Artificial intelligence and sports journalism: Is it a sweeping change? *Technology in Society*, 2018;54:47–51, ISSN 0160-791X, https://doi.org/10.1016/j.techsoc.2018.03.001.

[4]   H.S. Lee and J. Lee, Applying artificial intelligence in physical education and future perspectives. *Sustainability (Switzerland)*, 2021;13(1):1–16, [351]. https://doi.org/10.3390/su13010351.

[5]   D. Khurana, A. Koli, K. Khatter, *et al.,* Natural language processing: state of the art, current trends and challenges. *Multimedia Tools and Application,* 2023;82:3713–3744. https://doi.org/10.1007/s11042-022-13428-4.

[6]   K. Jiang and X. Lu, Natural language processing and its applications in machine translation: a diachronic review. In: *2020 IEEE 3rd International Conference of Safe Production and Informatization (IICSPI), Chongqing City, China,* 2020, pp. 210–214, doi:10.1109/IICSPI51290.2020.9332458.

Chapter 15

Machine learning and computer vision – beyond modeling, training, and algorithms

R. Ranjana[1], B. Narendra Kumar Rao[2], J. Raja[3], Nagendra Panini Challa[4] and K. Reddy Madhavi[5]

Machine learning is a branch of artificial intelligence (AI). Machine learning finds its application in different domains like healthcare, travel, and e-commerce, and has enhanced the working of the same. It makes use of statistical prediction and modeling. It takes the raw data as input, analyzes the data, and generates the output according to the analyzed data. This chapter provides an extensive overview of machine learning techniques and a basic conceptual briefing about this extensive topic. The chapter also aims to explain the types of machine learning including supervised learning, unsupervised learning, and reinforcement learning. Machine learning has the potential to produce consistently accurate estimates in this new era. This chapter is to basically understand the fundamental concepts of machine learning and its techniques. It tells about the techniques we generally use, and the places where these types can be applied, profuse algorithms. Here we also get to discuss the various languages that we are going to use, the framework of machine learning, the best tools or the efficient platforms that can support machine learning practices and to implement the concepts.

15.1 Introduction to machine learning

Machine learning is a field of study that is a sub-part of AI. The ultimate aim of machine learning is basically to absorb the framework of data and fit those data into the models and help people understand and employ it in their daily life. Computer science is used to solve a problem whereas machine learning relies on training the data and giving statistically analyzed data as a resource output. The decision-making

[1]Department of Information Technology, Sri Sairam Engineering College, Chennai, India
[2]Department of Artificial Intelligence and Machine Learning, School of Computing, Mohan Babu University, Tirupati, India
[3]Department of Electronics and Communication, Sri Sairam Engineering, Chennai, India
[4]School of Computer Science and Engineering (SCOPE), VIT-AP University, Amaravati, India
[5]School of Computing, Mohan Babu University, Tirupati, India

process is automated with the help of machine learning which facilitates in building models.

Machine learning has now become a widespread technology that has spread over all corners of the digital world and has become a virtue for doing many things. Machine learning is a part of AI and works in a way that can be changed and both are two different concepts where AI is used for solving problems like humans do and for learning new skills. Machine learning is enabled to learn new things from data independently [1,2].

As a human we have the ability to think by ourselves and make a decision and there are machines that we use to pass our instructions and get the output we want and it depends on the input we feed or relies on what we feed to the machine. But machine learning brings a new dimension to the world where we allow machines to learn from the data and get them trained by themselves. How does the machine learn by itself? It trains itself by learning from the data we feed, the more data we feed the more will be the performance. It gets trained by those past data and it can work on a larger amount of data than a human can handle which makes it more pragmatic.

15.2   Classification of machine learning algorithms

In machine learning, there are many types of classification algorithms depending on the dataset given. It is classified into mainly two categories [3]:

- Linear models
  - o   Logistic regression
  - o   Support vector machines (SVMs)

- Non-linear models
  - o   K-nearest neighbors (K-NNs)
  - o   Kernel SVM
  - o   Naive Bayes
  - o   Decision-tree classification
  - o   Random forest classification

15.2.1   Logistic regression

In logistic regression, the calculation is used to prophesying the outcome. We Analyze the independent variables to determine the binary outcome, and the outcome falls into one of the categories. The independent variable can be categorical or numeric, but the dependent variable is always categorical. Written like this:

$$P(Y = 1|X) \text{ or } P(Y = 0|X) \tag{15.1}$$

15.2.2   Support vector machines

The support vector machine is shortened as SVM. Here in this method, the degree of polarity mainly focused on training the models and classifying them.

15.2.3   K-nearest neighbors

K-NN is used to find the *k*-closest relative of the data. The datasets that are trained are used to find the *k*-closest relative and *k* nearest neighbor is an algorithm based on pattern recognition [4,5].

K-NN is used when it comes to the classification of the data, i.e., where the data is to be placed in a dataset is determined using this.

15.2.4   Kernel SVM

The use of kernel comes in with the use of mathematical functions' problems in the project along with SVM. This kernel basically changes the given set of training data to a linear equation which is at first a non-linear decision surface.

15.2.5   Naive Bayes

Naive Bayes is a classification algorithm that is used to calculate if a data or a data point belongs to a specific category or if it does not fall in that specification. This is how it is calculated:

$$P(A|B) = \frac{P(B|A) \times P(A)}{P(B)} \tag{15.2}$$

15.2.6   Decision tree

A decision tree is an algorithm that is similar to a flow chart that has multiple levels. It classifies the data point into two similar categories from a point. It creates categories inside other categories like having subclasses that bring it into a limited human supervision.

15.2.7   Random forest

Random forest technique is an extension of decision tree classification. Here multiple levels of decision trees are formed with the datasets. Then the new set of data is fed to any one of the decision trees and it forms a random forest [6,7].

15.3   Applications where machine learning enhances efficiency

15.3.1   Video surveillance

The major role played by surveillance cameras is to monitor the videos of several different video cameras. It is mainly used to detect the crime.

15.3.2   Social media services

People usually post the images or videos on social media, machine learning recognizes the picture of the posted image and gives the suggestions based on the search or the viewed one.

15.3.3   Health care

Machine learning potentially works for the growth of the medical field. In which, it detects the problem that occurred in the body of a human. It acknowledges by predicting the disease and treatments accordingly.

15.3.4   Online fraud detection

Machine learning works for the protection of money and transactions which are carried out between sellers and buyers. It actually makes a cyber-based safer place, it tracks and monitors the frauds [8].

15.4   Evolution of machine learning algorithms

Machine learning algorithms have been vastly developed. It is used in every activity from booking a ticket for anything to small games that we play all have some sort of hand in machine learning-based techniques. From getting trained one by one from scratch till now, it is in a position where it can beat its own master [9].

Business plans, research that organizations perform, and other service-oriented tasks give importance to machine learning in all the required aspects. Many tech-based companies now have developed their own centralized platforms to induce machine learning in their works.

15.5   Techniques and framework

There are 10 different types of machine learning frameworks, each is provided by different vendors.

15.5.1   Scikit-learn

Scikit is extensively used by Python programmers as it is built using scientific Python. It can support many machine learning algorithms and it is the library that is used among a large number of people as it gives easy access to NumPy and SciPy [10].

15.5.2   Amazon machine learning

This service can be used to build models with minimal knowledge about the model where not all details are needed. This service is provided by Amazon as a visualization tool.

15.5.3   MLib (Spark)

Mlib is a product developed by Apache Spark. Clustering, regression classification, and many other ML algorithms are supported by MLib [11].

15.5.4   *Azure ML Studio*

Azure ML Studio is a framework that allows the members to create and train their models and then use them as API's that can be used by other customers. It is created by the Microsoft team.

15.5.5   *Tensorflow*

This is used for calculating mathematical expressions and for working with deep learning and machine learning algorithms. Google was the one to frame Tensorflow [12].

15.5.6   *Veles*

Veles is a framework for deep learning which is constructed using C++ language, but it allows Python as automation is done using it.

15.5.7   *Caffe*

Berkeley Vision and Learning Center is the founder of Caffe. The main objective of Caffe is modularity and to attain speed.

15.5.8   *Torch*

Torch supports image processing, computer vision, and other community-driven packages in it. GPU is the first thing that Torch gives preference to.

15.5.9   *H2O*

The H2O framework allows us to use it for solving today's analytic and mathematical problems. The continuous and smooth easy functional properties of H2O can be extended when combined with Hadoop [13].

15.5.10   *Theano*

Like other frameworks, Theano is also used for mathematical calculations and it is built using Python.

15.6   Challenges in implementing machine learning

While adopting machine learning, business processes are automated and it increases the profit step by step. On the starting stage, it is a bit difficult for beginners to understand the algorithm and have an issue with the alignment of the business goals. The challenging stuff is that data is not represented and lacking in the excellence of the data its resources. Machine learning is actually a complicated process of understanding and implementing the products. The implementation part takes time to complete. The technical issue it deals with is the system security and the breaching of the data [14].

15.7   Emerging tools for ML

Machine learning is built and trained by many softwares. Tensorflow provides libraries to construct machine learning algorithms. It is the most powerful library. It enables the beginners and the users to use the technology and build the product efficiently. Using the tensorflow the developers and user can perform numerical computation. Machine learning is used to train the models in which it is efficient for deployment.

15.7.1   Scikit

Scikit is also one of the machine learning tools. It is the kind of unsupervised learning in which it performs many calculations on them. It is built on many platforms such as matplotlib, numpy, and SciPy. It can be reused in several contexts. The data analysis is easy and can be predictable. In which everyone can use this open-source library in an easy way. Scikit library is written to a great degree in python. The components of Scikit are regression, classification, clustering, supervised learning, unsupervised learning, and cross-validation.

15.8   Computer vision and relevant technologies

Computer vision concentrates more on face recognition, object detection, and image processing techniques. Computer vision is an AI technique. Frequently computer vision techniques of themes like

* Prediction
* Classification
* Summarization
* Recognition
* Reconstruction

Computer vision deals with two techniques efficiently namely deep learning and a convolutional neural network (CNN). The image of an object is broken down in the form of picture elements that are done by machine learning with the help of CNNs. A CNN understands an image and recognizes the shapes and the hard edges in the pictures. Convolutions are run by the neural network, they make a series of iterations to make predictions. Once the predictions are evaluated as true, they start to recognize the images or the objects [15,16].

15.9   Scope for ML in computer vision – use of CNN and DL algorithms

Machine learning is integrated with computer vision technology that focuses on visual classification and recognition. It also tracks the information by the effective methods of processing the objects and images. The field of AI is computer vision. It separately enables information from the visual images, videos, and inputs that are in the form of visuals. And machine learning automates and analyzes the data. Machine learning extracts the information from the image that is considered by the vision technology.

15.9.1 Uses

The CNN is an adaptable technique and the parameters of training are comparatively less than other algorithms. The recognition is efficient in this algorithm. It is useful in various fields like agriculture, diagnostics, etc.

Deep learning is also used to recognize the objects and it is applied to large datasets of images. Whereas deep learning needs some considerable knowledge to work with. The performance is improved by deep learning techniques and the data sets are trained efficiently. We can say that deep learning is a subset of machine learning. Deep learning is used in various fields of computer vision like health monitoring systems, disease detection, and decision making in tasks.

15.10 Applications of advanced machine learning algorithms and computer vision

At present, machine learning algorithms are widely utilized by varied applications of the software development system. For example, the electronic world contains a variety of data types and systems such as Internet of Things, cyber security, business data, and several more. Extracting information from this data is often used for creating various intellectual applications under the respective domains. For instance, if a person has to develop a machine-driven, cyber security-based system, they have to collect the relevant cyber security-based data and these relevant data are used to accomplish the process. The application of computer vision is spreading into many industries like image recognition, retail, healthcare, robotics, and such more [17].

- Image recognition
  It is one of the most important and common applications of machine learning. This is basically used for the identification of person, object, and so more.
- Voice recognition
  This tool uses voice input and assists the user by recognizing the voice. The voice instructions are sent to the cloud server and it is implemented using DL algorithms and ML algorithms.
- Medical analysis
  This is used to identify the disease and it recommends the user to be taken care of by the physicians. Medical technologies are enhanced a lot and they are designing 3D models to work on the process. Nowadays, many challenges are faced by healthcare applications in the field of medicine. To get rid of that computer vision has made many prospective changes using deep neural networks.

- Industrial robotics
  The evolution of robotics in computer vision has become one of the broadest of all. This is majorly used for processing the machine tools and for cutting and shaping the required tools. The storage of goods is taken care of by the warehousing agents [16].

Hence, the information management tools and techniques are capable of extracting useful information and insight from the data which are urgently needed.

15.11   Integrated ML and CV solutions

Computer vision plays a key role in modern AI and machine learning models. This ML-powered AI has provided solutions for many integrated data processing. You can also integrate computer vision-based machine learning into web applications to perform client–server activities and improve user experience. This ML–CV integration is one of the broadest concepts that can be easily implemented and mimicked in human traits. Machine learning models are also being integrated into deep neural networks that use artificial instances to train specific patterns, revolutionizing how software systems work [18]. Machine learning, a subset of AI that improves data integration performance and collects large amounts of data, appears in data recursion applications.

15.12   Data models and data set for CV

The digital systems have made computer vision models to interpret and integrate the information that are in the form of images, audio, and video. To gain the basic level of object recognition, computer vision models have gone through many stages of technologies like machine learning, deep learning, and some concepts of neural networks. Some data models are listed below.

- Image classification
  The image classification is mostly used to classify and identify the image dataset that is referred to by each object or class. For tracking the objects, we use the object detection model that enhances and upgrades the features of the classes.
- Image segmentation [18]
  In AI, image segmentation most probably supports semantic segmentation. This identifies the shape of the objects which are referred to an object or class.
- Object detection
  The object detection model is used for tracking the objects which are used in the classification of images. This maps the objects with the respective images. The dataset collects pieces of information and works on it. It is mostly used for analyzing and prediction of data. The datasets mentioned below are used in modeling the computer vision models.
- ImageNet
  This imageNet dataset is a common and well-known dataset that has many collections of human characteristics. This dataset is one and only developed for

the implementation of computer vision models. In Figure 15.1, the imageNet dataset has been picturized.

- MegaFace

  The dataset is mostly used for recognizing facial expressions and this has a vast collection of facial expressions. This is an open-source dataset that can be used by any commercial users. In Figure 15.2, MegaFace datasets have been picturized.

- MS Coco

  This dataset contains segmentation and object detection working models. It is used for shaping and accessing the objects also used in tracking of objects. This was introduced by Microsoft for designing the object models using computer vision algorithms.

Hence, we have seen detailed explanations of data models and datasets of computer vision models.

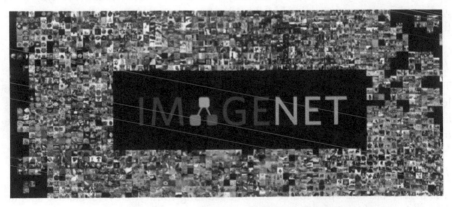

Figure 15.1   Picture of imageNet dataset

Figure 15.2   Picture of MegaFace dataset

15.13   Frameworks for integrating CV and ML

The framework has enabled the users to deploy and enhance the machine learning models easier. These frameworks have the same type of working libraries that simplifies the development of machine learning models. It has lots of pre-trained frameworks such as

- KERAS
- TENSORFLOW
- SHOGUN
- CAFFE
- OpenCV

15.13.1   Keras

It is an open-source framework based on tensorflow. The programming language used by keras is Python. It can efficiently be used on both central processing units and graphics processing units. Finally, after doing so much research, it has become the first choice for a high-level neural network [19].

15.13.2   Tensorflow

This is a previously trained model and it is one of the most popularized machine learning frameworks that help the creators and engineers to work on many algorithms and models, respectively. This tensorflow renders all the datasets and aggregates the machine learning and deep learning models to get rationalized results.

15.13.3   Shogun

It is a very old and open-source machine learning library. Developers use shogun for making large-scale production of machine learning models. It is a cluster of data structures and ML algorithms. It basically works on C++ programming language. It is mostly used for additive manufacturing.

15.13.4   Caffe

This is widely accepted on computationally constrained machine learning platforms. It is an open source framework and user friendly. It is mostly transmitted within CPUs and GPUs. It deals with computer vision and experimenting with many research methods and image processing techniques.

15.13.5   OpenCV

It is an open-source framework. It has well-developed computer vision and machine learning software libraries. It is mostly designed to aggregate computer vision applications and machine learning objects.

15.14 CNN architectures

CNN is the most well-known and often utilized algorithm. CNN's primary benefit over its portents is that it finishes the job without human intervention, automatically recognizing the pertinent elements. Many convolutional layers are present in a popular CNN variant, which is like the multi-layer perceptron (MLP), before sub-sampling (pooling) levels and FC layers.

15.14.1 Architectures

LeNet marked the beginning of the history of deep CNNs. The CNNs could only be used for handwritten digit recognition tasks at that time, which cannot be applied to all image classes. AlexNet is highly regarded in deep CNN architecture due to its ground-breaking achievements in the fields of image recognition and classification. Krizhevesky and others AlexNet were the first idea, and, as a result, it made CNN's ability to learn better by making it deeper and using several parameter optimization techniques.

15.14.2 Network-in-network

Two novel ideas were introduced by this network model, which differs slightly from the models that came before it. Utilizing multiple layers of perception convolution was the first. An 11 filter is used to perform these convolutions, allowing for the addition of additional nonlinearity to the networks. In addition, this makes it possible to increase the depth of the network, which can then be regularized using dropout. This concept is frequently implemented in the bottleneck layer of DL models. The GAP is also used in place of an FC layer. This is the second novel idea and makes it possible to significantly reduce the number of typical parameters. In accumulation, the network architecture is substantially updated by GAP. When GAP is applied to a large feature map, it is possible to generate a final low-dimensional feature vector without reducing the dimension of the map.

15.14.3 ZefNet

CNN learning is based on trial and error, it was impossible to know its exact purpose after the improvement. The deep CNN's ability to process complex images was hindered by this issue. DeconvNet, which is based on the multilayer model, de-CNN, was developed in response in 2013 by Zeiler and Fergus. ZefNet, built to measurably visualize the network, grew out of this approach. The network activity visualization is used to understand the neuron activation and monitor the CNN's performance.

15.14.4 GoogLeNet

GoogleNet (also known as Inception-V1) was named the winner of the 2014-ILSVRC contest. The primary objective of the GoogleNet architecture is to achieve high-level accuracy at a lower computational cost. Using merge, transform, and split functions for feature extraction, it combined multiple-scale convolutional transformations to create a novel CNN-specific inception block (module) concept.

15.14.5   Highway network

The network performs better when the depth is increased, particularly for difficult tasks. The network training, on the other hand, becomes challenging. The back-propagation of error may have small gradient values at lower layers in deeper networks where there are multiple layers [15]. To resolve this issue, a novel CNN architecture known as the Highway Network was suggested. The cross-connectivity idea serves as the foundation for this strategy. The guidance of two gating units within the layer, the Highway Network is able to allow for unhindered information flow.

15.14.6   ResNet

The Inception Network has been improved with ResNext. The Aggregated Residual Transform Network is another name for it. The word "cardinality," which was coined by [20], made efficient use of the divide, transform, and merge topology. The Inception network, however, improves the standard CNN's capacity for learning while also managing network resources more effectively.

15.14.7   DenseNet

DenseNet was offered similar to ResNet and the Highway system to address the issue of the vanishing gradient. ResNet has a few drawbacks, one of which is that many layers contribute less information, so it clearly conserves information through preserver individuality transformations. Because each layer has its own distinct group of weights, ResNet has a large number of weights. In an improved strategy to address this issue, DenseNet made use of cross-layer connectivity. Using a feed-forward method, it connected other layers in the network. Instead of adding features to the layers before it, DenseNet combines them. DenseNet, on the other hand, becomes parametrically expensive due to its slim layer structure and the increased number of feature maps. The information flow throughout the network is enhanced by the loss function's direct inclusion of all layers to the gradients.

15.14.8   WideResNet

WideResNet made use of the power of residual blocks by making the ResNet wider rather than deeper. By introducing an additional factor, k, which handles the network width, it increased the width. In addition, it indicated that, in comparison to deepening the residual network, layer widening is an extremely effective method for improving performance. Prior studies focused on expanding the depth; as a result, a number of new layers were required for even a modest performance boost. An experimental study demonstrated that WideResNet has twice as many parameters as ResNet.

15.14.9   Residual attention neural network

The Residual Attention Network's network feature representation was improved by Wang *et al.* (RAN). The main goal of adding attention to CNN is to enable the network to understand the features of the object that are aware. Stacks of residual blocks are also a component of the RAN in addition to the attention module. The bottom-up feedforward design also generates low-resolution feature maps and robust semantic data. Goh *et al.* were regularizing the usage of top-down attention mechanism of deep Boltzmann machines (DBMs) in the era of the reconstruction phase. It should be noted that a top-down learning strategy, in which the maps gradually output to the input throughout the learning process, can be used to optimize the network globally in a similar way.

15.14.10   Convolutional block attention module

The importance of the feature map utilization and the attention mechanism is supported by the SE-Network and RAN. The innovative attention-based CNN module known as the convolutional block attention was first created by Woo *et al.* (CBAM). The layout of this module is straightforward and resembles SE-Network. During image classification, SE-Network only takes into account the contribution of the channels and disregards the object's spatial location in the image. The spatial location of the object is crucial to object detection. The attention maps are inferred sequentially by the convolutional block attention module. To be more specific, the refined feature maps are obtained by employing channel attention prior to spatial attention. Using a spatial axis and pooling features is one way to create an effective feature descriptor.

15.14.11   CapsuleNet

When compared to cutting-edge handcrafted feature detectors, CapsuleNet CNN is an effective method for detecting object features and achieving well-behaved recognition performance. For instance, when taking into consideration an image of a face, the CNN does not take into account the various face components. A particular neuron or capsule of this kind is capable of effectively recognizing faces and various kinds of information. As a result, the capsule network is constructed using numerous layers of capsule nodes. The CapsuleNet or CapsNet, which was the first version of the capsule networks, is made up of an encoding unit with three layers of CapsuleNet.

15.14.12   High-resolution network (HRNet)

For completing tasks like segmentation, object identification, and pose estimation, HRNet is required. Modern frameworks, such VGGNet and ResNet, encode the input image as a low-resolution representation using a subnetwork that is constructed as a connected series of high-to-low resolution convolutions. There are two main components to this network, first a parallel connection is made between the high-to-low resolution convolution series; second, information is frequently transferred between the resolutions. A high-resolution representation is then created by recovering the low-resolution one. As an alternative, a High-Resolution Network (HRNet), a unique network, is used to retain high-resolution representations during the entire process.

15.14.13 Architectures

The development of deep CNNs began with LeNet. At the time, CNNs were limited to handwritten digit recognition tasks; therefore, they could not be employed for other image classes. Due to its revolutionary developments in the areas of image identification and classification, AlexNet is highly recognized in deep CNN architecture.

15.15 Conclusion

Machine learning is very important because it offers enterprises to read and collect the data from different sources. It is a powerful tool to make software development systems. Technology has to be developed so that the needs of society can be fulfilled. Machine learning algorithms are most commonly used to establish complex tasks and to predict the respective data. It has made significant progress in enhancing the development of new technologies. Computer vision is most probably implemented to make the software development process faster and simpler. Since there is a wide variety of machine learning libraries available, it provides some unique functionalities to the data scientists and machine learning engineers. Hope this detailed explanation effectively describes the richness of machine learning and computer vision integrated models.

References

[1] Chollet F. Xception: deep learning with depthwise separable convolutions. In: *Proceedings of the IEEE Conference on Computer Vision and Pattern Recognition*, pp. 1251–1258, 2017.

[2] Ranjana, T. Subha, N. Susila, R. Anushya, and S. Amritha, Predictive diagnosis of breast cancer using deep neural network. *Bioscience Biotechnology Research Communications*, 2021;14(5):218–224.

[3] R. Anushya, S. Amritha, S. Yuvasakthi, Ranjana, "Predictive diagnosis of cancer using machine learning.", *Test Engineering and Management*, 83, 7558–7567, 2020.

[4] B. Narendra Kumar Rao, P. Ranjana, "Text recognition from Images using deep learning techniques", *ICDIC-2021, December, 2021. Conference Proceedings.*

[5] B. Narendra Kumar Rao, Nagendra Panini Challa, A Mohan, "Automated detection of skin lesions using back propagation neural network", *ICDIC-2021, December, 2021, Conference Proceedings.*

[6] Fatima M, Pasha M, *et al.* Survey of machine learning algorithms for disease diagnostic. *J. Intell. Learn Syst. Appl.* 2017;9(1):1.

[7] Fujiyoshi H, Hirakawa T, Yamashita T. Deep learning-based image recognition for autonomous driving. *IATSS Res.* 2019;43(4):244–52.

[8] Ranjana R, Aadityan PR, Shubam Suryawanshi, "Survey on machine learning techniques for energy management in cloud data center", *IEEE International Conference on Engineering and Technology, Organized by*

Department of CSE, Rathinam Technical Campus, Coimbatore, August 30th and 31st 2018.

[9] Mohammed M, Khan MB, Bashier Mohammed BE. *Machine learning: algorithms and applications.* CRC Press; 2016.

[10] Yujin O, Park S, Ye JC. Deep learning COVID-19 features on CXR using limited training data sets. *IEEE Trans. Med. Imaging.* 2020;39(8):2688–700.

[11] Sarker IH. A machine learning based robust prediction model for real-life mobile phone data. *Internet Things.* 2019;5:180–93.

[12] Witten IH, Frank E. *Data mining: Practical machine learning tools and techniques.* Morgan Kaufmann; 2005.

[13] Witten IH, Frank E, Trigg LE, Hall MA, Holmes G, Cunningham SJ. *Weka: practical machine learning tools and techniques with java implementations.* 1999.

[14] Xu D, Yingjie T. A comprehensive survey of clustering algorithms. *Ann Data Sci.* 2015;2(2):165–93.

[15] Ranjana R, Susila N, Subha T. Application of machine learning techniques in data centre energy management. *Journal of Critical Reviews,* 7(14), 2020, 1938–1943, doi:10.31838/jcr.07.14.390. (Scopus Indexed)

[16] Drory, A. Computer vision and machine learning for biomechanics applications: Human detection, pose and shape estimation and tracking in unconstrained environment from uncalibrated images, videos and depth. 2017.

[17] Xie X, Ho JWK, Murphy C, Kaiser G, Xu B, and Chen TY. Testing and validating machine learning classifiers by metamorphic testing. *Journal of Systems and Software,* 84(4):544–558, 2011.

[18] Shree, G, Singh AK, Sarje AK, and Peddoju SK. Behaviour analysis of machine learning algorithms for detecting P2P botnets. *2013 15th International Conference on Advanced Computing Technologies (ICACT).* 2013: IEEE.

[19] García-Ordás MT, Alegre E, González-Castro V, and Alaiz-Rodríguez R. A computer vision approach to analyze and classify tool wear level in milling processes using shape descriptors and machine learning techniques. *The International Journal of Advanced Manufacturing Technology,* 2017. 90 (5–8): 1947–1961.

[20] Pedregosa F, Varoquaux G, Gramfort A, *et al.* Scikit-learn: Machine learning in Python. *Journal of Machine Learning Research,* 12:2825–2830, 2011.

Chapter 16

Assistive image caption and tweet development using deep learning

Parth Birthare[1], R. Maheswari[1], R. Ganesan[1] and P. Vijaya[2]

In this rapidly growing world and with the technological boom, there are a huge variety of applications and devices that generate an enormous amount of data every second. With unstructured data being the most difficult to manage and keep track of, there has been a drastic increase in the amount of visual data generation. To keep track of such data for further insights and use, a textual descriptor is often needed and getting it is the primitive step for any analytics. A manual description is subjective and not appropriate for larger data. This issue is addressed by automation, hence opening gates for computer vision and artificial intelligence in the domain. Another area that has changed multimedia communication and has seen a great deal of advancement is social media. Applications like Twitter have become an indispensable part of people's lives. Moreover, Progressive Web Application (PWA) is a term that has started to be implemented in various applications. It gives an on-par experience with native apps and has become more prevalent. This work Assistive Image Caption and Tweet (AICT) aims to set a new horizon by combining these applications, and setting a base for future applications and devices. It does so by using deep learning techniques such as convolution neural networks (CNN) and Long Short-Term Memory (LSTM) to generate captions for images within milliseconds, natural language processing (NLP) to generate the text in different languages along with the audio to assist visually impaired people, and an automated assistive tweet function that directly tweets the image with its caption in the language desired.

16.1 Introduction

Technology is fast improving and automation is taking a major role these days, from machines in agriculture to sophisticated artificial intelligence (AI)-driven cars

[1]School of Computer Science and Engineering, Vellore Institute of Technology, Chennai, India
[2]Modern College of Business and Science, Bowshar, Sultanate of Oman

and computers, technological, and mechanical enhancements have led to an increase in performance and a reduction in time and effort [1]. Also, there is a massive amount of data generated every year [2]. Storing and handling Big Data has many challenges associated with it [3]. Generating meaningful information from the visual data is feasible by human interaction by manually annotating and describing features, but it is quite a tiresome task and involves semantic gaps as different people have different views and opinions about an image. However, computing solutions have their limitations too. What appears to be a winning moment for a sportsperson where they smile and cry at the same time may be described by different algorithms differently. Since a simple computer program is not able to understand the context of an image, complex computer vision, and artificially intelligent algorithms must be implemented to consider every minute of detail. There are many methods to measure the semantic gap in image retrieval [4]. Therefore, to minimize human involvement, using efficient computer vision techniques, NLP and deep learning algorithms in the right manner solve the issue [5].

The structure of this work starts by discussing the algorithms and technologies used for developing AICT, theoretically comparing it with existing work, implementing an application, mathematically supporting the superiority of this work while comparing it with other state-of-the-art techniques, and concludes with inferences and future work. AICT serves to integrate the concept and methods of complex AI and deep learning-enabled techniques for image captioning with the increasingly popular modern social media applications to revolutionize the use and ease of access of such applications, as well as keep the technology up to date in their applications and working.

16.1.1   Deep learning models

Both CNN and LSTM are artificial neural networks. CNN takes in an input image, assigns importance or learnable weights, and biases to various aspects/objects in the image, and can differentiate one from the other [6]. It scans images to extract useful features and combines them to classify images. It is a Rotation, Translation, and Scaling (RTS) invariant like the Histogram of Oriented Gradients (HOG) features. LSTM networks are a complex area of deep learning and a type of recurrent neural network (RNN) that are capable of learning order dependence in sequence prediction problems. It is a type of behavior or constraint that is required in complex problem domains like machine translation, speech recognition, and more. These have internal mechanisms which are known as gates that facilitate the flow of information.

A typical LSTM unit consists of a cell, input gate, output gate, and forget gate [7]. The cell is for remembering values over random time intervals whereas the gates regulate information flow ingoing and outgoing from the cell. In simple words, based on the previous word, the next word can be predicted [8]. Unlike RNN which has short-term memory, it overcomes it by having a forget gate.

16.1.2 Additional technology used

In terms of the assistive nature of this work, important modules like the text-to-speech for the image caption generated, including the option to choose from different languages open possibilities for multilingual interaction for the description. An automatic tweet module further decreases the need for human interaction thereby leading to automation. Playing the audio description of an image to the user and creating a Twitter bot that automatically, based on the image, adds a tweet text to the image according to the users' choice, all lead to the efficient use of assistive technology. A similar implementation can be used in the case of various other social media applications. With voice-over features, visually impaired people would still be able to interact with the application and social media. Finally, being a PWA, AICT would be able to function as a website as well as a native application on mobile devices and even on desktops where they could be installed and be used just as a regular native application irrespective of the operating system. There is no need to maintain an application programming interface (API) for backward compatibility [9].

16.2 Literature review

Image captioning is a recent topic of study and research, which has witnessed some attempts to optimize the current algorithms that use computer vision and deep learning techniques to solve problems.

There are various methods that are used for image captioning. For example, it can be encoder and decoder based, attention based or novel object-based, or even using proximal policy optimization [10]. The choice of the method also depends on the type of dataset used and the number of images in the dataset. Even deep learning involves various methods and therefore one must keep every aspect into consideration while choosing an algorithm [11]. It is not the complexity and the quantity of algorithms put in to solve a problem, but the judicious and correct blend of the algorithms and thinking that lead to the most efficient and optimal solutions.

Among similar works, Sheshang Degadwala *et al.* presented a paper on the image captioning model where they used the Inception V3 model which is also an image recognition model [12]. Their paper proposed an Inception V3 image caption generator model using CNN and LSTM units. It involved removal from the Inception V3 model, the last classification layer for the dimension (1343,) vector. The embedded matrix was then used for vocabulary connections. However, in this work, the Xception model is used which is far better than the standard Inception model, as in the Xception model the Inception modules are replaced by depth-wise separable convolutions which lead to better performance.

A similar research work involved the use of the Inception V3 model where direct use of image embedding was done as an input to the LSTM network [13]. After that, an API returned the image caption from the image path.

Another research work in 2019 involved a review of image captioning by Raimonda Staniut and Dmitrij Šešok where they compared the performance of the models using the MS-COCO dataset and concluded that it is not enough to choose between the two datasets MS-COCO and FLICKR30k [14]. Other methods used generative adversarial network (GAN) and Inception models with different datasets such as the MSCOCO dataset and Flickr30k dataset.

A similar work involved research using the ResNet-50 model for the images which are 50 layers deep [15]. However, it only had a primitive and simple implementation of an approach to image captioning using CNN with minimal complexities and many major deviations from the accurate description were observed.

A research work by Charvi Jain and Neha Sharma involved using MSCOCO dataset for training the images [16]. Deep learning methods like CNN were used for training the model. Moreover, the dataset had a large number of images. But as for the implementation and the end results, two outputs were shown and it was mostly concerned with the implementation to get a caption for an image. Not much regarding the future aspects of the work or a real-life application was suggested.

This work holds its novelty in the sense of mitigating the problems discussed above by training the images using the Xception model and not the Inception model, combining CNN and LSTM to get the best of both the neural networks, and discussing more examples to portray the visual result of the work and its efficiency, implementing a novel application, ready to be deployed, that use NLP techniques, assistive technology while considering and integrating modern applications scope to generate image captions in milliseconds in the language of users' choice along with an audio description, and tweet it in the chosen language along with the image. Finally, a comparison with the state-of-the-art methods with scores supported by graphical representations, thereby covering both the application as well as the algorithmic part of the research.

16.3   Proposed system

After a careful study of the previous works, studying their drawbacks and future scope, and the role of social media applications, AICT is developed as an improved work by exploring and implementing novel methods and approaches, practically applying these methods to build an application while describing its future scope as well as the importance of such work. AICT not only efficiently determines an accurate description of the image using AI and deep learning but also provides the option to choose from different languages and share the same using social media and offers an ability to listen to the audio description in the chosen language to facilitate and help the visually impaired people. This is done using NLP and assistive technology. It also improves the current applications and promotes the use of AI, deep learning, NLP, and assistive technology. All of these aspects together lead to build next-generation applications.

16.4   AICT architecture

The methodology involves making an image caption generator using CNN and LSTM. The features will be extracted from a CNN-based model on the ImageNet dataset. Xception is a CNN that is 71 layer-deep. After processing through CNN, the features are then given to the LSTM model that generates the image caption.

CNN extract feature from the image where a pre-trained model Xception will be used. LSTM based on the information/output from CNN will generate a close description of the image. The architectures are thus merged for better efficiency in this work.

The features extracted from the image are pushed to the CNN model. The output from the CNN model is taken as an input to the LSTM model. Using that, it can then predict the next word from the previous word to generate an image caption.

A start and an end tag are also added to the description from which the model can detect the start and end of the description. From the developed model, it will be able to predict, for example, from the word dog, it will predict that the next word can be run, then from the word "runs" it will predict the next word – "through", from the word "through", it will predict the next word – "the" and then using it the next word – "grass" subsequently.

The assistive technology and concepts of NLP come to play when the text to speech is used, and, for implementing this, an audio file is generated that describes the image. The generated audio and the text description can further be translated to the language preferred by the user. There has been a huge boom in the speech interface in this decade in terms of human–computer interaction [17]. More and more applications are using voice-based assistance with devices and for interaction between them.

Also, an additional feature that implies assistive technology and automation in modern applications is automatic posts on social media. Automatic tweet generation can be added for improved human–computer interaction [18]. The tweet functionality here is an indication of the ways using which posts can be made to several social media apps automatically.

The architecture of AICT, from model development to image description generation and tweet, is shown in Figure 16.1.

Using the AICT architecture, modern applications can generate descriptions of images in different languages in both text and audio format so that the audially and visually challenged can still obtain the results by themselves and without external help, have a hassle-free and automated share functionality, and do all this within milliseconds, which is required the most in today's data-centered world, yet many commonly used applications lack it.

The work including the model development and interface implementation is sophistically divided into 10 parts:

1. Import relevant packages
2. Acquire and perform data cleaning
3. Extract feature vectors from images
4. Load dataset for training model
5. Tokenize vocabulary

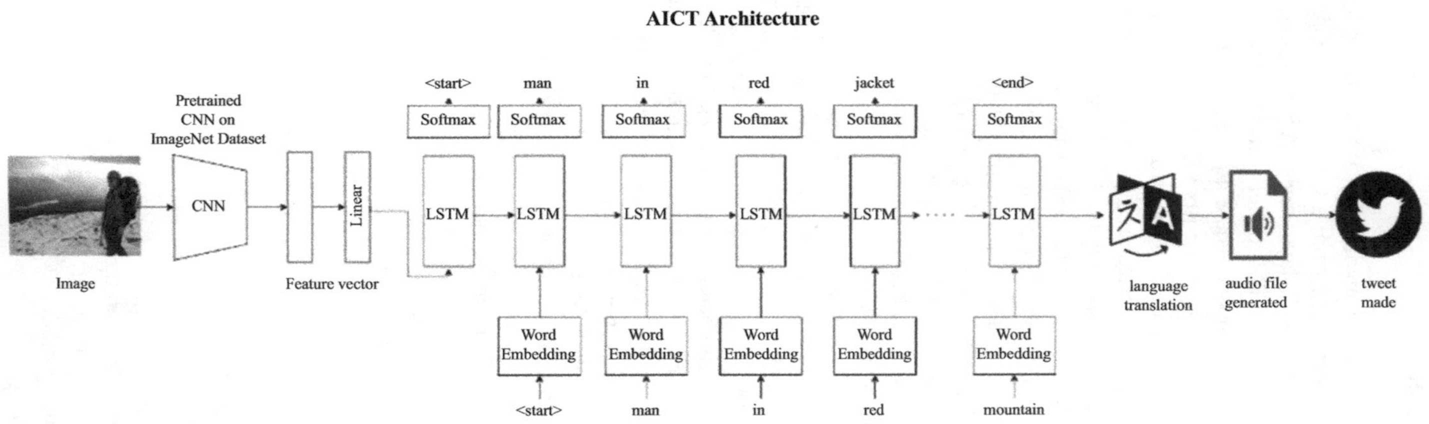

AICT Architecture

Figure 16.1   Architecture of AICT

6. Create a data generator
7. Define a CNN–RNN model
8. Train model
9. Test model
10. Implement interface

Furthermore, a comparison of performance with the existing methods is drawn for measuring the efficiency of image caption generation using BLEU-1 scores.

16.4.1   Import relevant packages

The important packages that are necessary for the work are imported including string, *NumPy, PIL, OS, pickle, neural network packages, Keras and tqdm* (for progress bar). These help in string formatting, for working with arrays and matrices, manipulating, and saving different image file formats, for system directory and files related tasks, for serializing, and deserializing python object structure, for neural networks and progress bar, respectively.

16.4.2   Acquire data and perform data cleaning

The main data files consist of the images and the captions separated by a new line. The captions file contains the image ID and five captions associated with that image. This step involves loading data into a string, mapping captions with their images, cleaning text, separating unique words to form a vocabulary, and storing pre-processed data into a descriptions file.

16.4.3   Extract feature vector from images

To extract the features from the images, transfer learning is used and a pre-trained Xception model is used which is trained on large datasets and extract features from that model. The features dictionary is dumped into the features file. The pickle object contains the image and its feature vector extracted from the Xception pre-trained CNN model.

16.4.4   Load dataset for training model

The model is trained for about 6,000 images out of around 8,000 images. With the unavailability of complex and efficient systems and due to low computational power, this ratio is kept. Using machines with better computational power yields accurate and better models.

16.4.5   Tokenize vocabulary

Since human-readable languages are not understandable by computers, the data is tokenized. Each word of vocabulary is mapped with a unique index value. These tokens are created from the vocabulary using the *Keras tokenizer function* and saved to the tokenizer file. The maximum length of descriptions is also calculated to know for stating the structural parameter of the model.

16.4.6   Create a data generator

Each image from the 6,000 images on which the model has to be trained, has a feature vector length of 2,048, and even the captions are represented as numbers. Since data for 6,000 images is not possible to be held in memory, a generator method that derives batches is used.

16.4.7   Define a CNN–RNN model

Defining the model, the features are extracted from the pre-trained Xception model. A word embedding layer is developed that handles text, followed by LSTM. Model 1 and model 2 are finally merged, this is done so to acquire better efficiency and is processed by the dense layer to make the final prediction since both the models produce a fixed-length vector.

16.4.8   Train model

Once the model is defined, the training images are used for training the model by generating the input and output sequences in batches and fitting them to the model using. This model is the final model which is saved in the models' directory and will be used for testing and implementing the application.

16.4.9   Test model

The model is then tested using the testing images. However, it might be noticed that the model inaccurately works for some of the images, this deviation is partly because of the choice of the dataset, the quantum of images, and the type of images in the dataset, while is accurate for most.

For an image with a little boy sitting on a bed, AICT generates the description as depicted in Figure 16.2.

As it can be clearly observed, AICT very accurately describes the image and provides the correct and exact description of the image. Image recognition module

small boy is sitting on bed

Figure 16.2   AICT description of an image of a little boy on bed

Figure 16.3   Image description for a dog running through the grass

Figure 16.4   AICT described an image of a man walking down the mountain

in this case can also include the name of the child which would be even more accurate.

A similar implementation is that of a dog running in the grass and the caption generated for that image is depicted in Figure 16.3.

In this scenario too, AICT is able to accurately determine the caption. AICT, however, very rarely gives a good description of the image but misses or wrongly interprets some minor details and example of which is shown in Figure 16.4.

It can clearly be perceived from the image description that the model describes some of the details accurately, like a man, wearing a jacket, walking down, snowy mountain, but wrongly interprets the color of the jacket. One reason for such an anomaly is the dataset containing more occurrences of the color red.

16.4.10   Test interface

The interface is implemented using *Flask*, which is a microweb framework and is used for building web applications. The PWA functionality allows the application to be used on any device, whether mobile or desktop and function as a native app that is installed.

AICT also creates an audio file for the generated image along with the caption. The caption as well as the audio can be translated to a different language of the user's choice. This audio can be played after the caption is generated using buttons. This function acts as an aid for visually impaired people to understand the context of the picture and get a closely matching description for it.

AICT would further provide users with an option to automatically post their images and descriptions to social media apps, here Twitter.

This opens up possibilities for implementing image recognition modules in further versions that would allow people to tag the people present inside the picture and include their names and details in the description too.

16.5   Implementation and interface

The home screen of AICT as an application displays what the application does. The home screen of AICT is displayed in Figure 16.5.

There is an about screen that displays the details about the work and its ownership. The About screen is depicted in Figure 16.6.

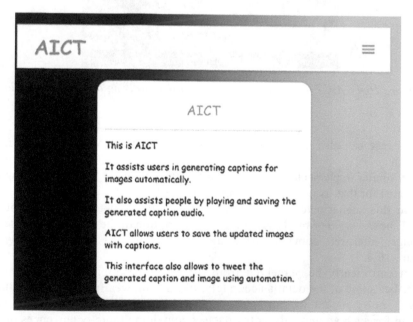

Figure 16.5   Home screen of AICT

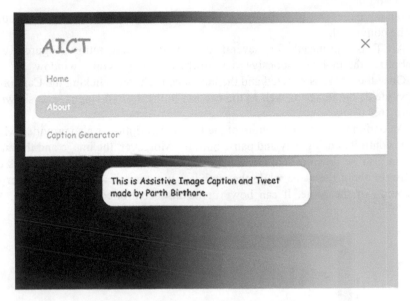

Figure 16.6   About screen of AICT

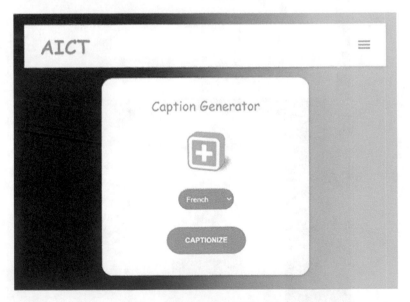

Figure 16.7   Image description generation window for AICT with the option to choose the language

The main screen which performs the functionalities listed is the Caption Generator. It takes the input from the user as an image and then generates the image caption in a matter of milliseconds. The Caption Generator window is displayed in Figure 16.7. The window also provides an option to choose from several languages in which the image description will be generated and the audio will be converted.

AICT is optimized for several device sizes and ratios (Figure 16.8). Symbolizes the mobile responsive view of the caption generator window.

Once the image is selected and the language is chosen, clicking the Captionize button yields the image as well as the caption in the desired language as shown in Figure 16.9.

An option to listen to the audio of the image description is also provided which can be controlled using play and pause buttons. Moreover, the image and the audio file can also be downloaded. Once the image description is generated, users can also tweet about the same while the application automatically opens up after the generation of the same. It can however be also controlled using a button. For

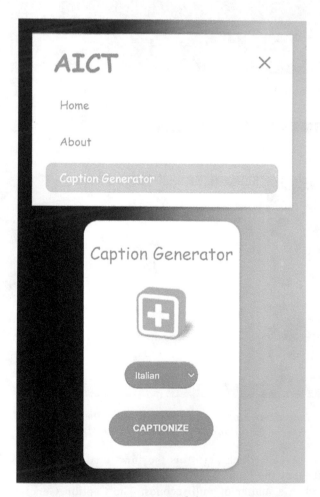

Figure 16.8   AICT in its mobile responsive state

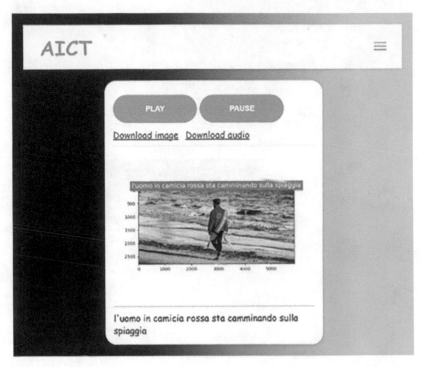

Figure 16.9   AICT generates image description and provides an option to download the audio and image along with play and pause functions for audio

visually impaired people and for enhanced assistance, a voice-over feature assists users when a touch or tap is detected near the button using audio instructions and support. The automatic tweet about the image and description in the selected language is shown in Figure 16.10.

Similarly, choices can be provided to post the image and the description on various social media platforms with improved features of tagging and identifying people.

When compared to the online services for image captioning, which are limited, AICT generates the image caption faster, and in the desired language too. Moreover, it has far better performance in terms of BLEU-1 score when compared with the existing methods. Only BLEU-1 scores are mentioned for comparison since some of the works do not have BLEU-2, and other scores are mentioned in their papers.

The scores can be observed in Table 16.1.

Figure 16.11 shows the superiority of the proposed model performance over other state-of-the-art methods using a line chart.

It can be clearly observed that the proposed method has a better performance compared to the existing works.

Figure 16.12 shows the same using a bar graph which is easier to interpret and makes it clear about the performance of the proposed method.

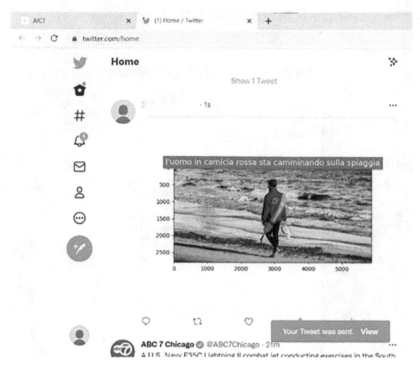

Figure 16.10   Automatic tweet of the description of an image in AICT

Table 16.1   BLEU-1 scores comparison of different methods

Model	BLEU-1 score
M-RNN [19]	0.5778
NIC [20]	0.6300
M-RNN [21]	0.5650
V-SM [22]	0.579
DL [23]	0.5335
NNM [24]	0.56
AICRL [25]	0.619
EL [26]	0.634
CL [27]	0.6373
CLA [27]	0.6532
Proposed method	0.6721

16.6   Trust in system

Trust in AI is a broad concept. All deep learning models use weights and features that are difficult to explain. Putting trust in AI systems mainly revolves around two concepts: fairness or low biasness, and explainability.

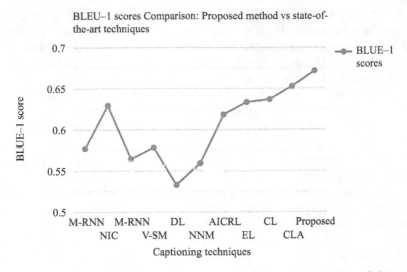

Figure 16.11 BLEU-1 scores of the proposed method and the state-of-the-art techniques using a line plot

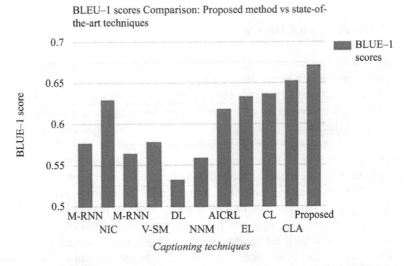

Figure 16.12 Various techniques performance plot considering BLEU-1 score

Fair systems mean developing and following practices that are not biased towards a particular class or group. Low biasness or more fairness in systems is achieved through explainability. As more information is available to the environment – be it users or any engine, it has more data to perceive and think and work upon, respectively.

In terms of AICT, in the image captions generated – the first word of the sentence finds the probability of the next word. That is, the first word predicts the most probable word in the caption. This is analyzed through the data. Furthermore, as more layers are added, it becomes difficult to track which words lead to a subsequent word. In AICT too, it was observed that increasing the complexity of the model, it became challenging to find the next word that will be predicted by the model, because of which, the model gave unpredictable reasons.

Therefore, adding more weights to the neural network, increasing the complexity of the model, does not always help. Even though the accuracy of the model is increased, the explainability is reduced, which makes it hard to identify the malfunctioning of the model.

In an example sentence, among the various captions generated for an image as shown in Figure 16.4, the sentence, "man in red jacket is walking down snowy mountain was the most suitable as given by the model". Other sentences like "man in red jacket is smiling and standing on a snowy mountain" had lesser probability, and therefore not identified by the model as the most suitable one. The reason behind this is – as the explainability of the model is increased, the complexity of the model is reduced, and so is the accuracy. The original caption had a probability of 0.43% while the latter caption had a probability of 0.29%. Clearly, the accuracy became less as the explainability of the model was focused on.

16.7   Inference and future work

The visual results and the scores show that the model generates captions for images considerably well with a better performance when compared with existing works. Moreover, the PWA works on any device and acts natively once installed on the device. AICT app can generate an image description along with an audio description in the preferred language selected by the user, which would be very beneficial for hearing-impaired and visually impaired people, and be helpful in this giant multilingual community. Furthermore, posting the images and their captions in their preferred language to social media is another boom in the fast-growing world and would allow the users to post their images and descriptions automatically to social media applications like Twitter which is even beneficial for visually impaired people to carry out activities like a normal person would which otherwise would not be possible as these media generally do not have such support.

It was also observed that there is a tradeoff between explainability and accuracy of the models. As the models increase in complexity and accuracy, explainability tends to decrease.

Future versions of AICT will include options for several social media platforms with an image recognition module that will successfully identify the people and the objects/entities present in the image, even tag them, and include their details in the descriptions. This introduces a plethora of opportunities in the field as a result of combining social media, AI, NLP, modern-day applications, and assistive technology that would totally change and shape up the working of future applications as well.

16.8 Conclusions

Therefore, AICT is implemented using deep learning techniques, NLP, and assistive automation and provides a solution to various problems faced by people by generating the image caption and narrating the same to the user in their desired language. The research findings conclude that CNN and LSTM used together yields a fast and efficient image description generator, NLP approaches lead to getting multi-lingual and multimodal results that benefit the physically challenged and the integration of the different technologies solves unsolved and challenging problems. The proposed work helps to automatically generate captions for images according to users' language preferences and share them on social media platforms based on their choice. Moreover, AICT also allows people to listen to the audio of the generated description as well which is very useful for visually impaired people. AICT being a PWA and mobile responsive, runs smoothly on any device whether mobile or desktop and functions as a native application when installed. Furthermore, increased accuracy does not always lead to more explainability. Moreover, a model being explainable does not mean more accuracy. There is always a trade-off between the two.

Acknowledgments

Deepest gratitude to Micah Hodosh and Peter Young and Julia Hockenmaier for providing the Flickr 8k dataset that was used in this research [28].

Funding

The authors received no specific funding for this study.

Conflicts of interest

The authors declare that they have no conflicts of interest to report regarding the present study.

References

[1]   S. Bhojak, V. Sharma, and P. Mishra, "Multipurpose manual agro equipment," *International Journal of Advanced Research*, 2020;8(6):302–307.

[2]   R. Devakunchari, "Analysis on big data over the years," *International Journal of Scientific and Research*, 2014;4:1.

[3]   U. Sivarajah, M. Kamal, Z. Irani, and V. Weerakkody, "Critical analysis of Big Data challenges and analytical methods," *Journal of Business Research*, 2014;70:263–286.

[4]   C. Liu and G. Song, "A method of measuring the semantic gap in image retrieval: Using the information theory," In *2011 International Conference on Image Analysis and Signal Processing*, 2011, pp. 287–291. doi:10.1109/IASP.2011.6109048.

[5]   R. Valencia-García and F. García-Sánchez, "Natural language processing and human–computer interaction," *Computer Standards & Interfaces*, 2013;35(5):415–416.

[6]   U. Bahety and S. Gupta, "Overview on image captioning techniques," *International Journal of Emerging Trends in Engineering Research*, 2021;9(8):1118–1123. doi:10.30534/ijeter/2021/15982021.

[7]   I. Sarker, "Deep learning: a comprehensive overview on techniques, taxonomy, applications and research directions," *SN Computer Science*, 2021;2(6):1–16. doi:10.1007/s42979-021-00815-1.

[8]   G. Sharma, P. Kalena, N. Malde, A. Nair, and S. Parkar, "Visual image caption generator using deep learning," *2nd International Conference on Advances in Science & Technology (ICAST)*, 2019. doi:10.2139/ssrn.3368837.

[9]   G. Kaushik, "Progressive web app - the future of web development," *International Journal for Research in Applied Science and Engineering Technology*, 20197;(7):495–498. doi:10.22214/ijraset.2019.7077.

[10] L. Zhang, Y. Zhang, X. Zhao, and Z. Zou, "Image captioning via proximal policy optimization," *Image and Vision Computing*, 2021;108:104126. doi:10.1016/j.imavis.2021.104126.

[11] P. Waghmare and D. Shinde, "Artificial intelligence based on image caption generation," *International Conference on Communication & Information Processing (ICCIP)*, 2020. doi:10.2139/ssrn.3648847.

[12] S. Degadwala, D. Vyas, H. Biswas, U. Chakraborty, and S. Saha, "Image captioning using Inception V3 transfer learning model," In: *2021 6th International Conference on Communication and Electronics Systems (ICCES)*, 2021, pp. 1103–1108. doi:10.1109/ICCES51350.2021.9489111.

[13] T. Wadhwa, H. Virk, J. Aghav, and S. Borole, "Image captioning using deep learning," *International Journal for Research in Applied Science and Engineering Technology*, 2020;8(6):1430–1435. doi:10.22214/ijraset.2020.6232.

[14] R. Staniūtė, and D. Šešok, "A systematic literature review on image captioning." *Applied Sciences*, 2019;9(10):2024.

[15] P. Diwakar, "Automatic image captioning using deep learning," *Proceedings of the International Conference on Innovative Computing & Communication (ICICC)*, 2021. doi:10.2139/ssrn.3833851.

[16] C. Jain and N. Sharma, "Image captioning using CNN long short-term memory network," *Proceedings of the International Conference on Advances in Electronics, Electrical & Computational Intelligence (ICAEEC)*, 2020. doi:10.2139/ssrn.3576373.

[17] L. Clark, P. Doyle, D. Garaialde, et al., "The state of speech in HCI: trends, themes and challenges," *Interacting with Computers*, 2019;31(4):349–371.

[18] E. Lloret and M. Palomar, "Analysing and evaluating the task of automatic tweet generation: knowledge to business," *Computers in Industry*, 2016;78:3–15.

[19] J. Mao, W. Xu, Y. Yang, J. Wang, and A. Yuille, "Explain images with multimodal recurrent neural networks," 2014. arXiv:1410.1090.

[20] O. Vinyals, A. Toshev, S. Bengio, and D. Erhan, "Show and tell: a neural image caption generator," *Proceedings of the IEEE Computer Society Conference on Computer Vision and Pattern Recognition*, 2015:3156–3164.

[21] J. Mao, W. Xu, Y. Yang, J. Wang, Z. Huang, and A. Yuille, "Deep captioning with multimodal recurrent neural networks (M-RNN)," 2014. arXiv:1412.6632.

[22] A. Karpathy and L. Fei-Fei, "Deep visual-semantic alignments for generating image descriptions," *IEEE Transactions on Pattern Analysis and Machine Intelligence*, 2017;39(4):664–676. doi:10.1109/tpami.2016.2598339.

[23] C. Amritkar and V. Jahade, "Image caption generation using deep learning technique," In: *Proceedings of the. ICCUBEA 2018*, pp. 1–4.

[24] A. Ghosh, D. Dutta, and T. Tiyasa, "A neural network framework to generate caption from images," In: *Emerging Technology in Modelling and Graphics*, J. Mandal and D. Bhattacharya (eds.) Springer, Singapore, 2020, pp. 171–180.

[25] Y. Chu, X. Yue, L. Yu, M. Sergei, and Z. Wang, "Automatic image captioning based on ResNet50 and LSTM with soft attention," *Wireless Communications and Mobile Computing*, 2020;2020:1–7. doi:10.1155/2020/8909458.

[26] H. Katpally and A. Bansal, "Ensemble learning on deep neural networks for image caption generation," In: *Proceedings of the 14th IEEE – ICSC*, 2020, pp. 61–68.

[27] S. Katiyar and S. Kumar, "Comparative evaluation of CNN architectures for image caption generation," *International Journal of Advanced Computer Science and Applications*, 2020;11(12):1–9. doi:10.14569/ijacsa.2020.0111291.

[28] M. Hodosh, P. Young, and J. Hockenmaier. "Framing image description as a ranking task: data, models and evaluation metrics," *Journal of Artificial Intelligence Research*, 2013;47:853–899.

Chapter 17

Explainable renegotiation for SLA in cloud-based system

Irving V. Paputungan[1]

17.1 Introduction

The excitement around cloud technology often leads people to believe that it can solve all problems, but this is not always true and the complexity of using the cloud is often overlooked by promoters. There is a significant difference between the adoption of cloud technology and the level of innovation that cloud consumers can achieve, which is a major concern for many cloud users [1,2]. They are questioning the ability of cloud computing to provide continuous service delivery [3].

The Service Level Agreement (SLA) is a crucial document in cloud computing that outlines the obligations of both the customer and the provider, including details about the expected service delivery and penalties for violations [4–6]. This document is essential for customers to trust the cloud provider's ability to handle their data and rely on the service [7]. Without strong assurances that their requirements and SLA will be enforced, customers will not outsource their data to cloud infrastructures. Thus, managing the SLA within a cloud-based system is crucial to ensuring service continuity.

Cloud providers typically offer two types of SLA: predefined and negotiated. A predefined SLA is a generic template that applies to all customers. However, some customers may have unique QoS requirements that are not covered by a predefined SLA. In such cases, the customer and provider engage in a negotiation process to establish a mutually agreed-upon SLA before service provision (negotiated SLA) [8,9]. In this context, negotiation refers to the process by which parties arrive at a mutually acceptable agreement on a particular matter [10].

In a typical scenario, the terms of an SLA are fixed upon construction and remain unchanged throughout the service period [11]. However, this approach conflicts with the dynamic nature of cloud computing, which is characterised by flexibility. The inability of current SLA management frameworks to accommodate this dynamic environment can negatively affect service delivery performance [12]. In this context, a framework refers to an abstract representation of functionality for

---

[1]Informatics Department, Universitas Islam Indonesia, Yogyakarta, Indonesia

managing the SLA. Service providers must be capable of accommodating changes in the needs and circumstances of cloud consumers over time [13]. Failure to address these factors can result in service violations that may impact the acceptance of a cloud service [14,15].

Existing frameworks for managing SLAs do not include provisions for adjustable SLAs based on customer preferences during operation [16–18], nor do they address service violation handling for cloud-based systems that can minimise such violations [19–21]. The focus of typical SLA renegotiation is limited to the initial phase of service delivery, and service violation handling only reacts after the violation has been detected. Consequently, there is a need for adjusting SLAs during service operation, considering the customer's changing preferences, the provider's current situation, and any occurrences of service violations.

17.2 Explainable artificial intelligence and cloud computing

Explainable artificial intelligence (XAI), also known as interpretable AI or explainable machine learning (XML), is a type of artificial intelligence (AI) where humans can understand how and why the AI makes certain decisions or predictions. This is different from traditional machine learning, where the reasoning behind the AI's decision-making process is not transparent, even to its creators. The term "Explainable AI" encompasses various methods and processes that enable humans to comprehend and trust the results produced by machine learning algorithms. It also acknowledges that these techniques can be applied to an existing system rather than being built into it from the start.

The goal of XAI is to enhance the performance of AI systems by providing users with a better understanding of how these systems arrive at their decisions. XAI could potentially fulfil the social right to explanation, even if there is no legal or regulatory obligation to do so. By explaining the decision-making process, XAI can improve the user experience of a product or service by increasing the trust that end-users have in the AI system. XAI aims to reveal what actions have been taken, what is currently happening, and what will happen in the future, as well as the information that is being used to make these decisions. This can help to validate existing knowledge, challenge preconceptions, and generate new assumptions.

XAI is a valuable resource for answering fundamental questions about AI systems, such as 'How?' and 'Why?', and can help to mitigate ethical and legal issues. As a result, researchers have recognised XAI as a crucial element of trustworthy AI, leading to an increase in attention towards explainability. The implementation of XAI is essential for organisations to establish trust and confidence in deploying AI models. Additionally, AI explainability assists organisations in taking a responsible approach to AI development.

There are several reasons why cloud computing should implement XAI: (1) increased transparency: cloud-based AI systems can process large amounts of data and provide insights that can inform important decisions. However, without XAI, it can be challenging for users to understand why certain decisions are being made. Implementing XAI increases transparency and helps build trust in AI-based decision-making; (2) better decision-making: with XAI, users can better understand the reasoning behind AI-based decisions, leading to better decision-making. This is especially important in complex decision-making scenarios, such as those involving multiple variables or factors; (3) improved accountability: XAI can help hold AI systems accountable for their decisions. If an AI system makes a decision that has negative consequences, the explanation provided by XAI can help identify where things went wrong and how to improve the system.

17.3   SLA renegotiation

In a cloud-based system, SLA parameters can be categorised into two types: functional and non-functional parameters. Functional parameters describe how the service is maintained and delivered in the environment, including aspects like security and protection. Non-functional parameters, also known as service level objectives (SLO), include measurable parameters like availability and throughput. SLOs provide specific characteristics of the service during delivery through these parameters.

Non-functional parameters are crucial for cloud-based services and consist of multiple SLO parameters that are regularly monitored and assessed to ensure that the service is effectively delivered. These SLO parameters vary based on the application, service, or outsourced data [22] and are intended to define the expected service between the customer and provider. SLO provides a quantitative way to establish the level of service a customer can anticipate from the provider. It may comprise one or more Quality of Service (QoS) metrics, with availability being composed of uptime and downtime. QoS refers to the measurement of a service's performance.

Renegotiating the SLA in cloud-based systems typically focuses on the non-functional parameters or SLOs, which are highly influenced by the network performance during service delivery. SLOs are a key feature of cloud computing that customers expect. It is assumed that the initial negotiation for the SLA has already taken place before renegotiation. The QoS used in this study is based on a private cloud storage prototype used in a research centre. The design for SLA renegotiation is based on the current implementation of the SLA management framework used in most SLA management research.

The process of SLA renegotiation involves modifying existing SLA clauses through subsequent negotiations [11]. Changes in service-based systems are inevitable, and SLA is no exception, as customer requirements or capability changes can lead to renegotiation [22]. During renegotiation, either the customer or the provider initiates modification in the established agreement before service or resource reconfiguration, such as resizing storage or adjusting throughput limits. Therefore, SLA renegotiation is necessary [23,24] to accommodate changing circumstances and should be carefully designed to maximise benefits for all parties involved. Flexible SLA terms also enhance the trustworthiness of cloud services [25], and in addition to security, reputation, and transparency mechanisms [3], SLA renegotiation can play an important role in the adoption of cloud technology. Such aforementioned explanation will become the notion of XAI within the cloud-based system in this chapter.

During SLA renegotiation, it is crucial to have a plan in place to ensure that the provider and consumer of the service can meet their service goals. These objectives are often tied to the agreed-upon price. To calculate the preferences of both parties, a utility function can be employed [26]. Various decision-making strategies, including those used in decision support systems, can be used to facilitate SLA renegotiation. Some of these strategies can be derived from bilateral negotiation strategies, with certain modifications [27].

In the renegotiation stage, the offer generation approach is considered more beneficial because it enables both parties to negotiate optimised SLA parameters. By providing multi-differentiated offers at the same time, it reduces the renegotiation time and offers various ways to meet both parties' interests [28]. To generate the offer efficiently and optimally, a range of values is set within an upper and a lower bound level, which can be obtained from learning the history of service level and assessing the current situation within the cloud environment. The initially agreed service level is also important to consider during renegotiation. However, determining which offer will be selected becomes another issue, as all offers generated using this approach will have the same utility value. Hence, negotiation preferences are evaluated using a utility function, and solutions are sorted using certain criteria to simplify the selection of the most suitable offer.

17.4 SLA violation

SLA breaches are common in cloud environments due to various factors such as workload changes, external conditions, limited resources, and hardware/software failures. These breaches can harm the customer's trust in the service provider and negatively impact their profits [15]. To address these issues, SLA renegotiation can be initiated proactively or reactively by either the service provider or the consumer. Proactive renegotiation involves proposing new SLOs when the customer needs to adjust their established SLA, or when the provider anticipates a breach. In contrast, reactive renegotiation occurs after a breach has been detected and may involve decreasing the service level and imposing a penalty charge. It is crucial to predict SLA breaches before they happen, using historical data and experience to inform decisions about which parameters to address during renegotiation.

The standard method of categorising delivered services in relation to SLA is by determining whether each parameter has been fulfilled, which results in a binary categorisation of either violation or compliance. However, this approach is inadequate due to the constantly changing network conditions within the cloud environment, as well as the varying importance and requirements of each SLO. To address this, a more comprehensive approach to SLA violation categorisation based on the Principles of European Contract Law has been proposed in reference [29]. This approach includes a broader range of categories for when a service is considered unfulfilled. They are:

● All-or-nothing provisioning – the service provisioning must meet all the SLOs for a successful delivery.
● Partial provisioning – the service provisioning meets some of the SLOs for a successful delivery.
● Weighted partial provisioning – the service provisioning meets SLOs that have a weighting greater than a threshold.

According to a report by the SLA@SOI European project on SLA Management, altering the QoS level can impact the likelihood of an SLA violation [30]. To minimise the occurrence of SLA violations and reduce the associated penalties, service providers must take steps to reconfigure the system based on SLA policies. In cases where penalties cannot be avoided, the severity of the violation should determine the penalty given. To ensure a fair and flexible system of penalties in the event of SLA violations, weighted SLOs are used.

17.5   Weightage for SLOs

The concept of using weightage in service-based computing was influenced by the utility function introduced in Ref. [26]. Utility, from an economic standpoint, is a measure of preferences for a set of goods, including services that fulfil human wants. In service-based computing, providers and customers are assumed to have preferences that represent their service objectives, which guide the behaviour of the service. Providers will strive to achieve the objectives that customers prefer the most. In many cases, a party's preference can be represented by a utility value [15,31,32], where a higher utility value corresponds to a greater preference.

As per Ref. [33], directly measuring or observing utility is not possible, so economists came up with a method to infer relative utilities from observed choices. They classified utility into two types – cardinal and ordinal utility. Cardinal utility considers the magnitude of utility differences to be important, whereas ordinal utility sees them as meaningless. For instance, if a soft-drink A has a utility value of 120, soft-drink B has a utility value of 80, and soft-drink C has a utility value of 40, cardinal utility suggests that A is better than B by the same amount that B is better than C. On the other hand, ordinal utility only tells us that A is preferred over B and C based on priority, but does not give any information about the magnitude of difference in preference.

Service-based computing involves customers considering their financial capability when deciding how they want a service to be delivered. Customers evaluate and select from a set of available preferences offered by the service provider based on their priority. To prioritise these preferences during the service period, customers adopt ordinal utility. This utility can also be used to generate the best possible offer.

17.6   Manifold learning for SLO violation detection

The conventional method of identifying SLA violations relies on pre-defined SLOs and their corresponding thresholds. However, this approach is inadequate for cloud-based services where multiple SLOs are used to measure performance, each with varying priorities depending on the desired outcome. To assess cloud service performance, various parameters with different measurement units, such as availability (percentage), response time (milliseconds), and throughput (bits per second), are employed. Some parameters may be independent of each other, making it more complicated to detect and predict violations across multiple SLOs. Additionally, it is possible for violations to occur in less critical parameters while not happening in essential ones.

To detect service violations within SLAs that involve multiple parameters, a manifold learning approach has been proposed. Manifold learning is a technique used in machine learning that has gained popularity due to recent advancements in data acquisition and high-rate information sources, which often result in large volumes of high-dimensional data. This technique involves constructing a manifold from sample data points or finding a mapping from a high-dimensional manifold to a low-dimensional Euclidean space. This approach shows promise because it can reduce the complexity of very high-dimensional or nonlinear datasets, which can be slow and difficult to work with for information retrieval algorithms, such as machine learning algorithms. For instance, grayscale images can have a dimensionality of over 10,000 pixels, which can slow down machine learning algorithms and make it challenging to find the global optimum. Moreover, high-dimensional datasets can be difficult to visualise, and reducing the dimensionality of the data while preserving as much information as possible is essential.

This chapter introduces an initial approach to detect performance violations in cloud-based systems using the concept of manifold learning. The network data within a cloud environment is characterised by high fluctuations and the need to measure multiple parameters simultaneously, which makes it challenging to detect and predict violations, particularly when only a few parameters are affected. By reducing the dimensionality of the network data involving multiple parameters and aggregating them based on their importance level, it becomes possible to detect and estimate the violations.

17.7   Support vector regression for SLO violation prediction

To predict SLO violation, data that is previously obtained by the monitoring system is analysed to estimate the upcoming ones within certain time intervals. The prediction will learn from historical data of violation level generated as in the previous section. This kind of data formed a sequential data point in time–space, which is called time series data.

Time series analysis involves the application of statistical methods to create models for a series of data points that are dependent on time. By using this data-focussed approach, it is feasible to predict future events based on past events that are already known. This type of analysis is different from regular data analysis problems, such as classical data mining or machine learning, where the data points are independent and the order of the data points within a data set is not significant. Time series analysis involves various techniques for examining time series data to extract useful statistics and other features of the data.

SVM is a regression analysis method that works by taking a set of input data and classifying the output into one of two possible classes. It identifies the best hyper-plane that separates each class in the input. SVM and other learning techniques, such as artificial neural network, have primarily been used for classification, but they can also be used for general regression analysis, which involves estimating a function by fitting a curve to a set of data points. This approach is called support vector regression (SVR) when SVM is used for general regression analysis. SVR involves assessing a function using observed data, which then trains the SVR. This is different from traditional time-series prediction methodologies where there is no strict model, and the prediction is determined solely by the data. Some important benefits of SVR are; it performs well even if there are very few cases on which to train the model, and, in addition, there is no local minimum. Such advantages make SVR suitable for SLO violation prediction.

17.8   Renegotiation simulation

The renegotiation framework as in Figure 17.1 is then simulated. The framework consists of:

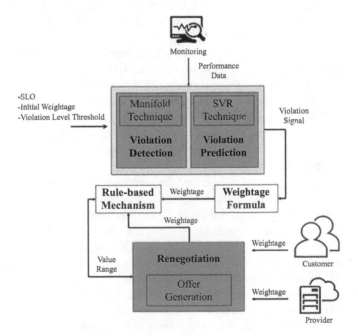

Figure 17.1   SLA renegotiation framework

(a)   Service violation detection and estimation.
(b)   Service assessment which evaluates the delivered service.
(c)   Mechanism to provide the range of SLO values where it can be renegotiated.
(d)   Timely manner bilateral renegotiation to give optimum multiple offers to the customer and avoid further violation.

Simulation on the SLA renegotiation then needs to be designed properly to be able to generate new SLO values based on several situations. The new SLO values must be a win–win solution for both the service provider and the customer. The renegotiation elements are first derived prior to designing each component within SLA renegotiation framework.

17.9   Service violation detection and estimation

SLOs used in this chapter are daily day availability, night availability, throughput, day response time, and night response time. Such SLOs are considerably the main features and performance measurements in any service-based system, especially on IaaS and used in several works [34–37]. Different types of services or environments may use different SLOs. In addition, due to the varying loads in the cloud storage at different times, the availability and response time are split into day and night. Both customer and provider then set such initial weightages prior to negotiation to identify how important such parameters are during service delivery. Violation thresholds are also set by the cloud customers during initial negotiation. Such customers must understand about their SLA before setting thresholds. Both are used to determine the violation class after obtaining the violation weightage.

In the violation handling section, manifold learning is used to address the challenge of detecting SLA violations across multiple parameters, which may be measured in different units of measurement. This involves reducing the dimensionality of the data, which is framed as an SLO data-mapping problem. Each SLO is treated as a dimension, with a weight assigned to reflect its importance in service delivery, as agreed upon during negotiation. The use of weightage is important to determine the relative importance of each SLO during service delivery. The number of SLOs represents the dimensionality of the data.

According to the thresholds input by the customer, the violation is then classified into none, low, medium, and high class. This classification is also based on what is commonly implemented by several cloud monitoring tools such as Cacti, Nagios, PRTG, and Zenoss. Instead of detecting the violation of each SLO, detection of the violation based on the aggregate importance level is more straightforward and meaningful. The historical data of daily violation level detection will then be used to predict the future violation level. Different levels of notification are expected to inform the user on the service delivery status before any severe violation occurs and prevents service interruption.

From the violation level that is obtained daily, prediction is performed to estimate the future violation level. Given the daily violation level as a set of time series data, SVR then maps the input onto a dimensional feature space using non-linear mapping, and a linear model is constructed in the feature space.

A new mechanism has been proposed to optimise the importance level of each parameter in a cloud-based system prior to renegotiation, considering the dynamic nature of performance. This mechanism uses predefined weightage and considers the service performance in the previous period to determine the new importance level for each parameter. In [38], it is mentioned that parameters that are more important during service delivery are more difficult to renegotiate from the user's perspective. To obtain the best weightage dynamically for the customer, the formula below uses the number of small violations that occur within a specified period. If a parameter has more violations, it will be considered more important during renegotiation. The new weightage will be bigger or smaller depending on the number of violations that occurred in the previous period. By using this formula, providers can acknowledge their own situation and reflect on their capability.

According to [39], a range of values can be generated for the areas of SLO that can be renegotiated before the actual renegotiation takes place. The nine rules that are derived from all renegotiation conditions are based on both the initial weightage and the new weightage. When the weightage of an SLO is higher than the average importance level, it is considered highly important. Such an SLO with a high importance level will have a smaller range of renegotiation options and possible values for renegotiation. Such boundaries are determined based on the importance level of the renegotiated SLO. If the SLO is very important, it is more difficult to be renegotiated.

To achieve the new objectives during SLA renegotiation, a negotiation strategy is necessary to benefit both parties. In this chapter, a technique called Genetic Algorithm (GA) has been proposed by [42] and incorporated as an offer generation-based negotiation strategy without any constraints. Essentially, GA is a heuristic agent that searches for the best negotiation offer in the form of SLO value combinations within a certain range based on a maximum fitness value. GA has also been used in recent works such as [27,40]. The GA generates one or more optimum offers based on certain criteria from both parties to obtain a certain level of acceptance. The offer generator provides a new SLO within a specific limit that was assessed earlier. With this mechanism, the customer can choose from among the optimum offers for the next period of service.

17.10 Simulation and result

In this chapter, only the SLA renegotiation part is covered, while the violation detection and prediction will be discussed in the future. The developed SLA renegotiation framework consists of four additional mechanisms to deal with the dynamic nature of cloud computing, they are (1) manifold learning approach for violation detection and prediction, (2) weightage formula to generate dynamic weightage for each SLO, (3) rule-based mechanism for generating a range of SLO values, and (4) genetic algorithm to generate optimised multiple offers during renegotiation. Those mechanisms will be simulated within the four scenarios:

(a) The cloud customer initiates renegotiation. First is when customers want to change their initial preferences. They occasionally need to change their preference following their e.g., business strategy. In this case, customers can update the weightage of each SLO in the next period (e.g., the following day or week).

(b) The cloud provider initiates renegotiation. The second scenario is when cloud service providers need to adjust their preference due to possibly upcoming infrastructure maintenance or any resource shortage that may affect the service delivery. Here, the provider will initiate renegotiation by modifying the weightage of the SLOs.

(c) Both cloud provider and customer initiate renegotiation. In the third scenario, both customer and provider adjust the weightage for the SLOs prior to renegotiation.

(d) Violation takes part and renegotiation is recommended. In the fourth scenario, if the cloud provider predicts an SLA violation, the provider will initiate renegotiation. The renegotiation will use weightage that is automatically redefined using a weighting formula based on violation occurrence prior to the renegotiation. For all scenarios, new SLOs will then be generated based on the new weightage and offered to the customer for them to choose one. The updated SLOs will be re-provisioned accordingly.

Several cases of renegotiation on Scenarios 1 and 2 have been simulated to investigate if the offer generation is able to provide multi-offers. From Table 17.1, multi-offers were successfully generated for three cases (cases 2, 3, and 5). As expected, GA can provide several offers during renegotiation for the customer to choose based on their new weightage.

In Table 17.2, the provider sets new important levels for each SLO. Renegotiated SLO values are then generated using GA. For example, in cases 2 and 5, the provider sets a higher weightage for daily availability, and there are two offers that the customer may choose during renegotiation. In case 2, the generated availability value for the day is lower than the initial one. It is because of a very high weightage for availability (day) that is set by the provider. However, the lower value on the response time is proposed to maintain the overall utility value.

A different situation can be seen in Table 17.3 where both customer and provider set new importance levels for each SLO based on their current requirement. From the simulation, GA can provide multi-offers for case number 5 while the rest of the simulation can only a generate single offer. Meanwhile, in scenario 4, the weightage formula is triggered based on service assessment to provide the importance level for each SLO prior to renegotiation. Using the new importance levels that are set for the provider as shown in Table 17.4, renegotiation was then simulated. The result showed that multi-offers could also be obtained using new importance levels in several cases compare with other scenarios.

Table 17.1 Simulation of scenario 1

#	Parameter	New w customer	New w provider	Parameter value possibilities	Offer 1	Offer 2	Offer 3	Offer 4	Offer 5
1	Availability day (%)	0.4	0.2	99 98.5 98 97.5	99				
	Availability night (%)	0.3	0.2	97 96.5 96 95.5	96.5				
	Throughput (kpbs)	0.1	0.2	5,000 4,500 4,000 3,500	3,500				
	Response day (ms)	0.1	0.2	400 450 500 550	550				
	Response night (ms)	0.1	0.2	400 450 500 550	550				
2	Availability day (%)	0.4	0.2	99 98.5 98 97.5	99	99			
	Availability night (%)	0.2	0.2	96 95.5	96	95.5			
	Throughput (kpbs)	0.2	0.2	5,000 4,500	4,500	5,000			
	Response day (ms)	0.1	0.2	400 450 500 550	550	550			
	Response night (ms)	0.1	0.2	400 450 500 550	550	550			
3	Availability day (%)	0.3	0.2	99 98.5 98 97.5	99	98.5			
	Availability night (%)	0.3	0.2	97 96.5 96 95.5	97	97			
	Throughput (kpbs)	0.2	0.2	5,000 4,500	4,500	4,500			
	Response day (ms)	0.1	0.2	400 450 500 550	550	550			
	Response night (ms)	0.1	0.2	400 450 500 550	550	550			
4	Availability day (%)	0.3	0.2	99 98.5 98 97.5	99				
	Availability night (%)	0.3	0.2	97 96.5 96 95.5	97				
	Throughput (kpbs)	0.1	0.2	5,000 4,500 4,000 3,500	3,500				
	Response day (ms)	0.2	0.2	400 450	450				
	Response night (ms)	0.1	0.2	400 450 500 550	450				
5	Availability day (%)	0.2	0.2	98 97.5	97.5	98	97.5		
	Availability night (%)	0.3	0.2	97 96.5 96 95.5	97	97	97		
	Throughput (kpbs)	0.1	0.2	5,000 4,500 4,000 3,500	3,500	3,500	3,500		
	Response day (ms)	0.2	0.2	400 450	400	450	450		
	Response night (ms)	0.2	0.2	400 450	450	450	400		
6	Availability day (%)	0.2	0.2	98 97.5	97.5				
	Availability night (%)	0.3	0.2	97 96.5 96 95.5	97				
	Throughput (kpbs)	0.3	0.2	6,000 5,500 5,000 4,500	6,000				
	Response day (ms)	0.1	0.2	400 450 500 550	550				
	Response night (ms)	0.1	0.2	400 450 500 550	550				

Table 17.2 Simulation of scenario 2

#	Parameter	New w customer	New w provider	Parameter value possibilities				Offer 1	Offer 2	Offer 3	Offer 4	Offer 5
1	Availability day (%)	0.2	0.4	98	97.5			97.5	97.5			
	Availability night (%)	0.2	0.3	96	95.5			95.5	96			
	Throughput (kpbs)	0.2	0.1	6,000	5,500	5,000	4,500	6,000	5,000			
	Response day (ms)	0.2	0.1	300	350	400	450	300	300			
	Response night (ms)	0.2	0.1	300	350	400	450	300	300			
2	Availability day (%)	0.2	0.4	98	97.5			97.5				
	Availability night (%)	0.2	0.2	96	95.5			95.5				
	Throughput (kpbs)	0.2	0.2	5,000	4,500			5,000				
	Response day (ms)	0.2	0.1	300	350	400	450	300				
	Response night (ms)	0.2	0.1	300	350	400	450	300				
3	Availability day (%)	0.2	0.3	98	97.5			97.5				
	Availability night (%)	0.2	0.3	96	95.5			95.5				
	Throughput (kpbs)	0.2	0.2	5,000	4,500			5,000				
	Response day (ms)	0.2	0.1	300	350	400	450	300				
	Response night (ms)	0.2	0.1	300	350	400	450	300				
4	Availability day (%)	0.2	0.3	98	97.5			97.5				
	Availability night (%)	0.2	0.3	96	95.5			95.5				
	Throughput (kpbs)	0.2	0.1	6,000	5,500	5,000	4,500	6,000				
	Response day (ms)	0.2	0.2	400	450			400				
	Response night (ms)	0.2	0.1	300	350	400	450	300				
5	Availability day (%)	0.2	0.2	98	97.5			98	97.5			
	Availability night (%)	0.2	0.3	96	95.5			95.5	95.5			
	Throughput (kpbs)	0.2	0.1	6,000	5,500	5,000	4,500	6,000	6,000			
	Response day (ms)	0.2	0.2	400	450			400	400			
	Response night (ms)	0.2	0.2	400	450			450	400			
6	Availability day (%)	0.2	0.2	98	97.5			98				
	Availability night (%)	0.2	0.3	96	95.5			95.5				
	Throughput (kpbs)	0.2	0.3	5,000	4,500			4,500				
	Response day (ms)	0.2	0.1	300	350	400	450	300				
	Response night (ms)	0.2	0.1	300	350	400	450	300				

Table 17.3 Simulation of scenario 3

#	Parameter	New w customer	New w provider	Parameter value possibilities								Offer 1	Offer 2	Offer 3	Offer 4	Offer 5
1	Availability day (%)	0.2	0.4	98	97.5	96	95.5					97.5				
	Availability night (%)	0.3	0.2	97	96.5	96	95.5					97				
	Throughput (kpbs)	0.3	0.1	6,000	5,500	5,000	4,500					6,000				
	Response day (ms)	0.1	0.2	400	450	500	550	600				550				
	Response night (ms)	0.1	0.1	250	300	350	400	450	500	550	600	600				
2	Availability day (%)	0.3	0.4	98.5	98	97.5	96.5					98				
	Availability night (%)	0.2	0.2	96	95.5	96	95.5					96				
	Throughput (kpbs)	0.2	0.1	6,000	5,500	5,000	4,500					6,000				
	Response day (ms)	0.2	0.2	300	350	400	450	500				400				
	Response night (ms)	0.1	0.1	400	450	500	550					600				
3	Availability day (%)	0.3	0.2	99	98.5	98	97.5					99				
	Availability night (%)	0.3	0.2	97	96.5	96	95.5					96.5				
	Throughput (kpbs)	0.1	0.3	5,000	4,500	4,000	3,500	3,000	2,500	2,000	1,500	1,500				
	Response day (ms)	0.2	0.1	300	350	400	450	500				300				
	Response night (ms)	0.1	0.2	400	450	500	550					550				
4	Availability day (%)	0.2	0.3	98	97.5	97.5						97.5				
	Availability night (%)	0.3	0.2	96.5	96	95.5	95					96.5				
	Throughput (kpbs)	0.3	0.3	5,500	5,000	5,000						5,500				
	Response day (ms)	0.1	0.1	250	300	350	400	450	500	550	600	600				
	Response night (ms)	0.1	0.1	250	300	350	400	450	500	550	600	600				
5	Availability day (%)	0.2	0.2	98	97.5	97.5	96.5	96				97.5	98	97.5	98	98
	Availability night (%)	0.1	0.1	97.5	97	96.5	96	95	94.5			94	97.5	94.5	97	97.5
	Throughput (kpbs)	0.3	0.3	5,500	5,000	5,000						5,500	5,000	5,500	5,000	5,000
	Response day (ms)	0.2	0.2	400	450	450						450	450	450	400	400
	Response night (ms)	0.2	0.2	400	450	400						400	400	450	400	450
6	Availability day (%)	0.2	0.3	98	97.5	97.5						97.5				
	Availability night (%)	0.1	0.2	96	95.5	95	94.5					94.5				
	Throughput (kpbs)	0.3	0.1	6,000	5,500	5,000	4,500					6,000				
	Response day (ms)	0.3	0.2	350	400	450	500					550				
	Response night (ms)	0.1	0.2	400	450	450	550					300				

Table 17.4 Simulation of scenario 4

#	Parameter	New w customer	New w provider	Parameter value possibilities			Offer 1	Offer 2	Offer 3	Offer 4	Offer 5
1	Availability day (%)	0.2	0.18611	98.5	98	97.5	98.5	98.5	98.5	98	
	Availability night (%)	0.2	0.18611	97	96	95.5	97	96	97	96	
	Throughput (kpbs)	0.2	0.18611	6,000	5,000	4,500	6,000	5,000	5,500	6,000	
	Response day (ms)	0.2	0.22083	400	450		450	450	450	450	
	Response night (ms)	0.2	0.22083	400	450		450	450	450	450	
2	Availability day (%)	0.2	0.19167	98.5	98	97.5	98.5	98	98.5	98.5	
	Availability night (%)	0.2	0.19167	97	96	95.5	97	96	97	96	
	Throughput (kpbs)	0.2	0.19167	6,000	5,000	4,500	6,000	6,000	5,500	5,000	
	Response day (ms)	0.2	0.2125	400	450		450	450	450	450	
	Response night (ms)	0.2	0.2125	400	450		450	450	450	450	
3	Availability day (%)	0.2	0.19444	98.5	98	97.5	98.5	98	98		
	Availability night (%)	0.2	0.19444	97	96	95.5	96	96	97		
	Throughput (kpbs)	0.2	0.19444	6,000	5,000	4,500	5,000	6,000	5,000		
	Response day (ms)	0.2	0.20833	400	450		450	450	450		
	Response night (ms)	0.2	0.20833	400	450		450	450	450		
4	Availability day (%)	0.2	0.18056	98.5	98	97.5	98	98.5			
	Availability night (%)	0.2	0.18056	97	96	95.5	97	96			
	Throughput (kpbs)	0.2	0.18056	6,000	5,000	4,500	6,000	6,000			
	Response day (ms)	0.2	0.22917	400	450		450	450			
	Response night (ms)	0.2	0.22917	400	450		450	450			
5	Availability day (%)	0.2	0.19167	98.5	98	97.5	98	98.5	98.5		
	Availability night (%)	0.2	0.19167	97	96	95.5	96.5	96	96		
	Throughput (kpbs)	0.2	0.19167	6,000	5,000	4,500	6,000	5,500	6,000		
	Response day (ms)	0.2	0.23333	400	450		450	450	450		
	Response night (ms)	0.2	0.19167	350	400		400	400	400		
6	Availability day (%)	0.2	0.18611	98.5	98	97.5	98.5	98.5	98.5	98	
	Availability night (%)	0.2	0.18611	97	96	95.5	97	96	97	96	
	Throughput (kpbs)	0.2	0.18611	6,000	5,000	4,500	6,000	5,000	5,500	6,000	
	Response day (ms)	0.2	0.22083	400	450		450	450	450	450	
	Response night (ms)	0.2	0.22083	400	450		450	450	450	450	

17.11 Analysis and conclusion

The objective of the renegotiation simulation is to determine if the proposed approach can generate optimised multiple offers from a single round of negotiation. This is seen from simulations of scenarios (Tables 17.1–17.4). The offers shown are generated optimally based on the consideration of the initial weightage and the new weightage at the first GA cycle. As GA works based on a random initial population, the multiple-offers solution is not always obtained in the first cycle. In some occasions, 2–3 more cycles are needed to obtain such multiple offers.

Comparing the results from each scenario, it can be seen from scenario 1 where the customer initiates the changing, more multiple offers are provided than the ones in scenario 2. To some extent, offering more flexibility to the customer when they require the renegotiation is better than when the provider initiates it. In scenario 3, where both parties modify the weightage, only 1 case that has multiple offers. There are five offers generated when the customer and provider set similar new weightage. More flexibility is generated when both parties have the same preferences. In scenario 4, more multiple offers are generated than in other scenarios. The occurrence of violation makes the renegotiation mechanism provides more options to the customer in order to balance the situation.

From the result, weightage plays an important role during renegotiation. The more important a parameter during renegotiation will result in the lesser possibility to renegotiate that parameter. This is in line with the statement from [41] that the more important the parameter, the more difficult it can be renegotiated.

The concepts mentioned earlier have been put into practice using MATLAB® and other simulation tools. The information is obtained from a prototype private cloud storage system located in a research centre. The effectiveness of this implementation has been thoroughly measured through quantitative evaluations. These experiments have demonstrated that the ideas presented in this study can manage the ever-changing conditions of cloud computing environments, particularly when there are typically breaches.

Moreover, the SLA renegotiation that has been developed is useful not only for service providers who wish to enhance their reputation but also for devoted cloud clients, particularly those who use IaaS and require long-term services. Rather than frequently switching to another service provider, which can be somewhat complicated in terms of system reconfiguration, they can continue using the service and renegotiate the conditions if required.

References

[1] K. Khan and Q. Malluhi, "Establishing trust in cloud computing," in *IT Professional*, 2010, vol. 12, no. 5, pp. 20–27. DOI:10.1109/MITP.2010.128

[2] K. J. Yao, S. Chen, C. Wang, D. C. Levy, and J. Zic, "Accountability as a service for the cloud," in *International Conference on Services Computing*, 2010, pp. 81–88.

[3]   I. Uusitalo, K. Karppinen, A. Juhola, and R. Savola, "Trust and cloud services - an interview study," in *2nd International Conference on Cloud Computing Technology and Science*, 2010, pp. 712–720.

[4]   D. Greenwood, G. Vitaglione, L. Keller, and M. Calisti, "Service Level Agreement management with adaptive coordination," in *International conference on Networking and Services*, July, 2006, pp. 45–50.

[5]   B. R. Kandukuri, V. R. Paturi, and A. Rakshit, "Cloud security issues," in *International Conference on Services Computing*, 2009, pp. 517–520.

[6]   W. Kim, "Cloud computing architecture," *International Journal of Web and Grid Services*, vol. 9, no. 3, pp. 287–303, 2013.

[7]   M. Alhamad, T. Dillon, and E. Chang, "Conceptual SLA framework for cloud computing," in *4th International Conference on Digital Ecosystems and Technologies*, April, 2010, pp. 606–610.

[8]   A. Galati, K. Djemame, M. Fletcher, *et al.*, "Designing an SLA protocol with renegotiation to maximize revenues for the CMAC platform," in *Web Information Systems Engineering 2011 and 2012 Workshops, LNCS*, vol. 7652, 2013, pp 105–117.

[9]   W. Mach and E. Schikuta, "A generic negotiation and re-negotiation framework for consumer-provider contracting of web services," in *14th International Conference on Information Integration and Web-based Applications & Services*, 2012, pp. 348–351.

[10] N. R. Jennings, P. Faratin, A. Lomuscio, S. Parsons, C. Sierra, and M. Wooldridge, "Automated negotiation: prospects, methods and challenges," *Group Decision and Negotiation, March*, vol. 10, no. 2, pp. 199–215, 2001.

[11] M. Parkin, P. Hasselmeyer, and B. Koller, "An SLA re-negotiation protocol," in *2nd Non-Functional Properties and Service Level Agreements in Service Oriented Computing Workshop*, Dublin, Ireland, 2008, pp. 6–11.

[12] S. Sharaf and K. Djemame, "Enabling service-level agreement renegotiation through extending WS-agreement specification," *Service Oriented Computing and Applications Journal*, vol. 9, no 2, pp. 177–191, 2015. DOI 10.1007/s11761-014-0159-5.

[13] J. Yan, J. Zhang, J. Lin, M. B. Chhetri, S. K. Goh, and R. Kowalczyk, "Towards autonomous SLA negotiation for adaptive service composition," in *10th International Conference on Computer Supported Cooperative Work in Design*, 2006, pp. 1–6.

[14] K. Lu, R. Yahyapour, P. Wieder, E. Yaqub, M. Abdullah, B. Schloer, and C. Kotsokalis, "Fault-tolerant Service Level Agreement lifecycle management in clouds using actor system," *Future Generation Computer System Journal*, vol. 54, issue C, pp. 247–259, 2016.

[15] A. Omezzine, N. B. B. Saoud, S. Tazi, and G. Cooperman, "SLA and Profit-aware SaaS provisioning through proactive renegotiation," in *15th International Symposium on Network Computing and Applications*, 2016, pp. 351–358.

[16] S. Bouchenak, "Automated control for SLA-aware elastic clouds," in *5th International Workshop on Feedback Control Implementation and Design in Computing Systems and Networks*, 2010, pp. 27–28.

[17] R. Buyya, C. S. Yeo, S. Venugopal, J. Broberg, and I. Brandic, "Cloud computing and emerging IT platforms: vision, hype, and reality for delivering computing as the 5th utility," *Journal of Future Generation Computer Systems*, vol. 25, no. 6, pp. 599–616, 2009.

[18] F. Faniyi and R. Bahsoon, "Engineering proprioception in SLA management for cloud architectures," in *9th Working IEEE/IFIP Conference on Software Architecture*, 2011, pp. 336–340.

[19] Y. Kouki and T. Ledoux, "SLA-driven capacity planning for cloud applications," in *International Conference on Cloud Computing Technology and Science*, 2012, pp. 135–140.

[20] M. Macias, J. O. Fitó, and J. Guitart, "Rule-based SLA management for revenue maximisation in cloud computing markets," in *International Conference on Network and Service Management*, Niagara Falls, 2010, pp. 354–357.

[21] V. Stantchev and C. Schrofer, "Negotiating and enforcing QoS and SLAs in grid and cloud computing," in N. Abdennadher and D. Petcu (Eds.), *Grid and Pervasive Computing 2009, LNCS*, vol. 5529, Springer-Verlag, Berlin, Heidelberg, 2009, pp. 25–35.

[22] ISO/IEC, "Information Technology – Cloud Computing – Service Level Agreement (SLA) Framework – Part 1: Overview and concepts," *International Standard*, ISO/IEC 19086–1, 2016.

[23] T. Labidi, A. Mtibaa, W. Gaaloul and F. Gargouri, "Ontology-based SLA negotiation and re-negotiation for cloud computing," in *26th International Conference on Enabling Technologies: Infrastructure for Collaborative Enterprises*, 2017, pp. 36–41.

[24] K. V. Patel, A. B. R. Khan, M. M. Sidnale, and D. L. D. Babu, "Advance strategies to understand the SLA's (Service Level Agreement) with specific Issues on Requirement Gathering," *International Journal of Advanced Research in Computer Science and Software Engineering*, vol. 4, no. 3, pp. 1199–1207, 2014.

[25] V. Spoorthy and C. Sreedhar, "Multi-level SLAs with dynamic negotiations for remote sensing data as a service," *International Journal of Scientific and Research Publications*, vol. 2, no. 10, pp. 1–5, 2012.

[26] J. Wilkes, *Utility Functions, Prices, and Negotiation, External Publication: Hewlett-Packard Development Company*, 2008.

[27] B. Pittl, W. Mach, and E. Schikuta, "Bazaar-extension: a cloudsim extension for simulating negotiation-based resource allocations," in *International Conference on Services Computing*, 2016, pp. 427–434.

[28] T. Alfredson and A. Cungu, "Negotiation theory and practice: a review of the literature," in *EASYPol Module 179*, Food and Agriculture Organization of the United Nations, 2008. http://www.fao.org/docs/up/easypol/550/4-5_negotiation_background_ paper_179en.pdf.

[29]   O. F. Rana, M. Warnier, T. B. Quillinan, F. Brazier, and D. Cojocarasu, "Managing violations in service level agreements," in *5th International Workshop on Grid Economics and Business Models*, 2008, pp. 349–358.

[30]   R. Yahyapour and P. Wieder, "State of the art analysis," in *Technical Report, no. FP7216556, SLA@SOI project*, 2009.

[31]   B. Pittl, W. Mach, and S. Schikuta, "A negotiation-based resource allocation model in IaaS-market," in *8th International Conference on Utility and Cloud Computing*, 2015, pp. 55–64.

[32]   B. Pittl, W. Mach, and S. Schikuta, "A classification of autonomous bilateral cloud SLA negotiation strategies," in *International Conference on Information Integration and Web-based Applications and Services*, Singapore, 2016, pp. 379–388.

[33]   A. Dasgupta and A. Prat, *Reputation and Asset Prices: A Theory of Information Cascades and Systematic Mispricing*, London School of Economics, 2005.

[34]   D. Battre, F. M. T. Brazier, K. P. Clark, M. A. Oey, A. Papaspyrou, O. Waldrich, P. Wieder, and W. Ziegler, "A proposal for WS-agreement negotiation," in *11th International Conference on Grid Computing*, 2010, pp. 233–241.

[35]   J. Bendriss, I. G. B. Yahia, and D. Zechlache, "Forecasting and anticipating SLO breaches in programmable networks," in *International Conference on Innovations in Clouds, Internet and Networks*, 2017, pp. 127–134.

[36]   N. Bonvin, G. Papaioannou, and K. Aberer, "Autonomic SLA-driven provisioning for cloud applications," in *11th International Symposium on Cluster, Cloud and Grid Computing*, 2011, pp. 434–443.

[37]   A. Galati, K. Djemame, M. Fletcher, *et al.*, "Designing an SLA protocol with renegotiation to maximize revenues for the CMAC platform," in *Web Information Systems Engineering 2011 and 2012 Workshops, LNCS*, vol. 7652, 2013, pp 105–117.

[38]   L. Wu, S. Kumar, and R. Buyya, "SLA-based resource allocation for software as a service provider (SaaS) in cloud computing environments," in *11th International Symposium on Cluster, Cloud and Grid Computing*, 2011, pp. 195–204.

[39]   S. Sharaf and K. Djemame, "Extending WS-agreement to support renegotiation of dynamic grid SLAs," in *eChallenges Conference*, 2010, pp. 1–8.

[40]   E. Benkhelifa, T. Welsh, L. Tawalbeh, A. Khreishah, Y. Jararweh, and M. Al-Ayyoub, "GA-based resource augmentation negotiation for energy-optimised mobile ad-hoc cloud," in *4th International Conference on Mobile Cloud Computing*, Oxford, 2016, pp. 110–116.

[41]   L. Wu and R. Buyya, *Service Level Agreement (SLA) in Utility Computing Systems*, Cloud Computing and Distributed Systems Laboratory, The University of Melbourne, 2010. arXiv preprint arXiv:1010.2881

[42]   X. Niu and S. Wang, "Genetic algorithm for automatic negotiation based on agent," in *7th World Congress on Intelligent Control and Automation*, Chongqing, China, 2008, pp. 3834–3838.

Chapter 18

Explainable AI for stock price prediction in stock market

*Pattabiraman Venkatasubbu[1],
Sharath Kumar Jagannathan[2], Anusooya Govindarajan[1]
and Maheswari Raja[1]*

In recent years, it has been observed that a lot of people invest their money into various stocks, and this growth is said to be exponential in the coming years as well. But people have to be careful in what they invest and how much they invest as the stock market is a high-risk and high-reward field. To cater to the need an explainable artificial intelligence (AI)-based methodology is proposed to create a model that could predict the future stock price which could help people mitigate losses and have a better chance of earning profits. In this work, the system is devised in such a way it first tests various models like K-nearest neighbours (KNN), moving average, linear regression and long short-term memory (LSTM) to understand how they respond to the data about any particular company that is listed on NSE India. Then the selected model's algorithm that produced the best accuracy is further used to find the price of any stock for the next 30 days. Since this is a software tool, for better user accessibility, a website using Django is created so that users can log in and check for any stock prices and predictions for the company in which they are interested.

18.1 Introduction

The stock market is a public exchange where people can buy and sell ownership stakes in publicly traded companies. Stocks, also called equities, are a representation of a part owner in a company. The intermediary that makes it possible to purchase and sell shares is the stock exchange. The stock market helps companies raise capital and also helps generate personal wealth by building savings and protecting people's money from inflation and taxes by maximising income [1]. It serves as an indicator of the state of the economy. Hence, it concludes how

[1]School of Computer Science and Engineering, Vellore Institute of Technology, Chennai, India
[2]Data Science Institute, Frank J. Guarini School of Business, Saint Peter's University, Jersey City, NJ, USA

important the stock market is for a country. But the stock market is not a steady income field, it has a lot of risks attached to it. People can lose all their savings if they do not invest properly or do not do any background study before they invest in any company. So how can we make sure that we invest in the right companies? Machine learning (ML) is an interdisciplinary field that brings together robotics, statistics and computer science. It is a component of academic research on artificial intelligence (AI) [2]. Making an automated system that can continually improve itself without human intervention is the main goal of ML. The only thing that it makes use of is data that it has collected and analysed to find specific patterns that are impossible for people to recognise [3]. ML has evolved into a powerful analytical tool that is widely used in the financial markets to assist with and manage investments more effectively. ML has been extensively utilised in the financial sector to offer a new mechanism that can assist investors in making better investment and management decisions to obtain better results and performance of their securities investment [4]. This new mechanism has been used to offer a new mechanism that can assist investors in making better investment and management decisions. Hence, a model is proposed that would help predict the future price of any company so that people can have a better chance of getting profits and mitigating losses [5]. In this work, we have taken four different models; KNN, linear regression, moving average and LSTM algorithms and checked which algorithm gives better accuracy for prediction. It was found that LSTM gave a better accuracy and that model was used to predict the stock price for the next 30 days for any particular company that is listed in NSE India. A user interface website is also created so that users can log in and select any company they want and find the approximate price for the next 30 days [6]. This can help people by helping them make profits as well as ensure that they do not invest in companies that have the potential to give losses.

Further, the stock market provides a snapshot of investors' and analysts' views on the economic and company growth prospects in the near future. Stock price changes have been caused by a wide range of factors, including but not limited to general economic conditions, market expectations and investor faith in the company's leadership and operations. The public can now get their hands on more information, and it can get it faster, thanks to technological advancements. Since a large amount of data needs to be processed in a short amount of time, stock analysis has become increasingly challenging. Investors anticipate improved stock-market analysis thanks to recent advancements in big data, particularly deep learning [7].

Changes in the stock and Forex markets have been the subject of extensive study and analysis by financial experts from around the world. As AI finds more and more uses, more and more investors are turning to deep learning models to analyse and forecast stock and Forex market movements. Stock and foreign exchange price fluctuations have been shown to be assumed [8]. The ability of deep learning to describe complex influencing factors sets it apart from conventional statistical and econometric models. We found that some of the existing methods predicted stock prices solely based on stock historical data, which only rarely introduced unstructured text data into the financial field. This was the case with the majority of the methods. Even though some of the methods took into account the significance of non-traditional data, all of the research focused on either financial news or information from social media. The traditional approach to analysing time series holds the belief that the movement of stock prices cannot be accurately predicted. However, behavioural finance theories demonstrate that the irrational investment behaviour of investors will affect the rise and fall of stock prices. This is because investors tend to overreact to market signals.

Data analytics refers to the data that can be extracted from reports (e.g., a recommendation for selling or buying a stock) that are provided by investment banks and research firms. These institutions conduct in-depth analyses of the business models, activities and competitions of various types of businesses.

These reports provide information on valuation, despite the fact that they may be expensive and shared among numerous customers, all of whom want to use this information to their advantage to make a profit. Out of the total number of prediction problems, 52 are daily classification problems, 54 are daily regression problems, 8 are intraday classification problems and 124 are intraday regression problems (11 of 124). The difficulty of collecting the necessary data may be at least partly to blame for this. Academics have much more access to daily historical price data and news titles than they do to intraday data.

To train a sophisticated neural network model, deep learning algorithms require massive amounts of input data. Since other types of data typically provide a smaller sample size, market data is the best option and most used for this purpose. The widespread adoption of social media and news websites online has increased the demand for text data, and web crawlers make it simple to collect this type of information. The analytics data is an extreme example; it is never used in the studies that were surveyed because of data scarcity and the high cost of access [9].

18.1.1   Explainable AI

Explainable AI, also known as XAI, is a group of techniques and methods that are applied to any ML techniques that mark it possible for the users to understand and obtain results/output produced by the algorithms. It can be utilised to describe an AI technique, along with its expected impact and potential biases. It provides assistance in characterising model accuracy, fairness, transparency and outcomes in decision-making that is powered by AI. Explainability in AI also assists organisations in taking a more responsible approach to the development of AI.

As XAI technology progresses, it becomes increasingly common to apply deep learning methods in a variety of contexts. Among the many possible uses are those in the fields of natural language processing, image recognition and medical prognostics. As deep learning has grown in popularity, so have the neural networks used in these programmes. For instance, since AlphaGo used reinforcement learning to beat the best chess player at the time, this technique has gained popularity and is now being used in the field of financial prediction. These advancements in technology have provided a firm footing upon which to build and expanded room for improvement in the stock and Forex prediction models.

The complete organisation of the chapter starts with a stock market and deep learning introduction, then the criteria and methods used to select articles for the literature review will be discussed, then the proposed system's architecture will be detailed, including an examination of the impact and analysis of various deep learning methods on stock markets and prediction, and finally, a conclusion and suggestions for future research will be offered.

18.2   Literature review

What people think has constantly been an essential piece of record for maximum folks all through the decision-making method. Technology has now (amongst different things) made it viable to discover approximately the reviews and stories of these withinside the substantial pool of humans who are neither our non-public acquaintances nor famous expert critics this is, humans have got in no way heard of. And conversely, increasingly more humans are making their reviews to be had by strangers through the Internet [10]. The hobby that personal customers display in online reviews approximately merchandise and services, and the capacity to have an impact on such reviews wield, is something this is a riding force for this vicinity of the hobby [11]. And there are numerous demanding situations concerned with this method that needs to be walked through in an effort to gain the right consequences out of them. In this survey, we analysed simple technique that generally occurs with this method and measures which are to be taken to conquer the demanding situations being faced [12].

The preliminary attention of our literature survey became to explore established online mastering algorithms and spot if they might be tailored to our use case, i.e., operating on real-time inventory rate data [13]. These protected Online AUC Maximisation, Online Transfer Learning and Online Feature Selection. However, as the user had been not able to discover any ability adaptation of those for inventory rate prediction, the system then determined to appear at the present systems, examine the principal drawbacks of the same, and spot if we should enhance upon them [14]. The system zeroed in on the correlation among inventory data (withinside the shape of dynamic, long-time period temporal dependencies among inventory prices) as the important thing difficulty that we wanted to solve. A brief seek of established answers to the above trouble led us to recurrent neural network (RNN) and LSTM [15]. After identifying to apply an LSTM neural community to carry out inventory prediction, we consulted a wide variety of papers to observe the idea of gradient descent and its numerous types [16]. We concluded our literature survey by searching how gradient descent may be used to chant the weights of an LSTM community and the way this method may be optimised [17].

In finance, international stock trading is one of the maximum essential activities. Stock marketplace prediction is an act of looking to decide the destiny fee of an inventory of different economic devices traded on economic exchange. This paper explains the prediction of an inventory of the usage of ML [18]. The technical and essential or time collection evaluation is utilised by the maximum of the stockbrokers whilst making the inventory predictions. The programming language used to are expecting the inventory marketplace the usage of gadget mastering is Python [19]. In this work, the system recommends an ML technique to be able to gain knowledge from the to-be shares records and benefit intelligence after which makes use of the received understanding for a correct prediction. This particular research endeavour makes its predictions regarding stock prices for both large and small capitalisations by employing a method of ML known as LSTM.

18.2.1 State of the art

18.2.1.1 Stock market prediction using AI techniques

The fragile version of the efficient market hypothesis (EMII) states that it is not possible to forecast the future price of an asset primarily based on the information contained with inside the historic prices of an asset. This is stated to be the case due to the fact the EMH states that it is impossible to forecast the future price of an asset. Because the market acts more like a random stroll, it is impossible to make accurate forecasts due to this [20]. In addition, economic forecasting is a challenging endeavour due to the inherent complexity of the economic machine. The purpose of this work was to apply synthetic EAI strategies to the model to forecast the future cost of an index that tracks stock prices [21]. Neural networks (NN) guide vector machines, and neuro-fuzzy structures are the three forms of AI that are utilised in the process of forecasting the future charge of a stock market index primarily based on the index's historic charge data [22]. Strategies based on AI have the potential to think about the complexities of economic machines, and they are also used as tools for the collection and forecasting of economic time [23].

The autoregressive moving average (ARMA) method, which is a linear modelling method, and the random stroll (RW) method are the two strategies that are utilised in the process of benchmarking the AI strategies. Based on the information obtained from the Johannesburg Stock Exchange, the experiment was eventually finished. The facts used became a chain of beyond the last expenses of the All-Share Index. The consequences confirmed that the three strategies have the capacity to expect the destiny fee of the Index with appropriate accuracy [24]. All three synthetic intelligence strategies outperformed the linear model. However, the RW technique completed all of the different strategies. These strategies display the capacity to expecting the destiny fee however, due to the transaction expenses of buying and selling withinside the marketplace, it is not feasible to expose that the three strategies can disprove the vulnerable shape of marketplace efficiency [25]. The consequences display that the rating of performances guides neuro-fuzzy systems, multilayer perceptron neural networks and vector machines depending on the accuracy degree used.

18.2.1.2 Artificial neural networks for stock market prediction

A stock marketplace is a platform that allows users to buy and sell shares of companies as well as derivatives for a fee that has been predetermined. The marketplace for inventory is driven by the supply of and demand for stocks. One of the industries with the greatest potential for growth is the stock market. In today's world, a significant number of people are connected to this industry in some direct or indirect fashion. As a result, having a good understanding of the trends in the market will become absolutely essential. Consequently, as a result of the development of the inventory marketplace, human beings are interested in making price predictions for inventory. However, because of the fluid nature of the situation and the possibility of momentary adjustments to the inventory fee, forecasting the inventory fee will be a challenging endeavour. Stock m Previous research has shown that it is possible to develop efficient methods for studying event representations that can capture syntactic and semantic data over a textual content corpus, demonstrating their usefulness for downstream tasks such as script event prediction [26]. On the other hand, events extracted from raw texts lack common-experience information, such as the intents and feelings of the event participants. This information can be helpful for distinguishing event pairs when there are best-diffused variations of the surface realisations of the events in question. To address this issue, the author of this paper suggests drawing on the outside common-experience information regarding the motivation behind the event as well as the general feeling associated with it.

Experimentations on three occasion-oriented concepts, namely, occasion similarity, script occasion prediction and stock marketplace prediction, ensure that the model achieved significantly higher occasion embeddings for the tasks, reaching 78% improvements on the difficult similarity task, yielding more specific inferences on subsequent activities beneath given contexts, and higher accuracies in predicting the volatilities of the stock market. The markets are, for the most part, deterministic chaotic system that is also noisy, non-linear and non-parametric. Inventory buyers are increasingly moving away from using fundamental analysis in favour of applying Intelligent Trading Systems to forecast the prices of stocks, as this provides them with the ability to make instant funding decisions. One of the primary goals of a dealer is to anticipate the inventory price in such a way that he can sell the inventory before its fee declines or buy the inventory before the rate rises. According to green marketplace speculation, it is not always possible to anticipate costs associated with inventory, and the behaviour of inventory is consistent with that of a random walk. It would appear that maintaining the professionalism of an experienced dealer to accurately predict inventory levels is a very difficult task. But now, as a result of the availability of an extraordinary quantity of data and the development of new technologies, we are in a position to devise the appropriate set of guidelines for prediction, the results of which can lead to an increase in profits for investors or investment firms [27]. Therefore, the accuracy of a set of rules is directly proportional to the profits that can be made through the utilisation of the set of rules.

Increasing integration of European economic markets is probable to bring about an even stronger correlation among fairness expenses in extraordinary European nations. This procedure also can result in convergence in financial improvement throughout European nations if tendencies in inventory markets impact actual financial components, inclusive of funding and consumption. Indeed, our vector autoregressive fashions advise that the effective correlation between adjustments fairness expenses and funding is, in general, significant. Hence, the economic government needs to display reactions of proportion expenses to economic coverage and their outcomes at the enterprise cycle [28].

18.2.1.3 Neural network approach for stock market prediction

To develop a ground-breaking neural community strategy for the purpose of improving one's ability to predict the stock market. Data have been collected from the stay inventory marketplace for real-time and off-line evaluation, as well as the effects of visualisations and analytics, to illustrate the Internet of Multimedia of Things for inventory evaluation. When attempting to evaluate the impact of market traits on inventory costs, conventional neural network algorithms may additionally incorrectly anticipate the inventory market. This is because the preliminary weight of the random choice hassle may be without difficulty liable to incorrect predictions. The development of phrase vectors in deep learning inspired us to present the concept of an 'inventory vector', which we illustrate here. The entry is not an index of a single inventory but rather of multiple inventories containing high-dimensional historic data [29]. To forecast the inventory market, we suggest the deep lengthy short-term reminiscence neural community (LSTM) with an embedded layer and the lengthy short-term reminiscence neural community with a computerised encoder [30]. In these models, we use the embedded layer and the automated encoder, respectively, to vectorise the data in an effort to forecast the stock using an LSTM neural network [31]. This was done in an effort to vectorise the data in a manner that the models could understand. The results of the experiments show that the deep LSTM that includes an embedded layer performs significantly better. For the Shanghai A-stocks composite index, the accuracy of fashions is exactly 57.2%, while it is 56.9% for the overall index. In addition, the corresponding numbers for personal stocks are 52.4% and 52.5% respectively.

18.2.1.4 An intelligent technique for stock market prediction

A stock market is an unfastened community of financial transactions among consumers and dealers primarily based totally on shares additionally called stocks. In inventory markets, shares constitute the possession claims on businesses. These can also additionally encompass securities indexed on an inventory alternate in addition to the ones simplest traded privately. An inventory alternate is an area in which agents should purchase and/or promote shares, bonds and different securities [32]. The stock marketplace is a completely prone region for funding because of its unstable nature. In the close to past, we confronted big monetary issues because of the big drop-in fee of stocks in inventory markets worldwide. This phenomenon delivered a heavy toll worldwide in addition to our countrywide monetary structure. Many humans misplaced their final financial savings of cash at the inventory marketplace [33]. In the 2010–2011 monetary year, the Bangladeshi inventory marketplace confronted a big disintegration. This phenomenon may be delivered below and managed specifically through strict tracking and example inventory marketplace evaluation. If we will examine the inventory marketplace successfully in time, it is able to end up a discipline of huge income and can end up relatively much less prone for the investors. The stock marketplace is all approximately prediction and fast choice making approximately funding, which cannot be completed without a thorough evaluation of the marketplace [34]. If we will be expecting the inventory marketplace by analysing historic statistics properly, we will keep away from the outcomes of significant marketplace disintegration and with the purpose to take vital steps to make marketplace proof against such situations [35].

18.3   Architecture

The gathering of accurate data to use as a foundation is the first step in the process of prediction. It is possible that the extrinsic data sources have more of an impact on the stock market than the intrinsic historical prices if we make the assumption that history will continue to repeat itself. According to the efficient-market hypothesis, the prices of assets already reflect all of the information that is available. To start the progression as shown in Figure 18.1, we first get the data about any stock from the NSE India website. In our case, we have taken the stock data of HDFC Bank. Then we only take useful features like the date and closing price each day. We then split the data into the training and valid datasets so that we can check the root mean squared error (RMSE) value obtained using different ML algorithms.

We then apply the LSTM, KNN, linear regression and moving average. We get an RMSE value of 187.00 for the moving average, 154.38 for the linear regression, 678.88 for the KNN and 58.09 for the LSTM. We take the model with the least RMSE value which is the LSTM model. We then scale the data by preparing it for

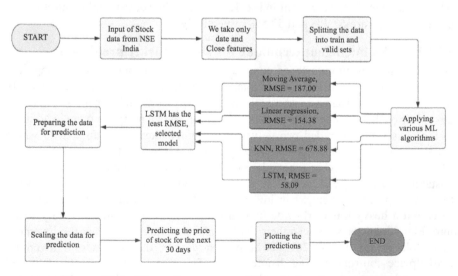

Figure 18.1   The entire process of the stock price predictions

the prediction. We use LSTM for predicting the price for the next 30 days and plot the predictions so that users can infer from the graph and take decisions.

18.3.1 *Pre-processing*

Predicting the price of a stock is an extremely difficult endeavour due to the wide variety of factors that can have an impact on the price. Therefore, it is necessary for us to capture these preconditions to the greatest extent possible so that we can understand the characteristics of the stock from a variety of perspectives and arrive at more accurate prediction results [36]. In the unstructured financial text data, this paper selects financial news and stock forum posts related to five listed companies and makes use of web crawler technology to collect sufficient data sets. Additionally, the selected companies are all publicly traded. According to the research that has been published in recent years, we are aware that the headline of a news article may contain more information than the actual text of the article. As a result of this, we also take news headlines as the object of our research [37]. The preprocessing of text data is an essential part of sentiment analysis, and once that step is complete, high-quality data sources can be obtained. Because sentences make up the majority of objects in natural language processing, it is necessary to break down sentences into single words. Additionally, the punctuation marks are taken out because there is no functional significance attached to them in the sentences. However, in Chinese text, only clear separators are found between sentences and paragraphs; there is no space between individual Chinese words. In English, the spaces between individual words serve as separators. To organise the unstructured data that comes from the financial industry, we segment it using the Jieba word segmentation algorithm. Jieba is a robust library for word segmentation that is written in the Python programming language. To segment every news title and stock forum post contained in the financial text data set, we make use of the precise model of this method [38]. After that, the Harbin Institute of Technology's stopwords dictionary is utilised to select the words that do not actually contribute anything to the meaning of the sentence and to acquire the wordset that results from the segmentation.

Document labelling is possible to break down sentiment analysis into three different levels of research: word level, sentence level and chapter level. The goal of sentiment analysis is to mine the opinions expressed by investors in speech or text. Analysis of an overall sentiment, tendency or polarity can be accomplished through the use of sentiment classification based on the chapter level. Before we can use deep learning for sentiment analysis, we need to label every piece of information that is found in news articles and forum posts so that we can collect training data sets [39]. The process of document labelling involves assigning positive and negative connotations to monetary text on the basis of previous transactional data. According to the research, there are two different ways to categorise news articles based on historical data: open-to-close (daytime return) and close-to-open. (overnight return). According to the research that has been done the return during the daytime contributes more to the overall return than the return during the nighttime does [40].

18.4   Model implementation

The system used four different models and compared them against each other to see which model gave better accuracy and the least root mean squared error. We have applied KNN, moving average, linear regression and LSTM algorithms to the data.

18.4.1   Data used in this analysis

We have obtained stock data of different companies from the NSE India website. We have utilised a package available in Python that extracts the data from the website and saves them as a table. We then use this table and store it as a CSV file so that we can use the pandas library against the data. Since **nsepy** package is not pre-installed into Python, we have to install the package using the command in the terminal *!pip install nsepy.* The sample data extraction is shown in Figure 18.2 which has been extracted using the command head(). This image shows the data that has been obtained after running the code by getting data from NSE India.

For predicting the future price, we will use the close variable and set the date variable as the index. Now split the entire dataset into two different data collections like the train set and valid sets using the new_data commands.

18.4.2   Applying the moving average algorithm

When making predictions about the stock market, one of the tools that are utilised most frequently is the moving average. On average, the number of previously observed values will be used to calculate the forecasted final price for each trading day. We are going to use the moving average technique, which takes into account the most recent set of values for each prediction, rather than the simple average, which is the method that most people use. To put it another way, at each succeeding step, the predicted values are taken into consideration, while simultaneously the value that was observed the longest is eliminated from the set:

$$\text{Simple moving average} = (A_1 + A_2 + \ldots\ldots + A_n)/n \qquad (18.1)$$

In this formula shown in (18.1), A is the data point and n is the number of observations taken into consideration. We will use the above-processed data as the input for this algorithm and the expected output would be the RMSE value and the appropriate prediction graph.

	Date	Symbol	Series	Prev Close	Open	High	Low	Last	Close	VWAP	Volume	Turnover	Trades	Deliverable Volume	%Deliverable
0	2015-01-01	HDFC	EQ	1135.90	1130.0	1131.15	1120.10	1125.90	1124.00	1124.23	401576	4.514650e+13	11804	128793	0.3207
1	2015-01-02	HDFC	EQ	1124.00	1127.3	1176.95	1125.35	1171.05	1171.90	1159.93	2019816	2.342845e+14	59071	1258847	0.6232
2	2015-01-05	HDFC	EQ	1171.90	1168.8	1175.00	1150.40	1154.95	1156.40	1159.24	2219458	2.572880e+14	57749	1414720	0.6374
3	2015-01-06	HDFC	EQ	1156.40	1148.6	1148.60	1096.10	1098.00	1101.95	1117.84	2531748	2.830100e+14	81436	1547523	0.6112
4	2015-01-07	HDFC	EQ	1101.95	1097.5	1114.15	1095.00	1097.65	1099.25	1105.58	2406880	2.660992e+14	133109	1533304	0.6371

Figure 18.2   Sample data extraction from NSE India

18.4.3   Applying linear regression

One of the most straightforward computational methods available is known as linear regression. This algorithm's primary purpose is to provide a solution in the form of an equation that analyses the nature of the relationship that exists between the independent variable and the dependent variable. Because our dataset does not contain an independent variable in the traditional sense, we are able to derive information such as the day, month or year and incorporate it into our model.

The formula for slope is given in (18.2), (18.3) and (18.4),

$$Y = mx + b \qquad\qquad (18.2)$$

$$b = \left(\left(\sum xy \right) + \sum x \sum y \right) / \left(\sum x^2 + \left(\sum x \right)^2 \right) \qquad (18.3)$$

$$m = (1/n) \left(\sum y - b \sum x \right) \qquad\qquad (18.4)$$

We will use the formula given in (18.2), (18.3) and (18.4) to compute the future stock data. The input will be the stock data that are processed accordingly and the expected output will be the RMSE value and the prediction graph.

18.4.4   KNN

The KNN algorithm makes the assumption that the newly collected data is similar to the data that was previously collected and then assigns the newly collected data to the category that is the most similar to it. We determine the distance between each row of the test data and the rows of the training data using a distance measure. When determining how far apart the two points are from one another, we will make use of the Euclidean distance. The value of k will be determined by taking the square root of the total number of observations in the dataset.

The Euclidean distance is given in (18.5),

$$d = \sqrt{\left[(x22 - x11)^2 + (y22 - y11)^2 \right]} \qquad (18.5)$$

The input will be the stock data that are processed accordingly and the expected output will be the RMSE value and the prediction graph.

18.4.5   LSTM

Analysis of time series can benefit from the use of LSTM. Memory for the long term and the short term is a form of recurrent neural network. The reason that LSTM is so effective is that it is able to remember past information that is significant while simultaneously forgetting information that is not significant. The architecture of an LSTM consists of three gates. The information that is added to the cell state is done so by the input gate. The forget gate is responsible for erasing any information from the model that is no longer necessary. The information that is displayed as output is determined by the output gate's selection.

The input will be the stock data that are processed accordingly and the expected output will be the RMSE value and the prediction graph.

18.5   User interface website for stock prediction

We have also created a website for our model so that the user can easily get the prediction for any stock that he/she wants. We have created our website using the Django framework using Python, HTML and CSS. On the website, we have a home page which is the main page, basically the first page when anyone opens our website. Then we have a contact page from where users can contact us. The next page will be the about us page where the users can get information about us. Then there will be a login page from which the users can log in, after the user logs in they will have a stock option. After the user clicks that option, he/she will have a text box to enter the company for which the user wants the stock prediction. After the user confirms the selection, a graph with the prediction for the next 30 days will be displayed.

18.6   Result and discussion

We have successfully implemented the four algorithms on our data and found the RMSE value and the prediction graphs.

Figure 18.3 represents the output obtained for RMSE value on the validation set and the corresponding graph obtained is shown in Figure 18.4 using the moving average model.

Figure 18.5 characterises the output obtained for RMSE value on the validation set and the corresponding graph obtained is revealed in Figure 18.6 using the linear regression model.

The output obtained for RMSE value on the validation set is presented in Figure 18.7 and the corresponding graph obtained is shown in Figure 18.8 using KNN model.

The yield obtained for RMSE value on the validation set is presented in Figure 18.9 and the corresponding graph obtained is made available in Figure 18.10 using LSTM.

The complete summary of the RMSE obtained by the various models was analysed and tabulated in Table 18.1.

The graphical analysis for the RMSE values compared in the table is presented in a graph and illustrated in Figure 18.11.

```
RMSE value on validation set:
187.00795055430112
```

Figure 18.3   The output RMSE for the moving average model

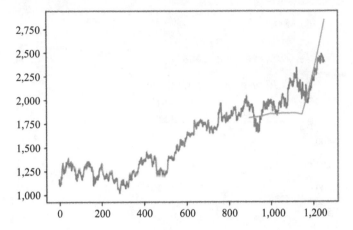

Figure 18.4   Graph for the moving average model

rms

154.3808738607781

Figure 18.5   RMSE for linear regression

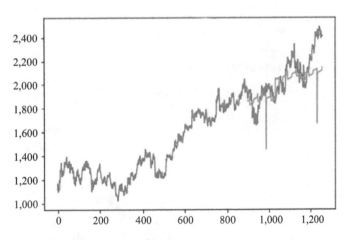

Figure 18.6   Graph for linear regression

Hence, from the above graphs and RMSE value, we can infer that the moving average (Figure 18.3) was able to predict the movement to an edict when there is a drop in the price but we can still aim for an even better model. In the KNN extent, but not accurately. In the linear regression model, the model was able to predict the models, i.e., the model was able to predict how the market is moving but the price

```
rms
```

`:   678.8880780635088`

Figure 18.7   RMSE for KNN model

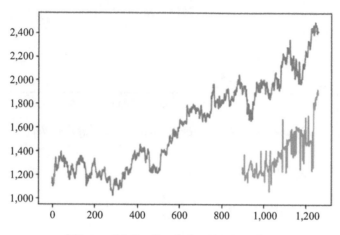

Figure 18.8   Graph for KNN model

```
rms
```

`58.095838753716265`

Figure 18.9   RMSE for LSTM

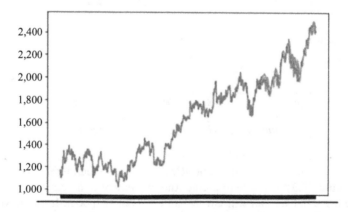

Figure 18.10   Graph for LSTM

Table 18.1   RMSE values obtained from different models

S. no.	Models	RMSE
1	Moving average	187.00
2	Linear regression	154.38
3	KNN	678.88
4	LSTM	58.09

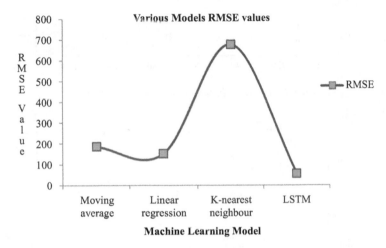

Figure 18.11   Comparative analysis of graph of various models

value hugely varied as we can see from the RMSE value. The KNN is a pretty convincing model but we can still aim for a better model. Now let us look at the LSTM model (Figure 18.6), the LSTM has predicted the price close to accurate! We can see that the predictions given by the LSTM followed the same movement as well as the price compared to the actual data. The RMSE value for LSTM model was the lowest compared to all the other models.

Hence, we can choose the LSTM model for future price prediction, now using the LSTM model we will predict the price for the next 30 days. We got the data from 1 January 2015 to 31 January 2020 for HDFC Bank. Now we will predict the price for HDFC Bank from 1 January 2020 to 1 March 2020. Figure 18.12 represents the graph that was obtained after prediction using LSTM model.

We can see that there is a price drop between January and March 2020 after applying our LSTM model. Now let us plot the actual graph from January to March 2020 timeline to see if our model has predicted the price to an extent. Figure 18.13 depicts the actual outcome of data being considered from January to March 2020 concluding the gradual drop in the price curve.

We can see that there was actually a price drop from January to March 2020 as illustrated in Figure 18.8. Our model might have not predicted the price accurately

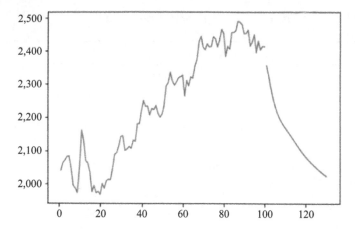

Figure 18.12   Prediction using the LSTM model

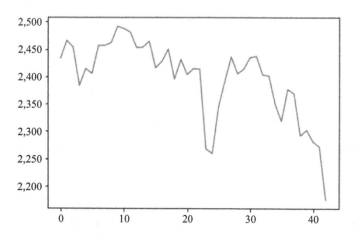

Figure 18.13   Actual data from January to March 2020

but it gave a general sense of whether the price will go up or down in the next few days.

18.7   Conclusion

The stock market prediction is something that has the potential to bear great importance in the future, keeping this in mind we decided to create a model that can predict the price for the next 30 days for any stock that the user wishes. We used a package that helped us get stock data from the NSE India website. We tested the dataset on four different models and used the best model to predict the price. The models that we used were moving average, Linear regression, KNN and LSTM.

Thus it was observed that the LSTM model gave the greatest outcomes with an RMSE value of 58 which was the lowest among all the other models used. So we then implemented the LSTM technique to make appropriate price predictions for the next 30 days; from the prediction graph that we obtained the model was able to predict the movement correctly, the model was not able to predict the price accurately, but it for sure gave an idea to the user on whether the price will go up or down in the future. This could be very helpful for the user to as it can also be another contributing factor upon which he/she can decide if they want to invest in the stock or not It can surely help the user to reduce the risk of losses to an extent and try to give the user profits. Of course, there is a huge scope of development for the model, we can add more LSTM layers to It so that the accuracy of the model also increases. This model also comes with a website through which the user can check the future price of any stock. It can also be noted that one of the biggest advantages of this model is that it can add an extra helping hand for novice traders as they are prone to making mistakes and face severe losses in the market compared to experienced traders. Hence, we would like to conclude by saying that we would consider this report a success if we were able to help even a single person by getting some profits by investing in stocks!

References

[1] Baek, Y., and Kim, H.Y. ModAugNet: a new forecasting framework for stock market index value with an overfitting prevention LSTM module and a prediction LSTM module, *Expert Systems with Applications*, 2018, 113, 457–480.

[2] Zhong, X., and Enke, D. Forecasting daily stock market return using dimensionality reduction, *Expert Systems with Applications*, 2017, 67, 126–139.

[3] Jafari, A., and Haratizadeh, S. GCNET: graph-based prediction of stock price movement using graph convolutional network, *Engineering Applications of Artificial Intelligence*, 2022, 116, 105452.

[4] Tao Yin, Chenzhengyi Liu, Fangyu Ding, Ziming Feng, Bo Yuan, and Ning Zhang. Graph-based stock correlation and prediction for high-frequency trading systems, *Pattern Recognition*, Volume 122, 2022, 108209,

[5] Emmanouil Platanakis and Andrew Urquhart, Portfolio management with cryptocurrencies: The role of estimation risk, *Economics Letters*, Volume 177, 2019, Pages 76–80,

[6] Hamid Eskandari, Ahmad Sadegheih, Hasan Khademi Zare, and Mohammad Mehdi Lotfi. Developing a smart stock trading system equipped with a novel risk control mechanism for investors with different risk appetites, *Expert Systems with Applications*, Volume 210, 2022, 118614.

[7] Zhao, Z.-Q., Zheng, P., Xu, S.-t., and Wu, X. Object detection with deep learning: A review. *IEEE transactions on neural networks and learning systems*, 30, 2019, 3212–3232.

[8]   Zhu, Y., Yang, H., Jiang, J., and Huang, Q. An adaptive box-normalization stock index trading strategy based on reinforcement learning. In *Proceedings of the International Conference on Neural Information Processing, Siem Reap, Cambodia, 13–16 December 2018*; Springer: Berlin/Heidelberg, Germany, 2018.

[9]   Kim, H.Y., and Won, C.H. Forecasting the volatility of stock price index: A hybrid model integrating LSTM with multiple GARCH-type models. *Expert Syst. Appl.* 2018, 103, 25–37.

[10]   Nikou, M., Mansourfar, G., and Bagherzadeh, J. Stock price prediction using DEEP learning algorithm and its comparison with machine learning algorithms. *Intell. Syst. Account. Financ. Manag.* 2019, 26, 164–174.

[11]   Chen, W., Yeo, C.K., Lau, C.T., and Lee, B.S. Leveraging social media news to predict stock index movement using RNN-boost. *Data Knowl. Eng.* 2018, 118, 14–24.

[12]   Wen, M., Li, P., Zhang, L., and Chen, Y. Stock market trend prediction using high-order information of time series. *IEEE Access* 2019, 7, 28299–28308.

[13]   Li, C., Song, D., and Tao, D. Multi-task recurrent neural networks and higher-order Markov random fields for stock price movement prediction: Multi-task RNN and higher-order MRFs for stock price classification. In *Proceedings of the 25th ACM SIGKDD International Conference on Knowledge Discovery & Data Mining, Anchorage, AK, USA, 4–8 August 2019*; Association for Computing Machinery: Anchorage, AK, USA, 2019; pp. 1141–1151.

[14]   Zexin Hu, Yiqi Zhao, and Matloob Khushi. *A Survey of Forex and Stock Price Prediction Using Deep Learning*. 2 February 2021.

[15]   Weiwei Jiang. *Applications of deep learning in stock market prediction*. 15 July 2021.

[16]   Hiransha, M., Gopalakrishnan, E.A., Vijay Krishna Menon, and Soman, K.P. *NSE Stock Market Prediction Using Deep-Learning Models*. 8 June 2018.

[17]   Nguyen, T. H., and Shirai, K. (2015). Topic modeling based sentiment analysis on social media for stock market prediction. In *Proceedings of the 53rd Annual Meeting of the Association for Computational Linguistics and the 7th International Joint Conference on Natural Language Processing* (Volume 1: Long Papers) (pp. 1354–1364).

[18]   Chen, M.-Y., Liao, C.H., and Hsieh, R.-P. Modeling public mood and emotion: Stock market trend prediction with anticipatory computing approach. *Comput. Hum. Behav.* 2019, 101, 402–408.

[19]   Mohan, S., Mullapudi, S., Sammeta, S., Vijayvergia, P., and Anastasiu, D. C. (2019). Stock price prediction using news sentiment analysis. In *2019 IEEE Fifth International Conference on Big Data Computing Service and Applications (BigDataService)* (pp. 205–208). IEEE.

[20]   https://www.analyticsvidhya.com/blog/2018/10/predicting-stock-price-machine-learningnd-deep-learning-techniques-python/

[21]   Rana, M., Uddin, M., and Hoque, M. Effects of activation functions and optimizers on stock price prediction using LSTM recurrent networks. In

Proceedings of the 2019 3rd International Conference on Computer Science and Artificial Intelligence, Beijing, China, 6–8 December 2019; Association for Computing Machinery: Normal, IL, USA, 2019; pp. 354–358.

[22] https://analyticsindiamag.com/hands-on-guide-to-lstm-recurrent-neural-network-for-stock-market-prediction/

[23] Shi, L., Teng, Z., Wang, L., Zhang, Y., and Binder, A. DeepClue: Visual Interpretation of Text-Based Deep Stock Prediction. *IEEE Trans.Knowl. Data Eng.* 2019, 31, 1094–1108.

[24] Wu, J.-L., Yang, C.-S., Liu, K.-H., and Huang, M.-T. A deep learning model for dimensional valence arousal intensity prediction in stock market. In *Proceedings of the 2019 IEEE 10th International Conference on Awareness Science and Technology (iCAST)*, Morioka, Japan, 23–25 October 2019,

[25] Kang, Q., Zhou, H., and Kang, Y. An asynchronous advantage actor-critic reinforcement learning method for stock selection and portfolio management. In *Proceedings of the 2nd International Conference on Big Data Research, Weihai, China, 27–29 October 2018*; Association for Computing Machinery: Weihai, China, 2018; pp. 141–145.

[26] Minh, D.L., Sadeghi-Niaraki, A., Huy, H.D., Min, K., and Moon, H. Deep learning approach for short-term stock trends prediction based on two-stream gated recurrent unit network. *IEEE Access* 2018, 6, 55392–55404.

[27] Li, C., Song, D., & Tao, D. (2019a). Multi-task recurrent neural networks and higher-order Markov random fields for stock price movement prediction: Multi-task RNN and higher-order MRFs for stock price classification. In *Proceedings of the 25th ACM SIGKDD International Conference on Knowledge Discovery & Data Mining KDD '19* (pp. 1141–1151). New York, NY, USA: ACM. URL: http://doi.acm.org/10.1145/3292500.3330983. doi: 10.1145/3292500.3330983.

[28] Zhan, X., Li, Y., Li, R., Gu, X., Habimana, O., and Wang, H. (2018). Stock price prediction using time convolution long short-term memory network. In W. Liu, F. Giunchiglia, and B. Yang (eds.), *Knowledge Science, Engineering and Management* (pp. 461–468). Cham: Springer International Publishing.

[29] Xu, Y., and Cohen, S. B. (2018). Stock movement prediction from tweets and historical prices. In *Proceedings of the 56th Annual Meeting of the Association for Computational Linguistics* (Volume 1: Long Papers) (pp. 1970–1979). Melbourne, Australia: Association for Computational Linguistics. doi: 10.18653/v1/P18-1183.

[30] Patel, J., Shah, S., Thakkar, P., and Kotecha, K. (2015). Predicting stock market index using fusion of machine learning techniques. *Expert Systems with Applications*, 42, 2162 URL: http://www.sciencedirect.com/science/article/pii/S0957417414006551. doi: https://doi.org/10.1016/j.eswa.2014.10.031

[31] Si, W., Li, J., Ding, P., and Rao, R. A multi-objective deep reinforcement learning approach for stock index future's intraday trading. In *Proceedings of the 2017 10th International Symposium on Computational Intelligence and Design (ISCID)*, Hangzhou, China, 9–10 December 2017.

[32]   Wei, D. (2019, October 17-19). Prediction of stock price based on LSTM neural network. *2019 International Conference on Artificial Intelligence and Advanced Manufacturing (AIAM)* IEEE, 544–547. https://doi.org/10.1109/

[33]   Lee, C.-Y., and Soo, V.-W. (2017). Predict stock price with financial news based on recurrent convolutional neural networks. In *2017 Conference on Technologies and Applications of Artificial Intelligence (TAAI)* (pp. 160–165). IEEE.

[34]   Matsubara, T., Akita, R., and Uehara, K. (2018). Stock price prediction by deep neural generative model of news articles. *IEICE TRANSACTIONS on Information and Systems*, 101, 901–908.

[35]   Nelson, D. M., Pereira, A. C., and de Oliveira, R. A. (2017). Stock market's price movement prediction with LSTM neural networks. In *2017 International Joint Conference on Neural Networks (IJCNN)* (pp. 1419–1426). IEEE.

[36]   Mohan, S., Mullapudi, S., Sammeta, S., Vijayvergia, P., and Anastasiu, D. C. (2019, April 4-9). Stock price prediction using news sentiment analysis. *2019 IEEE Fifth International Conference on Big Data Computing Service and Applications (BigDataService)* IEEE, 205–208. https://doi.org/10.1109/BigDataService.2019.00035.

[37]   Checkley, M. S., Higón, D. A., and Alles, H. (2017). The hasty wisdom of the mob: How market sentiment predicts stock market behavior. *Expert Systems with Applications*,77, 256–263. https://doi.org/10.1016/j.eswa.2017.01.029

[38]   Eapen, J., Bein, D., and Verma, A. (2019, January 7-9). Novel deep learning model with CNN and bi-directional LSTM for improved stock market index prediction. *2019 IEEE 9th Annual Computing and Communication Workshop and Conference (CCWC)* IEEE, 0264–0270. https://doi.org/10.1109/CCWC.2019.8666592.

[39]   Zhou, Z., Gao, M., Liu, Q., and Xiao, H. (2020). Forecasting stock price movements with multiple data sources: Evidence from stock market in China. *Physica A: Statistical Mechanics and Its Applications*, 542, 123389.

[40]   Wang, Y. (2017). Stock market forecasting with financial micro-blog based on sentiment and timeseries analysis. *Journal of Shanghai Jiaotong University (Science)*, 22(2), 173–179.

Chapter 19

Advancements of XAI in healthcare sector

Gudi Varaprasad[1] and J. Sheela[1]

Artificial intelligence (AI) has undoubtedly been a center for the latest advancements and has brought about significant developments in the medical field. However, the healthcare practitioners' and researchers' desire for an interpretation of the system's predictions based on the health statistics acquired through advanced machine learning models did not meet. So, the study of eXplainable AI (XAI) has been pursued through science establishment to give justifications for machine predictions and assure accuracy in the sophisticated medical framework. Because depending on artificial conclusions to rescue the health of an individual without an adequate knowledge of the underlying logic is unacceptable. Before applying the results to the patient, XAI helps the medical domain crew understand the reasons and keep the conclusions in check for a better cause. In this book chapter, we will emphasize the motives for espousing XAI in the medical domain and examine the basic principle behind it, as well as how it might help to dependent AI-based solutions in healthcare.

19.1 XAI in medical image analysis based on deep learning (DL) techniques

Automated picture analysis has greatly improved as a result of DL. In the past, systems wholly developed by human domain experts were typically used for image analysis. For instance, such an image modeling approach may have statistical classifiers that carry out a certain task using built-in picture properties or features. Features included basic picture characteristics like the corners and edges and more advanced picture characteristics like the potential boundaries of a tumor. A neural network from DL learns these attributes rather than building them to get the best results when given an input [1].

The most extensively employed technique today in medical image processing tasks is DL convolutional neural networks (DCNNs). Nevertheless, it has been regarded as black-box classifiers, with no description of the root causes. Explainable AI (XAI) is a new arena in AI that seeks to understand how models make decisions. We used can use XAI visualizations to obtain cognizance of the characteristics

[1]School of Computer Science and Engineering, VIT-AP University, Amaravathi, India

learned to assess estrogen receptor status (ER− vs. ER+) by a DCNN implemented in the breast using dynamic contrast-enhanced magnetic resonance imaging (DCEMRI) [2]. The AlexNet model trained on across the volume (spatial), across the collection sequence (dynamic) components, and ImageNet data of each DCE-MRI ROI may be used as an input to create a bespoke dual domain transfer-trained DCNN framework. To illustrate DCNN learning, we may apply XAI techniques to return on investments (ROIs) from a specific training set, such as the SmoothGrad noise reduction algorithm and the Integrated Gradients attribution method.

If a DL model is given an image of cancer as input, it may create the output "cancer." Many nonlinear entangled linkages frequently connect the various levels of neural networks. It is hard to fully understand how such a neural network came to its decision, even after all of the layers have been looked at and their connections have been documented. DL is commonly referred to as "the black box" as a result. There are growing concerns in a variety of consumption sectors that these black boxes may occasionally be biased in some way, and that any bias may go unnoticed [3].

It can have a lot more effects, especially in medical applications. A solicitation has been accredited for methods to understand the black box better. These methods are known as decipherable DL or XAI. The risks of medical decisions are frequently enormous. Not unexpectedly, doctors have raised concern about DL's "black box" feature, which is now quite advanced in the analysis of medical images. The main purpose of this topic is to provide a complete overview of concepts that use XAI in medical image analysis [4].

19.1.1   Enabling tools and technologies

The results of deep neural networks (DNN) in medical imaging can be explained in one of two ways: those that use typical attribution-based approaches and also that use unique, soft framework—or domain-centric methodologies. Numerous attribution methodologies have been created as a result of the difficulties in determining an attribution value, contribution, or importance to each input feature of a network. In a classification task, the target neuron is frequently the output neuron of the appropriate category. An attribution strategy aims to determine the impact of an input feature on this neuron. The heatmaps known as "attribution maps" are created by placing the attributions of various input attributes according to the shape of the input sample. A black-box convolutional neural network (CNN) may be used with the attribution methods without needing any modifications to the underlying architecture, molding them to a functional but dynamic XAI framework [35].

Perturbation methods such as Occlusion and Shapley value sampling can be used to explore the effect on an AI model's output of changing its input characteristics. This can be accomplished by masking, eliminating, or changing certain input properties, doing the forward pass (output computation), and then comparing the outcomes to the initial output. Backpropagation techniques are another option. Gradient, Saliency Maps, Guided backpropagation, DeConvNet, DeepTaylor, PatternNet, and DeepLIFT are several backpropagation-based attribution methodologies. With a single backward and forward transit via this neural network, these approaches calculate the criterion of all input attributes. We may argue that assessments of alternative attribution techniques by experts in a certain topic are potentially valuable for developing XAI models that are probably to be believed by the end clients, and so must be a vital aspect of this creation of an XAI model. Table 19.1 shows the types of XAI framework and its applications.

Table 19.1   Types of XAI framework and its application

Approaches	Algorithm	Application	Modality
Attribution	Gradient*I/P, GBP, LRP, occlusion	Alzheimer's detection	Brain MRI
	GradCAM, GBP	Grading brain tumor	Brain MRI
	IG	DR grading	Fundus images
	EG	Lesion segmentation for AMD	Retinal OCT
	IG, SmoothGrad	Estrogen receptor status	Breast MRI
	Saliency maps	Breast mass classification	Breast MRI
	GradCAM, SHAP	Melanoma detection [36]	Skin images
	Activation maps	Lesion classification	Skin images
	DeepDreams	Segmentation of tumor from liver	CT imaging
	GSInquire, GBP, activation maps	COVID-19 detection	X-ray images
	Mapping between images and reports	Bladder cancer	Tissue images
Attention	U-Net with shape attention stream	Cardiac volume estimation	Cardiac MRI
Concept vectors	TCAV	DR detection	Fundus images
	TCAV with RCV	Breast tumor detection	Breast lymph node images
	UBS	Breast mass classification	Mammography images
Expert knowledge	Domain constraints	Brain MLS estimation	Brain MRI
	Rule-based segmentation, perturbation	Lung nodule segmentation	Lung CT
Similar images	GMM and Atlas	MRI classification	3D MNIST, brain MRI
	Triplet loss, KNN	Melanoma	Dermoscopy images
	Monotonic constraints	Melanoma detection	Dermoscopy images
Textual justification	LSTM, visual word constraint	CNN	Mammography images
Intrinsic explainability	Deep hierarchical generative models	Classification and segmentation for Alzheimer's	Brain MRI
	SVM margin	ASD detection	Brain fMRI

Notes: GBP: gradient × input, guided backpropagation; LRP: layer wise relevance propagation; IG: integrated gradients; EG: expressive gradients; DR: diabetic retinopathy; AMD: age-related macular degeneration; OCT: optical coherence tomography; TCAV: Testing Concept Activation Vectors; RCV: Regression Concept Vectors; UBS: Uniform unit Ball surface Sampling; MLS: midline shift; GMM: Gaussian mixture model; KNN: K Nearest Neighbors; LSTM: long short-term memory networks; SHAP: DeepSHapley Additive exPlanations.

19.1.2   Use cases and applications

The use cases of XAI in medical picturizations are described here in two categories: those that use pre-existing attribution-based methodologies and those that use additional, typically unique methodologies. The methodologies are examined in relation to the XAI framework and the medical imaging application. Attribution-based use cases are brain imaging, retinal imaging, CT imaging, breast imaging, X-ray imaging, skin imaging, etc. Non-attribution-based includes attention-based, concept vectors, expert knowledge, similar pictures, textual justification, intrinsic XAI, etc.

Combining several modalities, such as patient data and medical visuals, in the decision-making process and assigning model decisions to each of them may be another study area. It might imitate a clinician's diagnostic procedure, in which visuals and physical characteristics of a patient are used to render a conclusion. It has the ability to increase accuracy but also explains in greater depth. To recapitulate, explainable diagnosis is gathering momentum, but it still has so far to go to fulfil the aspirations of governments, end clients, and the other sections at large [5].

19.2   XAI in clinical decision support systems using machine learning (ML) approaches

The potential for AI and ML in general to change almost every area of medicine is immense today and in the future. Although a need for disclosure in AI use cases has manifested more vexatious in numerous areas, including those outside of health, this is especially noticeable when users must understand the results of AI systems. Explainable AI (XAI) offers the reasoning that enables people to comprehend the rationale behind the system's generation of a specific outcome. The result can then be understood in light of the situation. Clinical decision support systems (CDSSs) are one application that might benefit greatly from XAI. These systems assist medical physicians in taking clinical decisions, but in the lack of explainability, they might raise worries about under or over including. Explaining how recommendations are made can enable clinicians to take further sophisticated, and under some circumstances, anti-retroviral conclusions.

The necessity for XAI concept in CDSSs, and the health industry in an unspecific, is exacerbated through certain requirements as fair and ethical decision analyzing, as well as the reality that AI edified on past data might operate as biases of prior actions and an augmented agent that must be identified. We can conduct a methodical assessment of previous contributions in the use of XAI concept in CDSSs [5]. Tabular data processing systems are the most frequent XAI-centered systems in the literature, but CDSSs with XAI are less common. Analysts are increasingly interested in providing local explanations, although there is virtually a mix of ante-hoc and post-hoc interpretations, as well as model-agnostic and model-centric methodologies. Some findings indicate positives of using XAI, such as greater decision conviction for doctors or for the generation of fatality hypotheses, which advances to increased credibility and acceptance of the structure and the possibility for its adoption into the medical system. However, we discovered an overall notable lack of use of XAI in the scope of CDSS, particularly a paucity of end-user concepts investigating those requirements of physicians. XAI in CDSS can use guidelines that will be provided, and potential issues and further research needs could be discussed [6].

19.2.1 Enabling tools and technologies

We may utilize XAI to assess the fairness and ethics of algorithmic judgments and determine whether predictions are skewed. Additionally, XAI can give some insight into causality, while it is acknowledged that genuine "causability" must go beyond causality and correlation. Medical professionals must be able to understand how and why a choice made by a machine has been made for it to bring value, which is at the heart of the application of XAI in medicine. Medical practitioners sometimes serve as interpreters for patients, explaining concepts that are too difficult for patients to grasp on their own and apply. It makes sense to have CDSS that helps medical professionals with this duty, as long as the CDSS facilitates the translation rather than getting in the way. Figure 19.1 shows the stages of clinical data analysis.

Additionally, techniques may be separated into post-hoc explainability approaches and ante-hoc explainability methods. Ante-hoc processes are explicable through a design or inherently explainable procedures, sometimes referred to as glass box/white box or transparent techniques. These techniques, which are by definition model-specific, include logistic and fuzzy inference systems, linear regression, decision trees, conditions-based learners, closest neighbors, Bayesian models, and generic additive models. Support vector machines (SVM), random forests, and neural networks (especially DL-based neural networks) are ML techniques that, within reasonable limitations, are essentially incomprehensible and are frequently referred to as "black-box" models. Black-box models may not be explained by post-hoc approaches, which are often model-neutral, but they may offer local reasons for a given decision. Building more straightforward limpid models that offer comprehensible more or less of the black box is one method to do this. Table 19.2 displays different XAI methods and models.

Global explanations, such as the model-neutral BETA method and the neural network-specific generalized additive model (GAM) method, may be distinguished

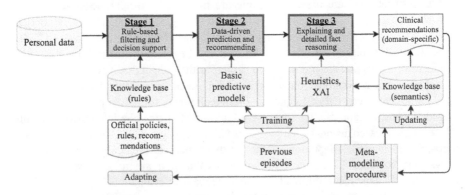

Figure 19.1   Stages in clinical data analysis

Table 19.2   Different XAI methods and model

XAI method	Model—agnostic/specific	Ante-hoc/post-hoc	Local/global
SHAP for attribution, LORE for counterfactual rules, MOEA/D for sensitivity analysis	Agnostic	Post-hoc	Local
Pre-processing to obtain regions, application of randomized DNNs on each region, and extraction of regional abnormality representations in the form of a map.	Specific	Post-hoc	Local
SHAP for summary plot and partial dependence plot.	Agnostic	Post-hoc	Global
BiGRU with an attention mechanism to show the contribution of each fragment of text to the prediction.	Specific	Ante-hoc	Local
Visualized the created preference model using rainbow boxes.	Agnostic	Post-hoc	Local
CLFNN, which autonomously generates fuzzy rules to provide human-like reasoning.	Specific	Ante-hoc	Local
Semantically interpretable FRBS with the integration of semantic ontology-based reasoning.	Specific	Ante-hoc	Local
Visual (using rainbow boxes and a polar multidimensional scaling scatter plot) case-based reasoning approach.	Specific	Ante-hoc	Local
RFGB, a statistical relational learning method that uses tree models and provides explanations in terms of features of interest.	Specific	Ante-hoc	local

LORE: Local Rule-Based Explanations; MOEA/D: Multiobjective Evolutionary Algorithm Based on Decomposition; BiGRU: bidirectional gated recurrent unit; CLFNN: complementary learning fuzzy neural network; FRBS: Fuzzy Rule-Based System; RFGB: Relational Functional Gradient Boosting.

from local explanations, which include model-neutral techniques like local interpretable model-agnostic explanation (LIME), SHAP, and anchors. These methods provide feature-level explanations by developing an interpretable model that seeks to mimic the actions of the indigenous model. Metrics that can be calculated statistically and assessments that are based on people are the two basic approaches to evaluate post-hoc procedures. These techniques can also give global explanations by condensing local explanations, such as using SP-LIME or SHAP summary graphs [7]. To develop local explanations that are backed by beguiling justifications that offer instances of inputs that are produced are similar to the indigenous input but for that the model produces a dissimilar outcome, model-agnostic approaches like CLEAR and CERTIFAI are used. Other frequently used techniques for DL model explanations include DeepLIFT and gradient-based attribution techniques like integrated gradients. CNNs may be seen using techniques like CAM, and gradCAM or class activation maps, deconvolution. Adaptations of each of these methods are being created and used in various contexts. Techniques for visual explanation are another way to offer explanations independent of models. As suitable ways of evaluation, approaches like—"goodness checklist, elicitation methods for mental models, computational measurements for explainer fidelity, explanation satisfaction scores, explanation trustworthiness, and model dependability" are proposed [8].

19.2.2   Use cases and applications

For instance, it has been established that some therapy suggestions made by "Watson for Oncology" (IBM) are unreliable and possibly hazardous. Another well-known example by Caruana *et al.* demonstrated how an ML-based model that was trained to predict which patients with pneumonia should be admitted to a hospital was able to recognize people with asthma as being at lower risk of dying from pneumonia. Asthma patients were less inclined to die from pneumonia, which was similar to the training data, however, this was because they frequently received more intensive care and were seamlessly connected to the intensive care units (ICU). Even so, if this model were applied in a legitimate clinical setting without understanding why this prediction was now being formed even without human or expert intervention, it is feasible that asthma cases would not be transferred to a clinic or would not receive the intensive treatment required to prevent death [9]. The adoption of explicable models could aid in avoiding such errors.

We may provide a novel XAI approach to evolutionary decision support for diagnostic purposes using decision trees. This technique enables AI systems to collaborate with human specialists, sharing information, and making decisions jointly. The approach can help doctors decide which test findings are most helpful given the available information. The system may also provide an explanation of a given choice, returning to the training data in its entirety. This offers the openness necessary for fostering patient confidence, adhering to regulations, finding, and fixing mistakes, and enhancing patient outcomes. A technique of expert-in-the-loop elucidation used to identify the activity of internal units in CNNs is another illustration of how humans and AI systems may cooperate. They show that several CNN models are capable of generating explanatory descriptions to aid in the categorization judgments at hand. Their research is a critical first step towards the categorization of sick tissue by XAI. In this chapter, our focus was directed towards exploring the significance of the XAI framework within Clinical Decision Support Systems (CDSS), particularly delving into the "how" and "where" aspects. We not only identified several notable advantages that have been realized but also identified areas where further improvements are needed within this domain [10].

19.3   XAI in healthcare

When incorporated into healthcare applications and intelligent wearables like Fitbits, this technology has the potential to anticipate the development of medical issues in end-users by collecting and analysing their health data. The incorporation of AI with intelligent wearable technology opens up a wide range of potential uses in smart healthcare, yet there is a hurdle in the AI model judgments' "black box" functioning, which has led to a lack of accountability and trust in the conclusions drawn. XAI is a field where strategies are created to demonstrate AI system predictions. Transparency, the tracking of outcomes, and model improvement are vital aspects within the healthcare industry. Smart healthcare is the application of technology including such as the Internet of Things (IoT), cloud computing, and AI to provide an economical, suitable, and tailored medical system. Such technologies provide a current health monitoring via medical software on phones or wearable/smart gadgets, empowering an independent to take charge of his/her health [11]. In this study, XAI is explored as a technology that can be employed in the processing and analysis of patient data through any intelligence model, and a recommended process to achieve accountability is offered. Medical information acquired regard to the end user perspective may often be staked with professionals for future diagnosis and must be employed in medical checks, prior illness detection, and curing its decision when combined with AI. The moral dilemma of transparency linked with AI, as well as a deficit of confidence in the black box functioning of AI systems, generates a demand for models which are articulated in the healthcare arena. To demonstrate these models and their predictions, XAI methodologies could be well sufficient.

This chapter recommends the use of XAI approaches to explain the logic behind AI-based system predictions to medical domain stakeholders concerning to get the below advantages:

1. **Model enhancement:** AI systems adapt from data to make predictions. At times, the taught protocols are incorrect, which advances to incorrect analysis and justifications. Decision-making justification provided by these techniques will aid in comprehending the learned rules, allowing mistakes to be recognized and models to be improved.
2. **Greater openness:** XAI techniques encourage openness in how AI systems work and can increase levels of trust since they explain how any intelligence system would make a certain decision.
3. **Output decision tracking:** XAI conclusions may be helpful to track the elements which influenced these systems to anticipate for an outcome [12].

19.3.1 Enabling tools and technologies

In this notion, we can suggest using current XAI models in combination with medical information to get further advantages from AI-centric solutions. The technique is explained as follows, as shown in Figure 19.2.

(a) Smart healthcare applications collect users' health information (1) and apply trained AI models (2) to forecast the likelihood of specific unusual or illnesses.
(b) XAI methods (4) create explanations based on the predictions (3) and health data (1) and (5).
(c) With the assistance of a clinician's understanding, these reasons (5) may be analyzed (6). This study will allow physicians to validate the AI model's predictions, allowing for more openness.
(d) If the predictions are right, explanations and clinical information may be combined to give significant insights and suggestions (7).
(e) If predictions are erroneous, the discrepancy between explanations and physician knowledge may be utilized to pinpoint the source of the error and allow adjustment (8) in the current AI model (2).

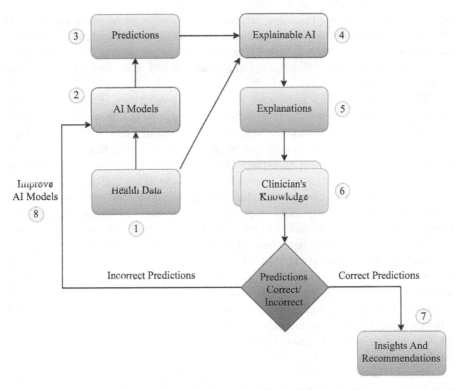

Figure 19.2   Steps in health data analysis

19.3.2   Use cases and applications

Over the past several years, many XAI-related solutions have been released, and numerous of them are deployed in the medical sector. Some AI models in the field of XAI, such as decision sets, which have been used by researchers to explain the prediction of illnesses (diabetes, asthma, and lung cancer) based on a health record of patient, are self-explanatory by virtue of their design. Decision sets are self-explanatory because they were created by mapping an instance of data to an outcome using IF-THEN rules. Decision sets, adduce, gain anticipate lung cancer utilizing the condition: IF the individual smokes and has a respiratory issue NOW anticipate lung cancer. The issue with straightforward AI models, though, is that they restrict the use of other models which are helpful to attain higher perfection. As far as concerned, a study shows a rise in interest in XAI approaches that can explain any AI system to justify the explainability concept in the wide spectrum of AI approaches. Model-agnostic XAI approaches are those XAI techniques that do not depend on the AI model that has to be described. One of the most popular model-agnostic techniques was developed by researchers, and it is called LIME [13]. LIME is a framework for explicating predictions that quantifies the contributions of all the components employed in prediction computations. Researchers are employed in LIME to expound how recurrent neural networks (RNNs) forecast heart failure, and its explanations helped to identify the most prevalent medical disorders, including renal failure, anemia, and diabetes, that increase a person's chance of developing heart failure. Future models independent of XAI techniques, such Shapley, and anchors values, have been created and implemented in the medical industry.

The concept behind a framework that was suggested was to apply the understanding of human reasoning in building XAI approaches to create preferable demonstrations by considering the reasoning objectives of a user. The methodology created is used for certain aspects like smart healthcare to produce intuitions that are approachable by humans to explain how AI-centric systems function utilizing these XAI methodologies across various levels to support clinical decision making. The use of XAI methods faces some difficulties. The end consumers of the explanations produced by XAI approaches, who may be professionals with knowledge of the medical field or regular people, should find them valuable. It is possible to create suitable user interfaces for the presentation of explanations. Research is still needed to address issues with model-agnostic XAI approaches' assumption-based operation and rising computing costs. If there is a spike in blood sugar levels, physicians will obtain a detailed outline along with data on body temperature, heart rate, and calorie consumption as an example implementation of this principle. The attribute principally responsible for this prediction, according to an XAI model, is calorie consumption. Medical professionals could examine the attributes of patients and prescribe relevant medicines/activities to be performed. In augmenting the utility of XAI, the justifications provided are usable and interpreted effectively, i.e., through a graphical user interface (GUI) for clients, who might be professionals with medical domain knowledge or general folks.

The expanding study in XAI is targeting the creation of methodologies, approaches, and models that aid in the interpretation and realization of AI model conclusions. Because ISO/IEC 27001 and the European General Data Protection Regulation (GDPR) require results created by autonomous systems employed in organizations to be trackable, XAI approaches would be utilized to decide AI-centric independent systems outputs explainable and identifiable. The adoption of XAI technology is fraught with difficulties. The field of XAI must be continually researched and implemented in AI-based solutions and services to enable improved advancements in its acceptance and utilization [7].

19.4 Healthcare framework based on XAI and global digital surveillance to prevent pandemic

An innovative strategy for combating infectious diseases throughout the world, like COVID-19, relies on or extends beyond XAI. Epidemics like COVID-19 may be efficiently handled by leveraging edge computation via the XAI and 5th-Generation wireless communication grid. The use of a multilayer edge computing approach has several benefits, including low latency, scalability, and the safety of software and retraining data of the model, allowing COVID-19 to be reviewed via a trustworthy non-global edge server. Furthermore, numerous DL methodologies endure from two critical drawbacks: for initial case, training needs a massive COVID-19 dataset made up of different strands, which adds complexity for non-global councils; and the other case is, to affirm the end result, DL disclosures require ethical acknowledgment and clarifying by the medical sector, and several other contributors. An idea of B5G substructure that uses the high bandwidth, and low latency capabilities of the 5G network to locate COVID-19 through CT scan pictures, or chest X-ray, as well as to construct a deep monitoring application that will surveillance mask wearing, social distance, and body temperature readings. The proposed framework investigates a few DL models like deep tree, ResNet50, Inception v3, etc. [14].

Additionally, blockchain technology is being utilized to secure healthcare data. Because of recent advancements in cellular connectivity and DL, numerous ISPs have been able to create profitable frameworks to please clients and end users. The 5G wireless network is built on three primary pillars that seek to deliver faster bitrates with low latency and a wide variety of IoT terms that allow. A quick spread of the COVID-19 worldwide pandemic revealed the critical nature and demands of these 5th-Generation underpinnings. Yet, current resources and advancement do not guarantee that all three pillars will be reached at once. Therefore, 6G and beyond 5G (B5G) wireless networks have recently emerged to address this problem. B5G provides vital answers to key pandemic advancements like as wireless consciousness, sensing, mapping, networking, and positioning. Furthermore, the three 5G foundations may be enhanced for COVID-19 via unsimilar distributed edge devices aid to an intelligent and adaptable dispersion of scaled network amenities in reply to node mobility. B5G and XAI combined with thorough COVID-19 lateral training could empower low latency, enhanced broadcasting for hospital staff to effectively monitor patients remotely, dramatically increase provincial access to medical data, allow medical clinicians outside locked down epicenters to define X-ray and CT samples obtained, and reduce the burden of diagnostics on local doctors [37].

19.4.1 Enabling tools and technologies

Leading a new generation that portrays on or goes above XAI provides an interesting method for worldwide contagious disease control, such as COVID-19. The illustration shows the suggested smart healthcare system to fight COVID-19-like pandemics. The structure is composed of three primary levels. Hospitals, decision-making, user homes, and surveillance entities, as well as other stakeholders and beneficiaries, make up the user layer, which is the lowest layer. Edge servers, edge nodes, and caches make up the middle layer's edge layer. The deep inner cloud, which houses the global storage and servers, is located on the top surface. In the lowest layer, particular data types from hospital tests (such as X-ray, CT scan, ultrasound, etc.) are obtained. Vital signs including blood pressure, body temperature, cough quality, and heart rate can be recorded at the user's house using an app [15]. A patient with infection suspicions may record and upload vital signs to a medical data center with a mobile phone application. An AI module would then determine if these signals were normal or required more examination. In the core cloud, a DL model is trained. High-performance servers with many GPUs are found in the cloud. Additionally, it features global storage, where various physiological signal kinds and hospital test signs are retained. The signals might incorporate chest X-rays, CT scans, protease sequences, photographs of the eye's surface, sounds of coughing, body temperature, blood pressure, and more. All hospitals that are registered and other stakeholders provide these signals. Deep trees, ResNet50 and Inception v3 are a few DL models we use. Images are used as input in these models.

Although there are numerous DL models, these three outperformed others in the compositions with regard to accuracy, information density, or a back-and-forth between the three. We transform temporal domain data into spectra for further processing. Each data stream in the parallel stream of the DL model corresponds to a particular kind of signal; for instance, consider a brook for CT scan pictures, a stream for X-ray images, etc as shown in Figure 19.3. At the point that decisions are made, each stream is combined after independently operating. In this approach, there would not be any problems with decision-making if any modality is absent. During after hours, the taught DL model is distributed from the cloud to the network edge and used by the intermediate layer. The specified hospital and community are nearby the edge server. The sample is delivered to the edge over Wi-Fi

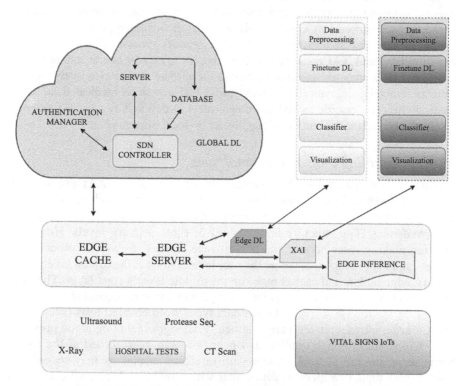

Figure 19.3   Smart healthcare system to fight COVID-19

when a test is available. The data is sent to the DL model after being encrypted using blockchain technology by the edge server. To help doctors comprehend the results of each layer of the DL model, the server additionally makes use of an XAI. The display of layers and confidence ratings can help to obtain the XAI. The DL model's learnable parameters are kept in edge caches for quick access. The outputs in the edge eXplainable AI section are created using a method depicted in the image. The multifaceted information sources, which include visuals from X-rays, CT scans, and ultrasounds, in addition to ocular surfaces, learnable, protease sequence data, and output probabilities (confidence metrics) parameters from various surfaces of the DL model, are all inputs used in inference delineating.

Local interpretable model-agnostic (LIMA) explanations are used in knowledge mapping. In this method, inputs are stopped to see how it affects the model's outputs. This enables us to develop a clearer picture of the inputs and methods the model employs to generate predictions. LIMA works by creating a distribution of the probability over the classes from an input picture using a black-box DL model. The feedback is then controlled in some way; here in the case of the image, this may include coloring the pixels white. To determine if the probabilities for the class it had previously anticipated have improved, this model-agnostic then feeds information to the black-box DL model. Here the main attributes that characterize the adjustments are derived using a decipherable (often linear) framework, such as an inference graph, from a dataset of probabilities and disturbances. The explanations are then produced via attention and imagery. To visualize, we employ the gradient-weighted class activation mapping (gradCAM) technique as it is shown in Figure 19.4.

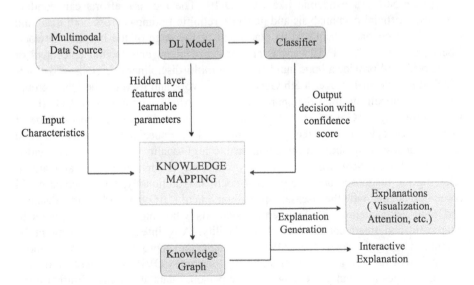

Figure 19.4   Gradient-weighted class activation mapping (gradCAM) technique

19.4.2 Use cases and applications

DNNs are really being widely used to manage massive volumes of epidemic data and anticipate epidemic emergencies in real time. A potential component of COVID-19 therapies using radiological inference has been identified in PET scan, CT scan, and MRI samples utilizing these neural networks lung disease inference. As an illustration, researchers have used image recognition-reliant neural network models that produced the maximum benefit for COVID-19 medical image processing by deploying COVID-19 datasets that are instantaneously reachable from accurate sources depending on the World Health Organization's data [16]. Therefore, these models may be useful in clinical studies utilizing COVID-19 real patients. Current research has demonstrated that neural networks model could successfully be verified to distinguish COVID-19 from various medical indications in addition to fluoroscopic media such as X-ray and CT scanning specimens. Examples include body temperature inspection using a mobile fingerprint sensor or a thermal camera to categorize people, the use of optical coherence tomography (OCT) to identify conjunctivitis or pink eye, and unstructured data (audio files) like cough signals. Because COVID-19 poses a threat to the epithelial cells that outline our respiratory tracts, clinicians utilize CT scans to evaluate the condition of their patients' lungs. Given that almost all hospitals have X-ray imaging equipment or CT scans, etc., tools might be employed for COVID-19 screening. It is a concern for patients who need a rapid corona disease diagnosis as alternative limitations of X-ray image processing and CT scanning that they take time and require domain-specialists. Therefore, to improve patient care and free up valuable time for medical professionals, an automated evaluation model must be created. There is a necessity for consolidated edge cloud-based DL infrastructure where research, assessment, monitoring, and inference may take place during a pandemic like COVID-19. The region's efforts can conduct significant official data analysis and generate reliable findings across both local and international channels thanks to its placement at the edge of the hospital network. Locations where COVID-19 victims are most prevalent, or infection epicenters or "hotspots," will provide a huge number of live multi-disciplinary versions of datasets which might be shared over a 5th-Generation network and used by the DNN group, and an AI globally to train the appropriate DNN. Along with extensive COVID-19 vertical training, B5G would be integrated [17]. This would allow doctors outside of locked-down epicenters to recognize X-ray and CT specimens, greatly improve regional access to medical information, enable high-quality with low-latency video streaming for medical staff to efficiently diagnose patients remotely, and aid in relieving the diagnostic pressure on local doctors. Additionally, fewer people could come into contact with the disease, especially medical staff who work from a distance and high-risk patients with long-term conditions who might have had access to diagnostic and treatment services at the facility. Any infectious illness might be diagnosed using the suggested COVID-19 diagnostic approach. To maintain anonymity, it will provide guidance for authenticating non-COVID-19 patients, reducing hospital congestion, and processing sensitive personal data at the edge. Furthermore, protease sequence analysis along with some DL models will be evaluated in the architecture in future aspects. Other potential future initiatives include including a time-series analysis model and a prediction model within the framework. Pervasive edge computing may also be employed for improved security and minimal latency.

19.5   Significantly enhance trust in health care with XAI

When it suggests a sequence of events that do not appear logical, you are using an AI model. Furthermore, because the model is illogical, you are unable to understand why the suggestion was made. There are just two options available to you: believe it or not. It is a frustrating but all-too-common scenario for most who deal with using AI systems, that in many cases operate as "black boxes" that cannot really be explained by their developers. Black box-style AI methods are great for specific purposes. In other cases, though, the ramifications of a bad AI judgment might be far-reaching and highly devastating. AI system errors in the legal system or medical services, for example, might damage a person's life or livelihood, eroding public and user faith in these processes and undermining their effectiveness. And that's why XAI seems to be so important in the healthcare business. Providers and patients must understand the reasoning behind major AI decisions such as surgical treatments or hospitalizations. XAI delivers interpretable justifications in natural language or other simple abstractions, enables physicians, patients, and other users to better comprehend the logic behind a suggestion and, if required, debate its validity. AI is being utilized by medical professionals to speed up and enhance a variety of functions, including decision-making, prediction, risk management, and even diagnosis, by analyzing medical pictures for abnormalities and patterns that the human eye cannot detect. AI has become a vital element for many doctors, but it is sometimes difficult to explain, leading to dissatisfaction among clinicians and patients, particularly when producing high choices. According to Ron Schmeltzer of Cognylitica, the most straightforward method to establish functioning XAI in medical services is through algorithms "that are naturally explainable." That is, rather than using complex DL or ensemble approaches like random forests, simpler solutions like decision trees, regression techniques, Bayesian classifiers, as well as other explicit algorithms can be utilized "without compromising too much efficiency or performance." According to several experts, the delayed acceptance of AI systems in health treatment is due to the near-impossibility of checking outcomes of black box-type systems. "Doctors are largely trained to detect outliers, or unusual instances that may not require normal therapies," says Erik Birkeneder, a digital medical health devices specialist, in Forbes. "If an AI system isn't properly trained with the right data and we don't know how it makes decisions, we can't be confident it'll spot outliers or otherwise appropriately diagnose patients." Bellio *et al.* do so to outline three aspects of sophisticated AI for health care that might be made more scientifically justified and trustworthy while still performing well:

1. **Better generalization error accounting:** Making it easier to discover deviations or generalization mistakes in the algorithm might assist users recognize when the model is not performing properly and offer information to help users assess if the model's suggestions are trustworthy.

2. **Function-dependent XAI:** The number of explanations required by an AI system is primarily determined by the user's role; for example, a doctor will likely demand more comprehensive context behind an AI proposal than an HR staffing planner. Customizing descriptions depending on the user roles and needs may result in more satisfying results.
3. **Interactive user interfaces:** Intuitive graphical user interfaces may assist consumers better grasp a system's accuracy while also helping them to acquire a more complete knowledge of the accuracy of a certain AI system.

According to Oxford University's Thomas Lukasiewicz, the limits of present XAI systems necessitate the development of a "third wave" of AI technology. The first-wave AI systems are rule- or logic-based, whereas the second-wave AI systems are ML and DL. According to him, the third industrial revolution of AI technology must blend the benefits and shortcomings of the first two kinds. "A very obvious concept is thus to mix them... where the first is strong at reasoning and the latter is good at statistics learning and prediction and to develop a third generation of AI systems known as neural-symbolic AI systems." This new type of AI, according to the professor, has a huge influence on health treatment, including enhanced disease control, more effective and less expensive diagnosis, and great design of treatment and healthcare applications—all while being inherently explainable to all kinds of users, from physician to hospital personnel, patients, and insurance companies. This is how XAI for healthcare builds user trust—even while making life-or-death decisions [18].

19.6 Skillful assessments of XAI techniques in the healthcare domain

A recent research area called XAI aims to provide human-comprehensible explanations for "black box" ML models. As diverse implementations with a black box paradigm are created, the necessity for assessment in examining their efficacy becomes unavoidable. This is particularly important in delicate industries like medical applications, where professional assessment is necessary to better understand how perfect the results of challenging ML are and update the models as necessary. The present concept's main goal is to quantitatively illustrate how expert-level evaluation of XAI technologies in a healthcare context may be used and connected to the clinician's true motivations. To that purpose, it is suggested to gather comments from expert individuals as they identify medical pictures using an eye-tracker and design a mechanism for comparing the findings to those acquired using XAI approaches. Several experiments show the usefulness of our strategy. ML models are in fact an essential component of contemporary technology since they may perform better than people in a variety of fields, such as ophthalmology, spam detection, autonomous robots, and healthcare [19]. Additionally, the ML model may be used to assist specialists in decision-making in areas such as medicine or risk assessments, where actionable answers could have catastrophic repercussions. Recent breakthroughs in ML promise to significantly enhance retinal disease screening and diagnostic accuracy. Systems built utilizing these methodologies have exhibited expert-level accuracy in diagnosing and monitoring the evolution of several eye illnesses, notably diabetic retinopathy; glaucoma, age-related macular degeneration (AMD), and other abnormalities associated with retinal diseases. The significance of such models in healthcare situations, however, is not well known. Prior attempts to use ML algorithms in a setting of computer-assisted diagnosis have run into a number of challenges, including under-reliance (ignoring correct algorithm predictions) and over-reliance (repeating model failures). If the computer-aided diagnostic system can support its black box intelligence predictions, some of these issues will be avoided [20].

The goal of XAI is to decode AI (ML or DL) decisions to a level that is understandable by humans. Consider the scenario where AI algorithms were used to categorize diabetic retinopathy (DR) signs from retinal fundus images. Due to the high level of risk involved, domain experts (clinicians) are typically hesitant to embrace interpretations produced by AI diagnosis tools in sensitive areas like clinical settings. However, if the efficiency of their assessment approach is examined when professional domain constraints are included, rather than generating multiple conclusions and methods for the tactful aspects, then AI diagnosis tools earn greater belief by the healthcare professionals. As a result, it is crucial to investigate the effects of expert review in the context of XAI techniques, as suggested by further expanding the transparency, tool accuracy, the notions of trust, and robustness. Application-centric assessment, human-specific evaluation, and functionally motive evaluations are the three basic classifications of XAI evaluation methodologies. The first classification type measures how effectively professional-generated explanations may assist other people in carrying out particular activities. Employing subject-matter specialists to carry out certain duties within the framework of an application allows us to gauge the effectiveness of this evaluation. For instance, while calculating the DR level from retinal fundus pictures, an ophthalmologist should assess the diagnostic method. On simpler jobs, non-expert persons do evaluative evaluations. Non-experts or users, for instance, could be given a variety of arguments, and the user ultimately decides which is best [21]. The functionally grounded evaluation described is essentially subject agnostic. The majority of cutting-edge techniques fall under this heading. For instance, to assess the accuracy of the XAI algorithms, the authors offered casual measures of deletion and insertion that are not dependent on people. The AI model will modify its judgment if the "cause" is removed or added as the main motive behind the deletion and insertion metrics. Functional and human-centered assessments would not be appropriate for such delicate medical areas, nevertheless. In actuality, all forms of appraisal are equally significant. The explanatory context affects the selection of the appropriate evaluation approach [22].

19.6.1 Enabling tools and technologies

We took into consideration the two most current visual explanation techniques while evaluating the visual explanation on the suggested dataset. They are referred to as SIDU and Gradient-weighted Class Activation Mapping (Grad-CAM) in short.

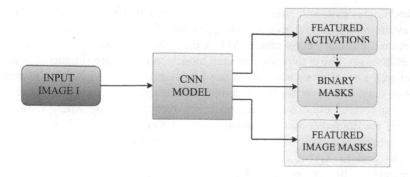

Generating Feature Image Masks From Last Conv Layer Of CNN

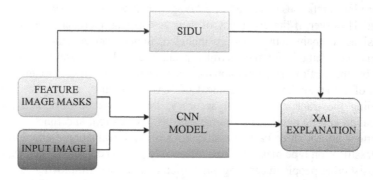

Figure 19.5   SIDU techniques

1. SIDU

    By removing the final convolutional layer from the deep convolution network architecture and constructing a similarity variant mask, a new visual explanation technique called SIDU that was recently described calculates the saliency of each pixel to produce an imaginary explanation of the prediction. Using the criteria for similarity, difference, and uniqueness, the approach generates a heatmap. First, a heatmap of an image's most conspicuous areas may be produced by comparing sets of features activation maps. Second, it evaluates the feature map's uniqueness. This method establishes how different a certain data point is from the rest. A feature map will be labeled as more prominent and given a greater weight if it is unique. The dot product of the two values yields the final score indicating the significance of the feature and is when utilized to compute the biased weighted total of entire feature activation picture masks and provide the graphical insights. The qualitative (human belief) and quantitative trials demonstrated that the SIDU technique outperforms state-of-the-art for both general and crucial medical data. SIDU is a well-suited approach to give clear insights and audit model results, which will be essential for delicate areas like medical diagnosis. This is because SIDU is capable of correctly restricting the domain of heed in the clinical eye fundus visuals as shown in Figure 19.5.

2. GRAD-CAM

Grad-CAM is a technique that uses gradient-based localization to produce visual explanations. It takes the gradients out of the network's final convolution layer. According to the theory underlying this approach, the layer preceding the classification reserves the data regarding attribute pertinence while sustaining spatial links, and, as a result, based on a weighted combination of activation maps dependent on gradient score, it produces a heatmap, which enlightens the attributes with a positive impact on the particular section that is picked as the prediction. Grad-CAM is a class-discriminative localization methodology that can produce graphical insights for any CNN model without needing architectural modifications or retraining [23].

We select the two typical metrics used in cutting-edge algorithms for evaluating saliency detection when comparing heatmaps. To guarantee that this colloquy of the outcomes is as unconventional from the selection of the measures as feasible, more than one assessment measure was used. In a practical situation, the ophthalmologists examine certain areas (regions of the heatmaps) of the eye fundus pictures to evaluate the image quality or DR levels. The GRAD-CAM and SIDU-produced heatmaps in columns show how well the visual explanation approaches match the knowledge of human specialists. Although the outcomes of the many assessment measures are not always the same, it is simple to understand the robustness of the approaches when two metrics exhibit commonalities. The area under ROC curve (AUC) and Kullback–Leibler divergence are two measures used to assess the effectiveness of XAI approaches in various types of trials (KL-DIV). So, it stands to reason that XAI-generated heatmaps will behave similar to those produced by human experts [27].

This concept demonstrates a suggested framework for assessing XAI techniques in the medical field, specifically for the detection and rating of retinal disorders and retinal picture quality as shown in Figure 19.6. It is made primarily for assessing XAI techniques in the medical field. Additionally, the suggested eye-tracker dataset is the first of its type for using human experts to assess the visual explanations in the medical area (ophthalmologists). Experimental findings employing two distinct datasets with various properties highlight the value of

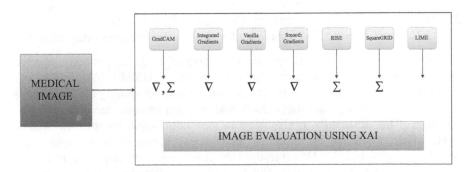

Figure 19.6   Image evaluation using XAI

incorporating human experts in the evaluation of XAI techniques. Human specialists are needed to evaluate XAI approaches in the medical field to increase trust and transparency.

19.7   An alternative viewpoint on healthcare and XAI

Modern AI systems lack explainability and transparency, which is one of the main reasons why they are not widely employed to solve a variety of real-world problems, including those relating to healthcare. Recent standards for the use of AI in healthcare were issued by the WHO, one of which is "ensuring explainability." Applications of AI in the medical field have the potential to save a significant number of lives by quick diagnosis or medical treatment, but they can occasionally provide new hazards and difficulties if they are not applied and used carefully. The AI models that collaborate along with people in the healthcare industry may help people make decisions, like diagnosis and prognosis. XAI models are particularly useful in this context since retaining AI models and assisted decision taking systems accountable is crucial for their application in the healthcare sector [24]. In the current backdrop, explainability is utilized for giving the methodology the ability to defend its results, which include judgments, forecasts, and occasionally even the reasoning process itself. This is a crucial aspect of a system's responsibility. The initial goal and key contribution of this study is to describe the findings from our literature review, also to develop an allocation that condenses numerous XAI-specific concepts since they are practical into a "simple" composition. The overarching goal is to classify and organize the wide domain of knowledge so that it can be addressed more quickly, promote collaboration and easier field comprehension, and enlighten the state-of-the-art for explainability and the difficulties, gaps, and opportunities XAI faces in the medical domain. The study has a propensity to ignore specific issues and domains in favor of examining explainability through a model-first lens approach. Examples of such a strategy include:

1. Black-box XAI approaches are applied without considering how to frame the problem for explanation after training.
2. Without considering the model's users.
3. Without considering the explanation's target audience.
4. Utilizing the similar XAI techniques for various issues across many sectors.

XAI and its use in medical zone are a new area of study that has been impacted by legislative initiatives and research initiatives including DARPA XAI, GDPR, and the upcoming AI Act. However, the current subject is never entirely the latest and is quite rapidly expanding since the DARPA XAI program was introduced in 2017. The recipient of the explanation is significant in the multidisciplinary research field of XAI, which is affected by education, psychology, human–computer interaction, sociology, and philosophy. However, this subject still has to develop in terms of how it applies to actual circumstances, and the research community needs to focus on creating consensus and degree for things like safety, definition, and measures [25]. For instance, "Interpretability" is described in the literature as the characteristic of a model that offers sufficient expressive data to comprehend how the model operates. On the other hand, "Explainability" may be characterized as a model's capacity to condense the causes of its behavior, win users' confidence, or generate insights into its actions. The definition of an explanation is necessary for explainability. According to the literature, an "explanation" is a claim, fact, or circumstance that explains how or why something occurred. Fidelity, accuracy, stability, consistency, certainty, relevance, and comprehensibility are a few of the desired facts for an explanation. A good explanation must be carefully crafted and thoroughly assessed.

19.7.1 Enabling tools and technologies

Starting with a "problem/domain lens" approach, this approach is used to (semi-)automatically identify the most suitable XAI model for a problem in a realm; if none has been discovered, a new model is created by combining or redesigning an existing one; or completely new challenge explainable models are created while considering pertinent justifications, performance, and safety metrics, etc. Although not each of the challenges mentioned will be resolved by the strategy, we anticipate improvements thanks to our approach's use of the problem's and the domain's expertise. This facilitates human and model collaboration and improves design quality, performance, safety level, and degree of needed explanations [26]. Let us examine a medical imaging example:

1. **Problem definition:** Using AI to identify and categorize the kind of white blood cells and any potential abnormalities in blood smear pictures of individuals suspected of hematological cancer.
2. **Potential ML algorithms:** The typical ML techniques used to solve these issues, such as CNN, Capsule Nets, Visual Transformers, etc. Be aware that also create inherently manipulable DL methods for recognizing images, like modified CNNs or alternative architectures.
3. **Potential XAI methods:** To ensure the model is selecting the appropriate patches or pixels in the visual for its decision-making, if we do not have an inherently interpretable model, we can employ some of the common XAI approaches, such as LIME, SHAP, gradient-based Grad-CAM, SIDU, or attribution-propagation, such as attention map, layer-wise relevance propagation (LRP), and others. Given the problem/domain, this is something that the technique may (semi-) automatically recommend.

We discovered a few somewhat dissimilar but connected categorizations of the XAI application approach in the literature. We may integrate the many viewpoints into the following classification of XAI, which is taken from:

- **Model design:** Intrinsic, post-hoc.
- **Scope:** Local (explaining just one instance of prediction) and global (explaining entire model behavior).
- **Relevancy to model:** Model-specific, model-agnostic.
- **Methodology:** Example-based, simplification-based, feature relevance-based, perturbation-based, backpropagation-based, gradient-based, ontology-based.

- **Timing:** Prc-model, in-model, post-model.
- **Presentation:** Visualization, text explanation, mathematical explanation.
- **Data type:** Text, tabular, image, graphs.

19.7.2   Use cases and applications

Due to their strength but also opaque nature, DL models have received the majority of XAI implementations so far, with the aim of facilitating simple model-agnostic explanations of models that have previously been developed. The majority of methods included in the study are post-hoc model agnostic, i.e., they are used to apply to "any" black-box model once it has been trained. For example, we notice a lot of XAI algorithms focusing on local instances in the literature, including feature relevance-based SHAP, LIME, or partial dependence plot, gradient-based attribution maps, or DeepLIFT, backpropagation. The fundamental advantage of post-hoc customized methods is that they are added to some new or existing ML model without the requirement to comprehend the model's underlying framework or operation. Intrinsically interpretable models, which may be utilized for explanation by the model itself, are the antithesis of post-hoc approaches. One of such is the visual transformers, which are becoming more popular in healthcare applications because of the explanations provided by their integrated attention map. Additionally, we observe a growth in the use of model-specific techniques for DL networks, such as SIDU and Grad-CAM. The majority of model-specific XAI approaches remove the last layer and provide a heatmap of the class activation to increase explainability. A DL model's explainability has to be provided to multiple stakeholders in different ways since they will each require a unique perspective and amount of depth.

Another possible limitation is to check the data quality used to guarantee that the data used to train the ML algorithms is not of poor quality, biased, or wrongly labeled, and that there is no confidentiality information leak. We think that because it is so challenging to get data in the first place, data availability is a major problem for XAI in medical and research in general. In fact, the explainability of artificial data in medical domain might be a fascinating subject for future research. We think that in addition to federated learning, more realistic-looking fake health data will be developed because it is difficult to acquire and share health data for study. Due to the challenges in obtaining and cleaning training data, and this could be a fascinating area to explore more. The research community will require to demonstrate the efficacy of training the model using simulated data and those models trained in this way develop quite well on live patient data without running the risk of disclosing any confidential information [31].

19.8   XAI techniques helpful to allergy diagnosis

Clinical diagnosis often relies on a disease's indications and symptoms. Given that many symptoms are shared by several diseases, making an early diagnosis based on the common signs and symptoms is tough and complicated. The severity of the symptoms and subsequent development of life-threatening illnesses are significantly impacted by the timing of the diagnosis. Because they overlap symptoms with a number of other medical conditions, allergies are one of the diseases that are challenging to detect in their early stages. The kind of allergy test to be used is decided upon depending on the patient's medical history, potential allergen triggers, and practical considerations like cost, time, and danger. In general, intradermal skin testing is regarded as the gold standard for determining whether an allergy is present and what its root cause is. However, it is less preferable due to the ambiguity and uncertainty surrounding the interpretation of the test's final results. In the absence of an immunologist, it is challenging for general practitioners and junior doctors to evaluate and communicate the results of the intradermal skin test. Currently, the decision of the subject–matter expert (immunologist) is regarded as the gold standard for disclosing the final test result; nevertheless, there are many places where there is a shortage of allergy experts who can finalize test results. Additionally, it is very challenging to guarantee uniformity in the administration and reporting of allergy tests across various medical facilities. Patients with comorbidities occasionally go to medical facilities. Junior clinicians are unable to consult computer-aided systems, compiled online medical data, or literary resources for making decisions. Because symptoms, laboratory tests, testing modalities, and equipment calibrations might differ from sickness to disease, it might not be viable to create a specific clinical support system for every illness [27]. However, it is conceivable to group a few illnesses together; physicians may do this thanks to their knowledge of medical data and expertise in treating patients. For instance, a patient with allergic rhinitis is more likely to develop asthma. It is preferable to integrate and give immunologists one support system rather than two separate ones for allergic rhinitis and asthma. Combining illnesses that can be treated by a doctor is a good idea.

Computer-aided systems are designed to support decision-makers in their work. CDSSs, diagnosis support systems, automated health diagnostics, healthcare information systems, electronic health record systems, intelligent healthcare systems, knowledge-based systems, medical expert systems, evidence-based systems, and many other types of computer-aided systems are reported in the literature as improving clinical diagnosis and decision support. These technologies help doctors deliver safe and dependable healthcare in a variety of specialties, including dentistry, ophthalmology, dermatology, cardiology, respiratory medicine, hepatology, nephrology, and many more. In the absence of subject–matter specialists, junior physicians might use the results and decisions to support their medical recommendations. With the proper application of CDSS, doctors may prevent inaccurate diagnostic choices and misinterpretations of test results, which are frequently caused by carelessness, observational mistakes, and occasionally even a lack of exposure and domain expertise. Additionally, using CDSS for clinical decision-making duties raises the standard of care delivered. To make rapid and better judgments, the CDSS was built based on cutting-edge methodologies like ML and AI. ML methods find patterns in complicated datasets to produce accurate predictions [28].

19.8.1   Enabling tools and technologies

A few categorization models are generally regarded as being "black boxes," yet physicians frequently need a clear grasp of the results. They are interested in learning the rationale behind the system's choice. The danger of utilizing projections that are not supported by evidence grows over time, as does the necessity for openness. Transparency and model performance do, however, trade-off. XAI principles are incorporated to prevent this trade-off. These ideas make sure that the CDSS supports all predictions made by a classifier with explicable medical knowledge and supportive reasoning. Additionally, this information and logic are simple for doctors to comprehend and understand [29]. Therefore, the major goal of this research is to create an allergy diagnosis support system (ADSS) that makes use of ML models so that it is possible to produce understandable justifications while keeping a high degree of model performance. The human-understandable format of the provided explanations will boost faith in the ability to believe the forecasts made by the support system. IF-THEN rules are typically used to describe the conclusions drawn from medical data to support illness predictions. Junior clinicians can have confidence in the forecasts and guiding principles offered by the ADSS since it is based on medical data and patient demographics, and it has been verified by medical professionals. Additionally, the employment of self explanatory IF-THEN rules to enable a variety of illness combinations may boost the reliance on these systems by doctors when making diagnostic decisions [30]. The two factors that are the subject of this study are as follows:

- First, the creation of CDSS to aid in the identification of many concomitant allergy illnesses. The emphasis is on providing comprehensible human logic for the CDSS forecasts. The doctor's confidence in the support systems will grow as a result of this argument. Instead of using several methods that are tailored to different diseases, immunologists may now diagnose allergies using a single, unified platform.
- The effectiveness of CDSS depends on the quality of the data; as a result, the second component focuses on improving data quality by addressing the issue of class imbalance. If there is at least one class in a dataset that has fewer samples than the other classes, the dataset is said to be unbalanced. Learning algorithms are biased in favor of classes with more samples when there is a class imbalance. The class imbalance issue is dealt with using data sampling strategies. The study involves adjustments to current sampling techniques to address issues with class imbalance by taking user preferences into account.

The graphic below depicts the conceptual design of the proposed CDSS in identifying multiple coexisting allergies. The system's inputs include information on allergy sufferers, such as the findings of an intradermal skin test. The three main components of the allergy diagnosis assistance system are the pre-processor, validator, and evaluator. Figure 19.1 presents the conceptual design of the proposed CDSS for the identification of numerous coexisting allergies. The system's inputs include (1) information on allergy sufferers, such as the findings of an intradermal

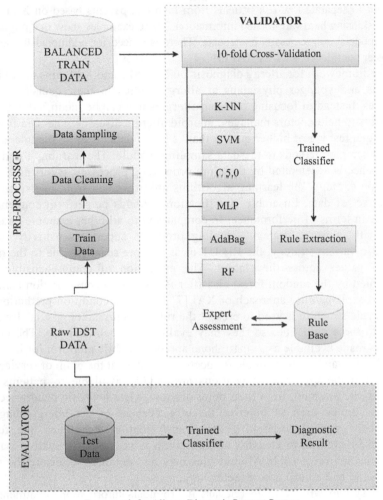

Framework for Allergy Diagnosis Support System

Figure 19.7   Framework for allergy diagnosis support system

skin test. The three main components of the allergy diagnosis assistance system are the pre-processor, validator, and evaluator as shown in Figure 19.7. A brief explanation of each essential mathematical representation that aids in comprehending the system's components opens this part. A growing number of high-performing black-box models have been exposed for incorporating incorrect or confounding factors to get their findings. For instance, a DL network that learned from a training dataset containing a sample of asthma patients who received active physician intervention discovered that patients with asthma had a low probability of dying from pneumonia. Another illustration shows certain ways a DL model is used to detect pneumonia in X-rays by using ambiguous information like the scanner's position. In the third instance, an ML model was built to separate low-risk patients from high-risk patients based on X-rays predicted risk using hardware-related information. These examples show that relying just on the models' correctness is inadequate. There is a need for additional frameworks that foster confidence, such as XAI [31].

The framework for allergy diagnosis built on ML and XAI aims to aid house surgeons and younger physicians at allergy clinics in their decision-making processes. Instead of focusing on basic allergies that can be identified with ease, the goal is to help doctors manage comorbid allergic diseases. The data from the intradermal test are of higher quality thanks to the data cleaning module and the updated sample methods in the data sampling module. The learning algorithms' performance is accelerated by these pre-processing processes. By using a cross-validation strategy, the learning algorithms are prevented from over-fitting the training set of data. Ensemble classification methods outperform conventional methods in terms of performance. In comparison to all other examples, random forest with constant strategy sampling produces superior sensitivity; nevertheless, in variant strategy, the RH UT class is more sensitive due to the difference in values across the classes. The extraction of comprehensible rules represented by the random forest classifier is taken into consideration using the post-hoc explainability approach of XAI [7]. A simple condition-prediction (IF-THEN) rule structure is used to present the rules. An immunologist is also given access to these guidelines so they may evaluate their clinical use. The created CDSS is made available as a smartphone app on a mobile platform for improved usage and portability. It is simple for doctors to access at the point of service. The reports and therapy recommendations are readily available to patients after installing the program, from their point of view. Meta-heuristic data-processing methods can be used to improve the effectiveness of the allergy diagnosis assistance system. Incorporating data transformation techniques like feature selection in addition to cleaning and sampling is possible. Innovative learning algorithms and responsible AI strategies may be combined to ensure the transparent, safe, and ethical use of technology.

The system will be more relevant if prognosis information, treatment outcomes, and patient comments are included. Junior clinicians and even professionals may use this as a source of information and a guide.

19.8.2   Use cases and applications

As there are a few alternatives that can fully address trust, accountability, and regulatory perturbs during fostering transparency and confidence in the AI technology, ignoring, or restricting XAI is harmful to its adoption in medicine. Explainable frameworks might be used to better match the goals of clinical recommendations with model performance. allowing for a more effective implementation of AI models in clinical practice [32,33]. For healthcare practitioners, using AI technologies can be made less dangerous by transparent algorithms or explanatory techniques. Explainable frameworks are already being used to promote openness and understanding across a variety of medical disciplines. The integration of AI medical systems and XAI can be

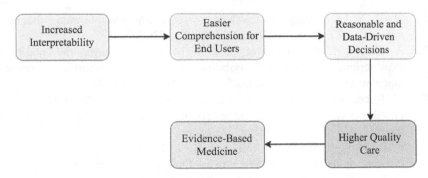

Figure 19.8 Uses of XAI

guided by these case studies. A next level of explainability and a number of advantages, such as enhanced interpretability, better understanding for clinicians leading to substantiated practice, and improved medical outcomes, can be attained through this integration [11–15,34]. Figure 19.8 shows the uses of XAI.

19.9 Conclusion

Sensitizing developers, healthcare workers, and lawmakers to the difficulties and constraints posed by medical AI's opaque algorithms is necessary to guarantee that the technology lives up to its potential. Due to several sources of inaccuracy, AI systems are unlikely to reach flawless accuracy despite their best efforts. Even if the AI system theoretically achieves 100% accuracy, there is no assurance that it is still bias-free, especially if the system was trained on diverse and complicated data, as is common in the medical field.

References

[1] E.-J. Lee, Y.-H. Kim, N. Kim, and D.-W. Kang. Deep into the brain: artificial intelligence in stroke imaging. *J. Stroke*, 2017;19(3):277–285.

[2] S. Lapuschkin, S. Wäldchen, A. Binder, G. Montavon, W. Samek, and K.-R. Müller. Unmasking clever Hans predictors and assessing what machines really learn. *Nat. Commun.*, 2019;10(1):1096.

[3] O. Kocadagli and R. Langari. Classification of EEG signals for epileptic seizures using hybrid artificial neural networks based wavelet transforms and fuzzy relations. *Expert Syst. Appl.*, 2017;88:419–434.

[4] L. H. Gilpin, D. Bau, B. Z. Yuan, A. Bajwa, M. Specter, and L. Kagal. Explaining explanations: an overview of interpretability of machine learning. In *Proceedings of the IEEE 5th International Conference on Data Science and Advanced Analytics (DSAA)*, Oct. 2018, pp. 80–89.

[5] A. Meldo, L. Utkin, M. Kovalev, and E. Kasimov. The natural language explanation algorithms for the lung cancer computer-aided diagnosis system. *Artif. Intell. Med.*, 2020;108:101952.

[6]   D. Gu, Y. Li, F. Jiang, *et al.* VINet: a visually interpretable image diagnosis network. *IEEE Trans. Multimed.*, 2020;22:1720–1729.

[7]   A. Holzinger, A. Carrington, and H. Müller. Measuring the quality of explanations: the System Causability Scale (SCS): comparing human and machine explanations. *KI Kunstl. Intell.*, 2020;34:193–198.

[8]   M. Rucco, G. Viticchi, and L. Falsetti. Towards personalized diagnosis of glioblastoma in fluid-attenuated inversion recovery (FLAIR) by topological interpretable machine learning. *Mathematics*, 2020;8:770.

[9]   P. R. Magesh, R. D. Myloth, and R. J. Tom. An explainable machine learning model for early detection of Parkinson's disease using LIME on DaTSCAN imagery. *Comput. Biol. Med.*, 2020;126:104041.

[10]   C. Shorten and T. M. Khoshgoftaar. A survey on image data augmentation for deep learning. *J. Big Data*, 2019;6:60.

[11]   P. Falcone, F. Borrelli, J. Asgari, H. E. Tseng, and D. Hrovat. Predictive active steering control for autonomous vehicle systems. *IEEE Trans. Control Syst. Technol.*, 2007;15:566–580.

[12]   D. Silver, A. Huang, C. J. Maddison, *et al.* Mastering the game of go with deep neural networks and tree search. *Nature*, 2016;529:484–489.

[13]   A. Holzinger, G. Langs, H. Denk, K. Zatloukal, and H. Müller. Causability and explainability of artificial intelligence in medicine. *Wiley Interdiscip. Rev. Data Min. Knowl. Discov.*, 2019;9:e1312.

[14]   E. M. Kenny, C. Ford, M. Quinn, and M. T. Keane. Explaining Black-Box classifiers using post-hoc explanations-by-example: the effect of explanations and error-rates in XAI user studies. *Artif. Intell.*, 2021;294:103459.

[15]   M. Jacobs, M. F. Pradier, T. H. McCoy, R. H. Perlis, F. Doshi-Velez, and K. Z. Gajos. How machine-learning recommendations influence clinician treatment selections: the example of the antidepressant selection. *Transl. Psychiatry*, 2021;11:108.

[16]   Y. Zhou, F. Tang, Y. Kawamoto, N. Kato. Reinforcement learning-based radio resource control in 5G vehicular network. *IEEE Wirel. Commun. Lett.*, 2020;9(5):611–614.

[17]   Z. Ali, G. Muhammad, and M. F. Alhamid. An automatic health monitoring system for patients suffering from voice complications in smart cities. *IEEE Access*, 2017;5(1):3900–3908.

[18]   B. Li, Z. Fei, Y. Zhang, and M. Guizani. Secure UAV communication networks over 5G. *IEEE Wirel. Commun.*, 2019;26(5):114–120.

[19]   M. S. Hossain and G. Muhammad. A deep tree model-based radio resource distribution for 5G networks. *IEEE Wirel. Commun.*, 2020;27(1):62–67.

[20]   M. S. Hossain and G. Muhammad. Emotion recognition using secure edge and cloud computing. *Inf. Sci.*, 2019;504:589–601.

[21]   L. Q. Zhou, X. L. Wu, S. Y. Huang, *et al.* Lymph node metastasis prediction from primary breast cancer US images using deep learning. *Radiology*, 2020;294:19–28.

[22]   K. Zhou, S. Gao, J. Cheng, *et al.* Sparse-gan: sparsity-constrained generative adversarial network for anomaly detection in retinal oct image. In

Proceedings of the IEEE 17th International Symposium on Biomedical Imaging (ISBI), 2020, pp. 1227–1231.

[23] Z. Zhu, X. Ding, D. Zhang, and L. Wang. Weakly-supervised balanced attention network for gastric pathology image localization and classification. In *Proceedings of the IEEE 17th International Symposium on Biomedical Imaging (ISBI)*, 2020, pp. 1–4.

[24] P. Zhu and M. Ogino. Guideline-based additive explanation for computer-aided diagnosis of lung nodules. In *Proceedings of the 2nd International Workshop on Interpretability of Machine Intelligence in Medical Image Computing, IMIMIC* 2019. doi: 10.1007/978-3-030-33850-3_5.

[25] Z. Zhu, E. Albadawy, A. Saha, J. Zhang, M. R. Harowicz, and M. A. Mazurowski. Deep learning for identifying radiogenomic associations in breast cancer. *Comput. Biol. Med.,* 2019;109:85–90. doi:10.1016/j. compbiomed.2019.04.018.

[26] K. Ma, K. Wu, H. Cheng, C. Gu, R. Xu, and X. Guan. A pathology image diagnosis network with visual interpretability and structured diagnostic report. In *Proceedings of the 25th International Conference on Neural Information Processing ICONIP*, 2018. doi:10.1007/978- 3- 030-04224-0_24.

[27] G. Maicas, A. P. Bradley, J. C. Nascimento, I. Reid, and G. Carneiro. Pre and post-hoc diagnosis and interpretation of malignancy from breast DCE-MRI. *Med. Image Anal.,* 2019;58:101562.

[28] S. Maksoud, A. Wiliem, K. Zhao, T. Zhang, L. Wu, and B. Lovell. CORAL8: concurrent object regression for area localization in medical image panels. In *Proceedings of the 22nd International Conference Medical Image Computing and Computer Assisted Intervention MICCAI*, 2019. doi:10.1007/978-3-030-32239-7_48.

[29] A. Malhi, T. Kampik, H. Pannu, M. Madhikermi, and K. Framling. Explaining machine learning-based classifications of in-vivo gastral images. In *Proceedings of the International Conference on Digital Image Computing: Techniques and Applications, DICTA,* 2019. doi:10.1109/ DICTA47822.2019.8945986.

[30] Y. Matsui, T. Maruyama, M. Nitta, *et al.* Prediction of lower-grade glioma molecular subtypes using deep learning. *J. Neurooncol.,* 2020;146:321–327. doi:10.1007/s11060- 019- 03376-9.

[31] J. Zhou, A. H. Gandomi, F. Chen, and A. Holzinger. Evaluating the quality of machine learning explanations: a survey on methods and metrics. *Electronics*, 2021;10:593. [CrossRef]

[32] G. Marcus. Deep learning: a critical appraisal. arXiv 2018, arXiv:1801.00631.

[33] B. Goodman and S. Flaxman. European Union regulations on algorithmic decision-making and a "right to explanation". *AI Mag.* 2017;38:50–57.

[34] Y. LeCun, Y. Bengio, and G. Hinton. Deep learning. *Nature*, 2015;521: 436–444.

[35] L. M. Zintgraf, T. S. Cohen, T. Adel, and M. Welling. Visualizing deep neural network decisions: prediction difference analysis. In *Proceedings of*

the 5th International Conference on Learning Representations, ICLR 2017. University of Amsterdam, Netherlands International Conference on Learning Representations, ICLR.

[36]   H. Zunair and A. B. Hamza. Melanoma detection using adversarial training and deep transfer learning. *Phys. Med. Biol.,* 2020;65:135005.

[37]   T. Mahmud, M. A. Rahman, and S. A. Fattah. CovXNet: a multi-dilation convolutional neural network for automatic COVID-19 and other pneumonia detection from chest X-ray images with transferable multi-receptive feature optimization. *Comput. Biol. Med.,* 2020;122:103869.

Chapter 20

Adequate lung cancer prognosis system using data mining algorithms

Loshiga Mohan[1], S. Usha[2] and N. Susila[3]

Data mining is the technique used by different algorithms to retrieve the necessary information from an immense amount of datasets. The main objective of this research is to predict the possible level of lung cancer. Several experiments have been conducted using data analysis methods to explain the estimation of lung cancer risks. Cancer is the deadliest illness now, causing a lot of deaths. That's because it is incurable in most situations. But it is not so the case if it is detected at an earlier stage. So an earlier diagnosis is necessary. However, to foresee the incidence of lung cancer, there are so many steps and actions needed. This research is therefore focused on using four data mining methods to forecast risks of lung cancer in patients without much effort using the naive Bayes, decision trees, k-nearest neighbors, and random forest algorithms based on basic parameters. To evaluate the most efficient and productive model, the efficiency of these classification techniques was measured.

20.1 Introduction

20.1.1 Motivations

Cancer is a disease caused in a part of the body by an unregulated division of unhealthy cells and by expanding into surrounding tissues. Cancer is caused by DNA modifications. In portions of DNA named chromosomes, most cancer-causing DNA modifications exist. Such variations are also considered genetic changes. Lung disorder, in nature, plays a significant role in health conditions [1,2]. Any prevalent types of lung diseases are caused mostly by breathing in some type of lung disease. Asthma, acute bronchitis, chronic obstructive pulmonary disease, chronic bronchitis, emphysema, lung cancer, and acute respiratory distress syndrome. There are numerous types of lung cancer, classified into two primary

[1]Department of Big Data Management and Analytics, Griffith College, Dublin, Ireland
[2]Research and Innovation, Rajarajeswari Engineering College, Bengaluru, India
[3]Department of Information Technology, Sri Krishna College of Engineering and Technology, Coimbatore, India

groups: small cell lung cancer and non-small cell lung cancer, with three subtypes: carcinoma, adenocarcinoma, and carcinoma of squamous cells. In the vital or final level, it is not easy to heal, causing mortal death. This experiment is to find a way to use the technology and expertise to make it easier for the medics to understand and treat it as early as possible.

20.1.2   Scope of data mining

The principles of data mining have been known for ages, but with the advancement of information technology, it has become even more prevalent nowadays [3]. By offering these capabilities, given datasets of sufficient scale and quality, data mining technologies can create new possibilities: Automated pattern and behavior analysis. Data mining automates the work of exploring predictive knowledge in vast databases. Complex data mining benefits from previous experiences and algorithms defined by existing software and packages, with some of these tools gaining a strong affinity or reputation for various techniques.

20.1.3   Objectives

The aim is to better understand which variables lead to the disease's complications. The models are constructed through the implementation of data mining techniques. In this project, we are developing multiple models to forecast the level of lung cancer. Data mining is the exploration of massive data to extract correlations that are hidden and previously unknown. The techniques of data science are simple and efficient ways of understanding and predicting future data. Manual handling of large data is almost impossible. Therefore, visual analytics is a very important step to have a general idea about given data. In many businesses, statistical techniques are popular and have an impact on different areas of study.

To be applied to these machine learning (ML) techniques and visualization, R, and Python were selected. The goal of this paper was to use data visualization and ML applications for breast cancer diagnosis to perform a comparative study. Here, for classification in our chapter, the R instrument is used. It is an interactive suite of data manipulation, estimation, and graphical interface program facilities. It requires powerful facilities for data handling and storage.

The method of finding hidden, interesting, and valuable patterns from datasets in data mining. This involves many concerns such as the dynamic nature and massive input data size that cannot be addressed by normal techniques or approaches.

The proposed method comprises two classification-based, efficient algorithms such as K-nearest neighbor (KNN), and random forest. Thus, it is important to reach a high degree of efficiency. The purpose of the work proposed is to use techniques known as KNN and random forest to predict lung cancer. The proper classification for a set of inputs can be evaluated on the second set of inputs with algorithms learned to see how well it classifies untrained patterns.

20.1.4   Research questions

To equate NB, decision tree, k-NN, and random forest habits. I performed an experiment that centered on testing the algorithms' efficacy and performance. More importantly, the testing questions asked for the experiment are: Which algorithm takes advantage of better efficiency? What is the more powerful algorithm? What algorithm offers higher precision?

20.2 Related work

Previous studies have also shown cancer detection with data mining techniques, and a few of them are listed below. The three popular data mining algorithms have been used to detect breast cancer, such as RepTree, RBF Network, KNN, and simple logistics [1]. The probabilities of developing breast cancer are broadly divided into modifiable and non-modifiable variables. Non-modifiable risk factors include age, gender, number of breast cancer first-degree relatives, history of menstruation, age of menarche, and age of menopause. The modifiable risk factors are BMI, age at first birth, number of infants, breastfeeding duration, alcohol, diet, and number of abortions.

In the test point, the ten-fold cross-validation approach was applied to the University Medical Center databases, Institute of Oncology, Ljubljana, Yugoslavia, to assess the performance of the proposed scheme. The correct classification rate for the proposed system is 74.5%. This research shows how basic logistics can minimize the size of the function space which can be used with the proposed Rep Tree and RBF network model to acquire fast automated diagnostic systems for other diseases. Data mining techniques have been explored in this paper: RepTree, RBF network, and basic logistics. They are using these algorithms to estimate a breast cancer dataset's survivability score. These three classification methods were chosen to find the most appropriate one to estimate the rate of cancer survivability.

They used libraries from the Weka ML environment. WEKA is a workbench for ML intended to help evolve methods of ML to several diverse problems. Each classification system has been used "as it is", in the Weka setting, asserting that no additional parameter tuning was performed before or during the classification results comparison. The research results specifically show that the evaluation features are not direct indicators of breast cancer patients. Here, compared to others, simple logistic is a more precise classifier, so it can quickly be seen that it has highly classified appropriate cases and incorrectly classified instances than RepTree and RBF network.

The best algorithm based on the patient's data is a simple logistic classification with an accuracy of 74.47% and the total time taken to build the model is at 0.62 sec. They proved that a simple logistic classifier can dramatically boost the traditional classification methods used in the analysis among the results suggested by the ML algorithm studied.

The next research, using KNN, support vector machine (SVM), and random forest [2], aims to predict breast cancer. They contrasted the three techniques. To construct a more complex classifier, all these approaches are used individually or with ensemble learning. In this study, the dataset was used to construct a classification model used to make an evidence-based inference. Using the classification model on medical reports, helped develop a system for future prediction.

To figure out the critical characteristics, they used LIME (local interpretable model-agnostic explanations). In a particular region of the role of specifications, this approach decides which Dataset features are important. This technique is more useful for evaluating a dynamic subject that has contributed significantly to its prediction. LIME is a common surrogate model. A proxy model is an explicitly interpretable model, such as a decision tree that is ready to mimic the behavior of the critical, complicated attention model. Locally inside LIME, it supplies certain surrogate versions. For a single prediction, LIME changes the values to produce new data points that are similar.

The outcome of this paper is based on the original Wisconsin Breast Cancer Dataset, an open-access web database accessed through the library of UCI ML. Dr. W.H. Wolberg compiled this dataset at the University of Wisconsin-Madison Hospital, consisting of 682 tests, rated as malignant and benign. Of all these trials, 458 cases were benign, and 241 were malignant (65.5% malignant and 34.5% benign). Clump width, cell size uniformity, call shape uniformity, marginal adhesion, single epithelial cell size, bare nuclei, bland chromatin, regular nuclei, mitoses, and class are the ten characteristics.

In this chapter, five ML techniques have been used, namely SVM, Logistic Regression, Neural Network, Gaussian Naive Bayes, and Voting Classifier. They identified their methodologies and their key features. The original Wisconsin breast cancer data collection was used to assess the efficiency of the approaches used in this article. The result obtained indicates that, depending on the chosen process, the performance of the classification varies. This paper reveals that the Voting Classifier has the best achievement in terms of precision, consistency, and accuracy.

Three of the most common ML techniques, SVM, random forest (RF), and Bayesian networks, which are commonly used for breast cancer detection and diagnosis, were contrasted by Bazazeh *et al.* in 2016 [17]. The Wisconsin initial breast cancer dataset was used as a training set to assess and compare the results of the three ML classifiers concerning important parameters such as accuracy, recall, accuracy, and operating characteristics of the receiver (ROC) area. A review of state-of-the-art ML approaches for diagnosing breast cancer is given in the results of this article.

The numerical simulations have shown that the performance of the classification varies based on the chosen method. Results have shown that SVMs have the highest performance in terms of precision, specificity, and accuracy. However, RFs have the highest probability of correctly classifying the tumor. Therefore, they showed that SVM is the best classifier used on the Breast Cancer dataset with 97% accuracy, 97.2% recall, and 97% accuracy score.

The main objective of the next study is to find out how precisely those very data mining algorithms can predict the likelihood of disease recurrence among patients based on critically indicated parameters [4]. The research highlights the performance of the dataset of different algorithms for clustering and classification. Experiments show that classification algorithms are better predictors than clustering of algorithms.

Diverse clustering and classification algorithms are used in this paper to identify the performance of these prediction models using data mining techniques.

Four clustering algorithms have been selected for this study (K-means, EM, PAM, and fuzzy c-means) and four classification algorithms (SVM, C5.0, naive Bayes, and KNN). They used the R programming tool, which provides a free data analysis software environment, for implementation purposes. This study intends to find the most promising algorithm for data mining that helps forecast cancer cases that could recur. The goal was to find the crucial characteristics that play a significant role in evaluating and forecasting breast cancer recurrence probability using the C5.0 algorithm in advance.

Their data collection consists of 198 patient records, out of which four records missed the value of the "Lymph node" status attribute. Although the lymph node's importance is a crucial factor in determining the status of breast cancer. Instead of deleting this attribute itself, the documents holding the missing data for this attribute were then excluded from the dataset. Thus, the final dataset comprises 194 documents, 148 of which were non-recurrent and 46 of which were recurrent events.

They have used four clustering algorithms: K-means, EM, PAM, fuzzy c-means, and four classification algorithms used: KNN, SVM, naive Bayes, and C5.0. Based on accuracy, sensitivity, and specificity, the efficiency of these algorithms is calculated. The chance of accuracy in the outcome is calculated in the 0 to 1 range, while 1 is 100% accuracy. Eighty-one percent accuracy is obtained by the two C5.0 and SVM classification algorithms, which is better than all the algorithms listed in this chapter.

Supreet Kaur and Amanjot Kaur Grewal examined the potential use of classification-based data mining techniques such as BFO, SVM, and neural networks to a massive volume of healthcare data [2]. This model aims to identify and accurately diagnose the disease early on, which will help the doctor save the patient's life. They used MATLAB® for implementing the algorithms. Each algorithm will be tested with lung cancer data as input data.

Their goal is to implement hybrid classification schemes and develop data mining techniques that are well-tailored to medical diagnostic systems' essential requirements. A substantial collection of analytical treatment approaches for these data was proposed to be developed. In data mining techniques and user interfaces, the approaches under review are varied and prove that the area and its technologies can be used entirely in biomedical research.

P. Bhuvaneswari and Dr. A. Brintha focused on the diagnosis of early-stage lung cancer [3]. For the identification of a non-parametric process, the genetic KNN (GKNN) algorithm is suggested. This optimization algorithm helps doctors in the early stage to recognize the nodules found in the CT lung images, hence lung cancer. Although the manual analysis of CT images of lung cancer is time intensive and very important, the genetic algorithm approach is paired with the KNN algorithm to identify cancer quickly and efficiently images to resolve this difficulty.

The implementation of the MATLAB® image processing toolbox and the classification of these images were performed on the CT lung images. The output measurements, such as the rate of classification and the false-positive rates, were analyzed. The distance between evaluation and training samples is initially established in the conventional KNN algorithm and more distant K-neighbors are begun taking for classification. In this proposed procedure, using the genetic algorithm, K (50-100) numbers of samples are selected for each iteration and 90% accuracy of the classification is obtained as fitness.

In three steps, they proposed the techniques. Originally, the CT lung images were preprocessed and segmented. The third phase was the extraction of the Gabor filter function, a KNN classification, and an optimized genetic algorithm. In this paper, a different technique was suggested to improve KNN classifier accuracy using the genetic algorithm (GA) to overcome the limitations of conventional KNN. The proposed G-KNN classifier was introduced and, for each iteration, identical k-neighbors were selected for classification using GA. The test samples were labeled with these neighbors, and the accuracy was determined to achieve high accuracy for different numbers of K values; hence, the KNN calculation time was decreased from the obtained results in this process.

In this chapter, a performance analysis between different ML algorithms was carried out on the Wisconsin Breast Cancer (original) datasets: SVM, Decision Tree (C4.5), Naive Bayes (NB), and KNN [5]. The fundamental purpose of the authors is to determine the quality of the data classification, in terms of accuracy, accuracy, sensitivity, and specificity, concerning the reliability and effectiveness of each algorithm. Here, ML strategies introduced in WEKA are lengthened to several real-world problems. The software provides a well-defined structure for experimenters as well as developers to make and test their models.

The Wisconsin Breast Cancer (original) datasets from the UCI Machine Learning Repository are used in this study. Breast-cancer-Wisconsin has 699 instances (benign: 458; malignant: 241), 2 classes (65.5% malignant and 34.5% benign), and 11 integer-valued attributes.

The classifiers were designed and evaluated and the ten-fold cross-validation test was applied, a technique used to evaluate predictive models that split the original set into a model training sample and a test set to evaluate it. They attempted to visually examine the data and determine the distribution of values in terms of quality and efficacy, after applying pre-processing and planning techniques.

SVM achieves 97.13% precision and, thus, outperforms all other algorithms. In breast cancer prediction and diagnosis, SVM has proven its efficiency and delivers the highest results in accuracy and low error rate.

Ahamed Lebbe Sayeth Saabith, Elankovan Sundararajan, and Azuraliza Abu Bakar conducted a comparative study on various classification techniques, such as decision trees, neural networks, and rough sets, using a breast cancer dataset. They evaluated classification accuracy with and without feature selection methods, demonstrating that the use of feature selection techniques is an important factor in diagnosing breast cancer [6]. When it removes redundant characteristics, the set of features improves the performance of the classifier. The experiment reveals that the set of features increases the efficiency of all three distinct classifiers, reduces the mean standard error (MSE), and enhances the ROC. Using data mining methods such as WEKA and ROSETTA, with and without feature selection techniques, the ultimate goal of this research is to evaluate and compare the output of three different classification techniques.

Experimental results showed that the above three classification algorithms of J48, MLP, and Rough were set without function selection techniques at 71.22%, 69.87%, and 58.36% accuracy. The accuracy of feature selection strategies was 79%, 75.3%, and 71.36%, respectively, for J48, MLP, and Rough sets. The accuracy of all three different classifiers was also improved under the feature selection techniques. The technique of feature discovery is also one of the essential explanations for diagnosing breast cancer faster.

The three classification techniques such as J48, MLP, and Rough set were used in this study to determine the percentage of accuracy with and without feature selection techniques for successful prediction of breast cancer. The UCI machine learning dataset has been used to reach the goal of the breast cancer dataset. Several experiments were conducted by adjusting the ratio of the evaluation and training dataset and obtained significant results under the methodology of function selection. The methods of feature selection are used to exclude certain features that have no meaning in classification. Therefore, the feature selection technique is the most effective way of enhancing the precision of various classification methods, reducing the MSE, and increasing the ROC to detect breast cancer disease. Aličković and Subasi introduced numerous data processing methods to detect breast cancer in this chapter [7]. To test the framework proposed in this report, two separate Wisconsin Breast Cancer databases were used. There were two steps to the proposed plan. In the first step, genetic algorithms were used to extract insight and the following characteristics to remove irrelevant characteristics. This method decreased the difficulty of programming and speeded up the process of data mining. In the second level, with two separate groups of subjects with or without breast cancer, many data mining methods were used to decide.

The purpose of this research is to create an effective, automatic diagnostic system that can discriminate between malignant cancers and benign tumors of the breast. To overcome this challenge, various data mining techniques were applied, and their performances were evaluated and compared. Logistic regression, decision trees, random forest, Bayesian network, radial basis function networks (RBFN), multilayer perceptron (MLP), and SVM networks.

These steps are followed into precise feature selection based on GA:

1. Pre-processing (scaling) data: Two advantages of scaling are the avoidance of attributes in a larger numeric range to control attributes in a smaller numeric range and the avoidance of numerical difficulties in calculating.
2. Genotype to phenotype conversion: We convert each chromosome feature here.
3. Subset feature.
4. Assessment of fitness.
5. The process is stopped if the termination criteria are met, or the process is continued.
6. Genetic surgery: In this step, genetic surgery searches for the best solution.

For the training data, two different experiments have been set up for two different WBC datasets. In the first example, the same training-testing dataset was applied. An open-source ML program called WEKA, which is freely accessible, was used in this observation to implement the algorithms and approach proposed in this report. Ten-fold cross-validation was included in the dataset for training. In the second example, where the best attributes were selected, they used GA feature selection a, and then they used tenfold cross-validation on these selected attributes.

Random forest and GA feature selection provided the highest precision of 99.48%. By using SVM, they also achieved good classification precision. This chapter proved that an ensemble of simpler classifiers could also be used instead of using complex methods based on strength classifiers to obtain vital classification accuracy, yielding remarkable results.

In the paper titled "Random Forests" by Breiman [8], it demonstrates that utilizing random inputs and features leads to positive results in classification, although this effect is less pronounced in regression. The study exclusively employs bagging and random features as forms of randomness. However, it is possible that employing different forms of injected randomness could yield superior results. The paper also discusses errors and residuals of the random forest model. Random forests consist of an ensemble of tree predictors, where each tree relies on values from an independently sampled random variable, all drawn from the same distribution. Similar to the behavior of the generalization error for forests, as the number of trees in the forest grows, the model converges towards a limit. The generalization error of a forest of tree classifiers depends on the intensity and similarity between the forest's individual trees. Using a random set of features to separate each node yields error rates that are more stable with respect to noise compared to Adaboost. Internal calculations monitor error, intensity, and correlation, and they are used to illustrate the reaction to increasing the amount of splitting features used. To assess the variable value, internal calculations are used.

Using the Strong Law of Large Numbers reveals that they still converge such that there is no problem with overfitting. Forests have implemented a random set of characteristics at each node to determine the split. First, random sampling from the initial inputs is used; the second utilizes random linear input combinations. The observations align favorably with Adaboost. It turns out that the effects are oblivious to the number of features chosen to separate each node. Usually, picking one or two characteristics gives near-ideal outcomes. In forecasting, random forests were a powerful instrument. Due to the Large Numbers Law, they should not overfit. It makes them effective classifiers and regressors by adding the correct kind of randomness. Additionally, the structure provides insight into the random forest's capacity to forecast in terms of the power of the individual predictors and their correlations. Using out-of-bag calculation makes the mostly theoretical power and correlation values real.

With boosting and adaptive bagging, forests give competitive outcomes but do not steadily alter the training package. Their precision suggests they are acting to minimize biased. The mechanism for this is not clear. It is also possible to consider random forests as a Bayesian procedure. In classification, random inputs and random features yield good outcomes, but less in regression. Bagging and random characteristics were the only modes of randomness used in this analysis. It could be that other kinds of injected randomness provided stronger outcomes.

The notion that current methods of predictive classification generated from computer analysis and deep learning methods such as neural networks, SVMs, and random forests can increase the precision, sensitivity, and specificity of forecasts of cognitive tests is advanced by De Mendon [9]. The study compared the performance of seven non-parametric classifiers, which were derived from data mining techniques (including Multilayer Perceptron, Neural Networks, Radial Basis Function Neural Networks, Support Vector Machines, CART, CHAID, and QUEST Classification Trees, as well as Random Forests), with that of three traditional classifiers (Linear Discriminant Analysis, Quadratic Discriminant Analysis, and Logistic Regression) in various aspects such as overall classification accuracy, specificity, sensitivity, Area under the ROC curve, and Press'Q. Ten neuropsychological tests is model predictors, widely used in the diagnosis of dementia. Statistical distributions of classified parameters derived from five-fold cross-validation were compared using Friedman's nonparametric test.

The result they got was a Q test by Press demonstrated that both classifiers worked better than chance alone ($p<0.05$). The greater overall classification accuracy (Median (Me) = 0.76) and area under the ROC (Me = 0.90) were seen by SVMs. This system, however, demonstrated elevated specificity (Me = 1.0) but low sensitivity (Me = 0.3). In total precision (Me = 0.73), the random forest ranked second with a high region under the ROC (Me = 0.73), specificity (Me = 0.73), and sensitivity (Me = 0.64). Linear discriminant regression also demonstrated reasonable average precision (Me = 0.66), with precision (Me = 0.66) and sensitivity (Me = 0.64) to an acceptable region under the ROC (Me = 0.72).

Random forests and linear discriminant analysis rated first of all classifiers evaluated using multiple neuropsychological measures to predict dementia when considering sensitivity, precision, and overall classification accuracy. Those approaches can be used to enhance the precision, sensitivity, and specificity of neuropsychological test predictions for dementia.

20.3 Methodology

The lung cancer dataset was acquired from the data universe. It contains 24 data attributes age, gender, air pollution, alcohol use, dust allergy, genetic risk, chronic lung disease, balanced diet, obesity, smoking, passive smoker, chest pain, coughing of blood, fatigue, weight loss, shortness of breath, wheezing, swallowing difficulty, clubbing of finger nails, frequent cold, dry cough, and snoring. It contains nominal data from 1 to 10 based on the intensity of those attributes. The class label is a level that contains the classification as high, medium, and low based on these attributes.

This application consists of three different phases, as follows:

- The datasets are pre-processed using Weka, which includes converting raw data into a readable format.
- To forecast lung cancer, R environment classification methods are used [19].
- To display the level of a single dataset, an Interface is developed.

R is a language and environment for mathematical computation and graphics. It is a GNU project close to the S language and work performed at Bell Laboratories by John Chambers and colleagues (formerly AT&T, now Lucent Technologies). R may be viewed as a distinct implementation of S. Any big differences occur, but much of the code written for S runs unaffected under R. R is extremely extensible and includes a wide variety of mathematical and graphical techniques (linear and nonlinear simulation, classical statistical studies, time series analysis, classification, clustering, etc.).

20.3.1   *Performance measures*

20.3.1.1   **Confusion matrix**

An uncertainty matrix includes information from a classification system regarding current and expected classifications. The efficiency of such structures is typically measured using the data in the matrix.

- A is the number of accurate predictions that a bad example is,
- B is the number of incorrect forecasts that an example is favorable,
- C is the number of incorrect predictions that are negative in an example, and c is the number of accurate predictions that an example is positive in d.

The accuracy is the proportion of the total number of predictions that were correct. It is determined using the equation:

$$AC = \frac{a+d}{a+b+c+d} \tag{20.1}$$

The recall or true positive rate (TP) is the proportion of positive cases that were correctly identified, as calculated using the equation:

$$TP = \frac{d}{c+d} \tag{20.2}$$

The false positive rate (FP) is the proportion of negative cases that were incorrectly classified as positive, as calculated using the equation:

$$FP = \frac{b}{a+b} \tag{20.3}$$

The true negative rate (TN) is defined as the proportion of negative cases that were classified correctly, as calculated using the equation:

$$TN = \frac{a}{a+b} \tag{20.4}$$

The false negative rate (FN) is the proportion of positive cases that were incorrectly classified as negative, as calculated using the equation:

$$FN = \frac{c}{c+d} \tag{20.5}$$

Finally, precision (P) is the proportion of the predicted positive cases that were correct, as calculated using the equation:

$$P = \frac{d}{b+d} \tag{20.6}$$

The naive Bayes algorithm provides the least efficiency among all. The decision tree algorithm provides lesser efficiency but is higher than the Bayes algorithm. The KNN algorithm and random forest provide better efficiency. Random forest is the best prediction model among all the algorithms with higher values.

20.3.1.2   Cross-validation matrix

Cross-validation is a well-known ML technique, and it is typically a part of the training phase that ensures that our models perform well on non-fitted results. There are numerous methods of doing cross-validation, but we forecast our fitted model on unfitted data in all of them [1,10,11]. Cross-validation is a procedure of resampling used on a small dataset to validate ML models.

The method has a single parameter called k that corresponds to the number of classes that are to be separated into a given dataset. As such, k-fold cross-validation is also called the method. If a particular value is picked for k, it can be used in the model comparison instead of k, such as $k=10$ being a ten-fold cross-validation.

Cross-validation is mainly used to estimate the ability of an ML algorithm on unseen data in advanced ML. That is, to use a small sample to approximate how, in general, the model is supposed to work when used to make assumptions about data not used during model testing. It is a common technique because it is easy to grasp and because it normally results in a model skill calculation that is less biased or less positive than other strategies, such as a simple train/test break. Cross-validation requires only the initial training set to be tuned to hyperparameters. This allows the test set to be held as a completely unseen dataset for the final model to be chosen.

20.4   System design

20.4.1   Statistical features

A broad range of statistical and graphical methods are introduced by R and its libraries, including linear and nonlinear modeling, classical statistical tests, time-series analysis, classification, clustering, and others. R is quickly extensible by functions and extensions, and in terms of packages, the R community is noted for its effective contributions. Many of the standard features of R are written in R itself, making it convenient for users to follow the algorithmic choices made.

C, C++, and Fortran code can be connected and named at run time for program-intensive activities. To modify R objects directly, advanced users can write C, C++, Java, .NET, or Python code. By using user-submitted packages for various functions or particular fields of analysis, R is extremely extensible. R has better object-oriented programming facilities than other statistical computer languages, owing to its S heritage. By its lexical scoping rules, Expanding R is also eased.

The highlights of R-Studio are:

1. An appropriate facility for data handling and storage.
2. Set of array calculation operators, in particular matrices.
3. A massive, coherent, interconnected set of data analysis intermediate tools.

Interactive data analysis and display facilities, either on-screen or on hard copy, and well-developed, simple, and effective programming language, including conditionals, loops, recursive functions defined by the user, and input and output facilities.

It is often the case for other data analysis software, the term "environment" is meant to describe it as a completely planned and coherent system rather than a gradual accumulation of very basic and inflexible devices. R is based on a real programming language, like S, which allows users to add extra features by specifying new features. In the R dialect of S, most of the system is itself written, which makes it easy for users to follow the algorithmic choices made. C, C++, and Fortran code can be connected and named at run time for computer-intensive activities. To directly modify R objects, advanced users should write C code.

R is conceived of by many people as a system of statistics. We like to think of it as an environment in which to apply statistical techniques. It is possible to extend R (easily) through packages. The R distribution is provided with about eight packages and several more are available via the CRAN family of Internet pages covering a very wide variety of modern statistics. R has its own Latex-like documentation format, which is used both online in a variety of formats and in hardcopy to supply proper data.

20.4.2   Data mining

Data mining, also widely referred to as Knowledge Discovery in Databases (KDD), refers to the nontrivial extraction from database data of implicit, previously unknown, and potentially useful information [1,2]. Although data mining and the discovery of information in databases (or KDD) are sometimes viewed as synonyms, data mining is simply part of the process of knowledge discovery. The method of Information Exploration in Databases consists of a few steps leading to some sort of new knowledge from raw data collections. The iterative method consists of the steps below:

- **Data cleaning:** Also known as data cleaning, it is a process in which the array eliminates noise data and irrelevant data.
- **Data integration:** Multiple data sources, often heterogeneous, may be merged into a common source at this point.
- **Data selection:** The data applicable to the study is settled on and collected from the compilation of data at this point.
- **Transformation of data:** Also known as aggregation of data, this is a stage in which the data selected is converted into forms suitable for the mining process.
- **Data mining:** It is the key stage in which clever methods are applied to potentially valuable pattern extraction.
- **Pattern assessment:** Based on given measurements, purely interesting patterns reflecting information are defined in this phase.
- **Information representation:** This is the final step in which the consumer is physically portrayed with the discovered knowledge. To help users grasp and view the data mining findings, this important step uses visualization techniques.

Combining both of these steps together is popular. For example, as a pre-processing stage to create a data warehouse, data cleaning, and data integration may be done together. Combining both of these steps together is popular. For example, as a pre-processing stage to create a data warehouse, data cleaning, and data integration may be done together. It is also possible to merge data collection and data transformation where the data consolidation is the outcome of the selection, or where, as in the case of any data warehouses, the transformed data is chosen. KDD is an iterative mechanism. The assessment measures can be changed, the mining can be further optimized, new data can be selected or further converted, or new data sources can be integrated to produce separate, more relevant outcomes until the discovered information is provided to the customer.

20.4.3 Data mining tasks

Descriptive and predictive data mining activities can be divided into two categories. The descriptive tasks in the dataset describe the properties of the data.

- **Informative task:** The general properties of the data contained in the database are present in these tasks. Descriptive activities are used to define data patterns, such as clusters, associations, trends and deviations, etc.
- **Predictive task:** Predictive data mining activities forecast the value of one attribute based on values of other attributes, known as the target or dependent variable, which are known as independent variables for the attributes used to produce the prediction.

20.4.4 Data mining functionalities

To define the kinds of patterns to be identified in data mining activities, data mining features are used. Characterization, discrimination, sorting, association rule mining, clustering, and prediction are the different data mining functionalities [2,4] The potential effect, rather than current behavior, was calculated by the predictive model. The predictive characteristic may be geometric or categorical for a predictive model. For example, the ruling of a set of characteristics related to the attribute of interest and the prediction of the distribution of value based on a dataset similar to the chosen item that predicts the type of disease based on the patient's symptoms.

20.4.5 Classification

One of the essential methods of data mining is grouping. Classification is the processing of a collection of models or functions that define data classes or definitions and separate them. Inputs are presented with a collection of data in the classification, called a training set, in which each record consists of multiple fields or attributes. The class to which each dataset belongs is indicated by one of the attributes, named the classifying attribute. The goal of the classification is to create a classification attribute system based on the other attributes that are not from the dataset of the training.

20.5 Implementation

20.5.1 Naive Bayes algorithm

The framework will uncover secret information associated with diseases from past reports of patients with lung cancer by using Bayesian classifiers [12]. The class membership probabilities are predicted by Bayesian classifiers in such a way that the likelihood of a given sample belongs statistically to a particular class. The Bayesian classifier is based mostly on a theorem of Bayes. We may use the Bayes theorem to calculate the probability, provided the observation, that a suggested diagnosis is accurate. The appearance (or absence of a certain characteristic of a class) is treated as independent of the presence (or absence) of some other characteristic, according to the naïve Bayesian classifier.

$$P[H/E] = \frac{P[E/H]P[H]}{P[E]}$$

H is the hypothesis; E is the proof pertaining to hypothesis H, i.e. the evidence to be used to confirm hypothesis H (accept/reject); P(H) is the probability of the hypothesis (prior probability); P(E) is the probability of evidence, i.e., the state of the environment represented by the data collected;

P(E/H) is the (conditional) chance of evidence E provided that hypothesis H holds; P(H/E) is the (conditional) probability of the hypothesis H given the evidence.

CODES: NAIVE BAYES

```
#install.packages("ggplot2")
#install.packages("lattice")
#install.packages("rlang")
#install.packages("lava")
#install.packages("caret",dep = TRUE)
#install.packages("purrr")
library(ggplot2)
 library(lattice)
 library(lava)
 library(purrr)
library(caret)
 #install.packages("klaR")
 #install.packages("MASS")
 library(MASS)
 library(klaR)
 cancer<-read.csv("~/Desktop/LosProject/cancer-patient-data-sets.csv")
 View(cancer)
 table(cancer$Level)
 data<- sample(2,nrow(cancer),replace=TRUE,prob = c(0.8,0.2))
 trainD<- cancer[data==1,2:25]
 testD<- cancer[data==2,2:25]
 nrow(trainD)
 nrow(testD)
#install.packages("rminer")
library(rminer)
#install.packages("e1071")
library(e1071)
naive_model<-naiveBayes(Level~ .,data=trainD)
naive_model
testmodel<-predict(naive_model,testD)
testmodel
testmodel<-predict(model,testD)
confusionMatrix(testmodel, testD$Level )
```

20.5.2 Decision tree algorithm

Identify all the options to be made (and their alternatives) and the sequence in which they must be made [9] (Figures 20.1–20.3). Create a tree diagram displaying the progression of decisions and chance events to classify the chance events that will occur after each decision [13,14]. From the left, the tree is built and moves to the right. The decision tree algorithm is part of the supervised learning approach and can be used to solve problems with classification and regression [18]. By learning basic decision rules deduced from training results, this algorithm predicts the goal variables. When constructing the decision tree, the attributes in the dataset are chosen to be categorical.

$$E(S) = \sum_{i=1}^{n} -pi - \log 2, \tag{20.7}$$

- where S is a set of training examples,
- c is the number of classes, and
- pi is the proportion of the training set that is of class i.

For our entropy equation $0 \log 2\ 0 = 0$. The information gain is represented by $G(S,A)$ where A is an attribute. $G(S,A) \equiv E(S) - \Sigma v$ in Values(A) $(|Sv| / |S|) * E(Sv)$.

Algorithm steps:

---

1. Assign to the root of the tree all the training examples and set the current node to the root node.
2. Partition each attribute with the value of the attribute at the node.
3. Calculate the data acquisition with all the attributes.
4. Making the highest-gain attribute as a decision node or root node. If the highest data gain is 0, make the present node the leaf node and return it.
5. Partitioning all instances of an attribute (decision node) according to the value of the attribute
6. Specify each partition as a node child of the current node.
7. For each child node, repeat the procedure until one of the following conditions matches.

- If the attribute value of all the tuples is the same.
- If the remaining characteristics are no longer.
- And when there are no remaining cases.

CODES: DECISION TREE

```
#install.packages('caret')
#install.packages("ggplot2")
#install.packages("lattice")
library(ggplot2)
library(lattice)
library(caret)
#install.packages('rpart.plot')
#install.packages("rpart")
library(rpart)
library(rpart.plot)
```

```
liver<
read.csv("~/Desktop/LosProject/cancer- patient-data-sets.csv")
View(liver)
set.seed(250)
intrain<- createDataPartition(y=liver$Level, p=0.6, list = FALSE)
training <- liver[intrain,2:25]
testing <- liver[-intrain,2:25]
anyNA(liver)
trctrl<-trainControl(method="repeatedcv", number = 10, repeats = 3)
set.seed(250)
dtree_fit <- train(Level ~., data = training, method = "rpart", parms = list(split =
    "information"),trControl=trctrl,tuneLength = 17)
dtree_fit
    prp(dtree_fit$finalModel,box.palette="Reds", tweak = 1.2)
    predict(dtree_fit, newdata = testing[1,])
#' Levels:1 2
library(tree)
test_pred <- predict(dtree_fit, newdata = testing, type- "raw")
test_pred=factor(c(test_pred))
str(test_pred)
testing$Level=factor(c(testing$Level))
str(testing$Level)
confusionMatrix(test_pred, testing$Level)
```

Screenshots:

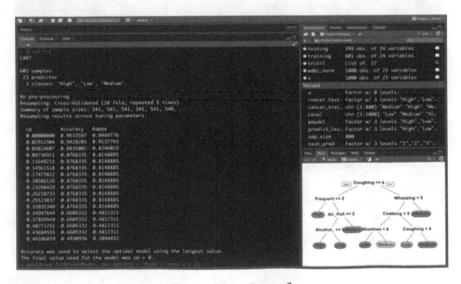

Figure 20.1   Dtree_fit

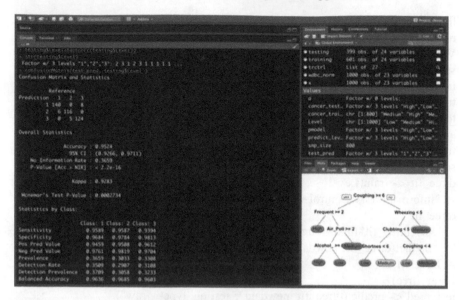

Figure 20.2   Dtree_confusionmatrix

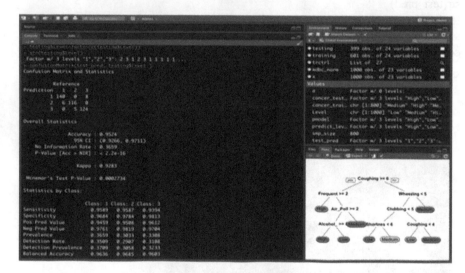

Figure 20.3   Dtree

20.5.3   KNN algorithm

The algorithm KNN is a non-parametric approach used to identify and regress. In both instances, the input contains the *k* training examples nearest to each other in the function space [2–4]. If KNN is used for the classification or regression depends on the output (Figures 20.4–20.7):

Algorithm steps:

In KNN, the performance is membership of a class [3]. An object is graded by its neighbors' majority votes, with the object allocated to the class more common among its closest neighbors (*k* is a positive integer, typically small). If *k* = 1, then the object is simply allocated to the closest neighbor's class.

- In KNN, the output is the object's property value. This value is the average of its closest neighbor's *k* values.
- The Euclidian distance is determined using the Distxy = sqrt(mk=1 xik-xjk)^2 formula.

CODES: KNN

```
cancer<- read.csv("~/Desktop/LosProject/cancer-patient-data-sets.csv")
View(cancer)
dim(cancer)
#table(cancer$Level)
x=subset(cancer,select=-c(Patient.Id,Level))
View(x)
dim(x)
data_norm <- function(x) { return((x) - min(x))/(max(x) - min(x))}
data_norm
#data(wdbc)
wdbc_norm<-as.data.frame(lapply(cancer[2:24], data_norm))
View(wdbc_norm)
summary(wdbc_norm[,2:5])
#summary(wdbc_norm[,1:4])
smp_size <- floor(0.8*nrow(cancer))
set.seed(123)
train_ind<-sample(seq_len(nrow(cancer)),size = smp_size)
cancer_train<-wdbc_norm[train_ind,]
cancer_test<-wdbc_norm[-train_ind,]
dim(cancer_train)
dim(cancer_test)
cancer_train_labels<-cancer[train_ind,25]
cancer_test_labels<-cancer[-train_ind,25]
length(cancer_train_labels)
length(cancer_test_labels)
library(class)
wdbc_test_pred<-knn(train=cancer_train,test=cancer_test,cl=cancer_train_labels,
    k=21)
length(cancer_train)
#install.packages("gmodels")
```

```
library(gmodels)
library(ggplot2)
library(caret)
#table(wdbc_pred,cancer[8001:10000,1])
cancer_test_labels=factor(c(cancer_test_labels))
str(cancer_test_labels)
str(wdbc_test_pred)
confusionMatrix(wdbc_test_pred,cancer_test_labels)
CrossTable(x= cancer_test_labels, y = wdbc_test_pred, prop.chisq = FALSE)
```

Screenshots:

Figure 20.4   K-nn_wdbc_norm

Figure 20.5   K-nn_confusionmatrix

Figure 20.6   K-nn_crosstable1

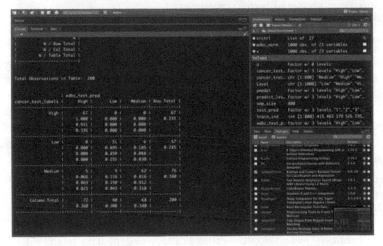

Figure 20.7   K-nn_crosstable2

20.5.4   Random forest algorithm

A random forest is a classifier consisting of a set of organized tree classifiers, where individual random vectors are identically distributed and each tree casts a unit vote at input *x* for the most common class [2,3,15,17]. The training algorithm for random forests applies to tree learners the general bootstrap aggregating strategy, or bagging. Provided the training set $X = x1, ..., xn$ with answers $Y = y1, ..., yn$, bagging repeatedly (B times), a random sample is selected to replace the training set and matches the following samples with trees:

For b = 1, ..., B:

1. Sample, with replacement, *n* training examples from *X*, *Y*; call these *Xb*, *Yb*.
2. Train a classification or regression tree fb on *Xb*, *Yb*.

- Predictions can be made after practicing for unseen samples x "by combining the predictions on x" from all the individual regression trees. A random vector that is independent of the previous random vectors of the same distribution is generated and a tree is generated using the training test. An upper bound is extracted for random forests to get the generalization error in terms of two parameters given below:

1. The accuracy of individual classifiers.
2. Dependence between each of the classifiers.

There are two segments in the generalization of error for the random tree. The segments are listed below.

1. The intensity of the individual forest classifiers.
2. In terms of the raw margin feature, the correlation between them.

There are attractive features in the class of procedures, as described below:

- Accuracy is great and better sometimes.
- Relatively robust to sound and outliers.
- Quick and conveniently parallelized.

The principle of bagging and boosting is included in this project, so as to improve the algorithm's performance. Bootstrap aggregating, also referred to as bagging, is a meta-algorithm for ML to boost the consistency and precision of ML algorithms used in statistical classification and regression (Figures 20.8–20.12). It also lowers variation and assists in preventing overfitting. It can be used for any form of method, but it is typically extended to decision tree systems. A special case of the model averaging method is bagging.

CODES: RANDOM FOREST

```
#install.packages("randomFrorest")
library("randomForest")
cancer<- read.csv("~/Desktop/LosProject/cancer-patient-data-sets.csv")
View(cancer)
#bagging
library(ipred)
#install.packages(ipred)
cancer$Level <- as.factor(cancer$Level)
cancer_bagging <- cancer[2:25]
cancerbagging<-bagging(Level~ .,cancer_bagging)
predict_level<-predict(cancerbagging,cancer_bagging)
cancer_bagging$prediction<-predict_level
head(cancer_bagging)
with(cancer_bagging,table(Level,prediction))
#end og bagging
set.seed(250)
library(ggplot2)
```

```
library(caret)
intrain<-createDataPartition(y =cancer$Level, p= 0.8, list = FALSE)
training <- cancer[intrain,]
testing <- cancer[-intrain,]
dim(training)
rf<- randomForest(Level ~ .,training)
rf
pmodel <- predict(rf,testing)
pmodel
table(testing[,24],pmodel)
mean(testing[,24]==pmodel)
confusionMatrix(pmodel, testing$Level)
```

Screenshots:

Figure 20.8   Randomforest

Figure 20.9   Rf_model

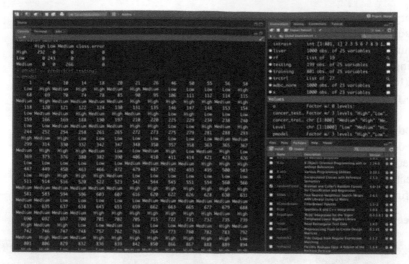

Figure 20.10   Rf_pmodel

Figure 20.11   Rf_confusionmatrix1

20.5.5   WEKA

Weka [16] is a tried and tested open-source programming language framework that can be used through a graphical interface, organizational environment programs, or a Java API. It is widely used for training, research, and industrial applications, provides a variety of built-in tools for standard ML activities, and offers easy access to well-known toolboxes such as SCI KIKI. There are often unnecessary items in the data obtained from the field that contribute to incorrect interpretation. Data that contain null fields, columns that are unrelated to the

Figure 20.12   Rf_confusionmatrix2

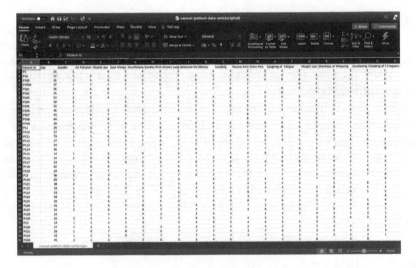

Figure 20.13   Missing_datasets

current research, etc. Thus, to satisfy the criteria of the sort of analysis you are searching for, the data must be pre-processed. The samples of the missing data are shown in the file cancer-patient-data-sets(original).csv (Figures 20.13 and 20.14).

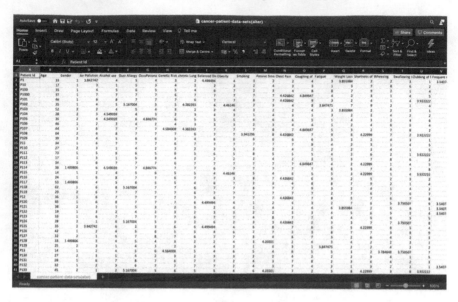

Figure 20.14   Corrected_datasets

20.6   Testing and evaluation

20.6.1   Results

To evaluate the selected tool using the lung cancer dataset comparisons are performed. In comparison, we have applied classification algorithms such as naive Bayes, KNN, decision tree, and random forest. Random forest achieves the highest efficiency of 1% (Table 20.1).

When cross-validation is performed in the case of naive Bayes algorithm, the train() function implements normal and non-parametric distributions on the training data. The below graph (Figure 20.15) shows the variation of accuracies for each of the distribution types obtained while training the dataset with naive Bayes algorithm. It can be seen that if the selected data is distributed normally, the naive Bayes algorithm provided an accuracy of 89.09%. However, if the data has non-parametric distribution, the algorithm outperformed by providing an accuracy of 98%.

Table 20.1   Accuracy

Algorithms	Accuracy
Naive Bayes	98%
Decision tree	99.2%
KNN	99.5%
Random forest	1%

When cross-validation is performed in the case of a decision tree algorithm, the train() function calculates the complexity parameter for each node of the decision tree. The value of the complexity parameter indicates the amount of improvement that the built model requires at each of its nodes (Figure 20.16). The below graph

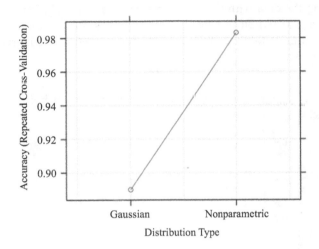

Figure 20.15   NB_Accuracy

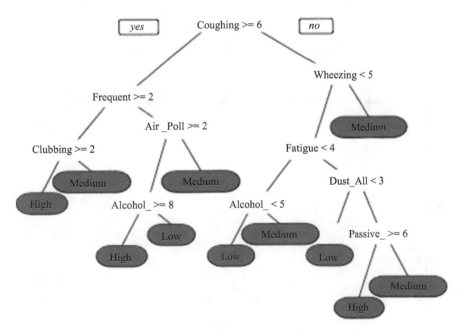

Figure 20.16   Decision tree

(Figure 20.17) shows how the value of accuracy varies with the different values of complexity parameter at each node. It can be observed that at cp = 0.0, the accuracy obtained is 99.2%, while the accuracy is lowest for cp = 0.414 (Figure 20.18).

The below graph (Figure 20.18) shows the graph plotted for accuracy against the number of folds selected in the process of k-fold cross-validation while training the data with the decision tree algorithm. This process of cross-validation was carried out for three iterations, thus the variation of accuracies against each value of fold for each iteration is represented in red, green, and blue lines, respectively.

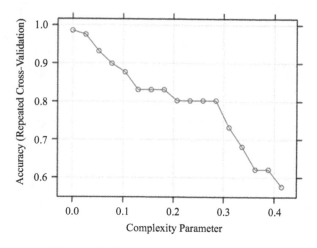

Figure 20.17   Decision_Tree_Accuracy

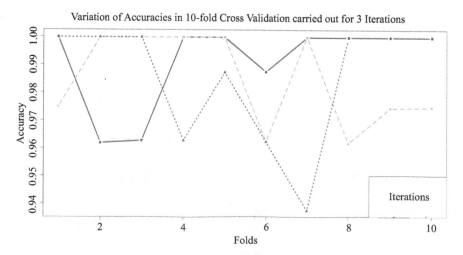

Figure 20.18   Dt_foldcv

When cross-validation is performed in the case of KNN algorithm, the train()
function obtains various accuracies for different values of *k*. It is observed that for
k = 5, the model provided the highest accuracy of 99.5% (Figure 20.19).

When cross-validation is performed in the case of the random forest algorithm,
the train() function randomly selected the set of predictors for building multiple
decision trees that constituted the whole of the random forest model. Irrespective
of which and how many predictors are selected the random forest algorithm
outperformed by giving a constant accuracy of 100% for all combinations of
predictors (Figure 20.20).

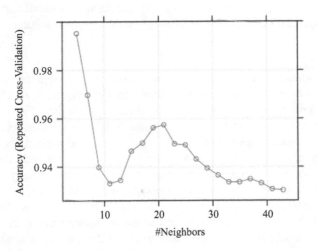

Figure 20.19   Knn_Accuracy

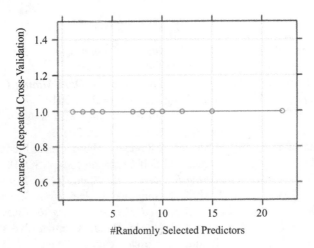

Figure 20.20   Rf_Accuracy

20.7   Conclusion and future work

20.7.1   Conclusion

To summarize, this research was conducted to perform a comparative analysis of the performance of various ML algorithms for predicting the severity of Lung cancer. To achieve the objectives of the research, the dataset was obtained from the repository and was cleaned and pre-processed. Based on the literature review that was conducted, four ML algorithms, namely, decision tree, random forest, KNN, and naive Bayes were selected to predict the severity of lung cancer. All the algorithms performed accurately at the individual level by giving accuracies above 95%. However, if their performance was compared, it was found that the random forest algorithm outperformed the rest by giving the highest accuracy of 100%.

20.7.2   Future work

It is possible to further expand the proposed method. There are some functions in an algorithm used by each method which are useful for detecting the level of lung cancer. These algorithms, but with higher computational costs, give higher efficiency values. To maximize the performance of the projected model with lower computational costs, even with a large amount of data collection, the different steps and methodologies should be applied. There are many types of cancer, worldwide. In this research, though we are detecting the severity of lung cancer, future studies can predict many other various cancers and their severities. Nevertheless, the application of this methodology in a large-scale sparse dataset will be a path in which to develop in the future. So far, there is no universal rule for selecting the number of patterns for tumor types in the diagnosis of cancer. A way should be built in the future to assess the number of symbolic tumors. This would reduce the time for the extraction of features and encourage doctors to draw inspiration from data mining approaches to understand the cancers based on the pattern.

References

[1]   P. R. Radhika, *A Comparative Study of Lung Cancer Detection Using Machine Learning Algorithms*, India: IEEE, 2019.

[2]   S. Kaur and A. K. Grewal, *A Review Paper on Data Mining Classification Techniques for Detection of Lung Cancer*, IRJET, 2016.

[3]   P. Bhuvaneswari, *Detection of Cancer in Lung with K-NN Classification Using Genetic Algorithm*, India: Science Direct, 2015.

[4]   H. Bharathi and T. S. Arulananth, A Review of Lung cancer Prediction System using Data Mining Techniques and Self Organizing Map (SOM), *International Journal of Applied Engineering Research*, vol. 12, no. 10, pp. 2190–2195, 2017.

[5]   H. Asri, H. Mousannif, H. Al Moatassime, and T. Noei, *Using Machine Learning Algorithms for Breast Cancer Risk Prediction and Diagnosis*, Elsevier, 2016.

[6]   S. Saabith, E. Sundararajan, and A. Abu Bakar, Comparative study on different classification techniques for breast cancer dataset, *IJCSMC*, vol. 3, no. 10, pp. 185–191, 2014.

[7] E. Aličković and A. Subasi, *Breast Cancer Diagnosis Using GA Feature Selection and Rotation Forest*, Springer, 2015.

[8] L. Breiman, Random Forests. *Machine Learning* 45, pp. 5–32, 2001. https://doi.org/10.1023/A:1010933404324.

[9] D. Silva, A. Rodrigues, M. Guerreiro, I. Santana and de M. João Maroco, *Data Mining Methods in the Prediction of Dementia: A Real-Data Comparison of the Accuracy, Sensitivity and Specificity of Linear Discriminant Analysis, Logistic Regression, Neural Networks, Support Vector Machines, Classification Trees and Random Forests*, NIH, 2011.

[10] M. Stone, An asymptotic equivalence of choice of model by cross-validation and Akaike's criterion, *JSTOR*, vol. 39, no. 1, pp. 44–47, 1977.

[11] D. M. Allen, The relationship between variable selection and data augmentation and a method for prediction, *JSTOR*, vol. 16, no. 1, pp. 125–127, 1974.

[12] Y. Ji, S. Yu, and Y. Zhang, *A Novel Naive Bayes Model: Packaged Hidden Naive Bayes*, IEEE, 2011.

[13] F.-J. Yang, *An Extended Idea about Decision Trees*, CSCI, 2019.

[14] H. Xie and F. Shang, *The Study of Methods for Post-Pruning Decision Trees Based on Comprehensive Evaluation Standard*, IEEE, 2014.

[15] S. R. Joelsson, J. A. Benediktsson, and J. R. Sveinsson, F*eature Selection for Morphological Feature Extraction Using Random Forests*, NORSIG, 2006.

[16] A. K. Pandey and D. S. Rajpoot, *A Comparative Study of Classification Techniques by Utilizing WEKA*, Noida: ICSC, 2016.

[17] D. Bazazeh and R. Shubair, *Comparative Study of Machine Learning Algorithms for Breast Cancer Detection and Diagnosis*, USA: IEEE, 2016.

[18] D. V. Patil and R. S. Bichkar, *A Hybrid Evolutionary Approach to Construct Optimal Decision Trees With Large Data Sets*, IEEE, 2006.

[19] M. L. F. Cheong, J. Poh, and A. Gunawan. *An Essential Applied Statistical Analysis Course Using RStudio with Project-Based Learning for Data Science*, Australia: TALE, 2018.

Chapter 21

Comparison of artificial intelligence models for prognosis of breast cancer

Anish Samantaray[1], C. Saravanan[1], Meghana Bollam[1], R. Maheswari[1] and P. Vijaya[2]

Breast cancer is the most common cancer not only affecting women but also men. Diagnosis and treatment are crucial stages in the cancer treatment process. However, even after treatment, individuals often experience ongoing challenges, including the regular need for painful procedures such as biopsies, MRIs, and scans as part of their journey towards recovery. We propose that in this case, machine learning (ML) and deep learning analyses may be used to perform longitudinal studies of women with breast cancer. We do a comparative analysis of three situations, in the first situation, we apply ML algorithms just after the primary preprocessing steps, in the second situation, we add balanced class weights hyperparameters, and in the third, we do principal component analysis (PCA). In the first situation, the light gradient boosting machine (LightGBM) gives the best accuracy of 87.87%, and the random forest (RF) gives an accuracy of 87.87% after the hyperparameter of balanced class weights is given. After PCA, logistic regression gives a maximum accuracy of 84.84%.

21.1 Introduction

A kind of cancer known as breast cancer arises when cells begin to multiply uncontrollably. While it may also affect men, it is one of the cancers that most usually affects women worldwide. Recurrences of breast cancer are those that come back after the first treatment. Breast cancer that has spread from its original site might return to the original breast or to other organs such as the liver, bones, or lungs. The stage of the illness at the time of diagnosis, the size of the tumor, whether it has spread to nearby lymph nodes or other body parts, and the type of therapy received all have an impact on the likelihood of breast cancer recurrence [1].

Despite improvements in diagnosis and treatment, some breast cancer patients still have a recurrence, which can be challenging to manage and significantly affect a

[1]School of Computer Science Engineering, Vellore Institute of Technology, Chennai, India
[2]Modern College of Business and Science, Bowshar, Sultanate of Oman

patient's quality of life. Continuous surveillance and monitoring are essential for patients who have undergone breast cancer therapy to identify and treat recurrence [1]. The stage of cancer at the time of diagnosis, the grade of the disease, the patient's age and overall health, the kind of breast cancer, genetic alterations such as BRCA1 and BRCA2, and the response to therapy are the most crucial details in breast cancer prognosis.

The process of identifying the extent of the cancer and whether it has spread to neighboring lymph nodes or other places of the body is known as staging. The appearance of the cancer cells under a microscope determines the grade, and high-grade malignancies tend to develop and spread more quickly and have a worse prognosis than low-grade tumors. The patient's age and general health are also important factors in breast cancer prognosis. The kind of breast cancer is also an important determinant in prognosis, as are genetic abnormalities such as BRCA1 and BRCA2. Ultimately, therapy responsiveness is an important component in breast cancer prognosis [2]. Hence, time and lymph nodes are two of the most crucial features to describe the prognosis of the disease.

With 685,000 deaths predicted in 2020 and 2.3 million women impacted, it is a significant issue in both India and the rest of the globe. With 7.8 million women receiving a diagnosis in the past 5 years, it is the most prevalent illness in the world. A woman in India receives a diagnosis of breast cancer every 4 min, accounting for 14% of all female cancer cases. 1,62,468 new cases of breast cancer were identified in 2018, while 87,090 people lost their lives to the disease. Fifteen women out of every 100 are diagnosed with breast cancer again as a result of the disease spreading to the adjacent lymph nodes (within a span of 10 years) [3].

Analyzing raw datasets for trends, conclusions, and improvement opportunities is part of data analytics. Healthcare analytics employs both recent and old data to produce macro and micro insights to help business and patient decision-making [4]. An abundance of resources is at our disposal nowadays for many different topics, and this information can be useful to understand, predict, and prevent many things in the healthcare sector [4].

There are multiple hospitals at this stage that are continuously monitoring breast cancer patients and hence a lot of data about their medical records can be generated, this data would be analyzed and modeled to get various results. Breast cancer prognosis is a complex and multifactorial aspect of patient care. Early detection, appropriate treatment, and careful monitoring are essential for improving breast cancer prognosis and ensuring the best possible outcome for patients. Based on parameters such as tumor size, grade, and lymph node involvement, ML can assist estimate the chance of breast cancer recurrence and patient survival. This data can help doctors make more educated treatment decisions and enhance patient outcomes.

The objective of the research is to analyze and infer from various visualizations using exploratory data analysis and find the best accuracy to classify if the person would be getting breast cancer or not in the near future. This may be integrated with a software and can be used by doctors to reduce the number of biopsies. Biopsies are a painful process and doing it again and again does not seem to be a good idea, so in this research, we propose to have an ML/deep learning model so that the doctor would be able to have an estimate about the future.

21.2   Related work

The authors, Chaurasia and Pal in 2014, used data mining techniques to make survival predictions for SEER dataset patients with breast cancer. Decision tree, RF, and support vector machine (SVM) were only a few of the classification algorithms evaluated to determine which one was best in predicting breast cancer patients' chances of survival. According to the authors, the RF algorithm has the highest levels of accuracy, sensitivity, and specificity compared to the others [5].

Li *et al.* (2016) compared the findings of three commonly used gene tests to the use of magnetic resonance imaging (MRI) radiomics signatures for predicting the risk of breast cancer recurrence. The authors used a radiomics technique, which involves extracting quantitative information from MRI scans and developing prediction models using ML algorithms. They discovered that radiomics signatures had a significant connection with gene test findings and could accurately predict the probability of breast cancer recurrence. The study showed the promise of MRI radiomics for predicting breast cancer prognosis as a non-invasive and cost-effective alternative to gene tests. Larger patient cohort validation studies are needed to corroborate their findings and prove the clinical value of MRI radiomics for breast cancer therapy [6].

In 2018, Al-Quraishi *et al.* introduced an RF algorithm-based model for predicting breast cancer recurrence. The scientists used data from UCI's Machine Learning Library to determine what factors best predict breast cancer recurrence. High accuracy and AUC values were found for the RF model while predicting breast cancer recurrence, proving the efficacy of the RF algorithm in finding the relevant characteristics. Overall, the study shows promise for the RF algorithm in recurrence prediction for breast cancer and illustrates the significance of feature selection in enhancing the precision of diagnosis and therapy. The clinical use of the suggested RF model for recurrence prediction in breast cancer is feasible [7].

In 2019, Chakradeo *et al.* used a dataset from the UCI ML repository to apply ML techniques to the problem of predicting the recurrence of breast cancer. Logistic regression, RF, and SVM were only a few of the ML methods utilized to make the recurrence of breast cancer forecasts. In terms of accuracy, sensitivity, and specificity, the RF algorithm was found to be the most effective, as described by the authors [8].

Zain *et al.* (2020) compared the performance of PCA with two other feature selection techniques, recursive feature elimination (RFE) and ReliefF, to identify the most effective method for predicting breast cancer recurrence. The study used the Breast Cancer Wisconsin Diagnostic dataset and applied three classification algorithms, including SVM, K-nearest neighbors (KNN), and RF. The PCA-based model achieved good accuracy using the SVM algorithm, suggesting that PCA can be an effective technique for feature extraction in breast cancer recurrence prediction [9].

The Grasshopper Optimization Algorithm (GOA) and SVM classification were proposed by Rahmani and Katouli (2020) as a means of detecting breast cancer. The findings demonstrated that the suggested GOA-SVM method provided superior classification accuracy, sensitivity, and specificity compared to alternative feature selection approaches. Also, the classification model's computational performance was enhanced by the lower dimensionality of the dataset. The results of this study show that the GOA-SVM approach has the potential to increase the accuracy of breast cancer detection and provide a useful tool in the diagnosis and treatment of this disease [10].

Sheth and Giger's (2020) paper focuses on the application of artificial intelligence (AI) in the interpretation of magnetic resonance imaging (MRI) breast cancer. The essay opens by emphasizing the shortcomings of human interpretation of MRI scans, such as observer variability and the possibility of missing lesions. It then goes on to talk about how AI algorithms, notably deep learning models, can help with MRI image interpretation for breast cancer detection and prognosis. The authors present an in-depth analysis of current research and breakthroughs in the application of AI for breast cancer diagnosis on MRI, including the use of convolutional neural networks (CNNs) for lesion detection, segmentation, and classification. They also go through the possible clinical implications of AI-assisted MRI interpretation, such as increased diagnostic accuracy and efficiency, as well as the problems and limits of adopting AI in clinical practice [11].

Kabiraj *et al.* in 2020 did a research to predict the risk of breast cancer using ML algorithms such as XGBoost and RF. The dataset was gathered from the Wisconsin Breast Cancer Diagnostic Database, which includes clinical and demographic information on patients as well as biopsy findings. Both models were trained on the dataset and their performance was assessed using measures including accuracy, sensitivity, specificity, and F1 score. In terms of accuracy and F1 score, the findings revealed that the XGBoost model beat the RF model. The scientists found that ML algorithms may give reliable estimates of breast cancer risk and that such models can help medical practitioners make better patient care decisions [12].

Duggento *et al.* (2021) investigate the use of deep learning in the field of computational pathology for the diagnosis and prognosis of breast cancer. Deep learning approaches, according to scientists, can aid in the identification of patterns and characteristics in histopathological pictures of breast tissue samples, allowing for more accurate diagnosis and prediction of disease development. The chapter presents an overview of deep learning techniques used in breast cancer pathology, including as CNNs and generative adversarial networks (GANs). The authors examine the benefits and drawbacks of these approaches, as well as how they might be combined with other clinical and genetic data to generate more accurate and individualized cancer diagnoses and treatment strategies. The study also discusses some of the difficulties and limits of using deep learning in breast cancer pathology, such as the necessity for big, diverse datasets and the possibility of bias in the training data. According to the scientists, more studies in this area might lead to better accuracy and reliability of deep learning models for breast cancer detection and prognosis [13].

An ML algorithm for estimating when breast cancer tumors may return is presented by Gupta (2022). In all, 569 cases of breast tumor samples representing a wide range of clinical and pathological characteristics were employed in the analysis, all sourced from the Breast Cancer Wisconsin collection. The results demonstrated that, compared to the other algorithms, the Gradient Boosting method provided the most accurate estimates of when breast cancer tumors will return. As compared to the Cox proportional hazards model, the suggested ML model performed better in terms of prediction accuracy and dependability. Overall, the results show that ML algorithms have the potential to improve clinical decision-making in the treatment and management of breast cancer, and they imply that the suggested model may be utilized to do so [14].

21.3 Proposed work

21.3.1 Dataset

So, in the present research, we take the dataset from the UCI ML repository, i.e., the WPBC dataset [15]. This dataset has about 34 features and 198 records. The features typically describe the time, recurrence, lymph node status and the mean, standard deviation, and worst-case situation of the cell's size, radius, area, perimeter, texture, smoothness, concavity, compactness, concave points, symmetry, and fractal dimension. We read this data as a CSV file. The table has four values which are given as "?". These question marks are the null values and must be replaced or has to be handled.

The Id number of the patients is also given with these. The outcome is given in terms of N and R, where N stands for non-recurrent and R stands for recurrent, i.e., whether patients are getting breast cancer again or not. The time component says about the recurrence time if the breast cancer's disease has recurred and the disease-free time after he has recovered. The radius says about the mean of distances from the center to points on the perimeter. The texture talks about the standard deviation of grayscale values. The smoothness talks about local variation in radius lengths. The compactness is perimeter^2/area $-$ 1.0. The concavity tells us about the severity of concave portions of the contour whereas the fractal dimension is the parameter for "coastline approximation" $-$ 1. The analysis has been carried out in a system with 512 GB SSD, 4 GB graphics, and 16 GB RAM.

21.3.2 Data pre-processing

We first replace the null values (which are given here as "?" in the lymph node status column) with the mean value of that column. Then we find the correlation of each column with the other and if the correlation is greater than 0.8 and less than -0.8 with the other column, we remove the column. The highly correlated columns are highlighted in Table 21.1. The feature 2 from Table 21.1 has been dropped. Then to check if the number of recurrent patients' data is balanced or not, we plot a bar graph between the number of recurrent patients and non-recurrent patients shown in Figure 21.1. Then we check for skewed columns and if there are any highly skewed columns, we normalize them using logarithmic transformation.

Eliminating columns based on correlation coefficients is an ML data preparation technique used to remove redundant characteristics from a dataset. It entails

Table 21.1   Correlation coefficients between two columns in the dataset

Feature1	Feature2	Correlation coefficient
perimeter_mean	radius_mean	0.995933
perimeter_mean	area_mean	0.990699
perimeter_mean	perimeter_worst	0.923659
perimeter_mean	radius_worst	0.921552
perimeter_mean	area_worst	0.889344
radius_se	perimeter_se	0.973267
radius_se	area_se	0.956929
concavity_mean	concave points_mean	0.909990
concavity_mean	compactness_mean	0.836015
texture_worst	texture_mean	0.86205
compactness_worst	fractal_dimension_worst	0.847403
compactness_worst	concavity_worst	0.835064
fractal_dimension_se	compactness_se	0.845176
fractal_dimension_mean	fractal_dimension_worst	0.838737

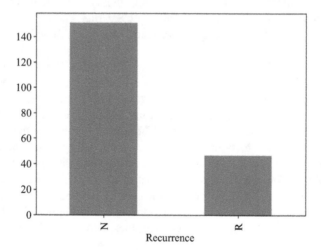

Figure 21.1   Unbalanced nature of recurrence data

computing the correlation coefficient between each pair of characteristics in the dataset and deleting one of the two strongly correlated (i.e., having a high correlation coefficient) variables since it does not contribute any extra information to the model. The correlation coefficient is a statistical metric that measures the link between two variables. It goes from −1 to 1, and a value of −1 implies a complete negative correlation (i.e., as one variable increases, the other decreases). Highly linked features can cause overfitting in ML, where the model performs well on training data but badly on test data. As a result, it is critical to detect and eliminate highly correlated characteristics from the dataset to enhance the model's performance.

Logarithmic transformation is a data transformation technique used in ML to convert non-normally distributed data to normal data. It entails applying the logarithmic function to the given values. This is frequently done when the data has a skewed distribution, which means that the majority of the data is concentrated at one end of the range, with few observations at the other. A logarithmic transformation can assist to minimize skewness and make the data more symmetric in such circumstances.

The following is the definition of the logarithmic transformation:

$$new\_feature = \log(feature)$$

The logarithmic function is a mathematical function that compresses large numbers while expanding tiny values. As a result, applying the logarithmic function on skewed data compresses the range of the bigger values while expanding the range of the smaller values, resulting in a more symmetric distribution.

Then we apply seven ML and deep learning algorithms to the data (20 columns left after removing correlated columns and 198 rows) and accuracy performance metrics defined in Section 21.3.5. The seven algorithms that we have used are logistic regression, KNN, SVM, LightGBM, Xgboost, RF, extra tree classifier, and artificial neural network (ANN) [9].

Then we know since the data is unbalanced as shown in Figure 21.1. We apply a hyperparameter existing in the Skicitlearn Library [16] called lass_weight= "balanced" and then we again apply the algorithms and compare the accuracy performance metrics defined in Section 21.3.5 (only five out of the eight algorithms have the hyperparameter).

While attempting to solve a classification problem, it is not uncommon to encounter unbalanced data, in which the number of examples in one class is disproportionately greater or lower than the number of instances in another class. Many drawbacks, including inaccurate interpretation of data and biased model performance, might come from this. When a model is trained on imbalanced data, it may become biased in favor of the majority class, leading to subpar results for the minority. It is also possible that models trained on imbalanced data would not generalize well to new data, which might lead to subpar results and inaccurate predictions. Overfitting can also reduce the results' interpretability and the model's ability to generalize to fresh data. Accurate and trustworthy predictions may be made with the use of data balancing and performance-enhancing approaches like resampling, cost-sensitive learning, and ensemble methods.

PCA is a technique for reducing dimensionality in data analysis and ML. It operates by converting the input into a new collection of orthogonal variables known as principle components (PCs). The number of PCs equals the number of dimensions in the original data, and the transformation is performed by determining the eigenvectors and eigenvalues of the data's covariance matrix. PCA may be used for a variety of tasks, including data visualization, noise reduction, and feature extraction. Nevertheless, PCA has certain disadvantages, including assuming a linear connection

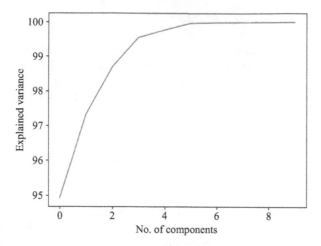

Figure 21.2   Explained variance by components after PCA

between variables, making interpretation of the principal components difficult, being susceptible to outliers, and performing poorly on small datasets.

PCA is one of the effective approaches for finding the necessary patterns and reducing the dimensionality of high-dimensional data. Therefore, before using PCA in a given situation, it is critical to evaluate its limits and underlying assumptions. Unbalanced data can result in poor performance and inaccurate forecasts, especially for minorities. Moreover, overfitting can impair model performance and reduce the interpretability of model findings. Techniques like resampling, cost-sensitive learning, and ensemble approaches can be used to balance the data and enhance the model's performance to avoid these negative effects.

Also, since the number of parameters is we can try dimensionality reduction. This, we have done it using PCA. So, we first fit the data frame and reduce it into yen components and now we see the cumulative sum of variance explained by each of the features. So, as we can see in Figure 21.2, 99% of the variance of the dataset is given by the first four features itself. So, we drop the other columns and consider these transformed columns and again we apply these algorithms and check the accuracy, precision, recall, and *F*-score again.

21.3.3   Algorithms used

1.   Logistic regression: A statistical model for two-sample classification issues. A logistic function is used to model the likelihood of an occurrence. The logistic regression model has several applications outside of medicine and business [17].
2.   Xgboost: Supervised learning tasks, including classification and regression, are ideal applications for the ML method Xgboost (Extreme Gradient Boosting). An ensemble of very ineffective decision trees is used in this gradient-boosting approach to construct a robust prediction model. Xgboost's superior precision and scalability have contributed to its rising popularity [18].

3. RF: To boost its prediction abilities, RF is an ensemble ML technique that employs a forest of decision trees. The method involves generating a collection of decision trees, each of which is educated using a different subset of the training data and attributes. The forest's collective wisdom is used to make the ultimate forecast. For both classification and regression issues, RF is a robust algorithm [19].

4. LightGBM: Tree-based learning techniques provide the basis of the LightGBM gradient-boosting architecture. It is optimized for speed and scalability, making it a good fit for issues requiring massive amounts of ML data. To shorten the training period and boost the model's accuracy, LightGBM employs a cutting-edge method called gradient-based one-side sampling (GOSS) [20].

5. Extra tree classifier: The ExtraTrees Classifier is an ML ensemble algorithm that works in a manner analogous to that of RF. To produce the final forecast, it generates a huge number of decision trees without pruning them. When compared to RF, ExtraTrees Classifier does not seek out the optimal split but instead randomly chooses the splits at each node. As a result, it is quicker than RF, however, the resulting model may be less accurate [21].

6. KNN: For classification and regression purposes, KNN is a non-parametric ML technique. The method uses the labels or values of the K training data points that are most like the input data point to make predictions about the label or value of the input data point. Although KNN is a straightforward technique, it can be time-consuming to run on big datasets [22].

7. SVM: SVM is a well-liked approach for ML, typically employed in the areas of classification and regression. The method finds the hyperplane that most effectively divides the data into its component classes. Using a kernel method to shift the data into a higher-dimensional space where it may be separated, SVM is a potent algorithm that can handle non-linearly separable data. Bioinformatics, text categorization, and picture recognition are just a few of the areas where SVM has found widespread application [23].

8. ANN: ANNs are a type of ML algorithm that takes their cues from biological neural networks in terms of both form and function. In an ANN, data processing and transmission are handled by layers of linked nodes (neurons). Classification, regression, and unsupervised learning are just some of the ML tasks that benefit from their utilization. Among the areas where ANN has been particularly effective include image recognition, NLP, and autonomous driving [24].

9. PCA: PCA is a method for reducing the number of dimensions in a dataset. To increase the variance of the data along each axis, the data is transformed into a new coordinate system. This minimizes the number of dimensions in the data without losing any useful information. Signal processing, picture identification, and even the financial sector all make use of principal component analysis [25].

21.3.4 Hyperparameters used

The default hyperparameters given by sci-kit learn [15] are used in the algorithm for logistic regression, SVM, KNN, RF, Xgboost, and extra tree classifier. The

LightGBM algorithm also uses the default hyperparameters given by the LightGBM library [26].

The balanced class weight hyperparameter is also used later on to make the data balanced and compare the performance metrics. During model training, it gives larger weights to minority class samples and lower weights to majority class samples, allowing the model to focus more on the minority class and avoid bias towards the majority class. In binary classification, for example, if there are 90 samples of "0" and only 10 instances of "1," the model trained on this dataset may classify all samples as "0" since it is the majority class. When the balanced class weight hyperparameter is applied, the model gives more weight to "1" class samples and less weight to "0" class samples during training, allowing the model to learn patterns in the "1" class samples and make better predictions for the minority class. Most ML frameworks, in reality, allow you to set the class weight hyperparameter during model training. Overall, the balanced class weight hyperparameter is a good strategy for dealing with unequal class distributions and can aid in boosting the model's performance on the minority class.

The ANN layer from the TensorFlow Library [27] that we have taken has about four layers, one input layer, one output layer, and two hidden layers. The output layer has only one perceptron as it needs for binary classification with a sigmoid activation function. The other three layers are given with the relu activation function. In the first situation before the PCA was applied and after the PCA was applied. In the situation before PCA was applied the number of perceptron in the three layers are 11, 7, and 6 whereas after PCA since the number of perceptron cannot be greater than the number of columns, so the number of perceptron is 3, 2, and 2. We also have used early stopping as a callback and so if the vanishing gradient problem occurs, i.e., if the change in accuracy is less than 0.001 for 20 epochs, it stops irrespective of the number of epochs given.

21.3.5   Performance metrics

Some of the most often used assessment measures for binary classification tasks include accuracy, precision, recall, and *F*-score.

The fraction of correctly identified cases among all examples is measured by accuracy. It is calculated by dividing the total number of instances by the number of true positives (TP) and true negatives (TN). Nevertheless, for unbalanced datasets where one class dominates the other, accuracy alone may not be an effective statistic. In such instances, models that merely forecast the majority class may attain great accuracy.

$$Accuracy = (True\ positive + true\ negative)/(total)$$

Precision, on the other hand, is the percentage of true positive forecasts among all positive predictions. It denotes a model's capacity to reduce false positives. Precision is calculated by dividing TP by the total of TP and false positives (FP).

$$Precision = (True\ positive)/(true\ positive + false\ positive)$$

The fraction of genuine positive predictions among all real positive cases is measured by the recall, also known as sensitivity or true positive rate (TPR). It indicates a model's capacity to recognize all positive cases. The ratio of TP to the total of TP and false negatives is used to calculate recall (FN).

$$Recall = (True\ positive)/(true\ positive + false\ negative)$$

The *F*-score is a symmetrical mean of accuracy and recall. It generates a single score that accounts for both measures. $F - score = (2 * Precision * Recall)/(Precision + Recall)$ yields the *F*-score. It is scored on a scale of 0 to 1, with a higher score signifying better performance.

In summary, when the classes are balanced, accuracy is a helpful statistic, however, precision, recall, and *F*-score are useful when the classes are imbalanced or the cost of false positives and false negatives is not equal.

21.3.6 Summary of the proposed work

So hence the dataset is taken and after the pre-processing steps are given to the ML/DL models after splitting the given dataset into a ratio of 67:33, 67% is the training dataset and 33% is the test dataset, and the respective performance metrics are noted. Then the data is given to the five algorithms where balanced class weight is given as a hyperparameter and then again, the performance metrics are noted. The same thing is done after applying PCA and transforming the data into data of four columns and again the performance metrics are noted. Then the performance metrics of all three situations can be compared. The necessary working of our proposed work is clearly shown in Figure 21.3.

21.4 Results and discussion

So after applying all the models to the pre-processed data, the maximum accuracy was achieved by LightGBM algorithm with an accuracy of 87.87% and precision, recall, and *F*-score of 81.81, 77.93, and 79.62. RF and Xgboost were behind it with accuracies of 84.84% and 83.83% followed by ANN and logistic regression as seen in Table 21.2 and Figure 21.3.

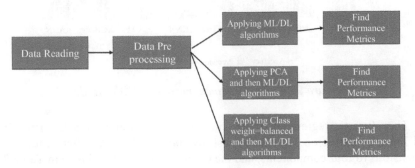

Figure 21.3 Work flow of the project

Table 21.2   Performance metrics of the algorithms initially

ML algorithms	Accuracy (in %)	Precision (in %)	Recall (in %)	F-score (in %)
Logistic regression	80.3	67.8	64.51	65.77
LightGBM	87.87	81.81	77.93	79.62
RF	84.84	82.62	64.44	67.83
Extra tree	80.3	74.6	56.7	57.3
KNN	75.75	54.96	52.97	52.85
SVM	78.78	62.95	57.76	58.75
XGBoost	83.33	74.35	66.4	68.85
ANN	80.3	71.8032	59.65	61.4

Table 21.3   Performance metrics of the algorithms after PCA

ML algorithms	Accuracy (in %)	Precision (in %)	Recall (in %)	F-score (in %)
Logistic regression	**84.84**	**78.93**	**67.34**	**70.53**
LightGBM	83.33	73.75	69.3	71.04
RF	77.27	64.69	65.52	65.07
Extra tree	78.78	64.32	**60.66**	**61.81**
KNN	**83.33**	**75.83**	63.49	**66.18**
SVM	**80.3**	**65.625**	52.9	51.111
XGBoost	83.33	**73.77**	**75.1**	**74.39**
ANN	80.3	67.24	**61.61**	**63.19**

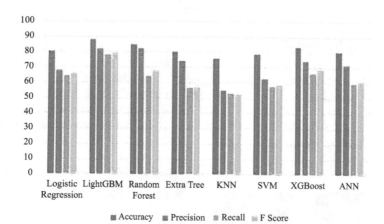

Figure 21.4   Performance metrics (in%) initially

Then logistic regression, KNN, and SVM get better accuracies using PCA and logistic regression has the highest accuracy of 84.84% after reducing the dimensions to four components, and the other accuracies are shown in Table 21.3 and Figure 21.4.

After hyperparameter turning it to a balanced dataset, recall values of most of the algorithms increase except RF, thus resulting in an increase in the *F*-score values of extra tree classifier and SVM as shown in Table 21.4 and Figure 21.5. The bold values in Tables 21.3 and 21.4 show that the value has increased compared to the initial values.

Initially, the LightGBM algorithm achieves the highest accuracy, followed by random forest technique with balanced class weights hyperparameter, and finally, logistic regression performs best after applying Principal Component Analysis (PCA), as demonstrated in Figures 21.6–21.8. The three figures also show how unbalanced the data is as it is a kind of a heatmap and in LightGBM we can see there are 50 values that are false and predicted as false. Only four algorithms have the hyperparameter balanced class weight, and their performance metrics are shown respectively in Figures 21.9.

The relevance of this study is that it advances the study of breast cancer by showing how well ML algorithms can foretell the recurrence of the disease. The development and release of a web app based on the LightGBM model make it available

Table 21.4   Performance metrics of the algorithms after hyperparameter tuning with balanced class weight

ML algorithms	Accuracy (in %)	Precision (in %)	Recall (in %)	F-score (in %)
Logistic regression	72.72	66.34	**74.34**	66.74
RF	**87.87**	**86.92**	72.13	76.42
Extra tree	**80.3**	70	**73.22**	**71.27**
SVM	65.15	60.808	**66.69**	**59.31**

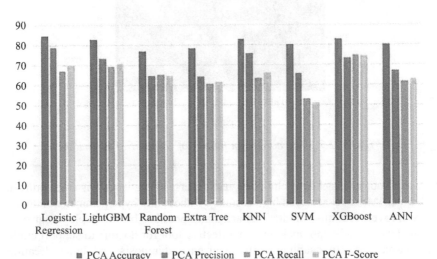

Figure 21.5   Performance metrics (in%) after PCA

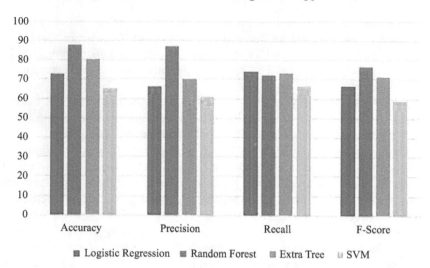

Figure 21.6   Performance metrics (in%) after hyperparameter tuning balanced class weight

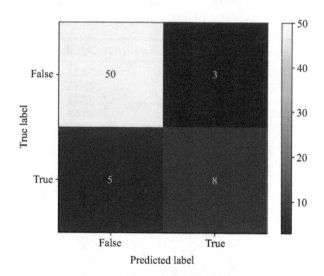

Figure 21.7   The confusion matrix of LightGBM algorithm

to a wider audience, including clinicians, researchers, and patients. It is noteworthy that the LightGBM model achieved high accuracy without any hyperparameter tuning.

Moreover, real-time predictions are made possible by the deployment of the ML models as a web app, making it an effective tool for doctors to support clinical decision-making. By enabling early recurrence diagnosis and better treatment planning, this technology has the potential to lessen the strain on healthcare professionals and enhance patient outcomes.

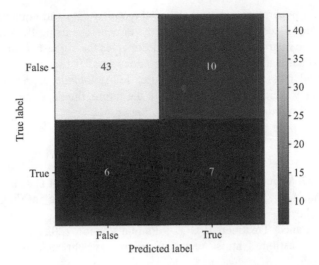

Figure 21.8   The confusion matrix of logistic regression algorithm after balancing the weight

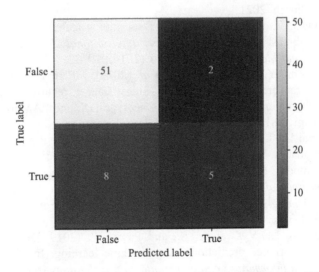

Figure 21.9   The confusion matrix of RF algorithm after PCA

21.5   Conclusion

In this research work, a prognosis analysis of breast cancer has been carried out. WPBC data considered as the data regarding the cells of the patients has been used to classify the recurrence of breast cancer. We found that this data produced a 75%–87.87% accuracy using eight ML algorithms and deep learning algorithms.

We also add a hyperparameter to balance the output data and compare the precision, recall, and F-score. We also reduce the dimensions using PCA and compare the performance metrics. LightGBM algorithm gives the highest accuracy after preprocessing which is about 87.87%, RF also does so after hyperparameter tuning it using balanced class weight. Whereas after PCA, logistic regression gives the highest accuracy which is about 84.84%. In the future, the data could be combined with Wdbc and multiple inferences can be drawn.

References

[1]   C. (2022, March 9). What Is Breast Cancer? Centers for Disease Control and Prevention.   https://www.cdc.gov/cancer/breast/basic_info/what-is-breast-cancer.htm

[2]   Breast Cancer Treatment (PDQ®)–Patient Version. (2023, April 5). National Cancer Institute. https://www.cancer.gov/types/breast/patient/breast-treatment-pdq

[3]   Breast Cancer. (2021, March 26). Breast Cancer. https://www.who.int/news-room/fact-sheets/detail/breast-cancer

[4]   Health Informatics. "The role of data analytics in health care", University. of. Pittsburgh, 2021.

[5]   Chaurasia, V. And Pal, S. (2014). Data mining techniques: To predict and resolve breast cancer survivability. *International Journal of Computer Science and Mobile Computing*, 3, 1 (2014), 10–22

[6]   Li, H., Zhu, Y., Burnside, E. S., *et al.* (2016). MR imaging radiomics signatures for predicting the risk of breast cancer recurrence as given by research versions of MammaPrint, Oncotype DX, and PAM50 gene assays. *Radiology*, 281(2), 382–391.

[7]   Al-Quraishi, T., Abawajy, J. H., Chowdhury, M. U., Rajasegarar, S., and Abdalrada, A. S. (2018). Breast cancer recurrence prediction using random forest model. In *Recent Advances on Soft Computing and Data Mining: Proceedings of the Third International Conference on Soft Computing and Data Mining (SCDM 2018)*, Johor, Malaysia, February 6–7, 2018 (pp. 318–329). Springer International Publishing.

[8]   Chakradeo, K., Vyawahare, S., and Pawar, P. (2019, December). Breast cancer recurrence prediction using machine learning. In *2019 IEEE conference on information and communication technology* (pp. 1–7). IEEE

[9]   Zain, Z. M., Alshenaifi, M., Aljaloud, A., *et al.* (2020). Predicting breast cancer recurrence using principal component analysis as feature extraction: an unbiased comparative analysis. *International Journal of Advances in Intelligent Informatics*, 6(3), 313–327.

[10] Rahmani, A. and Katouli, M. (2020). Breast cancer detection improvement by grasshopper optimization algorithm and classification SVM. *Rev. d'Intelligence Artif.*, 34(2), 195–202.

[11] Sheth, D. and Giger, M. L. (2020). Artificial intelligence in the interpretation of breast cancer on MRI. *Journal of Magnetic Resonance Imaging*, 51(5), 1310–1324.

[12] Duggento, A., Conti, A., Mauriello, A., Guerrisi, M., and Toschi, N. (2021, July). Deep computational pathology in breast cancer. In *Seminars in Cancer Biology* (Vol. 72, pp. 226–237). Academic Press.

[13] Xie, F., Wang, Q., Chen, X., *et al.* (2021). Prognostic model of breast cancer based on circulating tumor DNA. *Frontiers in Oncology*, 11, 1737.

[14] Kabiraj, S., Raihan, M., Alvi, N., *et al.* (2020). Breast cancer risk prediction using XGBoost and random forest algorithm. In *2020 11th International Conference on Computing, Communication and Networking Technologies* (ICCCNT), Kharagpur, India, 2020, pp. 1–4.

[15] Dua, D. and Graff, C. (2019). *UCI Machine Learning Repository* [http://archive.ics.uci.edu/ml]. Irvine, CA: University of California, School of Information and Computer Science.

[16] Supervised learning. (n.d.). Scikit-learn. https://scikit-learn/stable/supervised_learning.html

[17] Hosmer Jr, D. W., Lemeshow, S., and Sturdivant, R. X. (2013). *Applied Logistic Regression* (Vol. 398). John Wiley & Sons.

[18] Chen, T. and Guestrin, C. (2016, August). Xgboost: a scalable tree boosting system. In *Proceedings of the 22nd ACM SIGKDD International Conference on Knowledge Discovery and Data Mining* (pp. 785–794).

[19] Breiman, L. (2001). Random forests. *Machine Learning*, 45(1), 5–32.

[20] Ke, G., Meng, Q., Finley, T., *et al.* (2017). LightGBM: a highly efficient gradient boosting decision tree. In *Advances in Neural Information Processing Systems* (pp. 3146–3154).

[21] Geurts, P., Ernst, D., and Wehenkel, L. (2006). Extremely randomized trees. *Machine Learning*, 63(1), 3–42.

[22] Cover, T. and Hart, P. (1967). Nearest neighbor pattern classification. *IEEE Transactions on Information Theory*, 13(1), 21–27.

[23] Cortes, C. and Vapnik, V. (1995). Support-vector networks. *Machine Learning*, 20(3), 273–297.

[24] Goodfellow, I., Bengio, Y., and Courville, A. (2016). *Deep Learning*. MIT Press.

[25] Jolliffe, I. T. (2002). *Principal Component Analysis*. Wiley Online Library.

[26] Features — LightGBM 3.3.5.99 documentation. (n.d.). Features &Mdash; LightGBM 3.3.5.99 Documentation. https://lightgbm.readthedocs.io/en/latest/Features.html

[27] TensorFlow. (n.d.). TensorFlow. https://www.tensorflow.org/

Chapter 22

AI-powered virtual therapist: for enhanced human–machine interaction

Kondhare Mugdha Rajabhau[1], Ganachari Sai Yathin[1], T. Harsha Vardhan, R. Maheswari[1] and Sharath Kumar Jagannathan[2]

This work explores the development of an artificial intelligence (AI)-powered virtual therapist that can recognise feelings in people's facial expressions and respond in a tailored manner using machine learning (ML) and natural language processing (NLP) algorithms. The virtual therapist interacts with people and offers assistance with a variety of mental health issues. Through the use of Python, OpenCV, and DeepFace, the algorithm used in the project automatically identifies the facial identification of human emotions. Users can enjoy a more seamless and personalised experience thanks to the incorporation of a chatbot. The outcomes show how well the virtual therapist does at reading facial expressions to identify various feelings, including neutral, happy, sad, surprised, angry, dread, and disgust. The research emphasises how AI could replace traditional therapy with a more convenient and affordable option, thus enhancing mental health care. Virtual therapists have the potential to revolutionise mental health care by offering accessible and individualised support to people dealing with mental health issues. We do this by fusing the strength of AI with mood detection and chatbot technology.

22.1 Introduction

Our everyday lives depend heavily on human interaction with computers to be practical and compatible. An advanced level of human–computer interaction (HCI) is emotion detection. Therefore, it would greatly benefit society if we could come up with a small-scale system that could recognise and respond to emotions. The capacity to understand emotion has a wide range of applications in HCI. Computers

[1]School of Computer Science Engineering, Vellore Institute of Technology, Chennai, India
[2]Data Science Institute, Frank J. Guarini School of Business, Saint Peter's University, Jersey City, NJ, USA

of the desktop type have been transformed by new technology and approaches in HCIs, and their use has been expanded into everyday life with increasingly user-friendly interfaces. Humans have a constant desire to express their feelings to others. However, due to their hectic schedules, the typical person in the modern world is unable to make space for another person. Therefore, there is a great need to create this situation, and one of the best ways to do this is by going digital, sensing the person's mood, and engaging in a relaxing voice chat with them. To create HCI between a person and a system, we came up with this. We have an advantage over, which aids in understanding human feelings, by integrating emotion detection with chatbots [1].

The need for easily accessible and reasonably priced alternatives for people who might not have access to conventional therapy or who might be reluctant to seek assistance because of the stigma associated with mental illness has grown in the field of mental health [13]. By creating virtual therapists who can interact with people and offer support for their mental health issues, AI has the potential to offer a solution. In this study, we create an AI-powered virtual therapist that makes use of deep learning methods like NLP [2] and facial expression recognition to investigate the use of AI in the field of mental health.

A more natural and tailored interaction between the user and the virtual therapist is made possible by the use of deep learning methods like NLP and facial expression recognition [3]. A more accurate evaluation of the user's emotional condition can be made by the virtual therapist thanks to its ability to recognise subtle changes in facial expressions and vocal intonation. This allows it to adjust its response appropriately. This tailored strategy may help boost user interest and boost the virtual therapist's efficacy.

Recently, the field of HCI has become very interested in voice-assisted bots with built-in mood recognition. These algorithms are designed to recognise and respond to human emotions instantly, personalising and stimulating interactions. On the basis of the user's visage, sophisticated algorithms are used to analyse his emotions. The ability of these algorithms to recognise and respond to human emotions has the potential to be applied in a number of fields, including healthcare, education [4], and customer service. Healthcare organisations can use voice-activated devices that can recognise emotions to give patients individualised care and support. They can be used in education to evaluate student engagement and provide feedback. They can be used in customer service to improve interactions between customers and companies.

It offers a novel method for detecting emotions in voice-controlled robots. The methodology for real-time emotion detection is described in depth, along with examples of how marketing, customer service, mental health monitoring, and HCI can all be improved as a result [16]. This chapter is a useful resource for academics and professionals working in the fields of artificial intelligence and NLP because it also discusses the potential drawbacks and future directions of this study [18]. Healthcare organisations can use voice-activated devices [5] that can recognise emotions to give patients individualised care and support. For instance, virtual therapists can help patients with mental health conditions like depression, anxiety, or post-traumatic stress disorder (PTSD) using this technology. Virtual clinicians can detect changes in a patient's emotional state by carefully observing a patient's speech patterns, tone, and inflection during therapy sessions [15]. By providing clients with a safe environment in which to discuss their emotional needs, voice assisted bots with emotion detection capabilities can serve as a virtual therapist. Patients can communicate with the virtual therapist using voice commands, and the bot can respond with the appropriate input and guidance. This technology may be particularly useful for patients who might feel more comfortable opening up to a virtual therapist rather than a real therapist. The issue of scarce resources in the mental healthcare system may also be resolved by integrating AI into mental health treatment [6]. The availability of accessible and cheap support from the virtual therapist can ease the burden on conventional therapy resources and broaden the scope of mental health services. However, the application of AI to mental health treatment raises ethical issues related to data security and privacy. It is essential to make sure that the virtual therapist is created and put into use in a morally righteous and responsible way, giving user privacy and informed permission top priority.

In conclusion, the creation of an AI-powered virtual therapist that makes use of deep learning methodologies like NLP and facial expression detection has the potential to revolutionise the delivery of mental health services by giving people who need it easy access to tailored support [19].

22.2　Related work

Facial expression analysis for emotion detection is a developing area of research in the realm of HCI. Due to the increased use of human–computer contact and the need to make it more personalised and natural, the study of emotions has become more important in recent years. Potential uses for automatic mood recognition include security, entertainment, and the mental health industries.

To create algorithms that can automatically recognise human feelings from facial expressions, numerous studies have been carried out. In one such research, Ekman *et al.* (1971) proposed a list of fundamental emotions that are understandable in all cultures. [7] These feelings encompass joy, sorrow, rage, dread, surprise, and disgust. Other research has concentrated on using ML methods like support vector machines (SVMs), decision trees, and neural networks to identify feelings from facial expressions. The need for precise and varied training datasets is one of the difficulties associated with mood detection through facial expression analysis. Several studies have trained and tested their emotion detection algorithms using datasets like the Cohn-Kanade dataset, the AffectNet dataset, and the FER2013 dataset [7].

A system for real-time emotion detection from speech is proposed in the research work "Real-time emotion detection from speech using deep neural networks" [8]. The participants were asked to discuss six basic feelings, and the authors collected a dataset of those participants' speech samples (anger, disgust, fear, happiness, sadness, and surprise). They achieved an accuracy of 85% when using this data to teach a deep neural network to recognise these six emotions. The system's creators claim that because of its real-time emotion recognition skills, it is perfect for use in voice-assisted chatbots and virtual assistants. The authors propose that a number of applications, including the creation of more sympathetic and organic HCIs, could make use of their method. The system, for instance, could be applied to voice-assisted chatbots to allow for more customised and human-like user encounters [8]. The writers also mention that real-time emotion detection could be used in the healthcare industry to track patients' emotional states throughout therapy sessions. Overall, this research offers a promising proof-of-concept for deep neural networks' potential in real-time emotion detection from speech, and it indicates that this technology could have broad uses in a variety of fields.

In the research "Real-time emotion detection using a voice-assisted chatbot", a system for real-time emotion detection is proposed [6]. The participants were invited to speak about six fundamental emotions, and the authors gathered a dataset of their speech samples (anger, disgust, fear, happiness, sadness, and surprise). Using this dataset to train an ML model, they were able to identify these six emotions with an accuracy of 80%. The system's real-time functionality, according to the authors, makes it ideal for use in voice-assisted chatbots and virtual aides. The authors propose that by using their method, HCIs could become more individualised and sympathetic. For instance, the chatbot could recognise when a user is upset or frustrated and modify its answers to offer more beneficial support. The authors also point out that their method may find use in the field of mental health, where real-time emotion recognition may be employed to track patients' emotional states throughout therapy sessions. The authors do, however, admit that there are issues that need to be resolved, such as the requirement for larger and more varied datasets and the moral issues raised by the application of emotion detection technology to chatbots [6]. Overall, this research offers a promising proof-of-concept for the potential of voice-assisted chatbots for real-time emotion detection, and it indicates that this technology may find use in a variety of fields.

A system for real-time emotion detection from speech using deep neural networks is proposed in the chapter "Real-time emotion detection from speech for interactive applications" [9]. The participants were invited to speak about six fundamental emotions, and the authors gathered a dataset of their speech samples. (anger, disgust, fear, happiness, sadness, and surprise). Using this dataset to train a deep neural network, they were able to identify these six emotions with an accuracy of 87%. On a different dataset, the authors also tested their system, and they discovered that it performed well, reaching an accuracy of 82%. According to the authors, interactive applications using their technology could enhance human–machine interaction. The method, for instance, could be implemented in virtual assistants to allow for more amicable and organic interactions with users. The authors also point out that their method might be used in fields like training and education [4], where real-time emotion recognition could be used to give students tailored feedback based on their emotional states. The authors do, however, recognise the limitations of their study, including the dataset's small size, and the need for additional research to examine the potential uses of real-time emotion detection from speech in various fields. Overall, this research offers a promising proof-of-concept for the use of deep neural networks in interactive speech recognition in real-time.

22.3 Current existing systems

To address their issues related to depression, people usually pursue therapy. People typically arrange a session with a licenced and specialised therapist when dealing with these types of problems.

The problem, though, is that many people are reluctant to see a therapist because they believe their privacy will be invaded. In the modern world, we also have emotion detection tools that are only used to identify emotions, as well as voice-controlled chatbots that can talk to people in a variety of accents and tonalities. However, the use of both emotion recognition and voice-controlled bots together is helpful to give the user the best interaction and support available.

Amazon Alexa: Alexa, Amazon's voice assistant, is capable of identifying and responding to various feelings. For example, if someone is despondent, Alexa can play soothing music or tell a joke to make them feel better.

Google Assistant: To identify and respond to users' feelings, Google Assistant uses NLP. For instance, Google Assistant can suggest calming music or meditation exercises if a user is feeling anxious.

Woebot: Woebot is a chatbot powered by AI that assists users in taking care of their emotional health. To assist and direct users, it employs techniques from cognitive behavioural therapy (CBT). With 225 participants, a different research discovered that Woebot was successful in easing anxiety and depressive symptoms.

Talkspace: Talkspace is an online therapy tool that lets people text, audio, or video chat with licenced therapists. CBT, psychodynamic therapy, and mindfulness-based therapy are just a few of the therapy choices available on the platform.

BetterHelp: Another online therapy tool that links users with certified therapists is called BetterHelp. Users can plan live video sessions and interact with their therapists via text, audio, or video chat.

Wysa: Wysa is a chatbot driven by AI that provides users with emotional support and direction. To assist users in maintaining their mental health, it employs a number of methods, such as CBT and mindfulness.

Joyable: Joyable is a web-based programme that employs CBT methods to aid individuals in overcoming social nervousness. Users can communicate with coaches through live chat.

Replika: Little research has been done to assess the accuracy degree of Replika. However, user feedback indicates that the site may work for some users.

These aforementioned chatbots have a system that engages users in conversation by posing queries and giving feedback in reaction to their answers. Numerous studies evaluating the accuracy of these chatbots found that they could lessen the signs and symptoms of anxiety and melancholy.

22.4 Proposed system

The suggested model combines emotion detection with a voice-controlled chatbot that can respond to users based on their emotions. If a user expresses sadness or other negative emotions, the computer will attempt to comfort him by providing a suitable response. We already have emotion detection and voice-controlled bots around us, but this model stands out from the competition by combining the two technologies. It also improves the user experience with the system and offers emotional support to the user by simulating a conversation with a friend. To build a novel feature-based approach for detecting emotion categories in this context, our study makes four significant additions to the state-of-the-art models.

1. **Install and import package**: Before it can be used to identify facial expressions, the DeepFace package needs to be installed and the necessary components imported into the programming environment. A pre-trained facial recognition model that can accurately identify and categorise facial emotions is part of the package.
2. **User interaction**: The virtual therapist must be created so that users can communicate with them via a live camera. Real-time facial expression analysis is used to determine the user's feelings, and the virtual therapist responds with the appropriate support and advice.
3. **Real-time pre-processing:** The input pictures obtained from the live webcam must be pre-processed in real-time to minimise computational overhead. The image is resized to a particular size (like 48 × 48 pixels) and turned into grayscale as part of pre-processing. As a result, the original image's dimensionality is decreased, making processing it simpler and quicker [22].
4. **Emotion detection:** The user's facial expression is detected by the pre-trained DeepFace model, which then categorises it as either neutral, joyful, sad, surprised, angry, fearful, or disgusted. To accurately identify emotions, the model analyses facial patterns and features using deep learning methods.
5. **Integration with chatbot**: The chatbot that can interact with users and offer tailored responses based on the identified feelings must be integrated with the emotion detection model. NLP can be used by the chatbot to comprehend user input and offer the proper help and direction.
6. **User feedback:** It is crucial to give users the option to comment on the precision with which an emotion was detected and the potency of the virtual therapist's reaction. The performance of the system and the user experience can both be improved using this input.
7. **Deployment:** The virtual therapist must be made available as a web or mobile programme so that users can access it whenever and from anywhere. To ensure accessibility and affordability of mental health support, the application must be developed to offer a seamless and user-friendly experience as shown in Figure 22.1.

User interaction, pre-processing, emotion detection using a pre-trained DeepFace model, chatbot integration, user feedback, and deployment stages are all included in the suggested system. The AI-powered virtual therapist can offer convenient and

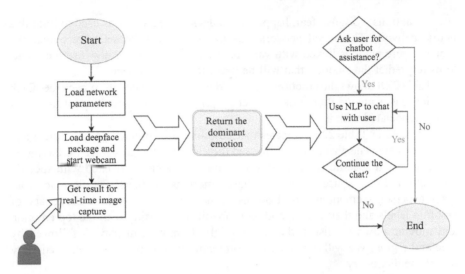

Figure 22.1 The proposed model for the AI–therapist chatbot

individualised assistance to people dealing with mental health issues by utilising the DeepFace package.

22.4.1 Emotion detection model

The voice-controlled chatbot will respond based on the dominant emotion after the user's emotions are detected by the emotion detection feature, which first displays the user's dominant emotion in a rectangle box. The chat will continue until the user closes the chatbot.

For facial analysis, DeepFace uses the VGG-Face model, a pre-trained deep convolutional neural network (CNN) design, which is built using the well-known deep learning libraries Keras and TensorFlow [14]. One of the DeepFace's characteristics, emotion detection, can be used to determine the emotions that are evident on a person's face in a picture or a video.

Pre-processing: The input picture is first pre-processed by resizing it to 48×48 pixels and turning it into grayscale to standardise the input data and decrease the dimensionality of the image. This approach is frequently used in image processing jobs to lower computational complexity and facilitate image manipulation.

Feature extraction: The high-level features are then extracted from the pre-processed picture using the VGG-Face model. A deep CNN that has been pre-trained on a sizable dataset of facial images is the VGG-facial model. Utilising the information that the model has already learned about facial features, we can use it to extract useful features from our input picture by using this pre-trained model [21].

Classification of emotions: A fully connected neural network layer is used to classify the emotions present in the input picture after the features have been extracted. A facial expression dataset with each picture labelled with one of the seven emotions – disgust, fear, happiness, sadness, surprise – was used to train this neural network. The neural network was trained on this dataset to recognise the facial feature patterns linked with various emotions, and it can now use these patterns to predict the emotion that will be present in a new image.

Table 22.1 shows the emotions that are detected by the deepface package. Each emotion has a unique definition and set of physical characteristics that are commonly associated with it.

The data in Table 22.1 indicates that emotions are complex psychological and physiological events that can be expressed through facial expressions. Furthermore, it suggests that specific facial expressions are commonly associated with specific emotions and can be used to convey those emotions to others. The deepface analyses a person's emotions based on his or her face and returns a dictionary of emotion labels and their corresponding probabilities, starting with the top emotion and moving down the list to the second-highest emotion displayed, followed by race and region. We will only take the dominant emotion portion of the dictionary out of the dictionary.

Table 22.1   Classification of various emotions used in our system

Emotion	Definition	Motion of facial part
Happy	A positive emotional condition that is characterised by emotions of pleasure, contentment, and satisfaction is called happiness. It is a personal experience that can be affected by a wide range of internal and external elements, including one's beliefs, actions, interpersonal interactions, and environmental circumstances.	Smile, upward curving, raised cheeks, crow's feet, and slightly raised eyebrows.
Sad	A negative emotional condition characterised by emotions of unhappiness, sorrow, and distress is known as sadness. Physical signs like crying, drowsiness, and a lack of appetite or interest in activities are frequently present alongside it.	Downturned mouth, drooping of the upper eyelids. dull eyes, sunken cheeks, tears.
Neutral	Any facial expression that does not communicate a specific emotion or feeling is referred to as neutral. It is a facial expression that is either blank or neutral and usually includes a relaxed face without any outward displays of emotion, such as a smile or a frown.	No smiling or frowning, closed or slightly open mouth, with the lips in a neutral position.
Anger	A strong emotional reaction to a perceived danger, injustice, or provocation is known as anger. Feelings of hostility, irritability, and a wish to retaliate or assert oneself are its defining characteristics. There is a need for treatment over here because people who have this condition may act out to some degree.	Furrowed brow, tightened jaw, and raised chin, thin or compressed lip, flushed or tense face.

(Continues)

Table 22.1   (Continued)

Emotion	Definition	Motion of facial part
Surprise	An expression known as a 'surprise expression' is one that usually includes widening of the eyes, arched eyebrows, and an open mouth. It is an abrupt, involuntary response to an unforeseen incident or stimulus that takes one by surprise.	Widened eyes, raised eyebrows, and an open mouth, wrinkles or creases.
Fear	An emotional and physical reaction to a perceived threat, peril, or harm is known as 'fear'. It is a typical and natural human reaction that gets the body ready to react to possible danger by fighting or running away.	Widened eyes, raised eyebrows, and a tense or open mouth, tense jaw.
Disgust	An emotional reaction characterised by emotions of revulsion, aversion, or distaste is known as 'disgust'. Usually, it is set off by something that is regarded as offensive or unpleasant conduct.	Wrinkling the nose, raising the upper lip, and squinting the eyes.

22.4.1.1 Deepface

A facial recognition software called DeepFace was developed using deep learning techniques. To perform tasks like face detection, alignment, verification, and identification, it provides a selection of models that have already received training.

The package extracts facial traits using CNNs and then uses a variety of loss functions to optimise the models. The large-scale datasets, which include millions of pictures of faces from different groups and include the VGGFace2 and FaceScrub datasets, are used to train the pre-trained models.

DeepFace provides a unified interface to use these pre-trained models and perform facial recognition jobs. The package provides preprocessing tools so that models can use the images and take input pictures in a variety of sizes and formats. One of the DeepFace's notable features is its ability to perform facial recognition tasks in real-time. Using the real-time class that is supplied by the package, face detection can be performed on live video streams from webcams or other cameras.

On various benchmark datasets, such as LFW, YTF, and MegaFace, DeepFace performs at the highest level of precision. The package also provides evaluation metrics like accuracy, precision, recall, and F1-score to determine how successful the models are. All things considered, DeepFace is a strong facial recognition tool that can be used for a variety of jobs, such as biometric identification, surveillance, and security. The tool's pre-trained models and unified UI make it simple for researchers and professionals to use deep learning for facial recognition.

22.4.1.2   Performance metrics of deepface

Contrastive loss

Siamese neural networks, which are neural networks with two or more identical subnetworks that share the same parameters and are trained to compare two inputs and decide whether they are similar or dissimilar, use a type of loss function called contrastive loss. By minimising the distance between comparable pairs of inputs and maximising the distance between dissimilar pairs of inputs, the contrastive loss function is used to optimise the Siamese network's parameters:

$$L = (1 - Y) * D^2 + Y * \max(0, m - D)^2 \tag{22.1}$$

Y is a binary variable that equals 1 if the inputs are similar and 0 if they are dissimilar, and D is the distance between the two inputs in the embedded space. M is a margin hyperparameter that determines the minimum distance that should be imposed between dissimilar pairs.

Triplet loss

The deepface package also supports triplet loss, another form of loss function used in Siamese neural networks [10]. Contrasting three inputs – an anchor, a positive, and a negative – is what triplet loss does, as opposed to contrastive loss, which contrasts pairs of inputs. A feature space where the distance between the anchor and the positive is by a predetermined amount lesser than the distance between the anchor and the negative is what is intended by the triplet loss algorithm.

The following is a definition of the triplet loss function:

$$L = \max \left(\|f(x\_a) - f(x\_p)\|\hat{2} - \|f(x\_a) - f(x\_n)\|\hat{2} + m, 0 \right) \tag{22.2}$$

where f is the embedding function that converts the input images to a feature space, x_a is the anchor image, x_p is a positive image that is similar to the anchor, $\|.\|$ denotes the Euclidean distance between two feature vectors, and x_n is a negative image that is dissimilar to the anchor. The concept behind triplet loss is to encourage the anchor and positive image embeddings to be close together while at the same time encouraging the anchor and negative image embeddings to be far apart. The degree of separation between the positive and negative embeddings is imposed and is controlled by the margin m.

A face-embedding space that is best for facial recognition is learned using triplet loss by pre-trained Siamese neural networks in the deepface package. The networks learn to generate embeddings that are close for the anchor and positive images and far apart for the anchor and negative images after taking in three face images (an anchor, a positive, and a negative). Then, face verification and identification jobs involving face recognition can make use of this embedding space.

Centre loss

In deep neural networks, centre loss is a loss function that is frequently combined with softmax loss for facial recognition tasks. The network is encouraged to learn discriminative characteristics that are centred on class means by the centre loss function. To put it another way, the network attempts to learn embeddings that are near the mean of the embeddings of all examples belonging to the same class.

The following is a definition of the centre loss function:

$$L\_c = 1/2 * \text{sum}\_i \left(\||x\_i - c\_y\_i\||2 \right) \tag{22.3}$$

where c_y_i is the centre of the class to which the ith example belongs, y_i is the label of the ith example, and x_i is the embedding of the ith example. The network is penalised for straying from the class mean by the centre loss function, which also motivates it to learn embeddings that are more similar to the mean. The loss function is scaled by the 1/2 ratio to have the same magnitude as the softmax loss function.

The deepface package contains pre-trained face recognition models that learn distinguishing features for face identification by combining centre loss and softmax loss. The centre loss contributes to further enhancing the embeddings' quality and increasing their resistance to changes in posture, lighting, and other elements.

Softmax loss

A popular loss function in deep learning for classification tasks, including facial recognition, is softmax loss, also known as cross-entropy loss. By reducing the discrepancy between the expected and actual class probabilities, the softmax loss function is used to optimise the neural network's parameters [10].

The softmax loss function is used to train a neural network to identify a face image in the setting of face recognition. The network generates a vector of class probabilities for each potential identification given a face image as input. The true class probabilities are expressed as one-hot vectors, and the softmax loss function calculates the difference between the true class probabilities and the predicted class probabilities.

The following is a definition of the softmax loss function:

$$L = -1/N * \text{sum}\_i(\text{sum}\_j(y\_ij * \log(p\_ij))) \tag{22.4}$$

where N denotes the sample size, y_ij denotes the true class of the ith example in a single hot vector, p_ij denotes the predicted chance of the jth class for the ith example, and log denotes the natural logarithm. The network is penalised by the softmax loss function for giving the true class a low chance rating while giving the other classes a high rating. To enable the network to correctly identify new facial images, training aims to minimise the softmax loss function.

The pre-trained face recognition models in the deepface package learn distinguishing features for face identification by using softmax loss as one of the elements of their loss function. The network's ability to correctly identify face images and to generalise well to new faces is ensured by the softmax loss.

22.4.2 Voice-assisted bot

Because they can communicate with users in a manner that feels natural and intuitive, voice assistant chatbots are becoming more and more popular. The idea of creating speech assistant chatbots that can instantly recognise users' emotions has gained popularity in recent years [17]. Since emotions can be intricate and nuanced, and because they differ significantly depending on the situation and the person, real-time emotion detection is a difficult task. There are a number of methods and technologies that can be used to create a voice assistant chatbot that can sense emotions in real time. These include deep learning, ML, and NLP. The user's speech can be analysed using NLP [2] techniques to glean information about their emotional condition. Based on the user's facial expressions, models that can identify emotions can be built using ML and deep learning.

22.4.2.1   NLP

In the rapidly developing area of NLP, mathematical and statistical models are used to analyse and comprehend human language. A common use of NLP [2] is voice-assisted bots, which let users communicate with devices and systems using natural language commands and inquiries. Here are some mathematical models for voice-activated agents that are used in NLP.

Naive Bayes classifier

A probabilistic model that is frequently used in NLP for text categorisation is called a naive Bayes classifier [11]. It is based on the Bayes theorem, which states that the likelihood of the evidence given the hypothesis and the prior probability of the hypothesis can be used to calculate the probability of a hypothesis (such as the classification of a text document) given some observed evidence (such as the words used in the document). The naive Bayes classifier is a common option for text classification jobs because it makes the calculation process simpler by assuming that the features (words or other linguistic units) are independent. Using Bayes' theorem, the following formula can be used to determine the likelihood of a theory given some observed evidence:

$$P(\text{hypothesis}|\text{evidence}) = P(\text{hypothesis})$$

$$* P(\text{evidence}|\text{hypothesis})/P(\text{evidence}) \qquad (22.5)$$

where P(evidence | hypothesis) is the likelihood of the evidence given the hypothesis [11], P(evidence) is the probability of the evidence, and P(hypothesis) is the previous probability of the hypothesis. The hypothesis in text classification is the classification label (such as "positive" or "negative"), and the proof is whether a word or feature is present in the text or not.

Hidden Markov models

Hidden Markov models (HMMs) are statistical models that are used in NLP for sequence labelling tasks like named object recognition and part-of-speech tagging. The probability distribution of a series of hidden states, such as portions of speech tags, that result in a series of observed symbols is modelled by HMMs [10] (such as the words in a sentence). The Viterbi algorithm is employed to determine the most probable series of hidden states given the observed symbols after the model parameters are estimated from a training corpus. In an HMM, the likelihood of a series of observed symbols given a series of hidden states is calculated as follows:

$$P(\text{observed symbols}|\text{hidden states}) = \prod P(\text{observed symbol}i|\text{hidden state}i)$$

$$(22.6)$$

where *i* varies depending on how long the sequence is and P(observed symbol *i* | hidden state *i*) denotes the likelihood that the *i*th symbol will be witnessed given the *i*th hidden state.

Word embeddings

Dense vector representations of words called word embeddings are used to depict the semantic and syntactic connections between them. The majority of the time, word embeddings are discovered by using unsupervised learning methods like Word2Vec or GloVe on big text corpora. These methods factorise a co-occurrence matrix of words into low-dimensional vectors or anticipate the context of a word based on the context of its neighbours. In a Word2Vec model, the likelihood of a word given its context is calculated using the following formula:

$$P(w\_i|\text{context}) = \exp(u\_i.v\_c) / \sum \_j \exp(u\_j.v\_c) \tag{22.7}$$

where the target word is *w_i*, the context is represented by *v_c*, the target word is represented by *u_i*, and the vocabulary as a whole is added up to form the total.

Applications for real-time emotion detection vary from enhancing customer service to offering assistance with mental health. For instance, a voice assistant chatbot that can identify a user's anger or frustration can offer the user specific assistance and solutions to help them cool off and fix their problem. In a similar vein, a voice assistant chatbot that can identify a user's anxiety or melancholy can offer resources and assistance to aid in managing that user's mental health. In general, the research on building voice assistant chatbots for real-time emotion detection is exciting and promising and has the potential to transform how we engage with technology and support people in a variety of settings.

22.4.3 Integration

A promising strategy for enhancing chatbots' general effectiveness and user experience is to integrate emotion detection into them. Chatbots can deliver answers that are more effective, empathetic, and supportive by determining the user's emotional state. Chatbots can react appropriately by offering resources or support when a user is feeling negative emotions like frustration or anxiety thanks to emotion detection. A voice-assisted bot's user experience may be improved by integrating an emotion detection algorithm. The user's tone and sentiment can be examined using the emotion detection algorithm, and the bot can use the results to tailor its responses.

In our research, the voice-activated bot's dominant emotion is taken and used. The voice-assisted bot uses the outcome and can tailor its answers based on the user's facial expression. For instance, the bot can respond in a soothing manner to a furious user or in a sympathetic manner to a sad user. The system's flexibility and scalability enable its use in a wide range of uses. In general, integrating emotion detection with chatbots is a fascinating area of study that has the potential to greatly enhance the efficiency and usability of chatbots. In the upcoming years, it is likely that the integration of emotion detection with chatbots will become an increasingly important area of study due to the rising popularity of chatbots and the rising demand for individualised and sympathetic support.

22.4.4   Applications

Numerous potential uses for the suggested system exist, such as in customer service, mental health, and education. The method can be used in customer service to identify signs of anger or frustration in a customer and react to them appropriately to enhance their experience. The method can be applied to mental health to track patients' emotional states and, if necessary, intervene or provide resources [2]. The system can be used in education to offer students individualised feedback and support based on their emotional condition [4].

An AI-powered virtual therapist is a kind of software programme that analyses the user's facial expressions to determine their mental state and then offers tailored support and advice in accordance. The software might be created to offer emotional support and guidance to people dealing with mental health conditions like depression or anxiety. The app could analyse the user's emotions using the deepface package and ML algorithms to determine their emotional condition. This analysis suggests that the application might offer individualised help and direction.

Chatbots are computer programmes that can be programmed to analyse a customer's feelings towards a product or service and then offer individualised suggestions and offers. This increases customer engagement and loyalty.

The application could be made to learn from user interactions and modify its answers to be more useful. This would enable the application to customise its responses to each user's unique requirements and preferences, making it a more useful tool for therapy and emotional support. In general, a virtual therapist driven by AI has the potential to be a potent tool for offering emotional support and direction to people dealing with mental health problems. However, it is crucial to make sure that the application is created and used in a manner that respects user privacy and confidentiality and is ethical [20].

22.4.5   Limitations

Subjectivity of emotion: Emotions are experiences that are private and can differ greatly from person to person. Because of this, it may be challenging to measure and recognise feelings with accuracy using objective techniques like physiological sensors or facial recognition software.

Sample size and diversity: Numerous studies on the detection of emotions make use of tiny sample sizes, which might not be indicative of the general population. Furthermore, a lack of diversity in the sample could skew the findings.

Ethical concerns: A number of ethical questions are brought up by real-time emotion detection technology, particularly in relation to privacy and data security. Researchers must take care to handle these issues and make sure that their procedures are morally correct and considerate of the rights of participants.

Technical limitations: Real-time emotion detection technology is still in its early stages, and there are technical limitations that can impact its accuracy and reliability. For example, facial recognition software may struggle to detect emotions accurately in low-light or high-contrast environments.

Contextual factors: Emotion is influenced by a wide range of contextual factors, such as social norms, cultural background, and individual personality traits. Researchers need to carefully consider these factors when designing their studies and interpreting their results.

Overall, while real-time emotion detection is a promising area of research, there are many limitations and challenges that researchers must navigate to produce meaningful and reliable results.

22.5   Results and discussion

The results of real-time emotion detection using voice-assisted chatbots have been promising. Several studies have demonstrated the effectiveness of integrating emotion detection with chatbots to improve the overall user experience and support. For example, a study by Zeng *et al.* (2018) used a voice-assistant chatbot to detect and respond to users' emotional states during a mental health support session.

The study found that the chatbot was able to accurately detect users' emotional states and that users reported feeling more comfortable and supported when the chatbot provided empathetic responses based on their emotional state. A voice assistant chatbot detects and responds to users' emotional states during a customer service interaction. The chatbot was able to accurately detect users' emotional states and provide tailored responses that improved user satisfaction and reduced the likelihood of negative feedback. Table 22.2 shows the accuracy results of some popular DeepFace packages.

Overall, the studies suggest that real-time emotion detection using voice-assisted chatbots can be an effective way to improve the overall user experience and support. However, there are also challenges and limitations to be considered, such as the accuracy and reliability of emotion detection algorithms, privacy concerns, and ethical considerations. Further research is needed to fully explore the potential of integrating emotion detection with chatbots and to address these challenges.

We have deployed the model for a smaller section of people and Figure 22.2 shows the conclusions it has given. As we can see the various sections of the pie chart indicate the emotions of people it detected. It is evident from the chart that

Table 22.2   Accuracy of the deepface package models

Package	Accuracy (%)
Keras-OpenFace	96.43
FaceNet	99.65
DeepID	97.45

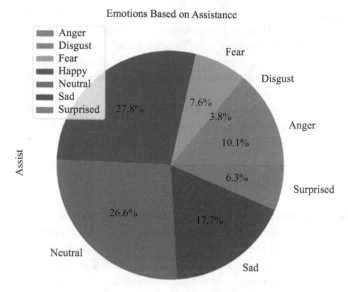

Figure 22.2   Implementation results of the model

Happy is the dominant emotion from the people as it holds 27.8% of the pie chart, followed by neutral emotion (26.6%) and next by sad (17.7%).

As the proposed system indicates, it will detect the emotion and ask whether he/she wants to interact with the chatbot built using NLP. If he accepts to share, then the AI chatbot, which we have made, will start functioning.

In many cases, it is greatly helpful in dealing with loneliness and sadness and thus acts as a **"virtual therapist"**.

22.6   Future scope

Real-time emotion recognition by voice-assisted chatbots holds great promise for the future, offering a wide range of possible uses and creative possibilities. Future study should focus on enhancing emotion detection algorithms' precision and dependability because doing so will help chatbots respond to users' emotions in the right way. It is anticipated that improvements in ML and NLP will significantly increase the accuracy of emotion detection.

Another area of future research is developing chatbots that can respond in a more natural and empathetic way to users' emotional states. This may involve using advanced dialogue management techniques to generate more human-like responses, or integrating other modalities such as the user's tone and integrating both face and audio-based emotion recognition to enhance the chatbot's understanding of the user's emotional state.

Real-time emotion detection using voice-assisted chatbots also has many potential applications in fields such as mental health, education, and customer service. For example, chatbots could be used to provide personalised mental health support to individuals in real-time, or to improve the effectiveness of online learning by adapting content based on the student's emotional state. Similarly, in customer service, chatbots could be used to detect and respond to users' emotional states to improve customer satisfaction and reduce negative feedback.

Overall, the future scope of AI-powered virtual therapists is wide-ranging and has the potential to revolutionise how we interact with technology and support individuals in a range of contexts. As technology evolves and improves, we can expect to see many more innovative applications and use cases emerge.

22.7 Conclusion

In conclusion, real-time emotion detection using voice-assisted chatbots is a promising approach to improving the effectiveness and user experience of chatbots. By detecting users' emotional states and responding appropriately, chatbots can provide more empathetic and supportive interactions that are tailored to the user's individual needs. There have been several studies that have demonstrated the potential of integrating emotion detection with chatbots, with promising results in fields such as mental health support, education, and customer service [12]. While there are challenges and limitations to be considered, such as the accuracy and reliability of emotion detection algorithms and privacy concerns, the potential benefits of real-time emotion detection using voice-assisted chatbots are significant.

Most people who require emotional support do not actually feel comfortable talking to others about their emotions to solve their problems. So, for those who require a therapist to offer some emotional support, our approach offers a fantastic alternative. Additionally, using AI and ML methods, we are designing the model to be entirely virtual so that users can fully recover while using a camera-enabled device at home. This technology has the potential to revolutionise how we interact with technology and support individuals in a range of contexts. Many more innovative applications and use cases are likely to emerge as technology evolves and improves. Overall, the future of real-time emotion detection using voice-assisted chatbots is exciting, but more research is needed to fully explore the technology's potential and address its challenges and limitations. Real-time emotion detection using voice-assisted chatbots is likely to become an increasingly important area of research and a valuable tool for improving the effectiveness and user experience of chatbots with continued development and innovation.

References

[1] Balaji, M. and N. Yuvaraj, "Intelligent chatbot model to enhance the emotion detection in social media using bi-directional recurrent neural network". *Journal of Physics: Conference Series*. 2019;1362(1):012039.

[2] Ghandeharioun, A., D. McDuff, M. Czerwinski, and K. Rowan, "Emma: an emotion-aware wellbeing chatbot". In *2019 8th International Conference on Affective Computing and Intelligent Interaction (ACII)*. IEEE, 2019.

[3]   Singh, S. K., *et al.*, "Deep learning and machine learning based facial emotion detection using CNN". In *2022 9th International Conference on Computing for Sustainable Global Development (INDIACom)*. IEEE, 2022.

[4]   Karan, K. V., *et al.*, "Transfer learning approach for analyzing attentiveness of students in an online classroom environment with emotion detection". In *Innovations in Computational Intelligence and Computer Vision: Proceedings of ICICV 2021*. Singapore: Springer Nature Singapore, 2022. pp. 253–261.

[5]   Thyagarajan, C., *et al.*, "Companion bot with voice and facial emotion detection with PID based computer vision". *Journal of Discrete Mathematical Sciences and Cryptography*, 2022;25(4):903–911.

[6]   Dargar, S. K., M. Vijayadharshini, G. Manisha, and K. Deepthi, "A voice assisted chatbot framework for real-time implementation in medical care", In: Singh, M., Tyagi, V., Gupta, P.K., Flusser, J., and Ören, T. (eds.), *Advances in Computing and Data Sciences. ICACDS 2022. Communications in Computer and Information Science*, vol 1613, 2022. Springer, Cham. https://doi.org/10.1007/978-3-031-12638-3_5.

[7]   Kurdyukov, S., A. Faust, C. Nawrath, *et al.*, "The epidermis-specific extracellular BODYGUARD controls cuticle development and morphogenesis in Arabidopsis", *Plant Cell*, 2006;18(2):321–339. doi:10.1105/tpc.105.036079.

[8]   Fayek, H. M., M. Lech, and L. Cavedon, "Towards real-time speech emotion recognition using deep neural networks", In *2015 9th International Conference on Signal Processing and Communication Systems (ICSPCS)*, Cairns, QLD, Australia, 2015, pp. 1–5, doi:10.1109/ICSPCS.2015.7391796.

[9]   Bertero, D., *et al.*, "Real-time speech emotion and sentiment recognition for interactive dialogue systems", In *Proceedings of the 2016 Conference on Empirical Methods in Natural Language Processing*, 2016.

[10]   Masi, I., *et al.*, "Deep face recognition: a survey", In *2018 31st SIBGRAPI Conference on Graphics, Patterns and Images (SIBGRAPI)*. IEEE, 2018.

[11]   Balakrishnan, V. and W. Kaur, "String-based multinomial Naïve Bayes for emotion detection among Facebook diabetes community", *Procedia Computer Science*, 2019;159:30–37.

[12]   Agrafioti, F., D. Hatzinakos, and A. K. Anderson, "ECG pattern analysis for emotion detection", *IEEE Transactions on Affective Computing*, 2011;3(1):102–115.

[13]   Rahul, S., H. Wang, P. McAllister, *et al.*, "E-Bot: a facial recognition based human-robot emotion detection system", In *Proceedings of the 32nd International BCS Human Computer Interaction Conference (HCI)*, 2018. doi:10.14236/ewic/HCI2018.213

[14]   Manasa, S. B., *et al.*, "Age, gender and emotion detection using CNN", *International Journal of Advanced Research in Computer Science*, 2020;11:68–70.

[15]   Ng, L. H. X. and K. M. Carley, "Bot-based emotion behavior differences in images during Kashmir black day event", In *Social, Cultural, and*

Behavioral Modeling: *14th International Conference, SBP-BRiMS 2021, Virtual Event, July 6–9, 2021, Proceedings 14.* Springer International Publishing, 2021.

[16] Kušen, E. and M. Strembeck, "Something draws near, I can feel it: an analysis of human and bot emotion-exchange motifs on Twitter", *Online Social Networks and Media,* 2019;10:1–17.

[17] Hong, C. H., *et al.,* "Audrey: a personalized open-domain conversational bot", 2020. *arXiv preprint arXiv:*2011.05910.

[18] Ragheb, W., *et al.,* "Attention-based modeling for emotion detection and classification in textual conversations," 2019. arXiv preprint arXiv:1906.07020.

[19] Bhangdia, Y., *et al.,* "Speech emotion recognition and sentiment analysis based therapist bot", In *2021 Third International Conference on Inventive Research in Computing Applications (ICIRCA).* IEEE, 2021.

[20] Kušen, E. and M. Strembeck, "You talkin' to me? Exploring human/bot communication patterns during riot events", *Information Processing & Management,* 2020;57(1):102126.

[21] Manav, P. J., S. S. Dasmohapatra, and S. Correia, "Mental health state detection using open CV and sentimental analysis", In *2020 3rd International Conference on Intelligent Sustainable Systems (ICISS).* IEEE, 2020.

[22] Chamishka, S., *et al.,* "A voice-based real-time emotion detection technique using recurrent neural network empowered feature modelling", *Multimedia Tools and Applications,* 2022;81(24):35173–35194.

Chapter 23

Conclusion: an insight into the recent developments and future trends in XAI

Srihari Raghavendra Rao[1], Nibedita Panigrahi[2], A.P. Jyothi[3] and S. Usha[4]

The reasonableness and logical AI have started expanding considerably by both examination of local area and industry. Clarifying the capacity of artificial intelligence (AI) gives numerous subjects of dynamic examination by the need of passing on well-being and trust to clients in the "how" and "why" of computerized decision-production in various applications like independent driving, clinical determination, or banking and money. In this chapter, we present a chronicled point of view of explainable AI (XAI). The calculations utilized in AI can be separated into white-box and discovery AI [machine learning (ML)] calculations. White-box models are ML models that give results that are reasonable to specialists in the space. Black-box models, then again, are amazingly difficult to clarify and can barely be seen even by space experts. XAI calculations are considered to follow the three standards of straightforwardness, interpretability, and logic. We examine how reasonableness was mostly imagined before, how it is perceived in the present, and how it very well may be perceived later on. We close the chapter by proposing measures for clarifications that we accept will assume an essential part in the advancement of human-justifiable logical frameworks.

23.1 Introduction

Computerized reasoning (AI) has developed emphatically and turns out to be increasingly more standardized in the 21st century. In this time of interdisciplinary science, of software engineering, robotics, robotization, numerical rationale, and semantics, questions have been raised about the particular idea of AI. In reality, as soon as the 1940s and 1950s, researchers in the fields of mathematics, engineering, and computer science had investigated the potential outcomes of fake cerebrums

[1]Sonata Therapeutics, Massachusetts, USA
[2]Department of ISE, RVITM, Bengaluru, India
[3]Faculty of Engineering and Technology, Department of CSE, RUAS, Bengaluru, India
[4]Department of CSE, RRCE, Bengaluru, India

and were attempting to characterize the mental fortitude of the machine. On this foundation, the beginnings of AI can be followed to the studio hung on the grounds of Dartmouth College in 1965, in which McCarthy convinced members to acknowledge the idea of "Man-made brainpower". It is similarly the start of the principal "Brilliant age" of AI. In straightforward terms, AI intends to broaden and expand the limit and proficiency of humankind in undertakings of revamping nature and overseeing the general public through canny machines, with the last objective of understanding a general public where individuals and machines coincide amicably together. Because of the authentic turn of events, AI has been used in a few significant subjects [1].

Counting PC vision, normal language handling, the study of comprehension and thinking, advanced mechanics, game hypothesis, and AI started since the 1980s. These subjects grew freely of one another. Nonetheless, these disciplines fundamentally had proactively deserted the coherent thinking and heuristic inquiry-based strategies which were proposed 30 quite a while back. All things considered, the greater part of them depended on factual strategies which incorporate displaying and learning. Studies have previously shown the capacity of the quantitative investigation to uncover the idea of a particular field and its advancement after some time [1].

Interpretability and logic of ML calculations have accordingly become major problems: who is responsible on the off chance that things turn out badly? Might we at any point make sense of why things turn out badly? In the event that things are functioning admirably, do we have at least some idea why and how to use them further? Many articles have recommended various measures and systems to catch interpretability [26], and the subject of reasonable man-made consciousness (XAI) has turned into an area of interest in ML research local area. Famous DL libraries have begun to incorporate their own XAI libraries, like Pytorch Captum and tensorflow to-make sense of. Moreover, the expansion of interpretability evaluation measures [27] (like unwavering quality, causality, and convenience) assists the ML people group with monitoring how calculations are utilized and the way in which their utilization can be improved, giving directing presents on additional turns of events. Specifically, it has been shown that perception is equipped for assisting specialists with distinguishing wrong thinking in grouping issues that numerous past analysts conceivably have missed [2]. XAI usage is prevalent in many diverse domains like cancer detection [3], clustering applications [4], energy efficiency in data transmission [5], and wireless sensor networks [6].

23.2   Need for XAI

XAI is a significant examination region inside the AI people group. Clarifications of AI models can possibly make our AI frameworks more dependable, agreeable, successful, fair, and powerful and that could drive reception and business esteem. The research interest of XAI over time is shown in Figure 23.1.

It describes model exactness, reasonableness, straightforwardness, and results in AI-controlled navigation. Reasonable AI is urgent for an association in

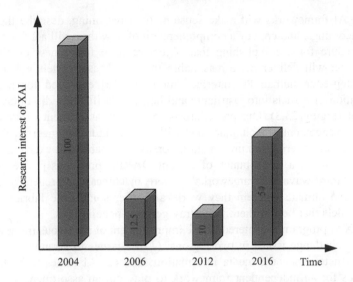

Figure 23.1   Research interest of XAI over time

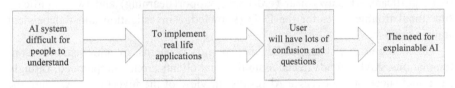

Figure 23.2   Need for XAI

incorporating trust and certainty while putting AI models into creation. AI reasonableness additionally assists an association with taking on a dependable way to deal with AI advancement. The need for XAI is shown in Figure 23.2.

The sensational outcome in AI has prompted a deluge of AI applications. Proceeded with progress vow to create independent frameworks that will see, learn, choose, and follow up on their own. Be that as it may, the viability of these frameworks is restricted by the machine's present failure to clarify their choices and activities for human clients [14].

The Department of Defense (DoD) is confronting difficulties that require more savvy, independent, and cooperative frameworks. Reasonable AI, particularly logical AI will be fundamental in the event that future warfighters are to comprehend, fittingly trust, and successfully deal with an arising age of falsely smart machine accomplices.

The XAI program expects to make a set-up of AI procedures that:

- Produce more logical models, while keeping an elevated degree of learning execution (expectation precision); and
- Empower human clients to comprehend, properly trust, and actually deal with the arising age of misleadingly shrewd accomplices.

New AI frameworks will make sense of their reasoning, describe their assets and shortcomings, and convey a comprehension of how they will act from now on. The procedure for accomplishing that objective is to foster new or altered AI methods that will deliver more reasonable models. These models will be joined with cutting-edge human–PC interface methods [13] equipped for making an interpretation of models into justifiable and helpful clarification discoursed for the end client (Figure 23.3). Our procedure is to seek an assortment of strategies to create an arrangement of techniques that will furnish future engineers with a scope of plan choices covering the presentation versus-reasonableness exchange space.

XAI is one of a small bunch of current DARPA programs [16] expected to empower "third-wave AI frameworks", where machines comprehend the unique situation and climate wherein they work, and after some time fabricate hidden logical models that permit them to portray genuine peculiarities.

The XAI program is centered on the improvement of numerous frameworks by tending to challenge issues in two regions: (1) AI issues to arrange occasions of interest in heterogeneous, media information; and (2) AI issues to build choice approaches for an independent framework to play out an assortment of recreated missions. These two test trouble spots were decided to address the crossing point of two significant AI draws near (order and support learning) and two significant functional trouble spots for the DoD (knowledge investigation and independent frameworks).

In the context of business benefits, morals concerns, or administrative con-templations, XAI is fundamental assuming that clients are to comprehend, fittingly trust, and successfully oversee AI results. In view of the investigated writing, the requirement for making sense of AI frameworks might originate from (at any rate) four reasons (Figure 23.4), despite the fact that it might create the impression that

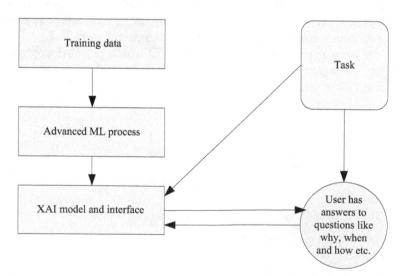

Figure 23.3   XAI concept

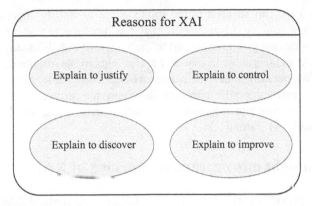

Figure 23.4   Reasons for XAI

there is a cross-over between these four reasons, from our angle, they catch the various inspirations for logic.

(1) Explain to legitimize: Beyond quite a long while have seen different debates over AI/ML-empowered frameworks yielding one-sided or biased outcomes. That suggests a rising requirement for clarifications to guarantee that AI-based choices were not made mistakenly. Whenever we talk about a clarification for a choice, we by and large mean the requirement because of reasons or supports for that specific result, as opposed to a depiction of the internal functions or the rationale of thinking behind the dynamic interaction overall. Utilizing XAI frameworks gives the necessary data to legitimize results, especially when unforeseen choices are made. It likewise guarantees that there is an auditable and provable method for guarding algorithmic choices as being fair and moral, which prompts building trust.

(2) Explain to control: Explainability is not only significant for defending choices. It can likewise assist with keeping things from turning out badly. For sure, seeing more about framework conduct gives more prominent perceivability over obscure weaknesses and imperfections and serves to quickly distinguish and address blunders in low criticality circumstances (investigating). In this way, empowering an upgraded control.

(3) Explain to move along: Another justification for building reasonable models is the need to further develop them persistently. A model that can be made sense of and comprehended is one that can be all the more effectively moved along. Since clients know why the framework created explicit results, they will likewise know how to make it more brilliant. Consequently, XAI could be the establishment for progressing cycles and improvement between humans and machines.

(4) Explain to find: Asking for clarifications is a useful instrument to learn new realities, to assemble data, and consequently to acquire information. Just logical frameworks can be valuable for that. For instance, considering that

AlphaGo Zero can succeed at the round of go obviously superior to human players, it would be advantageous that the machine can make sense of its learned methodology (information) to us. So it will not shock anyone if, in the future, XAI models show us new and secret regulations in science and physical science. We presume that logic is an incredible asset for legitimizing AI-based choices. It can assist with checking forecasts, for further developing models and acquiring new bits of knowledge about the main issue, which leads toward more reliable AI frameworks.

23.3   An insight into operational working of XAI

In view of the previously mentioned propositions, we recommend three headings of exploration for XAI in the process business: client-focused research as a significant movement to approve and refine a few of the theories presented in the past segment; research on unambiguous calculations and strategies that address the requirements examined inside the postulations; and clarifications that are dynamic and determined utilizing multi-instruments to provide food for the shifting necessities of various clients.

- **Client-centered approach to XAI:**
  In the plan of robotized frameworks in the process business, generally, the robotization is at the core of the framework with the assumption that the clients will adjust to the mechanization. It is notable that the outcome of this approach is restricted. Progressed robotization does not be guaranteed to further develop administrator execution. Human-centered AI [15] is a convincing possibility that empowers individuals to see, think, make, and act in remarkable ways, by joining powerful client encounters with installed AI techniques to help benefits that clients need. It inverts the story and treats the clients' requirements, objectives, and capacities as the center around which computerization is assembled. The demonstration of clarification is innately friendly. Independent of the explainer being human or a calculation (as in XAI), the clarification should be adjusted to the setting of the beneficiaries for an effective correspondence of the clarification. In the event that a clarification is not significant to the client, their impression of the framework may be impacted adversely. Clarifications with a couple of subtleties and an excessive amount of detail can make clients lose trust in the framework. Indeed, even the requirement for clarifications is setting subordinate. Sometimes, clarifications do not affect navigation. To get what qualifies as a significant clarification to the client, we want to get the client and their specific situation. Strategies like mental model elicitation, cognitive task analysis, and logical request assist us with understanding how master clients absorb data and simply decide. Co-creation and participatory plan approaches can assist with modifying clarification to explicit areas. A client-focused approach established in human variables, mental science, and client experience can assist with designing easy to understand AI answers for process businesses.

- **XAI methods for industrial data:**
A few well-known XAI techniques, for example, SHAP values [7], LIME [8], or include significance plots, give clarifications by highlighting attribution—recognizing the elements with the most elevated pertinence. The use of these strategies to multi-variate signal information, perhaps of variable length, which is normal in process industry applications, is testing. Despite the fact that there exist utilizations of SHAP and LIME to time-series information, they are normally fit to univariate time-series [9]. Of course, an assessment of XAI techniques [24,25] for time-series information [10] likewise raises the requirement for more theoretical portrayals and to foster more complex ways to deal with XAI for time-series information. Both SHAP and highlight significance plots depend on changing the info highlighted across the element conveyance acquired from the informational index. Gullibly applying this to flag information—and exclusively changing each point in each sign—will yield tests that are ridiculous or even infeasible. What that will mean for the unwavering quality of the element attribution stays hazy. LIME and the connected technique and Anchors [11] use include irritation and fluctuating highlights in agreement with the instruments of the information-creating space. In any case, the topic of how to acquire great component annoyance appropriations for modern cycles that are likewise inside the time necessities is an open exploration question. Reasonableness in view of case-based thinking or models seems, by all accounts, to be a superior way to deal with help ML use in the process business. Nonetheless, the creators do not know about any application to multi-variate time-series or even interaction industry. Model-explicit strategies like saliency maps for profound learning organizations or shapelet-based clarifications for arbitrary woods are fascinating techniques, assuming that comparing ML models are utilized. For use cases in the process industry, shapelet-based methods could be an exceptionally fascinating way to deal with making worldwide substitute models (e.g., in light of choice trees). Creating approaches that install space mastery into ML pipelines can be extremely gainful in the process business. While such procedures might be hard to straightforwardly scale to bigger datasets, they enjoy the benefit that the subsequent clarifications are designed by the space specialists themselves and are in this manner, liable to be more significant to them.

- **Dynamic and multi-mechanism explanations:**
Various clients have fluctuated prerequisites that are affected by variables, for example, time tension and experience. Computer-based intelligence arrangements should be placed into setting for various clients and a one-fits-all AI arrangement is in this manner not adequate. Dynamic or intelligent clarifications ought to permit clients to perform drill-downs or to browse different clarification instruments. As indicated, this kind of XAI is, by and large, a white spot in the exploration scene. A couple of models are that predominantly examine prerequisites. The improvements to dynamic clarifications additionally back differentiation forecasts with models from the chronicled information is a significant examination heading with importance past the application region of the cycle business.

23.4   Challenges of XAI

Reasonableness is an intelligently entrancing and socially huge subject. What's more, XAI is an extraordinarily strong graphic apparatus that can give understanding a long way past what was conceivable with customary direct models.

The difficulties of XAI include:

1. Secrecy:
   At times, a calculation is classified, or a proprietary innovation or it would be a security chance to uncover it. Since AI does not get the instruments of society, ethical quality, and classification, calculations might uncover delicate information, corporate proprietary advantages, or individual data without understanding that there is any issue with doing as such. Furthermore, the more mind-boggling AI methodologies are perceived, the more open doors will open up for double-dealing and the openness of private information.

2. Intricacy:
   Now and again calculations are surely known, yet are profoundly perplexing. Along these lines, a reasonable comprehension by a layman is ridiculous and here XAI approaches might be helpful. Since XAI has the choice to make elective calculations that are more straightforward to make sense of. Most AI calculations are complicated to such an extent that it is hard to make sense of them adequately for laypersons to comprehend, and, surprisingly, the people who make the calculations observe them trying to separate them for others to grasp. The degree of understanding about XAI is not entirely settled by the foundation of the individual endeavoring to comprehend the XAI application as the clarification has been made by an individual with a foundation in AI.

3. Outlandishness:
   Calculations that utilize typical genuine information often settle on choices that are not sensible, biased or inaccurate. How to affirm that the choices made are fair assuming that it is made in the light of an AI framework? Sensibility is consistent and has a substitute perspective dependent upon the particular data input given to the AI calculations.

4. Treachery:
   We might comprehend the manners in which a calculation is working; however, we want an explanation for how the framework is steady with a legitimate or moral code.

5. Transparency:
   AI processes are frequently intricate to the point that it is hard to "eliminate" them from the "black box" of obscurity. Also, how profoundly do individuals reserve the option to have the option to get the systems of AI?

6. Reasonableness:
   How can one know if the choices AI makes are fair and evenhanded? While decency is by and large relevant, the choices AI makes depend on the information it has been taken care of.

7. Safety:
    Are the choices that AI makes ok for everybody? Do clients have a solid sense of reassurance when they do not have the foggiest idea of how the AI reached the resolutions it did?
8. Trust:
    Closely attached to somewhere safe, people are continuously going to be wary with regard to believing the choices that AI makes. We have all seen Terminator and 2001: a Space Odyssey, and, however, we perceive that they are fictitious, trust in AI should be procured and demonstrated, again and again.
9. Causality:
    When "this" happened, for what reason did the AI do "that"? Are there the right derivations as well as clarifications for the basic exercises?

Programming: When everything the work is done, would we say we are ready to troubleshoot any inaccurate results, predispositions, and so on?

23.5   Benefits of XAI

- Lessening cost of mistakes: Decision-touchy fields like medicine, finance, legal, and so forth, are profoundly impacted in the case of wrong forecasts. Oversight over the outcomes decreases the effect of incorrect outcomes and recognizing the main driver prompts working on the basic model.
- Diminishing impact of model biasing: AI models have shown critical proof of inclination. Models incorporate orientation Bias for Apple Cards, Racial Bias via Autonomous Vehicles, Gender, and Racial predisposition by Amazon Rekognition. A reasonable framework can diminish the effect of such one-sided forecasts that is caused by making sense of dynamic models.
- Obligation and accountability: AI models generally have some degree of blunder with their expectations, and empowering an individual who can be mindful and responsible for those mistakes can make the general framework more productive.
- Code confidence: Every induction, alongside its clarification, will in general build the framework's certainty. Some client basic frameworks, like autonomous vehicles, medical diagnosis [28,29], the finance area, and so forth, request high code certainty from the client for more ideal use.
- Code compliance: Increasing tension from the administrative bodies implies that organizations need to adjust and execute XAI to rapidly consent to the specialists.
- Further developed logic and straightforwardness: Businesses can comprehend complex AI models better and see the reason why they act in some ways under unambiguous circumstances. Regardless of whether it is a black-box model, people can utilize a clarification point of interaction to comprehend how these AI models accomplish specific ends.

- Quicker reception: As organizations can comprehend AI models better, they can trust them with more significant choices
- Improved troubleshooting: When the framework works out of the blue, XAI can be utilized to distinguish issues and assist engineers with investigating the issue.
- Empowering reviewing for administrative prerequisites

Building reliability: Humans are better ready to believe the AI model when the qualities and reasoning of the AI yield have been made sense of.

- Fulfilling lawful necessities: Financial and medical services businesses might be expected to join AI models into their mind-boggling risk appraisal techniques to satisfy administrative prerequisites for successful gamble the board.
- Giving morals-related support (and eliminating oblivious predispositions): Because XAI is straightforward and ready to all the more effectively be fixed, oblivious inclinations can be taken out, and moral choices made sense of.
- Inferring significant and vigorous bits of knowledge: AI and ML give the capacity to infer noteworthy and hearty experiences, be that as it may, XAI empowers people to comprehend how and why the XAI calculation had the option to decide the "following best activity." Figure 23.5 depicts the benefits of XAI.

The XAI program means to make a set-up of AI methods that:

- Produce more logical models, while keeping an elevated degree of learning execution (expectation precision); and
- Empower human clients to comprehend, properly trust, and really deal with the arising age of misleadingly canny accomplices.

The XAI program is centered on the improvement of numerous frameworks by tending to challenge issues in two regions: (1) AI issues to group occasions of interest in heterogeneous, interactive media information; and (2) AI issues to develop choice strategies for an independent framework to play out an assortment of reenacted missions. These two test pain points were decided to address the convergence of two significant AI draws near (arrangement and support learning) and two significant functional trouble spots for the DoD (insight examination and independent frameworks).

Figure 23.5   Benefits of XAI

23.6   Recent developments in XAI

23.6.1   Generative AI for content creation and chatbots

Current AI models can produce text, sound, and pictures in an extremely great, practically indistinct from non-manufactured genuine information.

At the core of text age stands natural language processing (NLP). Quick advances in NLP [32–34] have prompted the rise of language models. For example, Bidirectional Encoder Representations from Transformers (BERT) model is effectively utilized by Google and Microsoft to supplement their web indexes.

By what other means does the improvement of innovations connected with NLP support organizations? Above all else, joining NLP and AI instruments permits the making of chatbots. As indicated by Business Insider, the chatbot market is supposed to arrive at USD 9.4 billion in 2024, so we should underscore the manners in which organizations benefit from AI-driven chatbot execution.

Chatbot attempts to get the expectations of individuals, rather than simply performing standard orders. Organizations working in various regions utilize the AI-driven chatbot to furnish their clients or clients with human-level correspondence. Uses of chatbots are generally seen in the accompanying industry spaces: medical care [17–20], banking, showcasing, travel, and accommodation.

AI-driven chatbots help to mechanize administrator assignments. For example, in medical services, they decrease how much manual work. Here, chatbots help to put together arrangements, send updates connected with taking medications, and furnish patients with replies to inquiries. In different regions, chatbots are acquainted with conveying designated messages, further, developing client commitment and backing, and furnishing clients with customized offers.

Other than chatbots, NLP lies at the core of other state-of-the-art mechanical arrangements. One of the models is NLP text age which can be utilized in business applications. An NLP-based Question Generation framework introduced in the video underneath is utilized in a safe verification process.

The fresh introduction of the GPT-3 model permits AI specialists to create a normal of 4.5 billion words each day. This will permit an enormous scope of downstream utilization of AI for both socially valuable and less helpful purposes. It is additionally making analysts put resources into innovations for distinguishing generative models. Note that in 2022 we will observe the appearance of GPT-4—"misleadingly for the most part keen AI."

Returning to generative AI, we need to focus on GANs, or generative adversarial networks, that are currently fit for making pictures unclear from human-delivered ones. That could be pictures of non-existent individuals, creatures, objects, as well as different kinds of media, like sound and text. Presently it is the best second to execute GANs acquiring from their capacities since they can display genuine information circulations and learn accommodating portrayals for further developing the AI pipelines, getting information, tracking down abnormalities, and adjusting to explicit certifiable cases.

The logotypes in the image underneath were made with the assistance of GANs, you can track down more data in the examination.

23.6.2   *Man-made intelligence driven QA and investigation*

The most momentous part of computer vision is AI investigation. Lately, this bearing has been thriving as a direct result of the rising exactness and execution. Organizations began to contribute both computational and monetary assets to create computer vision frameworks [12] at a quicker rate. The concentrated improvement of AI examination is likewise associated with a fast advancement in the area of item identification in video outlines.

Computerized assessment in assembling infers the examination of items concerning their consistency with quality principles. The strategy is additionally applied to gear observing.

The following are not many used instances of AI examination:

• Recognizing imperfections of items in the mechanical production system
• Recognizing imperfections of mechanical and vehicle body parts
• Things screening and airplane support
• Investigations of thermal energy plants

23.6.3   *Game-changing AI leaps forward in medical services*

The following pattern connected with the execution of AI in the medical services industry [21–23] has been seriously examined over the late years. Researchers use AI models and PC vision calculations in the battle against COVID-19, including regions like pandemic identification, antibody advancement, drug disclosure, warm screening, facial acknowledgment with veils, and breaking down CT filters.

To balance the spread of COVID-19, AI models can identify and break down expected dangers and make precise expectations. Likewise, AI assists with creating immunizations by recognizing essential parts that make them effective.

Computer-based intelligence-driven arrangements might be applied as a proficient instrument in The Internet of Medical Things and for taking care of privacy issues that are well defined for the medical care industry. Assuming we arrange to use instances of AI in medical services, obviously, they are joined by one point—to guarantee that the patient is analyzed rapidly and precisely.

23.6.4   *No-code AI stages in something like three regions*

No-code AI stages have empowered even little organizations to apply strong advances that were beforehand accessible just to huge undertakings. We should figure out why such stages are a key AI pattern for organizations in 2022.

Creating AI models without any preparation calls for time use and significant experience. Reception of the no-code AI stage improves the assignment since it diminishes the passage boundary. The benefits are:

- Fast execution—contrasted and composing code without any preparation, working with information, and troubleshooting, efficient spans 90%.
- The lower cost of advancement—through mechanization, the organizations killed the requirement for enormous information science groups.
- Ease of purpose—intuitive usefulness works on programming improvement and empowers the formation of applications without coding.

No-code AI stages are sought after in medical care, monetary area, and advertising—however, created arrangements could not be exceptionally redone. Among the most pursued no-code AI stages, you can track down Google Cloud Auto ML, Google ML Kit, Runaway AI, CreateML, MakeML, Super Annotate, and so on.

Undertaking estimated organizations, as well as average-size organizations, influence no-code stages for programming arrangements focusing on picture grouping, perceiving postures and sounds, and item location.

23.6.5   Diversity in AI

The absence of variety in AI can add to the rise of racial and orientation inclinations. By variety, we mean an assortment of individuals who foster AI models. As per NYU's exploration, 80% of teachers engaged with AI improvement are men, and just 10% of scientists who work with AI at Google are ladies. A similar examination shows that not even 5% of staff at Google, Facebook, and Microsoft are Black laborers.

The quantity of female alumni of AI PhD projects and software engineering resources has stayed at a low level for quite a while. Be that as it may, the requirement for variety in AI ought to impact what is going on, which is one of the arising patterns. Besides, ladies in AI can pursue huge choices impacting the turn of events and execution of AI frameworks. Thus, to find out about females in AI, read the article committed to the splendid profession way of an AI engineer at MobiDev. We value variety and incorporation that empower MobiDev groups to foster AI programming pursuing exact and proficient choices and staying away from predisposition.

23.7   Future trends of XAI

1. **More noteworthy cloud and AI cooperation:**
   Rico Burnett, the overseer of client advancement at legitimate administrations supplier Exigent, says that AI will assume a critical part in the expansive reception of Cloud Solutions in 2021. Through the organization of man-made brainpower, it will be feasible to screen and oversee cloud assets and the tremendous measure of accessible information.
2. **Man-made intelligence answers for IT:**
   The quantity of AI arrangements that are being produced for IT will increment in 2021. Capgemini's Simion predicts that AI arrangements that can

identify normal IT issues all alone and self-right any little glitches or issues will see an expansion in the forthcoming years. This will lessen vacation and permit the groups in an association to chip away at high-intricacy tasks and concentrate somewhere else.

3. **AIOps turns out to be more famous:**
   Throughout the most recent couple of years, the intricacy of IT frameworks has expanded. Forrester as of late said that merchants would need stage arrangements that consolidate more than one observing discipline like application, framework, and systems administration. IT activities and different groups can work on their key cycles, independent direction, and undertakings with AIOps arrangements and further developed examination of the volumes of information coming in its direction. Forrester encouraged the IT chiefs to find AIOps suppliers who will engage the get group coordinated effort through start-to-finish advanced encounters, information connection, and a mix of the IT activities in the executives' toolchain.

4. **Simulated intelligence will help in organizing information:**
   Later on, we will see more unstructured information organized with regular language handling and AI processes. Associations will use these innovations and make information that RPA or mechanical cycle robotization innovation can involve when they need to mechanize value-based movement in an association. RPA is one of the quickest developing regions in the product business. The main limit that it faces is that it can utilize organized information. With the assistance of AI, unstructured information can undoubtedly be changed over into organized information, which can give a characterized yield.

5. **Man-made brainpower ability will stay tight:**
   The stock of ability is supposed to be an issue in taking on computerized reasoning in 2021. There has been a persevering hole in AI ability, and associations have at long last understood this potential. It is fundamental to address this hole and guarantee that a more extensive gathering learns computerized reasoning. Guaranteeing that a more extensive arrangement of clients approach computerized reasoning to zero in on innovation, learning techniques, and supporting an adjustment of it is fundamental in the 2021 workplace.

6. **Enormous scope reception of AI in the IT business:**
   We have seen consistent development in the reception of AI inside the IT business. In any case, Simion predicts that associations will involve AI underway and begin utilizing them at a huge scope. With the assistance of man-made reasoning, an association can get ROI continuously. This implies that associations will see their endeavors being paid off.

7. **AI ethics is the concentration:**
   Natalie Cartwright, fellow benefactor and COO of Finn AI, an AI banking stage, predicts that in 2021, associations will convey ability on the most proficient method to use computerized reasoning against major worldwide issues, invigorate advancement and monetary development, and guarantee incorporation and variety. As AI morals [30,31] become more vital to

associations, straightforwardness of information and calculation decency are two of the issues that are at the center of attention.

8. **Expanded processes become progressively well known:**
   Man-made consciousness and information science will end up being a piece of a greater picture with regard to advancement and robotization in 2021. Information environments are adaptable, lean, and furthermore give information on schedule to heterogeneous sources. Be that as it may, it is important to give an establishment to adjust and cultivate advancement. As indicated by Ana Maloberti, a major information engineer at Globant, organizations will go above and beyond in upgrading their increased business and improvement processes. Utilizing AI, programming advancement cycles can be streamlined, and we can search for a more extensive aggregate knowledge and further develop coordinated effort. We should encourage an information-driven culture and outgrow the trial stages to move into a feasible conveyance model.

9. **Computerized reasoning will turn out to be more logical:**
   The ranking executive of item at client information center point Tealium and Dave Lucas, expresses that there will be a greater spotlight on reasonableness. As more information guidelines become an integral factor, the confidence in AI will be crucial. To plainly comprehend and verbalize how every trademark will add to the end expectation or the consequence of the AI model.

10. **Voice and language-driven knowledge:**
    Especially in client care focus, the expansion in remote working has driven an extraordinary chance to take on NLP or ASR (robotized discourse acknowledgment) abilities. Under 5% of all client contacts are regularly checked for quality criticism as per ISG's Butterfield. Because of the absence of one-on-one training, associations can utilize man-made brainpower to finish routine quality keeping an eye on client understanding and goal to guarantee preceded with consistency.

Reasonableness is depicted as being essentially as old as the subject of AI itself instead of being an issue that emerges through AI. In the beginning of AI research, the models frequently comprised of thinking strategies, which were sensible and representative, bringing about restricted execution, adaptability, and relevance. Nonetheless, such sort of AI frameworks conveyed a reason for clarification as they played out some kind of coherent deduction on images that were meaningful for people.

Conversely, the AI frameworks of today are more mind boggling why reasonableness is seriously difficult. Hence, research in XAI and computer-supported validation underscores the need to align with applied AI research to address research gaps that might hinder practical implementation. We contend that this does not just allude to the improvement of new XAI techniques, yet additionally requires a socio-specialized point of view. There are henceforth different open doors for additional examinations on the subject of reasonableness in data frameworks.

23.8   Conclusion

XAI is a collection of procedures and strategies that allow human users to understand and trust machine learning algorithms' findings and output. The term "explainable AI" refers to a model's predicted impact and probable biases. It aids in the evaluation of model correctness, fairness, transparency, and results in AI-assisted decision-making. XAI is a new and growing approach that aids people in comprehending the consequences and decisions that their AI technology suggests. With the constant advancement and application of new technologies, the ability to adapt to and comprehend these changes becomes increasingly important for businesses. Many sectors will require XAI to comprehend AI and machine learning systems' insights, answers, and forecasts. It is now more vital than ever to embrace and learn XAI.

References

[1]   W. Samek, G. Montavon, A. Vedaldi, L. K. Hansen, and K. R. Muller, *Explainable AI: Interpreting, Explaining and Visualizing Deep Learning* (Springer Nature, 2019).

[2]   O. Biran and C. Cotton, Explanation and justification in machine learning: a survey, Paper presented at the IJCAI-17 Workshop on Explainable AI (XAI), Melbourne, Australia, 20 August 2017.

[3]   A.P. Jyothi, C. Megashree, S. Radhika, and N. Shoba, Detection of cervical cancer and classification using texture analysis. *Journal of Contemporary Issues in Business and Government,* 2021; 27(3):1850–1856.

[4]   U. Sakthivel, A.P. Jyothi, N. Susila, and T. Sheela, Conspectus of k-means clustering algorithm. In *Applied Learning Algorithms for Intelligent IoT* (Auerbach Publications, 2021), pp. 193–213.

[5]   A.P. Jyothi and U. Saktivel, Technique to Balance Energy Efficient Clustering with Data Transmission in Large Scale Sensor Network, 2016.

[6]   A.P. Jyothi and U. Sakthivel, Trends and technologies used for mitigating energy efficiency issues in wireless sensor network. *International Journal of Computer Applications,* 2015;111(3):32–40.

[7]   C. Olah, A. Mordvintsev, and L. Schubert, Feature visualization. *Distill,* 2017;2(11):e7.

[8]   A. Vellido, The importance of interpretability and visualization in machine learning for applications in medicine and health care. *Neural Computer Application,* early access, Feb. 4, 2019, doi:10.1007/s00521-019- 04051-w.

[9]   S. M. Lundberg and S.-I. Lee, A unified approach to interpreting model predictions. In *Advances in Neural Information Processing Systems 30,* I. Guyon *et al.,* (eds.) (Red Hook, NY: Curran Associates, 2017), pp. 4765–4774.

[10]   Y. Xie, G. Gao, and X. A. Chen, Outlining the design space of explainable intelligent systems for medical diagnosis. *CoRR,* 2019;abs/1902.06019:1–5. http://arxiv.org/abs/1902.06019.

[11] K. Kallianos, J. Mongan, S. Antani, *et al*, How far have we come? Artificial intelligence for chest radiograph interpretation. *Clinical Radiology*, 2019;74 (5):338–345.

[12] H.J. Escalante, S. Escalera, I. Guyon, *et al*, *Explainable and Interpretable Models in Computer Vision and Machine Learning* (Springer, 2018).

[13] V. Bellotti and K. Edwards, Intelligibility and accountability: human considerations in context-aware systems. *Human-Computer Interaction*, 2009;16:193–212.

[14] T. Kulesza, M. Burnett, W. Wong, and S. Stumpf, Principles of explanatory debugging to personalize interactive machine learning. In *Proceedings of the 20th International Conference on Intelligent User Interfaces* (ACM, 2015), pp. 126–137.

[15] D. Wang, Q. Yang, A. Abdul, and B.Y. Lim, Designing theory-driven user-centric explainable AI. In *Proceedings of the 2019 CHI Conference on Human Factors in Computing Systems*, paper no. 601 (ACM, 2019).

[16] D. Gunning, Explainable artificial intelligence (XAI), DARPA/I2O; www.cc.gatech.edu/~alanwags/DLAI2016/(Gunning)%20IJCAI-16%20DLAI%20WS.pdf.

[17] E.-J. Lee, Y.-H. Kim, N. Kim, and D.-W. Kang, Deep into the brain: artificial intelligence in stroke imaging. *Journal of Stroke*, 2017;19(3):277–285.

[18] O. Ronneberger, P. Fischer, and T. Brox, U-Net: convolutional networks for biomedical image segmentation. *CoRR*, 2015;abs/1505.04597(3):234–241. http://arxiv.org/abs/1505.04597

[19] L. Chen, P. Bentley, and D. Rueckert, Fully automatic acute ischemic lesion segmentation in DWI using convolutional neural networks. *NeuroImage, Clinical*, 2017;15:633–643.

[20] J. Irvin, P. Rajpurkar, M. Ko *et al.*, Chexpert: a large chest radiograph dataset with uncertainty labels and expert comparison. *CoRR*, 2019;abs/1901.07031:4–7. http://arxiv.org/abs/1901.07031.

[21] F. Milletari, N. Navab, and S. Ahmadi, "V-Net: fully convolutional neural networks for volumetric medical image segmentation." *CoRR*, 2016;abs/1606.04797:7–9. http://arxiv.org/abs/1606.04797 4810. IEEE Transactions on Neural Networks and Learning Systems, vol. 32, no. 11, November 2021.

[22] L.-C. Chen, G. Papandreou, I. Kokkinos, K. Murphy, and A.L. Yuille, Deeplab: semantic image segmentation with deep convolutional nets, atrous convolution, and fully connected CRFs. *CoRR*, 2016;abs/1606.00915:7–11. http://dblp.uni-trier.de/db/journals/corr/corr1606.html.

[23] C.J. Kelly, A. Karthikesalingam, M. Suleyman, G. Corrado, and D. King, Key challenges for delivering clinical impact with artificial intelligence. *BMC Medicine*, 2019;17(1):195.

[24] S. Lapuschkin, S. Wäldchen, A. Binder, G. Montavon, W. Samek, and K.-R. Müller, Unmasking Clever Hans predictors and assessing what machines really learn. *Nature Communication*, 2019;10(1):1096.

[25] M.T. Ribeiro, S. Singh, and C. Guestrin, 'Why should I trust you?': explaining the predictions of any classifier. In *Proceedings of the 22nd ACM*

SIGKDD International Conference on Knowledge Discovery and Data Mining (New York, NY: Association Computing Machinery, Aug. 2016), pp. 1135–1144.

[26]   G. Montavon, W. Samek, and K.-R. Müller, Methods for interpreting and understanding deep neural networks. *Digital Signal Processing*, 2018;73: 1–15.

[27]   W. Samek, T. Wiegand, and K. Müller, Explainable artificial intelligence: understanding, visualizing and interpreting deep learning models. *CoRR*, 2017;abs/1708.08296:1–6. http://arxiv.org/abs/1708.08296.

[28]   S. Meacham, G. Isaac, D. Nauck, and B. Virginas, Towards explainable AI: design and development for explanation of machine learning predictions for a patient readmittance medical application. In *Intelligent* Computing, K. Arai, R. Bhatia, and S. Kapoor, (eds.) (Cham, Switzerland: Springer, 2019), pp. 939–955.

[29]   B. Heinrichs and S.B. Eickhoff, Your evidence? Machine learning algorithms for medical diagnosis and prediction. *Human Brain Mapping*, 2020;41(6):1435–1444.

[30]   M. Brundage, S. Avin, J. Wang, *et al.*, "Toward trustworthy AI development: Mechanisms for supporting verifiable claims," European Commission, Brussels, Belgium, Tech. Rep., 2020. https://ec.europa.eu/digitalsingle-market/en/news/draft-ethics-guidelines-trustworthy-ai.

[31]   Ethics Guidelines for Trustworthy AI, Nov. 2019. https://ec.europa.eu/digital-single-market/en/news/ethics-guidelinestrustworthy-ai.

[32]   B. Zhou, D. Bau, A. Oliva, and A. Torralba, Interpreting deep visual representations via network dissection. *IEEE Transactions on Pattern Analysis and Machine Intelligence*, 2019;41(9):2131–2145.

[33]   L. Arras, F. Horn, G. Montavon, K. Müller, and W. Samek, What is relevant in a text document? An interpretable machine learning approach. *CoRR*, 2016;abs/1612.07843:1–17. http://arxiv.org/abs/1612.07843. Tjoa and Guan: Survey on Xai: Toward Medical XAI 4811.

[34]   O. Eberle, J. Buttner, F. Krautli, K.-R. Mueller, M. Valleriani, and G. Montavon, Building and interpreting deep similarity models. *IEEE Transactions on Pattern Analysis and Machine Intelligence*, 2020;1:1–13.

Index

Printed in the USA
CPSIA information can be obtained
at www.ICGtesting.com
JSHW011501061223
53301JS00012B/4